PLUTARCH'S PRISM

Throughout the early modern period, political theorists in France and England drew on the works of Plutarch to offer advice to kings and princes. Elizabeth I herself translated Plutarch in her later years, while Jacques Amyot's famous translations of Plutarch's *Parallel Lives* led to the wide distribution of his work and served as a key resource for Shakespeare in the writing of his Roman plays, through Sir Thomas North's English translations. Rebecca Kingston's new study explores how Plutarch was translated into French and English during the Renaissance and how his works were invoked in political argument from the early modern period into the eighteenth century, contributing to a tradition she calls 'public humanism.' This book traces the shifting uses of Plutarch in the Enlightenment, leading to the decline of this tradition of 'public humanism.' Throughout, the importance of Plutarch's work is highlighted as a key cultural reference and for its insight into important aspects of public service.

REBECCA KINGSTON is Professor in the Department of Political Science at the University of Toronto. She is the recipient of three Social Science and Humanities Research Council of Canada grants, and has been awarded research fellowships at Clare Hall, Cambridge, the Bodleian Library Centre for the Study of the Book, and the Jackman Institute for the Humanities at the University of Toronto. She is the author of *Montesquieu and the Parlement of Bordeaux* (1996), which was awarded the Prix Montesquieu by the Académie Montesquieu, and *Public Passion: Rethinking the Grounds for Political Justice* (2011). She is editing the forthcoming *Plutarch: Selected Writings*, with the translator Elizabeth Sawyer for the series 'Cambridge Texts in the History of Political Thought.'

T0384773

IDEAS IN CONTEXT

Edited by DAVID ARMITAGE, RICHARD BOURKE and JENNIFER PITTS

The books in this series will discuss the emergence of intellectual traditions and of related new disciplines. The procedures, aims and vocabularies that were generated will be set in the context of the alternatives available within the contemporary frameworks of ideas and institutions. Through detailed studies of the evolution of such traditions, and their modification by different audiences, it is hoped that a new picture will form of the development of ideas in their concrete contexts. By this means, artificial distinctions between the history of philosophy, of the various sciences, of society and politics, and of literature may be seen to dissolve.

A full list of titles in the series can be found at: www.cambridge.org/IdeasContext

PLUTARCH'S PRISM

*Classical Reception and Public Humanism in France
and England 1500–1800*

REBECCA KINGSTON

University of Toronto

CAMBRIDGE
UNIVERSITY PRESS

Shaftesbury Road, Cambridge CB2 8EA, United Kingdom

One Liberty Plaza, 20th Floor, New York, NY 10006, USA

477 Williamstown Road, Port Melbourne, VIC 3207, Australia

314–321, 3rd Floor, Plot 3, Splendor Forum, Jasola District Centre, New Delhi – 110025, India

103 Penang Road, #05–06/07, Visioncrest Commercial, Singapore 238467

Cambridge University Press is part of Cambridge University Press & Assessment, a department of the University of Cambridge.

We share the University's mission to contribute to society through the pursuit of education, learning and research at the highest international levels of excellence.

www.cambridge.org
Information on this title: www.cambridge.org/9781009243469

DOI: 10.1017/9781009243490

First published 2022
First paperback edition 2023

A catalogue record for this publication is available from the British Library

ISBN   978-1-009-24348-3   Hardback
ISBN   978-1-009-24346-9   Paperback

Contents

v

Figures

Preface

This book, like perhaps most books, has many points of origin. One account begins with a photograph.

A young girl, just five years of age, holds a bouquet of hand-picked flowers (poppies perhaps) sitting in the sun. Her sister will remind her that the staging of the photograph was a consolation prize. Her family had travelled to Rome from Oxford for the school holiday. Her two brothers were enrolled in the Christ Church Choir school where they were immersed in the ABCs of British public culture, jackdaws, knights in shining armour and the 'heroes' of the ancient world. Arriving in Rome was a moment not only to test that knowledge but to imbue it with something of a material and embodied reality. The statue of Julius Caesar was a special draw for school-age boys only beginning to grapple with the iconic status of the man. The parents of the young girl who made a fuss at not being photographed with her brothers in front of a Julius Caesar statue tried to appease her. They took a picture of her at another site, the Curia of Pompey. It was close to the spot where Julius Caesar, seated and speaking to Roman Senators, famously met his death, stabbed by his close associates. The young girl, most interested in the wildflowers and stray cats, was not aware of the events which had taken place there 2,000 years before. She didn't know that the public history that gave Julius Caesar renown included a ruthlessness and violence highlighted in precisely that location. Of course, it was also that place and the circumstances surrounding that event, that have shaped and inspired countless volumes of literature, history, and political reflection. The seeming allure, and threat, of Caesarism still loom large on public consciousness today.

Still, the gap between the resounding historical importance of that site and the ignorance of the person in the photograph can be thought of as symbolic of an ongoing and perennial gap between the ethos of our contemporary era and the world of the ancients. At some level, the disregard is both an insult and an affirmation that glory seeking and all that was associated with it was rightly overtaken by a concern for individual comfort and personal happiness. A cursory measure of that historical gap could also be found through a simple mathematical calculation of the number of lives mentioned by Plutarch, not as the focus of his narrative, but as the victims of the countless battles and slaughters peppered throughout each page. What were the stories of those lives of captives, willing soldiers, ambitious aristocrats and poor peasants just trying to live or to survive from the booties of war and whose lives were ended prematurely and in horrible violence? What does Plutarch's consistent invocation of the praiseworthy quality of _humanité_ mean in the face of such carnage? The girl in the photograph may not have even survived in that ancient world, given the life-threatening conditions of childbirth for both mothers and children at the time. Yet the photograph is taken _there_, and the site continues to be photographed by travellers partly due to the textual tradition that has issued from reflection on its significance, texts that continue to form a core of ongoing cultural and political narratives in the west. The historical gap persists but it is also mediated and partly bridged by traditions of writing and reflection that continue to engage with related themes. Still, the picture itself, I think, raises the question of the pertinence of the site to the life and cultural meanings of the society in which that child grows up and through which she seeks to define herself.

Of course, that child is me. I am still far removed from a full understanding of that world represented by the ruin. The purpose of this book is not to bring that world to life, but rather to try to shed light on a thread through which an interpretation of that ancient world, especially as it pertains to public life, helped to shape our understandings of politics in the early modern period in Europe. It is but one thread in a much broader story about how the gap between the world of the ancient past and our contemporary outlooks was shaped, in part through ongoing engagement with the stories and artefacts of that same past.

Acknowledgements

This book has been a journey in several respects. So many people have helped me along the way, and I could not have done it without them. My thanks go out to a vast number!

Thanks to various ancient Greek teachers, tutors and classicists over the years who have helped me to unpack Plutarch, learn the basics of ancient Greek and who have offered good advice and support, especially as I began this project. These include the late Elaine Fantham, Barrie Fleet, Noreen Humble, Christopher Pelling, Susan Jacobs (and other scholars of the International Plutarch Society who welcomed me to their meetings), Elizabeth Sawyer, Sara Monoson, Jeff Tatum (who assured me that Amyot's translation was excellent), Brad Hald, Emily Mohr, Alexandra Boleyn, Nada Conic and Lee Sawchuck. I also am very grateful for the thoughtful guidance and support of the classicist Alison Keith of the University of Toronto.

Thanks also go to the following for their great help in reading and offering suggestions for the revising of my manuscript in various stages of the process, including in a book manuscript workshop: Edward Andrew, Ryan Balot, Jeffrey Collins, Isabela dos Santos, Mark Jurdjevic, Erica Kunimoto, Mary Jo Macdonald, Andy Sabl and Jean Terrel. Thanks also to James Carley, Alexandra Franklin and David Howarth for both practical help and advice.

Many thanks to the countless staff members of several libraries, including The Fisher Rare Books Library and Robarts Library in Toronto, the Bodleian Library, the Cambridge University Library and the Arsenal library and Bibliothèque nationale in Paris, as well as staff in the Department of Political Science at the University of Toronto, without whom faculty would be adrift.

Thanks is due to the Social Sciences and Humanities Research Council of Canada who helped to fund this project. I am thankful for an RBC fellowship that helped to fund a term of research at the Bodleian Library in

Oxford. In addition, I am exceedingly grateful to the Jackman Humanities Institute which awarded me a faculty fellowship for a year allowing me to complete the first draft of the manuscript. The warm community of fellows at the Institute also provided me with a welcome and intellectually stimulating environment in which to do my work.

I also wish to thank the reviewers and editors at Cambridge University Press, especially Liz Friend-Smith, who ensured that my best efforts were reflected in my work. Of course, all deficiencies here are due to my own limitations.

Our community of scholars at the University of Toronto over the years has been an important source of inspiration and support. These include Nancy Bertoldi, Joe Carens, Arturo Chang, Joseph Dattilo, Nate Gilmore, Kelsey Gordon, Ran Hirschl, Ryan Hurl, Peggy Kohn, Kanta Murali, Emily Nacol, Jennifer Nedelsky, Carla Norloff, Clifford Orwin, Catherine Power, Ayelet Shachar, Torrey Shanks, Grace Skogstad, Dale Turner, Constantine Vassiliou, Rachel Wagner, Matthew Walton and Melissa Williams.

I acknowledge the use of Figure 1 from Freyja Cox Jensen, "The Popularity of Ancient Historians," *The Historical Journal*, 61 (3), 578. Reproduced with permission from Cambridge University Press.

I want to thank my son Gabriel who has always kept me on-task, gives invaluable advice and assistance, and offers me incalculable joy each day. I also thank my siblings Fred and Cap, Liz and Andrew, and Paul (who know I am always trying to get back into the picture!). Kai Nikko Zhi-ai Beiner and Hayden Michael Kingston Hayes also offer hope for the future. Unfortunately, my mother Pauline and father Frederick Temple passed away before this book came to light, but they were supportive of me every step of the way and I will be forever grateful to both. Of course, love and thanks also go to Ronnie who has helped me to persevere and who is an exemplar, in the best sense, of a dedicated and thoughtful scholar and loving partner.

Introduction

They are mistaken who think that engaging in public affairs is, like going to sea or to a war, something undertaken for an object distinct from itself and ceasing when that object is attained; for engaging in public affairs is not a special service which is ended when the need ends, but is a way of life of a tamed social animal living in an organized society, intended by nature to live throughout its allotted time the life of a citizen and in a manner devoted to honour and the welfare of mankind. Therefore, it is fitting that men should be engaged, not merely have ceased to be engaged, in affairs of State, just as it is fitting that they should be, not have ceased to do, right, and that they should love, not have ceased to love, their native land and their fellow-citizens.

Plutarch, "Old Men in Public Affairs" 791 c

With a key focus on virtue ethics, Plutarch is a writer who once had a privileged place in traditions of political reflection and the history of political thought, as well as broader trends of historical, cultural and moral thinking.[1] His readers have ranged from Ralph Waldo Emerson, Elizabeth I, and Shakespeare, to Frankenstein's monster and Charlotte Corday.[2] And

---

[1] Up to now the classic study of Plutarch reception has been Rudolf Hirzel's *Plutarch* (Leipzig: Theodor Weicher, 1912). *Plutarch's Prism* traces reception with greater emphasis on the early modern period in both England and France (and drawing on digital bibliographic sources to identify a broader array of significant texts) and with concerted focus on the history of political ideas, with special attention to depictions of the norms and ethos of public life.

[2] In the words of Frankenstein's monster: "The volume of Plutarch's *Lives* which I possessed, contained the histories of the first founders of the ancient republics. This book had a far different effect on me from the *Sorrows of Werther*. I learned from Werther's imaginations despondency and gloom; but Plutarch taught me high thoughts; he elevated me above the wretched sphere of my own reflections, to admire and love the heroes of past ages. Many things I read surpassed my understanding and experience ... this book developed new and mightier scenes of action. I read of men concerned in public affairs governing or massacring their species. I felt the greatest ardour for virtue rise within me, and abhorrence of vice, as far as I understood the significance of these terms, relative as they were, as I applied them, to pleasure and pain alone. Induced by these feelings, I was of course led to admire peaceable lawgivers, Numa, Solon and Lycurgus, in preference to Romulus and

while Simon Goldhill offers an account of the relative abandonment of the reading of Plutarch for broad moral and cultural education, he may not be as irrelevant as we might consider at first glance.[3] Still, to discern this we will need to explore the exact nature of this long tradition in political theory that has only been partially explored in existing scholarship.

The history of political thought offered in this book traces a series of reflections about public life drawing from the work of Plutarch. As we will see, there are many ways his thought was appropriated and adapted to the dominant concerns of the times. Thinkers having recourse to Plutarch did not use his work in the same systematic way and for the same purposes. Still, as I try to demonstrate, there are some guiding principles that tend to shape the various iterations of his work in the history of political thought. Appropriations of Plutarch in Renaissance France and England often highlight a sense of the nobility, importance and dignity of public life. Linked to this, the authors studied here offer some account of a unique ethos associated with public office, an ethos which incorporates both high

---

Theseus." Mary Wollstonecraft Shelley, *Frankenstein* (Berkeley: University of California Press, 1984), 133–134. Charlotte Corday is said to have read Plutarch the day before her journey to assassinate Marat, or even carried a copy of Plutarch in her pocket on the way there. Jean Cocteau, *Theatre* (Paris: Grasset, 1957), vol. 1, 50 cited in Francesco, Manzini. "Plutarch from Voltaire to Stendhal," in Sophia Xenophontos and K. Oikonomopoulou eds., *Brill's Companion to the Reception of Plutarch* (Leiden: Brill, 2019), 515–527. Emerson wrote a famous essay on Plutarch serving as an introduction to revised editions of *Plutarch's Morals* in late nineteenth-century America. See Ralph Waldo Emerson, "Introduction," in William Goodwin ed., *Plutarch's Morals* (Boston: Little, Brown and Company, 1874) and Edmund G. Berry, *Emerson's Plutarch* (Cambridge MA: Harvard University Press, 1961).

[3] Simon Goldhill, "The Value of Greek. Why Save Plutarch?" in *Who Needs Greek? Contests in the Cultural History of Hellenism* (Cambridge: Cambridge University Press, 2002), 246–293. One example of the direct contemporary relevance of Plutarch can be found in Ukraine. Volodymyr Zelensky won the presidential election in April 2019, a notable event due to his lack of political experience. As a comedian and actor, he made his way on to the ballot through his starring role in the television series "Servant of the People." There Zelensky plays a lowly history teacher by the name of Vasyl Petrovych Holoborodko who is caught on video complaining of corruption within the political elite. His students post the video on-line; it goes viral and catches the sympathy and imagination of citizens catapulting this fictional teacher into a fictional and then ultimately real presidential office. On the screen the character is an honest humble fellow and the first time we meet him in the fictional series, four minutes into the first episode, he is reading Plutarch's *Lives*. Indeed, in the second episode, Plutarch himself has a cameo in a dream sequence where he is discussing with Herodotus the challenges and implications of the election. The sculptural bust that is a permanent fixture of the history teacher's classroom is more than likely meant to be that of Plutarch.

Presumably the writers of the series chose Plutarch to emphasise the moral uprightness and honesty of the lowly teacher now elected as president, in contrast with the corruption of the established elites and of the political culture more generally (given the immediate expectations of even Holoborodko's own family to share in the wealth that access to political power could allow for). Of interest is that Plutarch is invoked in this context not through the trope of heroism or greatness, but as a representative of a morally judicious, prudent and well-intentioned approach to public life and as a defender of an earnest commitment to public service.

expectations of public service and awareness of trade-offs and compromises that public accommodation can require, all in the spirit of moderation, concord and pursuance of the public good. It is a set of ideas and expectations that together I call *public humanism.* While the contours and balance of these tendencies shift historically, through the tradition of Plutarch reception traced here, politics is regulated by an overriding conception of justice, and the public official bound by a commitment to an idea of the public good (of course, understood beyond the confines of a restrictive economist definition and used to invoke what responds best to the needs of the whole) and a conception of the dignified and distinct nature of their role. At the same time, this is subject to expectations of prudential judgement and practical reasoning, all constrained by an understanding of the limits beyond which politics can become noxious and corrupt. This exploration of intellectual history and the evolution of political reflection in England and France 1500–1800 through the lens of Plutarch reception will demonstrate key moments in the development of this ethos of public service as well as key moments of its decline in the eighteenth century.

Three Objectives of the Book

I have three overriding objectives in the writing of this book. At one level it is a contribution to the field of reception studies with a focus on the reception of Plutarch in the history of European political thought. I provide an account of the different ways in which Plutarch's work related to political reflection and was translated into the vernacular languages of French and English from 1500 to 1800 by key thinkers who also wrote essays and treatises on politics. I explore some of the possible links between an interest in and interpretation of Plutarch and broader reflections on politics. Given that a seminal translation of Plutarch was made available in French by Jacques Amyot by the end of the sixteenth century, a work which was subsequently translated into English vernacular by Thomas North, I also explore the work of political theorists who drew from Plutarch's work (and those vernacular translations available to them) after the late sixteenth century. So, this account at the level of reception begins with a story of translation into the vernacular, with a focus on selective translators of the early modern period (with special attention to those who went on to write treatises in the history of political thought). Then, the narrative shifts to explore reception in a slightly different sense, namely the various ways the new canonical translations and subsequent ones were used and cited and interpreted by key thinkers in the history of political thought (broadly conceived) in both France and England. Thus, this book stands partly within more traditional hands-on approaches to classical reception (certainly more than works in the history of political thought have tended to do), and partly within a more general practice of assessing the legacy of classical ideas within the history of political ideas, but with a focus on the work and legacy of Plutarch, and through the theme of the nature of public life.[4]

So why a focus on Plutarch for this study? As any historian of political thought will know, Plutarch is an important resource and reference for key thinkers in the development of the tradition from medieval times to the nineteenth century. Indeed, it has been shown that his work was in circulation more than previous scholarship assumed. The research of Freyja Cox Jensen has helped in the launching of this study, benefitting from more sophisticated research tools offered by initiatives in the digital humanities, including recourse to the new Universal Short Title Catalogue (USTC), and thereby correcting an authoritative picture of the distribution of works of classical historians in early modern Europe.[5] You can see in Figure 1 how her findings regarding the availability of the works of classical historians in early modern Europe challenge the 1966 findings of Peter Burke, findings which had served to guide the field of intellectual history for several decades.[6]

---

[4] Because of my purpose in exploring the development of themes in the history of political thought, traditions largely though not exclusively written up in vernacular languages, I focus less on philological questions of nuanced translation, except in a few key moments where it is of relevance for the theme I am discussing. I do not dwell much on competing theories of translation in various historical periods, nor do I study the life of Plutarch's texts more generally within Latin culture of early modern Europe, significant as it may be. (Thanks to Keith Sidwell for reminding me of the enormous importance of this side of Plutarch reception. Because I focus on references from Plutarch in the history of political thought and in the vernacular, I have not been able to focus on broader commentaries on his thought in Latin. I acknowledge that this detracts from the comprehensiveness of my account, but many rulers in early modern Europe were not well trained in classical languages. As far as the history of political thought is concerned, a vast majority of relevant texts in this regard could be found in vernacular languages.) I will not explore how the reading and study of Plutarch for traditions of political reflection intersect with the reading and study of other ancient authors, such as Xenophon or Lucian, whose centrality in the education and formation of political thinkers in the early modern period has yet to be fully explored. (Thanks goes to Noreen Humble for this very pertinent point. I look forward to her forthcoming work on Xenophon reception. It should be noted that there is a similar pattern with Xenophon as with Plutarch – namely, that a good number of thinkers associated with traditions of political reflection took it upon themselves to translate Xenophon, thereby demonstrating his central importance to their own development as thinkers.) While these questions are of interest, to linger too long in these matters would detract from the specific narrative I am developing here.

[5] Freyja Cox Jensen, "The Popularity of Ancient Historians, 1450–1600," *The Historical Journal* 61.3 (2018), 561–595.

[6] Peter Burke, "A Survey of the Popularity of Ancient Historians, 1450–1700," *History and Theory* 5.2 (1966), 135–152.

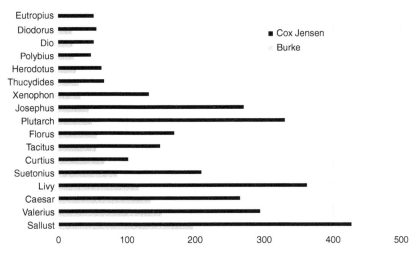

Figure 1 Comparison of Peter Burke and Freyja Cox Jensen on the availability of the works of classical historians 1450–1599
From Freyja Cox Jensen, "The Popularity of Ancient Historians 1450–1600," *The Historical Journal* 61.3 (2018).

As Cox Jensen notes, this Table brings to light three key points: more books of the ancient historians were printed from 1450–1599 than previously acknowledged; Peter Burke's conclusions concerning the ranking in popularity of ancient historians in this period requires serious revision; and there has been severe underestimation of the popularity of several key authors, especially Josephus and Plutarch.[7]

This table does raise some further questions. For example, the line between historical works and more broadly moral works, especially in the cases of Xenophon and Plutarch, is not always clear so that the category of the 'historical' for purposes of this table may be subject to some degree of contention, thereby having an impact on which editions are to be counted and which not. In addition, as in most research drawing from the USTC, there is a great deal of reliance on how the works explored have been catalogued by their home institutions, so that certain variations of method or of accuracy in cataloguing may affect the end results. This is all to say that reliance on the USTC allows the researcher to draw a general picture of broad trends. Regardless, clearly the work of Burke on the matter of the prevalence of editions of ancient historians needs substantial revision and, considering

---

[7] Cox Jensen, "Popularity," 574.

this, the work of Plutarch was clearly much more central to the book collections and to the education of the literate in the early modern period than has previously been accounted for. Of course, the revelation of the *quantitative* presence of Plutarch begs the question of its *qualitative* impact, something this study seeks to address.

Challenges nonetheless emerge in considering the history of political thinking from the perspective of Plutarch's work. These include: Plutarch's debt to a number of earlier political thinkers, including Plato and various Hellenistic philosophers, influences which may at times obscure where the lines of influence are to be drawn in an accurate way; some similar themes among Plutarch and other important classical sources for early modern political thought, including Aristotle, Cicero, Sallust, Tacitus, Xenophon, etc.; certain disputes, some ongoing, concerning whether Plutarch was actually the author of the works and treatises claimed or believed to be written by him in an earlier period; and perhaps most importantly, the myriad ways in which works of his vast corpus were taken up and used in political thinking and justification in early modern thought. Despite these challenges, there is ample reason for the need and significance of such a study. Given the findings of Cox Jensen there is clearly good reason to seek to understand the impact of the pervasiveness of Plutarch in early modern book culture, especially as it pertains to political reflection.

This leads to the second objective of this book: to use the lens or prism of Plutarch to revise our current understandings of the evolution of the history of political thought through the early modern period. At present, there exist competing narratives about the place of classical strands of thought in the development of our political thinking, and these narratives, of course, not only add to our understanding of the past, but also feed into a certain number of dominant accounts of how we should or do under-stand ourselves as moderns in relation to the unfolding of those classical ideas. One approach focuses on the importance of strands of Stoicism, Epicureanism and Scepticism in the development of early modern thought.[8] In their origins, those strands of Hellenistic thought looked to individual self-regulation as the key to moral behaviour often, arguably, with suspicion or at least an attitude of personal indifference towards the

---

[8] Relevant studies (to give very few examples) include Christopher Brooke, *Philosophic Pride. Stoicism and Political Thought from Lipsius to Rousseau* (Princeton, NJ: Princeton University Press, 2012), John Christian Larsen and Gianni Paganini, eds. *Skepticism and Political Thought in the Seventeenth and Eighteenth Centuries* (Toronto: University of Toronto Press, 2015), Jeffrey Edward Green, "Solace for the Frustrations of Silent Citizenship: the Case of Epicureanism," Citizenship Studies, 19.5 (2005), 492–506, Catherine Wilson, *Epicureanism at the Origins of Modernity*, (Oxford: Oxford University Press, 2008).

inherent importance and worth of a life of public service.[9] It is easy to acknowledge strands of anti-politics quite prevalent today that may stem in part from those Hellenistic roots.[10] Another important (and indeed dominant) strand of thinking about the legacy of classical ideas in the history of political thought has been the longstanding focus on republicanism or civic humanism, said to have been inspired by either Aristotelian or Roman thought and inspirational from the Renaissance on for a whole tradition of argument prioritising liberty and collective self-rule.[11] Yet, more recently, James Hankins has questioned the argument that republicanism is the clear legacy of the Italian Renaissance for the history of political thought. He argues convincingly for the overriding thrust of what he calls 'virtue politics' in Italian Renaissance political thought, or the idea that what was most important to those political thinkers was *character* and *not institutions*, focused on education (*paideia*) and the need to promote an attachment to justice in the heart of the rulers and a desire and respect for justice in the ruled.[12]

This project offers a distinct perspective while building on the Hankins argument. Instead of a focus on Italy, I look to both the French and English traditions of political reflection, beginning in 1500 and reaching up to 1800. Also, instead of a broad treatment of all strands of political thought in this period, I focus on those which reflect significant engagement with and interpretation of the work of one classical thinker, namely Plutarch. I argue that his work, at least initially, resounded in French and English political thought in different ways, though both within a broader perspective that could be characterised as virtue politics. However, and here is where I most acutely diverge from Hankins, I argue that the way in which Plutarch was received in the French tradition led at first to a more pointed political reflection, and with a more applied if not realist bent.[13] English thinkers of the sixteenth century received Plutarch as a traditional

---

[9] I will address the central question of Cicero's *On Duties*, much inspired by the Stoic Panaetius in Chapter 1. Cicero's defence of public engagement of course can be seen as an exception to this general characterisation.

[10] For a general discussion of contemporary anti-politics, see Eliane Glaser, *Anti-Politics: On the Demonization of Ideology, Authority and the State* (London: Repeater Books, 2017).

[11] J. G. A. Pocock, *The Machiavellian Moment* (Princeton, NJ: Princeton University Press, 1975), Quentin Skinner, *The Foundations of Modern Political Thought* (Cambridge: Cambridge University Press, 1978).

[12] James Hankins, *Virtue Politics* (Cambridge, MA: Belknap, 2019).

[13] The application of the term 'pragmatic' to characterise Plutarch's *Lives* more generally has been invoked in Susan Jacobs, *Plutarch's Pragmatic Biographies* (Leiden and Boston: Brill, 2018). I do not address in this book the question of the relative weight of moral and pragmatic advice within the *Lives* itself, only sticking to analysis of differential aspects in Plutarch reception.

virtue theorist arguing for good character and a standard account of the
virtues for those with ambitions to serve in public office (much like
Hankins argues for the broad Italian Renaissance project). However, the
reception of Plutarch in the French case offered distinct twists on this
approach. French Renaissance thinkers, as shaped by Plutarch reception,
developed an awareness of the unique status of the public figure, meaning
not only that the moral challenges of public office were greater and more
significant, but also that the very nature of the public sphere affected how
the virtues were to be understood. We see in the French case of the
sixteenth century, with greater focus on the *Lives*, either a strong tendency
to celebrate the singular achievements of Plutarch's subjects as heroes in
a category of their own (so treating the classical source as encomium to
serve the cause of emergent absolutism), transforming the critical reflection
on character, or using the text to shed light on the features and challenges
of public responsibility. In both cases, French reflection invoked a logic of
public uniqueness, of public persona or of public office, as a lens through
which Plutarch's lessons for public life were filtered and understood.

To some degree we could envisage Plutarch's sixteenth-century legacy as
triple. The English focus exclusively on virtue politics was matched by
a French tendency to consider public life as driven by unique and specific
norms along with considerations of virtue. In effect, French political
reflection as engaging with Plutarch combined a need for an overall
commitment to justice with attention to the special context of public life
that could impact the application of traditional virtues. At times this could
shift into yet another form which came to elevate Plutarch's subjects to the
level of heroes – that is, as objects of admiration and public emulation. The
broad set of ideas focused on the unique ethos of public life as articulated
through the tradition inspired by Plutarch is what I call *public humanism*.

Given this depiction, it may become clearer how this project seeks to
shed new light on the existing narratives in the evolution of early modern
French and English political thought. There are strands of political reflection in the French and English context drawing inspiration from the work
of Plutarch and acknowledging the importance of public life as well as
the norms, ethos and demands specific to it. For many of the French
thinkers I explore in this work, a commitment to justice was not *sufficient*
as a guarantee of good politics because certain knowledge of the nature
of public life was also thought to be required to be effective. Being in
a position of political power and responsibility brought into play various
considerations of expectations, duty, perception and attributions that all
had an impact on how one should act. However, I argue that despite

attention to the uniqueness of public life and responsibility, French thinkers drawing on Plutarch differed from both Machiavellian and reason of state thinking partly through considerations of the inner life of the public figure (including their motivation and justifications) and thus by not fully replacing the language of virtue with that of utility or effectiveness. In other words, while the public sphere was treated as a unique realm with its own specific norms and ethos, the goals of public action were still dictated by an overriding need to pursue justice (rather than solely ambition or maintaining the state or staying in office) and a concern for the public good with no blurring between the goals, practices, and motivations of the good political leader and that of the tyrant. The major thrust of my argument is that Plutarch served as a source through which early modern political thinkers could reflect on very practical questions of virtue politics in their application. Plutarch brought to traditions of later political reflection an idiom through which a certain form of virtuous prudence, tailored to the specific needs and challenges of public life, became apparent to early modern readers, especially as the intended audience grew. And while, as we will see, the thrust and significance of this idiom shifted in stages of reception – focusing at times on the virtuous character of the ruler or the need for an overriding commitment to the public good, and at others on the ways in which the specific nature of the public sphere shifted prudential application of the virtues, or on the need to avoid the greatest evil of political life, namely tyranny – all are unified by recourse to Plutarch as a source of both moral theory and example and by an overriding concern to balance considerations of pursuit of the good, the avoidance of tyranny, and a thoughtful exercise of prudence and a sense of pragmatic reason in the development of a model for political rule and advice. To put it another way, it is possible through Plutarch to envisage the distinct nature of relations in the public sphere and the way in which norms and rules apply without having to collapse into reason of state thinking.

Some might ask why Plutarch as a source and not Cicero? Despite some of the overlap in themes (an issue that I will address more systematically in Chapter 1), I am suggesting that there is a uniqueness to the tradition stemming from Plutarch, most evident in the French tradition of reception, which allows for insights not possible with a focus on Cicero. Part of my case lies with the dynamic of transmission and reception in the French case, and part on the substance or emphasis of the theory. There is no doubt that Cicero was an important inspiration in both the English and French context, and that his work was both widely available in Latin and read by all with formal education in the classics. Indeed there is no doubt

that his work was more broadly available in the Latin culture of early
modern Europe than that of most Greek thinkers, barring Plato and
Aristotle.[14] Still, Plutarch was also an author of choice for translation
into vernacular French by a long list of French political thinkers and
intellectuals in a way unmatched in the case of Cicero, at least for the
sixteenth century. Further, Plutarch's vernacular reception in the French
case has an early trajectory that was largely unmet in England. This is
significant because while the educated public often were immersed in
Cicero, the French monarchs of the Renaissance did not read Latin well,
as their education was focused on state and military matters. Thus, French
vernacular translations of Plutarch were often first completed by political
theorists for rulers who did not have the skills for ready access to works of
political reflection in Latin. Seyssel and Budé worked on translations of
Plutarch (and not Cicero) so that they could be read to the king and court,
to offer them direct instruction in matters of state. Only later were these
translations issued in published form for a broader public. Subsequently
the published vernacular translations ensured the circulation of these ideas
beyond the usual circles where education in Latin was a given, opening
access to literate noble women for example. So, Plutarch's work appeared
in the early sixteenth century in France as a popular source of stately advice
for those in close association with the king and court.

In addition, Plutarch's work offered an array of historical examples
speaking to a need for practical advice and provided a set of observations
based on experience rather than deductive reasoning. Plutarch also offered
deeper analysis of the various aspects of moral psychology associated with
the challenges of governance. While Cicero's *On Duties* was couched in
loose Stoic principles, Plutarch offered a more emotionally engaged model
of political action and stewardship. It may be these features which help to
account for a continued resonance of Plutarch in the French tradition, as
we will see, with a figure like Montaigne confessing greater attachment to
the work of Plutarch over that of Cicero.

I suggest in the early chapters that Plutarch was read differently in the
early modern English and French traditions of political reflection. In the
case of England, Plutarch is predominantly taken to be a moralist, with few

---

[14] See, for example, William Altman, ed., *Brill's Companion to the Reception of Cicero* (Leiden: Brill,
2015); Daniel J. Kapust and Gary Remer, eds., *The Ciceronian Tradition in Political Theory*
(Madison: University of Wisconsin Press, 2020); Quentin Skinner, *Hobbes and Republican Liberty*
(Cambridge: Cambridge University Press, 2008); Quentin Skinner, *Machiavelli* (Oxford: Oxford
University Press, 2019); Catherine Steel, ed., *The Cambridge Companion to the Reception of Cicero*
(Cambridge: Cambridge University Press, 2013);

direct lessons for political life, although there were some rather awkward exceptions to this rule. I surmise, then, that in terms of a narrower form of political reflection, the presence of Cicero is singularly dominant in early modern English political thought. The case of French political thought of the sixteenth century is somewhat distinct.

Plutarch stood as an ancient Greek thinker and moralist through whom a certain amount of Roman history was filtered for early modern readers, meaning that his presentation of key players in the drama of Roman politics tamed those examples to a degree, largely due to the moralist lens through which they were explored. Still, in terms of political life, there was also a realist dimension to Plutarch's treatment, a tone that was filtered into later European reception. Plutarch reception gave rise to a vision which offered careful adjudication of the need for an understanding of the good, the necessity of prudence, an insight into the practical or pragmatic, and a vision of bad politics to know where to draw the line between the acceptable and the unacceptable in public life. A focus on Plutarch reception in the history of ideas helps to highlight themes concerning the nature of public life, the importance of civic duty and public service, as well as the relation between morality and politics, and in ways not fully or accurately presented if we rely solely on narratives highlighting other aspects of the legacy of classical traditions in early modern thought.

Thus, this narrative offers an alternative to civic humanist and republican readings of the history of early modern political thought, including Eric Nelson's account of the legacy of Greek philosophy in early modern political reflection.[15] While it builds on the important contributions of both J. G. A. Pocock and Quentin Skinner, through the lens of Plutarch we can also see ways in which those pictures of the evolution of early modern political thought may require further precision or qualification.[16] My argument in this book suggests that there was an ongoing conversation in early modern Europe concerning the nature and ethos of public life separate from both civic humanism or the life of citizens – as it was linked to strands of Aristotelianism or neo-Roman thought – and from constitutionalism often drawing resources from Roman law.[17] In more general terms, my contention is that previous accounts have privileged Anglo-American traditions and their links to currents of Italian Renaissance

---

[15] Eric Nelson, *The Greek Tradition in Republican Thought* (Cambridge: Cambridge University Press, 2004).

[16] Pocock, *Machiavellian Moment*; Skinner, *Foundations*.

[17] On constitutional traditions as related to the history of European political thought, see Benjamin Straumann, *Crisis and Constitutionalism* (Oxford: Oxford University Press, 2016).

humanism but have missed the unique aspects of the French tradition. By exploring Plutarch reception in the French context in the Renaissance offering a contrast with that of England at least through the early part of the sixteenth century, and by showing how those aspects of reflection concerning politics informed by Plutarch were subsequently taken into traditions of political reflection in England (partly in the wake of Jacques Amyot's translations), I will demonstrate how reflection on the special ethos and nature of relations within a public realm became a key focus for traditions of early modern political thought. This strand of thinking distinguishes itself from both civic humanism and constitutionalism. Focus on the distinct nature of the public sphere and the public realm does not offer substantial consideration of a better form of regime structure (or of how to align social and military interests and political power), nor of the preferred nature of fundamental law, nor indeed provides an argument for liberty as the supreme political value, rather it accentuates the spirit in which public power is exercised alongside a consideration of its own moral and psychological dynamics. It emphasises neither citizens, nor legal and judicial infrastructure, but instead the power and responsibilities of the public servant and the norms, ethics and responsibilities associated with them, acknowledging a certain spirit of prudence and pragmatism that abjured both moral absolutism as well as the corrupt politics of tyranny and domination lacking any conception of the good. My contention is that there is a long tradition of reflection on these aspects of politics that have remained somewhat obscured by reigning paradigms in the history of ideas and that a focus on Plutarch and Plutarch reception allows us to reconsider that history and recognise additional resources available to early modern political theorists.

A third objective of this work is to reflect on the theoretical space between the idea that public life is about the reaching of a singular moral ideal and the notion that any moral purposes in public life are not only anachronistic but can lead to tyrannical practice. We might call moral absolutism an approach that does not acknowledge some of the uniquely demanding dilemmas of public life and which assumes a singular maxim or set of principles applied consistently through all human relations as a guarantee of goodness and ethical propriety. Michael Walzer demonstrated in a seminal article the ways in which this stance does not do justice to some of the specific moral challenges presented by public life.[18] An

---

[18] Michael Walzer, "Political Action: The Problem of Dirty Hands," *Philosophy & Public Affairs*, 2.2 (Winter, 1973), 160–180.

alternative to moral absolutism in conceptualising the place of morality in politics is that which holds the public realm to be so unique and its demands so esoteric, that any effective conception of justice is beholden to the ability of the ruler and the state to establish and maintain order. It tends to be driven by a politics of crisis and driven by a logic of political survival. So, in contrast to the public official largely occupied by consequences and effectual outcomes, I place an emphasis on the public official who not only has in mind constantly a sense of the better as well as the morally deficient, alongside a sense of prudence and certain pragmatism, but who also has cultivated sensibilities towards the complex moral psychology of political life both among peers as well as in relation to the public, and is aware of the emotional costs of policy choices. Such sensitivities are crucial for informing judgement because they indicate what persons and the public are capable of and how principles meet the real contours and limits of public life. In the tradition informed by a reading of Plutarch, personalities and moral sensitivities do matter and the political challenge consists in part in seeking to pursue justice and the public welfare in a sphere where the parameters of this are not always easily discernible. The unique contribution of Plutarch is not only a focus on the specific nature of public life, but an emphasis on both the complex psychological and moral considerations in relation to it.

I would hope that my account offers new and helpful insights into the broader story of the reception of Plutarch's work overall in the development of European ideas. My ambition here, however, is not to provide a fully comprehensive account of Plutarch reception in France and England with regard to vernacular translations, but rather to provide an account of one strand of Plutarch reception that was particularly significant for the development of political thinking overall in the European context. I also seek to offer a broad narrative that allows for a more accurate understanding of the evolution of political thought in the early modern period, one that revises our current understandings of the main currents of reflection.

Nuances and Shifts in the Tradition of Plutarch Reception: A Broad Overview

Scholars rarely read Plutarch anymore, and this may account for why his place in the history of ideas has been often neglected. It could be suggested that what constituted the strength and the appeal of Plutarch's work throughout the Renaissance and the early modern period is precisely what explains the relative weakness and neglect of his work today, namely the eclecticism of his work and the challenge of classifying it. While he wrote histories, or at least 'lives' (βιοί), Plutarch is not an historian's historian (Thucydides was more often deemed to be closer to the desired model of the historian in the eighteenth and nineteenth centuries) and while he wrote moral essays, he is not a philosopher's philosopher. The appeal of his work in the past is precisely his ability to bring the two together, to allow ethical frameworks and considerations to infuse his study of key historical figures and events, and to consider ethical issues in the context of their application, whether as approaches to be taught or matters to be discussed, or reconciled, such as the ethical demands of distinct spheres of friendship and public life. While the breadth of his work (and the sheer physical mass of his extant corpus) does constitute a challenge to the contemporary scholar seeking to trace his place in the history of ideas (which perhaps only a lifelong scholar of Plutarch could fully command), this breadth allows one to trace a complex pattern of cultural appropriation that can perhaps do better justice in capturing significant twists and turns in the development of European thought.

In thematic terms, a central challenge in reading Plutarch and in exploring the reception of his work in early modern and modern thought is the need to come to terms with the notion of the 'public' and its ethical priority. While espousing a basic 'virtue ethic' framework it is also clear that for Plutarch public service takes on an ethical importance for even less-than-perfect regimes in a way unmatched in the work of Plato and Aristotle. Perhaps surprisingly, Plutarch's own plea for public spiritedness was voiced at a time (for a first century CE Greek living under Roman dominion) when opportunities were few and fragile. In traditions of early modern reception, Plutarch's work included competing depictions of public life. The following account of these differences and shifts draws on a number of factors, including the motivations ideally required for effective public service (self-interest, honour, glory or duty), the parameters for defining what constitutes good public action, the question of whether public action is a form of theatre or a realm of deeper authenticity for the subject, the particular ethical questions specific to action in the public realm, the place of critical thought and contestation in conceptualising the public, the way to differentiate between public status and power, and the ethical questions of the relation of public action to other fields of human life.

As I demonstrate in Part II, while earlier theorists taking up Plutarch appeared to be quite optimistic about the ways in which well-intentioned rulers could negotiate the good, the prudent and the practical in public life, by the late 1500s many taking up these themes were more sceptical about how this fine balance might play out in practice. Thus, for example, Montaigne (and Shakespeare following him) was much more pessimistic about the possibilities of good politics, though not abjuring the public realm and the need for well-intentioned action altogether. In Part III we see much more loose appropriation of Plutarch's thought, especially in eighteenth-century France, with interpretation often tethered to either a more dogmatic moralism or doctrines of utility. One could characterise these latter appropriations of Plutarch as the decline of the tradition of political humanism found earlier in France. Why decline? Because they tend to deny the specificity of the public realm and the more situated and context dependent types of prudential reasoning associated with it.

This book looks to Plutarch and his legacy in the history of political thought to portray a tradition that does not forgo the idea of a public good and the personal qualities needed to further it, but develops and refines its meaning through the course of interpretation and appropriation. What I seek to explore through this account is an evolving and complex tradition that comes to grips with an understanding of the particular qualities of public life while at the same time acknowledging, short of a model of philosophical perfection, the skill, character and disposition required to fulfil those offices properly. An ethos of commitment to a deeper under-standing and practice of public good, even at a cost to private tranquillity, can be seen to issue historically in part from engagement with Plutarch's work.

The ethos of public life and public service discussed in this book applies broadly. While initially relevant to rulers as explored in Renaissance polit-ical treatises invoking Plutarch and written expressly for kings, later theor-ists of public life invoked the theme of public service via Plutarch to apply to a wider range of state officials and public activities. This narrative, or genealogy, serves as a background from which to understand the historical origins and development from the early modern period to the aspects of contemporary norms that frame ongoing discussions of public service delivery.[19] Indeed, it could be suggested that the salience of efficiency, fairness, responsiveness and respect, which have been deemed to character-ise the delivery of public service in the modern era, are grounded in a deeper set of concepts which set the activity of public service apart

---

[19] See for example, Bernardo Zacka, *When the State Meets the Street* (Cambridge MA: Harvard University Press, 2017) and Michael Lewis, *The Fifth Risk* (New York: Norton, 2018).

from other forms of activity.[20] This book looks at some of the early modern roots of public service as an activity best suited to pursue the public good along with reflection on other ethical norms unique to it.

Summary of the Chapters

The work explores the traditions of reception chronologically while going back and forth between the English and French traditions. In Part I, I lay the foundations for the analysis. Chapter 1 provides a brief and general introduction to Plutarch for those who have little or no previous knowledge of his work. I identify main lines of interpretation of his work from the secondary literature and offer an overview of a few key *Lives* that play an important role in reception. I also offer an analysis of the distinct nature of Plutarch's contributions in relation to Cicero.

Chapter 2 is a prelude to the main account of reception but offers some analysis of the first great reference to Plutarch in the post-classical world in John of Salisbury's *Policraticus* (c. 1159). Despite the apocryphal nature of John's Plutarch, the association of Plutarch as tutor to Emperor Trajan was a trope which did a great deal to provide greater weight to the authority of Plutarch's writing in the subsequent history of political thought. In the latter part of this chapter, I provide a brief synopsis of a couple of essays ("On Homer" and "On the Education of Children") which are now deemed as apocryphal but which for many early modern scholars formed a legitimate part of Plutarch's corpus. I discuss how we should consider these texts in the context of a history of Plutarch reception.

Part II begins with Chapters 3 and 4 offering a study of the first printed vernacular translations of Plutarch's work in French with special attention paid to political thought. After an initial discussion of the 1530 translation of Plutarch's essay *Precepts of Statecraft* by the Royal Printer Geoffroy Tory (c. 1480–1533), a translation which invokes the French term of *la chose publique* in relation to Plutarch's idea of politics, I explore Plutarch translations in the French context by scholars who went on to draft important treatises in political theory, namely Claude de Seyssel (1450–1520) and Guillaume Budé (1467–1540). I also explore some of Antoine du Saix's (c. 1504–1579) translations of Erasmus's (1466–1536) Latin translations of Plutarch's *Apophthegmata* (or *Sayings of Kings and Commanders*) here shedding light on an important dialogue among these

---

[20] These are the norms invoked by Zacka in *When the State Meets the Street*, chap. 3.

thinkers regarding the specific and unique nature of public life with reference to Plutarch's work.

Through this study I develop an account of four key features characterising this French Renaissance understanding of the specificity of public life forged in part through an engagement with Plutarch's work, a set of features that together constitute what I call *public humanism*: (1) a concern with a mode of governance, focusing on how to govern, rather than a language of citizenship (or concerning who governs), with greater emphasis on *la chose publique* as the target or object of public action, and advocacy for the French vernacular as a new tool of political communication; (2) an emphasis on the particulars of political prudence and on how to conduct oneself in public life (rather than on the concept of *libertas* that justifies participation) with discussion surrounding appropriate models or examples of political rule; (3) attention to the important and unique psychological considerations for a person holding public office both in terms of relationships with peers and other public officials as well as relationships with the public at large, and how these considerations come into play with a realistic appreciation and consideration of the important ethical challenges of public office. This includes reflection on the relationship between prudence and the other virtues (the arguments generated in the case of French Renaissance humanism often acknowledge the very special demands of public office); (4) an importance of history that often stresses the specificity of the French context distinguishing it from both ancient Roman and contemporary Italian traditions, and which celebrates the historical legacy of the Gauls.

Chapter 5 explores the distinct dynamics of Plutarch reception in England prior to the famous 1579–1603 translations of Thomas North (1535–1604). I suggest that in England at this time Plutarch's work was read largely through a Ciceronian lens that looked solely to the motivation and character of the public official for good political outcomes (rather than a focus on the nature of public office which was predominant in the French case). I reflect on the vernacular translations of Plutarch's moral essays by Thomas Wyatt (1503–1542), Thomas Elyot (1490–1546), Thomas Blundeville (1522–1606), Richard Taverner and Queen Elizabeth I (1533–1603) as well as explore the place of Plutarch in Thomas More's *Utopia* (1516). I argue here that prior to the translations of Thomas North, Plutarch was read predominantly in England as a thinker whose political insights were secondary to his moral ones. I also demonstrate how the Plutarch translated by Erasmus took on a different face in the vernacular in France and England at this time. There were distinct patterns in the way

Erasmus's Latin translations of Plutarch were subsequently translated into
French and English respectively. While the increasing precariousness of the
English realm into the latter sixteenth century changed the tone of political
thought to a certain degree, the English never read their Plutarch in the
vernacular with the same attention to the nature of public office and the
public realm in the way prevalent in France earlier in the century.

Chapter 6 continues an account of the reception of Plutarch's work in
the mid- to late sixteenth century in France with reference to the translation work and political reflection of figures including Georges de Selve
(1508–1541) (now famous as one of the figures in Holbein's famous painting
"The Ambassadors"). The latter part of the chapter discusses what is
perhaps the best-known moment of Plutarch reception, the French vernacular translations of the *Lives* (1559–1565) and *Moralia* (1572) by Jacques
Amyot (1513–1593). I discuss how the advent of the Wars of Religion (1562–
1598) in France affected the themes through which Plutarch was received
and read in Renaissance France, partly through an examination of the
paratext of Amyot's translations in the late sixteenth century. I also explore
Jean Bodin's (1530–1596) discussion of the reliability of Plutarch as a source
as noted in his *Method for the Easy Comprehension of History*.

Chapter 7 examines Plutarch translations by Du Haillan and offers
a discussion of strands of Montaigne's (1533–1592) political thought given
the importance of Plutarch on its development.

Part III begins with Chapter 8 where I explore key moments of the
reception of Plutarch in England of the sixteenth and seventeenth centuries. I look at key aspects of the resonance of Plutarch in the work of Francis
Bacon (1561–1626). I also discuss the significance of Philemon Holland's
(1552–1637) translation of Plutarch's essay "How to Profit from your
Enemies." I show how this essay (which Hobbes of course could read in
the original Greek and Latin translations but could also consult in
Holland's version) can shed new light on Hobbes' *Leviathan* (1651).

Chapter 9 discusses the use of Plutarch in drama understood as
a mode of political reflection. I provide a brief analysis of the political
implications of Shakespeare's (1564–1616) famous use of Plutarch in
a series of plays devoted to key figures of the classical era. I explore how
Shakespeare's depiction of public life shifted between his first Roman play
Titus Andronicus, deemed to have been written before his close study of
North's translations of Plutarch, and his latter plays focused on key Greek
and Roman historical figures (*Timon of Athens, Coriolanus, Julius Caesar*
and *Antony and Cleopatra*) for which his use of North is heavily documented and discussed. I then explore political themes and argument

stemming from Plutarch and as relayed through Pierre Corneille's *Pompée* and Jean Racine's *Mithridate*.

Chapter 10 studies the broad contours of Plutarch's place in political argument in English and Irish thinkers of the later seventeenth and early eighteenth centuries, including the significance of the Dryden translation and the work of Jonathan Swift.

Chapter 11 studies the evolution of Plutarch reception in political reflection with a focus on three important figures of the French Enlightenment: the Abbé de Saint-Pierre (1658–1743), the Abbé Mably (1709–1785) and Jean-Jacques Rousseau (1712–1778). Rousseau is the culminating figure in my study, and Plutarch's place in Rousseau's political reflection is a highly complicated one. Rousseau's encounter with Plutarch not only shaped his intellectual development and the content of many features of his moral and political philosophy, it also, as he recounts in *The Confessions*, played a role in his own emerging sense of self as a child and the formation of some of his basic moral intuitions. Indeed, it could be suggested that Rousseau's broader intellectual project was developed on the pillars derived from fundamental Plutarchan tenets of moral education in virtue, exemplarity as a central aspect of moral thinking, and political right as the pursuit of justice and the common good. I explore the ways in which Rousseau's knowledge of Plutarch had a profound impact on elements of his thought. In a concluding section to the chapter, I also demonstrate, partly in dialogue with contemporary scholarship on Rousseau in political theory, how Rousseau's political vision as developed in the *Social Contract* can be regarded in certain ways as a turning away from the ideas of public humanism with which Plutarch's work was associated in the period covered by my overall analysis in this book.

In my conclusion, I pull together various threads of the account and provide a restatement of what I see as the most significant findings of my account and the implications of this new attention to arguments in our traditions focusing on the specific qualities of the public realm.

For those who think that Plutarch and Plutarch's legacy may have nothing to say to us because history has already had its say on these matters or because all the past is tainted, I can do no more than cite the authority of Francis Bacon on the need to revisit the past:

> Another error . . . is a conceit that of former opinions or sects, after variety and examination, the best hath still prevailed and suppressed the rest . . . . . .
> [T]ime seemeth to be of the nature of a river or stream, which carrieth down

to us that which is light and blown up, and sinketh and drowneth that which is weighty and solid.[21]

In the spirit of Bacon, we go mudlarking and seek to uncover the 'solid and weighty' that may have become hidden in the flow of intellectual history.

---

[21] Francis Bacon, "The Advancement of Learning," in Brian Vickers ed., *The Major Works* (Oxford: Oxford University Press, 1992), 145.

PART I

Setting the Stage

A Brief Introduction to Plutarch and a Comparison of Cicero and Plutarch on Public Ethics

Plutarch (c. 45–120 CE) is rarely referred to or read today among political theorists, despite his towering presence as a reference in the history of ideas and in political thought. This chapter serves as an overview of his work as relevant for the themes of this book.

The chapter is divided into three sections. In the first section, I discuss Plutarch's life and work in the general context of the first century CE. Following this, I provide a short analysis of six of Plutarch's *Lives*, Lycurgus, Numa, Alexander, Caesar, Antony and Phocion, to demonstrate some of the key themes highlighted by scholars of his thought, and to introduce readers to some accounts which figure among the most prominent as references in Western intellectual traditions.[1] In the concluding section, I offer a comparison and contrast of Cicero's *On Duties*, and the themes of Plutarch's *Lives* and a few of his moral essays devoted to questions of public life to highlight what distinguishes Plutarch's contribution and to signal what could be identified as his unique contribution to traditions of political reflection on public life and public service.

Apart from Plutarch's moral essays directly offering advice to those in public life, I leave discussion and broad summary of other of his moral essays for the subsequent chapters in this book. In the course of intellectual history, while the arguments of the moral essays have tended to offer an earnest articulation of Plutarch's stance, the *Lives* have been used in a much more varied way. Those having recourse to Plutarch for arguments in

---

[1] Of course, the six selected for summary here do not exhaust the list of those lives most read and referred to throughout the early modern period. Martha Shackford suggests that the most popular of Plutarch's *Lives* during the Renaissance were the following: Alexander, Lycurgus, Caesar, Brutus, Antony, Pompey, Cicero, the two Cato's, Marius and Sulla. See her *Plutarch in Renaissance England* (Wellesley, MA: Wellesley College, 1929), 8. Here the Roman lives garner more attention than the Greek, but part of this was due to intense interest in the period of the late Republic and early principate. Going into the seventeenth century there was interest in themes of civil religion leading to greater attention to the life of Numa, and the French of the eighteenth century saw special value in the life of Phocion who represented an independent-minded public figure.

political thought have tended to read his *Lives* as a collection of anecdotes to be chosen at random without a great deal of attention to or reflection on the broader import of the work from which they were taken. This may be related in part, as we will see, to Plutarch's own reticence in spelling out in the most obvious terms the lessons of his *Lives* to encourage the active reflection of his readers. Still, what this more sophisticated literary device meant in practice is that his works have often been harnessed by competing schools and arguments.

In the *Lives* Plutarch often engages in what critics have called 'descriptive' or 'exploratory' moralism, that is, offering a description of the moral psychology of subjects to reveal general facets of human behaviour without providing the precise moral lesson for readers. This allows readers to reflect independently on the material, and to work the lesson out for themselves. However, many traditions of reception provide a much more explicit account of the lesson they wish to draw from the *Lives* as a means to guide conduct, engaging in what has been called 'protreptic' or 'expository' moralism.[2] And while the latter does appear in parts of Plutarch's work including the *Lives*, material from the *Lives* in the process of reception has often been distilled more readily by either an unrepresentative focus on those passages where counsel appears to be more explicit, or by adapting and interpreting matters of descriptive moralist import in a more packaged form of moral precept.

It is also the case that in this process of selection and appropriation in reception, certain writings of Plutarch figure more prominently than others. Throughout this book, I focus on writings that appear more frequently and consistently in Plutarch reception. In broad terms that set includes lives of the founders and great reformers in the ancient history of the various regimes of Greece and Rome, key Roman officials at the time of the decline of the republic and the founding of the principate, and a selection of moral essays focused on questions of character and moral psychology as well as on public life.

In this chapter, I present select *Lives* drawing on conventional readings as discussed by scholars today to provide a background for the reader and many historians of political thought for whom Plutarch is relatively new.

---

[2] On the distinction between descriptive and protreptic moralism in Plutarch, see Christopher Pelling, "The Moralism of Plutarch's Lives," in D. Innes, H. Hine and C. B. R. Pelling eds., *Ethics and Rhetoric. Classical Essays for Donald Russell on his Seventy-Fifth Birthday* (Oxford: Oxford University Press, 1995), 205–220, reprinted in Christopher Pelling, *Plutarch and History: Eighteen Studies* (London: Classical Press of Wales, 2002 and 2011).

This background in turn serves as a context for the ways in which the text was put to new uses in reception and appropriation.

1.1 Who was Plutarch? An Introduction to his Life and the *Lives* and *Moralia* for the Uninitiated

What we know of Plutarch's life comes largely from what he chose to tell his readers through fleeting references in his works. As Plutarch was averse to self-congratulation, as Lamberton tells us, he does not offer us many clues.[3] Born almost mid-way into the first century, he spent most of his life in Chaeronea, a town which was famous for a battle that helped to determine the fate of the Greeks vis-à-vis the growing power of Macedonia under Philip II, Alexander the Great's father. By Plutarch's time, roughly 400 years later, Chaeronea was largely a backwater and subject to the imperial force of Rome (rather than Macedonia). Plutarch travelled in elite circles in the community, working in public administration in various capacities. He hosted dinner parties with leading members of the community in his home, as is evident from his dialogue "Table Talk" which was inspired by those gatherings.

We do not know a great deal about Plutarch's public activities. He tells us that he chose to stay in Chaeronea for most of his life (so as not to make it even smaller than it already was, as he tells us with his tongue firmly in his cheek). Yet we also know that he travelled to Athens and to Rome where he was granted citizenship.[4] As a young man Plutarch had access to the social circles of those with power and influence, possibly attending the Isthmian games where the Roman emperor, Nero, acknowledged the autonomy of Greece under Rome, and later it is thought that he embarked on a diplomatic mission to Alexandria.[5] Plutarch's friendships with L. Mestrius Florus, a prominent Roman Senator and friend of the emperor Vespasian, as well as Sosius Senecio, attest to his social networks including notable members of the Roman Imperial order (we know of his connection to these men because Plutarch travelled with Florus to the north of Italy and he dedicated *Table Talk* and the *Lives* to Senecio). In addition, starting

---

[3] Robert Lamberton, *Plutarch* (New Haven, CT: Yale University Press, 2001), 12.

[4] For a good overview of Plutarch's life and his interactions with the Romans, see Philip Stadter, "Plutarch and Rome," in Mark Beck ed., *A Companion to Plutarch*, (London: Wiley Blackwell, 2014), 13–31.

[5] Philip Stadter, "Plutarch: Diplomat for Delphi?" in Lukas de Blois et al. eds., *The Statesman in Plutarch's Works. Vol. 1: Plutarch's Statesman and his Aftermath* (Leiden and Boston: Brill, 2014), 22. See also C. P. Jones, *Plutarch and Rome* (Oxford: Oxford University Press, 1971).

c. 92 CE he spent many years in Delphi as a priest of Apollo, which brought other public responsibilities, including a seat on the Amphictyonic Council (a gathering of regional representatives to oversee the keeping of the temple). By this point in history an appointment at Delphi may have been no more than a mark of elite status and social respect since the oracle had long been silent. Indeed, it is suggested that his connections in Rome may have helped to sway certain decisions in Delphi's favour and to bring new construction projects to the site.[6] Later in his life he received an honorific title from the Emperor Trajan giving him consular rank and privileges.[7]

The single most important pervasive contextual fact of Plutarch's era, as noted by Lamberton, was the "pax Romana" or the dominance of Rome.[8] And while this gave the Greeks some modicum of self-government, there were also clear limits as to what could be demanded and asserted by individual Greek city states. The constraints in place due to the power of Rome over its territories were compounded by a wavering and sometime uncertain status of philosophy and philosophising vis-à-vis Roman Imperial rule. During the years of the Flavian dynasty (69–96 CE), when Plutarch was in his mid-twenties to early fifties, many Hellenistic thinkers and their disciples were either exiled or executed for their opposition to imperial rule.[9] In this context Plutarch reflected and wrote on a broad number of topics as well as on the lives and moral psychology of a large array of statesmen and generals of Greco-Roman heritage. The broader aim was educating his readers, often political elites, in the appropriate questions and terms by which to adjudicate character and moral development. To a degree he was also coming to terms with the complex identity of Greeks at that time who looked to their specific ethnic historical past with a degree of pride, and who acknowledged themselves to be part of a broader Greco-Roman world or classical *oikoumene*.[10] His writing, it would appear, gave him a greater reputation in his own time than his administrative and political roles. A compilation of his extant essays has been handed down to posterity through a later collection now known as the *Moralia*, and most of what has survived from his studies of historical figures has been relayed

---

[6] Stadter, "Plutarch: Diplomat," 29.   [7] Stadter, "Plutarch and Rome," 20.

[8] Lamberton, *Plutarch*, 2.

[9] See John Penwill, "Expelling the Mind: Politics and Philosophy in Flavian Rome," in A. J. Boyle and W. J. Dominik eds., *Flavian Rome. Culture, Image, Text* (Leiden: Brill, 2003), 345–368.

[10] See Rebecca Preston, "Roman Questions, Greek Answers: Plutarch and the Construction of Identity," in Simon Goldhill ed., *Being Greek Under Rome* (Cambridge: Cambridge University Press, 2001).

to us under the title the *Lives* or *Parallel Lives*. Despite the extensive nature of both these works, it is thought that they represent only about a half of what Plutarch produced as a scholar.[11] In terms of literary categories, Plutarch's life and work are often acknowledged as lying the cusp of a movement called the Second Sophistic which celebrated and sought to revive in certain ways the robust rhetorical culture of fifth- century BCE Athens.[12]

Plutarch considered himself a Platonist and a great number of his works fall within the broader genre of moral philosophy, with a concern for central questions of how to live, the quality of one's soul and the nature of the virtues. But while Plato's moral theory is often thought to present a complicated and sometimes tangential relation to the politics of his time by virtue of an overriding metaphysical framework, Plutarch's recourse to historical examples and public figures in discussion of the virtues suggests a more straightforward account of the direct applicability of Platonic virtue theory to politics. This is evident in at least three ways: that the public figure as known and visible offered a common cultural reference for identifying and discussing the virtues; that the public figure, or at least one worthy of admiration, was generally regarded as part of a cultural elite which prided itself on a type of education through *paideia* through which virtuous conduct was promoted; and that the public figure had special responsibilities including those of promoting virtue and justice among the populace.[13] This applied even if Plutarch's chosen examples were drawn from the past rather than the present. It is perhaps easier to discern general themes of Platonism that are distilled throughout Plutarch's work, includ-ing a broad attachment to virtue ethics as developed through a particular form of education, a standard for judging public life according to its ability to bring about moral outcomes, and a vision of philosophy and the intellectual life that surpasses ends of self-regulation to include social and political goals. What is more difficult is to identify the precise ways in which Plutarch's sensibilities take up Platonic themes to make them his own. Still, what is evident is that Plutarch is more interested in past Greek and Roman cultural tradition than Plato gave evidence of (it is difficult, for instance, to think of Plato embarking on the writing of *Lives*), and that

---

[11] M. J. Edwards, *Plutarch. The Lives of Pompey, Caesar and Cicero* (London: Bristol Classical Press, 2003), 1.

[12] For an overview of the movement, see Tim Whitmarsh, *The Second Sophistic* (Cambridge: Cambridge University Press, 2005).

[13] The classic work on the evolution of the idea of *paideia* in the classical world is Werner Jaeger, *Paideia: The Ideals of Greek Culture* (Oxford: Basil Blackwell, 1939).

Plutarch has a fascination for earthly particulars such as individual actors and public figures in a way unmatched by Plato. One might say that while Plato was focused on the nature of the human soul, Plutarch was concerned with souls in the plural, that is, in the various manifestations and permutations of the earthly presence of humanity in the face of Plato's eternal ideal. What this also entails for Plutarch is a much more complex and variegated analysis of both positive and negative traits of individual and collective psychology.

1.2   A Brief Overview of Six Lives

A recent study suggests that Plutarch was a champion of the Spartan way of life, and that the highest praise Plutarch offers is to his Spartan heroes.[14] In this section, I contest that reading and offer readers an introduction to his work of moral biography. Plutarch does not champion any one individual or actual regime wholeheartedly, although he does acknowledge that some lives are better lived than others. As a Platonist, he harbours an ideal of human development and behaviour that would appear never to have been met. In addition, given his affinities with Aristotle, he does not look for human virtue or perfection in the exercise of just one quality, such as honour (*philotimia*), but in a complex balance of virtues and moral capacities, with praise of both moderation and humanity. He approaches the study of human behaviour and history with great insight into defects as well as strengths of character. And while philosophical training in a classical and practical way appears to be a key to good character and good politics, at least as far as politics are concerned there can be, as has been noted by Christopher Pelling, "too much of a good thing"; in other words, a philosophical disposition without a quality we might call moderation or gentleness can be, as in the examples of both Cato and Brutus, ineffective or even disastrous in public life.[15] Neither is good education

---

[14] Hugh Liebert, *Plutarch's Politics* (Cambridge: Cambridge University Press, 2016) and Hugh Liebert, "Plutarch's Critique of Plato's Best Regime," *History of Political Thought* 30.2(2009), 251–271. Liebert suggests: "In...Lycurgus ... Plutarch claims Sparta not only as a model for the best regime, but a city superior to that imagined in the Republic" (254).

[15] Christopher Pelling, "Political Philosophy," in Mark Beck ed., *A Companion to Plutarch* (Oxford: Wiley Blackwell, 2014), 149. Indeed, one might suggest that in the same way that for Plutarch the uncompromising Cato was seen to be defective as a political actor, so too the Spartan regime, given its uncompromising attitude to the development of a certain vision of excellence for the few at the expense of the many, may be considered defective as a model for political organisation. As Pelling notes, Plato in *The Republic* acknowledged that the spirited part of the soul (*to thumoeeides*) requires not only harsh discipline and singlemindedness but also gentleness. It is the qualities that Plato

sufficient for a fully praiseworthy character, as the example of Alcibiades shows us.[16] Because such a complex and nuanced account of moral psychology may not lend itself well to distilled nuggets of practical advice without some degree of transformation, it is thus already possible to see the challenge of reception.

Perhaps most important for those not acquainted with Plutarch's work, and something that the evolution of his work's reception sometimes obscures, is that he never intended for his *Lives* to be considered as stand-alone accounts. Plutarch writes of the moral psychology of his chosen historical actors in parallel chapters, with an emphasis on moral psychology that justifies his insistence that he is writing *lives* as a genre rather than historical biography. Twenty-two of the original twenty-three pairs have survived (along with some singular lives from his earlier scholarly work) and eighteen of the summarising comparisons (*synkriseis*) offering a more general statement of how to understand the two lives set alongside the other. Unfortunately, we lack what appears to be Plutarch's very first pair (scholars think Scipio and Epaminondas), which might have given his readers a more explicit account of his intentions in framing the material in the way that he did.

As has been broadly acknowledged, the main purpose of the *Lives* was ethical and Plutarch's life-writing project was driven by the notion that the observation of others could be (and should be) edifying.[17] Still, exemplarity as a mode of education can function in different ways. In the first instance, the provision of *exempla* may mean that the action and principles informing one life become a template and aspiration for another. This form of mirroring action in practice characterises the moral psychology of a certain number of Plutarch's heroes and can serve as a means of insight into human possibilities as well as a tool of self-discipline in seeking to attain them. In the remarks opening the life of Pericles, Plutarch notes how the beauty of character and action in others may serve as an inspiration for the self. In the second instance, the complexity of moral character, both good and deficient aspects, in the lives of various individuals can serve as the material from which to draw moral lessons. A focus on actual individuals

---

(strangely) illustrates by analogy to dogs who not only need to know how to excel in defence but also be kind to those whom they protect. There may be sense in which that quality of gentleness identified by Plato when transcribed in broader political terms can be understood as a basic sense of civility and humaneness (both to oneself so that one is not always driven to avenge injury as in the case of Coriolanus, as well as to others).

[16] See Jacobs, *Pragmatic*, chap. 5.

[17] Simon Swain, *Hellenism and Empire* (Oxford: Clarendon Press, 1996), 138.

and the ways in which they handled themselves (rightly or wrongly) in certain circumstances adds a degree of realism to moral deliberation and can serve as occasions for testing, reflecting on and educating one's own disposition and moral intuitions. Of course, the broader assumptions in both cases include the view that there is something identifiable and discernible as good character which can be distinguished from bad character, better action from worse action, and that reflection and education can enhance moral development. Today we may tend to regard the tradition of exemplarity as a way of celebrating pathbreaking accomplishments, as in science, the arts as well as in public life. Still, for Plutarch, while accomplishments can be made easier due to certain personal qualities, his interest is less in what we might identify objectively as historical milestones and more in the types of character and personality that achieved recognition.

The idea of not just ethical goodness, but of the sort of education that promotes it, namely Greek *paideia* (a term spanning the formal goals of education such as good public speaking, cultural and historical knowledge as well as ethical formation and the more general cultural identity of the Greek elites that accompanied that training)[18] is infused throughout the work, with the result that those heroes, be they Roman or Greek, who have received such an education tend to fare better in terms of self-control and ethical standing. The ideal encompassed moderation (*sophrosune*) not through an effort of repression and internal struggle, but through an attachment to reason that would arise as second nature and express a balance in the soul. But instead of working out such ideals through allegory and philosophical argument (as in Plato's *Republic*), Plutarch sought to illustrate the need for good character through the practical examples of lives lived. In doing so he intertwines the question of character with other themes, including the forces of chance, circumstance, nature and individual spirit. There is also an overriding sense in Plutarch that those individuals with an appropriate education, and those who practice moderation and live in accordance with a strong sense of self-regulation and respect for reason and virtue, are those who in the end are more effective in their public lives. In a sense, it reflects a certain optimism that those who live with deep flaws of incontinence, excessive and blind

---

[18] Preston, "Roman Questions, Greek Answers," 89–90. As she notes, *paideia* not only differentiated educated Greeks of the imperial age from Romans who lacked training in Greek philosophy, but also offered an aristocratic ethos differentiating Greeks of high-standing and wealth from those who could not afford to or did not have access to such an education, thereby serving to legitimate the political authority of those associated with those elites in the various communities of Greece. It is also a mark of his Platonism.

ambition, lack of self-control, avidity and extreme irascibility will in the end become the victims of their own deficiencies. And while there are aspects of Plutarch's world and the classical world that remain obscure and foreign for us in the present, one might hope that there are aspects of this message that are not completely inapplicable in contemporary times.

So why does Plutarch choose figures with a certain renown? It may be that these figures provide a point of common knowledge and reference given the visibility of their actions for readers. But one should not confuse the choice of these figures with a celebration of blind heroism. It may be that a good number of the figures studied in the work were a source of fascination for Plutarch and his readers, but the broader thrust of the analysis was often not to highlight their singular natures, nor to give us more detail concerning the deeds for which they were best known. Indeed, to a certain degree a close study of the inner moral psychology of these figures brings them closer to the reader in a way that a pure focus on their deeds could not. And how Plutarch depicts that inner moral psychology of his subjects can often shed light on various weaknesses or deficiencies as well as strengths. This not only shows that moral psychology is complicated, but also that one should be careful not to conflate the entry into public consciousness with veneration.

To reveal those lessons, a certain art was required. The idea of the parallel goes beyond choosing a figure from Greek history for placement alongside and comparison with an analogical life from Roman history. Plutarch is thoughtful in his choices, seeking to pair figures from each cultural tradition not in terms of their measured historical achievements, but rather in terms of the patterns and challenges found within each character. So, for example, as discussed by Jeffrey Beneker, Plutarch pairs the Theban military leader Pelopidas with the Roman Marcellus, both of whom act out an inability to moderate or suppress deep sentiments of anger and animosity vis-à-vis the commander of their enemies, a moral deficiency that despite their other military skills lead them to overreach and end in their own demise in battle.[19] This suggests that one of the principles determining the choices for comparison is not the relative and proximate status of the figures compared, but rather the similarities in the contours and topography of their respective souls. From this perspective, then, the *Lives* offer not just a series of moral lessons to be teased out of the comparisons, they are built around a vision of moral psychology through

---

[19] Jeffrey Beneker, *The Passionate Statesman. Eros and Politics in Plutarch's Lives* (Oxford: Oxford University Press, 2012), chap. 2.

which the peoples and events of history are understood. Those who approach the collection as merely an account of various heroes of the ancient world may be blind to the deeper structure and logic of the work and will thereby miss an important aspect of its contribution to intellectual life, which was to offer an account that would deepen how we speak about moral psychology and how we might better understand the facets and diversity of human character in general. How this thrust of the work was transmitted or reconfigured in the process of reception and cultural transmission is significant.

It is beyond the scope of this study to discuss Plutarch's methods of research, but it should be noted that much of the historical detail was collected by Plutarch from other classical sources. This is one reason why Plutarch's cultural standing fell into such disrepute by the nineteenth century, as professional philologists began to regard his work as unoriginal and in certain ways unreliable. Still, as we have noted, Plutarch himself did not regard his own project as one of writing biography or history per se, even in a classical sense, but rather of writing 'lives' (βίοι), and what he meant by this was in part that he was attempting to reconstruct the moral psychology through which the actions of the various historical figures might be better understood. In terms of Plutarch's contribution to historical understanding, it should be noted that to a certain extent the very dismissal of him and his writings by nineteenth-century philologists has been subject to revision by contemporary scholars of Plutarch who acknowledge his artful and judicious use of those earlier sources, revealing an intelligent and purposeful pattern in his texts that may double as a hidden form of commentary on those same sources.[20]

Through these considerations we can begin to understand the strengths and weaknesses of Plutarch's account. One strength is that a psychological approach renders the material more vivid and offers an interpretation of events through a pre-existing moral template according to which actions can be more easily accessed and their significance more deeply felt. It is no wonder that the material of Plutarch's *Lives* lent itself well to dramatic appropriation and representation. However, on the other side, a weakness of the approach from a contemporary perspective is that as a matter of historical record some of the motivational discussions may be a matter of conjecture. In an epoque where the moral fabric of Plutarch's world is in

---

[20] On this point, see the papers presented at a meeting of the North American Plutarch Society entitled "Plutarch's Unexpected Silences," held at the University of Utah, Logan, UT, May 2019. The work of Christopher Pelling also provides a more positive account of the value of Plutarch's historical writing. See his *Plutarch and History*.

tatters (to borrow an image from Alasdair MacIntyre) one can more easily understand the relative neglect of contemporary Plutarch studies when neither its truth as a moral account, nor its veracity as a historical one can be defended without hesitation or qualification. Nonetheless, it is well worth considering given that the work offers insight into how Platonic ideas served to shed light on moral psychology and into how human beings lived and thought in Hellenistic Greece at the dawn of the Second Sophistic. Furthermore, the long history of its reception can shed light on how the roots of European culture were forged and can offer us tools for more sophisticated reflection on the nature of public life in the contemporary era. As I have noted in the introduction, my focus here is to explore how engagement with Plutarch's work helped to create certain traditions of political thinking in the West and indeed how, even if not the main focus for Plutarch himself, his work offered the material through which a more robust understanding of politics and of the public realm was developed.

I present here a brief analysis of two sets of parallel lives (Lycurgus and Numa; Alexander and Caesar), as well as two lives taken on their own, separate from their pair (Antony who is in Plutarch's work paired with Demetrius; and Phocion who in Plutarch's work is paired with Cato the younger). This is presented succinctly to give the reader new to Plutarch a more precise understanding of the nature of his writing and approach. We can see among these examples that Plutarch does not champion any one of these as a fully exemplary life although he can most readily acknowledge those lives which demonstrate greater deficiencies.

Still, prior to details of these select lives, it may be helpful to review in more general terms how Plutarch approached the study of his subjects. As we have noted, Plutarch begins his life of Alexander with a well-known statement regarding both the purpose and method of the larger work. He notes "that [his] intent is not to write histories, but only lives," meaning that his interest is not in the deeds of his subjects, nor their impact in world affairs, but rather in how to understand their actions and choices. He goes on to note that often it is most revealing of a person (in terms of knowing their virtues and vices, or dispositions and manners), not to explore the deeds they are most known for, but the quieter moments and sometimes offhand comments or actions. An example of this approach follows shortly after in Plutarch's discussion of how Alexander revealed both his intelligence and ability to think creatively by taming his horse Bucephalus as a young boy. Alexander's special insight at this moment was not just to consider the horse in terms of its nature and his need to tame it, but also from a wider perspective in exploring how the horse reacted to certain factors in its environment. By observing that the horse was disturbed by his own shadows, Alexander made sure to turn him towards the sun, allowing him to subdue and then master the horse. Thus, it was less Alexander's ferocity than his intelligence that allowed him to achieve the success that the force of the tamers could not. Alexander's ability to tame the wild animal has been said to serve as a double metaphor, reflecting both his early successes in personal self-control, as well as his later successes in subduing those enemies and adversaries who remained intractable for his father.

For the uninitiated reader, it should be noted that Plutarch is not seeking here to reveal distinct personalities or the inner individual in a more modern sense. He is approaching his subjects with a certain pre-established template of the soul and seeking to explore the motivating efficacy of reason and moderation over the course of a largely public career. As noted by Beneker, this approach may actually harbour some degree of homogenisation as a result of Plutarch's inference that his individual subjects can all be understood through recourse to a specific set of moral and psychological factors.[21] This broad account of Plutarch's approach to the analyses of his subjects with a distilled Platonic and Aristotelian understanding of the basic dynamics of moral psychology used to unpack, explore and explain motivations and behaviour allows us to make sense of the few examples singled out below.

1.2.1 Lycurgus and Numa

I begin with Lycurgus in part because Plutarch's depictions of Sparta have had an important resonance in political thought, especially French political thought, and in part because it demonstrates Plutarch's ambivalence towards the Spartan regime.[22] We have explored in general terms the

---

[21] Beneker, *The Passionate Statesman*.

[22] Liebert's position is perhaps driven by *Republic,* Book 8 placing Sparta as the best model of a timocratic policy, one notch below that of the kallipolis. Liebert states: "For Plutarch, Lycurgus's Sparta was the city par excellence. This fact alone set Plutarch apart from his philosophical forbears, the most prominent of whom looked upon Sparta as deeply flawed and ill-fated, owing to its inculcation of the love of honor (philotimia) rather than true virtue. Plutarch, by contrast, praises Lycurgus for recognizing that within the political form of the city, the desire for the esteem of one's fellow citizens can mimic true virtue so closely as to be indistinguishable from it." See *Plutarch's Politics,* 4. For Liebert, Lycurgus's manipulation of the love of honour is key, but this aspect is not evident from the text where, as is demonstrated below, the Spartans are taught not to think of themselves at all in isolation but only to consider themselves as part of an integrated and undistinguishable whole, much like bees in a hive. The psychological glue of Sparta as depicted by Plutarch is closer to Montesquieu's notion of love of the republic or intense civic loyalty than a love of honour.

degree to which Plutarch's focus and interest was primarily on the quality and features of character in a broader tradition of classical moral philosophy. What this means first and foremost is that concerns about a so-called best regime were not preeminent in Plutarch's reflections. To the extent that he did take an interest in the dynamics of politics and power, he sometimes came to note how circumstances of power either modified or most often revealed longer standing weaknesses of character. It may be that when Plutarch notes in his "Political Precepts" that the rules of visibility in politics make public actors more transparent, he means not only that people's characters are more evident because more people have their eyes turned toward public figures, but also that the circumstances and pressures of power themselves tend to lead public figures to reveal their latent weaknesses more readily than they otherwise would. Public expectations also play a role in this dynamic of visibility. Plutarch notes in the same essay that the broader public can tend to judge their public officials harshly, to the point of being prone to conspiratorial thinking.[23] It points to the risks of public life that both provides conditions where one's weaknesses become more apparent but also where those weaknesses may be more harshly judged. The unstated presumption is that public officials are held to a high standard so that all defects are regarded as important failures. In tandem with his moralism then, Plutarch can offer us insights of realist awareness.

The life of Lycurgus is one of a series that have more to do with myth than historical fact. Plutarch acknowledges this and rejects the more imaginative accounts while still retaining the more plausible details. Some have suggested that in the context of ancient historiographical commentary on the Spartan regime, there is not a great deal of his account that remains verifiable.[24] Plutarch begins with the circumstances leading to the rule of Lycurgus, including his self-imposed exile from the kingdom to ensure the rule of his young nephew. He travels to Crete, where he encounters the peace-inducing poetic oratory of Thales, to Ionia where he learns of the benefits of both discipline and pleasure through the work of Homer, and then on to Egypt where he learns about structuring military

---

[23] "The people in every city can be malicious and inclined to find fault with their political leaders. Moreover, unless they observe some partisanship or opposition, the people suspect many good policies of being implemented by conspiracy, which leads especially to criticism of their leaders' political connections and friendships." Plutarch, "How to be a Good Leader" [also known as "Political Precepts"] J. Beneker, trans. in *How to be a Good Leader* (Princeton, NJ: Princeton University Press, 2019), 141. The earlier points about visibility in public life are found on 69–71.

[24] See the work of Noreen Humble on Plutarch's Sparta, and her *Xenophon of Athens: A Socratic on Sparta* (Cambridge: Cambridge University Press, 2021).

and political power. On his return, seeing the kingdom in great disarray, he embarks on a famous project of reform becoming one of the first famous "founders" in a long tradition of political history.

The interest in Lycurgus for Plutarch is largely on his institutional innovations and how this might both reflect his own moral character and, at least in principle, produce what he regarded as good civic qualities. Plutarch likens the model of Sparta to that of a hive where citizens like bees were not to be thought of as individuals at all but rather as integral parts of a larger civic whole (s.25). Lycurgan constitutional reforms are well known given the iconic place this account has had in the history of political reflection. He is said to have introduced a Senate of elders to moderate political tendencies. Still, as Plutarch tells us (s.7), those reforms were not enough to curb the excesses of oligarchy, leading to a need to appoint the body of ephors in reform efforts a century later. A second set of innovations to address problems of massive economic inequality involved land redistribution, a highly cumbersome currency, the abolition of luxuries and the institution of common meals (though we are given hints that classes of rich and poor still existed in the wake of these reforms). The institutions associated with Lycurgus point to an effort to instil a particular form of civic, courageous and warlike character with the shaping of social norms, for example through the regulation of marriages; the introduction of intense military training, including the separation of young boys from their families for education in courage and stealth tactics (by encouraging successful stealing of food and supplies) often summarised under the term *agoge*; the granting of certain though limited forms of independence for women; encouragement of homosexuality between boys and men within the structures of military training; and periodic testing of a boy's knowledge of civic matters. Despite a clear interest in the particulars of the measures introduced, Plutarch does not present these reforms as an ideal portrait of a best regime, although he does appear to endorse the principle of education being organised and administered by the state (as opposed to being sole responsibility of families, as was common in the Roman Empire of his day).[25] Indeed, Plutarch suggests that warlike attributes of the training conflicted with Lycurgus's more peaceful nature (s.23). He criticises the harsh treatment of the helots (slaves who did all the agricultural labour) made even harsher by secret assassinations and cruel working conditions; and in the *synkrisis* he suggests that Numa's acknowledgement

---

[25] See Paolo Desideri, "Lycurgus: the Spartan ideal in the age of Trajan," in Philip Stadter and Luc Van der Stockt eds., *Sage and Emperor* (Leuven: Leuven University Press, 2002), 315–326.

of the dignity of slaves made him a more Hellenic, and hence better, lawgiver than Lycurgus (s.1). Plutarch suggests that Lycurgus consulted the Delphic oracle about the quality of the constitution, which is called good/beautiful, but not characterised with superlatives as the best (s.29). Plutarch also notes that while Numa, even as a foreigner was able to convince Romans of needed changes through wisdom and justice alone, Lycurgus needed to resort to a mobilisation of the nobles against the commons to begin his reforms. Indeed, Lycurgus' regime is depicted as arising from a set of particular social and political challenges Spartans were facing at that time (the need to "tighten the strings" which he found "relaxed with luxury" as he states in the *synkrisis,* s. 1), and it survived as a sort of regional policeman in the face of political calamities in neighbouring regimes, such as the rise of tyrannies and illegal oligarchies (s.30). So, while Sparta had some merit for Plutarch due to its stability in the context of broader political upheaval as well as its longevity accompanied by deep-seated institutions of education whose effects Plutarch compares to dye, these came with the imposition of harshness and a cruelty that did not fully respect the ideal of humaneness.[26] The deficiencies of Lycurgan Sparta are highlighted by Plutarch in the very thread of comparison with Numa.

Numa's life and character is acknowledged by Plutarch to exhibit a good deal in common with Lycurgus, including their moderation (*sophrosune*), piety, talent for governance and education, and their divine inspiration.[27] Lycurgus is said to have had a more difficult task in converting an ill-disciplined people obsessed with wealth to change their customs than did Numa, whose task it was to soften a fierce people. Nonetheless, as we have noted, Plutarch acknowledges Numa as the more Hellenic lawgiver (and hence better) given that his methods were more humane, effected through persuasion rather than violence, and were more favourable to the marginalised (e.g. slaves, craftsmen and women). In addition, his goal in shaping civic qualities was directed toward producing a love of righteousness in the Roman people rather than Lycurgus's objective of producing brave warrior

---

[26] The reference to dye in education appears to invoke Plato's own metaphor in Book IV of the *Republic*, but as argued by Ryan Balot, Plato himself appeared to repudiate the Spartan model of courage for its link to deep-seated unreflective mechanisms rather than to belief and cognitive evaluation (and re-evaluation) as tied to a culture of deliberation in Athens and foundational for the virtue of the guardians. See Ryan Balot, "Virtue and Emotional Education in Ancient Greece," in Kiran Banerjee et al. eds., *Emotions, Community and Citizenship* (Toronto: University of Toronto Press, 2017), 35–51.

[27] Plutarch, "Comparison of Lycurgus and Numa," *Lives*, vol. 1, s.1.

citizens.[28] The *synkrisis* thus reaffirms Plutarch's clear preference for the rule of Numa over Lycurgus.[29]

It is curious that in light of Plutarch's preference for the Roman Numa, future thinkers in the history of political thought, such as Abbé de Mably, who champion Lycurgus's innovations (as we shall explore in a later chapter) are not more guarded in their praise. It can only be surmised that they were drawn to the radical, uncompromising, and wide-ranging nature of Lycurgus's reforms, which sought to infuse his political objectives into the very heart of all relations and into the education of sons. Perhaps it also speaks to the depths of corruption those modern thinkers found in their own contemporary context and to the ultimate principles those reforms were meant to instil. In Lycurgus's model, all social relations were regarded as instrumental to the production of highly efficient and self-disciplined warriors.

In a certain sense, just as Plutarch himself may have used some guess-work to build a model of Sparta based on a set of principles (given the lack of uncontested and verified accounts), so too do later thinkers in the history of political thought falsely assign a sort of reconstructed ideal status to the Spartan model. It is depicted as a social order with little distinction between public and private realms, and one where the domestic sphere is fully fashioned and infused by predetermined and externally imposed public norms. The lack of any spirit of compromising moderation in this enterprise, or to put it another way, the basis for a political thought experiment of wholesale reform disregarding the humanity of those who are being governed, may have appealed to certain radical reformers through the ages, but this is what also draws Plutarch's criticism. The implication in Plutarch's own stance is that governance is done well when driven by good intention and with ethical goals in mind and when it is still normatively subject to considerations of humanity and dignity that dictate the need for moderation and compromise vis-a-vis the structure and reality of problems one faces.

In addition to the more moderate and humane spirit of Hellenism that Numa represents for Plutarch, Numa also represents, perhaps to a greater degree than does Lycurgus, the art of summoning divine sanction and religious piety in the service of civic goals. Although this aspect of Plutarch reception will not be explored thoroughly in this book despite its evident importance (for reasons of space it was not possible to explore themes surrounding the idea of civil religion as in part influenced by Plutarch's

---

[28] Plutarch, "Comparison of Lycurgus and Numa," ss.1–4.   [29] Cf. Liebert, *Plutarch's Politics*.

work), it does nonetheless bear mentioning. The figure of Numa will later be invoked famously by Rousseau, not only for reasons of civil religion, but also as the mysterious figure he calls the "Legislator" and who, as an outsider or foreigner, is brought in to create a new regime when the old one is in disarray and on the verge of civil war. Despite his crucial role in shaping the regime, the one aspect that Numa was not able to control effectively enough for Plutarch was the legacy of his reforms. While moderate as well as moderating and praiseworthy, Plutarch does acknowledge that the impact of the reforms lasted for a much shorter time than the changes introduced by Lycurgus, largely due to the lack of educational rigor for the very young in Numa's system.

1.2.2 Alexander and Julius Caesar

There is a unique challenge in coming to terms with Plutarch's analyses of both Alexander and Julius Caesar given that the notoriety of both make them somewhat larger than life, and their deeds appear to upstage and overwhelm any commentary one might have, moral or otherwise, on the character of the person. From a contemporary perspective both represent much of what is considered reprehensible in the wielding of military and political power. Placing such contemporary considerations aside, Plutarch did not always choose his subjects as ideal models of virtue but as complicated and often flawed examples providing fuel for thought. Plutarch does not let a sense of awe at the military accomplishments of Alexander and Caesar get in the way of a critical assessment of character. As noted by a recent commentator, the account of Alexander reads like a tragedy of epic proportions, and that of Caesar has obvious iconic cultural status as a tragedy.[30]

Alexander is depicted by Plutarch, even in his early development, as having an extraordinary *persona*. What is also apparent is that character is not a set of fixed qualities but the *summa* of features that are subject to change over the course of a life (and in this recognition Plutarch diverges from Aristotle). And despite the truism that moderation comes more easily as one gets older, the case of Alexander offers an exception, demonstrating that large amounts of worldly acclaim, power and wealth once gained can undermine the self-control needed to obtain it. It may not be that power always corrupts, according to Plutarch, but the story of Alexander

---

[30] Judith Mossman, "Tragedy and Epic in Plutarch's Alexander," in Barbara Scardigli ed., *Essays on Plutarch's Lives* (Oxford: Clarendon Press, 1995), 209–228.

demonstrates that power can exacerbate the occurrence and effects of immoderate tendencies.

Plutarch's account begins with anecdotes that reflect Alexander's ambition and his desire for recognition of a lasting sort. This is illustrated by his unwillingness to compete athletically with anyone but kings and his adolescent need to surpass all the accomplishments of his father (s.4). What is perhaps most remarkable about Alexander from Plutarch's perspective is his combination of a desire for great things (one that lasted his whole, albeit short, life) and his ability from an early age to harness his appetites and efforts to achieve those goals, an ability that was not instilled but certainly cemented by his education. At the same time, following the account that Aristotle served as a tutor to Alexander, Plutarch invokes Alexander's growing suspicion of Aristotle as a clue to the moral weakness that will become apparent by the end of Alexander's life.

Initially at least, Plutarch appears not to flinch in his recital of Alexander's acceptance, at twenty years of age, of the reins of power after his father's death, or his work to subdue the rebelliousness of neighbouring territories. The notably cruel devastation of the city of Thebes (335 BCE) is understood by Plutarch as, at least in part, a personal response of anger to the city's proud defiance, though more predominantly as a means to instil a fear of similar treatment in all Greeks (s.11). In noting that Alexander came to feel remorse about it, Plutarch suggests Alexander acknowledged his moral defect. Indeed, a key dramatic tension of the life is that the same strong spiritedness (*thumos*) to which Alexander partly owed his military successes was also the source of the excessive anger that would often, especially when combined with drinking, lead him to do things he would come to regret.[31] Despite the intensity of his desire for domination and control, Alexander was not blind to the fact that the excessively cruel treatment of Thebes was a mistake, one that drove him to subsequent acts of leniency and clemency in an impossible quest, it would appear, to expunge his excess (s.13).

Plutarch does appear to admire the display of courage, determination and forceful leadership that Alexander demonstrates in his crossing of the river Granicus, despite the challenges of the current, the topography of the area and the reluctance of his own troops, to defeat the Persian army of Darius. But having gained the edge in military terms, Alexander's anger vis-à-vis Greek mercenaries on the Persian side, led him to call a charge in which he lost his horse and presumably almost his own life (s.16). We are

---

[31] Mossman, "Tragedy," 213.

once again shown how the atmosphere of battle and intensity of conflict can lead an ambitious leader to misjudgement through excessive anger. Elsewhere, however, Plutarch remarks on Alexander's extraordinary capacity for self-control, in moments of greater calm and outside of battle, at least in the first stages of his conquests. His moderation is demonstrated in his considerate treatment of Darius's mother, wife and daughters after his victory over the Persians at the battle of Cilicia (s.21).

In later conquests, as narrated by Plutarch, Alexander's favouring by fortune, especially with the defeat of Darius at Gaugamela, appeared only to boost his pride and sense of personal glory, a reaction which eroded his moderation and enhanced his moral weaknesses. Alexander engaged in simulation, taking on the persona of being fathered by a god, even if he did not personally believe it to be true (s.28). Furthermore, having advanced into Persia where he stationed himself in Xerxes's palace and sat in his throne, Alexander indulged his mistress Thais's vengeful fantasy of burning the palace of Persepolis to the ground, a deed he quickly regretted. This speaks to an increased impulsiveness and loss of self-control. As the wealth of his associates grew with both the extent of Alexander's conquests and his greater propensity to generosity with each success, many of his followers grew softer and less loyal. In the wake of his military successes, his cruelty towards critics and potential enemies of his inner circle increased, and the escalation of his increasing loss of moderation came to a head when, in a drunken rage, he murdered his friend Cleitus (ss. 50–51). After Alexander's conquests in India the band of fighters began to march back to Macedonia in a dissolute parade of drunkenness and excess; but the challenges he had faced to that point, including large losses among his troops, led those of his wider kingdom to doubt his safe return and thence to various acts of rebellion and sedition. The undoing of his own self-control was matched by uprising in his political domain. His dissolution increased with his grief at the loss of his close companion Hephaestion, which led him into battle with the Cosseaans no longer for noble reasons but for a motive of outright slaughter (s.72). Near the end of his life Alexander was suspicious of his entourage and mistrusting of the gods; he perceived bad omens everywhere, and ultimately died at a premature age, possibly of poisoning.

Alexander is paired with Julius Caesar, who offers a similar story of great ambition, great aspirations at a young age, and intimations of challenges in maintaining an ethos of moderation when faced with continued military success and increased political influence and power. In terms of later Plutarch reception, the life of Caesar is often placed alongside his historical peers – that is, key political actors of the late republican period in Rome – rather than read in tandem with the life of Alexander. Because of the relative scarcity of historical sources covering the late republican period, and the drama that inevitably characterises Plutarch's accounts, Caesar's life, along with those of Antony, Pompey, Brutus and Cicero have become the most famous of Plutarch's collection. Beginning in Renaissance Italy, many scholars turned to Plutarch to shed light on the events leading to the principate; as a result, his work became an important reference in debates about the relative merits of republicanism and monarchy.[32]

For those with deep understanding of the text and its historical context, and in the work of Christopher Pelling in particular, Plutarch's life of Julius Caesar is notable for what it does not say as much as for what it does; thus, it has been noted that the life provides no reference to aspects of Caesar's career that bear resemblance to, and indeed were celebrated by, Emperor Trajan at the time this life was written.[33] For my purposes, a deep dive into an analysis of the details of the life or the nuances in the presentation of the biographical detail are not necessary. Rather, I will highlight only some of the particularities of Plutarch's own rendition of this life, particularities that are most significant for the history of reception.

Plutarch's reflections on Julius Caesar are not limited to what is written in the "Life of Caesar," for Caesar appears as a figure in various other of his lives written about key actors in the politics of the late Republic. This also means that early modern thinkers who reflected on the example of Caesar also did not limit their sources to this life. For example, Shakespeare drew from the life of Caesar for his famous play as well as the lives of Brutus and Antony.[34]

Like Alexander, Plutarch tells us, Caesar singles himself out as a leader at a young age, but one who was capable of great cruelty. In the wake of the authoritarian reign of Sulla his popularity grew because of his gifts of rhetoric, his charm and generosity and his staging of lavish public displays. At first it was only Cicero who sensed Caesar's own tyrannical ambitions (s.4). The contrast of a figure like Alexander, born to inherit power, with one who had to achieve it would not be missed by the attentive reader.

After serving as praetor Caesar was sent to serve in Spain. As evidence of his great ambition Plutarch gives an account of Caesar's own tendency to

---

[32] As we will see briefly in Chapter 2, the work of Marianne Pade sheds a good deal of light on this period of reception in this regard.
[33] Christopher Pelling, "Introduction," in C. Pelling ed., Plutarch *Caesar* (Oxford: Oxford University Press, 2011), 2–3.
[34] Pelling, "Introduction," 68.

compare his life with others. He famously notes Caesar's tears on reading that Alexander had at the same age already conquered much of the world (whereas Caesar felt that he had accomplished very little, s. 11). This, anecdote it would appear, serves two purposes. It demonstrates that Plutarch is invoking the trope of comparison of lives as an extension of what might be considered a natural or common mechanism in moral self-regulation – in other words, individuals tend to compare their own lives with others to assess themselves. In addition, whereas Plutarch writes lives so that readers come to an understanding of both the moral strengths and weaknesses of others and to better assess their own moral psychology, Caesar reveals his own unique moral psychology by invoking the trope of comparison for purposes of self-deprecation, not on moral terms, but in terms of historical accomplishment. Thus, Caesar demonstrates his own vainglory in his misuse and distortion of the function of comparison. Still, as we shall see, for certain Renaissance authors, the grand sense of pre-eminence displayed by Caesar in comparing himself with Alexander provided evidence of how all rulers should come to perceive themselves.

Plutarch acknowledges Caesar's crafty manoeuvring to gain Pompey's friendship, win the office of consul and break the aristocracy, and he reviews how, once in the office, Caesar and his friends passed a series of laws to stir up the people and target his political enemies among the elite, including Cato and Cicero (s.14). From there he was appointed to preside over Cisalpine and Transalpine Gaul (s.15). His military interventions in the Gallic Wars to quell revolt not only cemented his military reputation, but also inspired soldiers and gave him access to the military and financial resources through which he could bolster support from citizens in Rome (s.17). Overall, Plutarch demonstrates how Caesar embarked on a concerted strategy to win power, a project for which he had trained himself from a young age and which he pursued with multiple strategies that employed discipline, daring, uncommon focus and a sense of purpose.

The same spirit of boldness and strength of purpose is depicted in Plutarch's account of Caesar's return to Italy: his crossing the Rubicon in defiance of convention and the start of civil war in violent conflict against the supporters of Pompey and his allies as Caesar slowly advanced with his troops toward Rome (s.32). The interest of Plutarch's account is his unique description of the character traits and psychology evoked in various anec-dotes, which help the reader understand the deeper personal forces behind world-shaking events. And while some might consider the text as verging on hagiography, the tone is not always one of praise in its recognition of how Caesar was more concerned for his own victories in the face of a national disaster and of how the Roman people accepted what they knew to be tyranny only because of the modicum of peace and respite from civil war that it brought them. There is also a general sense that his powerful drive for power and glory in the end brought Caesar very little. Both the ends and the means by which he sought power stirred up extreme hostility and culminated in his death by assassination at the hands of his closest allies and previously loyal friends. Plutarch's account is not a celebration of Caesar's achievements so much as a cautionary tale of the results of uncompromising ambition.

Still, the paired lives of Alexander and Caesar leave the reader with questions. Both lives offer an account of moral development in the context of highly ambitious aspirations and unprecedented access to military and political power (and the loss of a staggering number of lives: Plutarch estimates that Caesar was responsible for a million deaths during his less than a decade long campaign in Gaul, s.15). The notoriety of Alexander and Caesar, as prominent figures in the shared Greco-Roman heritage of Plutarch's day, made them obvious case studies for character. Their political prominence is clearly treated like a stage on which their display of character traits was made more manifest; but in addition, it also appears that Plutarch was interested in demonstrating how both responded to and dealt with the impact of important military and political success. A slightly different question, though no less relevant and important for the tradition of Plutarch reception, is the degree to which that military and political success, or more succinctly, the dynamics of political power itself, helped to shape how those characters evolved. As I will show, in European reception of Plutarch, and particularly the earlier years of his French vernacular reception, we see a fascination for the unique dynamics of political power. So, while many of Plutarch's initial readers may have approached this pair with reflections concerning what they reveal about character, over the course of Renaissance reception a certain number shifted the focus to ask what these examples reveal about the nature of politics and the requirements of character within that realm.

1.2.3   Antony

Antony stands out in Plutarch's collection as he forms one of a pair of lives (with Demetrius) that is singled out as a largely negative example for readers. The moral comparisons offered by the analysis of figures like Alexander and Caesar, while not perfect, are presented as offering some positive messages regarding self-discipline and self-motivation. We are told, however, that the pair of Antony and Demetrius are to serve as deterrent examples, perhaps to create an effect analogous to the Spartan practice of dissuading young warriors from abuse of alcohol by showing them the drunken brawls of the helots.

The life of Antony also stands out because it has been the subject of a great amount of attention and commentary in Plutarch reception, suggesting perhaps that the flaws of human nature in the end garner more attention in the modern era than calls to virtue. The life of Antony has also lent itself to the most dramatic appropriation of the themes and subject of the *Lives*, and again this may be in part due to a focus here on deficiencies and weaknesses of character. Whatever the case, a summary is offered here as a background to subsequent discussions of how this life would be taken up in the early modern period.

Plutarch begins the life by acknowledging Antony's propensity to gen-erosity as well as his early initiation into excess (drink, spending, sexual promiscuity) and his development of a style of speaking that reflected his propensity for boastfulness and misguided ambition (s.2). In the initial stages of the civil war with Pompey and the aristocratic forces pitched against Caesar and the popular forces, Antony chose the latter and served as tribune to help further the cause of Caesar (s.5). At the time of the conspiracy to kill Caesar there was some discussion about killing Antony as well, given his closeness to Caesar, but some argued against it (s.13). He gave the eulogy for Caesar, but in the context of the subsequent struggle for power he negotiated with Octavian and Lepidus to carve up areas of influence in the empire and for each to do away with their most virulent enemies (s.19). From Greece Antony went further east, seeking goods, riches and pleasures, and during his preparations for the Parthian war he met and fell in love with Queen Cleopatra (s.25). As conflicts among the leading powerful figures in the empire grew, and as Antony's love led him to spurn his legal wife, Octavia, the sister of Octavian, his previously astute military judgement began to falter (s.37). Relations with Octavian became strained. Antony was stripped of his authority in the east and war on Egypt was declared (s.40). At the Battle of Actium, in Plutarch's account, Antony reveals the priority of his blind devotion to Cleopatra's needs over military exigencies. Defeat led to their eventual capture; Antony took his own life in the belief that Cleopatra had died, and Octavian, while seeking to keep Cleopatra in custody to bring to Rome, was defied in his orders by Cleopatra who managed to expose herself to the deadly snake which killed her (s.86).

It is a famous story best known, of course, through Shakespeare's dramatic rendition and numerous modern film adaptations.[35] But while the modern era (and even Shakespeare himself) tends to regard these events through the lens of tragedy as a conflict between the demands of love and the demands of politics, for Plutarch it was largely a tale of weakness and character decay. While Antony's nobility in intelligence and capacity for self-discipline was demonstrated through early military and political success his achievements were wasted by his later pursuit of personal pleasures. Plutarch's reading of the life of Antony also brings to light the highly gendered assumptions in his underlying notion of classical virtue. The reception of the story of Antony (and the changing conception of Cleopatra within it) offers insight into shifting sensibilities over the course of cultural and intellectual development within Europe.

1.2.4 Phocion

In contrast to Antony, Phocion is a clearly positive example of character in Plutarch's selection of lives. Despite the clear distinction between the philosopher and the statesman, Phocion is likened in explicit terms to Socrates as a worthy individual unjustly put to death by the Athenian public. Phocion stands as a good example of virtuous moderation and self-control, and for this he is paired in the Lives with Cato the Younger. As Plutarch tells us at the outset of this life, despite the positive attributes of a character it can still sometimes be very difficult to achieve the best outcome in one's deeds. While a character may appear in him or herself to be almost flawless, such as Cato, if an individual is not received or respected in the proper spirit due to the temper of the times, they may be subject to poor treatment by fortune. Thus, through Phocion we are introduced to the spirit of Plutarch's political pragmatism. He acknowledges that characters are not to be judged only by the contours of their moral disposition in the abstract but must also be assessed on the basis of their judgement and ability to work with the people and times in which they live.

Phocion was a devoted servant to the city of Athens in the roles of general (with notably heroic service at the battle of Naxos 376 BCE), ambassador and politician. While moderate of temper, humble, courteous, and even kind and civil to his public enemies in private, he could also, as Plutarch tells us, be sharp and determined in public deliberations to those opposing him. He served in Athens through the period when Macedonia

---

[35] The WXYZ four o'clock movies planted some seeds for this book!

was on the ascendant and Athens on the decline, what Plutarch calls "a shipwreck" (s.1). While counselling the Athenians not to engage Philip of Macedon directly in battle, he also advised caution once Philip wished to impose a peace. In both instances Phocion was opposed by the city, which then came to regret its refusal to follow his advice. He similarly came to loggerheads with Demosthenes regarding Athenian strategy against Alexander, especially in the battle of Thebes. His own encounter with Alexander is said to have softened Alexander's mind so that Athens was spared the worst of Macedonian subjection, and its democratic institutions were largely preserved under Alexander's rule. Paradoxically, under the revival of those same democratic institutions, Phocion was charged with conspiracy and sympathy for the Macedonians for which he was put to death in 318 BCE.

According to Plutarch, Phocion's Platonic education served as an important foundation for qualities of character (like those of Cato) combining humanity with austerity, bravery with caution, and care for others with fearlessness for himself as well as a drive to avoid evil and follow justice.[36] The strength of his internal virtue was symbolised by his laconism and supposed asceticism, perhaps a literary device to enhance the reader's association of Phocion with Socrates.[37] His ethical excellence was accompanied by a suitability for politics, which included good oratorical skills, directness and good judgement. While Phocion provides a clear example of how bad fortune and unfortunate circumstances can lead a worthy character to a tragic end, he is not unbending in his principles (as Cato was). In defending the interests of Athens as a public figure, he advocates compromise with various leaders who threaten Athens, such as Philip of Macedon. Indeed, as Timothy Duff notes, Phocion is criticised in the life of Demosthenes for compromising his values to preserve the state.[38] As again noted by Duff, it may be that Plutarch is saying something here about the nature of virtue, perhaps that in times of crises a case can be made for both unbending principle and for compromise, both of which might reflect a differing virtuous path; or it may be that he is suggesting that in less than ideal circumstances and in the political realm virtue is best exemplified through the exercise of moderation or compromise because otherwise no good could be achieved.[39] So while the fates of Phocion and Cato were in the end similar (both died prematurely), there is a sense in the

[36] Timothy Duff, *Plutarch's Lives Exploring Virtue and* Vice (Oxford: Oxford University Press, 1999), 141.
[37] Laurence Tritle, *Phocion the Good* (Beckenham: Croom Helm, 1978), 9–10.
[38] Duff, *Plutarch's Lives*, 133.   [39] Duff, *Plutarch's Lives*, 134 and 139.

narrative that in his ability to deal with the Athenian people reasonably and without excessive severity, Phocion dealt better with his lot. In an adaptation of Platonic metaphor of the sun, Plutarch provides an evocative image: the good statesman, in less-than-ideal circumstances, should adopt a course like that of the sun, which bends in the sky to the arc of the earth in a smooth manner and in doing so preserves all things. In short, there are some circumstances where it is better to seek a mixture of austerity and reasonableness.[40]

While the figure of Phocion has faded from the contemporary cultural lexicon, he was an important cultural reference in the seventeenth and eighteenth centuries, especially in France. This was strengthened further by the famous 1648 painting of Nicholas Poussin (1594–1665) which depicts Phocion's funeral and his widow's reception of his ashes.[41] As we will see in Chapter 11, Phocion commanded attention as a classical figure devoted to the public good, one who suffered as a martyr as a result of his civic mindedness (though also represented falsely as an advocate of a strict Spartan regime of education for Athens). Symbolically, his name was invoked by public-minded figures who were put to death by guillotine during the Terror (invoked to tap into the notion that they understood themselves to be part of a long line of political martyrs).[42] Foreshadowing my discussion of French eighteenth-century Plutarch reception, what is of special interest here is that the French often looked to Phocion rather than Cato as a model of an independently minded and virtuous public figure. In Plutarch's account part of what distinguishes Cato from Phocion is that while Cato took stances on principle and showed himself to be consistent and uncompromising in public matters, Phocion acknowledged that good public judgement would require him at times to advocate confrontation and at other times peace and conciliation in ways determined by what he reasoned that virtue and the public good required.

1.3   Plutarch and Cicero

The context of Plutarch's writing (the first century of the Imperial era) as well as some of the themes of Plutarch's work (adjudicating the merits of various schools of Hellenistic philosophy, reflections on public service, distilled Platonism and reflection on the relation between philosophy and

---

[40] Duff, *Plutarch's Lives*, 139 and Plutarch, *Life of Phocion*, s. 2.
[41] On this painting, see especially Joseph Geiger, "Death of a Statesman: Poussin's Phocion," in *The Statesman in Plutarch's Works*, vol. 1 (Leiden and Boston: Brill, 2004), 287–296.
[42] As noted by Lamberton, *Plutarch*, 158.

the active life) offer clear potential for a comparison with Cicero. This is even more relevant in matters of classical reception given that Cicero's works were widely circulating in early modern Europe and were a source of Latin education for much of the educated elite. This section offers an analysis of what is shared by these two thinkers, but also what makes Plutarch distinct. Attention to the unique nature of Plutarch's contribution in relation to Cicero is a first step in determining Plutarch's contributions to early modern political reflection, especially in France. Nonetheless, how Plutarch was taken up in the early modern period does not necessarily reflect all that Plutarch represented for his own era.

Given a paucity of commentary comparing the practical ethics of Cicero and Plutarch, despite the centrality of both in traditions of reception, I will compare them here based on key passages from selected primary texts.[43] In *On Duties* (*De Officiis*) Cicero is most concerned with themes of public service, and this offers clear overlap with his Greek counterpart.[44] Nonetheless, despite a shared adherence to Platonism, the spirit of Plutarch's discussion of public service is distinct from that of Cicero and those differences are also evident in traditions of political reflection drawing from Plutarch from the sixteenth century onward. In this section, I draw mainly on three of Plutarch's moral essays, "To an Uneducated leader," "Political Precepts" and "Should an Old Man Engage in Politics?"[45]

Both Cicero and Plutarch were prominent political figures of their time, combining a devotion to philosophy with engagement in and indeed defence of the active life, though the first in the context of the latter years of Roman Republicanism and the second in the context of limited autonomy under Roman Imperial rule.[46] In their intellectual work, both

---

[43] Jacobs in *Pragmatic* offers a brief discussion of Cicero and Plutarch on practical ethics, but with the purpose of demonstrating that Plutarch was part of a broader tradition giving both moral and practical advice to rulers. Here my focus is on what differentiates the two.

[44] Cicero, *On Duties*, eds. M. T. Griffin and E. M. Atkins (Cambridge: Cambridge University Press, 1991).

[45] While these essays are available in the Loeb series, which I use for most other citations from the *Moralia*, for purposes of this comparison I use the translation of these essays most recently available in Plutarch, *How to be a Leader*, ed. Jeffrey Beneker (Princeton, NJ: Princeton University Press, 2019).

[46] Cicero predated Plutarch living at a time when republican Rome was beset by crises. Cicero was an active defender of republican institutions and the ideal of civic freedom associated with it. As a prominent lawyer, quaestor, consul and public speaker he wrote numerous tracts and letters and delivered numerous speeches through which his republican commitments were justified and defended. He also was a prominent commentator on the various schools of practical ethics which had taken hold in late republican Rome, so much so that his work is still regarded as one of the main sources for learning about the contours of those competing doctrines. Cicero, *Tusculan disputations*, trans. J. E. King (Cambridge, MA: Harvard University Press, 2014).

were disciples of Plato in their own way, and both adopted a general virtue theory approach to ethics and politics. In addition, both adapted their Platonic sympathies to somewhat more pragmatic concerns, either discussing principles of applied ethics, as in Cicero, or reflecting on virtues and character in their unfolding and disclosure, as in Plutarch. Cicero reflected on the idea of the best regime and wrote his *Republic* following the lead of Plato, defending republicanism in his active politics. Plutarch in his writing was most often focused on the lives of historical subjects rather than the respective merits of institutional settings, but he did acknowledge the benefits and the relative intransigeance of the imperial structures of power under which he lived and worked.

A first clue about deeper differences between Plutarch and Cicero is the recognition that Plutarch wrote a *Life of Cicero*, comparing him with the Greek rhetorician and public figure Demosthenes. It is often the case that Plutarch prefers the character of his Greek exemplar to that of his Roman one (because the Greek ideal of *paideaia* or education in culture and virtue was often better met in the Greek contexts), and the case of Cicero-Demosthenes is no exception. While acknowledging some of the benefits of eloquence always associated with Cicero, especially when used to defend the right and reasonable path as opposed to flattering the multitudes, his life was not fully exemplary for Plutarch. Plutarch was critical of Cicero's hyper-inflated sense of self-worth and his exaggerated ambition and desire for honour, which formed a tone of self-congratulation that was judged to pervade and sully his written work.[47] For Plutarch, of course, it was this ambition that led to Cicero's demise. Plutarch's last word is that his deference to Caesar nurtured a greater tyranny than the one he had earlier opposed, undermining his defence of republican principles and in the end precipitating his death.

Perhaps Plutarch's judgement of Cicero's active life is not sufficient as an indicator of their differences. Another clue comes from the history of political thought, most notably the work of Montaigne. As we shall see in more detail in Chapter 7, Montaigne offers an expressed preference for the work of Plutarch over that of Cicero. While due in part to Montaigne's criticism regarding Cicero's public persona, a preference for Plutarch also carries over into the substance of their philosophy. For Montaigne, Plutarch dives much deeper into the facets of individual motivation and

---

[47] As noted in the Amyot translation: "Toutefois l'être extrêmement joyeux de se sentir loué et l'être passionné du désir d'honneur lui demeura toujours tant qu'il vécut jusques à la fin, et le fit plusieurs fois dévoyer du droit chemin de la raison." "Cicéron," *Les Vies des hommes illustres*, trans. Amyot, vol. 2 (Paris: Gallimard, 1952), 746.

the complex psychology that informs action, something I expand on in this section.

With regards to practical Hellenistic ethics, both Cicero and Plutarch engaged with Stoicism and Epicureanism. Cicero's scepticism, along with his recourse to traditional rhetorical methods, led him to weigh their relative merits (although he was harsher on Epicureanism). In *On Duties*, for example, Cicero expounds on principles of middle Stoic ethics developed earlier by Panaetius. Plutarch, in contrast, tended to offer more critical commentary on the schools of Stoicism and Epicureanism, and he developed his ethical analysis by looking first to lived examples and by the exercise of individual virtues. It could be suggested that Plutarch's greater Peripatetic sympathies, acknowledging the role of Fortune in the fashioning of the good individual, the complicated manifestations of character and the essentially social and political nature of human life, made him more critical of the broad Hellenistic schools of his day.

In terms of their overall approaches to ethics and to social and political questions, Cicero offers his readers a triangulation among rhetoric, republicanism and liberty. For Cicero, speech is an expression of the essential sociality of human life, but also a tool for persuasion and argument in fashioning the forms of collective existence most conducive to human happiness (1. 22–23 and 1. 49). Rhetoric and speech offer practical applications of reason and when well used advance the welfare of all. Tyranny, in contrast, is defined by a rejection of fellowship on the part of the ruler who deprives others for the sake of their own advantage and neglects the general welfare (III. 28–31). Liberty, as both the absence of tyranny and a commitment to the preservation of private property, can support the broader and fundamental principles of a life in common. Thus, for Cicero, republican commitments informed by a certain idea of liberty are direct consequences of his idea of basic human sociality. The virtues serve to express and deepen this sociality, hence the invocation of both the honourable and the beneficial as central to making sense of ethical behaviour. Of course, more broadly all this is conceived as guided by principles of reason, of nature and of happiness (understood as tranquillity of individual soul) as well as of the normative concern at a collective level to pursue the common benefit.[48]

It is important to emphasise the degree to which Cicero's *On Duties* is rooted in a basic Stoic outlook, albeit with some modifications (1, 6). The

---

[48] For a further elaboration of these precepts, see eds. D. Kapust and G. Remer eds., *The Ciceronian Tradition in Political Theory* (Madison: University of Wisconsin Press, 2021).

Stoic view justifies public action through an acknowledgement of the rational capacities shared by all and it is supported conceptually through the idea of duty. Public action and service is seen as one aspect of a continuum of responsibilities in social life starting with the family and branching out to the human community at large. The noble individual, at least in fundamental terms, is not motivated primarily by emotion or by a sense of warm sympathy and solidarity with other human beings, but by what they are bound to do as a rational individual. Indeed, in *On Duties* Cicero refers twice to his admiration of a need to perform public duties alongside a display of disdain for human affairs (1.61 and 1.72), largely implying that it is the ideal of rational motivation that drives and grounds the goodness of the dutiful action at the level of the state, rather than any particulars of the human existence it may impact. So, while the public actor must seek an outcome of justice and advancement of the public welfare, they must also be of, or develop, a disposition that allows them "freedom from anguish" (1. 72). At the same time, acting effectively in the public realm is a cause for personal honour, open to those unique individuals who have a "greatness of spirit" but who also share in the more general human predisposition of "an impulse towards pre-eminence" (1. 13). The type of republican commitment issuing from this vision of duty is secondary to a focus on rational self-command as the cornerstone of Stoic ethics.

In basic terms, public service for Cicero is done in view of the most fundamental principles of human sociality, meaning that because humans can only flourish in an organised social life, politics is an important and necessary instrument to ensure that social life is conducted in the most effective way and with justice. In discussing the application of the principles of public duty, Cicero also acknowledges that context and circumstances play a role in determining how they are applied and concedes that these are not often an easy calculation. He singles out certain rules that may facilitate awareness of where reason lies, such as properly assessing the needs of relevant parties and judging who is in most need of our help (1, 59). While military exploits seem most suited to fulsome praise and admiration, as demonstrated by the multiple statues of those dressed in military attire, military commands are to be shunned as an entry into public life as they tend to stir desires for the wrong sort of glory (1, 70). Perhaps one of the greatest challenges in public life is to ensure that the individual most suited to the greatness of spirit or "a brave and great spirit" that the position requires is not to be carried away with themselves to the point of neglecting the pursuit of justice.

A brave and great spirit is in general seen in two things. One lies in disdain for things external, in the conviction that a man should admire, should choose, should pursue nothing except what is honourable and seemly, and should yield to no man, nor to agitation of the spirit, nor to fortune. The second thing is that you should in the spirit I have described, do deeds which are great, certainly, but above all beneficial, and you should vigorously undertake difficult and laborious tasks which endanger both life itself and much that concerns life. (1, 66).

Cicero does not advise a career in public life for all his young readers, but only those who have a capacity for this greatness of spirit and rational self-control. Duties of justice trump even the pursuit of knowledge given that there is nothing more sacred than human fellowship. Those who help to preserve that human community should be acknowledged as providing some of the greatest benefits to humanity. In turn, those who do this in the right way and in the pursuit of justice are most likely to achieve glory (II, 38 and 42). He suggests earlier in the same work that the greatest achievements are often associated with men who rule the republic because their government "reaches extremely widely and affects the greatest number." (1, 92)

In sum, Cicero's philosophy of public life focuses on the important work of rhetoric or oratory – that is, the skill of the public figure to persuade and bring one's fellow citizens to justice as an extension of the basic virtues required by a basic sociality of human life. In political terms, these conditions are best met by a republican regime committed to a principle of liberty including the preservation of property. Through the invocation of reason and its dictates in natural law the public figure is driven by a vision of the honourable life that responds firstly to the rational demands of justice and secondly to what the beneficial requires. His account of ethics is not limited to the political realm but encompasses realms of commerce and other activities that impact the lives of a broad number of citizens. While conundrums of ethical reasoning may arise, as is evident through the text of *On Duties* itself, such puzzles should not impact the public figure who is to act in accordance with reason in a spirit of relative imperturbability (1, 80). The general spirit of Ciceronian advice is that public ethics is just one arena where the work of justice is played out. While some of the challenges of ethical reasoning may be more pointed for the public figure, the demands of justice appear to be everywhere the same.

Plutarch's approach differs in important ways. In the first instance it should be noted that while Cicero in *On Duties* is writing a treatise to cover in a comprehensive way the ethical issues associated with embarking on a life of public service, Plutarch writes about public service in several essays written for different audiences and different purposes; thus, his ideas are not expressed in quite as systematic a way, and some with a more pragmatic tone than others. In addition, while Cicero appears concerned to demonstrate how the pursuit of honour can stay tethered to the pursuit of justice in the context of public service, Plutarch appears to be more interested in the exact contours of inner motivation as well as the more general way the moral psychology of individuals and groups affect the ethics of governance.

While Cicero speaks of public service as a duty in the service of the more fundamental principles of sociality, Plutarch speaks of public service as itself natural, and in certain ways as adhering to order of the cosmos. For Plutarch it is not only that human beings need others to flourish, as a theory of sociality would hold, but that public service itself "is a way of life for a tamed, political and social animal, one that by its nature must live its whole life interacting with its fellow citizens, pursuing what is good, and caring for humankind."[49] Public service is not functional to a social need, rather it incorporates all those activities through which individuals demonstrate the intrinsic connection between their quality of life and that of the whole. This can lend itself to a more capacious understanding of public life.[50] Plutarch makes a more expanded notion of statesmanship explicit beginning at 796c in *Old Men in Public Affairs*:

> In addition to stating all these things, we must mention that practicing politics does not consist only in holding office, leading embassies, shouting loudly in the assembly, and raging around the speaker's platform while giving a speech or proposing a law. Most people think that those activities are the sum of politics, however, just as they doubtless think that practicing philosophy is only a matter of conducting dialogues from a chair and reciting lectures from books. But the continuous practice of both politics and philosophy, which may be observed on a daily basis in deeds and actions, escapes those people . . . But practicing politics is just like practicing philosophy. Socrates, for instance, did not set up desks for his students, sit in a teacher's chair, or reserve a prearranged time for lecturing and walking with his pupils. No, he practiced philosophy while joking around (when the chance arose) and drinking and serving on military campaigns and hanging

---

[49] Plutarch, "Should an Old Man Engage in Politics?" in Beneker ed., *How to be a Leader*, 273.

[50] Plutarch gives us a justification of the political realm in *To an Uneducated Ruler*. He suggests that the goods of the earth can only be enjoyed and used in a climate of law and justice shaped by the work of a political leader. "Now justice is the aim and end of law, but law is the work of the ruler, and the ruler is the image of God who orders all things." (δίκη μεν ουν νόμου τέλος εστι νόμος δ' άρχοντος έργον άρχων δ'εικων θεου του πάντα κοσμουντς 780e). So, at one level, politics serves as an activity that allows all human beings to take full advantage of the goods of the earth.

around the marketplace with some of his students, and finally, even while under arrest and drinking the hemlock. He was the first to demonstrate that our lives are open to philosophy at all times and in every aspect, while experiencing every emotion, and in each and every activity.

This, then, is how we must also conceive of the public life. *Foolish people practice politics* not by serving as generals, secretaries, or popular leaders, but *by inciting the mob, giving public speeches, fostering discord, or performing public service out of obligation*; and conversely, those who are civic-minded, philanthropic, devoted to the city, attentive, and truly political are always practicing politics by the promotion of those in power, the guidance of those needing direction, the support of those deliberating, the correction of those causing harm, and the reinforcement of those who are sensible. It is clear that these people attend to public business not only as a side-line; that they go to the theater and the council chamber not merely to take pride of place when there is important business at hand or they are summoned there; that when they come to meetings, moreover, they attend not simply for their amusement as though they were attending a show or a lecture; and that even when they are not physically present, they nonetheless participate by thinking about the business at hand and inquiring about what occurred, approving of some of the actions taken and expressing dissatisfaction with others. For Aristides at Athens and Cato the Elder at Rome did not hold office very many times, but they did constantly dedicate their whole lives to serving their citizens. Epaminondas had many great accomplishments as general, but no less worthy of memory is what he accomplished in Thessaly while serving neither as general nor elected leader.[51]

We see here that good forms of politics are defined, whether effected through public office or not, as those which reflect public spiritedness, love of mankind and of the state, and care for the public welfare (τον δε κοινωνικον και φιλάνθρωπον και φιλόπολιν και κηδεμονικον και πολιτικον αληθως 796e). Plutarch here rejects those who perform public service out of obligation, or duty, it would seem in direct contrast with Cicero. Trapp suggests this passage highlights a convergence of politics and philosophy in Plutarch, at least insofar as both carry a claim of instantiating the good life.[52] Most notably for my analysis here, what politics and philosophy

---

[51] Plutarch, "Should an Old Man Engage in Politics?" 327–331. I call the essay *Old Man in Public Affairs* as the name it is more frequently given. My emphasis.

[52] Michael Trapp, "Statesmanship in a Minor Key?" in Lukas de Blois et al. eds., *The Statesman in Plutarch's Works. Vol. 1 Plutarch's Statesman and his Aftermath*, (Leiden: Brill, 2004), 195. "Plutarch seeks to make the choice of political engagement seem like just that choice of the right way to live which philosophy claims to promote. This point is not exactly that he is thus trying to change politics into something else ... but rather that he wishes to claim that there is a version of politics that turns out also to satisfy the criteria that philosophy lays down for the good life; and that his version of politics thus turns out to be the only truly fulfilling form of the activity."

clearly share for Plutarch is their nature as vocations, and it is from this principle, I think, that Plutarch makes an identification of the two. Public service, as exercised in the best sense, is associated with a specific type of disposition that accompanies speaking, acting, reasoning and judging well in view of seeking the general welfare with constant attention and in all matters. It is not something one should do for instrumental reasons, out of duty, or as a past-time just when matters are of interest, or largely for purposes of honour seeking, because those reasons and motivations have a negative impact on how public responsibility is conceived and exercised.

There is independent ethical value to the political actor who enhances the general welfare through stewardship and service. Politics is invoked as a natural good, because it is defined normatively as an activity through which the "honour and welfare" of humankind is pursued, which brings together the noble motivations of the good statesman and the pursuit of noble things for one's fellow beings (φιλοκάλως και φιλανθρώπως ζην 791d). This suggests that outcomes of action are also of ethical relevance. The underlying assumption is that noble things (i.e. the honour and welfare of mankind) do not generally come about on their own or inadvertently in other spheres, such as the household. Rather they require some form of coordination and organisation among like-minded individuals. Furthermore, political service is important and unique in Plutarch's philosophy because those who serve are seen not only as the source of law, but also as a sort of icon or symbol of the divine (here a metaphysical Platonic principle) seeking to institute justice, much like the sun offers light and life in the natural world. In this way, Plutarch offers quite an elevated vision of the nature of public office, which can be deemed under proper circumstances as the place of those who offer a pale image of divine benevolence and virtue, and who can rule with some resonance of "order, justice, truth and mildness."[53] This notion resonates in a more practical piece of advice in his essay "Political Precepts" where he notes: "Above all, we must honor every public office, treating it as a great and sacred thing."[54]

Alongside this vision of the more elevated spirit of public service, at least in relation to Cicero, Plutarch offers a much more mundane understanding of the actual content of public service. Plutarch refers to Epaminondas who, when appointed to an insignificant office by the Theban people with the intent to insult him, took on the tasks of overseeing the clearing of

---

[53] Plutarch, "To an Uneducated Leader," in Beneker ed., *How to be a Leader*, 19.
[54] Plutarch, "How to be a Good Leader," in Beneker ed., *How to be a Leader*, 167. I call the essay "Political Precepts" in this book.

dung and diverting of water from the streets and in doing so with a spirit of care and concern, brought new honour to the office.[55] Similarly, Plutarch speaks about his own work overseeing construction, including the measuring of tiles and delivering of stones, activities that can take on a dignified quality if done with great care and concern because they are done on behalf of the city and as an act of public service.[56] This is not a question of a measure of their utility, as evoked for instance in Cicero's example of measuring the costs and benefits of the importation of corn. The moral worth of the activity in these instances is reflected in the justification for *why* one is doing them which in turn affects *how* it is done and *how* it is perceived. So, while the content or direct outcome of the tasks involved may not always seem worthy of great honour, the purpose for which they are done and the spirit in which they are done can elevate them much higher than they might be in ordinary life.

This idea filters into the issue of how to work with others in public life. For Plutarch, the suggestion is that a certain sharing of responsibilities and tasks in public life is recommended, in other words avoiding an excessive concentration of power at the top. However, this is not suggested as a matter of collective liberty but rather for reasons of effectiveness in meeting public goals. He gives the examples of both a sailing ship, where the goal of navigation is better met through a division of responsibilities, and the hand, where acts of dexterity (including the typing of this very phrase) is better met when each finger is doing its specialised task. Here a sharing of power in the public realm is effected to meet the public goals in the best way.[57]

Nonetheless, the dignified nature of acts of public service is not something automatically conferred by the holding of public office; for Plutarch it is also connected with the personal qualities of the office holder. It is the quality of the agent in conjunction with the public office they occupy that can elevate and give a special quality to those public actions. In turn those qualities may ensure that individuals continue to play an important role in terms of counsel and help in times of crisis. For Plutarch, the virtue of the person in public office is a crucial consideration in the quality of rule. Character is also an important feature for Cicero, of course.

Both Cicero and Plutarch acknowledge that for those in public office, a sense of justice or primacy of the general welfare should be an overriding principle of good rule. It also means for both that despite the existence of

---

[55] Plutarch, "How to be a Good Leader," 127.   [56] Plutarch, "How to be a Good Leader," 129.
[57] Plutarch, "How to be a Good Leader," 135–137.

conflict among social groups and players, some of which may even have positive consequences, the seeking of concord through pursuit of the common benefit should always be the overriding normative and driving feature of political life. Still, unlike Cicero, Plutarch does not invoke liberty as an essential feature of social and political order (nor does he invoke the preservation of property as a key feature of liberty) but rather the idea of the humane (as we have seen in Plutarch's criticism of the Spartan treatment of the helots) and the need for well-intentioned and effective leadership. Cicero is a defender of republican institutions as better suited to the promotion of collective liberty. Plutarch is less concerned with institutions to prevent tyranny than the need for good education, suitable motivation and good counsel for those occupying public office to avoid a misuse of political power.

Cicero also recognises the need for good motivations for those entering public service. They must have no intentions to do harm and seek to serve the common advantage (1, 32) with a commitment to let reason guide actions. If one is driven to mete out justice to achieve glory, they must do so with an appropriate understanding of glory. Like Plutarch, Cicero suggests that an entry into public life should be an intentional decision. Both call on the importance of reason in ruling in the soul as a mark of good character and virtue. However, Cicero's distilled Stoic principles also distinguish him from Plutarch in his thinking about how good character manifests itself in public life.

In the first instance, Plutarch suggests that the robust pursuit of personal honour and good public service do not always align. He suggests in "Political Precepts" that the individual who seeks honour excessively in public life becomes contemptible.[58] It can be a vice in politics: "the love of honour, although it is a more impressive quality than the love of profit, is no less ruinous to a political system. For a love of honour makes people bolder and more reckless; it is a natural component not of sluggish and humble policies, but of those that are especially vigorous and impetuous; and the wave of praise that surges from the mob often helps to elevate and inflate one's love of honor, rendering it uncontrollable and unmanageable."[59] In "To an Uneducated Leader" he raises the example of Theopompus who *reduced* the powers of his office to reduce public envy and enhance public welfare for future regimes. His wife (wives often serve as a voice of unreason in Greek philosophy . . .) objected that he was dishonouring himself by this action, but Theopompus and Plutarch

---

[58] Plutarch, "How to be a Good Leader," 133.   [59] Plutarch, "How to be a Good Leader," 181–183.

defend the action as one of great political insight that served to enhance the future concord of the state.[60] While Cicero does suggest that glory-seeking can be excessive, he associates it with such things as pursuit of military victory. Cicero has a much more capacious idea of the acceptable degree of honour seeking in a public position.

In addition, Plutarch allows for a much more nuanced appreciation of the emotions for the person of good character in public service. For example, Plutarch suggests a better ruler is one who fears harming the governed, and there are times when he actively praises the sentiments of anguish of those in public life related to the often-difficult choices that must be made.[61] This, of course, provides a sharp contrast with Cicero's injunction that the ruler rid themselves of anxieties and anguish. They also diverge on the important issue in the classical world regarding the place of anger. In line with general Stoic precepts Cicero suggests that "anger should be denied on all occasions" (1, 88). In contrast, closer to the Peripatetics, Plutarch praises the way Phocion used his anger to defend the public welfare, while knowing how not to hold personal grudges and to remain friendly and civil with his colleagues outside of the public realm.

In discussing how the person in public office should relate to others, Cicero often invokes the idea of "being seemly" and "seemliness" (1, 99, 100). This relates to the ideas of moderation and restraint which he advocates, but it also invokes a form of self-regulation based on the expectations of status and class. Thus, he also suggests this aligns with "the appearance of a gentleman." What this suggests, then, is that the behaviour of the public official should also be governed by internalised norms of socially generated expectations regarding how a man of elite status should act. The individual here is to be concerned about social reputation which is judged not only by what one does but also by how one acts. Acting with respect towards others and not indulging in the excessive shaming of another, even if they are of a lower status, is part of what it means to act in a seemly way.

This mode of self-regulation through internalising of traditional social expectations in Cicero is distinct from the study of the inner lives of his subjects, including emotions, that we find in Plutarch. The moral essays together with the *Lives* highlight the central importance for Plutarch of a deeper *internalist* account, allowing him to describe detailed features of a specific character, rather than just a generalist idea of what principles

---

[60] Plutarch, "To an Uneducated Leader," 7.
[61] Plutarch, "To an Uneducated Leader," 23 and 27.

might govern public service. As we saw in the passage cited above, Plutarch rejects the idea of embarking on public service through a sense of obligation or duty (as Cicero's rationalistic account would hold), which ends with the term of office. Instead, he considers appropriate political motivation as a deeper concern about public welfare that is manifested throughout one's activities and that is an extension of one's personal attributes. And while more interested in manifestations of good character, Plutarch also demonstrates a fascination for human weaknesses. In sum, Plutarch is more interested in plotting wide and deep manifestations of the internal life of his subjects (as we have seen in the various summaries of select lives) and by extension the intersubjective moral psychology of public action.

We get a glimpse of their respective considerations when we examine what they see as significant in the actions of the same historical figure. In the texts I am exploring here both refer to the famous suicide of Cato the Younger. For Cicero, the actions of Cato are looked at through the lens of the "seemly," and he specifies that one must seek to be consistent and project an evenness in life and action (I, 112). Cato's suicide, rather than being captured by Caesar, was regarded as consistent with his "extraordinary seriousness" and "unfailing constancy" and thus was deemed admirable in view of his own adopted purpose (so others who surrendered should not be condemned if they were gentler and more easy-going). Cicero is concerned here with projecting constancy as a feature of the "seemly." Plutarch also refers to the events at Utica but views them in a somewhat different way.[62] He suggests that after his defeat in battle Cato first ensured that the troops were embarked onto ships and sent away safely before his suicide, demonstrating that his first thoughts were for the welfare of those who fought and that he did not want to impose on them the end he saw for himself. While in some ways saying the same thing, that Cato was an extraordinary individual, they also do so with a different sensibility and purpose which may capture some of their differences. Plutarch is attentive to action and behaviours that reveal some of the content of the inner workings of the individual mind, namely Cato's concern and sensibility for the priorities of his followers which may not have matched his own.

As an extension of this, Plutarch pays closer attention to the social psychology of the regime in which the public leader functions. One of the first things noted by Plutarch in "Political Precepts" is the need for the ruler to know the ethos of those they govern, to discern their aptitudes,

---

[62] Plutarch, "To an Uneducated Leader," 25.

capabilities and limits. This will greatly impact what public leaders can achieve in public life in terms of shaping their community. For Plutarch, like the metaphor of the sun arching in the sky in the life of Phocion, the task for the public figure is to find the appropriate calibration of moderation in consonance with justice and the public good, a stance which requires a good reading of the situation as well as the capacities and feelings of the broader public. The reciprocity required of a Plutarchan public figure is less that of a participant in a broader public dialogue and more of one who is capable of knowing their public and is sensitive to the various parameters of the circumstances. In addition, Plutarch unlike Cicero offers insight into how to manage some of the competitiveness and possible envy and love of honour that governs relations among those within public service.[63]

In relation to a greater attentiveness to matters of social psychology, another feature that distinguishes Plutarch's approach to public life from that of Cicero is his consideration of the special features and optics of public life, something I will focus on more concertedly in Chapter 3. Plutarch recognises how small faults can appear larger in public life, and even how the public can be prone to deep criticism and conspiratorial accusations against public figures, something that may require careful management in policy deliberation.[64] He also acknowledges how power can encourage depravity by giving those of bad character the ability to act on their emotions in a way they might otherwise avoid.[65] So while Plutarch shares with Cicero a commitment to justice in political life, which includes a certain knowledge of philosophy, Plutarch also pays concerted attention to moral psychology, something not found in the same way in Cicero. Attentiveness to moral psychology makes one a better judge of strengths and weaknesses of character and will better equip an individual to take on responsibilities. A good disposition will include an awareness of the elevated work of public service if done in the proper spirit to enhance the general welfare and to strive for basic humaneness and the avoidance of tyranny.

The more insightful and complex portrait of human psychology offered by Plutarch may make the attainment of justice in public life an even greater challenge than that set forth in Cicero. Individuals are often portrayed as not having full command over themselves nor indeed do

---

[63] Plutarch, "How to be a Good Leader," 135–137, 181 and "Old Men in Public Affairs," 249–251.
[64] Plutarch, "How to be a Good Leader," 71 and 141–143.
[65] Plutarch, "To an Uneducated Leader," 33.

they always have full responsibility for their characters. If we include his writing from the *Lives*, Plutarch's work offers a contextual appreciation of political challenges with a consideration of a much wider range of situations than Cicero.

In relation to this, what will be of relevance for the analysis in this book is how these two thinkers compare in their treatment of the unique challenges of public life. For Cicero, alongside the question of knowing what honour requires, something that philosophy can offer insight into, is the question of how to act in those circumstances where honour and benefit appear to conflict. These are issues that may sometimes arise in politics, though not uniquely in political life, and which Cicero takes up for the most part in the third section of *On Duties*. He offers the example of tyrannicide (in the not-so-veiled allusion to the killing of Julius Caesar) which violates the rules of honour by committing murder of a close friend but rids the people of a tyrant (III, 19). In the discussion that follows Cicero suggests that laws protecting life and property can in certain instances be violated if the act is done not for the benefit of self, but for the maintenance and saving of human fellowship, and as a condition for justice. The tyrant is acknowledged as an enemy to human fellowship and thus their murder is justified by the great benefit to the community. Cicero points to other situations where the principles of honour and benefit might appear to conflict, such as dealing with friendships. He suggests that commitment to friends should never lead us to act contrary to the interests of the republic (III, 43). In the main, though, these are situations that can arise in all arenas of life. While he notes that in public affairs there is a propensity to wrongly judge what is to the benefit of the community, in general the relevant ethical calculation for Cicero is the public as the collective beneficiary (or victim) of the action, whether it be performed by a private entrepreneur (III, 59 concerning the corn merchant) or the public official. The general idea to be emphasised here is that Cicero's notion of justice as relevant to public matters relates to the invocation of the whole community as the *object* of ethical calculation in reference to general notions of honour and benefit. While Cicero's work may have been written to young men thinking about taking up a career in public life, and while his ideas were engaged with by such as Machiavelli, who is sometimes thought to be at the root of reason of state thinking, it is important to stress that there is nothing in Cicero's texts and in the principles he invokes to suggest that public officials themselves are subject to any different sort of ethical calculation or experiential dynamics from any other individuals, such as merchants whose work and decisions might have an impact on the quality of collective life. Cicero's concern is with the principles that should be invoked by anyone who has a concern for justice, and how they should be applied. While the idea of *salus populi suprema lex* (taken from Cicero's *Laws*) might appear to privilege the public official, as we have seen in the case of Caesar it is as easily taken on by the people themselves or their advocates to rid themselves of a perceived tyrant to preserve the fellowship of the state.

What I will be invoking in relation to Plutarch is the potential for a different type of focus, one which was taken up and developed in a tradition of reception. The tradition I will be highlighting, first evident in the case of early modern French reception, is one that emphasises the unique *experiential* qualities of public life. With the *greater emphasis on individual and social psychology* in Plutarch's writing in general, we also see various ways in which *the unique features of being in a public position are highlighted and discussed*. With a more perspicacious outlook on the unique intersubjective dynamics of public life alongside a continuing adherence to the fundamental moral goals of politics, Plutarch opens a space for considering *the public realm as unique*, not because traditional ethical goals are suspended or reduced to a calculation of interest as in reason-of-state thinking, but because public space itself is characterised by distinct types of relation in which those ethical goals are pursued. Indeed, the pragmatic thrust of "Political Precepts", being one of the first published vernacular translations of Plutarch's essays in Renaissance France, contributed to a much greater sense of the applicability of Plutarch's writing to politics in an early modern context. This makes the account of the reception of Plutarch's work in the French case more complicated given a combination of a more traditional moralist thrust of much of the opus with overlying realist insights and concessions. I will be developing these themes more concertedly in Chapter 3.

1.4 Conclusion

The purpose of this overview has been in part to try to capture some of the spirit of Plutarch's analysis. Through a recounting of some of his most iconic biographies for the tradition of reception I have argued that Plutarch was not generally concerned with the question of the best form of government. Instead, his central focus was the essence of human character, how character is formed as well as how it manifests in an often- complex mix. Adjudicating character for Plutarch is a complicated affair, both because much of the *Lives* is pitched as an exercise in descriptive moralism, giving the readers leeway to sort out those judgements for themselves in many instances, and because the terms through which these characters are judged involve considerations of the good, the prudent, the pragmatic as well as the bad with the acknowledgement (perhaps in the spirit of Aristotle) that outcomes matter to the ethical worth of action and that an unbending principled actor demonstrates aspects of moral deficiency. Admittedly, I have illustrated this through a very general overview of a few pieces of a much larger work. Nonetheless, the selection here has been in part determined by the lives of Plutarch that appear to figure most in commentary and reception throughout the early modern period.

I also have compared the broad contributions of Plutarch with one of the figures most often cited in the literature of the history of political thought as shaping the contours of early modern political thought. By highlighting the uniqueness of Plutarch's work in relation to Cicero my hope is to supplement that earlier work, but also to demonstrate that the lines of reception from classical sources is not as straightforward as it might appear. Plutarch offered early modern political thinkers a set of sensibilities that were distinct from Cicero's.

This manner of understanding Plutarch's work also conflicts with the view that the central contribution of the work was mainly hagiographic – that is, uncritical praise and a pantheon of heroes offered as models for those engaged in public life with a focus on and celebration of some of their public actions and achievements.[66] Plutarch is not offering a pantheon of exemplars for ambitious young public figures to follow, a project that in itself would not require the parallel structure through which Plutarch's biographical work presents itself; instead, the forced intellectual work of comparison and contrast invites the reader to be more discerning and critical about the moral psychology of his subjects. As we have noted, his interest is less in the public contributions and actions of his subjects and more in the personal qualities and the evolution of character in both positive and negative manifestations that help to illustrate more basic principles concerning the practice of virtue and its relation to education and pressures of circumstance. Insofar as there is an exemplary dynamic in the work, it operates in the implicit attraction of the qualities of virtue, moderation and self-discipline and through a repudiation of excess in its various manifestations.

---

[66] An example of this perspective is the work by Robert Lloyd George, *A Modern Plutarch: Comparisons of the Most Influential Modern Statesmen* (New York: Overlook Duckworth, 2016). The implication here is that for Plutarch what is important is their influence and their deeds. As we have already seen, Plutarch may invoke his subjects as known figures, but it is not generally in a spirit of celebration but in a spirit of inquiry regarding what can be judged about their inner lives.

CHAPTER 2

The Secret History of Plutarch (and the History of Pseudo-Plutarch) and a Brief Account of Reception in Renaissance Italy

This chapter traces two aspects in the narrative of the retrieval of Plutarch's work in the medieval period through the early Renaissance. The first part explores the legacy of Plutarch in a canonical text of the medieval era: John of Salisbury's *Policraticus* (c. 1159). Despite the longstanding identification of John's work with that of Plutarch, the association has been judged by Plutarch scholars to be spurious. John (c. 1115–1180) is regarded as one of the foremost political and moral thinkers of the twelfth century known for his organic understanding of the political community. In *Policraticus*, it appears, he either directly concocted a letter from Plutarch to Trajan along with a summary of political advice, or he leaned heavily on a manuscript falsely attributed to Plutarch or fragments of the same.[1] Whichever story is true, the letter and advice took on a life of their own and were recopied and recited countless times in the history of political thought as the work of Plutarch. The claims in John's text about Plutarch are so influential in the history of ideas, and the notion of Plutarch as tutor to Emperor Trajan so pervasive in the minds of early modern readers that it would be remiss to tell a story of Plutarch reception in Europe without acknowledging the place and influence of this work.

Of course, this adds greater challenges to the story of reception, not only because the origins here are murky. We may also need to come to terms with the fact that those early modern scholars who were reading authentic works of Plutarch along with this and other works ascribed falsely to Plutarch (works whose authorship we refer to collectively as pseudo-Plutarch), were still reading their authentic Plutarch through this lens, believing that he had been a tutor to the emperor and had written these other spurious works. The question of pseudo-Plutarch is not one of delving into an additional strand of a large and varied tradition. In this

---

[1] Marianne Pade, "The Reception of Plutarch from Antiquity to the Italian Renaissance," in Mark Beck ed., *A Companion to Plutarch* (Oxford: Blackwell, 2014), 532.

case, the work of pseudo-Plutarch helped to shape the very suppositions and contours of the whole tradition of interpretation. We must consider not just *what* representation of Plutarch it offered but also *how* this strand might have had an impact on a longer tradition of Plutarch reception.

Analysis of relevant aspects of the *Policratus*, together with examination of pseudo-Plutarch works that constitute an important part of the narrative of the reception of Plutarch in Europe, are the main thrust of this chapter. This core is framed, front and back, by two brief historical accounts of the transmission of Plutarch's work as recounted in existing literature on Plutarch reception. The first account highlights the ways in which Plutarch's work survived into the medieval era, largely through the work of key scholars of Byzantium. As a summary of existing research this first account is meant to provide a broad introductory background for those readers with little previous awareness of the issues concerning Plutarch reception in the medieval era. In the latter and concluding account, I offer a brief introduction to some of the politics of Plutarch reception in early Renaissance Italy, where the first important transmission and translations of Plutarch from Greek to Latin occurred and where a new generation of humanists began to define themselves in relation to his work. I address here a few examples (Leonardo Bruni and Guarino) of a wider tradition of commentary in the Italian context. This short focus on the Italian case offers a backdrop for my argument concerning the singularity and significance of the reception of Plutarch in the French Renaissance for a set of ideas I call public humanism (as I will do in Chapter 3). While the focus of this book is on the reception of Plutarch in France and England and the translation of his work into the vernacular languages of French and English, it is important to acknowledge the increasing attention Plutarch's works were already enjoying in 1400s Italy and to build my case for the uniqueness of the tradition of French reception in contrast.

The broader dynamic addressed in this chapter is the process through which Plutarch, whose work focused to a large extent on matters of moral psychology and moral education as well as history, came to be associated more closely with politics. While it was not the case that every early modern person read Plutarch as a uniquely political thinker, we will see in subsequent chapters how various thinkers, especially in Renaissance France, drew on Plutarch for inspiration in the development of political ideas. That direction in Plutarch reception has something to do with earlier patterns of reception in both medieval Europe and Renaissance Italy, both of which I trace in broad strokes. This chapter provides some of the background that helps explain how it was possible for many thinkers in Renaissance France to presume to draw on Plutarch's work for special insight into political matters.

2.1 Plutarch in Byzantium: A Very Brief Overview

The best account of the early history of Plutarch reception through the Roman Empire and into the Renaissance period is Marianne Pade's *The Reception of Plutarch's Lives in Fifteenth-Century Italy*, an invaluable work.[2] The Lamprias Catalogue offered an inventory of 'books' – papyrus rolls – amounting to 227 titles copied and attributed to Plutarch sometime in the third to fifth century.[3] It is not without its errors: it lists books now attributed to Aristotle and other authors, and it excludes others that we know are attributed to Plutarch, but it does give us some clues regarding not only the breadth of Plutarch's work, but the fact that a great deal of his work remained accessible to scholars centuries after his death. Indeed, Pade notes that Plutarch was famous at the time of his death, and his work was known to a large number of the cultured elite, including Appian who drew on Plutarch in his writing of history.[4] She suggests that the interest of later Roman writers in Plutarch was largely focused on the *Moralia*.[5] Today we have access to roughly half of those works of Plutarch noted in the Lamprias Catalogue.[6]

While Plutarch's place in classical literature and the Roman world waned after the drafting of the catalogue, his work continued to receive attention in Greece and in the Byzantine Empire. Pade suggests that Plutarch's work was known to the educated public in the Eastern Empire until at least the sixth century, with another resurgence of interest in the ninth century.[7] In the thirteenth century Maxime Planudes (1255–1305) compiled Plutarch's extant work and reproduced it in carefully edited manuscript versions.[8] Plutarch scholars today owe much to Planudes for ensuring that a great deal of Plutarch's corpus survived into the age of the printing press. One copy made by Planudes that included the entire

---

[2] Marianne Pade, *The Reception of Plutarch's Lives in Fifteenth-Century Italy*, 2 vols. (Copenhagen: Museum Tusculanum Press, 2007). See also the more recent Sophia Xenophontos and Katerina Oikonomopoulou eds. *Brill's Companion to the Reception of Plutarch* (Leiden: Brill, 2019).

[3] The 'editio princeps' of this catalogue by D. Hoeschel can be found in the Loeb edition of Plutarch's collected works.

[4] Pade, *Reception*, 38.   [5] Pade, "The Reception of Plutarch," 532.   [6] Lamberton, *Plutarch*, 22.

[7] Pade, *Reception*, 59.

[8] See, for example, "Maximos Planoudes and the Transmission of Plutarch's Moralia," in Sophia Xenophontos and K. Oikonomopoulou eds., *Brill's Companion to the Reception of Plutarch*, 295–309.

Moralia was owned by Pace da Ferrara, one of a group of Paduan pre-humanists of the fourteenth century.[9] Still, as generally recognised, outside of Byzantium in the medieval period there was little knowledge of the Greek language, so there was little if any direct knowledge of Plutarch's work in the West.[10]

2.2 John of Salisbury's *Policraticus* and the Question of Pseudo-Plutarch

2.2.1 Policraticus *(c. 1159)*

Perhaps one of the most famous works ascribed to Plutarch is a short piece that he never wrote. It is a letter purportedly written by Plutarch to his supposed pupil Trajan, emperor of Rome, and the summary of an accompanying text. The letter first appeared in publication at the start of Book v of one of medieval Europe's most well-known political treatises: John of Salisbury's *Policraticus* (a work which predated Planudes's manuscript editions of Plutarch). The letter, also referred to as the *Institutio Traiani*, is a bit of a mystery because although it is very well known there is no trace or evidence of any reference to it prior to the publication of John's work.[11] Most Plutarch scholars reject the idea that Plutarch ever taught Trajan, suggesting that the image of the philosopher-tutor was the product of a vibrant medieval imagination eager to see Platonic themes re-enacted in history. The explanation for the letter is that either John of Salisbury made it up, citing an invented Plutarch source to bolster his message (something that was not so uncommon in the medieval world), or that some form of manuscript tradition around this letter existed just before the completion of this work from which John drew believing in its authenticity.[12] Once

---

[9] Pade, *Reception*, 66

[10] Guiseppe di Stefano, "L'Hellénisme en France a l'Orée de la Renaissance," in Anthony Levy ed., *Humanism at the End of the Middle Ages and in the Early Renaissance* (Manchester and New York: Manchester University Press and Barnes and Noble, 1970), 29–42.

[11] Pade, "The Reception of Plutarch," 537.

[12] For a discussion of the debate over how John came to invoke Plutarch (i.e. whether there was a pre-existing apocryphal manuscript or not), see Janet Martin, "John of Salisbury as Classical Scholar," in Michael Wilks ed., *The World of John of Salisbury* (Oxford: Blackwell, 1994), 194–196. Martin argues John's account of the manuscript is manufactured. It is not an isolated case in John's work. Still, there is another dedicatory letter to Trajan in Plutarch's extant corpus that prefaces a collection of *Sayings* or *Apophthegmata*. While many have thought this letter also to be spurious, there are some Plutarch scholars who see it as authentic and evidence of Plutarch's high standing at the time. See Mark Beck, "Plutarch to Trajan: The Dedicatory Letter and the *Apophthegmata* Collection," in Philip Stadter and Luc van der Stock eds., *Sage and Emperor: Plutarch, Greek Intellectuals, and Roman Power in the Time of Trajan (98–117 AD)* (Leuven: Leuven University Press, 2002), 163–174.

presented by John, the myth of Plutarch as Trajan's educator grew as a matter of common knowledge throughout the medieval period and was repeated so often that even today it is sometimes cited as fact in learned circles.[13]

This is perhaps the most famous example of a pseudo-Plutarch text, but it is not the only one. I will first explore the nature and significance of John of Salisbury's Plutarch before tying it in with other examples of false attribution related to Plutarch in the history of ideas. This includes pseudo-Plutarch's essay on Homer which became one of the most important sources on Homer for a long period of European intellectual history, as well as "On the Education of Children" (often also referred to in its translated Latin title *De liberis educandis*). The latter is a spurious work attributed to Plutarch that was widely circulated in the Renaissance.

We might say that John's *Policraticus* incorporates two pieces attributed to Plutarch. The first is the letter to Trajan the Emperor, a letter which is cited verbatim, and which later was transmitted independently or included in other compilations of works attributed to Plutarch, and the second is a summary of a text offering a theory of government. According to Pade these two parts of the *Institutio Traiani* were broadly accepted as genuine works until late into the fifteenth century.[14]

While a long and multifaceted work, in broad terms *Policraticus* is John's attempt to articulate a theory about the coordination and interrelation of temporal and ecclesiastical institutions and priorities. The important metaphor of unity is that of the body and soul, which work together for the good of the whole, but which also have distinct purposes and goals. In this context, striving for earthly justice is a duty for all individuals in their temporal life, a goal which neither undermines nor conflicts with a seeking of eternal life in heaven.

His ethics are largely Aristotelian in inspiration and a prime example of philosophical naturalism as well as recognition of the autonomy of politics that can be found in medieval scholarship long before the translation and transmission of Aristotle's *Nicomachean Ethics* and *Politics* c. 1250.[15] He defends moderation and strongly denounces tyranny (especially in Books III and IV of the treatise), defining the tyrant as "any person who weds the ambitious desire to curtail the liberty of others with the power to

---

[13] It was cited once as a historical fact in a seminar I attended as a visitor at Cambridge.

[14] Pade, "The Reception of Plutarch," 537.

[15] On this discussion of Aristotelianism before Aristotle (at least insofar as the medieval period is concerned), see Cary J. Nederman, "Aristotelianism and the Origins of 'Political Science' in the Twelfth Century," *Journal of the History of Ideas* 52.2 (1991), 179–194.

accomplish this goal," a phenomenon he regards as possible in private and ecclesiastical life as well as in public life.[16] It is nonetheless public tyrants who are to be feared the most as they threaten the promise of security and liberty in all realms of life, and so all parts of the body politic are obligated to enforce justice and do what they must to condemn and stop tyranny.

John begins his discussion of Plutarch in Book v of the treatise. Chapter 1 offers the text of the presumed letter written by Plutarch to his former pupil Trajan.[17] In this letter there are allusions to some of the earlier themes of the book, namely a denunciation of ambition (with a need to cultivate humility) and the important theoretical and practical distinction between kingship and tyranny. His general message upholds a conjunction between the virtue of the ruler and the virtuousness of the rule. "If you first of all compose yourself, if you dispose all your affairs towards virtue, everything proceeds properly for you."[18] Plutarch acknowledges that his own reputation will be affected by the ultimate reputation of Trajan, and therefore in the closing of the letter Plutarch declares that he absolves himself of any responsibility and association if Trajan does not follow the advice.

The substance of Plutarch's teaching in the work sent to Trajan is then claimed to be summarised by John in the subsequent chapters. He justifies this way of proceeding by suggesting that it carries greater intellectual integrity. "One who follows everything in the text syllable-by-syllable is a servile interpreter who aims to express the appearance rather than the essence of an author."[19]

He begins with the famous depiction of the 'body politic.' In this instance, the soul of the community refers to the institution of religion and all that is done to assure salvation of the people. The head of the body is identified with the person of the prince; the heart with the senate; the ears, eyes and mouth with judges and governors of provinces; hands with officials and soldiers or knights; flanks to those who always assist the prince; stomach with the treasurers and record keepers; and feet with the peasants "perpetually bound to the soil, for whom it is all the more necessary that the head take precautions, in that they more often meet with accidents while they walk on the earth in bodily subservience; and those who erect,

---

[16] This synopsis is based on Nederman's excellent summary of John of Salisbury's arguments in "Introduction," to John of Salisbury, *Policraticus* (Cambridge: Cambridge University Press, 1990), xv–xxxvi. The quote is taken from xxiv.

[17] This letter was independently translated and attached to other editions of Plutarch, most notably to Sekoundinos's edition of the pseudo-Plutarch *De Politica* to be discussed later.

[18] John of Salisbury, *Policraticus*, v.1, 66.   [19] John of Salisbury, *Policraticus*, v.2, 67.

sustain and move forward the mass of the whole body are justly owed shelter and support."[20] As an invocation of a metaphor of body politic, it is still quite different from the fable of the belly (invoked in Aesop, Livy, as well as in Plutarch's *Life of Coriolanus*) used to demonstrate the interdependency of the governors and the governed as well as the indispensability of the state.[21] While certainly invoking a sense of interdependency, this metaphor goes further in ascribing to the prince a deeper function in helping to coordinate the whole and in acting with moral intent so that each part is attended to in the most appropriate way. According to Liebeschütz, this is simply a vivid restatement of a conventional medieval conception of the need for the secular and spiritual authorities to work together harmoniously, and it is one among many invocations of the notion of *corpus* or *corpus mysticum* invoked in philosophical and institutional argument in high medieval society as discussed by Kantorowitz.[22]

The focus for the prince is to develop an appropriate practice of virtue, with the understanding that there is a direct correlation between the virtue of the prince and good rule, in other words, that good leadership can be reduced to good morals. Still, the ruler does have special moral exigencies demanded of them, something that Salisbury identifies in four precepts: reverence for God, self-discipline, education of officials and of those in power, and love for and protection of subjects.[23]

Legitimacy in princely office for John depends to a large degree on moral conduct, meaning seeking wisdom and good advice in ruling, looking out for the welfare and liberty of subjects, and conducting oneself with moderation. "I do not hesitate to prefer Trajan, who built the majesty of his reign solely upon the practice of virtue."[24] The practice of good politics also requires that those in subordinate positions perform their function well and with integrity, so John, following Plutarch, examines the various types of officials in the state, from senators, governors and soldiers, explaining not only their duties, but the spirit in which these duties should be performed (e.g. tax collection without intimidation), with special attention paid to the need to avoid various forms of

---

[20] John of Salisbury, *Policraticus*, v.2, 67.

[21] David Hale notes that John of Salisbury appeals to this fable in the context of his wider metaphor of the state as corpus, but he does not allude to the philosophical distinction between the two. See "Intestine Sedition: The Fable of the Belly," *Comparative Literature Studies*, 5.4 (1968), 377–388.

[22] H. Liebeschütz, "John of Salisbury and Pseudo-Plutarch," *Journal of the Warburg and Courtauld Institutes*, 6 (1943), 33 and Ernst Kantorowicz, "*Pro patria mori* in Medieval Political Thought," *The American Historical Review* 56.3 (1951), 485.

[23] John of Salisbury, *Policraticus*, v.3, 68.   [24] John of Salisbury, *Policraticus*, v.8, 79–80.

corruption. Special responsibility falls on the prince to ensure that his officials are appropriately constrained and led to act according to a principle of moderation.

The lowliest in the political community, those who are represented by the feet, are those peasants, farmers, craftsmen, and other groups who supply the various needs of the population. These, as suggested by John through Plutarch, should govern their activities according to the principle of public utility within the boundaries of the law.

> For inferiors must serve superiors, who on the other hand ought to provide all necessary protection to their inferiors. For this reason, Plutarch says that what is to the advantage of the humbler people, that is, the multitude, is to be followed; for the fewer always submit to the more numerous. Therefore, magistrates were instituted for the reason that injuries might be averted from subjects and the republic itself might put shoes, as it were, on its workers. For when they are exposed to injuries it is as if the republic is barefoot; there can be nothing more ignominious for those who administer the magistracies ... The health of the whole republic will only be secure and splendid if the superior members devote themselves to the inferiors and if the inferiors respond likewise to the legal rights of their superiors, so that each individual may be likened to a part of the others reciprocally and each believes what is to his own advantage to be determined by that which he recognises to be most useful for others.[25]

In broad terms, then, the vision of public activity and public good here corresponds to a sense of stewardship for the whole in a broad framework of welfare and justice, with some degree of reciprocity among the various corporate entities of both state and society. As an alternative metaphor to the body, John – again through Plutarch – invokes the model of the hive, and in the form of a poem (surely a key point of reference in eighteenth-century Mandeville's ironic undermining of a corporatist vision of social order).

This work of John of Salisbury is not commonly what we identify as pseudo-Plutarch, although if he was working from an actual manuscript that predated his work, then we might identify the manuscript as such. In any case, knowing what scholars know now of Plutarch's extant works, we can say for certain that whatever John's source, a pre-existing manuscript or his own creative thought processes, the picture of the political community that he develops in Books v and vi under the name of Plutarch does not actually cohere with Plutarch's texts. We know this not only because

[25] John of Salisbury, *Policraticus*, VI.20, 126.

there is no manuscript (attributed to either Plutarch or pseudo-Plutarch) with this content predating the work, but also because there is no indication in the various stages when Plutarch's work was catalogued (e.g. the Lamprias Catalogue) that a manuscript with this supposed content ever existed. We must pause and consider then the significance of this, apart from the reference providing the weight and thereby the rhetorical power of classical authority.

Drawing on Nederman, I think it is noteworthy that we find in this work an alliance between the name of Plutarch and a broader work that espouses an independent theory of politics, suggesting that politics is neither a subordinate branch of theological matters, nor an extension of individual ethical considerations, but that there are issues of justice and welfare that are specific to politics. In other words, John highlights the fact that the function of leadership, or being the 'head' of state involves factoring in concerns and considerations beyond those in one's immediate vicinity. In broad terms it involves greater *breadth* and *depth* of ethical concern, though not tenor. The fact that Plutarch's name can be so easily invoked with an approach that is clearly identified as Aristotelian may shed some light on Plutarch's complex relation with Plato, for clearly Plutarch was not fully unknown (otherwise he would not have been cited as an authority).

Nonetheless, while providing greater basis for theories which would develop the notion of the relative autonomy of politics, what we do not find in John's Plutarch is any recognition of the specificity of 'the public' as a domain in which the individual actor is subject to distinct ethical dilemmas, concerns and restraints. In other words, while John's political leader needs to have a wider ethical sphere of concern than most, looking out for the feet as well as the hands, and with a concern for justice overall, it suffices for John's Plutarch that the ruler be a good and virtuous human being in accordance with traditional virtues for them to be able to exercise their functions properly and avoid tyrannical behaviour. The invocation of Plutarch with a doctrine of the relative autonomy of politics from theology was a step in the direction of a new consideration of the specific nature of the public, but it is not until the advent of Renaissance humanism that we will find a more robust and challenging account of the spirit and constraints of exercising public office.

What is the most lasting feature of John's invocation of Plutarch is the attribution to the role of Trajan's tutor. The story linking the two certainly contributed to Plutarch's reputation as a thinker with insights into the nature of politics and public life. But the effect of this association, however misguided, on top of a pre-existing tradition regarding Trajan as the most just of Roman emperors, has been one which has brought a heavier sense of moral *dirigisme* to the reading of Plutarch than it perhaps deserves.

2.2.2   On Homer

While not often acknowledged by Plutarch scholars, but clearly on the radar of many scholars of the history of French and English literature, two influential essays on the life and poetry of Homer were incorrectly attributed to Plutarch until the end of the seventeenth century.[26] The research required to confirm the identity of author and work is not always easy. In the case of these essays, it was through identification of vocabulary which only began to be in circulation roughly 100 years after Plutarch's death that the attribution was discredited, combined with the recognition that the literary style of the essays, working somewhat like a fingerprint, was quite different from anything else found in Plutarch's known work. What may have caused confusion was a reference in the Lamprias catalogue to works entitled "Four Books of Homeric Studies," along with Planudes's decision to include these essays in his own compilation of the *Moralia* in the thirteenth century, leading to the proliferation of copies. There are some who suggest that these essays may have some link to an earlier writing of Plutarch on the same theme, but with "substantial excerpting and editing."[27] Because in general the literary style is unlike Plutarch's, despite some examples reading more closely to his style, it is thought that the author may have known Plutarch's work well and borrowed from him.[28]

According to the work of Mark Bizer, French Renaissance scholars often became acquainted with the work of Homer through these two essays.[29] It had some implications for thinking about monarchy also. There was a tradition clearly present in the sixteenth century but starting much earlier (invoked for example in Christine de Pizan's *Epistre d'Othea*) linking the

---

[26] According to Keaney and Lamberton, the first printed edition of this essay accompanied a 1488 edition of Homer and a 1570 edition of Plutarch's *Moralia*. J. J. Keaney and R. Lamberton, "Introduction," in J. J. Keaney and R. Lamberton eds., *Essays on the Life and Poetry of Homer, by [Plutarch]* (Atlanta, GA: Scholars Press and American Philological Association, 1966), 1.

[27] Keaney and Lamberton, "Introduction," 7.

[28] In addition, the silence on a salient controversy concerning the relation of Homer to Plato suggests that the writer did not see themselves within the Platonic tradition, and hence could not have been Plutarch. "Introduction," in *Essays on the Life and Poetry of Homer*, 10.

[29] Marc Bizer, *Homer and the Politics of Authority in Renaissance France* (Oxford: Oxford University Press, 2011).

origins of the French monarchy to Troy and giving France an original Trojan heritage rather than an Italian or Roman one.

The politics of Homer references and interpretation were not straightforward, and they often led to both praise and criticism of the monarch, as Bizer discusses.[30] Nonetheless, in terms of alternatives in epic poetry, Virgil's *Aeneid* was often read through the lens of Landino, who offered a much more distinct neo-Platonist reading of the epic, highlighting the base side of politics. In certain contrast, then, Homer, as presented through the lens of these essays of pseudo-Plutarch, offered a more positive vision of public life.

Homer became an important literary ally for French monarchs claiming their descent from the Trojans, but also, because of the panegyrics concerning Homer's own wisdom in a multitude of fields, his work became an active source of knowledge on all matters of governance. Indeed, the search for kernels of political wisdom from Homer was in part motivated by these very pseudo-Plutarch essays in which it is written that "Homer was the first to speak analytically about the state."[31] The moral psychology of Homeric heroes was also singled out in these essays as providing lessons for political behaviour. Hence, the way Achilles submitted his anger to reason, or the account of the struggle between Nestor and Ajax, as well as the web of Penelope as attributed to Odysseus became allegories of the virtues and skills needed for effective political rule as highlighted by pseudo-Plutarch, and these were in turn taken up by humanists such as Budé and Erasmus.[32]

The essays suggest that Homer's *Odyssey* offers us an account of the 'nobility of the soul,' with the author sounding decidedly Peripatetic in his praise of the active virtues and lauding Homer for "taking true happiness to lie in acting with wisdom and restraint while enjoying good things."[33] Homer is also praised for associating the craft of politics with the art of rhetoric. Indeed, the evidence that Homer should be considered as one of the first analysts of political life is that he presents his readers with the image of the shield of Hephaestus, "for in the shield which Hephaestus (that is, the power of spirit) made as an image of the entire universe, he included two states, the one living in peace and happiness and the other

---

[30] Bizer, *Homer*, 6. [31] Bizer, *Homer*, 36
[32] The suggestion is that Budé reinterprets Penelope's weaving and undoing as an allegory of male practices of reassessment in practical leadership (thus, self-examination and revision). Bizer, *Homer*, 47
[33] [Plutarch], "Essay of the Life and Poetry of Homer," eds. Keaney and Lamberton, s. 137. Subsequent references to or citations of this text will be indicated by the section number in parentheses in the body of this text.

occupied with war. He elaborated material appropriate to each, indicating that there is on the one hand a civic life and on the other a military life" (s. 176).

The analysis of Homer here also indicates practices of good governance, including Agamemnon's call for a congregation of elders before war as an endorsement of a deliberative council meeting in each city before the people are assembled (s. 177); the extra concern of the king for the safety of all, through the advice to Agamemnon that a leader in counsel must not sleep through the night (s. 178); the need to "win over the people of rank with gentle words while berating those in the crowd more severely" (s. 178); and the appeal to punish only those crimes which are deliberate (s. 181). The impact of these essays, it would appear, is that the educated French and English of the early modern period were inclined to read Homer with much closer attention to political messages in the actions and sayings of the characters, and in this regard may have been led to develop a deeper political sensitivity. The author of this treatise also suggests that readers of Homer look to heroes appropriate to their stage in society and life:

> there are in Homer examples of exemplary deeds of people of all ages, with which absolutely everyone might be encouraged: those at the peak of their powers look to Achilles, Ajax, and Diomedes; younger men to Antilochus and Meriones; mature men to Idomeneus and Odysseus; those who are old, to Nestor. Kings look to all of these and to Agamemnon. Such are the profitable examples of political discourse and actions to be found in Homer. (s. 199).

Despite the invocation of a singular political message by the author of this essay, the work of Homer was taken up with competing lessons in the work of scholars of the French Renaissance. For example, while Penelope became an exemplary figure for the practice of self-reflection and re-evaluation in public life for Budé, she was an icon of futile repetition for Erasmus. Later, Etienne de la Boétie takes Homer up not as a guide for kings, but for the nobility.[34]

What can we distil from this overall? In the first instance, the attribution of these essays to Plutarch provided a basis for understanding Plutarch as a thinker with important insight into practical politics, including the identification of virtues best suited for those in public life, as well as advice on matters of institutional practice and political judgement. From this point, then, his *Lives* as well as his moral essays were often read with

---

[34] These examples and others concerning the cultural play of Homer as a reference in Renaissance France, including the uptake of these pseudo-Plutarch essays, is done masterfully by Bizer.

attention to their lessons for politics and public life. To demonstrate this one only need look at the correlation between major writers in the history of political thought tradition and the translators of Plutarch (or humanist translators of Plutarch and writers in the history of political thought tradition) prior to the famous editions of Amyot. The overlap is notable, encompassing the figures of Seyssel, Erasmus, Budé, and La Boétie. In contrast, a quick survey of sixteenth-century French translators of Cicero reveals not one political theorist of note.[35]

This link to Homer's work (first made clearly in 1488) may have contributed to making Plutarch a privileged reference in political commentary throughout the early modern period in France. In addition, it allied Plutarch with Homer in a project to cultivate a special link between the French monarchy and the Greek past, a move that was not without significance in the context of geopolitical issues of the later Renaissance.

2.2.3   On the Education of Children

Another essay thought until recently to have been written by Plutarch has had an immeasurable influence in the history of ideas – namely, "On the Education of Children." The uptake and reworking of this essay and its themes in the history of ideas warrants a completely independent book treatment, but I will dwell on the impact of this essay as it relates to matters of governance and public life in political theory.

The essay has been repeatedly included in collected essays by Plutarch since the medieval era and into the contemporary period, though scholarly consensus now deems it spurious (this claim is based less on questions of vocabulary, as in the Homeric essay, and more on stylistic considerations). Still, it had an enormous influence throughout the Renaissance and beyond, especially on Erasmus, Montaigne, Milton and Rousseau. It was edited and translated numerous times in the English tradition, starting with Thomas Elyot in 1532 (this will be taken up in Chapter 5).

The essay, in brief, offers a general defence of *paideia* or education in character. While good action requires a concurrence of nature, reason and habit, habit by far is most important for the development of moral virtue and can effectively compensate for deficiencies of nature. To illustrate this fact the author draws on the famous tale of Lycurgus who emphasised the

---

[35] A comprehensive list of sixteenth-century French translators of Cicero is offered in chapter 1 of Valerie Worth's *Practicing Translation in Renaissance France* (Oxford: Clarendon Press, 1988). None in that list are known as canonical political thinkers.

central importance of education by showing the Spartans' two puppies from the same litter who had subsequently been raised in completely different ways giving rise to opposite temperaments. (This was an anecdote taken from Plutarch's *Sayings of the Spartans*.)

The focus of education, referring to social influences as well as teachers, should be moral philosophy, with an effort to draw children towards wisdom and away from showy displays of rhetoric. Only with a firm foundation of the rule of reason can one achieve the admirable model of a combination of politics and philosophy:

> I regard as perfect, so far as men can be, those who are able to combine and mingle political capacity with philosophy; and I am inclined to think that these are secure in the possession of two things which are of the greatest good: a life useful to the world in their public position, and the calm and untroubled life in their pursuit of philosophy. For there are three forms of life, of which the first is the practical life, the second the contemplative life, and the third the life of enjoyment. The last, which is dissolute and enslaved to pleasure, is bestial and mean, but the contemplative life, which falls short in practice, is not useful, while the practical life which has no portion in philosophy, is without culture or taste. One must try, then as well as one can, both to take part in public life, and to lay hold of philosophy so far as the opportunity is granted. Such was the life of Pericles as a public man, such was Archytas of Tarentum, such was Dion of Syracuse, such was Epaminondas of Thebes, of whom the next to last was the associate of Plato.[36]

This offers a reading of Plutarch that is quite removed from conventional understandings of a traditional disciple of Plato in its defence of public life not only as a means for applying wisdom, but as a very forum of the good life due to its practical features.

Education of the whole person in morals, in the practical arts as well as in knowledge of culture, is a theme found across Plutarch's works, including the essays "How a young man should listen to poetry" and "On listening to lectures."[37] The emphasis in the passage above appears to diverge from Plutarch's insistence in certain passages in the *Lives*, such as "Themistocles," that individuals can be born with natures that shape their attitude to education and can demonstrate a less fully malleable model of

---

[36] [Plutarch], "On the Education of Children," in *Plutarch's Collected Works Loeb* (Cambridge, MA: Harvard University Press,), s. 10, 37.

[37] See Sophia Xenophontos, *Ethical Education in Plutarch: Moralising Agents and Contexts* (Boston and Berlin: de Gruyter, 2016).

character.[38] This observation, among other things, has led contemporary scholars to judge that this essay should not be attributed to Plutarch.

By assuming that "On the Education of Children" was written by Plutarch, early modern readers might have been led to read and perceive Plutarch as someone who did not wrestle with some of the complexities of character and who offered more of an unproblematic developmental model of character than was actually the case.[39] For example, some of the Enlightenment optimism in the unlimited power of education to shape individuals and society may have stemmed in part from the centrality of this work as a reference in the early modern period. This is a feature to keep in mind as we progress in our narrative, and another reason why consideration of spurious literature can be just as important as those works later identified as authentic.

From the understanding of both authentic and pseudo-Plutarch works that were beginning to circulate in the early Renaissance, I will now offer some indication of the process through which these works were brought back into Europe and translated into French and English.

2.3   The Politics of Plutarch Interpretation in Early Renaissance Italy (as relevant to later reception)

Not all the channels through which Plutarch's work was brought back into the West in the Renaissance are known. His fifteenth-century appearance in Europe is one aspect of what has been called a second wave in the reception of Greek thought (the first coinciding with the recovery of Aristotle's thought in the High Middle Ages).[40] The general pattern appears to be that in the late medieval period some scholars and others came to be interested in learning Greek in addition to conventional Latin (very few, apart from scholars in Byzantium, having that knowledge at all).[41] The reasons for this new interest included: closer access to scripture; ongoing theological debates with the Eastern Church (the papal court in Avignon had a program to train missionaries in dialogue with the Orthodox Church and by 1439 with the Council of Florence there was

---

[38] For a more thorough discussion of Plutarch's theory (or theories) of education, see Timothy Duff, "Models of Education in Plutarch," *The Journal of Hellenic Studies* 128 (2008), 1–26.

[39] This distinction between a 'developmental model' and a 'static' model is raised by Duff in "Models."

[40] Hankins, *Virtue Politics*, 364.

[41] Of course, there is the prior question of why Latin remained the conventional scholarly language in the late medieval period and not Greek. This question and other related ones are address by James Hankins, in "The Study of Greek in the Latin West," in *Humanism and Platonism in the Italian Renaissance, vol. 1* (Rome: Edizioni di Storia et Letteratura, 2003), 274–291.

an attempt to impose a union of the two); increasing interest in Greek philosophical sources to deepen understanding of Latin literature (e.g. Cicero); an interest in Greek historical sources that might shed better light on certain periods of Roman history for which there was relatively little comprehensive Latin commentary; and a sense of opportunity in increased commercial and diplomatic interactions with the East as a result of the expansion of Venetian interests throughout the Mediterranean. In this context and for these various motives, Plutarch's texts were sometimes used to gain better command of the Greek language, as well as to gain insight into history and philosophy. Of course, one should also not discount the possible motives of those coming from Byzantium to disseminate knowledge of the Greek heritage. In the cases of Manuel Chrysoloras and Jean Lascaris, for instance, there is strong evidence that both were patriots of the East.[42] Indeed it is argued that Lascaris, as counsellor to French kings, was a continued influential and powerful advocate for support for the Eastern Empire, and throughout his life lobbied for a new crusade against Constantinople (after its conquest by the Ottomans in 1453).

Chronologically speaking, Avignon was the first scholarly centre in the West where a humanist interest in Plutarch originated. Petrarch (1304–1374), one of the first humanists, did not know Greek but was said to have had his curiosity in Plutarch sparked by a reference to the essay "On Controlling Anger" in Aulus Gellius *Attic Nights*.[43] Curiosity within the papal court in Avignon led to the translation of this essay into Latin by Simon Atumanos in 1373, which is considered the first known authentic Plutarch translation. This led to another project at the papal court in Avignon to translate Plutarch's *Lives* from Greek into Aragonese.

As the literature demonstrates, while the first more systematic translations of Plutarch's work can be traced to Renaissance Italy, there is no direct lineage between this early Renaissance interest in Plutarch and the scholarship that began a century later in the French context. Associates of

[42] Hankins supports Ian Thomson in this view regarding Chrysoloras, and he provides additional evidence to support it. See Ian Thomson, "Manuel Chrysoloras and the Early Italian Renaissance," *Greek, Roman and Byzantine Studies*, 7 (1966), 63–82 and James Hankins, "Manuel Chrysoloras and the Greek Studies of Leonard Bruni," in *Humanism and Platonism in the Italian Renaissance, vol. 1 Humanism*, 244. On Lascaris, see the fascinating biography by Borje Knos, *Un ambassadeur de l'hellénisme Janus Lascaris et la tradition Greco-Byzantine dans l'humanisme Français* (Uppsala and Paris: Almquist and Wiksells and Les Belles Lettres, 1945).

[43] Walter Berschin, "Plutarque en France xIVe–xVIe siècle," in Charles Brucker ed., *Traduction et adaptation en France. Actes du colloque organisé par l'Université de Nancy II 23–25 mars 1995* (Paris: Honoré Champion, 1997), 295–298.

Petrarch, and especially the circle of humanists in Florence surrounding Coluccio Salutati (1331–1406) took on more concerted study of Greek literature, in part due to the excellent teaching of Byzantine diplomat and scholar Manuel Chrysoloras (c. 1350–1415).[44] Indeed, it was through the enthusiasm and skills of Chrysoloras, whose life mission was to revive interest in ancient Greek authors in Italy, allied with Salutati, that Plutarch became one of the most widely read authors in Italy in the fifteenth century.[45] This shift may have been part of the reason, if not an explanation, for Hans Baron's thesis of a distinctly 'civic' form of humanism that came to Italy after 1400.[46]

In the wake of the teaching of Chrysoloras and Salutati, Guarino Veronese (1374–1460) undertook a large number of translations into Latin and thereby provided an array of Plutarch's texts which spread throughout Europe.[47] Surprisingly, among the first translations of

[44] Chrysoloras was preceded by Leontius Pilatus, first professor of Greek in Florence from 1360–1362. According to Pade, Salutati was sent a copy of Plutarch's treatise on anger, *De cohibenda ira*, a work translated from the Greek by Simon Atamanus during his stay in Avignon. It was received by Salutati in Florence sometime between 1373 and 1395, but Salutati felt that the translation was inadequate, and he sought to revise the wording without reference to the original Greek text. Salutati's version was subsequently translated into French by Nicolas de Gonesse in 1400–1401. Pade, *Reception*, 73, See also her "The Reception of Plutarch," 538. Pade claims that Petrarch did have an active interest in the Greek world and discussed Greek literature with scholars he met in Avignon. Still, he never learned to read Greek. "The Reception of Plutarch," 538.

[45] Pade, *Reception*, 94–95.

[46] Hans Baron, *Crisis of the Early Italian Renaissance* (Princeton, NJ: Princeton University Press, 1966).

[47] His dedication to ancient Greek language and culture stemmed from his study in Constantinople in 1403–1408 and his teacher Chrysoloras. See Ivayla Popova.

"Manuel Chrysoloras (1350–1415), Érudit et Diplomate Byzantin, et Sa Syncrisis" *Études balkaniques* 3 and 4 (1998), 153–157. Chrysoloras was also teacher to Jacopo d'Angelo (1360–1410) whose "Brutus" was the first published Latin translation of any of Plutarch's *Lives* directly from the Greek, as well as the teacher of Leonard Bruni (1374–1444), Palla Strozzi (1372–1462) and Poggio Bracciolini (1380–1459) among other humanists. Because of this, Chrysoloras is perhaps the one person most responsible for the opening of humanist work to Greek sources and for this, Guarino compared his teacher Chrysoloras to the sun. Popova, "Chrysoloras," 154. Chrysoloras also considered Plutarch one of his favourite authors, and this love of Plutarch was passed on to Salutati and others. Andrew Taylor, "The Translations of Renaissance Latin," *Canadian Review of Comparative Literature* 41.4 (2014), 332–333.

On returning to Italy from Constantinople, Guarino brought several important manuscripts, and given his long association with Plutarch's work we can hypothesise that these included a Plutarch manuscript. As well as writing the first Renaissance Latin grammar book in 1418, Guarino taught Greek in Florence (1410) and Venice (1414) before becoming a private tutor to the son of the Lord of Ferrara in 1430.

Guarino translated and published numerous *Lives* of Plutarch as well as several moral essays. In contrast to some of his contemporaries, Guarino took an active interest not only in Greek language but also Greek history, choosing to translate Plutarch's Greek figures, such as "Alexander" (1408). His style is reportedly closer to the looser end of approaches to translation than some other Renaissance humanists (a translation style he shared with Salutati and others of the circle), that is, adding rhetorical figures and new syntax to better communicate the force of the message in the

Plutarch there were several in vernacular languages alongside the Latin versions .[48] As an early anomaly to the Byzantine connections through which vernacular translations of Plutarch in French began to appear (as I will demonstrate later), Salutati's Latin version of the essay "On the Controlling of Anger" became the basis for the first translation of Plutarch into the French vernacular by Nicolas de Gonesse in 1401.[49]

In broad terms, Italian humanists appeared to take much more interest in the *Lives* over and above the *Moralia*. The famous Aldine press in Venice (run by Aldus Manutius 1449/52–1515) produced a Greek edition of Plutarch's *Moralia* in 1509 (with some help from Erasmus), but few of these essays were translated subsequently by scholars into Latin (apart from Erasmus himself whom we will see offered his Latin translations to various patrons in England). Individual *Lives* were translated into Latin (e.g. Guarino's *Alexander*) followed by two full Latin editions of the *Lives* published within two years of each other (1517–1519), the first in Florence and the latter by Aldus.

Contrary to civic republican approaches, James Hankins has convincingly argued that writers of the Italian Renaissance were engaged in a general project of advocating for virtue and wisdom in the ruling class with less concern for precise institutional distinctions or promotion of any

---

original language into the idiom of the new. Similarly, Leonardo Bruni who published the first theoretical discussion of translation in European history according to Hankins, entitled *On Correct Translation*, argued for the *ad sententiam* method (according to the sense) as opposed to *ad verbum* (or word for word). See James Hankins, "Leonardo Bruni: Life and Works," in *Humanism and Platonism in the Italian Renaissance, vol. 1. Humanism*, 12.

[48] The Aragonese translation of the *Lives*, referred to above and commissioned by Juan Fernandez de Heredia was completed 1387–1388. This Aragonese version was then translated into Tuscan. The first Italian vernacular translation dates to 1518, with Jaconello's *Le vite di Plutarcho*, complete with quite fascinating engravings. One might note especially that which accompanies the life of Solon. Here Solon is depicted as Christ, naked and poor, surrounded by well-dressed nobility. Here is an attempt to identify Solon's policies in abolishing debts with a broader Christian ethos.

While there were several vernacular translations of Latin classics into Italian and French in the thirteenth and fourteenth centuries, before 1400 few Greek texts were translated into the vernacular, either from their original Greek or from a Latin translation. Hankins, "Translation Practice in the Renaissance," in *Humanism and Platonism in the Italian Renaissance, vol. 1 Humanism*, 189. This probably has to do with limited knowledge of Greek at the time. The translations to Latin were more than likely done by scholars from Byzantium, but these scholars may have lacked the knowledge of European vernacular languages for purposes of translation. Of course, this changes significantly in the fifteenth century when Greek began to be taught more extensively in Europe.

[49] Berschin, "Plutarque en France," 297. Despite a broad humanist project favouring the study and translation of classical texts, there was no one conventional theory in the Renaissance of what a proper translation should be. Erasmus gave himself great latitude in providing elucidation and additional commentary in his translations of Plutarch's *Apophthegmata*, as he found Plutarch's own expression much too economical. Angelo Poliziano (1454–1494) reportedly also began translation with a practice of greater elucidation when rendering the text in another language, only to shift later in his career to a much more streamlined and literal approach. Taylor, "Translations," 340.

singular constitutional framework.[50] Nonetheless, as Pade demonstrates, translations of Plutarch in Italy at this time were often done with specific patrons in mind, meaning that the choice of what texts or selections to translate could often have some relation to the established regime (even if not driven fundamentally by an institutional argument).[51]

There are a vast number of ways in which Plutarch figures in Italian Renaissance thought. My purpose here is only to select a few examples that help to set the stage for the somewhat different spirit in which Plutarch was taken up in France. Specifically, Italian political thinkers tended to use Plutarch's historical examples to argue for a virtue politics, be it in republican or monarchical form. The idea was that through learning and the exercising of the virtues as traditionally understood, one could usher in good politics and promote the cause of liberty. (In the French case, as we will see, there was no appeal to an overriding notion of liberty in humanist argument, and there was greater attention to the unique and specific way the traditional virtues were to be exercised in the special context of public office.)

A quick overview and contrast between the historical claims of Guarino Veronese (1374–1460) and Leonardo Bruni (1370–1444) as in part informed by their reading of Plutarch will at least provide a small taste of some of the wider issues at stake in reception during the broader Italian Renaissance period. It bears highlighting that this example is chosen not because of its status or significance within the broader field of Italian Renaissance political thought and literature, but because it offers a rather interesting and tidy example of ways in which Plutarch's work was used (or put aside) for purposes of political debate. It demonstrates two very different ways of engaging with Plutarch in the context of the Italian Renaissance, but both still share certain features in common that stand in contrast to what we will generally find in early sixteenth-century French and English Plutarch reception.

Both Guarino and Bruni shared an early interest in Plutarch and embarked on a practice of translation, emphasising cultural and not just literal translation, that had been handed down to each by Chrysoloras; their interactions with the material led to quite different results, however.[52] In the first instance, these two scholars differed to a degree on what part of

---

[50] Hankins, *Virtue Politics.*   [51] Pade, *Reception.*

[52] It could be argued that these thinkers radicalised the notion of *conversio ad sententiam* (translation of both style and content) that was handed down to them by Chrysoloras. According to Pade, it is possible to consider Guarino's rendering of Dio going even beyond what Chrysoloras advocated, as it takes on certain qualities of an independent Latin humanist text.

Plutarch's oeuvre they chose to translate.[53] Bruni, a loyal citizen of
Florence, for the most part chose to translate lives of famous statesmen
and generals of the Roman Republic.[54] In contrast, Guarino took an active
interest in the substance of Greek history (for Pade this may have something to do with his links to Venice and the city's own tendency to perceive
itself as a descendent of ancient Greek culture) and he translated Plutarch
more broadly, including essays of the *Moralia*.[55]

---

[53] Hankins, in "Leonardo Bruni," 11, Bruni translated the lives of Marc Antony (before March 1405),
Cato the Younger (1405/13), Aemilius Paullus (before August 1409), the Gracchi (before
March 1410), Sertorius (1410), Pyrrhus (1412), and Demosthenes (1412). See also David Rundle,
"Book Review of Marianne Pade's *The Reception of Plutarch's Lives in Fifteenth-Century Italy*,"
Renaissance Studies 23.1 (Feb. 2009), 129–131. Guarino translated at least thirteen lives by 1435. Pade,
Reception, 165. Some humanists like Bruni took exclusive interest in the *Lives* whereas others took
more interest in the essays from the *Moralia*, so the question remains as to why those essays of the
Moralia were overlooked by some in the Renaissance for translation, but not by others.
  The point is even more salient when looking at the history of published editions in France prior to
the work of Amyot. Through consultation with the *Universal Short Title Catalogue* (the closest we
have to a comprehensive account of all published materials in the Renaissance) of 100 known printed
editions of Plutarch's work in France from 1505 (the first) to 1558 when Amyot's edition appeared for
the first time, sixteen (including Amyot's) were devoted to the *Lives*. The first is the *Illustrium
vivorum vite* published by J. Bade, which first appeared in 1514 and was reissued in 1520 with four
more editions sold under the name of separate bookstores (the records identify the bookseller rather
than the editor so one can suspect that they refer to the same version but reprinted under different
guises) in 1521 and then once more in 1532. The first vernacular translation of any of the *Lives*, (*Les
Vyes des huicts excellens et renommez personages grecs et romains*, trans. George de Selve, Paris,
Vascosan, 1543) and this is a selected version, was not until 1543. It is identified as the work of
George de Selve and was sold by Michel de Vascosan, the famous bookseller of Amyot's version. De
Selve's translation was reissued in three versions in 1547 and again one in 1548. Another Latin version
of the *Lives* appeared in Lyon under the name of Paul Miralliet in 1548. In 1554 Louis Marchant
translated the Life of Cato the Younger and four years later Philippe Des Avenelles translated
Epitome ou abrégé des vies de cinquante et quatre notables et excellens personnaiges tant grecs que roman
(Paris: Philippe Danfue and Richard Breton, 1558). One hypothesis is that in the relative tranquility
of the early sixteenth century, the moral essays, and particularly those devoted to questions of
women and the nature of marriage, appeared to be the more salient for French sensibilities, but as
the religious and political crisis deepened there was a growing interest in seeking the political lessons
of good leadership that might be gleaned from Plutarch as a way of leading the country out of crisis.
[54] Gary Ianziti, *Writing History in Renaissance Italy. Leonard Bruni and the Uses of the Past* (Cambridge,
MA: Harvard University Press 2012), 31. Bruni states in his preface to his translation of St Basil's letter
Ad adolescent, cited and translated by Hankins: "For when we read in Plutarch, a man of high
authority, of the deeds of distinguished Greeks and Romans, whom he selects and arranges as paired
rivals, we are surely grieved to notice the great loss of Latin authors, with the result that we now
know neither the deeds nor even the names of the men for whom Italy won a glorious name
throughout the earth. Hence, having devoted such study to Greek letters as not to be entirely
ignorant of them, we have it in mind, as time allows, to translate into Latin all these lives of Plutarch,
and to renew the fame and glory of great men, so that we may join the utility we have ourselves
received from the knowledge of Greek to the utility of our men." See James Hankins, "Manuel
Chrysoloras and the Greek Studies of Leonard Bruni," *Humanism and Platonism in the Italian
Renaissance, vol. 1. Humanism*, 257.
[55] Pade, *Reception*, 165. As Pade argues: "Guarino was instrumental in developing the specific trait of
Venetian civic, or patrician, humanism that used ancient Greece as a cultural model. The strong
Byzantine influence on Venetian culture had long been evident; Guarino and his students merged

From the beginning, how one chose to engage with Plutarch's work could signal political commitments and allegiances. Indeed, Bruni was not always in agreement with Plutarch, as is evident from his work on Plutarch's life of Cicero. When Bruni began to translate this life in 1413, he became frustrated with Plutarch's apparent inability to see Cicero in a better light, or at least to better appreciate his political accomplishments. To address this Bruni shifted his project, offering commentary on Plutarch's work as well as drawing from other writings, including those of Cicero and Sallust, to provide a new perspective on the events. This was especially true for his treatment of the Catilinarian conspiracy in which he made Cicero much more central to swaying the decision of the Roman Senate on the punishment.[56] What started as an exercise in translation ended up as a completely independent work and a counter-narrative to Plutarch.

Most importantly, Bruni objected to the parallel schema not only because it tended to diminish Cicero in relation to Demosthenes, but more importantly because the comparison of lives led to special emphasis on character and moral virtue as a measure of historical acclaim and as causal factors for success and failure. According to Gary Ianziti, Bruni, being motivated primarily by his allegiance to the oligarchic families who ruled Florence, came to recognise that Cicero's ambition was not a liability or something that should be curbed, but an important motive in shaping his more effective political strategies. Similarly, according to Bruni, Cicero was not brought down by his own faults or inability to see the resentment of others due to his degree of pride, but rather by the threat he posed to others with his increased prestige.

With his *Cicero,* Bruni wrought a new sort of biographical narrative. The crux of the novelty lies in the compartmentalisation he proposed, where matters moral are relegated to the sphere of personal idiosyncrasy. The political narrative (*res gestae*) attains a status of independence: it operates as an instrument for presenting, justifying and explaining the career of the individual concerned. The explanation does not refer to doctrine regulating standards of behaviour, whether moral, religious or legal. It instead develops its own logic through an examination of the

---

the ideas of current Florentine humanism with the traditional Venetian orientation towards the East. The result was a group of civic-minded patricians who saw the followers of Plato as more attractive models for the educated ruler than the Stoics of the late Roman Republic, and the construction of Sparta and the Delian League as more relevant historical examples than the Roman Empire." Pade, *Reception,* 208.

[56] Ianziti, *Writing History,* 50–51.

political elements as they came into play: power struggles, factionalism, treachery and deceit are not condemned as evil but are seen rather as so many factors in the political equation.[57]

For Ianziti, Bruni develops a sense of history on a uniquely and pointedly realist ('political' is the term Ianziti uses, but I think 'realist' is more accurate) plane, in contrast to either a 'scientific' or a 'civic' mode of historiographical writing. Ianziti sees Bruni as a precursor to Machiavelli's approach to history, driven by an engaged political stance rather than by a concern for scientific or objective treatment of the subject, and this for the author was also presumed to involve a rejection of the moralism found in the historical writing of Plutarch. Still, when it came to making prescriptions for his own state of Florence, as argued by Hankins, Bruni fell within the general virtue politics camp by championing the middle classes' greater tendency to virtue and moderation (whereas Machiavelli championed institutional approaches with the management of productive forms of *tumulti*).[58] It might therefore be said that Bruni represents a form of virtue politics that nonetheless was in dialogue with more salient features of realism.

As I will demonstrate in Chapter 3, the French political theorists who translated Plutarch in the early sixteenth century neither repudiated Plutarch (as Bruni came to do in writing about Cicero) nor rejected certain aspects of political realism. While the challenge for Bruni was coming to terms with ambitious motivation in politics, the challenge for the French thinkers I examine was how virtuous prudence might function in real terms within a public setting. This meant that the French were able to develop a nuanced political realism in their arguments, combining it with virtue politics in a different way than Bruni.

A second point of difference between Guarino and Bruni that also offers an important point of contrast with later French reception of Plutarch, concerns debate over the life and politics of Julius Caesar. As James Hankins has shown, the figure of Caesar was important in Italian Renaissance political reflection because it raised challenging questions concerning the nature of political power and its abuse, including how virtue should be manifested in political office, and how much strong popular support can justify an undermining of the rule of law and upending of an established constitution.[59] One famous example is found in the

---

[57] Ianziti, *Writing History*, 60.   [58] Hankins, *Virtue Politics*, chap. 10.

[59] Hankins, *Virtue Politics*, chap. 4. In this chapter Hankins summarises a wider debate concerning Caesar and Cicero's condemnation of him as taken up by Petrarch, Salutati, Guarino and Poggio. Hankins argues that the point of division was not largely one of allegiance to regime type, but rather

exchange of letters between Guarino and his fellow humanist Poggio Bracciolini (1380–1459).[60] Poggio provoked the debate with a letter written in April 1435, suggesting that Caesar was to be blamed for helping to destroy the Roman Republic. In reply a few months later, Guarino defended Caesar, suggesting that he was a man of virtue who should be admired for founding the Roman Empire which brought peace and great benefits to the people. Guarino was ultimately concerned about the quality rather than the structure of rule. The rule of one person in itself need not be condemned, but in distinguishing between kings and tyrants one must pay close attention to the quality of the rule and its impact on people's lives.[61] Guarino lived and worked in the latter part of his life as tutor to the son of the duke of Ferrara, Niccolo III d'Este and then as professor of rhetoric in Ferrara. In defending the legality of Caesar's rule at the end of Rome's republican period it might be suggested he was defending a form of monarchical legitimacy, if exercised by a ruler of virtue. Guarino's position led to further attacks by Poggio.[62]

Although not a party to this exchange, Bruni, in his *Panegyric to the City of Florence* like Poggio also condemns Caesar as a usurper of power.[63] While it is argued that Bruni did not always reject the legitimacy and possible benefits of one-person rule, he made an important distinction (like his predecessor Salutati) between legitimate and illegitimate rule. Caesar, according to Bruni, fell clearly on the side of an illegitimate ruler and therefore deserved condemnation. Bruni's argument was a legal one, but it was supplemented by observation that the rule of the Caesars was not benevolent. Given Bruni's clear allegiances to the republic of Florence and his hostility to the Ghibellines, his arguments are often placed in the context of the Florentine republic's continued battles against the claims of the Holy Roman Empire.[64]

over what type of person Caesar was and whether his actions were to be regarded as self-serving and tyrannical or as a manifestation of virtue in pursuance of the public good. The broader point is that the crux of Renaissance Italian political thought was a concern for a politics of justice led by public officials practicing the traditional virtues, and a public who through education became aware of the need for a virtuous politics.

[60] See Davide Canfora, *La Controversia di Poggio Bracciolini e Guarino Veronese du Cesare e Scipione* (Florence: L. S. Olschki, 2001).

[61] The argument resembles an earlier defense of Caesar in Salutati's *On Tyranny* (c. 1400), where Salutati argues that Caesar took his position lawfully and brought peace to Rome only to be unjustly killed. Coluccio Salutati, "On Tyranny," in Stefano Baldassarri ed., *Political Writings*, trans. Rolf Bagemihl. (Cambridge, MA and London: Harvard University Press, 2014).

[62] See also Hester Schadee, "Caesarea Laus: Ciriaco d'Ancona praising Caesar to Leonardo Bruni," *Renaissance Studies* 22.4 (2008), 435–449.

[63] See Brian Jeffrey Maxson, "Kings and Tyrants: Leonardo Bruni's translation of Xenophon's Hiero," *Renaissance Studies* 24.2 (2010), 188–206.

[64] Maxson, "Kings and Tyrants," 198.

So Guarino and Bruni came to different assessments of the politics of Julius Caesar, and these assessments were arrived at in part through a reading of Plutarch's life of Caesar (one of few classical accounts available). This is significant for our later discussion of French Plutarch reception for two reasons. In the first instance, the differing allegiances of Guarino and Bruni, one to a monarchical regime and the other to a republic, did have some impact on their assessment of Caesar's politics, even if they were agreed on the need to avoid tyranny and the importance of virtue politics. For Bruni, the need to save the republic was a paramount consideration in assessing Caesar's rule, as opposed to considerations of mere stability and efficiency of the state invoked by Guarino. This is just one instance of a broader characteristic in Plutarch reception of the Italian Renaissance in that both what was chosen for translation and how that history was interpreted did have some links to the political context and intense rivalries among advocates of republican independence, monarchical and imperial rule. The existing networks of patronage and support for scholarship are clearly relevant in this context.[65] Of course, in the French context, as we will see, as far as the early sixteenth century was concerned, there was no prominent deliberation concerning the relative merit of republics and monarchies.

To say that there appeared to be difference of opinion between Guarino and Bruni concerning the rule of Caesar that may have reflected aspects of their political allegiances does not imply a challenge to the account of Hankins concerning the centrality of virtue politics for understanding the Italian Renaissance context.[66] He acknowledges that by the second half of the fifteenth century, republics and monarchies were understood as being in a binary opposition to one another, even if the meaning of republic was somewhat sketchy (indeed he avoids the term republic altogether preferring to replace it with 'oligarchy').[67] The background to Hankins argument is that since the 1970s at least, historians of political thought have tended to put

---

[65] Indeed, as discussed by Pade, there appears in Guarino's translation of Plutarch's *Life of Dion*, completed prior to his arrival and service in Ferrara, a willingness to support the idea of a mixed constitution with a strong aristocratic element modelled on Sparta or Crete, a model of government that Dion himself wished to introduce into Syracuse and to which Guarino added the marginal gloss on the manuscript: "like in our time the glorious government of the Venetians." These notes, as argued by Pade, were intended for Barbaro, an aristocrat and senior official in Venetian affairs to whom the manuscript was dedicated. In the marginal notes to this translation Guarino appears to side always with Dion the aristocrat against both tyrants and democrats. Pade, "'I Give you Back Plutarch in Latin': Guarino Veronese's Version of Plutarch's Dion (1414) and Early Humanist Translation," *The Canadian Review of Comparative Literature*, 41.4 (2014), 354–368. Pade's analysis is based on his 1414 translation of Plutarch's *Life of Dion* found in manuscript form at the Bodleian Library in Oxford, Bywater 38.

[66] Hankins, *Virtue Politics*.   [67] Hankins, *Virtue Politics*, 87.

regime adjudication, and the argument for republicanism in particular, at the forefront of Italian Renaissance political thought. Hankins seeks to unravel this depiction in part because the previous accounts relied on an imprecise and inaccurate picture of republicanism, and in part because a focus on the need for justice through the good character of the ruler and ruled is a more accurate depiction of the crux of debates in the period. What we find then with Guarino and Bruni, is a debate that centres explicitly on the assessment of the relative virtue of Caesar, but with links to differing modes of governance in the Italian context. While Plutarch is invoked in an argument largely centred around questions of virtue in politics, the different contexts from which this debate proceeded did offer implicit support for one type of regime over another. I argue that despite a common focus on virtue politics when French political thinkers took up Plutarch they often did so in a somewhat distinct spirit and application. Within the French tradition of virtue politics, what I will call public humanism, there were debates concerning how best to exemplify and act on traditional moral ideals in a uniquely public setting.

A final consideration offering a point of contrast with the later French tradition of Plutarch reception concerns the broader outlook through which politics and history are assessed. As we have seen with Guarino and Bruni on Caesar, as well as Bruni on Cicero, there was a tendency to see Plutarch as a source for assessing specific historical figures in ancient history as read through a classical moralist lens. For the most part, as part of a wider set of literature used to develop a model of virtue politics, Plutarch here is not read as a writer who is thought to offer particularly valuable insight into politics, but rather as an author whose subject in the *Lives*, important political and military leaders of ancient history, offers certain material from which political argument can be forged. One exception to this is Francesco Patrizi's *De Regno* which focuses on kingly virtues, and perhaps not coincidentally, does so with reference to Plutarch's *Moralia*. Patrizi's sensibility to delve into the way the virtues are manifest in public life accompanies his key concern that princes be educated in the humanities.[68] This is closer to the spirit in which Plutarch was first taken up in France. Otherwise, a consideration of the ethos within the court and among those who serve in the Italian context, was developed in the work of Castiglione, but through largely an appropriation of Cicero rather than Plutarch.[69] I will explore in future chapters the distinct resonance of Plutarch vis-à-vis Cicero in reception.

---

[68] Hankins, *Virtue Politics*, 419–421.
[69] Baldesar Castiglione, *The Book of the Courtier* (London: Penguin, 1967).

With the early translation by Geoffrey Tory of Plutarch's "Political Precepts", among other vernacular translations of Plutarch by political thinkers, there was a certain shift in the status of Plutarch who came to be regarded in France as an author offering special insight into politics. This was facilitated by linguistic shifts through which the matter of politics or political affairs understood in the plural and in a general way came to be understood via the Latin into French as matters concerning *la chose publique*, something which could be rendered literally in English as "the public thing," thereby suggesting an understanding of political life that was separate and having special and unique status. The reception of Plutarch in France in relation to political thought of the Renaissance period will appear distinct from many earlier Italian iterations. Plutarch became a privileged classical thinker for reflection on politics in France in a way unmatched in Italy or later England. Reflection on Plutarch's work in the French context gave way to a particular form of discourse I call public humanism highlighting the special and unique form of relations associated with public life, relations which did not invalidate the claims of traditional ethical thinking, but which required their subtle reconsideration in light of those specific and unique features.

2.4 Conclusion

The purpose of this chapter has been to set the stage for understanding the deeper historical context from which Plutarch's work began to be read and translated into the vernacular in early modern France and England. As we have seen, there are several factors at work here that must be kept in mind. The first is recognising the importance of key references to Plutarch that were not always a fully accurate understanding of his historical place. The work of John of Salisbury provided a backdrop against which Plutarch came to be read as a thinker whose work offered useful material for reflection on politics given the assumption that he had served as a tutor to the Emperor Trajan. This was reinforced by a false attribution to Plutarch of a couple of influential essays on Homer which also stressed the important political messages of the *Odyssey*. This led some scholars to approach the *Lives* as offering special insight into politics and the state. When various humanist writers of the Renaissance began to translate, compile, and repackage excerpts from Plutarch's work, passages offering subtle insights into the unfolding of the character of a particular individual of public prominence began to take the form of authoritative statements with more generalisable applicability as lessons for those in politics.

But there were different ways this could be done. As we have seen, in the case of the Italian Renaissance through the work of Bruni and Guarino, Plutarch could be harnessed to debates concerning the relation between virtue and models of governance (republics vs monarchies). The contested terrain had to do with adjudicating institutions and their political effects for virtue politics. There is a different sensibility that arises, as we will see, in how Plutarch was invoked for insight into politics in the French case. There Plutarch's work was appealed to often with different questions in mind: who stands as a good exemplar for Renaissance kings? What is an appropriate psychological disposition for a good monarch? What are the key attributes of political prudence?

It took about fifty years for the teaching of Greek to spread from Italy into other parts of Europe.[70] By the 1520s the study of ancient Greek had been integrated into the university curriculum in northern Europe. Hankins suggests that Girolamo Aleandro, a humanist scholar from Venice who came to Paris from 1508 to 1517, should be credited as the true initiator of Greek education in France.[71] It is generally reported, however, that the first teachers of ancient Greek in France were not competent. As we will see in Chapter 3, it was only with the work of Guillaume Budé through the university, and the mentorship of Jean Lascaris, counsellor and adviser to the monarch, that the concerted learning of Greek took hold. These two figures also played important roles in spreading interest in, as well as material access to, works of Plutarch for translation and dissemination. Through this, the work of Plutarch was about to take on even greater significance for the development of the history of political thought.

---

[70] On the early teaching of Greek in France, see di Stefano, "L'Hellénisme," 29–42.
[71] Hankins, "The Study of Greek in the Latin West," in *Humanism and Platonism in the Italian Renaissance, vol. 1 Humanism*, 288.

PART II

Plutarch in Renaissance France and England

Plutarch in Early French Renaissance Public Humanism: Geoffroy Tory and Guillaume Budé

Many early modern political thinkers often translated classical works in addition to writing political treatises. Recently, this translation work has been studied as an integral component of the development of political reflection.[1]

This is noteworthy especially given that despite a continuous and over-arching goal of *fidelity* to the text, the norms and practices of translations have shifted over time.[2] As the art of translation developed from the fourteenth century, translators sometimes regarded translation as communicating the spirit of the text and thus moving away from close literalist translations. In one case, Thomas North (1535–1603) provided his Plutarchan heroes with items of clothing very close to Elizabethan fashions rather than invoking ancient Greek and Latin terms.[3] Likewise, Desiderius Erasmus (1466–1536), in some translations, thought it proper to provide an elaboration of the meaning of various passages in the original work to aid the reader in comprehension.[4] Even aside from the very important question of choosing what was to be translated along with more technical questions in the translation of specific terms, we can find in early modern translations a plethora of material that allows us to consider these works of formal translation as moments of political reflection. Study can reveal meaningful gaps between a literal reading and the interpretative reading in and through translation.

---

[1] See, for example, Robin Sowerby, "Thomas Hobbes's Translation of Thucydides," *Translation and Literature*, vol. 7, no. 2 (1998), 147–169; Jean S. Yolton, "John Locke as Translator" in *Studies in Voltaire and the Eighteenth Century* (Oxford: Voltaire Foundation, 2000); C. R. Thompson, *The Translations of Lucian by Erasmus and Sir Thomas More* (Ithaca, NY: The Vail-Ballou Press, 1940).

[2] See, for example, Peter Burke, "Cultures of Translation in Early-Modern Europe," in Peter Burke and Po-Chia Hsia eds., *Cultural Translation in Early-Modern Europe* (Cambridge: Cambridge University Press, 2007), 7–38.

[3] John Denton, *Translation and Manipulation in Renaissance England* (Florence: Firenze University Press, 2016), 56.

[4] Erika Rummel, *Erasmus as a Translator of the Classics* (Toronto: University of Toronto Press, 2012) and Elaine Fantham and Betty Knott, "Introduction," *Collected Works of Erasmus*, vol. 37.

For some writers, such as Erasmus, I will explore those gaps in conjunction with their works of political reflection in order to draw direct links between their scholarly work as translators of Plutarch and their broader political theory. In other instances, like that of Claude de Seyssel (d. 1520), it is also possible to connect the themes of the Plutarch works chosen for translation and the broader themes of their political theorizing. In various ways, then, I will demonstrate how Plutarch, channelled through translation, was integrated into broader traditions of reflection in the history of political thought.

Before turning to Geoffrey Tory (c. 1480–c. 1533), Guillaume Budé (1467–1540), Seyssel and Erasmus, whose work will be the focus of my analysis in this chapter and the next, it is important to dwell briefly on the broader context. Plutarch translation in the Renaissance offers an interesting case for exploring the relation between the broad movement of humanism and the currents of political thinking that developed in its wake.

Despite the early caution of Paul Oskar Kristeller, many scholars since have argued that the humanist shift carried important implications for not just philosophy but political philosophy in particular.[5] As noted in Chapter 2, Hans Baron famously argued that the work of Florentines in the fifteenth century demonstrated a distinctly *civic* form of humanism, something that was tailored more to the public life of Italian communes championing their independence from the Holy Roman Empire. This thesis was revised by Quentin Skinner and James Hankins who suggest that arguments defending independent republics are found much earlier. Juristic defences of the free life of communal Italian states date back to the mid-twelfth century.[6] This theme, taken up perhaps most famously in the history of political thought with John Pocock's *Machiavellian Moment*, holds that civic humanism/republicanism became a leitmotif of political argument throughout the development of European political thought.[7] For Pocock, civic humanism was rooted in Aristotelianism. It found its first authentic articulation in the work of Italian humanists and Machiavelli before spreading through Europe and adapting to new circumstances, most notably in the Anglo-American world.

Baron, Skinner and Pocock not only share the general view that civic humanism/republicanism is the dominant political philosophy issuing

---

[5] See, for example, Paul Oskar Kristeller, *Renaissance Thought the Classic Scholastic and Humanistic Strains* (New York: Harper and Row, 1955).

[6] James Hankins, "Humanism and the Origins of Modern Political Thought," in Jill Kraye ed., *The Cambridge Companion to Renaissance Humanism* (Cambridge: Cambridge University Press, 1996), 118–141.

[7] Pocock, *The Machiavellian Moment*.

from Renaissance humanism, but also that it arises from the Italian context – or more narrowly, the Florentine one – and that it has important ties to the broader geopolitical struggles of the region, namely struggles for independence from the forces of empire and hegemony. It has meant that humanism in the history of political thought has most often been identified with a prioritising of freedom and all that implies for institutional design and regime focus (notwithstanding a few dissenters who drew from an explicitly Platonic strand of thinking where issues of equality were also salient).[8]

However, this depiction of political thinking in humanist thought has never *fully* captured the distillation of humanist thinking in French political thought, in part because it ignores just how important Plutarch was for that tradition. In addition, Plutarch reception in the French Renaissance offers a different pattern than is generally held about the reception of classical works. The standard account suggests that various classical texts were first 'received' or rediscovered – or more accurately, re-evaluated and appreciated – in the Italian context, and subsequently brought in manuscript form to the 'north' in their newly packaged Latin versions. The recognition that Petrarch was based in Avignon reveals a more complicated reality, but the broad thrust of this accepted account does apply for a large number of works in the Latin tradition.[9] In terms of the reception of the Greek tradition, Venice has been rightly privileged as an important point of reception and transmission given its crucial position in all forms of east–west relations.[10] Still, despite the crucial role of Venice and the Aldine Press in particular, these narratives do not account for some of the features through which Greek and Byzantine learning (barring a few notable exceptions, including Aristotle of course) was filtered.[11]

---

[8] For a discussion of those civic humanists seen to be drawing on a Greek model, as opposed to a Roman one, see Nelson, *The Greek Tradition*.

[9] For a discussion of the cultural links between France and Italy in the late 1300s and throughout the 1400s and the subsequent transmission of humanism into France, see Craig Taylor, "The Ambivalent Influence of Italian Letters and the Rediscovery of the Classics in Late Medieval France," in David Rundle ed., *Humanism in Fifteenth Century Europe* (Oxford: The Society for the Study of Medieval Languages and Literatures, 2012), 203–236.

[10] Deno Geanakoplos, "Erasmus and the Aldine Academy of Venice," *Roman and Byzantine Studies*, 3.2 (1960), 107–134. One prominent example of new research acknowledging Venice's place in a web of east–west interactions in the Renaissance can be found in Noel Malcolm's, *Agents of Empire: Knights, Corsairs, Jesuits and Spies in the Sixteenth-Century Mediterranean World* (London: Allen Lane, 2015).

[11] Geanakoplos suggests the project of Aldus Manutius and his associates was to print in systematic fashion all the major Greek classics of the ancient world. "Erasmus," 113. Indeed, as Linton Stevens acknowledged as early as 1961, "it was the Byzantine scholars who introduced [Plutarch] to France." While accurate, some of the broader analysis of Stevens is due for revision, and in particular the

While a printed Latin version of Plutarch's *Lives* was available as early as 1470 and a Greek version of the *Moralia* printed by 1509, in the French case one notes the ongoing presence of Byzantine intermediaries in the process of reception. It should alert us to the *possibility* of a distinct tradition of reception and interpretation of Plutarch in the French case. Indeed, while there was a good deal of engagement with the texts of classical Rome, the texts of ancient Greece, and Plutarch in particular, were also central to the development of humanist political argument in France in ways quite distinct from other appropriations of classical Greek political thought. Plutarch was often taken up for his ability to speak to very practical political concerns as opposed to the more utopian spirit in which other thinkers often took up Plato.

As noted in Chapter 2, Hankins has suggested that the tradition of linking the political legacy of humanism to a specifically *republican* or *civic humanist* project is too narrow and indeed a mischaracterisation of the broader thrust of the humanist legacy for politics.[12] The privileging of Machiavelli for this republican account is evidence of this partial perspective, given his marginal place in the broader scope of humanist scholarship. Hankins suggests that the most important political legacy of Renaissance humanism as it evolved in the Italian context was a focus on individuals, and indeed on the importance of individual character as both necessary for good politics, as well as a desired object of policy in the form of moral education. In short, for Hankins, *virtue politics* should replace civic humanism as the dominant leitmotif of humanist political thought and certainly as more representative of the political legacy of humanism in the Italian Renaissance context.

Still, as I explore the development of political argument in the French context, I demonstrate that the legacy of humanism for French political thought as far as Plutarch was concerned rested *neither on the institutional ideals of civic humanism, nor on the largely individualistic ideals of virtue politics*. A focus on the French tradition of 'public humanism', offers a conversation on the unique role and specific ethos of public life in reference to either kings in high office or those working within

---

assertion that the impact of Hellenism on the political tradition in France was only manifest at the end of the sixteenth century through the work of Bodin and La Boétie. Of course, Aristotelian influence was pervasive in French political thinking throughout the medieval and Renaissance period, and there was a vibrant tradition of political reflection throughout the sixteenth century and much of which, as will be discussed, reflects the specific impact of Plutarch. See Linton C. Stevens, "A Re-evaluation of Hellenism in the French Renaissance," *Studies in Philology*, 58.2 (April 1961), 115–129.

[12] Hankins, *Virtue Politics*.

a monarchical administration. In early vernacular translations of Plutarch, public life was often referred to by the term "la chose publique" which invoked an array of features including a sense of the nobility of office, a deep sense of public purpose and an understanding of the serious nature of political responsibility. Along with this came an awareness that public service often required a unique mix of virtues, prudence and practical insight as well as a grasp of their limits and a regulative and clear vision of the type of politics to avoid. I will demonstrate that political thinkers involved in the translation and dissemination of Plutarch in France emphasise the distinctiveness of the public realm *without* seeing freedom as independence and participation or as tied to republican institutions (found in traditional accounts of Florentine civic republicanism), nor are their arguments pitched as a broad call to virtue for both rulers and citizens. Political argument in the French context of early sixteenth-century humanism offers competing accounts of "la chose publique" (we might translate it as the public realm or the public sphere) and how best to qualify and characterise the ethos, norms, relations and expectations of those who wield political authority.

As I hope to show, the uniqueness of the French argument is neither a form of Ciceronian rhetorical flourish adapting an inherently northern Italian argumentative trope to a monarchical reality, nor a Gallic version of the 'monarchical republic' sometimes used to refer to Tudor England.[13] There are four interrelated structural features that distinguish this political strand of French humanist argument influenced by engagement with the work of Plutarch. Its important distinctive feature from the numerous mirror-for-princes texts circulating in Europe throughout the late medieval and Renaissance period is a focus on the unique ethical, emotional and rhetorical challenges of a public role. The four unique features of the arguments found in the works of French Renaissance humanist thinkers can be summarised as follows: (1) its initial articulation is as a mode of governance, focusing on *how* to govern rather than a language of citizenship (or concerning *who* governs), with greater emphasis placed on *la chose*

---

[13] See Patrick Collinson, "The Monarchical Republic of Queen Elizabeth I," *Bulletin of the John Rylands Library*, 69.2(1987), 394–424. In a somewhat similar way, Orest Ranum suggests the invocation of the term *chose publicque* [sic] in later French Renaissance historiography is something akin to the mixed regime. Still, as will become apparent in our discussion, this was not the way the term was used by Tory, and it appears that it had shifting meanings over the century. See Orest Ranum, *Artisans of Glory* (Durham, NC: North Carolina Press, 1980), as well as James Collins, "Dynastic Instability, the Emergence of the French Monarchical Commonwealth and the Coming of the Rhetoric of *l'état*, 1360s to 1650s," in Robert von Friedeburg and John Morrill eds., *Monarchy Transformed* (Cambridge: Cambridge University Press, 2017), 87–126.

publique as the target or object of public action; (2) it provides an emphasis on the particulars of political prudence and on *how* to conduct oneself in public life (rather than on the concept of *libertas* that justifies participation) with discussion surrounding appropriate models or examples of political rule; (3) it offers a focus on the specific qualities and nature of the public role, and a realistic appreciation and consideration of the important ethical challenges in the exercise of public office. This includes reflection on the relationship between prudence and the other virtues as well as the place of practical considerations in public life alongside a regulative conception of good government. In contrast to a broadly Ciceronian inspired approach which considers exceptional and specific situations both public and private, where general ethical norms may be applied in unconventional ways, the arguments generated in the case of French Renaissance public humanism stress the full uniqueness of public office alongside its deeper ethical responsibilities, the more complex factors of public and collective psychology, as well as a more general sense of exceptionalism verging on distinct normative frameworks and concerns; (4) finally, these texts demonstrate advocacy for the French vernacular as a new tool of political communication and tend to emphasise the importance and specificity of the French historical context, distinguishing it from both ancient Roman and contemporary Italian traditions, and celebrating the historical legacy of the Gauls.

This chapter and the next will demonstrate the important and distinct patterns in the way key French political thinkers of the Renaissance chose to read, and in many cases translate, their Plutarch. I will demonstrate how in the process of translation and reflection on Plutarch's work these thinkers came to integrate into their political thought concerted reflection on the qualities of public life that broadly conform to the four features identified above. For some, the ethical demands of those in power are greater, for others in certain instances the ethos of politics is distinct, though still driven by a concern for justice overall. Despite their differences, and despite differing patterns of focus on either *Lives* or essays from the *Moralia*, all appear in a general way to converge on the idea that *a public role entails distinct social psychological features that help to shape unique ethical considerations (in intensity or kind) for the individual who acts publicly.* I argue that this is the core of the tradition of Plutarch reception to the history of political thought.

Before exploring the first translations of Plutarch into French, it is helpful to have an idea of what works of Plutarch were available to scholars in print both in Latin and in Greek. The fact that many of the first French humanist translators of Plutarch into the vernacular were often working with Byzantine translations or scholars is important for my argument.

As noted, the first print edition of the *Lives* appeared in Latin in Rome in 1470 (the Campano edition), and it served for many years as the basis for subsequent editions. The first printed Greek edition of the *Lives* appeared in Florence in 1517. The edition princeps of the *Moralia* in Greek (based on a thirteenth-century manuscript) was published by the Aldine Press in Venice in 1509 (with some help from Erasmus). Compilations of selected essays of Plutarch translated by different authors began to appear in Latin by the 1540s (under the title *Ethica, sive Moralia* or *Opuscula*), including the essay "De Pollitica" (i.e. "Precepts of Statecraft" or "Political Precepts") translated by Nicolaus Sekoundinos, which spearheaded the edition. For most of the first half of the sixteenth century then, for a Renaissance reader relying on print editions, and especially for one whose knowledge of Greek was not strong, the *Lives* were more accessible than most of the essays of the *Moralia*. Exceptions were those essays singled out and translated by scholars, most notably by Erasmus. These essays were selected for their special insights, and a select few were beginning to circulate more widely in France. The essays published separately and translated first into Latin and only subsequently into the vernacular included most notably: "On the Education of Children" (now regarded as spurious), "How to Tell a Friend from a Flatterer" (translated by Erasmus into Latin and by Antoine du Saix into French), "Advice on Marriage" (issued six times in often different translations from 1535 to 1550), and "On the Bravery of Women" (with three different translations from 1538 to 1546).[14] In addition to this were Plutarch's "Sayings of Kings and Commanders," which was widely circulated at the time, especially in France (there is some debate as to whether this work was fashioned directly by Plutarch himself or by someone else seeking to compile lessons and list anecdotes from the *Lives* for ready access for speeches etc.).

Still, despite the availability of the *Lives* in Latin by the early sixteenth century, it can be argued that the French of the early sixteenth century owe more to Byzantine scholars, especially Nicolaus Sekoundinos (1402–1464) and John Lascaris (1445–1535), for the strong resonance of Plutarch in sixteenth-century French political thought than they do to the earlier scholarly work of Italian Renaissance humanists. Sekoundinos (one of

---

[14] This derives from a study of the entries of the *Universal Short Title Catalogue*. Post-Amyot the *Moralia* was reissued in 1572 along with the *Lives* by Henri Estienne (known by most Plato scholars as Stephanus) and the *Moralia* was again issued in Greek in 1574 by Xylander.

a very wide range of spellings of his name) is a fascinating figure in his own right. He was born in Chalcis, Euboea and was captured in 1430 by the Turks in their conquests in Salonika. On his release he served in various administrative posts for Italian city states. Given his sound knowledge of both Latin and Greek, he served as official translator at the Council of Ferrara-Florence (1438–1439) and subsequently served as ducal secretary and ambassador for the Venetian republic. He was on the first Western mission to speak with the Sultan Mehmed II to discuss the release of prisoners after the fall of Constantinople in 1453. He described the sultan as intellectually curious with a special interest in the lives of Alexander and Julius Caesar.

Sekoundinos was also a scholar and promoter of Greek texts. He may have been best known in his own lifetime as the translator of Onasander's text on military strategy (*De Optima Imperatore*) which exists in about fifteen extant manuscript copies. His translation of Plutarch's "Political Precepts" into Latin does not appear to exist in any recorded extant manuscript copy but was published after his death in the first decade of the sixteenth century. The apocryphal letter of Plutarch addressed to Emperor Trajan, discussed in Chapter 2, was attached to this publication.[15] It was "La Pollitica" that was included in a number of editions collecting various Latin translations of Plutarch's essays and began to be circulated in the early sixteenth century. This translated essay into Latin was significant enough for Jacques Amyot to allude to it in his dedicatory letter to readers in his vernacular edition of Plutarch's *Lives* published in 1559. It was also through Sekoundinos's translation that Plutarch's political thought came to be introduced to France in one of the first editions of a translation of Plutarch into the vernacular through the work of Geoffroy Tory (c. 1480–c. 1533).

Jean Lascaris was the second exile from the east who had an important impact not only on Plutarch reception in France, but on the development of Renaissance humanism in France as a whole.[16] Having escaped Constantinople shortly after it fell in 1453, Lascaris spent much of his

---

[15] My judgements regarding the manuscripts of Sekoundinos come from searches through the online data base *Iter Italicum* (http://cf.itergateway.org/italicum/) accessed 11 May 2016. His name appears in the database in the form Secundinus (with one other entry for Segundinus). See also note 32 in this chapter.

[16] Gerald Sandy recognises the importance of Lascaris for the development of French humanism, which became a beacon for Greek reception. He appears to suggest that Lascaris was part of more a general trend through which humanism moved from Italy to France. However, the work of Lascaris in France was quite distinct from other ways in which Italian humanism was received in France, in part because he encouraged the French to read Plutarch and also because he brought manuscripts to France to encourage scholarly work on Plutarch in different directions to what had

career in Italy promoting the study of Greek and working as a book collector for famous patrons, including the Medici. His Byzantine identity remained important to him throughout his life, and he was a persistent advocate through his patrons for a renewed crusade against the Turkish occupation. During the French occupation of Florence he was invited to return to France with King Charles VIII, where he stayed in 1495–1515 and again in 1518–1535, to organise the royal library and to advise on scholarly matters.[17] He became a close acquaintance of Guillaume Budé and Claude de Seyssel and facilitated the work of the latter in translating Plutarch.[18] His arrival in Paris had a decisive impact on the reception of Greek literature in France, beyond the sheer number of manuscripts he either brought with him or helped the king to acquire.[19]

A third scholar from the east, Georges Hermonyme (d. c. 1510) who served as one of the first teachers of ancient Greek in Paris, came to France, it is believed, from somewhere in the Peloponnesus (hence his known name Hermonyme of Sparta). He is also known to have transcribed certain Greek manuscripts for Budé's use.[20] While these three individuals did not come directly from Constantinople to France, they all came from various regions of the former Byzantine Empire and they were devoted to the encouragement of Greek learning and the spread of knowledge about the Greek tradition, with Plutarch playing a prominent role in the west. Their knowledge of Plutarch and the Greek tradition appeared to come directly from their immersion in scholarly traditions of the east rather than via traditions of translation and Latin scholarship in early Renaissance Italy, though in certain cases they contributed to those same traditions.

When examining the act of translation at this time it should be noted that while the Renaissance is known for the concerted retrieval of ancient texts, not all humanists may have had the same intent in their work. Many

---

been done in the Italian context. His scholarly contribution to Seyssel's translations allowed Plutarch to be picked up in new and significant ways, and his association with Budé also brought attention to Plutarch and new traditions of reception. See Gerald Sandy, "Resources for the Study of Ancient Greek in France," in Gerald Sandy ed., *The Classical Heritage in France* (Leiden: Brill, 2002), 47–78.

[17] George J. Kovtun. "John Lascaris and the Byzantine Connection, "*The Journal of Library History (1974–1987)*, vol. 12, n. 1 (winter 1977), 17–26.

[18] In 1494, Lascaris published the Greek Anthology of Maxime Planudes, the Byzantine scholar responsible for the reassembling and recopying of all of Plutarch's work.

[19] As suggested by di Stefano there were only a small number of Greek manuscripts in the royal library at the beginning of the sixteenth century, but this had grown to 546 by the time of the death of François I. See "'L'Hellénisme," 29.

[20] Luigi-Alberto Sanchi, "Budé et Plutarque," in *Moralia et Œuvres morales à la Renaissance* (Paris: Honoré Champion, 2008), 93.

texts were translated and then dedicated to powerful patrons to impress and establish a relationship, or to sustain it.[21] Some, such as we will see below with Seyssel, will have chosen excerpts to translate with a particular philosophical purpose in mind, as the choices of texts in translation could function as a soft form of power and influence towards patrons and rulers. Some humanists may have been struck by the literary or philosophical beauty of the manuscripts or classical texts they discovered and translated them to ensure they would be read more widely. Yet others, and here we include Erasmus to a certain degree, looked upon the practice of translation as a way of improving and exercising linguistic skills, skills that needed to be perfected in order to take on the most challenging of tasks, the Greek Bible and the writings of the Church fathers (although language training may also have served in offering mental respite in times of more heated scholarly disputes).[22] Furthermore, these purposes and intents were not necessarily exclusive and could be combined in the same exercise. Also, whatever the intent, the work of translation could impact broader patterns of reflection in sometimes unforeseen ways.

Many humanist scholars who contributed to reflection in political theory shared a set of key characteristics. As humanists they were scholars who had their strongest footing in the world of scholarship and translation. However, because they were scholars with no independent source of income their fortune was closely tied to kingly courts where nobility might serve as both readers and patrons. Many of these thinkers developed an account and justification of good monarchical rule, drawing on classical texts.

These thinkers were also faced with a challenge in developing a political theory that spoke to the age. They were in a context where rulers and states were seeking to consolidate their control over persons and territories and to establish their authority by replacing practices of trial by ordeal and personal vengeance with an institutionalised system of justice. The dangers of badly exercised state power and tyranny were also apparent. The challenge was to develop a theory that would allow a king with good intentions and good judgement to flourish, to expand his influence and

---

[21] This is suggested by Fred Schurink in "Print, Patronage and Occasion: Translations of Plutarch's Morals in Tudor England," in *The Yearbook of English Studies*, vol. 38, no. 1–2 Tudor Literature (2008), 86–101. "In particular, writers often translated works to seek a reward, or (more commonly) some form of preferment from a patron, or to express gratefulness for the dedicatees support of the author in the past – often presented to patrons at the time of the new year or for a birthday" (87). See also Warren Boucher, "The Renaissance," in Peter France ed., *The Oxford Guide to Literature in English Translation* (Oxford: Oxford University Press, 2000), 45–55.

[22] Rummel, *Erasmus*, 4 and 81.

power and to achieve good outcomes for the state, while hemming in the legitimacy and power of the ruler who lacked the intention or the capacities to rule wisely and in the interests of the whole. In doing so, many thinkers drew their paradigmatic account of good kingship from Aristotle, but Plutarch's work was used to fill in the details of this broader framework.

In comparing the work of Budé, Erasmus and Seyssel through the prism of Plutarch we see the emergence of key debates in Renaissance thought concerning the nature and norms of public life. Furthermore, in the works of political theory examined here and informed in part by translations of Plutarch, the reflections are not grounded in the kind of metaphysical discussions of human nature and human community or public service that one might find if Cicero was the primary influence. Rather, the focus is more practical. Given the necessary and important work of politics, and the types of relationships and expectations that it generates, the task was to find the best framework for understanding the ethical contours in which public figures act.

Bradshaw has suggested that in terms of political thought the current of 'transalpine humanism' to which these three thinkers belong is drawn from a largely idealised notion of politics that was grounded in texts of classical antiquity and applied towards competing visions of political reform.[23] While it is clear that each of these thinkers offer visions of reform, whether through the education of rulers and patronage of the arts or the minimisation of violence in politics, it is less clear the extent to which their visions were actually informed by idealism. It is true that behind these theories we see a general commitment to the Aristotelian picture of the ruler as the ultimate distributor of justice. What is also striking is the degree to which their visions of good political rule and the nature and demands associated with public life are illustrated and informed by history and historical figures, and indeed a certain sense of realism.

For Budé, public life, in the context of monarchical government, was the sphere in which individuals could demonstrate extraordinary capacities, and where heroic virtues could be recast in light of Aristotelian philosophy and Christian orthodoxy. As such virtues were developed in part through the study of history, the search for renown became an appropriate motivation in public life. In contrast, Erasmus explicitly renounces the heroic vision of and inspiration for monarchical leadership, while still

---

[23] Brendan Bradshaw, "Transalpine Humanism," in J. H. Burns ed., *The Cambridge History of Political Thought 1450–1700* (Cambridge: Cambridge University Press, 1991), 100.

acknowledging that the capacities for holding a position of rule are unique and significant. He stresses the importance of responsibility that extends beyond that of good intentions, noting that rulers are ethically responsible for the consequences of their actions and that they require specialised knowledge of possible impacts of their decisions as well as a sophisticated awareness of themselves and of how to manage conflict. Despite this, Erasmus with certain greater psychological insight, acknowledges that the good ruler will not achieve *apatheia* but will be inwardly torn with anxiety, and that the effects of differential status and power brought on by leadership need to be acknowledged and managed wisely. Thus, given the need for flexibility, an understanding of the effects of one's rule in terms of potential harm (to be minimised), fostering public good through education or promoting various facets of the public welfare, including peace, the ethical demands of public life will not always correspond to those of private life.

Seyssel provides us with another way of thinking about the distinct nature of public life through the lens of Plutarch. Seyssel's translations of the lives of Antony and Demetrius suggests a certain allegiance with Erasmus in his scepticism towards a heroic model of political leadership, since public figures who appear at first to demonstrate capacity for great political virtue may also be susceptible to acting out vices in politics in ways that have important negative impact on the community. And while both Erasmus and Seyssel draw on the metaphor of the 'political body' to shape the ruler's understanding so that their function and purpose is tied to a broader sense of attunement to the whole, Seyssel is more explicit in how this understanding should offer an essential normative and practical restraint (*frein*) on the will of the ruler. While not yet articulating a formal constitutional response to the challenge of potential tyranny, Seyssel provides us with an important rendering of an institutional theory as a rejoinder to the earlier models of personal rule. Overall, the first half of the sixteenth century in France offers a discussion surrounding the norms, merits, and pitfalls of personal rule. All this refracted through the lens of Plutarch.

Before embarking on an analysis of the Plutarch translations and political reflection of these three key figures, it is important to shed light on a lesser known but highly significant predecessor in Plutarch reception in France. Arguably the force and tone of 'public humanism' as I have presented it would not have been the same without the translation work of Geoffroy Tory.

3.1 Geoffroy Tory: Publishing Plutarch in the French Vernacular

While not a political theorist in the narrow sense of the term, Geoffroy Tory's (c. 1480–c. 1533) scholarship had important implications for the history of political thought in France, as well as its politics. Tory was a Renaissance man in the full sense of the term. He was a humanist scholar with knowledge of both Latin and Greek and an accomplished translator of various texts, including some pseudo-Plutarch. He was more widely known as an engraver and printer and was appointed Royal Printer in recognition of the beauty and skill of his work. Finally, and perhaps most importantly, he was a theorist of language and of the graphic arts. His most famous work, *Champ fleury* (1529) provides an eloquent defence of the French language as a noble and worthy medium of communication, an argument for its special origins in the Greek (as opposed to the Latin) tradition, and a theory of the appropriate graphic presentation of Roman letters based on proportions derived from the human form. An understanding of the appropriate shaping of letters (i.e. font) and expression of the French language, given its origins in ancient Greek, would, he believed, ensure the language as a powerful tool in the flourishing of French culture.[24] Tory brings together classical scholarship and contemporary technology (in the form of engraving and printing) to bolster a culture and ultimately consolidate a deeper sense of political community though vernacular language, one that would overshadow diverse local linguistic variations within France as well as strengthen the French identity as distinct from others within Europe.

Tory was not the first Frenchman to translate Plutarch into the vernacular (Seyssel had already done so in 1510, and there are other extant manuscripts of French vernacular translations of selected *Lives*), nor was he the first to *publish* a *French* translation of Plutarch (a French edition of a translation by Francois Sauvage of Plutarch's essay "How to Tell a Friend from a Flatterer" had been produced in 1520), but Tory's edition of Plutarch (among a number of his translations of classical works), along with his strong theoretical defence of the French vernacular, ushered in

---

[24] J. W. Jolliffe, "Introduction," to Geofroy Tory, *Champ Fleury* (East Ardsley, New York and Paris: S. R. Publishers, Johnson Reprint Corporation and Mouton et Co, 1970 and 1529). Tory's defence of the beauty of the French language was followed by Du Bellay's *La Defense et Illustration de la Langue française* (1549) and then Henri Estienne's *La Precellence du Langage françois* (1579). Du Bellay begins his essay with the suggestion that the history and merits of the Gauls had been unjustly silenced through active suppression by envious Romans. Etienne Pasquier begins his *Recherches sur la France* with a similar position. There appears to be a link between the defence of the French language for contemporary purposes, and hostility to the Roman conquest of Gaul.

a transformation in humanist trends of publication in France.[25] Indeed, his promotion of the French vernacular served as a precursor to the 1539 *Ordonnance de Villers-Cotterêts, ordonnance sur le fait de la justice*, which made it necessary for all official acts to be written in French (rather than in the traditional Latin) and is today the oldest standing law in France.

What was the spirit in which Tory embraced and defended greater use of the French vernacular in scholarship? On the one hand, it was perceived as a way in which to ennoble and develop a sense of the possibilities of higher cultural achievement in France; on the other, it served to open access to cultural production beyond the narrow array of educated humanist scholars. In an act of subtle subversion of standard humanist tropes and practices, Tory did not dedicate his *Champ fleury* to any individual patron or person of political eminence and power. Instead, the work is dedicated "to all true and devoted Lovers of well-formed Letters," placing all those who love letters on the same footing.[26]

---

[25] The first printed and published edition of a translation of Plutarch in the French vernacular as identified by the USTC is: Plutarque, *Le livre moult utile et profitable a tous roys, princes, gens d'auctorite et generalement a toutes gens de quelque estat qu'ilz soient pour cognoistre et scavoir discerner ung vray amy d'avecques ung flatteur*, Francois Sauvage trans. (Yves Gallois: Paris, 1520). This translation was based on a Greek to Latin translation by Erasmus. This was the only published vernacular Plutarch translation in the decade 1520–1529, whereas in the next decade there were thirteen.

Gallica offers examples of a few sixteenth-century scholars who effected manuscript translations of select *Lives*. These include: Georges de Selve, Arnauld Chandon, and Symon Bourgouyn. On this latter translator, see James P. Carley and Myra D. Orth, "Plus que assez: Simon Bourgouyn and his French Translations from Plutarch, Petrarch and Lucian," *Viator* 34 (2003), 328–363. Carley cites Sturel in suggesting that Bourgouyn may have been the first to translate Plutarch from the Latin to vernacular prose. See René Sturel, *Jacques Amyot traducteur des Vies parallèles de Plutarque* (Paris: Joseph Flock, 1908 and 2006), 8–9. Bourgouyn's early translations were completed by 1503, the year of the death of one of his patrons, and he is known to have translated the lives of Pompey, Demosthenes, Cicero and Cato, largely by choice of his patrons. It appears that there was an earlier vernacular translation of Plutarch, but of the essay "On Anger" from the *Moralia*, translated by Nicolas de Gonesse in 1400–1401 as a gift to Jean de Berry, as identified by Giuseppe di Stefano. See his, *La Découverte de Plutarque en Occident* (Turin: Accademia delle Scienze, 1968).

[26] "Dedication," in Geofroy Tory *Champ fleury* (London: Johnson Reprint Corporation, 1529 and 1970), iii. The English translation of the Dedication reads : "Poets, Orators and other learned in Letters and Sciences when they have made and put together some product of their studious diligence and toil, are wont to present it to some great lord of the Court or the Church, lifting him up by letters an laudation to the knowledge of other men; and this to flatter him and to the end that they may be always so welcome about him, that he seems to be bound and obliged to give them some great gift, some benefice or some office as reward for the labours and vigils they have put to the making and composition of their said works and offerings. I could easily to the like with this little book; but, considering that, if I should present it to one rather than to another, some feeling of envious despite might be caused, I have thought that it would be well of me to make of it a present to you all, O devoted Lovers of well-made letters, and is more at home in virtuous things. Thus the Prelates and great Lords, who are eminent, all, in goodly virtues, will have their part therein, whilst you will not lose yours." Geofroy Tory, *Champ fleury*, trans. and ed. by George Ives (New York: The Grolier Club, 1927), v.

In the beginning of this work, Tory comments on a passage taken from Lucian regarding a painting in which the Celtic God Ogmios is depicted as an elderly Hercules, who draws towards him a crowd of men and women attached by the ears to chains that lead to his tongue. The image is explained to Lucian by a Gaul who sees it as demonstrating the secret of the god's power in his eloquence and persuasiveness. Indeed, for Tory it demonstrates that the French language "est si gracieux, que sil est pronounce dung homme discret, sage et age, il a si grande efficace, quil persuade plustost et myeulx que le latin, ne que le grec." [is so full of grace that, if it be spoken by a discreet and wise man, of mature age, it has such great efficacy that it persuades better than Latin or Greek.][27] In other words, language, and particularly well spoken and well written French language, is power and not just the reserve of those with an education in the classics.

Andreas Alciatus (widely known and celebrated as one of the first French legal humanists bringing to the study of Roman law the new methods of more historically sensitive analysis) also evoked this image in verse and engraving five years after Tory in his *Emblematum libellus* (1534), giving birth to the emblematic literature tradition (as well as coining the term 'emblem').[28] It was translated into French by Jean LeFevre in 1536 with the following rendition of Alciatus' verse:

> "Eloquence vault mieulx que force."
> L'arc en la main, en l'autre la massue,
> Peau de lyon estant cy aperceue,
> Pour Hercules me faict ce vieillart croire.
> Mais ce qu'il a marque de si grand gloire:
> Que mener gens enchainez a sa langue
> Entendre veult, qu'il feist tant bien harengue,
> Que les Francois pour ses dits de merveilles,
> Furent ainsi que pris par les oreilles.
> Si donc il a par loix & ordonnances
> Rangé les gens, plustost que par vaillances:
> Dira l'on pas (comme est verité)
> Que l'espee a lieu aux livres quicté?
> Et que ung dur cueur par sages mieulx se range,
> Que gros effort son aspreté ne change?
> Pour ce Hercules ne fait pas grandes forces:
> Et si sont gens, apres luy grandes courses.[29]

---

[27] Tory, *Champ fleury*, Biii. The English translation is found in Tory, *Champ fleury*, ed. G. Ives, 7.
[28] See, for example, Aurelio Perez Jimenez in "The Reception of Plutarch in Spain," in Mark Beck ed., *A Companion to Plutarch* (Oxford: Blackwell, 2014), esp 563–567.
[29] Andreas Alciatus, *Livret des emblemes mis en rime francoyse*, trans. Jacques LeFevre (Paris: 1536).

[Eloquence is worth more than force: The bow in one hand and the club in the other, along with the lion's pelt, all of this leads me to believe this old man is Hercules. But what marks him with great glory is that he can lead men who wish to hear him and chained to his tongue given that he speaks so well the French are so charmed by his words that they are led by their ears. Hence, he can shape and order a people by laws and ordinances rather than by force: will not one say (that which is true) that the sword has yielded to books? And doesn't a strong heart of wisdom order things better than what the harshness of physical force changes. For this Hercules is not wielding great physical strength: yet people will follow his lead.]

For the broader community of humanists in France, it was evident that the work of Tory was not just a celebration of the beauty of the French language, but of its intrinsic link to a community governed by the rule of law, as opposed to fear through the threat of force.[30]

Tory's translation of Plutarch's "Political Precepts" from the Latin, "La Pollitica", first published in 1530 (the same year that François I established *le Collège royal* for the teaching of Latin, Greek and Hebrew), provides a reading of Plutarch that is focused on the French term *la chose publique*.[31] Tory's work was based on a Latin translation of the essay by Nicolaus Sekoundinos, the diplomat and scholar mentioned earlier (he is also sometimes referred to as Nicole Sagundin).[32] The Latin version of this essay was published repeatedly in the compilations *Opuscula* or *Opuscula moralia*, which included a number of previously translated essays by a number of prominent humanists including Budé, Guarino and

---

[30] For a broader treatment of the place of the image of l'Hercule gaulois in French Renaissance humanism, see the article by Claude la Charité, "Henri III rhéteur, nouvel Hercule gaulois," in Laurent Pernot ed., *New Chapters in the History of Rhetoric*, (Boston, MA: Brill, 2009), 269–286.

[31] I have consulted two different editions of Tory's translation of Plutarch. They are as follows: *Politiques de Plutarche, cest a dire civiles institutions et enseignemens pour bien Regir la Chose Publique* Iadis composes en Grec par Plutarche, et de puis translates de Grec en Latin par le Seigneur Nicole Sagundin, 1532 and *Politiques ou civiles institutions pour bien regir la chose publicque*. (Lyon: Boulle, 1534). I cite the passages in the latter edition, as the first does not contain page numbers. I also use the name Plutarch as the author even though the name is cited 'Plutarche' or 'Plutarque' in the French editions. There is note of the 1530 edition in the USTC. On Tory, see also my "Thinking about the Public Realm in Early Sixteenth Century France through Plutarch and Geoffroy Tory (1480–1533)," in David Carter et al. eds., *Brill's Companion to the Legacy of Greek Political Thought* (Leiden: Brill, forthcoming). Some of the analysis used for this chapter is also found in my article devoted to Tory.

[32] On Sekoundinos see Marios Philippides, "The Fall of Constantinople 1453: Classical Comparisons and the Circle of Cardinal Isidore," *Viator* 38.1(2007), 361–362 as well as A.-M. Talbot, "Sekoundinos, Nicholas," *Oxford Dictionary of Byzantium* 3 (Oxford: Oxford University Press, 1991), 1865. Sekoundinos's *Plutarchus de pollitica et imperatoria institutione ad Traianum imperatorem. Plutarchus de liberis educandis. Epistola Nicolai Sagundini ad Marcum Donatum patricium Venetum. Epistola Plutarchi ad Traianum imperatorem* was published in Venice by Bernardino Benali c. 1500–1509. Only a few copies of this work are extant in various libraries in Italy.

others.[33] Tory both translated and produced the edition of this one Plutarch essay. Beginning with a translation of the apocryphal letter by Plutarch written to Trajan, "Political Precepts" is dedicated by Tory to the Dauphin, Francois de Vallois. This reflection on the nature of *la chose publique* was the first significant published introduction to Plutarch's political thought in the vernacular French. Given the importance of the subject matter, as well as its being promoted in the printing work of Tory, it became a popular edition with three editions in four years. As noted, Jacques Amyot, in his "Avis aux lecteurs" in the first edition of his translation of Plutarch's *Lives*, alluded to this essay, suggesting that his literate public may already have been acquainted with it.[34]

Here was a text from an author whose works were new to a wider public – including the king, whose command of Latin was imperfect – but whose fame had been celebrated throughout the medieval era at a time when the printed book was still somewhat of a novelty. It is significant that this was the work through which many sixteenth-century Frenchmen first became directly acquainted with Plutarch for, as we will see, it consolidated a tradition in which Plutarch was identified as offering significant insights for rulers and providing wise instruction on the nature of public life. In addition, and most significantly, within the opus of Plutarch the essay chosen by Tory for vernacular translation is distinguished by its largely practical focus on the demands and ethos of public life. What this meant was that the standard moralist thrust of Plutarch's political advice was now represented in ways that were tempered by concessions to both realism and pragmatism. The focus of this work was not on political education of the

[33] The edition I consulted was Plutarch, *Opera moralia* (Basile: Mich. Isingrinium, 1541). Sekoundinos's translation appears to have been dedicated to a Marcus Donatus of Venice, presumably a Venetian patrician.

[34] "Si l'homme vieil se doit entremettre du gouvernement de la chose publique: et qui jadis eut cest heur et honeur, que d'estre precepteur de l'Empereur Traian, ainsi qu'on tient communement, et qu'il est expressement porte par une missive, qui se lit au devant de la traduction Latine de ses Politiques." Jacques Amyot, "Avis aux lecteurs," *Les Vies des Hommes Illustres grecs et romains compares l'une avec l'autre par Plutarque* (Paris: l'Imprimerie de Ieremie des Planches, 1583). Amyot doubts the authenticity of the Letter to Trajan, something contemporary scholars suggest is a credit to his scholarly skills, as he is one of the first to do so. Also significant is that Amyot identifies the letter to Trajan not with John of Salisbury's *Policraticus* but with the work he calls "Ses Politiques," presumably referring to the Sekoundinos Latin translation of "Political Precepts" published under the title "Pollitica", which always was accompanied by the letter to Trajan. We can ascertain that Amyot has the Sekoundinos translation in mind in part because he calls it "Ses Politiques," using the terms of Tory's French vernacular translation of the essay "Pollitica", and not "La Polycratique," which had been the vernacular title of John of Salisbury's work translated into French in the medieval era. Another clue that Amyot is referencing Sekoundinos is his mention of the accompanying letter to Trajan, which was always included in the widely circulated Sekoundinos translation.

young to help fashion the soul best suited to devotion to justice (à la Telemaque), but rather on advice for those entering politics so that those with a commitment to justice could navigate the challenges of perception, enmity, power dynamics and competition that shaped the practice of politics and the public realm. Here was moralism with a realist edge.

Before addressing the substance of the argument, it is important to highlight a couple of things regarding the translation. In the first instance, Tory was translating the text from a Latin translation by Sekoundinos from the previous century. This was not unusual during the Renaissance. Even in France, which tended to lead the continent in knowledge and scholarship of ancient Greek texts, resources for learning ancient Greek were not always easy to come by.[35] Clearly, and independent of the translator's theoretical and methodological commitments in terms of translation, the fact that Tory (and others) were translating texts already translated into Latin from the original Greek was a structural condition that could lend itself to a certain amount of innovation. In addition, we see that in the context of debates in Renaissance translation theory between what is deemed to be a more literalist approach and what has been deemed an anti-literalist approach, Tory is not easily peg-holed. Norton has recognised that, at least in his statements concerning basic theoretical commitments in his practice of translation, Tory both rejects excessive servitude to the letter of the text and also, perhaps as the articulation of an ideal, suggests that a close version of the original can be reconstructed in the new idiom. In suggesting that style of expression must remain an important conveyor of sense, he does provide some space for innovation.[36]

There is a further layer (or layers) of complication, especially concerning one of the key terms of interest here, and one that is frequently repeated in the text – the term *la chose publique*. As is clear, this is how Tory translated the Latin term *res publica* which Sekoundinos invoked when Plutarch in the manuscript used the term πολιτεία or κοινός or one of their variants, and most often in the plural. It would appear that Sekoundinos was following the lead of Leonardo Bruni who had first invoked the Latin term *res publica* as a translation for the Greek term πολιτεία.[37] In the first instance, given that it derived from a fully different political context, the

[35] Sandy, "Resources for the Study of Ancient Greek in France," 77.
[36] Glyn Norton, *The Ideology and Language of Translation in Renaissance France and their Humanist Antecedents* (Geneva: Droz, 1984), 143–144.
[37] Claudia Moatti, *Res publica: histoire romaine de la chose publique* (Paris: Fayard, 2018), 11. Moatti suggests in ancient Rome the term *res publica* never had a stable uncontested conceptual meaning but was invoked at crucial political junctures to serve different political purposes.

Latin term *res publica* was a rather awkward translation for the Greek; in the second instance, it was a term that even in the Roman context was subject to quite contested and competing meanings. Recent scholarship has tended to reject the notion that there was any consistent and stable meaning for key political concepts in the Roman context, suggesting in particular that the term *res publica* could be invoked to denote a number of ideas: the things or affairs implicating citizens and about which decisions were made, the processes through which decisions were made, a recognition of contestability that defined the realm of politics, and, from the eyes of subjected peoples, the Roman people taken as a whole who exercised imperium over other non-Roman territories.[38] It often served as a rhetorical trope infused with different connotations depending on the context but through which agonistic political struggle took shape. Still, it was generally, though not always, associated with a combative and somewhat broadly based political community with mechanisms for the representation of the interests of the poor.

In the transition from the Greek (πολιτεία or κοινος) to the Latin (*res publica*), and then again from the Latin to the French (*la chose publique*), particularly in the context of sixteen-century monarchy and nascent absolutism, there were numerous unacknowledged hermeneutic leaps. Notably, *la chose publique* is invoked in a way that imbues it with a sense of an objective and reified reality. The Greek terms invoked in the original text of "Political Precepts" refer to the things of the city, or things that are common to all, and while by implication these are the things which concern public life, the nuanced implication is that those things are political by virtue of having a shared sense of importance for those in the city rather than political due to the position of public responsibility through which they can be addressed. With the shift from issues that concern the whole and those who manage them, to the 'public thing' (via the Latin *res publica*) comes a reification of public life. Furthermore, through Tory's substitution of contemporary French institutions (such as the *parlements* and the sovereign courts) in translation for Plutarch's appeal to his own institutions (Greece under the thumb of an imperial power), there is an implicit claim that despite the circumstances and context in which the essay was originally written (and indeed translated into Latin with the invocation of republican vocabulary), it has a meaning that not only transcends that context but can be judged as directly relevant to the

---

[38] Also, see Joy Connolly, *The Life of Roman Republicanism* (Princeton, NJ: Princeton University Press, 2017).

French context. In these shifts in meaning, *la chose publique* is now invoked in the translation to imply a sphere with its own norms and rules of behaviour. For Tory, we find throughout the translation a repeated invocation of various expressions alluding to the relation between the individual in public life and their relation to *la chose publique*, such as "the regime of *la chose publique*," the "superintendence of *la chose publique*," the "administration of *la chose publique*," the "governing of *la chose publique*" and even "presiding over *la chose publique*." What these various expressions portray, as in Jacques Amyot's later use of the term, is certainly not the agonistic politics of Rome and not just a relation of power, or even strict public/private division, but a stewardship of a kind. As we will see, this is associated not only with the idea that stewardship is best taken on by someone with a certain type of motivation and character, but also that the nature of the relation offers its own ethical considerations. Significantly, what is brought to light through the uses of *la chose publique* as a stand-in for the invocation of politics, is the idea that it is here not only a question of what statesmen must do to succeed, but also *a discussion of the particular and distinct features of public life to which statesmen, if they are to succeed, must adapt.*

In this essay, and the inflection of the translation as offered by Tory, one can discern distinctions among four key categories: the good, the prudent, the practical or pragmatic and the bad. The good refers to the overarching goals of public life most often referred to as justice, but sometimes cast in the language of public good; the prudent refers to the virtues or actions that are recommended as helping to lead towards that good, and the types of judgements that can be deemed specific to public life but which do not clash substantially with what are more generally called the civil virtues, although they can be justified as means as well as aspects of good character; the practical refers to those areas or instances in which public norms, given the unique nature of public life, may require some disjuncture between the requirements of virtue in civil life and the demands of public life; and finally, the bad refers to the approach to public life that the statesman is to avoid. I will demonstrate that both Plutarch and Tory in this essay focus on both the second and third, with Tory, via the Latin of Sekoundinos, infusing his translation with a subtle emphasis enhancing an already existent theme of expediency found in the original text. The point is not to depict all public life through the theme of expediency, but rather to offer important distinctions where a small window for pragmatic consideration is necessary given the demands of public life, while still acknowledging that there are clearly overriding goods to pursue as well as clear parameters of bad politics to avoid. In other words, through Tory's translation we are shown a vision of political life that offers a clear moral commitment and framework, but which allows for practical concessions given the unique nature of the political sphere.

Plutarch's essay as translated by Tory begins with a focus on the need for more practical understanding in public matters. Speculative philosophers are compared to those who in seeking light focus on trimming and preparing the wick but neglect to put any oil in the lamp.[39] The question then posed at the outset is what sort of non-philosophical knowledge or insight is necessary to administer *la chose publique*. It raises the issue of inner motivation as a factor in judging an individual's potential and suitability for public life in terms of sustaining an individual's efforts and of shaping their effectiveness as a public actor. To a certain degree, this approach offers a greater emphasis on themes of practical effectiveness than is apparent in Plutarch's other writing and specifically his *Lives*. Classical commentary tends to stress the rather narrow intent motivating Plutarch in writing this essay, giving advice to an ambitious young man in the cultural and political context of Greece under Roman imperial rule.[40] Still, it was presented by Tory as a reflection on public life with application to his own Renaissance context.

In terms of an overall good for political life and the virtues, Plutarch via Tory suggests at the outset that someone taking on the caring for *la chose publique* needs to have strong resolve and will. Certain emotional states are noted as inappropriate as motivations for public office: fear, a sense of strong anger over a particular cause, desire to please, an excessive sense of honour and ambition, or a wish to avoid boredom. Some think that public office is an easy thing which brings honour without a great deal of effort, yet many of these individuals navigating on rough seas become muddled in their understanding and, continuing the metaphor, are afflicted with nausea and headaches. These men are harmful not only to themselves because they do not find the honour they seek, but also to others because

---

[39] "On peult dire ainsi sembler faire les philosophes quant ils veullent esmouvoir quelquun a quelque chose ils ladmonestent assez mais ils ny donnent aucune ayde ne semblent bailer raison comment il convient faire ce quilz dysent et veullent estre faict. Ils resemblent certes a ceulx qui pour bienfaire esclairer leur lampe mouchent et purgent la meiche et au rest ny mettent point dhuylle." Plutarch, *Politiques*. One must remember that this translation was published before his *Champ fleury* and indeed before Tory successfully dedicated himself to introducing accents and apostrophes into written and printed French.

[40] See, for example, Christine Trego, "Do as I Say and as I Do: Lessons on the Use of History for the Civic Statesman in Plutarch's *Praecepta*," *Classical World* 109.3(2016): 357–379, Blois et al. eds., *Statesman* and Phiroze Vasunia, "Plutarch and the Return of the Archaic," in A. J. Boyle and W. J. Dominik eds. *Flavian Rome. Culture, Image, Text* (Leiden: Brill, 2003), 369–390.

they have no true good in sight. The emphasis on the need for appropriate motivation in entering public affairs is a theme that also emerges forcefully in the latter part of the essay where the need for moderation and virtue is stressed, although with emphasis on rejecting the force of ambition and the allure of sumptuous living, for the ruler himself as well as for the people (822c; 823a). This is a position clearly in the broad Platonic and Aristotelian tradition with which Plutarch identifies himself philosophically, relayed with flourish and strength by Tory. Given the Renaissance precedent of Leonardo Bruni, who in his rewriting of Plutarch's *Life of Cicero* (1415) took issue with Plutarch's repudiation of Cicero's excessive ambition, Tory's apparent endorsement of Plutarch on this point is not without significance.[41] For Plutarch a firm resolve with a good sense of purpose is crucial in order to withstand the challenges of public office.

So how is public life conceptualised? We see this depiction of public life in the following passage from Tory's translation:

> Il en y a plusieurs autres venans de cas adventure *a la chose Publique* qui souddain estant faschez de la grande fascherie des choses on merveilleuse-ment desire de eulx retirer du negoce en repos laquelle chose ils nont peu faire (my emphasis).[42]

> [There are some others who come to *la chose publique* in an impromptu way and in finding themselves flustered by the intense and complicated nature of these matters desire greatly to pull back from the fray and to find a place of calm but without success (my translation from the French).]

Tory is articulating Plutarch's notion that if an individual comes to *la chose publique* more by chance than by reflection, they may often find themselves bothered or frustrated by the difficulty of achieving anything in public life. Here clearly *la chose publique* is invoked as referring to public life, or life in politics, in general. It is not a reference to a specific type of regime or to the state as a whole, but rather to the particular set of relations and concerns that constitute public life.

In another passage, we see the same meaning of *la chose publique*, this time in the plural, and placed in opposition to the matters of private life.

> Le Peuple ayme ainsi escheoir es choses privees que es choses Publiques. En quoy il advient que daucuns ayment et estiment lun et hayssent lautre et ne lestiment aucunement.[43]

---

[41] On Bruni's famous repudiation of Plutarch on ambition, see Ianziti, *Writing History*.
[42] Plutarch, *Politiques*.   [43] Plutarch, *Politiques*.

[The people thus like to take sides in private as in public matters. And so it appears that some like and honour one and hate and do not honour the other at all.]

In addition to being a realist concession, we also see again that *la chose publique* invokes a certain category of human relations that is not reducible to regime type. It also places emphasis on its distinct nature as public life in general, rather than as the politics of one ancient state.

In addition to invoking character through consideration of individual motivations in entering public life, there is also a strand of argument in the text focusing on what those in public life need to do to be effective. These elements alluding to features of utility and expediency as forms of political prudence are subtly emphasised in Sekoundinos's Latin translation and carried forward into Tory's translation, reinforcing a tendency in Plutarch's text to invoke special demands and norms of appropriateness and effectiveness in public and political life. This broader logic is revealed shortly after the passage discussing the motivations of individuals entering public life. Some are condemned for imprudence leading to both harm and ineffectiveness. Those who are motivated by an excessive sense of honour seeking or ambition tend to be either excessively beholden to those whom they seek to please, or they anger those whose support they need.[44] Similarly, entry into *la chose publique* should not be considered as an extension of the market or an opportunity to get rich by pillaging public stores or by using public institutions for personal gain.

In an apparent effort to resonate more strongly with his readers, Tory substitutes specific French institutions of his time for Plutarch's invocation of the stone where speakers addressed the assembly (τὸ βῆμα) – a reference which had been transformed in the Sekoundinos translation to an invocation of the Roman tribunal and curia (798f.):

> Je t'asseure que ceulx qui entreprenent la superintendence de la Chose publique ny doivent aller comme ceulx qui vont aux feres et petites assemblees de marchandise. Comme nous avons entendu que Stratocles et Dromoclides se invioyent l'un l'autre daller a la moysson dor. Ils appelloyent ainsi en raillerie le Parlement et la Souveraine cour de Justice.

---

[44] "Ceux aussi qui par Emulation et Ambition sont telz quilz se y iectent comme font ceulx qui en maniere de joeurs de ieux et Spectacles se composent dhabit et Grimaces. Tels pour la fascherie de leurs negoces sont enfin necessairement tres faschez. Car pour vray ou ils sont contrainctz destre subiectz a ceulx soubz qui ils veulent imperer ou ils font desplaisir et oultragent ceux a qui ils estudient grandement pour complaire." Plutarch, *Politiques*, 4–5.

> [I emphasise that those who take on public matters should not do so in the
> same way as those who go to market and for profit. Stratocles and
> Dromoclides invited each other to go to the golden harvest. It is thus that
> they mockingly called the Parlement and the Sovereign Court of Justice.]

The argument in the text is on the level of moral principle as well as
prudence or political effectiveness. Certain types of motivation can cause
the public actor to be blind to key factors, partly through neglect of their
own sense of honour, and partly through lack of adequate knowledge and
preparation for what they face. In this discussion, the shift from an
invocation of political activity in Plutarch's own time to the more abstract
notion of *la chose publique* in Tory's translation provides a more reified
sense of public life as a distinct sphere governed by its own specific norms.

If the will is solid and the motivation free from individual preoccupations which can cloud judgement, then the person entering public life can
be more attentive to the actual qualities, demands and aspirations of the
relevant public:

> En ceste voulente en ces belles et bonnes manieres en ce solide et incom-
> mutable iugement fault quel homme se conferme et puys apres quil se
> tourne a povoir congnoistre les meurs de ses Citoyens et a povoir esprouver
> et traicer leurs voulentez et esperitz (799b).[45]

> [It is necessary that the man adopt this good will and good and beautiful
> manners and solid and unwavering judgement and then he can turn to being
> able to know the morals of the citizens and to be able to feel and gauge their
> wills and minds.]

Still, Plutarch is not suggesting that the popular will or the manners of *le
menu peuple* be followed, but that a deep knowledge of the people is
required as an important starting point or at least as a consideration in
public matters, to guide them towards that which is better. The focus here
is on being attuned to the psychology and the concerns of the governed.

A broader lesson of governance is that of slow change and moderation. In
passages reminiscent of Montesquieu, Plutarch is translated here as requiring
the public figure not to change the *moeurs* and spirit of a people suddenly by
new laws, but to do so gradually through an appreciation of their current
customs, something he illustrates through a contrast between the spirit of the
Athenian people and that of the Carthaginians.[46] This is not a merely

---

[45] Plutarch, *Politiques*, 5.
[46] "Certes vouloir incontinent sefforcer de changer les meurs et Esperitz du Peuple et les vouloir
    moderer soubdain par nouvelles Loix nest seulement chose difficile mais est tres dangereuse

imitation as a form of flattery; rather it indicates a basis for understanding the means by which subjects can be led to that which is better.[47] Again, he insists that one should not seek to rally the people, but merely to ensure that they tolerate being governed.[48]

The work of a public figure involves important efforts in understanding citizens and subjects, something which excessive individualistic preoccupations can hinder, as well as an ability to work with those characteristics towards changing broad practices for the better. In doing so, the life of a public figure becomes an open spectacle. While perfection is not possible, self-awareness of public perception can help the individual in public life to self-regulate.

> Tu doibs si bien toute ta vie regarder que tut e pense et saiche que tu doibve user toute ta vie en pleine veue au milieu dun Spectacle et devant les yeulx de tout vivans sans en celer aucune choses a homme quelconque. En laquelle chose sil ne test par aventure possible de pouvoir oster tous les vices que tu as en toy et les emaculer du tout il t'est expedient et necessaire de oster et diminuer ceulx qui sont tres apparens et qui sont occurrens de premiere veue.[49]

> [You should also examine your whole life well including what you think and know, for you need to think that your life is in full view in the middle of a spectacle and in front of the eyes of every living person without hiding anything from anyone. In this state if it is not at all possible for you to remove all the vices that you have and to rid yourself of them all, it is expedient and necessary for you to remove and diminish those which are the most visible and which can be seen at first glance.]

There is a slight difference of nuance between the Greek, the Latin and the French versions. The Greek appears to command the statesman to temper

---

entreprise comme chose qui est indigente a mettre en effect par long temps et par grande force . . . . Tout ainsi celluy qui veult bien commencer a regir la chose publique doibt par temps vivre selon ses Citoyens et consentir a leur maniere de faire. Pareillement se accommoder a leur nature et saigement use de bonne coniecture our ensuyure et faire les choses lesquelles le peuple a coustume se delecter." Plutarch, *Politiques*, 5–6.

[47] "Certainement les Gentilzhommes (ou doibs je dire gens de cours flateurs) ressemblent Oysseleurs a dire paroles doulces comme vient les pititz Oyseaulz et se faignent apres a toutes autres choses de tout leur pouvoir n pour autre chose que pour decevoir les Roys a se metter en leur grace. Pour vray le Seigneur qui veult droit et iusetment administrer la Chose Publique ne doibt en facon quelconque imiter ne ressembler les meurs et manieres de vivre du menu peuple. Mais doibt seullement savoir et écongnoistre sur tout par quelle Raison ung chascun peult estre gaigne et du tout persuade." Plutarch, *Politiques*, 8.

[48] "Certes il nest facile a chascun de alleicher et attiser a soy par Raisons salutaires le commun peuple ne la multitude des hommes et les scavoir bien contenir en leur office. Il suffit si le peuple comme une beste sauvage de nature suspicieuse et variables laisse et permet le Regime et le fraing ne se rebellant a la vois ni au regard de son recteur." Plutarch, *Politiques*, 9–10.

[49] Plutarch, *Politiques*, 8.

their persona and, if it is not easy for them to entirely remove the vice from their soul, they are commanded to remove and prevent those faults that show themselves most conspicuously (ἐξάσκει καὶ κατακόσμει τὸν τρόπον· εἰ δὲ μὴ ῥᾴδιον ἀπαλλάξαι παντάπασι τῆς ψυχῆς τὴν κακίαν, ὅσα γοῦν ἐπανθεῖ μάλιστα καὶ προπίπτει τῶν ἁμαρτημάτων ἀφαιρῶν καὶ κολούων, 800b). In Sekoundinos's version, followed by Tory, this instruction is subtly softened. In the Latin and the French versions (in addition to enhancing the visual imagery) it is advocated that the statesman remove or *diminish* those conspicuous faults (*minuenda* or *diminuer*), rather than remove and prevent them, and thereby the injunction is softened slightly.[50] In addition, in the French (and not the Latin) we see an invocation of the expedient and necessary (*il t'est expedient et necessaire*). The nuance reflects the issue of motivation: does a political leader modify their behaviour due to a sense of moral command (i.e. because their life is in full public view, they must do their best to eliminate those vices which are most noticeable to come as close to a moral ideal as possible because a good character is good for politics), or with other goals in mind (i.e. a full elimination of vice may not be possible so leaders must regulate their behaviour to be perceived as virtuous)? The nuance of the Tory (and Sekoundinos) translation appears to emphasise the latter because a limited visibility of faults is still tolerated as long as it does not interfere excessively with public image. The upshot in all versions is that the public figure is not to hide or to erase all vices, but in the spirit of awareness of public perception which appears to demand that leaders be free from any imperfection or eccentricity, to embark on a concerted strategy of self-regulation to avoid acting out those vices while in public life. Public officials are instructed to follow the examples of Themistocles and Pericles who once in office avoided situations which would bring out their vices, instead taking on new habits to enhance their own practice of good living as well as to project an image of virtue to others. A counterexample is that of Alcibiades who exercised discipline and skill in battle, but in the household, despite being a public figure, succumbed to luxury and immoderate behaviour which led to his downfall. The point, then, is not to make princes fully virtuous but only to suggest that they rein themselves in while in power since the public has a magnifying effect on even small faults and errors.[51] (In passages elsewhere in his work Plutarch suggests that the broader public can be very harsh

---

[50] Here I am indebted to Bradley Hall for helping me to make sense of the subtleties in wording from the Greek to the Latin translation.

[51] "les petites faultes et erreurs y sont notes et reputes pour tres grandes." Plutarch, *Politiques*, 11.

judges of their governors.) The broader point being made here is that in Tory's version we have a direct invocation of expediency (and a slightly milder moral injunction, i.e. to diminish rather than to remove those vices) that is heightened in relation to the original text.

According to Plutarch, some cities have been drawn to public figures of dubious character and outrageous behaviour. He depicts it as a form of collective pathology (likened to random unhealthy cravings brought on by pregnancy) whereby often through lack of better alternatives or because of the luxury of their lives, people come to support candidates they are entertained by while loathing them at the same time. The implication is that such exceptions are short lasted.

The treatise continues with a defence of rhetoric, along with good habits (or *moeurs*), as central features of good public performance. Indeed, speaking well is a necessary condition of good rule:

> En bonne verite lhomme prive ne pourra jamais regir une Cite de sa robe et habit populaire ne detourner le vouloir du people ne mettre ordre de meurs dune multitude sil nest de sain langaige et deloquence fonde. Laquelle eloquence admoneste esmouve convertist attire et maine icelle multitude.[52]

> [In good truth the private man cannot ever manage a city with his popular dress and manners nor shape the will of the people nor put order in the morals of a multitude if he does not have good language and eloquence. This eloquence chastises, moves, converts, draws and leads this multitude.]

The reason here is not moral but one of effect. As the story of two masons in Athens demonstrates, a better builder will not win the contract if his competitor provides a more convincing account of what will be done. In this regard, an important distinction is made in the French translation of this text between ambition and popularity.[53] While ambition leads one to

---

[52] Plutarch, *Politiques*, 14.

[53] "Aussi ne peut on facilement gouverner un peuple ne restant rude et mal gracieulx en parolle comme font ceulx qui ne sont exercez en Eloquence et cherchent gratifier a quelque Multitude pour la tirer a leur volunte en luy donnant gros Banquetz, gros Denier, Offices, Jeux, Denses, Moziques, Tournois, iouxtes, et autres Spectacles et finablement de plusieurs autres sumptueuses Impenses. Esquelles choses ceulx qui y sont intentifs me semblent plus estre Ambitieux que populaires, car Popularite est cette vertu qui par Raison et saine Oraison persuade au Peuple." [there is a common saying that one cannot easily hold a wolf by the ears. Also, one cannot easily govern a people being rude and ungracious in speech as do those who are not trained in eloquence and who seek to gratify the multitude to attract their goodwill in giving them big banquets, lots of money, holidays, games, dances, music, tournaments, jousting and other spectacles and finally other matters requiring sumptuous expenses. It appears to me that the people who are intent on such things are more ambitious than popular, because popularity is that virtue which persuades the people through reason and good oratory.] Plutarch, *Politiques*, 16–17.

flatter the people and to descend to their level by enticing them through bribes, entertainment, spectacles and popular music to win support, popularity uses elevated and moderate speech through which persuasion is nonetheless possible, in part through the telling of stories, fables and examples that can move the audience, all while maintaining a certain tone of gravity. Reminiscent of the theme of *l'Hercule gaulois*, the idea of leading people by their ears through eloquent speech (διὰ λόγου) is a strategy appropriate to political leadership, unlike attempts, made more forceful in the original Greek, to pull people by the belly, which is the strategy of the ambitious. This clear statement of the normative features of public life guiding the appropriate strategies of leaders, is carried into Tory's account, which offers a nuanced defense of eloquence.

Again, in the spirit of political prudence, the type of speech recommended for a public figure does not involve excessive abstraction and reasoning or overworked prose which, as Plutarch states, smells too much of the lamp (*la meiche de lampe et chandelle*), nor should it be too theatrical. Instead, he recommends unaffected speech (unlike, we might suggest, the eloquence of a Cicero), which is distinct from juridical discourse and can move the audience through narrative (with *exempla* presumably) and metaphors, like Pericles himself, evoking, if necessary, disparagement, but not insult (which makes the speaker appear to be motivated by malice).

> Il convient certes que loraison civile soit proferee dune douceur naturelle et favoureuse ayant en elle belles Sentences plaines de verite et vray simplesse. En icelle est requise une liberte de langaige convenable a ung prince debonnaire plain de providence de Cure et de prudence qui saiche gratifier et admonester par honneste et bon moyen ... Et aussi quelle ne soit dicte par trop grande scurilite cest a dire par trop grand desir que les auditeurs en rient ne mettant raison a la vergoigne ou dignite de sa personne.[54]

> [It is appropriate certainly that civil speech be delivered with a natural and pleasant softness having lovely phrases full of truth and simplicity. This requires a freedom of speech appropriate to an honoured prince full of favour, care and prudence and one who knows how to both praise and blame in an honest and good manner ... It should not be delivered with too much drollery, that is with too great a desire that the listeners laugh at it thereby casting doubt on the innocence and dignity of one's person.]

This is echoed near the end of the essay. Plutarch suggests that one does not need to hold back blame where it is due; but blame when mixed with praise and containing nothing abusive is more honest and honorable.

---

[54] Plutarch, *Politiques*, 17.

Another consideration of political prudence concerns the dispersal of power that is necessary for every good regime. Plutarch defends the sharing of responsibilities, acknowledging that, like on a ship, it is impossible for the captain to perform all the tasks and to sail well. A good distribution of authority and force among some will ensure that the public good is best achieved. This message is further reinforced by a recognition that different people will bring different skills to a regime and that a distribution of power may therefore also improve the overall effectiveness of the use of public power. Similarly, in cases of public dispute the prince should not rule on these matters alone but in council and with some form of deliberation as a means to maintain public confidence.

This ties in with a longer discussion near the conclusion of the essay recommending sharing the exercise of power in the name of the public good:

> Sans faulte la distribution dauctorite et de force ainsi esparce en plusieurs, ne efface ne diminue tant seullement Enuye, mais faict et donne que les choses concernans le faict et utilite du Bien Publique, sont plus commodement et beaucoup myeulx parachevees.[55]

> [Without fault the distribution of authority and of force being divided among many does not only erase or diminish the trouble, but also ensures that the things related to the doing and utility of the public good are more easily and much better achieved.]

Those involved in public service can specialise to some degree and work to their strengths, such as the division of power between Pericles who governed internally in Athens, and his ally Cimon who took charge of the war. Similarly, he suggests that some contentious matters may best be worked out through a great deal of consultation and discussion to lighten the suspicions of *le menu peuple,* and that some matters should be left to the decision of citizens themselves to help generate faith towards statesmen.

Again, in the spirit of prudence, towards the end of the essay it is noted that an overriding principle of an effective ruler is the pursuit of justice and avoidance of stirring up dissent and sedition to exacerbate division. Recommendations also include a careful use of funds. One should avoid seeking to buy the public's favour in all things (822) as this will only make one more beholden in all things: spending without expecting anything in return may be more effective; or spending to make a show of piety – honouring, as

---

[55] Plutarch, *Politiques*, 34.

noted in the French text, "God and his saints" (822b, as opposed to just a god or τὸ θεῖον).

For Plutarch, as translated by Tory in the closing passages of his essay, the health of the polity is compared to a balanced and moderate state of bodily health; it is also compared to a state of peace and concord (823f.):

> Tout ainsi celluy que Dieu a estably et mis au gouvernement de la Chose publique doit par civile raison estre ioyeux sur toutes choses de veoir son peuple estre en repos de paix et mansuetude qui luy est souveraine felicite.

> [Thus, the one whom God has established and placed to preside over la Chose publique must by civil reason be joyous above all things in seeing his people resting in peace and gentleness that is to him the highest happiness.]

The public figure has special tasks and responsibilities to ensure the health of the whole, and indeed it is that special perspective of looking out for the advantage of the whole that brings to public responsibility its own special quality of honour (*dignité et maiesté* in the French), which seen as more valuable than riches (823a). The special standing associated with administering *la chose publique* implies that the justifications for public action and behaviour are driven by a concern for effectiveness along with a sense of justice, and that the knowledge of governing the body politic is a specialised one. The acts of public statesmanship praised in the final passages of the essay are those that seek to mitigate the effects of division and faction, bringing some elements of concord. Thus, it may not always be wise to invoke the Solonian policy of forcing citizens to take sides in public disputes, but instead to follow the model of Theramenes who sought to converse in earnest with both sides (824a–b); or, better yet, to pre-empt division and do all one can to hold off factional discord by fostering a spirit of accommodation, conciliation, mildness and nobility of character.

Alongside these considerations of what I have called political prudence, we see a distinct tone in certain passages to a more practical counsel with special attention to the unique dynamics of public office. After discussing the importance of speech for a public figure, Plutarch considers how a young person might gain a good public reputation. He notes that the possibilities for distinguishing oneself in battle are minimal given a climate of relative peace (805b). While Plutarch singles out the continued possibility of public lawsuits and embassies to the emperor, which can single out an individual for his temperament, courage and wits, Tory translates with an eye to the public possibilities of his own time. He refers not to the emperor but to "souverains princes," namely the various courts of Europe, where it is possible to distinguish oneself not only by temperament but also by rhetorical skills.[56] The intention, which was to apply the message to a European and modern humanist context, could not have been made more clearly.

A subsequent focus of the text revolves around the best means to reach public office. Plutarch suggests that there are two paths. The first is for an individual to capitalise on some work or achievement that has attained great attention from the public and to use this as a basis on which to embark on a political career. This can be quick, but it is also more difficult and dangerous given the phlegmatic nature of the people. It is also less likely to achieve results in a time when there are fewer grand military expeditions against formidable enemies or fewer occasions to overthrow domestic tyrants, actions through which immediate glory is often won. One exception in a time of peace was to distinguish oneself in an important court case. A second, slower path to political success involves an individual slowly building a reputation, following the examples of Aratus or Alcibiades as well as Pompey and Scipio, often with the help of a highly regarded public figure and through a long career of service to them.

A more fully fledged shift to practical considerations is evident when the discussion turns towards a consideration of the way in which certain virtues are applied in public life, such as the virtue of friendship. Plutarch acknowledges that those in public office should approach friendships carefully (806f–809b). In the language of Tory, and through the lens of the concept of *la chose publique*, it becomes a more entrenched form of precept: to treat one's friends from a public position in the same manner as one might in private is corrupt and unfair. The nature of public life and public position is that competing preferences must be considered and the public good may oftentimes override individual and personal loyalties.[57] And just as friendships are to be managed carefully and uniquely in public life to avoid corruption, so may similar considerations apply to enemies. Public office should not be used to harm personal enemies, but only those who are regarded more broadly as enemies to public welfare. The deeper message is that a position of public power cannot be regarded as a tool for furthering one's personal preferences but only be occupied with a broader and deeper sense of what public considerations may require. An inability to distinguish

---

[56] Plutarch, *Politiques*, 8.

[57] For an in-depth discussion of these passages in the context of Plutarch's wider opus see Luc van der Stockt "ΚΑΡΠΟΣ ΣΚ ΦΙΛΙΑΣ ΗΓΕΜΟΝΙΚΗΣ (Mor. 814c): Plutarch's observations on the 'old-boy' network," in Philip Stadter and Luc van des Stockt eds., *Sage and Emperor* (Leuven: Leuven University Press, 2002), 115–140.

between the two is evidence of unsuitability for public office. One might say that, through the language of Tory, the discussion shifts from a mere question of effectiveness in public life and gestures towards a more substantial and specific form of public ethics. In other words, while suggesting that the words of Plutarch in this essay have a direct application to his own era, Tory also highlights the special qualities of public life (e.g. visibility) that impact not only what a ruler needs to embrace or avoid to be effective, but also how traditional ethical expectations, such as those regarding friendships, are to be applied with special consideration and revision.

In the spirit of political effectiveness, Plutarch suggests that some conventions may be overridden in broader pursuit of the public good. The example invoked in the text is that of Epaminondas, who in a time of war extended his term of office four months to allow him to follow through with his campaign on Messina. As Tory has Plutarch state (817f.):

> Pour ces raisons cy deudit dictes on peult honestement innouver quelque chose extraordinare affin que subs couverture de necessite on se puisse bonnement excuser sil advient quon en soit accuse. Du quon puisse commodement compenser son entreprinse par la magnitude des honneurs a cas advenu.

> [For these reasons here said one can honourably innovate in something extraordinary so that under justifications of necessity one can well excuse oneself if you are accused by anyone. In this manner one can suitably compensate for one's actions by the magnitude of honourable things they bring.]

One should be careful here not to overestimate the meaning. This is not a defence of extreme actions of violence and illegality as a general practice. What is conveyed here, as also relayed by Tory in the French translation, is that an overzealous scrupulous attachment to rules may not always work for the good in political life. The text notes prior to this that iniquitous public officials who lack any sense of the public good should be denounced to protect public norms. The question of limited exceptionalism alluded to here takes places against a background of proven commitment to a broader sense of public welfare and a deep and honourable sense of service to the public, and not the primacy of oneself or of a particular faction in public life.

On perhaps a less controversial note, Plutarch invokes the story of Phocion, who when faced with public pressure to go to war, instituted measures that would make such a policy less desirable for the people (819a). He did so with the conviction that on reflection people would change their minds. Thus, as noted in the French by Tory:

> Il y a maintes incommoditez que tu peux oster et detourner par secrete dissimulation et par artifice de sembler sen vouloir aller . . . En ceste maniere

tu pourra retarder lardeur de ton people quant tu verras quil voudra quelque foys te importuner de faire quelque chose qui te semblera nestre gueres a propos ne de raison.

[There are several difficulties that you can remove or skirt around by secret dissimulation and by false indications of your intention . . . In this way you can delay the ardour of the people when you see that they at times will pressure you to do things that seem to you both inappropriate and irrational.]

In the Greek the language is one of turning or bending, or of creating a distraction (καμπῆςκαὶ περιαγωγῆς). In the Latin of Sekoundinos, one sees a similar invocation of the terms of curving or going around, although with a sense of artifice and cunning added (*insinuatione et ambiundi artificio opus fit*). The Tory translation appears to have heightened the theme of expediency (with its reference to 'secret dissimulation' and false representation), or at least made it more explicit along with a sense of distinct justification for resorting to special measures to ensure a good outcome in public policy. The precise example invoked is that when Phocion was enjoined to lead a military expedition into Boeotia he commanded that all men between fourteen and sixty follow him, and by entreating the elderly on the mission, he made the policy which he disapproved of on principle much more unpalatable to the people.[58]

A similar appeal to a unique ethos of public life is invoked where the text addresses how to relate to colleagues. Plutarch in this essay offers his readers a rare account of his own experiences in diplomacy. In the service of a general ethos to "conciliate his superior [in office], add prestige to his inferior, honour his equal, and be affable and friendly to all" (816b), he follows his father's advice to share the honours for a successful ambassadorial mission even if the colleague who was supposed to join him in an

---

[58] The remarks of Francis Bacon (1561–1626) almost a century later are relevant here. Bacon makes a distinction among secrecy, dissimulation and simulation. [See Francis Bacon, "Of Simulation and Dissimulation," in *The Major Works* (Oxford: Oxford University Press, 1996), 349–352.] The first, secrecy, is understood as being silent or not forthcoming about a certain matter so it is unclear what you are or where you stand; the second, dissimulation, is understood as dropping hints suggesting that you are other than what you are; and the third, simulation, is understood as outright duplicity in presenting yourself in a way that is fully different and false from what you are. For Bacon, while the latter is understood as morally wrong, the first two are not condemned and are acknowledged to have their appropriate place in certain circumstances in public life. Thus, with the invocation here of dissimulation in the Tory translation (despite the possible dislocation of meaning between Renaissance French and early modern English) one can see through this schema how the invocation of 'dissimulation' could be acknowledged as not an outright reprehensible lie or abrogation of the law, but a pragmatic way to follow the order all the while letting one's opposition to it have an impact on its implementation.

important meeting did not do so. Mention of the absent colleague in the report is, according to Plutarch, not only the honourable thing to do but also a way to manage and soften the envy that is an inevitable part of public and professional life. Again, the broader ethical consideration is that the honour of those whom one works alongside should be respected and promoted if they are not iniquitous or enemies of the public good. The action participates in a more general ethos of foregoing unmitigated self-promotion in dedication to a broader public enterprise and public service. Plutarch via Tory is acknowledging that there are norms of service and collegiality in public life that may be different from the demands of virtue in other settings. Thus, what might be viewed from one perspective as embellishing the record, might also under certain circumstances be regarded as an act of collegiality through a strong sense of a need to ensure equity and mitigate jealousy among co-workers. This attention to specific features of social psychology as it relates to public life is a unique aspect and contribution of Plutarch to traditions of political reflection.

Knowing that the public realm allows for more effective governance also means knowing the dignities as well as the specific constraints of institutions. Plutarch invokes aspects of his own public and professional experience. On the one hand, he recognises that some of the actual duties he has been involved in, such as overseeing construction, could appear to be trivial and mundane, but because of their association with public duty and service their ethical importance should be elevated and their value more important than the same activities in a more restrained private context (811c–d). On the other hand, he highlights the subordinate status of Greece under the rule of Rome, noting that public leaders in Greece must not seek to unsettle the political and military hierarchy. As he famously states, the public figures in Greece of his own day must know their limitations in terms of institutional powers and position and see "the boots above their head" (813f). Tory eloquently invokes Plutarch's image of the theatrical prompter "speaking behind the ear" of the actor, making sure they follow the preordained script while they nonetheless draw on their character and feelings; but there is a less eloquent invocation of the possible consequences (813f.): "transgression a faict plusieurs hommes avoir la teste trenchee" [transgression has led several men to have their heads cut off]. Where Plutarch cites Sophocles, Tory tells us bluntly the consequences of overstepping the powers of one's office in the institutional hierarchy. It is not clear how or if Tory saw this cautionary advice of Plutarch's as having any clear application or purchase in his own political context.

This translation of Plutarch's "Political Precepts", published in the vernacular in the early French Renaissance for an educated public that was eager to receive new and particularly novel Greek classical ideas, was positioned to have an impact. While it may not be easy to measure the full extent of it, we can at least consider that it provided some of the parameters around which considerations of *la chose publique* and public good were based. The first, as we have seen, denotes the specific nature of the public realm in which authoritative decisions are made and politically significant rituals are performed; and the second is a way to identify one principle through which those decisions, actions and symbols were either justified, motivated, or normatively defended.

We see here first and foremost a consideration of the very special and important nature of the public realm, which is driven by unique rules of access, of vision and of expectation. We see an emphasis on the importance of speech for the public, as well as a consideration of the interplay between public role and morality, both for the individual public actor and for the people who are governed. We also see less emphasis on the actual institutional nature of power, with only focused concern on the need to avoid tyranny, and indeed no consideration of the legal or judicial means by which power is exercised and enforced. In contrast, the focus is on the attitude, behavioural practices, and the social psychology of both the general public and those driven by honour and ambition in public life, as well as the customs with which one must come to terms so that a better form of public rule can be made possible. We have singled out distinctions among modes of ethical argument that weave together considerations of the good, the prudent, the practical (or efficient) and the bad while invoking the special and unique nature of public life.

The discourse is neither juridical, nor republican, but neither is it reductively moral in the medieval and early Renaissance tradition of the mirror for princes. For example, if we compare the tone of this work to that of Christine de Pizan's *Le Livre du corps de policie* (1406–1407) or *Le Livre de la paix* (1414), written a century earlier and following a general model of political argument in the mirror for princes tradition, we find quite a different approach to the question of rule.[59] For Pizan and others in that genre or mode of political argument, the focus is on the exact list and nature of the virtues required of a ruler if he (or she) is to live up to basic Aristotelian

---

[59] Christine de Pizan, *The Book of Peace*, ed. Karen Green et al. (University Park, PA: 2008) and Christine de Pizan, *Le Livre du corps de policie* (Geneva: Droz, 1967). The edition of *The Book of Peace* noted here includes the text of Pizan's work in the original medieval French. The third section of that work is explicitly devoted to how "bien gouverner le people et la chose publique" (257), so it allows for a direct comparison of the use of the term 'la chose publique' with later uses. Pizan's invocation of the term here and elsewhere in the text did not hold a great deal of weight for her, but it was invoked as a way of identifying public matters in general.

goals of ruling as a good dispenser of justice. There we find a list and an appeal to such political virtues as clemency, honesty and liberality with some reference to the classical authorities (Seneca, Cicero and Aristotle among others) to help illustrate the exact nature of those virtues. In broad terms, the project of this earlier political genre is one of focusing on the character of the prince and seeking their conversion and good will in an exercise of moral improvement. This is a characterisation invoked by James Hankins for all fourteenth- and fifteenth-century humanist political thought.[60]

In contrast, the shift that we find in this translation is a move away from the dialogue of the prince with his own conscience (hence the image of the mirror) towards the nature of the public realm in which the prince is a participant. Here we have a new question about the nature of public life and what is required to effectively hold office with a consideration of how the virtues can be applied in a context marked by its visibility and its unique dynamics of social psychology. Given its important moral foundation (and indeed in certain instances such as regulating friendships a demand for even more scrupulous considerations), it is not reason of state discourse. It gives special attention and concessions to the unique ethos and demands of public service, alongside recognition of some of the hard choices and dissension involved in public office. This sensitivity to the special nature of the public and its requirements forms the basis for the set of debates that characterise French public humanism.

What is perhaps of greatest significance is that within Plutarch's broader opus, his "Political Precepts" may be considered one of the most practically minded of his writing concerning politics. The fact that this was the work that introduced Plutarch to a literate public in France in the early sixteenth century arguably had an important and discernible impact on how Plutarch's works more broadly came to be perceived. He could be regarded as a writer who offer not only a great deal of historical knowledge and insight but did so with an astute understanding of the practicalities of public life without abandoning moral commitments, and in ways perhaps unmatched by other classical writers.

3.2   Guillaume Budé

Guillaume Budé's legacy is often overshadowed by that of Erasmus and Seyssel. However, he preceded Tory in translating Plutarch (both in Latin

---

[60] As Hankins states: "the primary moral interest of humanists in the 14th and 15th centuries lay in improving the level of prudence and wisdom among members of the ruling classes." In "Humanism," 119.

and in the vernacular, though the latter only appeared after his death) and his advocacy for the importance of Plutarch's work helped to inform his political theory. Budé did not write in French as a celebration of the language, but as an instrument of advocacy to François I to strengthen his commitment to the flourishing of the study of the classics (François I had imperfect command of the classical languages). For Budé this meant not only attention to the style of eloquence made singularly possible through a good knowledge of Greek and derivatively Latin, but also attention to the lessons of classical thinkers among whom Plato, Aristotle, Plutarch, Livy, Suetonius, Cicero and Hortensius stand out as the most valuable. Plutarch has a special place in Budé's work through Latin translations of several essays among his first published works, and of special interest here, as translated and commented on in the French vernacular, is his *Institution du Prince* (1519). In this work Plutarch is used to portray a distinct understanding of monarchy, political power and *la chose publique* more generally. As we will see, in terms of his political argument and his use of Plutarch, Budé offers a discussion of *la chose publique* to depict a quasi-heroic status for the figure who occupies the highest position in the public realm. Within this vision of politics, all actions of the ruler are subsumed under the idea of prudence, for given the lack of clear external restraints (and even the historical exemplars provide little moral direction in this regard), it is up to the noble character of the ruler himself to exercise restraint according to the broader implied framework of justice as a guiding ideal.

Budé was an advocate not only for the study of Plutarch, but also for the study of history as a requirement for those in public life.[61] He is often called the father of French humanism, at least insofar as the instigation for the study of ancient Greek language and history is concerned, and he helped in the founding of what was to become the Collège de France.[62] He was also an associate of John Lascaris, initially as a student of Greek, and later as beneficiary of his manuscript collection. What is sometimes less emphasised is Budé's ongoing role of service to the French monarchy (Charles VIII, Louis XII and François I). He worked for the chancellery, was sent on diplomatic missions in Italy in 1501 and 1505 and served as *maître des requêtes* from 1523 and *maître de la librairie du roi*.[63]

---

[61] For a discussion of Budé's broader championing and engagement (including translation) with Plutarch's work, see Sanchi, "Budé et Plutarque."

[62] David O. McNeil, *Guillaume Budé and Humanism in the Reign of Francis I* (Geneva: Droz, 1975).

[63] Robert B. Rigoulot, "Guillaume Budé," *Sixteenth-Century French Writers* of the *Dictionary of Literary Biography*, vol. 327 (2006). Online at http://go.galegroup.com/ps/retrieve.do?inPS=true&userGroupName=oxford&prodId=DLBC&docId=GALE|PKJAGR102182797. Accessed 6 May 2016.

Budé's first Plutarch translations (Greek to Latin) were from the *Moralia*. In 1503 his translation of "On the Opinions of the Philosophers" (now deemed to be a spurious work of Plutarch) appeared followed by "On the Tranquillity of Mind," "On the Fortune of the Romans" and "On the Fortune or the Virtue of Alexander" in 1505.[64] Lascaris, who had arrived in France in 1495, was an important advocate of Greek thinkers and Plutarch in particular and a friend of Budé, so he more than likely had some role to play in these choices, even if the original Plutarch manuscripts on which two of these translations were based were copied for Budé by George Hermonymus.[65] Indeed, the translation of Plutarch into Latin, as in the case of Erasmus who also was acquainted with Lascaris quite early on in his intellectual development, may have been a project recommended by teachers of Greek to help students develop a deeper sense of the finer points of semantics and form. As a self-proclaimed example of an opsimath and in poor health for much of his life, Budé perhaps did not see himself as so far removed from the aging *Hercule gaulois* who appealed to others through the power of words (here written) rather than through his vigour.

Budé also became well acquainted with Plutarch's historical work. Perhaps one of Budé's most important contributions to scholarship is his research into ancient systems of weight, measures and coinage presented in his work *De Asse* (1514). Here, Budé treats Plutarch's *Lives* and *Sayings of Kings and Commanders* as valid sources of useful historical information (sources whose usefulness for historical analysis will be later disputed by Bodin), alongside the work of Pliny and Suetonius. He acknowledges the weakness of relying on more recent Latin translations of Plutarch's work, suggesting that translators did not adequately understand the monetary systems of classical antiquity and thereby misrepresented some of the details.[66] He supports Plutarch's analysis that the Gallic wars were an important source of wealth for Caesar, allowing him to buy influence and access that contributed enormously to his rise to power. He

---

[64] The choice to translate Plutarch's moral essays rather than excerpts from the *Lives* suggests for McNeil that Budé may have had Christian humanist and even reformist sympathies. In his work *De Asse*, Budé had already condemned corruption in the Church and expressed need for reform. However, Budé remained within the fold of the Catholic Church all his life and was critical of Luther. McNeil, *Guillaume Budé*, 110–115.

[65] Gerald Sandy, "Guillaume Budé: Philologist and Polymath. A Preliminary Study," in *The Classical Heritage in France* (Leiden: Brill, 2002), 82–83. Indeed, Sandy goes on to relate "[Budé's] mentor Janus Lascaris helped to edit the first printed edition of the Moralia (1509) and sent it piecemeal from Italy to Budé as the fascicles appeared in print." (87)

[66] Guillaume Budé, *Extrait ou abrégé du Livre de Asse* (Lyon: Thibauld Payne, 1534), 83.

acknowledges that the opulence of the empire, gained through its tributes from conquered territories, was an important factor in the corruption of ancient morals and discipline, but he nonetheless praises the Augustan era as one that combined great wealth and order.[67]

One of two works written in the vernacular, *L'Institution du Prince* celebrates a strong conception of monarchical power focused on the king's role to distribute honours and appointments.[68] In this work devised as a personal gift in manuscript form, Budé was gathering insights from classical works, most notably Plutarch, to offer advice to the king in the art of ruling. The selections from Plutarch also serve to illustrate more general lessons from classical literature acknowledging the need for royal patronage of classical learning and a vision of the king's independent power over and above subordinates illustrated by the example of King Solomon.[69] As distributor of justice in the tradition of ideal Aristotelian one-person rule, the monarch is not deemed subject to the laws and ordinances of the realm in the same manner as the subjects, for he must apply laws for the benefit of all and is judged perfect in prudence, nobility, justice and equity.[70] The translations from Plutarch are rearranged in thematic order but often without attribution.

---

[67] Budé, *Extrait*, 136.

[68] McNeil, *Guillaume Budé*, 39. See also Rigoulot, "Guillaume Budé." The work was first drafted by Budé and presented to François I in 1519 with the title *Le Recueil d'Apophthegmes*. As a manuscript it was reworked by Budé over several years and then posthumously by others. It was not published in print form until 1547 (after his death) and the extant manuscripts offer us no clear indication where Budé's work ends and that of his posthumous editors begin. Despite being edited posthumously, and therefore not the last version to have met with the author's approval, a standard rule in editing for determining the definitive edition, I base my analysis on the 1547 version, because this is the version that was published (the earlier versions remaining in manuscript form) and therefore it was only this version with which Budé's name was associated for his interlocutors and successors in the political theory tradition. Guillaume Budé, *De l'Institution du prince* (Paris: Maistre Nicole Park, 1547 and Farnborough: Gregg Press, 1966). Also, despite the mysteries surrounding how the final version of the text in 1547 came to be, with some concerns as to whether Budé was even responsible for writing some of the material that went into the final edition, I will continue with the standard form of identifying the author as Budé given his responsibility for at least a large portion of the work.

Of course, the second work written by Budé in the vernacular French is his summary of *De Asse* mentioned in in notes 66 and 67 above.

[69] Nannerl Keohane, *Philosophy and the State in France* (Princeton, NJ: Princeton University Press, 1980), 59.

[70] "les Roys sont exaltes en honneur, et ont souveraine puissance, et dons de prerogatives: et prennent profict et emolument sur le populaire, par dessus touts aultres, et telle et si raisonnable portion qu'il leur plaist: et si'il ne son sujets aux Loix, ny aux Ordonnances de leur Royaulme, comme les aultres, si bon ne leur semble. Car il est a presumer qu'ils sont si parfaicts en prudence, si eminens et eleues par noblesse, si imbus et porveus de Justice et de Equite, qu'il ne leur fault point de reigle, ny de forme escripte, pour les estreindre par creinctes de peines, ou de muletes, qu'on appelle condemnations pecuniaires, ou par arrests de leur biens ou persones, ou aultre correction, ou necessite d'obeissance, comme il fault aux aultres subjets. Et doibt suffire pour leur commander la Loy divine

In an insightful article, Basset and Bénévent acknowledge that while the form of Plutarch's *Apophthegmata* and *Sayings of Kings and Commanders* generally highlights the historical figure to whom the sayings and deeds are attributed, Budé's reorganisation and presentation of his selected examples from Plutarch's work places more emphasis on the reader and the thematic lessons of the examples.[71] Like Erasmus after him, Budé completes his presentation of the passage from Plutarch with his own commentary on its meaning.[72] In general terms, the presentation and repackaging of examples drawn from Plutarch in Budé's *Institution* brings the material of Plutarch's history away from *illustrations of moral character* (perhaps best illuminated though not specific to public figures) and towards a more didactic form as *precepts of specifically political prudence.*

There is irony in this use of Plutarch by Budé, given that the most prudential features of Plutarch's own opus are those writings devoted to advice to statesmen in the local politics of Greece under Rome. What was for Plutarch a more detached and expository depiction of political character in the *Lives* and distilled in more summary form in the *Sayings* becomes for Budé the basis for more practical political advice. He begins the treatise

seulement, qui a authorite de Dieu legislateur souverain, et non pas des hommes; selon laquelle, tous hommes sont egaulx, sans distinction ou pre-eminence, quant a l'obeissance qu'on doibt porter a icelle Loy." Budé, *Institution*, 20.

[71] "De Plutarque à Budé, un déplacement s'opère, peu perceptible dans l'image du miroir, plus manifeste dans celle des semences. Le premier met en effet l'accent sur l'auteur du dit: l'apophtegme joue le rôle de révélateur de son âme dont il offre une image pure à contempler, débarrassée de ce qui ne lui appartient pas en propre. Budé déplace l'attention vers le lecteur des dits: ce sont ses vertus intrinsèques qu'ils vont venir révéler, ce sont ses actions qu'ils vont guider et éclairer. L'apophtegme est dès lors envisagé dans sa dimension pragmatique. Cela n'est pas sans incidence sur les dits que Budé emprunte à Plutarque et qu'il réécrit. De fait, le miroir n'est pas seulement une image, il est aussi un dispositif textuel où se déploie un espace qui invite à 'l'exercice spirituel.'" Bérengère Basset et Christine Bénévent, "Les apophtegmes de Plutarque et la tradition des miroirs du prince au XVIe siècle: l'exemple de *l'Institution du prince* de Guillaume Budé," *Littératures Classiques* 84.2 (2014), 63–96.

[72] For example, what appears in Plutarch as the following in reference to Augustus thinking about Alexander the Great: "Ayant entendu qu'Alexandre, à l'âge de trente-deux ans, après s'être rendu maître de la plus grande partie du monde, se demandait ce qu'il ferait le reste de sa vie, il se montra surpris qu'Alexandre n'eût pas considéré comme une plus grande tâche d'organiser un si vaste empire." becomes the following in Budé's rendition : "Auguste en ce propos poursuyvant dist en cette maniere, quant à moy je m'esmerveille d'ung si grant roy et de si grant avis comme estoit le roy Alexandre, qui après avoir conquis la Grece, l'Egypte, et toute l'Asie, pensoit desormais n'avoir que faire s'il n'entreprenait choses nouvelles en querant passe temps de guerre. N'entendoit il point que c'est aussi grant chose et autant à priser et matiere d'aussy grant gloire, bien ordonner le regime et gouvernement d'ung grant empire quant on l'a ja tout paisible, comme c'est de le conquerir au commencement. Laquelle parole me semble bien à noter pour l'exemple des grans princes, car ils peuvent aussy bien accroistre leur renommee et plus seurement en exerçant actes de paix que de guerre, et mesmement au jour d'huy les princes chrestiens, qui ne doibvent souhaiter guerre sinon contre les infideles pour augmenter la foy catholicque et orthodoxe et soustenir l'honneur de Jesucrist." Basset and Bénévent, "Apophtegmes," 35–36.

with a general discussion of the nature of monarchy and this understanding of monarchy is sustained throughout the work. While the king is considered formally unbound by his own laws, Budé suggests that through love of honour in both immediate reputation and renown after death, a predominant motivation of all in public life, the ruler will be encouraged not only to follow his own laws but to develop the skills of eloquence and prudence through study to allow him to attain honour while effectively demonstrating love for his subjects.[73] Renown, as a step towards immortality, also requires that history be written down, so the king's drive for honour and recognition should also include support and recognition for the learned classes.[74]

As evidence of a singular conception of political leadership he suggests near the end of the work that royal virtues are akin to heroic virtues, bringing more authority and power to the individual. Through translated passages from Plutarch and other authors, he offers brief accounts of key moments in the lives of several ancient rulers seeking out examples of admirable and exemplary action and suggesting that while knowledge is important for good governance, it is not metaphysical knowledge, but practical knowledge or prudence. Pompey stands out as a particularly good example for leaders to follow:

> la gloire de Pompeie le grand, semble (selon le tesmoignaige des Histoires) estre une vraye, bonne, et pure source de renomee, sans estre aulcunement entachee de vergoigne et reproche. Et me semble la vie de luy estre un vray exemplaire de vertu et conditions necessaires a touts grands personnaiges, qui ont desire d'avoir en leur vie la faveur et amour du Monde: .... Et ne peulx comprendre (quant a moy) ny concevoir chose, dont un grand Prince accomply par accumulation de dons et de graces de Dieu, de Nature et de Fortune, peust mieulx et plus facilement meriter et acquerir grand loz, que de suivre, imiter et prendre par bon exemple digne d'estre suivy ce, que dict Lucian de Pompeie ... Car j'estime vertu souveraine et heroicque a un homme ayant entier pouvoir et faculte (sans aulcune limitation ou reserve) en un si grand Empire (comme estoit celluy, auquel Pompeie avoit toute authorite) de se maintenir constamment, et avoir une honneste et bien fondee volunte en toutes ses operations.[75]

---

[73] Budé, *Institution*, chap. 5 and 6 "nous n'avons rien si estime et recommende en toutes les puissances de l'ame (quant est des choses temporelles) que l'honneur en la vie, et bonne et honorable reonmmee apres la mort" 33.

[74] "l'esperance de tous les scavants est remise sur vostre infinite Liberalite: et quilz se confient, que vous estenderes voz bontes envers eulx." Budé, *Institution*, chap. 6, 34.

[75] Budé, *Institution*, chap. 47, 194.

[... the glory of Pompey the great seems (according to historical accounts) to be a true, good and pure source of renown, without being in any way tainted with shame or reproach. It appears to me that his life is a true example of virtue and of the conditions necessary for every great personnage who desires to have in their life the favour and love of the world: ... As for me I cannot understand nor conceive of anything that a great Prince favoured by the gifts and graces of God, nature and fortune, can better and more easily merit and acquire great praise, than by following, imitating and taking as a good example worthy of being followed, that which Lucian says of Pompey ... For I judge it to be a sovereign and heroic virtue for a man having full power and means (with no limitation or reserve) to maintain himself with constancy and to have an honest and well grounded will in all matters ...]

Important and indeed unique to a model of excellent exercise of political power for Budé is that the public realm provide no formal constraint on the leader in terms of laws or institutions, for this is the precise condition that allows the ruling excellence of the individual to be revealed in his constancy and good will (while they themselves are motivated by honour) such that he may inspire a broader array of public officials to follow his personal example. The inspiration of exemplary leadership (accessed through reading) is emphasised by Budé who mixes a tale about Caesar from Suetonius, Dio and the *Sayings* (as well as s. 11 of Plutarch's *Life of Caesar*) in which Caesar, on one of his earlier campaigns in Spain, weeps when he reads that Alexander had conquered half of the world and was memorialised by his age.[76]

The argument is developed on several levels. At an institutional level is the position that monarchy is a regime based fundamentally on Aristotelian premises, in which the king is expected to govern according to a conception of justice through which each is given their due, being ordained directly by God without the intermediary of the Church.[77] For

---

[76] Budé, *Institution*, chap. 33, 139. As Christopher Pelling points out, the details of Caesar being in Spain at a temple of Hercules are significant for the fact that they play into important Trajanic motifs, and so it is of note that Plutarch left these details out of the story, leaving Caesar to read about Alexander rather than contemplate his statue. Budé follows Plutarch's account here. See Pelling, "Introduction," *Plutarch's Caesar*.

[77] "Justice consiste et est une volonte constant et propos non muable, rendant a un chacun ce, qu'il lui appartient" and "les rois sont exaltés en honneur et ont souveraine puissance, et dons de prerogatives: et prennent profit et émolument sur le populaire, par-dessus tous autres, en telle et si raisonnable portion qu'il leur plaist: et s'ils ne sont subjects aux loix, ny aux Ordonnances de leur Royaulme comme les autres, si bon ne leur semble. Car il est a presumer, qu'ils sont si perfaicts en prudence, si eminens et eleves par noblesse, si imbus et proveus de Justice et de equite, qu'il ne leur fault point de reigle, ny de forme escripte, pour les estreindre par creinctes de peines, ou de multes, qu'on appelle condemnations pecuniaires, ou par arrests de leurs biens ou personnes, ou aultres

Budé this requires no formal limits to the power of the king. He offers a version of monarchy unbounded in its power, indeed a version which even goes beyond the limits defined and defended by a later political tradition of absolutist monarchy.[78]

Nonetheless, for kingly power to be exercised well, a king will have a high sense of honour and concern for his own reputation as well as good judgement to appreciate how a good reputation in posterity is developed. In a broad way Budé advocates that a ruler should be well-versed in classical languages and knowledge of the classical texts, and this as a condition for good rule, something that was less than true in his own day (which is why he had to make the pitch to the king in French, a language he knew less well than Latin). Indeed, he explicitly takes up the theme of *l'Hercule gaulois*, but here it is no longer a defence of the French vernacular, nor even necessarily the superiority of speech over force, but merely the importance of knowledge, particularly knowledge of the past, for effective speaking and political judgement.[79] While self-serving in many regards – who else but one of the emerging pre-eminent classical scholars of France could play the role of classical tutor to the king? – it also points to some notion of a classically informed normative

correction, ou necessite d'obeissance, comme il fault aux aultres subjects. Et doibt suffire pour leur commander la loy divine seulement, qui a authorite de Dieu legislateur souverain, et non pas des hommes." And again, "[les roys et princes] sont Commissaires de la souveraine iustice, establiz pour regir et gouverner par superintendence, les biens et possessions seculieres, qui sont soubz la main de la Providence divine, ainsy comme les Evesques Rommains et aultres sont Fideicommissaires du spirituel." Budé, *Institution*, 81.

[78] For Bolgar, the fact that Budé along with other humanists shared this general picture of a ruler motivated by glory and holding the force of all executive and administrative power in their hands, while also exhorted to be restrained in the actual exercise of that power, was not only a truism but also lacking in insight. "The humanists were for the most part blind to the obvious fact that freedom and respect for law depend on a wide distribution of political power." R. R. Bolgar, "Humanism as a Value System, with Reference to Bude and Vives," in A. H. T. Levi ed., *Humanism in France at the End of the Middle Ages and in the Early Renaissance* (Manchester: Manchester University Press, 1970), 201. While not fully off the mark, this comment assumes that freedom was an important political value for Budé and other humanists, but certainly in the case of Budé it was not. What I am suggesting is that Budé is significant less for some of the specific political prescriptions he advocates and more for the sharing of a general depiction of the public realm that was a focus of discussion among political thinkers of his day, and which was linked to concerted engagement with the work of Plutarch.

[79] In reference to the gold and silver chains of *l'Hercule gaulois* Budé notes: "Car par l'argent, qui est clair, il fault entendre elegance de langaige, qui resplendit en la bouche de l'homme, ou au stile d'escripture, qui est le vicaire du parler, ainsi que souvent l'argent est poly et resplendissant. Mais par l'or, est entendue la science, d'où vient la gravité des sentences, et l'authorité de l'oraison, qui donnent le pris, estimation et reputation au beau langaige." Budé, *L'Institution*, 60. Also cited in La Charité, "Henri III Rhéteur, nouvel Hercule gaulois," 274.

framework for determining the contours of the just exercise of power and of Budé's minimally critical stance vis-à-vis his own monarch.

Prudence is an important virtue for those who rule, and this can be most readily acquired through the study of history.

> vous pouvés avoir une grande Maistresse, qui equipolle toute seule à plusieurs grands Precepteurs ensemble, et si enseigne par grand Plaisir et douceur ceulx, qui s'addonnent a sa doctrine. Et se nomme ceste maistresse que vous aurés au lieu de Maistres, Histoire.[80]

> [you can have a great Mistress, who is on her own the equivalent of several great teachers together, and who teaches with great pleasure and sweetness for those who give in to her doctrine. And this mistress who you will have in the place of teachers, is History.]

and

> Prudence vient pour la plus part, par experience et observation des exemples du temps passe, dont Histoire (comme je l'ai predict) est le registre.[81]

> [Prudence comes for the most part, from experience and the observation of examples from times past, of which History (as I have said earlier) is the register.]

The history that is the privileged focus of study for the development of prudence is that written by the ancient Greeks.[82]

It appears that for Budé, prudence or wisdom (sapience) are interchangeable terms.[83] For Aristotle, practical wisdom can be developed through experience, but not through observation. In a move that implicitly counters this view, Budé invokes the authority of Afranius, a Roman poet (as discussed by Aulus Gellius) who suggested that one could develop prudence by internalising the lessons of texts not just understanding them, and this could be achieved with a more thorough consideration of the precepts and lessons advanced by historical events. In other words, the study of history and reflection on the past judgements of others can substitute for experience as a basis for one's own moral development. Indeed, at one point further along in the text Budé suggests that the prudence acquired through study may be better than that acquired through

---

[80] Budé, *Institution*, chap. 9, 43.   [81] Budé, *Institution*, 66.

[82] "Histoire en Langue Grecque, comme enqueste et information de toutes choses advenues, dignes de mémoire, pour en faire le recit par escript, et rapport au plus pres de la verite que faire se peult. A ce, que par les choses passees, on iuge et estime plus certainement les presentes, qu'on preveoye les futures, et qu'on en soit saisy contre l'inadvertence." Budé, *Institution*, 43.

[83] Eshan Ahmed, "Wisdom and Absolute Power in Guillaume de Budé's *Institution du Prince*," *Romanic Review* 96.2 (2005), 173–185.

actual experience: "Vray est, que usaige et experience faict les gens saiges, quand ilz ont bon entendement. Mais la prudence acquise par doctrine, est plus seure, pour remedier à dommaige et deshonneur, et moins subiecte à estre oubliée." [84] [It is true that use and experience make people wise when they have good understanding. But the prudence acquired by doctrine is more certain, in avoiding harm and dishonour, and less liable to be forgotten.] As we will see later, for other Renaissance thinkers, the idea that political leaders or those preparing for political leadership can gain practical wisdom through the study of historical and theoretical texts is important especially for those who espouse a more moderate view of the boundaries of political power and who do not wish to make the political forum a field of potentially unlimited political experimentation for the prince. So, praise of history in Budé plays a double role, as the matter from which some forms of moral development are possible, as well as the forum in which great actions are celebrated and made known.

After praising the work of savants and orators in the ancient world, in chapter 23 Budé shifts focus to explore the ways in which history can shed light on the virtues. Budé does not just parrot the longstanding mirror for prince's tradition but adapts the genre beyond advocacy for the humanist enterprise. We will explore here some of the ways in which the virtues of rulers are singled out by Budé, as well as his understanding of the nature of prudence that emerges from the historical examples and the choice of historical episodes and figures that are deemed to be most useful in offering political wisdom. Still, it should be noted that Budé does not embark on a systematic analysis of princely virtues in this treatise; rather, his discussion of these virtues is dispersed among various passages and arguments sustaining the case for the importance of letters and oratory in political life.

As a first general observation, it is the broad contours of Greek history that are deemed most useful for instilling a sense of prudence for a ruling monarch of the Renaissance. The lives of heroic figures such as Artaxerxes, Alexander and Pericles are particularly relevant in providing lessons for kings, both for their strong sense of honour and preeminent excellence but also, although almost as an afterthought for Budé, because they cannot fully control their fate which is ultimately a matter of God's will.[85]

---

[84] Budé, *Institution*, chap. 28, 118.
[85] Budé compares the king to Artaxerxes in the opening dedication of the work. His conclusion to chapter 30 highlights the early death of Alexander and the downfall of Darius, signifying that even the most virtuous of leaders does not have control over their fate, given God's omnipotence. *Institution*, 129.

It is telling that while praising Alexander throughout the text, he also invokes the comments of Augustus Caesar who appears surprised that Alexander was only interested in conquering further rather than acknowledging the glory that can be achieved through the instauration of good order and good laws in a new political community, or newly pacified one. Budé emphasises the contemporary relevance of this reflection: "Laquelle parole me semble digne d'estre bien note et recite, pour server d'exemple aux deliberations des Princes puissants de mener la guerre. Car ilz peuvent aussy bien accroistre leur renommee, et plus seurement, en exerceant actes de paix, que de guerre." [86] [These words seem to be worthy of being well noted and repeated, to serve as an example for the deliberation of powerful Princes in waging war. For they can also increase their fame, and more securely, in exercising acts of peace, rather than war.]

In an invocation of the orator Demetrius's letter to Ptolemy it is suggested that the act of ruling requires the heroic virtues (*vertuz heroicques*), accessible to those of a higher breeding.[87] Yet what we see in the latter part of the text of *L'Institution*, is sometimes less a celebration of heroic virtues, than a complex and historically contextualised version of some of the traditional virtues recast for what are portrayed as very specific qualities of public office.

From the outset it appears that the traditional rules of ethics have more particular and contextualised applications given the specific nature and demands of political life. A first lesson from Budé concerning the specific public role of the king is the judgement that the king should not publicly give an indication of their faults in a way that would do damage to their reputation and the good opinion each should have of them. This plays on the notion of secrecy as we invoked it earlier. This is also a reflection of the theme we have seen in Tory's translation of "La Pollitica". "Il se doibt donc bien vigilamment garder, à ce qu'il ne donne aulcune apparence ou congnoissance sur luy mesme, par quelque faulte apparente, qui puisse endommaiger l'estime de sa reputation, et la bonne opinion que chascun doibt avoir de luy."[88] [He should therefore be very careful in not giving any hint or knowledge of himself, through any apparent fault, that might harm the honour of his reputation and the good opinion that each should have of him.] This is related to the great weight that the words and deeds of the king have on the populace, such that if the words and deeds were not worthy of honour, it would weaken the bonds of obedience and reverence required by the prince. It thus appears that the public position of the king requires the cultivation of

[86] Budé, *Institution*, chap. 34, 144.   [87] Budé, *Institution*, chap. 26, 104.
[88] Budé, *Institution*, chap. 20, 83.

a certain lack of transparency, a precept of prudence derived from the very function of being a public figure.

In a somewhat similar vein, further along in the text Budé suggests that for a good ruler it is important to "know oneself," as inscribed on the temple of Apollo and deemed a first principle of numerous ethical doctrines. To illustrate the principle of the importance of self-knowledge in chapter 30, instead of an ethical tale that one might expect to demonstrate a show of lucid humility of a person or ruler knowing their limitations or vices and thereby regulating themselves appropriately, Budé invokes Plutarch's tale of Alexander who is melancholy at the sight of his father's conquests thinking that there will be nothing left for him to do.[89] This is followed by a narration from Plutarch of Alexander's demand that if he were to participate in the Olympic games as his father suggested, he would do so on the condition that he compete with princes or kings as his own honour and capabilities dictate that he deserves nothing less.

> Monsieur (dist-il) ie feray voluntiers ce, que me commanderés, mais que vous faciés, que tout ceulx, qui vouldront esprover leurs forces, et disposition de corps avec moy, soient touts enfans de Roy, comme ie suis, ou qu'ilz soient Roys, ou qu'ilz ayent aussy bonnes arres de l'estres, comme moy.[90]

> [Sir (says he) I will willingly do what you command, but only if you ensure that everyone who wishes to compete with me be either children of a king, as I am, or that they be kings, or that they will be, as I will.]

---

[89] Here is a juxtaposition of the original Greek from the first paragraph of the Alexander section of Plutarch's *Sayings of Kings and Commanders*, the current Loeb translation of the passage and Budé's own adaptation of it:

" Ἀλέξανδρος ἔτι παῖς ὤν, πολλὰ τοῦ Φιλίππου κατορθοῦντος, οὐκ ἔχαιρεν, ἀλλὰ πρὸς τοὺς συντρεφομένους τρεφομένους ἔλεγε παῖδας, "ἐμοὶ δὲ ὁ πατὴρ οὐδὲν ἀπολείψει." τῶν δὲ παίδων λεγόντων ὅτι "σοὶ ταῦτα κτᾶται". "τί δὲ ὄφελος," εἶπεν, "ἐὰν ἔχω μὲν πολλὰ πράξω δὲ μηδέν;"

Loeb translation: "While Alexander was still a boy and Philip was winning many successes, he was not glad, but said to his playmates, 'My father will leave nothing for me to do.' 'But,' said the boys, 'he is acquiring all this for you.' 'But what good is it,' said Alexander, 'if I possess much and accomplish nothing?'"

The same passage integrated into Budé's *Institution du Prince* : "je veoy bien, que le Roy mon père gaignera tant de victoires, qu'il ne m'en lairra aulcunes à faire … Auquel respondirent les aultres ieunes Gentilzhommes: comment, Monsieur, vous melencoliés-vous de cela ? Le Roy, en ce faisant, ne faict-il pas voz besoignes, puis que tout ce, qu'il a conquis et conquerra, est pour vous? Lequel leur respondit: Que me servira ceste conqueste, ou de quoy vauldray-ie mieulx, d'estre grand Roy et puissant, si ie ne fais rien digne de mémoire, avec toute ma puissance, dont ie puisse acquerir honneur et réputation, pour estre iuge digne de la charge que i 'espère de tel Empire?" chap. 30, 124.

One can see how Budé inserts the term "roy" here to enforce the relevance for contemporary rulers; likewise, his greater emphasis on the motives of honour and reputation have a similar aim.

[90] Budé, *Institution*, chap. 30, 125.

The shift implemented here is important. In Budé's hands, the same incidents that were used by Plutarch to illustrate the *uniqueness* of Alexander as a historical figure (given the tremendous force of his ambition evident from a very young age), are now used to support a basic precept for all public leaders. The 'know oneself' as applied in political matters reinforces the deep sense of heroic leadership and preeminence which Budé suggests informs monarchical rule, thereby running close to the unarticulated maxim of 'think of yourself as.' Part of the public persona of the prince is to acknowledge their own stature as preeminent and to do nothing that might compromise their dignity and place.

Budé then provides a list of virtues associated with princely rule:

> Qu'ilz ayent Prudence, pour policer et regir ses Subiects: et Sapience, pour bien commander ce qui est utile en toutes choses: industrie, et vigilance perpetuelle sur le bien public: Liberalité reiglée, esloignée et d'avarice et de prodigalité: dignité et Maiesté en ses oeuvres, avec perpetuelle verité: bon advis et meure déliberation en entreprinses tant de guerre, comme de Paix, faisant iustice, et exerceant toutes aultres vertuz qui surpassent la condition moyenne de ses Subiects. Car aultrement, si les Princes ne sont provueuz de toutes ses vertuz: ilz ne seroient differents des aultres hommes, ny dignes d'avoir la superintendence par-dessus eulx, ny ne pourroient parvenir à la louange qu'ilz veulent acquerir en ce Monde.[91]

> [That they have prudence, to police and rule their subjects, and wisdom, in order to command well which is useful in all matters ; industry and perpetual watch over the public good; regulated liberality, far from both avarice and prodigality; dignity and majesty in his works with perpetual truth; good counsel and mature deliberation in matters of both war and peace, doing justice and exercising all the other virtues that go beyond the average condition of his subjects. For otherwise, if princes are not imbued with all the virtues; they would not be different from other men, nor worthy of having power over them, nor could they achieve the praise that they seek in this world.]

We have seen that Budé's conception of prudence, is virtually synonymous though rhetorically distinguished from 'sapience' and the conception of justice as the ultimate objective of political rule through the broad Aristotelian framework which informs his political thought. The virtue of liberality is treated in chapter 27. Here Budé cites the case of Vespasian who at the beginning of his reign developed the reputation of being miserly because of the great sum of money he accumulated in the treasury through the numerous extra taxes and tributes he imposed on the population.

---

[91] Budé, *Institution*, chap. 30, 125–126.

However, it is suggested that by the end of his reign his reputation had greatly shifted, in part because he avoided being cruel but also because he came to diminish the taxes and was able to distribute some of the collected funds to senators and men of science who had fallen on hard times due to their integrity and loyalty. This would appear to be a direct example of a 'regulated liberality.' The virtue of liberality is raised again in chapter 32 in reference to Alexander who virtually depleted his treasury prior to leaving for his conquest of Asia. When asked by a close friend what he had kept for himself, Alexander replies 'the hope of his future conquests.'[92]

In terms of the 'other virtues' noted here, in chapter 27 we are presented with the case of the King Artaxerxes who wished to demonstrate the virtue of clemency without revoking the laws of his predecessors which punished important mistakes in the administration of royal policy as capital crimes. He thereby instituted a form of punishment in effigy. (It is a move somewhat reminiscent of Phocion in the translation of "Political Precepts" by Tory.) Similarly, when being pressured by one of his attendants to bring about an unreasonable change in policy, he explored what may have been inciting his attendant to press for the changes and found that the attendant had been promised 30,000 pieces of gold to bring it about. Because Artaxerxes was attached to this attendant, he decided to give him the money without fulfilling the request. For Budé, this is deemed a virtuous action because the king was saving the honour and reputation of his own office of king by refusing to implement a policy he considered unjust.

These are puzzling examples because they do not really appear as examples as clemency at all. The first may be closer to an act of political moderation, and the latter one of expediency in the name of political integrity. While it is true that the king did not want to sully the public office by bowing to undue influence, the 'lobbyist' was retained in his service and indeed rewarded for his action. Pre-eminent in both, however, is the cultivation of a reputation for decency.

While invoking a normative understanding of 'le bien public,' as well as Aristotle's conception of the ruler as a distributer of justice, Budé's message may appear to waver concerning whether the monarch should be exempt from subjection to any laws but divine ones. He makes the case for the monarch's status above the law in the opening chapter of the work:

> l'une partie de Justice s'appelle distributive: par laquelle, les honneurs et profICts se doibvent distribuer, selon le merite et scavoir des hommes, qui

---

[92] Budé, *Institution*, chap. 32, 134–135.

peuvent proficter a la chose publicque, faire service et donner conseil et confort en commun, quent il en est necessite, ou que le besoing le requiert. Et pour cest cause, les Roys sont exaltes en honneur et ont souveraine puissance et dons de prerogatives: et prennet profict et emolument sur le populaire, par-dessus tous aultres, en telle et si raisonnable portion qu'il leur plaist: et s'ilz ne sont subiects aux Loix, ny aux ordonnances de leur Royaulme, comme les aultres, si bon ne leur semble. . . . et doibt suffire pour leur commander la Loy divine seulement.[93]

[one part of justice is called distributive; through which honours and profits should be distributed according to the merit and wisdom of men, who can benefit *la chose publique*, do service and give counsel and comfort together, in times of necessity or when needed. And because of this Kings are exalted in honour and have sovereign power and prerogatives ; and take profit and privileges over the common, in such and as reasonable a portion that they wish; and they are not subject to the laws, nor to the ordinances of their kingdome, as others, as they wish . . . and divine law is sufficient to command them.]

Yet in chapter 32 it might at first appear that a modified position is articulated:

. . . se doibt tout homme rendre subiect et obeissant aux Loiz: a fin que par icelles, il puisse vivre en franchise. Qui est la raison, pourquoy l'Empereur Theodore dict en une Loy, que c'est parole digne de Prince, que de se dire et maintenir estre subiect a la Loy: pour autant que l'authorite de Prince depend de la conservation de Iustice. Et a la verite, *dist-il,* le Prince ne peult plus exaulcer et authorizer sa Maieste, que de la soubzmettre a raison escripte.[94] (my emphasis)

[. . . it is necessary that each man be subject to and obey the laws: so that through this they can live freely. This is the reason, why the Emperor Theodore said in a law, that it is a word worthy of a prince, that he regards himself and maintains himself subject to the law: insofar as the authority of the prince depends on the preservation of justice. And in truth, *he says,* the prince cannot exercise and authorise his majesty but through submitting it to written reason.]

The 'dist-il' is telling. In this chapter Budé is extolling the virtues of King Antigonus, a successor to Alexander, for his commitment to reason and justice in the public realm and to the idea that good public administration requires that all, including the king, submit to law. Yet while praising this view Budé stops short of endorsing it.

---

[93] Budé, *Institution*, 20.   [94] Budé, *Institution*, 67.

Thus, despite a rather neutral invocation of 'la chose publique' in other matters, the implication for Budé is that the realm of political power, while governed overall by the virtue of justice, has a special status and a distinct type of relation. Whereas 'know yourself' has an important role to play in both personal and political ethics, as we have seen in the example of Alexander – and Budé sees this as a very puffed-up sense of 'self-knowledge,' -for a prince self-knowledge is not a sufficient condition of good and effective rule because the nature of public office requires that the prince also know those who are enforcing his will:

> C'est asses et beaucoup, que de se congnoistre, qui est l'un des trois commandemens escripts iadis au temple d'Apollo. Mais à un Prince, ou grand Prelat, n'est pas assés. Car il s'ayde des yeulx, des aureilles et des bouches de ses principaulx Serviteurs, Lieutenans, ou Vicaires. Parquoy, il les doibt congnoistre, avant que leur mettre en la main le pouvoir et authorite sur les Subiects. Ou aultrement, il ne peult avoir occasion de se reposer sur la fiance de leur diligence et preudhommie: et pourroit tomber en tel danger, comme un voiaigeur, qui a un passaige glissant et dangereux, ou il auroit besoing d'appuy, pour le soustenir: et se fiast a la force d'un foible baston demy rompu, qui ne seroit suffisant pour endurer le faix.[95]

> [It is enough and a great deal to know oneself, which is one of the three commandments once written on the temple of Apollo. But to a prince, or bishop, it is not enough. Because he has the help of the eyes, ears and mouths of his principal servants, lieutenants or vicars. Because of this he must know them, before giving them power and authority over the subjects. Or otherwise, he cannot rest with confidence in their diligence and honour; and he could fall into trouble, much like a traveller who on a slippery and dangerous path where he would need support to stand and seeks to secure himself on a weak and half-broken stick that is insufficient to carry his weight.]

A similar point is made at the start of chapter 32, though with the added idea that true friends can help the ruler gain knowledge of the shortcomings of his administrators to encourage effective governance:

> Il fault que les Roys soient advertiz par leurs plus fideles amys, de l'estat, et des choses qu'ilz ne peuvent scavoir par eulx mesmes. Car (comme dict Aristote en ses politicques) ilz s'aydent trop plus des membres et organes d'aultruy, que des leurs propres. C'est a scacoir, des yeulx, des aureilles, des mains, et des avertissemens de leurs Conseillers. Dont il advient, que si leurs Ministres, desquelz ilz se servent, ont les yeulx traversants ou hebetes, ou aultrement vicies, s'ilz ont la Langue mal diserte, si la main en est plus

---

[95] Budé, *Institution*, chap. 30, 123.

legiere . . . : Il ne se peult faire, que leur default et erreur qu'ilz commettent,
ne redonde au deshonneur du Prince, et detriment du bien public.[96]

[It is necessary that kings be warned by their most faithful friends concerning the state and of things that they are not able to know themselves. For (as
Aristotle says in his Politics) they depend more on the members and organs
of others than their own, in other words, the eyes, ears, hands and warnings
of their counsellors. Such that if their ministers have eyes that are shifty,
dazed or otherwise deficient, if their tongue speaks poorly, if their hand is
too weak . . . Whatever they do and whatever the faults and errors they
commit rebound to the dishonour of the prince and the detriment of the
public good.]

Of course, the loyal friend is also difficult to find amidst the flattery and
deception that surrounds the powerful.

We can see in this cursory look at Budé's political thought that the first
stages of the reception of Plutarch in the northern currents of humanism
offer various interpretive issues which each thinker will sort out in their
own way. A first question is whether some or all of Plutarch's historical
figures are to be considered heroes, and if so, to what degree does their
example provide guidance for rulers in contemporary times? In much the
same way as matters arising from the interpretation of Roman law (the *mos
italicus* vs. *mos gallicus* divide), there was also a question at the time of
which ancient examples and clear lessons of political rule could be invoked
to shed light on matters of contemporary leadership, if at all.[97] Political
theorists differed in their answers. Budé took from Plutarch and his praise
of Alexander the idea that politics is best suited for exceptional individuals
and heroic virtues, something which accompanied his defence of
unchecked power for the monarch. This will be something to which
Erasmus and Seyssel will be opposed. Still, Budé's understanding of what
those heroic virtues consisted of was also somewhat modified and adapted
from the ancient texts.

A second issue on which various Renaissance thinkers will differ in their
reflections on and adaptations of Plutarch is in how they conceptualise the
uniqueness of the public sphere. As we have seen for Budé, the public
sphere provides an occasion for those possessing heroic virtues to shine, yet
those noble and heroic virtues for Budé are recast in the light of Christian
orthodoxy and the primacy of Aristotelian justice as giving to each their
due, rather than in a celebration of courage and conquest. The primary

---

[96] Budé, *Institution*, chap. 32, 131–132.
[97] Myron Piper Gilmore, *Humanists and Jurists* (Cambridge, MA: Belknap Press, 1963).

motivation of those suitable for public life for Budé, as we have seen, is honour and a seeking of renown that will ensure the monarch will also be driven by a love for their subjects. Nonetheless, distinctive sensibilities for questions of individual and social moral psychology, whether it be in terms of self-conception, how to manage the ambition of others in the public realm, how to negotiate friendships and public commitments, or how to think about the moral qualities of the people as a whole as well as their own expectations and perceptions about those who govern, form a common thread throughout and can be traced to Plutarch as a major source and inspiration.

A third issue is how these good qualities for public life are developed. Budé stresses eloquence, which will be enhanced by close study of ancient Greek and Latin, to help distinguish the monarch and other public elites in their public roles, but as we have seen, an eloquence that is rooted in deeper understanding and knowledge as well as the study of history is also a medium for developing the virtue of prudence (and presumably an enhanced sense of honour). Budé's translations of some of Plutarch's essays will have taught him that while Fortune can be an important force in human affairs, virtue and knowledge achieved through individual effort also have an important role to play in history.

CHAPTER 4

Plutarch in Early French Renaissance Public Humanism: Desiderius Erasmus and Claude de Seyssel

In Chapter 3 we explored significant moments in the reception of Plutarch's work in French vernacular during the first half of the sixteenth century. The figures studied in this chapter, Desiderius Erasmus and Claude de Seyssel, were known to Tory and Budé, and while their translations of Plutarch, either into Latin (in the case of Erasmus) or French (in the case of Seyssel, as well as du Saix who translated Erasmus's Latin version) were completed around the same time, they were *published* in the vernacular French at a later date. My analysis of Plutarch reception in early sixteenth-century France will focus here on the paradigm of public humanism as an ongoing discussion among the thinkers discussed, particularly for questions concerning the good, the prudent, the practical and what was to be avoided in public life while also paying attention to matters of individual and social psychology in the public realm.[1]

4.1 Desiderius Erasmus (c. 1469–1536)

The name and work of Desiderius Erasmus towers over not only the Renaissance, but indeed the whole of European history for both his admirable scholarly accomplishments and his rigorous project of fashioning the modern conception of intellectual culture.[2] While best known in political theory (apart from his translation of the Bible) for his work *Education of a Christian Prince*, he was a regular translator of Plutarch, and indeed Plutarch figured among his

---

[1] While it is significant that these thinkers produced translations of Plutarch, either directly or indirectly published in the French vernacular, my focus is less on the mechanics and theory of translation, and more on the possible links between the works translated and the broader theoretical commitments voiced by these thinkers in either commentary or independent treatises of political reflection. In other words, I explore how knowledge of Plutarch played a role in the development of their political theory, and more specifically, how they conceptualised the nature and norms governing public life.

[2] See Lisa Jardine, *Erasmus, Man of Letters: The Construction of Charisma in Print* (Princeton, NJ: Princeton University Press, 1993 and 2015).

favourite classical authors.[3] In addition, while not a French national, nor indeed writing in French vernacular, he has been identified as the most influential humanist for the French Renaissance tradition.[4]

Erasmus's introduction to Plutarch took place during his stay in Venice (1507–1508) while working on the *Adages* (the expanded version going by the title *Adagiorum Chilieades*) at the Aldine Press under Aldus Manutius.[5] During his time at the press Erasmus became acquainted with Byzantine exiles who worked with Aldus on the broad project of editing and producing Greek texts of the ancient world. Jean Lascaris, who later played a key role in the introduction of Plutarch to France, was among the exiles in Venice at this time. Greek manuscripts of both Plutarch's *Lives* and *Moralia* were loaned to Erasmus, and the latter text was in the process of being edited and published by the press under the supervision of Demetrius Ducas.[6] Presumably, the Plutarch that Erasmus was reading in Venice served to inspire late additions to his *Adages*, which was in production at the press. Indeed, Erasmus's engagement with Plutarch's work was so significant that he remained at the press a few weeks after the publication of his *Adages* in part to correct the proofs of Plutarch's *Moralia* which was then in production.[7]

It is not surprising then that while teaching at Cambridge just a few years later (1511–1514) Erasmus embarked on full translations of Plutarch's essays. He translated and published eight full essays of Plutarch into Latin, one of the first to do so, during his years in England. And more than ten years later in 1525, he turned to a translation of Plutarch's *Sayings of Kings and Commanders* or *Apophthegms* (the same work that had inspired Budé).[8] These were works translated by Erasmus from Greek into Latin, but they sometimes contained personal elaborations and embellishments. When translating *Sayings*, for instance, he added other passages from Plutarch's work that were not in the existing manuscripts, as well as pithy sayings and observations from the work of other ancient authors.

Three of Erasmus's translations of Plutarch essays were presented to English patrons as gifts, including *De Tuenda sanitate praecepta* (*Advice on*

---

[3] Patricia Thomson, "Classical Philosophy and English Humanism," in *Sir Thomas Wyatt and His Background* (London: Kegan Paul, 1964), 85.

[4] "If Erasmus played a determining role in the making of this Erasmus, Erasmus played an even more determining role in the shaping of the Renaissance in France. It was Erasmus, more than any of the great Italian humanists of the fourteenth and fifteenth centuries, who inspired in the French a belated enthusiasm for antiquity." Edwin Duval, "Erasmus and the 'First Renaissance' in France," in Christopher Prendergast, ed., *A History of Modern French Literature: From the Sixteenth Century to the Twentieth Century* (Princeton, NJ: Princeton University Press, 2017), 49.

[5] Geanakoplos, "Erasmus."   [6] Geanakoplos, "Erasmus," 122.   [7] Geanakoplos, "Erasmus," 131.

[8] Rummel, *Erasmus*, 73.

Health) given on New Year's day 1513 to diplomat John Yonge; *Quomodo adulator ab amico internoscatur* (*How to Distinguish Flatterers from Friends*) presented to Henry VIII in July 1513; and *De Capienda ex inimicis utilitate* (*How to Profit from your Enemies*) presented to Thomas Wolsey for New Year's in 1514.[9] In broad terms, Erasmus's choices reflect a turning away from the narratives of a single king or political leader and their extraordinary and complex characters, as found in Budé's conception of political leadership. The essays translated invoke concern for practical ethics with application to public life (questions of flattery and dealing with public enemies).

Erasmus's key work in the political theory canon, *Education of a Christian Prince*, was written in 1515, just a couple of years after his first Plutarch translations and shortly after his departure from England. Indeed, as Lisa Jardine notes, the first print edition of this treatise included some of his translations from Plutarch, suggesting an intimate connection between the subject of the book and the lessons coming from the essays.[10] The book was initially written with Charles V, king of Spain, in mind, but it was also sent to Henry VIII of England who was looking for a replacement for the recently deceased Latin scholar in his court.

Clearly Erasmus was not French, although he did live in Paris for a short while as a student and kept up an extensive correspondence with Budé.[11] Still, while most of his translations were from the Greek into Latin or English, his work reached a broad public in France in the vernacular through the translation work of Antoine du Saix (1505–1579).[12] Saix's vernacular translation of Erasmus's translation of Plutarch's essay on

---

[9] Rummel, *Erasmus*, 73. The other Plutarch essays translated and published at this time were "That a Prince needs Knowledge," "That it is Most Necessary for the Philosopher to Converse with Princes," "Whether the Ills of the Soul are more Serious than the Ills of the Body," "Whether the Saying Lathe Biosas is Correct," and "About the Desire for Riches."

[10] Lisa Jardine, "Introduction," *The Education of a Christian Prince* (Cambridge: Cambridge University Press, 1997), xii.

[11] See Guillaume Budé and D. Erasmus, *La Correspondance d'Erasme et de Guillaume Budé*, trans. M. de la Garanderie (Paris: Librairie Philosophique J. Vrin, 1967).

[12] Antoine Du Saix came from Brittany to become the tutor to the children of Charles III of Savoie. He is perhaps best known for his work on the education of children, *L'Esperon de Discipline* where of course he engaged directly with the work of pseudo-Plutarch on the subject. His approach to child-rearing is based on a need to reign in the impulses of children:

> Mais il n'y a hydeux monstre en Affricque
> Lion, Gryphon, Crocodile, ou liepart,
> Si dangereux et de maulvaise part,
> Comme la rage horrible et furibunde
> D'ung jeune enfant, qu'on laisse vagabonde
> Touttallement suivre sa volunte, (...)'
>
> (Esp., II, XIV, 88–93)

friendship and flattery appeared first in 1537 [*La Touche naïfve pour eprouver l'amy et le flateur* (Paris: Simon de Colines, 1537)], and had at least four editions in eight years, expanding the already established reputation for Erasmus in the early French Renaissance. In addition, Antoine Macault translated the first five books of Erasmus's *Apophthegmata* (which was begun as and structured around a translation of Plutarch's *Sayings*) into French. Others embarked on similar projects so that no less than twenty-eight editions of either the full work or selected parts (according to the Universal Short Title Catalogue) appeared from 1539 to 1557.[13] The importance of the Erasmus–Macault editions is also highlighted by a poem by Clement Marot, one of the most eminent poets in France at this time. The poem was in praise of both Macault and Erasmus and it headed a number of those editions.[14] French readers were also no strangers to Erasmus's main work of political theory, appearing in French under the title *Brief recueil du*

Cited in Marie-Luce Honest, "Antoine du Saix, Pédagogue humaniste émule d'Erasme," *Bibliotheque d'Humanisme et Renaissance*, 54.3 (1992), 661–689.

[13] This figure derives from searches in the USTC. Macault's edition and translation of the first five books was later completed by a certain E. Des Pl.There were also French poets who offered versions of Erasmus's *Apophthegmes* in verse. Margolin suggests that there were four different vernacular translations circulating in France in the mid-sixteenth century (amounting, he suggests, to twenty-two editions from 1539 to 1574), and it appears that all were based on the same Erasmus Latin translation, though clearly the Erasmus-Macault edition was pre-eminent. See J-Cl. Margolin, "Guillaume Haudent, poète et traducteur des Apophthegmes d'Érasme," *Revue de Littérature comparée*, 52 (1978), 202–222. For a more in-depth discussion of the circumstances of the French translations of this work in the early sixteenth century, see Louis Lobbes, "Les *Apophthegms* d'Erasme," *Seizième Siècle* 1(2005), 85–97. According to Lobbes, Macault and his successor took a few liberties in translating Erasmus including skipping some of the apophthegms as well as integrating some stylistic changes, such as the addition of redundant synonyms to give more emphasis to certain points, or to modernise some of the references, in terms of currency etc. The history of this translation may also be complicated by the fact that Erasmus himself added on to his Apophthegmes in succeeding editions. For a full history of Erasmus's Latin version of the text, see the introduction to the two volumes devoted to the *Apophthegmata* in the *Collected Works of Erasmus*, ed. Betty I. Knott and trans. Elaine Fantham and Betty Knott (Toronto: University of Toronto Press, 2014).

[14] Clement Marot's (1496–1544) poem in praise of Macault's work on Erasmus's translations of Plutarch:

Clément Marot aux lecteurs François.
Si sçavoir veux les recontres plaisantes
Des sages vieux, faites en devisant,
O tu, qui n'as lettres à ce duysantes,
Graces ne peux rendre assez suffisantes
Au tien Macault, ce gentil traduysant.
Car en ta langue orras (icy lisant)
Mille bons motz, propres à oindre et poindre
Ditz par les Grecz et Latins: t'avisant,
Si bonne grace eurent en bien disant,
Qu'en escrivant, Macault ne la pas moindre.
Luy encores.

livre de l'enseignement du prince chrestien translated and published 1548 and 1549. And yet another French vernacular edition of a summary of Erasmus's reflections on the education of a Christian prince appeared in 1665 with another edition the following year. Perhaps surprisingly, it appears that there was no English vernacular edition of Erasmus's *Education of a Christian Prince* throughout the sixteenth and seventeenth centuries (although part of the reason for this may have something to do with the pervasiveness of Latin learning and culture in the English context). The broader conclusion here is that for the public who may not have had facility in reading Latin, Erasmus as political thinker was in the main a French phenomenon, whereas in the English vernacular he remained a moralist.

So while Erasmus may not have been in active dialogue with all of the French thinkers publishing translations of Plutarch, his long association with Budé and the pervasiveness of both his Plutarch translations and his own works of political thought in the French context meant that he was nonetheless an important voice in the evolving understanding of the nature of public life in France in the first half of the sixteenth century. Those who translated Erasmus's Plutarch work into French would have already been acquainted with the style and vocabulary of the earlier work of Tory.

What in broad terms is Erasmus's political theory as developed in *The Education of a Christian Prince* and its French translation? And what might it owe to the work of Plutarch that Erasmus translated, either before or after the publication of this work? How, in turn, was the political theory of this treatise reflected or developed in Erasmus's later translation of and commentary on Plutarch's *Apophthegmata* and in its published version in France? More precisely, what does Erasmus contribute to a theory of what is specific to public service and action, drawing on Plutarch?

Jardine suggests that Erasmus is to be considered most substantially a defender of the status quo.[15] However, from the outset of this work one

> Des bons propos cy dedans contenuz,
> Rends à Plutarque, o Grec, un grand mercy:
> Soyez, Latins, à Erasme tenuz,
> Qui vous à tout traduit et esclarcy.
> Tous les François en doyvent faire ainsi
> Au translateur: car, en ce livre, apprennent
> De bon sçavoir autant (quant à cecy)
> Que les Latins et les Grecz en comprennent.
> La mort n'y mord.

[15] "Whereas Machiavelli set out to instruct the ruler who has seized power on how best to sustain it, Erasmus is candid in his commitment to the hereditary monarchies of Europe, and forthright in his contention that the cost of disturbing the order currently in place, in terms of ensuing discord and social disintegration, is too high to be contemplated. Only outright tyranny justifies political

can see the expression of more radical thinking with which he is often associated (particularly when seen alongside Budé), and most significantly his advocacy of peace at the cost of personal status and ambition for a figure in public life. As Erasmus states in the preface: "You owe it to heaven that your empire came to you without the shedding of blood, and no one suffered for it; your wisdom must now ensure that you preserve it without bloodshed and at peace."[16] Perhaps this is sufficient in explaining why the *Lives* were of lesser interest to Erasmus.

Notwithstanding points on which he differed from Budé, concerning the good in public life, we find in *The Education of a Christian Prince* a commitment to an overarching Aristotelian framework, and a political commentary fused with Christian apologetics, made evident at the outset by a key distinction between the good ruler and the tyrant:

> Aristotle differentiates in his *Politics* between a prince and a tyrant by the criterion that the latter is concerned for his own interests and the former for the state. No matter what the prince is deliberating about, he always bears in mind whether it is to the advantage of all his subjects, a tyrant considers whether it will serve his own purpose. A prince is chiefly concerned with the needs of his subjects, even while engaged in his personal business. On the other hand, if a tyrant does ever do well by his subject, he turns this very fact to his private benefit all the same.
>
> Those who look out for their people only in so far as it redounds to their personal advantage are treating their subjects on the same level as the common people treat their horses and donkeys. For the latter do indeed take care of their animals, but they measure their attention by the advantage it brings to themselves. But those who despoil people in their greed and torture them with their cruelty or expose them to all sorts of perils to satisfy their ambition are giving free citizens a lower status than the common folk give to the cattle they buy or the gladiator-master give to the gladiators he owns.[17]

---

challenge from a ruler's subjects. The problem Erasmus sets himself in *The Education of a Christian Prince*, given this commitment to and support for, the *status quo*, is how to ensure that those born to rule are educated so as to govern justly and benevolently, and so that the prince's rule never degenerates into oppression." Jardine, "Introduction," vii. Still, it would be inaccurate to suggest that Machiavelli in *The Prince* is advocating political challenge on behalf of subjects, or even encouraging the seizure of power on behalf of would-be rulers, especially where hereditary monarchies are concerned. Indeed, it could easily be argued that social and political discord beyond a certain threshold and civic disintegration were considered as great if not a greater evil for Machiavelli than for Erasmus himself.

[16] Erasmus, *The Education of a Christian Prince*, ed. Lisa Jardine (Cambridge: Cambridge University Press, 1997), 3.

[17] Erasmus, *Education*, 25–26.

In terms of the nuances of distinction among the good, the prudent, the practical and what is to be avoided in public life, for Erasmus the ideal of the good has a predominant role in his reflection. This is solidified by the analogy with the Christian deity:

> Although there are many kinds of state, it is pretty well agreed among the philosophers that the most healthy form is monarchy; not surprisingly, for, by analogy with the deity, when the totality of things is in one person's power, then indeed, in so far as he is in this respect in the image of God, he excels everyone else in wisdom and goodness, and, being quite independent, concentrates exclusively on helping the state. Anything different from this would have to be the worst type of state, since it would be in conflict with that which is best.[18]

While this may appear to be an unquestioned appropriation of the classical and religious sources, we should be aware of some of the interpretative work going on beneath the surface. For Aristotle, as is generally known, while there is a model of perfect monarchy in which the person of the good king and the good man coincide, for the vast majority of states, one may say for all practical purposes, for every state, there will be a disjuncture between the high demands of ethics and philosophy and the need for competent rule. For Aristotle, this carries the necessity to supplement his concern for good judgement in office with certain prudent institutional recommendations, such as the rule of law, a largely agricultural economy and muted inequalities of wealth or, at the least, a large middle class. For Aristotle these are conditions which precede and help to structure and moderate the exercise of power. While political relations for Aristotle are defined and identified as having a unique quality of reciprocity, the power imbalances issued by political rule often require certain institutional or socio-economic conditions to offset the deficiencies of prudence in the ruler to ensure the promotion of common interests.

In a departure from Aristotle, Erasmus does not invoke the ideal of perfect rule, but rather that of 'healthy' rule, in other words, covering a rather broad swath of actual empirical examples. The key to good rule in a vast number of states for Erasmus, more than in Aristotle, will depend largely on the rulers themselves. While certain institutions and practices are recommended, these for the most part are seen to flow from the good judgement of the ruler, rather than preceding and helping to structure or moderate that judgement.

---

[18] Erasmus, *Education*, 37.

What is required of the good ruler for Erasmus, and what claims does he make about public service? A first requirement, it would appear, is a good understanding of one's role. To conceptualise the place of public service in relation to the broader whole, Erasmus invokes four key analogies for the prince. The first flows from his invocation of health. Erasmus superimposes an adaptation of the body politic metaphor (originally taken from Livy with the fable of the limbs versus the stomach, though taken up as we saw earlier and adapted by both Plutarch and John of Salisbury) with the prince as the *heart* giving life to the whole.[19] While on the surface benign, this supplement can be seen as a subversion of the Platonic metaphor. For Plato, of course, the living function of the soul or 'mere life,' was something that Plato ascribed to appetite. In the context of the state, or the ideal state, there was no suggestion for Plato that the ruler or philosopher kings animated the state, but only structured and guided the energies of all to a just outcome. Erasmus invokes this ruling principle in a distinct way, one which in turn impacts on the conception of the public which underlies his analysis:

> be sure to remember how the pagan philosophers themselves understood an expounded them: that the prince's authority over a people is the same as that of the mind over the body. The mind has control over the body because it is wiser than the body, but its control is exercised for the great advantage of the body rather than for its own, and the happiness of the body consists in the rule of the mind.
>
> What the heart is in the living body the prince is in the state. Since it is the fount of the blood and of the spirits, it imparts life to the whole body, but if it is impaired, it debilitates every part of the body. Just as that organ in the living body is the last one of all to be affected by disease and is thought to retain the last vestiges of life, so the prince ought to remain quite uncontaminated by any taint of foolishness if that sort of condition overtakes his people.[20]

While carrying the message communicated by Plato in Books 8 and 9 of *The Republic* that the integrity of the state depends to a large degree on the integrity of the rulers, there is also a shift in the conception of rule presented in this way. In the case of philosophic rule, judgements are made in the interests of the whole, but in ways that from competing perspectives may abuse and manipulate the public. The analogy with the heart suggests a connection to the whole that is not only harmonious but in principle sympathetic, prudent and wise. It also posits a much greater

---

[19] Erasmus, *Education*, 39.   [20] Erasmus, *Education*, 39.

interdependency of ruler and ruled. While Aristotle's ruler and Plato's philosopher can stand alone, and in this sense can be indifferent to the longer-term prospects for their rule, for Erasmus's ruler, whose status is no longer separable from their civic and political function, there is much more at stake.

Erasmus's other analogies for the position of ruler invoke not just this important theme of interdependency of ruler and people, but also themes of the nobility of rule and the ethical (as opposed to philosophical) requirements of political leadership. Another image is that of the father, "for what else is a kingdom but a large family and what is a king but the father of very many people? For he is set above them and yet he is of the same kind: a man ruling man, a free man ruling free men and not wild beasts."[21] This sets a minimal threshold of respect and concern. This image is superseded by yet another, that of the ship of state:

> the man at the helm cannot be a sleepyhead, so can the prince go snoring on in such perilous conditions? No sea ever has such severe storms as every kingdom constantly experiences. And the prince must therefore always be on his guard against going off course in some way since he cannot go wrong without bringing disaster to thousands.
> The size of his ship, the value of his cargo, or the number of passengers are not the source of greater pride, but of greater vigilance in a good ship's captain. So the more subjects a good king has, the more alert he must be, not the more arrogant.[22]

Again, while reminiscent of the Platonic analogy, the passage also subtly subverts it, for the point of greatest reference is not the stars and science of navigation, as invoked in *The Republic* (488e–489d), but in vigilance for the welfare and wellbeing of the passengers with attention to particulars. Knowledge of the course to follow also requires an ability to recognise how it is being followed and when the ship is diverting from that course. Arrogance of the man at the helm is an impediment to just rule. Thus, Erasmus is constructing a picture of the expectations of conduct and character in the public sphere that distances itself to a certain degree from the Platonic legacy.

A fourth and final set of images invoked in the text is taken directly from Plutarch and relates to ancient iconographies of power. The images here are threefold: an eye superimposed with a sceptre, a sceptre with a stork on top and a hippopotamus on bottom (symbolic of the greater importance of

---

[21] Erasmus, *Education*, 34. [22] Erasmus, *Education*, 47.

love of country over good fortune and material success in rule) and the Theban sacred image of magistrates without hands seated with their chief who is without eyes. The need for a calm and balanced temperament is symbolised by the sitting pose, the lack of hands (as discussed by Erasmus) is symbolic of blamelessness and the absence of (or incapacity to accept?) corrupting bribes, and blindness is symbolic of not being deceived by appearances.[23] The implication may be that if left to our natural capacities and desires, human nature will lead us to neglect the qualities important for good public service. The measure and standard of the character needed for good public service is not perfection of nature, as posited by classical philosophy (as good leaders are blinded and maimed), but the exercise of strategic self-management (aided by iconic representation) that works to overcome human desires of greed, arrogance and revenge in favour of devotion to a whole beyond the self.

While this discussion of Erasmus gives us some indication of the features to be avoided in public service, it does little to elucidate how exactly we are to think of the nature of public service, what motivation is necessary to do it well, and how we judge performance in the public sphere. Is the standard of good service that of the character of the public actor, or the effects of their actions and policies on a public? And if the judgements of the public differ, how are we to discern what makes for good and appropriate public service? What is the reason for and the significance of acts of public service; what is their cost and why should individuals engage in them despite the costs?

In terms of how to distinguish good rule from bad, Erasmus is clear that the best judges are not to be found close to the king nor even among the ruler's contemporaries. Although the ruler should seek the good will of the public, and this through the performance of benevolent actions, as discussed by Plutarch in his essay, "How to Distinguish a Friend from a Flatterer" it is not always easy for a king to gain broader perspective from his entourage. As Erasmus suggests: "a plague of a flatterer does more damage to the state by corrupting and contaminating those first years of a prince with the ideas of a tyrant than does someone who steals from the public treasury."[24] He suggests that it is the nature of those who surround the ruler, even tutors, to want to flatter those in power. The challenge for the prince, therefore, is how to cultivate virtue and a good sense of self in a social setting devoid of true and constant sincerity.

---

[23] Erasmus, *Education*, 49.   [24] Erasmus, *Education*, 56.

Even books can do more damage than good for individuals of a certain temperament. For this reason, Erasmus suggests that the reading of the lives of ancient heroes such as Achilles, Alexander, Xerxes and Julius Caesar should be limited, as they can incite those of a certain disposition to tyranny. While Plutarch's *Lives* are not fully rejected as a source of learning, Erasmus suggests that such reading is best done after a study of the Proverbs and Gospels of the Bible. Even then, the wisdom of Plutarch's *Moralia* is said to be preferable to that of the *Lives*, at least insofar as the education of rulers is concerned.[25] In his later *Apophthegmata*, Erasmus gives a more muted defence of moral philosophy over history with the suggestion that in the study of deeds most of the credit can be given to Fortune whereas noble words are fully the property of those who pronounce them.[26] However, the type of moral philosophy recommended is not the metaphysical thinking associated traditionally with Plato, which cultivates systematic reflection, but rather sayings and maxims that distill lessons and wise practical advice. "Everything included under proverbs, maxims, striking sayings, striking actions, is particularly relevant to men in positions of authority, who are so busy with the practicalities of government that they cannot devote much of their lives to books."[27]

Perhaps especially illustrative of Erasmus's wariness of a focus on the heroism of ancient leaders in relation to Budé is his contrasting interpretation of a passage from Plutarch. As we saw in Chapter 3, Budé in his *Institution* invokes a scene from Plutarch's *Sayings* [and also found in his *Life of Caesar* (11.5–6)] in which Caesar cries while reading about Alexander because Alexander had accomplished greater things at a younger age. Budé uses this to praise Caesar and to tell the reader that this moment was a crucial motivating event that propelled him to greater and better things. In Budé's eyes, Caesar was a courageous and virtuous leader whose 'cruel and undignified' end was an unmerited and unfortunate blow by Fortune. Budé is sure that had Caesar lived he would have become the equal of Alexander. The reading of Erasmus is wholly different. While recognising that his account differs to some degree from that of Suetonius, Erasmus provides his own brief editorial commentary that it would have been better had Caesar felt drawn to imitate a modest prince rather than a great one.[28]

---

[25] Erasmus, *Education*, 62.   [26] Erasmus, "Dedicatory Epistle," *Education*, 6.
[27] Erasmus, "Dedicatory Epistle," *Education*, 14.
[28] Here are the various accounts starting with the Greek from Plutarch's Life of Caesar:
    "ὁμοίως δὲ πάλιν ἐν Ἰβηρίᾳ σχολῆς οὔσης ἀναγινώσκοντά τι τῶν περὶ Ἀλεξάνδρου γεγραμμένων σφόδρα γενέσθαι πρὸς ἑαυτῷ πολὺν χρόνον, εἶτα καὶ δακρῦσαι· τῶν δὲ φίλων θαυμασάντων τὴν

Distinct then from some of the leaders of Plutarch's *Lives*, for Erasmus the good ruler is identified by a certain type of good character, someone who not only instantiates some of the classic virtues, but exemplifies them in a way surpassing others, especially the virtues of wisdom, generosity, restraint and integrity. Furthermore, that which motivates individuals to virtue is not virtue or nature alone as in a Stoic or Epicurean framework, but the seeking of honour and good reputation. Here Erasmus endorses the remarks of the Spartan leader Anaxandridas:

> Someone put forward the view that glory and reputation were harmful things and that the happy man was therefore the one who shunned

αἰτίαν εἰπεῖν· "Οὐ δοκεῖ ὑμῖν ἄξιον εἶναι λύπης, εἰ τηλικοῦτος μὲν ὢν Ἀλέξανδρος ἤδη τοσούτων ἐβασίλευεν, ἐμοὶ δὲ λαμπρὸν οὐδὲν οὔπω πέπρακται;" (From Loeb edition)

Pelling translation: "And there is another story too, relating to his time in Spain. He had some time to himself, and was reading a book about Alexander. He fell quiet for a long time, then he began to weep. His friends did not know what to make of this, and asked him why. 'Don't you agree that it is a matter for tears?' he said. 'When Alexander was my age, he was already master of so many nations – and I have not yet done anything distinguished at all.'" (From Plutarch, *Caesar*, trans. and ed. Christopher Pelling (Oxford: Oxford University Press, 2011)

Budé's account with commentary from *Institution du Prince*: "Iules Cesar premier des Cesars, et celluy qui translata en monarchie le gouvernement de Romme, fut homme du plus grand cœur, franc couraige par Nature, et hault esperit sans insolence, dont il soit mémoire en histoire autenticque, et qui plus pres approchea des vertuz dignes d'Empereur, et de demener la guerre, ensemble de la forme et hardiesse du grand Alexandre. Quelque fois luy estant en Hespaigne encore peu renomme entre les Rommains, se preind à lire une histoire dudict Alexandre, comme se preparant, ou aulcunement proposant d'ensuivre ses grands et beaulx faicts: il larmoioit ainsy que s'il eust veu audict Livre quelque commiseration, ou aultre chose lamentable. Laquelle chose veoians ceulx, qui assistoient avec luy, luy demandairent, pour quelle cause il monstroit si triste visaige, et remply de pleurs. Ausquelz il respondit ces parolles: N'ay-ie pas grande cause de me douloir, quand ie pense, qu'en cestuy age ou ie suis, Alexandre a desia subiugue par sa prouessse et chevalerie, presque l'universel Monde: et ie n'ay encore rien faict digne d'estre mis en mémoire par les Escripvans ? Et sur ce propos, se delibera incontinent d'acquerir grand bruict et renommee, et de chercher moyens et occasions, pour faire parler et escripre honorablement de luy. Et oncques puis ne cessa de se travailler et veiller à ceste fin, iusques à ce, qu'il fut cruellement et indignement occis au Senat par ses plus proches parents, et ausquelz il vouloit faire plus de bien et d'advancement. Car tousiours tendoit et tenoit propos constamment, pour faire choses et mener a fin entreprinses equiparables a la gloire d'Alexandre. Et s'il eust vescu en ceste domination espace de temps suffisant: il eust par adventure surmonté." (chap. 33, 139)

Macault translation of Erasmus: "Lisant les gestes d'Alexandre le grand, il ne se peult tenir de plorer, et dist a ses amys: En cest aage que ie suis maintenant Alexandre subiuge Darius: et iusques ce iourd'huy ie n'ay faict aucun acte vertueux.

Suetone recite cecy estre aucun, quant Cesar estant preteur, tenoit les grans iours et les estatz en Espaigne, sur le destroict de Gilbathar, au temple d'Hercules, ou il veit la statue d'Alexandre le grand. Pleust à Dieu qu'un tel esprit se fust plustost dispose à l'imitation d'un modeste prince, que d'un grand." From Plutarque, *Les Apophthegmes, c'est-à-dire prompts subtilz, et sententieux dictz de plusieurs Roys, chefz d'armees, Philosophes et autres grands personnages, tant Grecz que Latins*, trans. Antoine Macault from Erasmus (Paris: Estienne Grouilleau, 1551), 228.

For an interesting discussion of the significance of Plutarch's account of this incident in relation to Suetonius, see Christopher Pelling, "Plutarch's Caesar: a Caesar for the Caesars?" in *Sage and Emperor*, 213–226.

them. "Well then" said Anaxandridas, "if what you say is true, then wrongdoers will be happy. For how can the man who commits sacrilege or some other crime possibly have any concern for reputation?"

This remark censured those who reject praise and then do nothing praiseworthy out of idleness. In fact, a great name naturally attaches itself to excellence and in noble souls a passion for praise is an inborn stimulus to great achievements.[29]

And again:

These two things, honour and disgrace, are of prime importance in maintaining discipline in any group of people. Honours nourish not only arts, as the proverb says, but also virtue.[30]

Of course, this also demonstrates why flattery is such a challenge for those in public life, for the solution is not to make oneself immune from the effects of praise, but to be able to recognise the good praise (and truthful praise) from the bad. One strategy suggested by Erasmus through Plutarch, is to assess the character of the one who is giving the praise through their prior patterns of judgement.[31]

So what qualities are sought by this somewhat selective array of influences? In accordance with his overriding notion of the good, Erasmus offers via Plutarch prudential advice on how public judgement may at times differ from other forms of moral practical ethics. There are also times in Erasmus's work where these suggestions border on the highly pragmatic. For Erasmus, though ruling requires knowledge, in accordance with demands of public prudence this knowledge is not the universal form sought by the philosopher but a form of practical ethics. Indeed, Erasmus suggests that knowledge of how to advance the good for public life is distinct and specialised. As he states early on in the work, "the prince must excel in the best kind of wisdom, namely, an understanding of how to administer the state justly."[32] And again, "a prince should not be praised for the same things as a subject, nor a person in public life for the same things as a private citizen."[33] What this means is that the qualities and knowledge that may determine

---

[29] Erasmus, *Apophthegmata*, 1.117, 69   [30] Erasmus, *Apopthegmata*, 1.299, 136.
[31] Erasmus, *Apophthegmata*, Book 1, 23–24 and 12 in the Macault edition in French.
[32] Erasmus, *Éducation*, 37. The spirit of this is reiterated in Erasmus's commentary on the apophthegm attributed to Agasicles: "a prince should not learn any and every art, but only those which teach the principles of good government." Erasmus, *Apophthegmata*, 20
[33] Erasmus, *Apophthegmata*, 1.326, 145.

goodness in a private and independent realm are not adequate for performing a public role well:

> the first obligation of the good prince is to have the best possible intentions; the next is to be on the look-out for ways of avoiding or removing evils, and, on the other hand, of achieving, increasing, and reinforcing what is good. It is perhaps enough for a private individual to be well intentioned, since he is guided by the law and the magistrates prescribe what is to be done. But in the prince, it is not enough to be well meaning and have the best intentions, unless they are accompanied by wisdom which demonstrates by what means he may achieve what he desires.[34]

From this perspective, Erasmus not only pre-emptively undermines the Stoic and neo-Stoic approaches to public service and duty, he also signals that it is a very specific knowledge set – namely, the knowledge of means, along with the ability to discern the evils and good in public life – that is required by the good and effective ruler. It is a form of practical knowledge, as opposed to reflective wisdom. A knowledge of the prudent and pragmatic are required alongside that of the good.

As a first requirement of prudence, those best suited for rule are not only those with good intentions and special knowledge of means, but also those with a fair amount of self-awareness and knowledge of their own capacities. As Erasmus comments on the translation of the words of Agesilaus:

> While Agesilaus was still a boy, the annual boys' athletics demonstration was taking place, and the organizer assigned him to a not very prominent position. He accepted this although he was already king designate saying, "That's fine by me. I shall show that position does not bring distinction to men, but men give distinction to position."
>
> These words demonstrate the boy's remarkable nobility of mind combined with self-control. It is persons like this who are best fitted to rule a kingdom.[35]

What Erasmus invokes here with the term nobility is not only that the boy had the qualities that would bring him distinction and that he knew he had these qualities, but that he chose to respect the initial decisions of the organisers and demonstrated respect for his competitors by acquiescing to them in the preliminary assignments. The anecdote demonstrates a willingness to see one's capacities for what they are, but not to deny

---

[34] Erasmus, *Education*, 50. Though note also what Erasmus remarks later: "It's a common enough excuse but a feeble one to say, 'I didn't intend to.' The person should have been taking care not to do wrong by mistake." Erasmus, *Apopthegmata*, 11.9, 156.

[35] Erasmus, *Apophthegmata*, 1. 24.

others the opportunities to be distinguished and proud, even if uncertain of
success. It also reveals a spirit in which status is always something that
needs to be earned.

In the French translation of Macault, this commentary by Erasmus is
embellished slightly. It reads: "Telle parole monstre en un ieune prince,
une merveilleuse excellence de courage, accompagnée de modestie et
tempérance."[36] In addition, the example stands in direct contrast to the
incident involving Alexander at the Olympic games. Alexander's refusal to
compete with anyone not a ruler was for Budé, as we have seen, an
indication of Alexander's self-knowledge. The verdict is presented quite
differently in the case of Erasmus. Here is the incident retold in Macault's
French translation:

> Comme luy mesme fust aleigre de corps et agile a bien courir, et que son père
> l'enhortast de courir es ieux Olympiques, dedans le stade, il luy dist: ie le
> feroye volontiers, si j'avois des Roys qui voulussent courir contre moy.
>
> En cecy congnoissez l'homme haultain et qui a peine eust voulu ceder
> a personne: en cas de louange et domination il n'estoit point encores Roy, et
> toutesfois il ne se vouloit mettre quavecques les Roys.[37]

> [As he himself was light in body and fit to run well, and as his father
> entreated him to run in the Olympic games in the stadium, he told him:
> I would be pleased to, as long as I had Kings who wished to compete
> against me.
>
> In this you can discern the haughty man who hardly wished to cede to
> anyone: in terms of power and praise he was not yet King, and yet he only
> wished to be placed among kings.]

Erasmus judges Alexander to be not just proud, but to be seeking recognition and praise beyond his appropriate station. This directly counters
Budé's reading, for it appears in Erasmus's commentary to be an exercise
in self-aggrandisement and not lucidity.

The demands of public life are greater than those of private life, not only
due to this required knowledge of means along with ends, but also due to
the inescapable exemplary dynamic that authority brings. As another
requirement of prudence, the public official must be aware that the public
nature of authority means greater scrutiny and a seeking of transparency in
the person of the ruler: "your life is open to view: you cannot hide. The fact
is that either you are a good man to the great benefit to all, or a bad one
bringing great disaster to all."[38] In addition, it means that the persona of

---

[36] Plutarch, *Les Apophthegmes*, trans. A. Macault, 12.
[37] Plutarch, *Les Apophthegmes*, trans. A. Macault, 192.   [38] Erasmus, *Education*, 21.

the ruler tends to set a tone for ongoing relations within the wider community.

> The common people imitate nothing with more pleasure than what they see their prince do. Under a gambler, gambling is rife; under a fighter, everyone gets into fights; under a gourmandiser, they wallow in extravagance; under a voluptuary, they become promiscuous; under a cruel man, they bring charges and false accusations against each other. Turn the pages of history and you will always find the morality of an age reflecting the life of its prince.

> No comet, or fateful power affects the progress of human affairs in the way that the life of the prince grips and transforms the moral attitudes and character of his subjects . . . the prince should take special care not to fall into wrongdoing, so as not to turn innumerable people to wrongdoing by his example; and for the same reason he will rather devote himself to setting a good example, so that many more good people may result.[39]

Erasmus, citing Plutarch, acknowledges that any such undertaking requiring good intentions, knowing how to achieve your ends through factors not always under your control and the ability to perform this constantly under the public eye, thereby setting a good example for all, is a very difficult one.

> it was very wisely said by one of the wise Greeks that what is excellent is also difficult. Consequently, it must be remembered that to prove oneself a good prince is indeed by far the finest thing of all, but is at the same time much the most difficult of all.[40]

It also requires a constant awareness that inequalities of power have significant impact on the economy of honour:

> it is not safe to provoke with insults those who have it in their power to do actual harm when they choose; also . . . the powerful should not let themselves be unduly angered by the words of lesser people – there is sufficient retaliation in the knowledge that they, the powerful, can exact vengeance whenever they will, whereas the others have nothing at their command but words of abuse.[41]

This prudential advice, acknowledges that part of the specialised knowledge of public life is knowing how to use hostility for improvement of oneself. The lessons of Plutarch's essay "How to Profit from your

---

[39] Erasmus, *Education*, 21–22. [40] Erasmus, *Education*, 45.
[41] Erasmus, *Apophthegmata*, 1.215, 105. This is how it is translated by Macault: "Les avertissant qu'il n'y a pas grande seurete d'iniurier ceux qui a l'effet peuvent nuyre quand ils veulent. Et aussi qu'il ne fault point que les grans se courroussent si fort du parler de leurs inferieurs et plus bas: car ils sont assez vengez de se pouvoir venger quand il leur plaist: veu qu'il ne reste aux autres que le mal parler." 56.

Enemies," an essay that Erasmus translated and offered to a patron, are repeated throughout his translations of Plutarch's *Sayings*:

> Philip used to say he felt very grateful to Athenian politicians because their abuse had made him improve in both eloquence and character, "as I tried to prove them liars both by my words and by my deeds."
>
> This king truly had a philosophical nature, in knowing how to derive benefit even from his enemies. Instead of behaving like most people, who aim only to harm those who abuse them, he aimed to improve himself, taking warning from their abuse.[42]

Despite the heavy demands on the ruler, and the specialised knowledge that is required, in other words the need for political prudence, Erasmus acknowledges that the ruler has particularly difficult challenges in learning the art of rule due to the riskiness of the field, in which mistakes are rarely tolerated and where time is often of the essence. While in other matters individuals may learn from their mistakes through experience, this is often not possible, or at least not advisable, in the realm of politics given how much is at stake.[43] Because of this, Erasmus suggests that some theoretical training can be good for the ruler: "the prince's mind will be educated in the first instance by established principles and ideas, in such a way that he gains his knowledge from theory and not practice." Their knowledge should then be supplemented by advice from older individuals as a substitute for the lack of experience.[44] While this may seem to be in contradiction with what Erasmus dictated in his earlier *Institution*, it can be acknowledged that theoretical training is something to be taught at an earlier stage when the prince is young and living in leisure, whereas in the midst of public duties a prince will only have time and energy for maxims and practical advice.

Regardless of the ever-present danger of excessive flattery that will fuel naturally tyrannical ambitions, Erasmus places great importance in the hands of the educator and advisor:

> Plutarch has good reason for thinking that no man does the state a greater service than he who equips a prince's mind, which must consider all men's interests, with the highest principles, worthy of a prince.[45]

---

[42] Erasmus, *Apophthegmata*, II.6, 337.

[43] "Darius, the father of Xerxes, used to say in his own commendation that he had learnt wisdom through battles and hardships.

But this kind of wisdom costs a state too much. It is better for a prince to derive discernment from the teachings of philosophy than to acquire from experience what they call a sad kind of wisdom." *Apophthegmata*, V.4, 457.

[44] Erasmus, *Education*, 20.   [45] Erasmus, *Education*, 2.

Perhaps it is no wonder that we have come full circle, placing the key to good rule in the very form of the advice book that seeks to lay out these principles for the prince. In a similar vein, the *Apophthegmata* sought to provide practical maxims already expressed by those in power to guide the public figure in matters of concrete decision-making.[46] So the function of a tutor and advisor is to ensure that the ruler has a commitment to virtue and an aversion to vice, and this through a vivid depiction of both good and bad types of rulers. Interestingly, the model of the good prince does not invoke any specific historical example, but only an outline of the contours of 'a celestial creature':

> more like a divinity than a mortal, complete with every single virtue; born for the common good, sent indeed by the powers to alleviate the human condition by looking out for and caring for everyone; to whom nothing is more important or more dear than the state; who has more than a fatherly disposition towards everyone; who holds the life of each individual dearer than his own; who works and strives night and day for nothing else than that conditions should be the best possible for everyone; with whom rewards are ready for all good men and pardon for the wicked if only they will mend their ways, for he wants so much to do well by his people of his own free will that is necessary he would not hesitate to attend to their wellbeing at great risk to himself; who considers that his own wealth consists in the welfare of his country; who is always on the watch so that everyone else may sleep soundly; who leaves himself no leisure so that his country has the chance to live in peace; who torments himself with constant anxieties so that his subjects may enjoy peace of mind. Let the happiness of whole people depend upon the moral quality of this one man; let the tutor point this out as the picture of a true prince![47]

The nature of this hypothetical example is quite extraordinary. It depicts an anxiety-ridden person, certainly not the eudaimonic soul of classical philosophy said to be most fit for rule. It is also someone for whom the idea of a public good and public service has real meaning, one which exists at great cost to personal goals. The exact definition and nature of public justice which supplies the substance to the ideal of public good remains quite vague in Erasmus's work up to this point (we have seen that good

---

[46] "those wrestling with the problems of peace and war need to have to hand specific thoughts which will help them to decide what is the appropriate course of action in the circumstances and what is not . . . .A man does great service to a busy ruler when he presents him with the gold ready refined and shaped, who offers him gems already selected, cleaned and mounted in gold or set in goblets. Many have sought to do this service but no one in my opinion performed it better than Plutarch." Erasmus "Dedicatory Epistle," *Education*, 4–5.

[47] Erasmus, *Education*, 26.

intentions are not sufficient for effective political rule), but there is no question that he articulates a stringent demand for commitment to public welfare over and against the wishes and desires of the self.

While the exemplum of good rule is a hypothetical and divine construction, that of bad rule invokes both the tyrants of classical history and mythology and the worst characteristics of the Platonic unjust soul.

> On the other side, let him thrust before his pupil's eyes a terrible, loathsome beast; formed of a dragon, wolf, lion, viper, bear and similar monsters; having hundreds of eyes all over it, teeth everywhere, fearsome from all angles, and with hooked claws; having a hunger that is never satisfied, fattened on human entrails and intoxicated with human blood; an unsleeping menace to the fortunes and lives of all men, dangerous to everyone especially to the good, a sort of fateful blight on the whole world, which everyone who has the interests of the state at heart curses and hates; intolerable in its monstrousness and yet incapable of being removed without great destruction to the world, because its malevolence is supported by armed forces and wealth. This is the picture of a tyrant unless something even more hateful can be depicted. Claudius and Caligula were this sort of monster; and so, as represented in the stories of the poets, were Busiris, Pentheus, and Midas.[48]

The inherently repulsive quality of the image is reinforced by Erasmus's claim that the historical and mythological examples of bad rulers are universal objects of hate. The monstrousness of the bad ruler is judged even worse than the work of the predators of the natural world because those of the human world attack their own kind.

What are the sought after virtues, or to be more precise, what is the content of justice from Erasmus's perspective? We know that the priority of the public good appears to be the overriding factor, but how is this reconciled with an objective sense of justice and right, in other words, how is the content of the public good defined?

One fundamental principle appears to be the minimisation of harm. Erasmus suggests that the ruler must at certain points tolerate injuries inflicted on his people if the cost of retaliation and avenging them will bring greater harm to more.[49] Indeed, if the possibility of great bloodshed is imminent in response to a military threat, Erasmus suggests that it would be better for the ruler to abdicate and accept defeat to avoid precipitating the loss of lives. As we have seen, Erasmus goes even farther in his dedication addressed to the young prince Charles, suggesting "you owe it

---

[48] Erasmus, *Education*, 27.   [49] Erasmus, *Education*, 19.

to heaven that your empire came to you without the shedding of blood and no one suffered for it; your wisdom must now ensure that you preserve it without bloodshed and at peace."[50] Taken at face value this is a radical suggestion that is highly at odds with the norms of the day.[51] "To a Christian prince every victory should be an occasion for sorrow when it involves the destruction of many men, even if they are enemies."[52]

Another principle is acknowledging the fundamental importance of the protection of the possessions and security of the subjects. Rule for the good of all for Erasmus involves ensuring the safety of property.[53] Linked to this is a need for the powerful not to treat the weak poorly. This is raised in Erasmus's commentary on remarks of Theopompus in the *Apophthegmata*:

> Many princes have been destroyed because they allowed their friends total liberty of action and ignored the injustices inflicted on the people. A middle course should be followed here: a ruler should neither alienate his supporters by tyrannical harshness, nor let them abuse their familiarity with him and do what they like to the common people with complete disregard for justice; for the common people, when goaded beyond endurance, have often thrown off their rulers.[54]

The same principle is raised more evocatively in relation to Agesilaus, king of Sparta, who, after watching a boy bitten fiercely by a captured mouse, says to his companions: "Since a little creature avenges itself like that on those who injure it, just think what men should do." Erasmus suggests that this could be understood as one of the many ways in which this king sought to inspire his troops to fight with more courage, but then he goes on to suggest from a perspective of prudential governance (questions of mercy aside) that the incident shows better "that no one, however powerful, should provoke someone weaker than himself by ill-treatment."

---

[50] Erasmus, *Education*, 3.

[51] There are a number of passages in the *Apophthegmata* where Erasmus comments on tendencies to violence and conflict in his own day: "war should not be embarked upon thoughtlessly....princes today often rush into hostilities without consulting, or indeed in opposition to, the will of the leading men and the cities." 1.12, 26

[52] Erasmus, *Apophthegmata*, 1.45, 40.

[53] "If you cannot look after the possessions of your subjects without danger to your own life, set the safety of the people before your own." Erasmus, *Education*, 19.

[54] Erasmus, *Apophthegmata*, 1.192, 96. For Macault this becomes even more emphatically a statement about the challenge of managing friendships in public life, echoing the comments made in Tory's translation of Plutarch's "Political Precepts": "Cela a este cause de la ruine de plusieurs princes, qu'ils ont permie toutes choses a leurs amys privez: et qu'ilz ne se sont aucunement souciez de l'iniure ou dommage fait a leurs suiectz: et en cela fault user d'un moyen c'est que le prince n'estrange point ses amys par une trop grande familiarite iusques a oser entreprendre toutes choses, oultre le droit, contre les subiectz particuliers. Lesquelz par trop irritez ont souventesfois chasse leurs tyranz." (50).

In broader terms, this raises Erasmus's sensitivity to the problems of inequality of power and status. Although he does not repudiate all inequality as a structuring principle of social and political order, he also states: "equality nourishes peace and tranquility, whereas inequality is a seed-bed of sedition; . . . there is no place for justice where greater power implies greater licence to oppress the weak."[55]

The virtue of generosity, while central to the work of the skillful and vigilant Erasmian prince is understood in a capacious way, not limited or defined by liberality in material terms, but also understood in terms of time and effort, through giving advice and using their authority to raise those cast down.[56] Again, prudence defines that the virtues as implemented in public life take on their own unique shape and application.

Fairness through the rejection of the selling of public office, intolerance towards bribery and corruption and vigilance to ensure one's personal enmities or desires do not get into the way of public judgement are also advocated as principles of conduct in public office, supplemented by and guarded with a strong sense of public honour.[57] One exception to this principle is in the exercise of clemency, where Erasmus suggests that there are times one should acquiesce to the demands of friends if it involves using your power to pardon.[58]

On a more general level, overall, the ruler must seek to avoid hatred and contempt, incited most often through displays of brutality, violence, insults, sullenness, obstinacy and greed.[59] The good will of the people, according to Erasmus, is fostered by the ruler's demonstration of mercy, friendliness, fairness, courtesy, and compassion (following the old Ciceronian adage that it is in a ruler's interest to act honourably). All these are relational qualities, describing how the ruler should act in interactions with others. Erasmus adds that good will is fostered through cultivation of ties with those who are most approved of by the people,

---

[55] Erasmus, *Apophthegmata*, 1. 239, 113.   [56] Erasmus, *Education*, 77.

[57] "So long as you follow what is right, do violence to no one, extort from no one, sell no public office, and are corrupted by no bribes, then to be sure, your treasury will have far less in it than otherwise. But disregard the impoverishment of the treasury, so long as you are showing a profit in justice. . . . Do your personal feelings as a man (such as anger provoked by insults, love for your wife, hatred of an enemy, shame) urge you to do what is not right and what is not to the advantage of the state? Let your regard for what is honourable win, and let your concern for the public welfare conquer your private emotions." Erasmus, *Education*, 19.

[58] "It is wicked to punish an innocent man, but occasionally to condone a guilty act as a favour to a respected person who speaks up for the accused is to show decent human feeling. Justice should always be tempered with clemency, but when a person of standing interposes, there is less resentment, more approval." Erasmus, *Apophthegmata*, 1.18, 30.

[59] Erasmus, *Education*, 69

including appointing them as associates and granting them honours. The good will of the people in turn leads them favourably to their own efforts of public service, especially if there is a possibility of royal recognition and reward.[60] So the ruler must not only follow an inner compass regulating the rules of honest and virtuous behaviour, but must be particularly sensitive to the tone and quality of their interactions and see their role in part as inspiring others to serve both through incentives as well as through their own example. Again, the nature of political prudence requires special sensitivity to interpersonal dynamics. One overriding objective in ruling is to encourage people in their pursuit of honour, but not to a degree that results in civil strife, which he calls a "virulent poison in the national body."[61] This suggests the need for a fine balance between supporting competition and encouraging concord.

Despite a predominant emphasis on the nature of political prudence in public life that allows for unique forms of application in a public setting, one also finds in Erasmus concessions to a more pragmatic outlook where the overriding norms of public life may deviate in certain ways with those of the civil realm. An important issue in this regard is honesty as a virtue in public life. This is evident in Erasmus's commentary on the sayings attributed to the Spartan king Archidamus: "There are times for speaking bluntly and times for being conciliatory; times for pleasant words, time for harsh ones. If no treachery is involved, this is sensible behaviour. Stupid men who do not know how to adapt to people and circumstances are called 'muttonheads.'" Furthermore, Erasmus suggests that the most important commitment of the ruler is to uphold their underlying obligations to the people, even if it means breaking a promise made in passing.

> A certain person kept badgering Agesilaus, relentlessly pursuing him with some petition and saying, "You promised," over and over again, as if that constituted some moral obligation not to deny the request. "Quite right," said Agesilaus. "If what you ask is justified, I did promise; if it is not, then I spoke but I didn't promise." (By these words he cut the ground from under the importunate fellow's feet.) He however was still not prepared to desist and brought in a new argument: "All the same, kings should honour anything to which they give their royal nod." "And petitioners to kings," said Agesilaus, "should just as much come with justifiable requests and legitimate appeals, choosing the right moment and bearing in mind what is right and proper for kings to grant."
>
> Some people spring on kings out of ambush, as it were, and demand something unjustifiable of them when they have been drinking or when they

---

[60] Erasmus, *Education*, 67–69.   [61] Erasmus, *Apophthegmata*, 1.346, 153.

are busy with something else, and so cannot consider properly what kind of request is being put to them. It is quite right to go back on a promise made to such people, and wrong of them, when refused, to demand that the promiser keep faith, since they did not remember their own obligations when making their requests.[62]

The broad point being made here is that general commitments to serve a broader public can and do trump certain promises made to individuals, especially if made in the heat of the moment and without regard to one's public responsibilities (or perhaps without a lack of adequate information). It suggests that one's public position can give rise to moral tension, but that the greater moral trump stands with a broader sense of obligation. It is a tension that plays out only for those in public office and is resolved by acknowledging the greater ethical force of public justification.

In addition, alongside a predominant rule of the need to minimise harm, Erasmus is aware that mercy and compassion can be exercised to excess, undermining the very grounds of authority.

> Cleomenes heard one of the citizens saying that a good king ought to be absolutely mild and gentle towards everyone. "Yes," he said, "but not enough to make them despise him."
>
> He meant that to show too much kindness towards the evildoer is of no use to the state. He was also referring to certain people who learn to despise outstandingly good and merciful rulers when they ought to be devoted to them. To be sure, approachability and gentleness in a ruler is a very fine thing; but because of the wickedness of people it has to be tempered, so that the prince retains his authority.[63]

This is reiterated in the case of Philip of Macedon:

> Philip used to advise his son Alexander to keep on friendly terms with the Macedonians, so as to win strength and power by acquiring general goodwill while someone else was ruling and he could still afford to be humane.
>
> He realized that nothing so sustained authority as the goodwill of citizens: but it was very difficult for anyone exercising a monarchy to be humane with all and sundry, not only because royal power is exposed to jealousy, but because a state cannot remain unharmed unless crimes are disciplined by punishment.

---

[62] Erasmus, *Apophthegmata*, 1.6, 23.

[63] Erasmus, *Apophthegmata*, 1.209, 107. Again, as translated by Macault the commentary reads: "Signifiant qu'entre les malconditionez, une trop grande douceur est damageable a la communaute: et que la coustume de plusieurs est que la ou plus ils devroient aymer leurs princes tres bons et clemens, ils apprennent a les despriser. Et certes, c'est une belle vertu a un prince que mansuetude et douceur: mais pour le malengin des mauvais, il la fault temperer de sorte, que l'auctorite en demeure au prince." (57).

So kings must dilute their humanity towards their citizens enough to preserve their royal authority. For too much kindness often breeds contempt.[64]

Thus, the need to preserve public authority requires a specific type of public ethic. Still, this does not mean a repudiation of humanity, but a prudential consideration bordering on the pragmatic of how that ethos must be approached with a broader perspective in mind, one that is specific to the occupation of public office and the wider demands to which one is subject.

A final addition in the spirit of Aristotle, though curiously included almost as a passing thought in the text, is the suggestion by Erasmus that a prince who lacks perfect virtues (i.e. all princes) would preferably rule in a monarchical regime that was mixed, in other words, combined with aspects of aristocracy and democracy, so as to guard against tyranny.[65] While an institutional consideration, it is a surprisingly limited and vague allusion to a broad tradition of thinking about various modes of mixed government. It offers the suggestion that institutional configurations are considered as means to an end, that is, a style and spirit of rule, rather than a central consideration in thinking about the art of governance. In his *Apophthegmata,* Erasmus suggests that the institutional configuration of a political community is less important that the more informal system through which honour and honours are distributed.[66]

---

[64] Erasmus, *Apophthegmata*, 11.15, 340. Again, in Macault's translation: "Sagement entendant qu'un empire ne peult estre mieux estably par aucune chose que ce soit, que par la benevolence des citoyens. Aussi qu'il estoit tres dificile que luy estant venu au royaume il se peust monstrer humain envers un chascun: non pas seulement pour ce que la puissance royale est suiecte a envie, mais aussi pour ce qu'une Republicque ne peult demourer saine, si les abuz ne sont restraintz par supplices et peines. Et certes les Roys doivent moderer envers les citoyens leur humanite iusques a la, que tousiours leur auctorite royale y soit gardee: car une trop grande bonte engendre souvent mespris et contennement." (185).

[65] "If it happens that your prince is complete with all the virtues, then monarchy pure and simple is the thing. But since this would probably never happen, although it is a fine ideal to entertain, if no more than an ordinary man is presented (things being what they are nowadays), then monarchy should preferably be checked and diluted with a mixture of aristocracy and democracy to prevent it ever breaking out into tyranny; and just as the elements mutually balance each other, so let the state be stabilised with a similar control. For if the prince is well disposed to the state, he will conclude that under such a system his power is not restricted but sustained. But if he is not, it is all the more necessary as something to blunt and break the violence of one man." Erasmus, *Education*, 37.

[66] "These two things, honour and disgrace, are of prime importance in maintaining discipline in any group of people. Honours nourish not only arts, as the proverb says, but also virtue. What is important is not whether we have monarchy, aristocracy, democracy, or some form of government combining elements of all three, but whether under any constitution a distinction is made at public level between those who contribute to the state and those who serve only their own base pleasures." Erasmus, *Apophthegmata*, 1.299, 136.

The goal of the ruler, it might be said, was to be emblematic, a living tribute to the principles by which he lived, perhaps best demonstrated by the words of Agesilaus along with Erasmus's commentary:

> The people who inhabited Greece at that time decreed that statues should be erected in his honour in all the chief cities, but he wrote back: "There is to be no representation of my person either painted or modelled or produced by any other technique."
>
> The general run of rulers was of the opinion that this kind of honour put them on a level with the gods, and considered it the supreme reward for their achievements. Agesilaus was content with honour itself and scorned such flatteries, for such they were, not real occasions of glory. He preferred to have his image carved on the hearts of wise and good men, rather than stand fashioned in bronze or gold in their public places. There is a special honour that naturally follows in the train of outstanding virtue. No statue can be as impressive as the admiring recollection of a life well lived.[67]

In sum, Erasmus contributes to a discussion of the nature of public life by providing a much more textured understanding of the psychological facets and ethical challenges of rule than his counterpart Budé. Both tend to focus on their own expansive notions of prudence, although Erasmus does allow for certain pragmatic considerations. While Budé alludes to the need for a special individual who instantiates the heroic virtues to ensure a glorious exercise of power, he provides little guidance for the development or channelling of such capacities. Erasmus acknowledges the danger of such an approach and cautions those in power to be aware of the broader impact of their decisions. In particular, he sheds light on the nature of the relations between the ruler and various groups of subjects, providing advice on the management of hostilities as well as the contours and limits in applying conventional virtues of honesty and compassion in public life.

4.2 Claude de Seyssel

Claude de Seyssel is one of the first among French Renaissance thinkers, and clearly the first eminent French political theorist, to translate Plutarch. He also appears to be among the first to work on a vernacular translation of selected *Lives*.[68]

Perhaps it is no accident that he made his home for a large part of his career in France despite his Savoyard origins. Scholars in France often

---

[67] Erasmus, *Apophthegmata*, 1.27, 33.

[68] As we have seen in note 25 of Chapter 3, Simon de Bourgouyn appears to have been the first as far as we can tell with the translation of at least three lives completed prior to the death of a patron in 1503.

placed their attention on Greek traditions, whereas in the Italian context there was a preference for the Latin classics, (with the exception of a few including Chrysoloras in Florence and Demetrius Chalcondyle in Milan).[69] Mombello suggests that Seyssel's stay in Milan in the early 1500s might have provided him an opportunity to develop an interest in the Greeks, along with a possible first meeting with Jean Lascaris who was there in April 1500.[70] However, we know that Seyssel's fascination with Greek historians was less scholarly in that he was not driven to learn ancient Greek well enough to translate the texts from the original sources.

On two occasions, Seyssel chose to translate excerpts from Plutarch into the vernacular to complete an historical account for which another classical historian was the primary focus. Plutarch's work was included in two of the seven works that Seyssel is known to have translated and presented to his employer Louis XII. In 1507 Seyssel translated the work of Appian of Alexandria on the *Wars of the Romans*, to which he added part of Plutarch's life of Mark Antony. In 1510 Seyssel offered a translation of three books from the work of Diodorus Siculus on the successors of Alexander the Great (Books 18–20 of the *Bibliotheca*), to which Seyssel added at the end an excerpt from Plutarch's life of Demetrius. Both works were published posthumously, and the first was subsequently translated into English by Thomas Stocker and published in London in 1569.

There are features that make Seyssel's choice of Plutarch for translation curious.[71] Given Seyssel's identification in the scholarly literature as either a constitutionalist or a pragmatic political realist focused on the science of conquest and advising Louis XII on the same, why take an interest in translating Plutarch at all, particularly Plutarch's *Lives* where he is most clearly a virtue theorist, or at least interested in individual characters and their successes and failures in the context of broader social and political conditions?[72]

---

[69] Gianni Mombello, "Du Doute a la conscience du succès: Le Cas de Claude de Seyssel (1504–1514)," in Charles Brucker ed., *Traduction et adaptation en France. Actes du Colloque organisé par l'Université de Nancy II 23–25 mars 1995* (Paris: Honoré Champion, 1997), 26.

[70] Mombello, "Seyssel," 26–27.

[71] I say ally of the humanists rather than a humanist himself because, as Rebecca Boone has pointed out, he had little connection or correspondence with the leading humanists of his day, such as Budé or Erasmus, apart from his collaboration with Lascaris, and he remained largely outside the community of writers at the French court. See her "Claude de Seyssel's Translations of Ancient Historians," *Journal of the History of Ideas* 61.4 (2000), 561–575.

[72] Keohane in *Philosophy and the State* as well as J. W. Allen [*A History of Political Thought in the Sixteenth Century* (New York: The Dial Press, 1928)] identify Seyssel within a broader constitutionalist tradition. Rebecca Boone in *War and Domination and the Monarchy of France. Claude de Seyssel*

In addition, using Plutarch to complete a more standard classical historical account was a rather awkward choice. As noted earlier, Plutarch himself never saw his work as comparable with that of other ancient historians because his focus in the *Lives* was on the revelation of character as opposed to historical chronology. He states explicitly at the outset of "Alexander" that his interest in his historical figures lies in the quieter moments when their full characters are revealed rather than in the great moments of public display and accomplishment. This sets Plutarch apart from the other historians with which he is paired in these two compilations.

A third curious feature is the recourse to the lives of Antony and Demetrius that Seyssel tacked onto the two respective translations noted here. These are not random choices but present a pair in Plutarch's work. We know that Jean Lascaris, the humanist scholar with whom Seyssel collaborated on these translations, had in his possession a full manuscript of Plutarch's *Lives* in Greek, so it was not the case that these were the only lives that were available to Seyssel. Plutarch presents this comparison as one with a novel twist in his work overall, one where he focuses on qualities that could be considered merits or deficiencies depending on the circumstances, but that in the end lead the subject of the narrative to their political downfall. It was the same feel for tragedy that must have inspired Shakespeare to take up Plutarch's account as an important source for his "Anthony and Cleopatra." These lives are moral dramas associated with tragedy and ultimate moral failure. What then did Seyssel intend in his use of these Lives to complete two separate translations based largely on other historical works?

A fourth question is why Seyssel did not choose to translate these lives in their entirety but only in excerpts. Of course, time may have been a consideration, for we know that Seyssel had many responsibilities as a counsellor to the king, as a bishop in the church and as a diplomat, just to name a few of his roles. Still, the choices of not only these lives, but also the events within them deemed most important for Seyssel may help us to gain a deeper sense of not only the purpose of these translations, but also the broader outlook of Seyssel himself.

I argue that his translations and political reflections need to be explored through a broader lens than as an extension of his diplomatic role advising

and the Language of Politics in the Renaissance (Leiden and Boston: Brill, 2007) explores Seyssel's thought in the light of political realism with particular interest in the consolidation of French territories in Italy and the consideration of possible threat emanating from Savoie.

Louis XII in the Italian campaigns. Indeed, despite Seyssel's status as a foreigner in France, his concern about the functioning of the French monarchy is already evident in his preface to the 1510 translation of Appian. The recourse to a translation of the lives of Antony and Demetrius provides a dramatic illustration of Seyssel's intuition that the good character of rulers is often insufficient as a basis for effective political rule, thereby signalling his departure from some of the humanist arguments of his time, arguments that he had recourse to in his 1508 *Louenges* but which he abandoned by the time of his drafting of *La Monarchie de France* in 1515. In broad terms, Seyssel's use of Plutarch in the lives of Antony and Demetrius can be understood as both informing and justifying a model of good government and no longer appealing to the good character of the monarch. From this point on, Seyssel invokes customs and practices that sustain the functioning of the regime, and which can provide potential institutional checks on the sovereign.

Seyssel's recourse to Plutarch cannot be made sense of through a conception of republicanism in early modern Europe as drawing from the Greek tradition of prioritising justice, nor through the jurisprudential lens of neo-Bartolist readings of Roman law (despite Seyssel's academic work as a neo-Bartolist law professor at the University of Turin) to give greater weight to the notion of imperium that was to enhance absolutist claims to monarchical sovereignty.[73] In Seyssel's case at least, the classical sources appear to offer an admirable but less than ideal set of practices from which to distill certain principles for practical advice in administering and managing a kingdom.

I will first explore notable features of Seyssel's translations of Plutarch completed in the early 1500s and then proceed to explore their significance within his broader political reflection, most notably their possible connection to major themes of his major work, *La Monarchie de France*.

According to Chavy, in the early Renaissance new editions of works of classical antiquity tended initially to be reissued versions of earlier publications, such as Oresme's translations of Aristotle. It was only after 1510, and particularly after 1526, most notably in France, that new editions of the classics no longer relied on the scholarship of translators from an earlier time. New scholars of ancient languages, including Erasmus, sought out the older manuscripts and worked on their own new translations of classical literature. Erasmus's translation of essays from Plutarch's *Moralia* opened several new avenues for reflection. Apart from the early

---

[73] Nelson, *The Greek Tradition,* and Skinner, *Foundations.*

translation of Plutarch's essay "On Anger" by Nic. De Gonesse in 1401, and published c. 1476, it would appear that many of the subsequent essays appearing in the vernacular between 1520 and 1540 were a direct result of Erasmus's work in Latin, including "How to Distinguish a Friend from a Flatterer," "How to Profit from One's Enemies," "Political Precepts," "On the Education of Children," "Exploits of Women," and "Apophthegmes," although some authors, like Thomas Wyatt, whose "Queyte of mynde," (1528) was one of the first English print versions of any Greek author, took their inspiration from the Greek to Latin transla-tions of Guillaume Budé.[74] Commentary on historical and political figures and distilled anecdotes as found in Plutarch's *Sayings* were taken up in Renaissance France much more readily than in England (where the moral essays took prominence in the vernacular for the most part) as a prelude to the famous translation of the *Lives* by Amyot 1559–1565.[75] While there had been a few editions of Plutarch's *Lives* in Italian and Spanish at the turn of the century along with some Latin editions, Seyssel was one of the first (and the first canonical political theorist) to translate any of Plutarch's *Lives* into the vernacular French.[76] It has been argued that Seyssel was not a scholarly humanist like others of his time (as he relied on his friend Lascaris to translate Plutarch from Greek to Latin as noted earlier), but it should be acknowledged that his contributions still place him on the cutting edge of humanist scholarship. The fact that one of his translations was taken up and retranslated into English is recognition of the value of his contribution.[77]

Seyssel's choices place him in front of another trend of humanist scholarship in France at the time, which was the translation of works from the Greek tradition rather than the Roman.[78] Some suggest that the French sought out Greek authors to cultivate some distance from the

[74] See Paul Chavy, "Les Traductions humanists au début de la Renaissance française: traductions médiévales, traductions modernes," *Canadian Review of Comparative Literature* (Spring 1981), 302. On Thomas Wyatt, see Susan Brigden, *Thomas Wyatt. The Hearts Forest* (London: Faber and Faber, 2012), 135–143

[75] See note 13.

[76] The USTC shows a 1482 Italian edition of Plutarch's *Lives* translated by Battista Alessandro Jaconello, and a 1491 Spanish edition by Alfonso de Palencia. Other editions of the *Lives* were issued in Italian in 1518 and 1525, although I could not determine if these are reissues of the earlier edition.

[77] Diodorus Siculus, *A Righte noble and pleasant history of the successors of Alexander surnamed the Great*, taken out of Diodorus Siculus, and some of their lives written by the wise Plutarch, translated out of French into English by Thomas Stocker, (London, Henrie Bynneman, 1569).

[78] Along with Appian, Diodorus Siculus and Plutarch, Seyssel also produced translations of Thucydides and Xenophon.

Italians, as it allowed the French to develop a distinct sense of cultural roots. In the sixteenth century we see a continuing trend of the early modern French monarchy actively promoting its cultural link to the Trojans. In addition, as we have seen in the case of Tory, it was felt that the Greek language had particular and unique qualities of image and tone that through translation could serve to beautify and embellish the French language. In the case of Seyssel, it might also have been a case of serendipity and curiosity. Seyssel encountered Lascaris during his diplomatic work and despite Lascaris's lack of good French he was brought back to the French court by Charles VIII, presumably to enhance humanistic studies there. Seyssel drew on his work and good will to make available, initially just for the court, various accounts from the Greek never before available in the vernacular in France.[79] Evidence of the close association of these two officials in Charles VIII's court is found not only in the lending and translating of manuscripts, but also by the fact that Seyssel ended his most important political treatise in promoting a cause central to the concerns of Lascaris: the need for Western powers, and particularly the king of France, to embark on another crusade to free the holy land from domination by the Turks.

The first excerpt from Plutarch translated by Seyssel is a passage (starting at s. LIII) of the "Life of Antony" which Seyssel appended to a longer translation of Appian of Alexander's *Wars of the Romans*. This excerpt which concludes the volume focuses on the sixth civil war, specifically the Battle of Actium, that helped to seal the transition from republican to imperial rule. It is suggested this translation dates from 1507. A few years later in 1511, Seyssel embarked on the translation of a portion of the "Life of Demetrius" (starting at s. XXIX) which he appended to his translation of Diodorus Siculus and again presented to the king and his entourage. Like in the first translation of Antony, this life of Demetrius also concluded the work.[80]

---

[79] As argued by Boone, "Between 1540 and 1550 French humanists including Amyot, Du Bellay, Ronsard, Dolet and Pasquier feverishly translated and imitated the works of ancient Greece in an effort to both improve and glorify the French language." *War, Domination and the Monarchy of France*, 94. According to Patricia Eichel-Lojkine, the interest in Greek studies at the French court dates from the arrival of Lascaris after the first Italian campaign of Charles VIII. The first work printed in Greek in France (chez Gilles de Gourmont) appeared in 1507. See *Claude de Seyssel. Écrire l'histoire, penser le politique en France, à l'aube des temps modernes* (Paris: Presses Universitaires de France, 2010), 7.

[80] Appian of Alexandria, Wars of the Romans and Plutarch, Life of Mark Antony. Paris, Bibliothèque Nationale, MS Fr. 713–714 (1507?). Another presentation copy dedicated to Louis XII exists in the Biblioteca Nazionale di Torino (L.III.1). This copy was severely damaged by a fire in 1904. And Diodorus Siculus, books XVIII, XIX, XX of Bibliotheca and Plutarch, Life of Demetrius. Paris, Bibliothèque Nationale, Ms. Fr. 712 (1511).

According to Boone, the nature and purpose of Seyssel's translations should be considered in a different light to the works of his humanist contemporaries.[81] Seyssel's translations were not published in his own lifetime. He wrote them for use at court with no immediate interest in their wider circulation for purposes of more general edification.[82] In addition, as Boone notes, Seyssel did not fit the ideal profile of many of the leading humanists of his time, given that he was a Savoyard in the employ of the French king as a royal councillor for much of his life and helped to coordinate French rule over the duchy of Milan. Even though he had been a legal scholar in his early years teaching at the University of Milan, when he made these translations his focus was not at all scholarly but political, seeking to secure France's hold within Italy. As suggested by Chavy and supported by Boone, the purpose of Seyssel's translations was to demonstrate his utility as a councillor to the king. Indeed, Boone goes further to suggest that these translations were done with two main aims: first, to provide illustrations of ancient military tactics, tactics still viable in Renaissance conquest; and second, to make rulers aware of the specific danger posed by republican military forces, including by extension, the Swiss in his own era.[83] In Boone's account, Seyssel was less interested in the working of the French monarchy itself, and more interested in the matters with which he was directly concerned in his political and administrative career, namely negotiations with the Swiss and consolidation of French rule over parts of Italy.

Boone's thesis seeks to make sense of Seyssel's translations as a whole. Still, if we look to the choices of Appian and Diodorus Siculus, to which the lives of Antony and Demetrius were added, we might find a different logic. First, why translate these authors? We can find evidence for his reasons in Seyssel's introduction to these works.

Seyssel's introduction to the translation of Appian (1511) demonstrates his concern with how best to avoid tyranny. Seyssel begins with a discussion of the best regime (based on a story of Herodotus), settling for a monarchical regime as the least pernicious option. A popular government is deemed to be disorderly, an aristocrat government is deemed too

---

[81] Boone, "Claude de Seyssel's Translations."

[82] That said, their subsequent post-mortem publication and circulation may have had effects not intended by Seyssel, including inspiration for other humanist translators at the time such as Etienne LeBlanc and Antoine Macault. On this point see V. L. Bourrilly, *Jacques Colin. Abbé de Saint-Amboise (14?–1547)* (Paris: Société nouvelle de Librairie et d'Edition, 1905), 45. Also cited by Carley, "Plus que assez," 344 n.91

[83] Boone, *War and Domination.*

agonistic and more susceptible to civil war, while a monarchy risks descent into tyranny. Seyssel suggests that to avoid dangers inherent to monarchy "qu'a un chacun soit garde sa pre-eminence et sa raison, selon son etat, et que le chef soit regle par bonnes lois et coutumes civiles, au bien de l'universalite, le plus que faire se peut ; pour obvier que sa royale et legitime puissance ne se convertisse en tyrannie et domination volontaire." [84] [that each preserve their status and reason, according to their state, and that the leader be ruled by good laws and civil customs, for the good of the whole, the most that it is possible to do; in order to avoid that his royal and legitimate power not transform into tyranny and willful domination] He goes on to suggest that the reason for the stability and endurance of the French monarchy can be found in its mix of the three forms within the monarchical regime. The king is limited by laws and ordonnances, by his council and eminent nobility, as well as by the powers and numbers of administrative officers who help to guard him from acting violently and contrary to the good of the realm. Seyssel praises the judicial structure and the Grand Conseil and the parlements who have been delegated a strong and enduring base of authority akin to that of the Roman Senate, a power which helps them curtail the effectiveness of any royal command that might seek to undermine the law. In addition, he acknowledges that certain principles of equity apply in the granting of administrative offices that allows for the representation of the nobility but also many qualified members of the third estate, thereby contributing to a more harmonious form of rule. The metaphor he invokes for the king is that of water, i.e. kings "qui sont la fontaine et la source de laquelle defluent et eminent tous les ruisseaux de bonnes polices et de justice." [85] [who are the fountain and source from which flow all the streams of good administration and justice] This discussion clearly focuses on the French monarchy.

Seyssel justifies his choice of Appian of Alexandria's history of the Romans to demonstrate the deficiencies of Roman governance and in particular the constant play of extra-institutional dissent that eventually led to the rise of tyranny. He also suggests that the vulnerable state of Italy in his own times is a long-term effect of bad governance: in other words, to avoid being Italy in the future, France needs to heed the lessons of Roman history and manage its internal deliberations well to avoid placing excessive

---

[84] Claude de Seyssel, "Proheme en la translation de l'Histoire d'Appien [1510]," in Jacques Poujol ed., *La Monarchie de France* (Paris: Libraire d'Argences, 1961), 79.
[85] Seyssel, "Proheme Appien," 84.

power in the hands of the king. Appian, of all ancient historians, is one who best brings to light the internal conflicts of the Romans.

So why include Plutarch at all? Seyssel states that only some parts of eleven of Appian's twenty-two books were extant, and their translations of poor quality. With the help of Lascaris, he was able to work from a new Latin translation of the Greek manuscript. Plutarch's account of Antony was the one extant account of the final battle between Octavian and Antony that appeared to be missing from the Appian manuscript, and Lascaris had access to it in a Greek manuscript. Still, there was a great deal more missing from the Appian manuscript than the account of that battle, and there were other possible sources to draw from to illustrate this conflict. So while the missing sections of Appian's work provides a proximate cause for the addition of Plutarch to this translation, it does not fully explain the need for Seyssel to complete the account and translation of Appian's history with a section of Plutarch's life of Antony.[86] In addition, the insertion of Plutarch's voice in the concluding portion of this account of the civil wars provides a particular inflection of the overall message of the translation and offers an especially powerful illustration of Seyssel's message in the introduction. In other words, the life of Antony helped to powerfully demonstrate the dangers of sustaining good government on the character of one ruler alone.

Seyssel chose not to translate the entirety of the "life of Antony" but instead took up Plutarch's narrative when he begins to give an account of the Battle of Actium. What is left out is an insightful narrative of Antony's retreat from Asia and from the forces of the Medes. Plutarch gives an account of the distinct military formations used by Antony to protect his forces in this retreat, something that might be useful from a military and strategic point of view; but Seyssel omits this in his translation.

What then of Demetrius and why was his life inserted at the end of Seyssel's translation of Diodorus Siculus on the successors of Alexander? As we have seen, Demetrius was paired with Antony in Plutarch's *Lives* and both were deemed by Plutarch to demonstrate examples of leadership and command that were deeply flawed and to be regarded as counterexamples. Again, the proximate cause of the inclusion of the life of Demetrius to Diodorus Siculus's account of the successors of Alexander was the lacunae in the available manuscripts. The third book of the historian's account of Antigonus and Demetrius did not include an account of Demetrius's death

---

[86] In addition, we could suggest that the significance of this, especially for the concluding chapter of this translation, may surpass the actual intention of the author.

which Seyssel then provided with his recourse to Plutarch. Still, by complementing and completing Diodorus with Plutarch's account, Seyssel may in fact have modified the overarching message of this text.

In his preface to this translation of Diodorus and Plutarch, Seyssel begins with a classic discussion of whether to attribute the great accomplishments of history to virtue or to fortune. He suggests that divine omnipotence has replaced the idea of fortune, but that the unfolding of human affairs still can appear mysterious, unpredictable and unknowable and so in this context a cultivation of virtue is needed to handle the blows of providence. In making allusion to the recent success of King Louis XII in his Italian campaign, but also to his moderation in holding back from seeking to conquer the lands held by the Holy See, Seyssel makes the case for the importance of virtue as an important force in history against a background of constant mutation and change given the basic fragility, instability and imperfection of things.[87] Here he acknowledges that insights into military strategy could be gained by a king reading the translated text, but the lessons were not limited to that, and indeed there is little allusion to those themes in the sections of Demetrius's life from Plutarch that complete the work.[88]

The content from Demetrius's life relates to another theme highlighted by Seyssel in his introduction, namely a warning for a powerful political actor who engages in excessive self-aggrandisement (we might suggest that this is a message and usage of Plutarch in direct opposition to Budé). Demetrius is a negative example in presuming to be immune to fortune. Seyssel begins Plutarch's account around the time where Fortune turns her back on Demetrius and where the exercise of power and its accompanying flattery had made Demetrius excessively proud and his downfall more precipitous.

These two lives together serve as capstones to Seyssel's two volumes, but they are also paired by Plutarch himself because they are for him examples of a coupling of moral and strategic failure. The errors of Demetrius in his dealings with the Athenians and Antony at the Battle of Actium are rooted in fundamental character flaws. For Plutarch, these examples show that without the makings of good character, strategic judgement can be greatly compromised, for the historical actor may enter the fray of battle with weak

---

[87] *L'Histoire des successeurs de Alexandre de Grand extraicte de Diodore Sicilien et quelque peu de vies escriptes par Plutharque*, trans. Claude de Seyssel. Paris: Iehan Barbe et Claude Garamont, 1545.

[88] "quand au cours des choses mondaines, vous y verrez des cauteles et strategemes en faict de guerre: ensemble plusieurs diverses batailles, sieges et entreprises, qui sont moult plaisantes a lire et ouyr: et y peult l'on apprendre quelque chose servant a celuy mestier." *L'Histoire des successeurs*, 6.

convictions or with the wrong end in view. For Seyssel, there appears to be a project of avoiding a discussion of moral ideals. Instead he offers a cautionary tale with a heightened emphasis on the category of the bad exemplar or the vicious ruler.

In the case of the Appian volume translated first, Seyssel takes up Plutarch's narrative as Antony was preparing for his final showdown with his former ally Caesar. For Plutarch, Antony is an extraordinary man with a great gift for leadership and military command, but whose excessive love for Cleopatra led to his downfall. As he states in his introduction to the pair of Antony and Demetrius, these are examples of lives not to emulate, but to reject.[89]

Likewise, Demetrius's life shows us that great natures, while capable of virtue, can also be capable of vice. With his father Antigonus, Demetrius helped to free Greece from the subjection of Cassander and Ptolemy. However, his accomplishments led Demetrius to become excessively proud and eager for domination. He and his father made poor judgements in diplomacy and Demetrius began to take advantage of public resources to fund the lascivious habits of his friends. He did not recognise that the public honours that he had enjoyed previously were not driven by love or deep respect from the people, but by constraint and fear. He was driven from power and spent the latter part of his life overindulging in food and wine. According to Plutarch, while Demetrius did not engage in the same degree of political injustice as Antony, who appeared to hinder the cause of liberty in Rome, he demonstrated a higher degree of cruelty and caused his followers to desert him.

These two cases suggest that an individual acknowledged as a public leader (either inherited or through their own efforts) may inevitably be one who through an expected or required force of personality can offer a mix of virtues and destructive vices. Furthermore, they show that certain vices of those in a position of power can erase or undermine any gains made by previously good strategic judgement and tactical ability, thereby thwarting success in both war and in political life. In the context of Renaissance France, the lesson of Plutarch's lives of Demetrius and Antony provide a sober reply to the humanist ideals of Erasmus and Budé concerning the humanist prince. The cultivation of virtue by the individual in power may not be sufficient to deter the presence and growth of vices. In the end,

---

[89] Demetrius, 1.5: "and although I do not think that the perverting of some to secure the setting right of others is very humane, or a good civil policy, still, when men have led reckless lives, and have become conspicuous, in the exercise of power or in great undertakings, for badness, perhaps it will not be much amiss for me to introduce a pair or two of them into my biographies, though not that I may merely divert and amuse my readers by giving variety to my writing."

a good regime cannot rely on the strength of character of one person alone. This is also the message that grounds Seyssel's reflections in the introduction to his 1510 translation of Appian and serves as a starting point for his more thorough institutional and administrative prescriptions of *La Monarchie.*

Thus, the choices of the lives of Antony and Demetrius, while supplementing the work of other historians, should not be regarded as ancillary either to the broader import of the translations, nor indeed to the intellectual trajectory of Seyssel himself. That Seyssel chose to place these Plutarch translations at the end of his two manuscripts suggests they had importance for the message he wished to convey to his monarch and employer. We now turn to Seyssel's major works of political theory, written after these translations, to explore how these themes carry over into his later work.

Roughly eight years after translating Appian, and four years after translating Diodorus Siculus for the king, Seyssel wrote his *La Monarchie de France.* This text may be read through a somewhat different lens, for whereas Seyssel's translations were written while he was still in the service of the king, and with an intent to remain in good favour with his employer, *La Monarchie de France,* as is well known, was presented to Francis I at a time when Seyssel was contemplating leaving his political and diplomatic career to take up ecclesiastical duties.

Philippe Torrens suggests that we can discern continuity between Seyssel's translations of ancient historians and his political theory.[90] He argues that there is a great deal of Appian that is reflected in the text of *La Monarchie de France,* even if his work is not directly cited. This includes attention to the weaknesses of the Roman republic (due, he suggests, to the power of the tribunes), to legislative processes and to the importance of military discipline. In addition, while some of Seyssel's arguments may not reflect the views of Appian and Diodorus Siculus, it is argued that he developed aspects of his outlook through deeper consideration of aspects of those classical histories, including his endorsement of social mobility that helped to relieve social pressure in the case of the Roman republic and the importance of an effective navy for geopolitical hegemony. Apart from a vague allusion to the theme of bridles having perhaps a connection to Plutarch's work, however, Torrens remains silent on the possible links between Plutarch and Seyssel.

---

[90] Philippe Torrens, "Claude de Seyssel traducteur des historiens antiques," in *Claude de Seyssel, Écrire l'histoire, penser le politique en France, à l'aube des temps modernes* (Paris: Presses Universitaires de Rennes, 2010), 183–200.

In general, Seyssel takes a long view of history, a long view that is directly inspired by classical history. While some have found it puzzling that Seyssel appeared to be excessively obsessed with civil discord and the dangers of civil war at a time when the French kingdom was relatively peaceful, he suggests early on in his preface to the work that even a cursory view of the longer history of the French regime demonstrates repeated instances of conflict and times when the monarchy was close to ruin (we need only to think of the time of Christine de Pizan). Much like the ancient historians he read and translated, Seyssel acknowledges the need to reflect on the requirements for viability regardless of the perception of immediate threats. As he states succinctly at the end of chapter 19 of part II: "mon propos et intention en ce traicte de parler de toutes choses plus pour ladvenir que pour le present ayant principalement regard au bien du prince et a la conservation de la monarchie."[91] [my words and intention in this treatise is to speak of all things more for the future than for the present having principally regard for the good of the prince and for the preservation of the monarchy.]

The longer-term view of politics and the themes of growth and decay are also invoked through Seyssel's invocation of the corporeal metaphor of the state. As noted by Keohane, Seyssel offers a particularly striking and complex vision of political harmony.[92] He not only acknowledges the rise and fall of political structure like many of his contemporaries, he also conveys that the best sort of regime forms organic harmony. The political community like a body, or mystical body, encompasses different forces that can work towards either health or decline. Like any mortal body, states are destined for decay and dissolution in the long run, but health in the body can be achieved if the differing forces in the body can be held in balance. As he states in his discussion of the case of Venice:

> mesmes ces corps mystiques, qui sont à la semblance des corps matériels humains, lequels (pour autant qu'ils sont créés et composes de quatre éléments et humeurs contraires), jaçoit que par aucun temps se puissant entretenir et conserver en vie (à savoir tant que lesdites humeurs s'accordent), toutefois est impossible qu'à la longue l'un ne surmonte les autres et par ce moyen que la masse ne revienne à sa première matière par la dissolution de ladite compagnie; car par ordre de nature, tous lesdits éléments et humeurs, après qu'ils sont assemblés, ont augmentation, état et diminution, advenant laquelle est besoin aider à la nature et secourir celui

---

[91] Claude de Seyssel, *La Grant Monarchie de France*, part II, chap. 19. Online at http://gallica.bnf.fr/ark:/12148/btv1b8626309q/f7.item.zoom. Accessed 22 May 2016

[92] Keohane, *Philosophy and the State*.

membre et celle humeur qui se trouvent les plus faibles; mais il advient que, quand l'on cuide aider à l'un, l'on nuit à l'autre. Tout ainsi advient aux corps mystiques de la société humaine; car, après qu'ils sont assemblés par une civile et politique union, ils vont par quelque temps en accroissant et multipliant, après demeurant en leur état quelque autre temps, puis- pour autant qu'ils sont composés de plusieurs entendements et volontés discordantes et répugnantes- commencent à decliner et finalement viennent à néant.[93]

[even these mystical bodies, which are similar to material human bodies, which (insofar as they are created and composed of four contrasting humours and elements) although for a certain time they can maintain and conserve life (that is as long as those humours are compatible), yet it is impossible in the long run that one does not overcome the others and by this means the mass returns to its first matter by the dissolution of the ensemble; for through the order of nature, all the said elements and humours, after they are assembled, increase, stabilise and diminish, thereby coming to the point where it is necessary to help nature and rescue a certain member or humour that finds itself the weakest; but it arrives that when one comes to help one, one also harms another. What transpires for mystical bodies also applies to human society; for after they are assembled by a civil and political union, they go along for some time growing and multiplying, and then stabilising for another amount of time, then – insofar as they are composed of several minds and wills that are discordant and repulsed by each other – begin to decline and finally come to nothing.]

In broad terms, mystical here has nothing to do with metaphysical, but means allegorical, with a strong sense of the interaction and interdependence of the elements of society (with elements being loosely identified with different classes) such that in the end each element depends on the health and viability of the others to survive in the long term as a collectivity.

This metaphor is not unique to Seyssel in Renaissance thought and indeed, in terms of the history of political thought, it can perhaps best be traced to Book v of John of Salisbury's *Policraticus* (1159). It also difficult to know whether Seyssel was directly aware of the origins of his invocation of the notion of the mystical body of state and its links to a myth concerning Plutarch. What we find in John and Seyssel, as perhaps moderated by an apocryphal Plutarch, is a notion that politics is not about resolving the tension within a political community, but about managing the tension within the whole and seeking to harmonise the parts so that the movements contribute to vitality rather than decay.

---

[93] Seyssel, *La Monarchie de France*, part i, chap. 3.

Perhaps most importantly for our purposes, despite the centrality of this organic metaphor in Seyssel through which he theorises the French state in more holistic and sociological terms with emphasis on the classes and their various position in the polity, he does so with full recognition of the specificity of the dynamics within a public realm. He begins in his first chapter with this remark:

> La monarchie est le meilleur tant quil y a bon prince qui a le sens lexperience et le vouloir de bien gouverner. Mais pource que cela ne se trouve pas souvent a cause de ce qui est bien difficile en telle auctorite a licence garder au long aller la raison et tenir la balance de iustice droite.[94]

> [Monarchy is the best as long as there is a good prince who has the sense, the experience and the will to govern well. But this is not found often because it is very difficult in such a position of power to preserve reason in the long term and to hold the balance of justice straight.]

In other words, he tells us here that the very nature of public authority, precisely because of its lack of constraints, makes it challenging even for a prince of good character to govern according to reason and a good sense of justice in the long run. The same point is echoed in part ii, chapter 8 with regard to counsel, with the suggestion that no adviser to the king should be given a monopoly of influence regardless of his character because "il est bien difficille en si grande auctorite garder equalite et en user entierement par la raison."[95] He later invokes the idea of the *chose publique* through the image of the chariot – that is, "le chariot de la chose publique," denoting the triple idea that public life has its own momentum that must be guided, that the science of guiding through public life requires an abundance of knowledge that it is impossible for one man to handle on his own and for which a number of good counsellors are needed, and that there is a broader normative framework working positively to keep the chariot moving in a good direction, and negatively to keep it from toppling.[96]

This point is reiterated in different terms in his opening remarks in part ii devoted to a discussion of the potential flaws and weaknesses of monarchy and how one might compensate for them. In chapter 3 of part ii, he likens his approach to that of a doctor who is aware of his patient's propensity for certain illnesses, in other words, he offers advice as a form of preventative medicine. This advice is not directed to a specific

[94] Seyssel, *La Monarchie de France*, part i, chap. i
[95] Seyssel, *La Monarchie de France*, part ii, chap. 8
[96] Seyssel, *La Monarchie de France*, part ii, chap. 6

personality or any named king, but to kings in general. The implication is that regardless of the character of the king (which had been the traditional focus of the mirror for prince's literature, a tradition called by Seyssel "les lunettes des princes"), it is the position of being king, and the social and psychological effects of the power and authority associated with it, that make certain tendencies more salient or possible. Given that the nature of public life makes actors in that sphere particularly susceptible to problematic tendencies, Seyssel is offering advice to help mitigate them. This includes advocacy for the importance of counsel. Of course, this theme is an important trope of Renaissance political thinking in general.[97] Nonetheless, one should be aware of shifts in the justification of a need for counsel: does its importance relate to the potential individual deficiencies of particular kings in living up to an Aristotelian ideal of perfect judgement, in which case the solution is idiosyncratic and linked to the particular strengths and weakness of the individuals occupying that office and perhaps the deficiencies of their own educational background? Or does its necessity derive from the very nature of public life, making counsel not a tailored solution, but indeed an institutional necessity? We can see here how Seyssel shifts that justification to this second plane, mirroring his depiction of monarchy as by necessity incorporating the working of the bridles (*les freins*).

In addition, as Seyssel points out in the same chapter, it is important that written advice be given succinctly and in an easily readable form (including vernacular), since neither virtuous and wise leaders, nor the young and willful, will have time to read and study long texts given that they are either preoccupied with important matters or taken up with vain occupations. Regardless of the character of the king, the nature of public office make it impossible for him to benefit from the traditional genres of advice literature. Seyssel's work is framed as a new practical guide to making important aspects of ruling easily accessible as required by the demands of public office.

To illustrate his principles, Seyssel embarks in chapter 2 on a brief analysis of Roman history, and he suggests that despite many who judge Rome to be the best polity of all, imperfections in the regime are apparent. He suggests the mixed nature of the Roman regime for a large part of its history, meant that the populist and democratic forces were granted an excess of influence which led to elites catering to popular forces to gain the

---

[97] See, for example, Joanne Paul, *Counsel and Command in Early Modern English Thought* (Cambridge: Cambridge University Press, 2020).

power they could no longer achieve through recognition of merit. Notable persons dedicated to the 'bien publique' were passed over for those who could woo the populace with gifts and promises. This eventually led to abuses of political power through a long line of rulers and generals, including Marc Antony and the triumvirate, a decline in respect for authority and a failure of military discipline. By giving some political power to the multitude, mixed government, it appears, can be used as a lever to promote unworthy and dangerous individuals into public office and thus can often be noxious to the public good. Because of this Seyssel concludes that monarchy is the best form of regime, especially when authority passes by succession rather than by election. The upshot is that the more undetermined and open the selection for public office, the more intrigue, plotting and underhanded unscrupulous individuals can be, which can lead directly to the undermining of the regime.

While there is nothing in Seyssel's account that points specifically to the work of Plutarch, apart from the invocation of Antony, it is a view which coincides with Plutarch's reading of the downfall of the Roman republic. While it is questionable whether Plutarch took any position on the question of a best regime overall, an issue further confused by mixed views over which writings should be ascribed to him, it is generally acknowledged that he was not hostile to the broad structures of imperial rule in Greece for his own time, and thus likely favoured a form of monarchy, or at least one that was tempered. In this regard we can see a similar political outlook in the two authors.

Most importantly, we see in Seyssel's *Monarchie* an attempt to build on the lessons demonstrated through the lives of Antony and Demetrius that despite the presence of good qualities in individuals with good leadership skills, these can often be combined with the greatest of vices. In this instance, then, the work of shaping the character of the king through education as advocated by other humanists such as Budé would most prove to be ineffective. In terms of political theory, it was necessary to find other means through which to bind the king to virtuous action and avoidance of the exercise of tyranny. Seyssel seeks this by offering a new institutional interpretation of the workings of French monarchy and the functions of the king within it.

The first bridle of the three famously discussed by Seyssel is that of religion. As perhaps the first glimmer of what will become a more important tradition of praising the Gallic roots of the French political community, Seyssel invokes the long place of religion in French history dating back to the power of the Druids.[98] In his own day, Seyssel suggests that not only does an attachment to Christian principles keep a king from tyrannical behaviour, the fact that people are led to obey their king through their devotion to the Christian faith dictates that the king should be inclined to act within the limits set by religion, even if the kings themselves are impious, for only in this way will they continue to be supported by the people. The power of the priest to condemn the king in the pulpit means that the king has an incentive to both confess their piety and act within the limits set by religion.[99] Plutarch's work is invoked (without directly naming him) in demonstrating an ancient application of this idea through an account of his lives of Numa and Alexander the Great.

> Et à la vérité, cette couleur et apparence de religion et d'avoir Dieu de son côté a toujours donné grande faveur, obéissance et révérence à tous Princes comme l'on peut voir par les anciennes Histoires. Et sans prolixité d'exemples, il appert par ce que fit Alexandre le Grand, lequel se disait avoir été engendré par le dieu Jupiter; et tous les anciens Rois et grands Capitaines de Grèce se disaient être descendus par droite lignée des Dieux; Numa Pompilius aussi réduit le Peuple romain à plus grande obéissances- parce qu'il feignait faire toutes choses par le conseil des Dieux et avoir conférence avec la déesse Egérie- que n'avait fait Romulus par ses hauts et chevalereux faits et par sa discipline militaire.[100]

> [And to tell the truth, this tone and image of religion and to have God on one's side has always given great favour, obedience and reverence to all princes as one can see in the ancient histories. And without a myriad of examples, it is clear by that which Alexander the Great did, who called himself the son of Jupiter; and all the ancient kings and great captains of Greek who said they were direct descendants of the Gods ; Numa Pompilius also subdued the Roman people to the greatest obedience – because he feigned to do all things by the council of the gods and to have spoken with the goddess Egerie – that which Romulus did by his grand and chivalrous deeds and military discipline.]

Similarly, the bridles of justice and 'la police' do not rely for their effectiveness on the good character of the king, but on his effective and

---

[98] Seyssel, *La Monarchie de France*, part 1, chap. 9

[99] "A cette cause, est très requis et nécessaire que quiconques soit Roi, fasse connaître au people par exemple et demonstration actuelle et extérieure, qu'il est zélateur et observateur de la Foi et Religion chrétienne et veut l'entretenir et augmenter de son pouvoir: car si le people avait autre opinion de lui, il le hytrait et par aventure lui obéirait mal, pourtant que tous les inconvénients qui adviendraient au Royaume, icelui people imputerait à la mauvaise créance et imparfaite religion du Roi " Seyssel, *La Monarchie de France*, part 1, chap. 9.

[100] Seyssel, *La Monarchie de France*, part 1, chap. 9

strategic sense of what will maintain him in power and influence. The *parlements* are the primary instrument of the bridle of justice, both in terms of the number and status of the magistrates, and in terms of their legal powers that allow them to pronounce of the legality of the king's declarations and resolutions. 'La police' as a bridle invokes the ordinances that set down institutional guidelines. A key example of the practical benefits is their help in restraining excessive liberality encouraged by the mere holding of public authority.

In addition to the three *freins* of religion, justice and 'la police', the rights and privileges of the three broad social groupings he identifies as 'la Noblesse,' 'le Peuple gros' and 'le Peuple menu' help to maintain a balance that contributes to the order of the regime.[101] Seyssel invokes the principle of social mobility, recognising the central importance for members of the third estate to move up in administrative rank in both the state and the Church if they demonstrate skill and quality in their work. Once again, Seyssel invokes the concept of *la chose publique* in discussing the process through which a person may rise from the second estate of the rich to the first estate of the nobility:

> car pour parvenir a lestat de noblesse est necessaire quil obtiegne grace et privilege du prince: lequel se rend a ce assez facile quant celluy a la demande a faict ou est pour faire quelque grant service a *la chose publique*.[102][my emphasis]

> [for to achieve the state of nobility it is necessary that he obtains the grace and privilege of the prince ; which is given relatively easily when he who asks for it has done or is willing to do great service to the *chose publique*.]

Here the term is evoked in both a general descriptive and slight normative sense, meaning the public life of the regime. The idea of the mystical body of the polity functions for Seyssel in accordance with the mobility of occupational advancement, ensuring that the ambitions of those in the third and second estates can find an outlet. He recognises that the principle of regime-sanctioned social mobility was a positive feature of Roman republican institutions, and he acknowledges the public utility of the practice of social advancement through the church hierarchy as well. His defence of the importance of the possibility of social advancement is voiced with force in the concluding chapter of Book II.

---

[101] This is similar to some Florentine discussions of social categories, taken up at roughly the same period by Machiavelli in his *Florentine Histories* written in the latter part of his life.
[102] Seyssel, *La Monarchie de France*, part I, chap. 17.

To some degree, his support for local militias or groups of men recruited locally to serve in the infantry for purposes of defence, particularly in border regions of the realm, also serves as a potential mechanism of advancement for those of the lowest estate.[103] In this part of the text, Seyssel diverges from the Platonism of Cicero that leads the ancient orator to praise knowledge over valour in his *Pro Lege Manilia*. Indeed, it is here where we can perhaps discover a wedge in the Platonism of Plutarch. In his admiration of some of the military accomplishments of leaders like Alexander, Plutarch's narratives clearly present a celebration of valour distinct from philosophic knowledge as it is traditionally understood. Seyssel concurs, suggesting that Cicero may be right only insofar as he may have assumed that a man with a longstanding military career might likely have already demonstrated a capacity for courage. He subsequently cites Plutarch as an important source for outlining the qualities needed for an effective military commander.[104]

In this discussion of military leadership, Seyssel gives one further justification for his efforts in translation and dissemination of classical texts.

> Une autre qualité me semble très requise à un chef, dont l'on ne tient point de compte en France, à savoir qu'il soit éloquent et ait vu plusieurs histoires anciennes et nouvelles. Car en un gros affaire, les sages remontrances d'un chef, bien fondées en bonnes raisons et en bons exemples, donnent moult grand coeur à toute une armée voire jusques à les faire hardis comme lions.[105]

> [Another quality seems to me to be necessary for a leader, and one which is not given much heed in France, and that is that he be eloquent and have read various ancient and modern histories. For in a big matter, the wise words of a leader, well founded in good reasons and good examples, give great courage to a whole army, indeed to the point of rendering them as formidable as lions.]

In other words, along with French humanists' growing interest in cultivating cultural links with ancient Greek traditions, as well as drawing from the Greek texts an infusion of tone and expression to embellish the French language, Seyssel suggests that the content of these ancient histories can aid leaders in motivating troops, and thus in promoting valour. In this age, prior to the development of a professional military, kings were often

---

[103] Seyssel, *La Monarchie de France*, part III, chap. 4.
[104] Seyssel, *La Monarchie de France*, part III, chap. 9
[105] Seyssel, *La Monarchie de France*, part III, chap. 8.

involved in the day-to-day work of battlefield strategy and troop management.

In broad terms, then, Plutarch's work can be seen to resonate at distinct levels in Seyssel's work. He clearly shares Plutarch's advocacy of a broad practical approach in his giving of political advice, as well as wariness towards more populist forms of politics, partly due to an awareness that tyranny and populism often go hand in hand. He advocates avenues of social mobility within institutional frameworks to guard against excessive resentment of the capable and the building of popular protest politics that can be taken advantage of by the tyrannically inclined. More significantly for our purposes, we see in Seyssel's work the idea that public life has its own dynamic that requires specialised considerations for those in power, considerations that are distinct from the mere adoption of traditional virtues for those in political authority. *La chose publique* is likened to a body or a chariot for which there are distinct normative practices of good functioning and which the good and effective prince is advised to obey.

4.3   Broader Questions in Conclusion

The invocation and appropriation of works of classical Greek historians, including Plutarch, in French Renaissance political thought offers broader challenges for the history of political thought. Eric Nelson has brought to light one way in which Greek philosophy served as a reference in the history of political thought for republicanism and for more radical visions of political justice, like that of Thomas More.[106] Still, we have also noted how there was increasingly an attempt in Renaissance France to cultivate ties to the ancient Greeks and the Trojans in particular, in order to generate a specific political and cultural understanding that would distinguish the French from their Italian neighbours and would bolster claims to royal authority and power. The increased interest in the works of the ancient Greeks, even in the context of early sixteenth-century France, did not serve a single political outlook. Thus, the politics of the appropriation of the works of the Greek classical tradition in Renaissance France is a complex one.[107]

Similarly, while Seyssel did express some admiration for Roman practices, he did not do so through the lens of Roman law, nor did he see the

---

[106] Nelson, *The Greek Tradition*. I will revisit this thesis when I discuss the work of Thomas More in the following chapter.

[107] For an account from yet another perspective, see Bizer's *Homer*.

Roman example as one to replicate.[108] In many ways, the Roman historical example offered two perspectives for Seyssel. Insofar as politics was deemed to be effective in Rome (such as allowing for a good degree of class mobility) it was regarded as the application of a principle that could be also effective in modern circumstances; however, there were also many indications for Seyssel that Rome served as a less than perfect ideal. As we have seen, Seyssel drew from his translations of Plutarch a lesson that given the complexity of human actors and the qualities of public life, good governance should not be uniquely dependent on a leader's moral character. In addition, the conditions of the Roman Republic led Seyssel to be dismissive of a mixed regime if its dominant ethos was to be republican. To a large degree, while there were things to be admired, Rome stands as a beacon of political pitfalls and warnings for Seyssel as regards his contemporaries.

Budé, Erasmus and Seyssel were contemporaries, and the articulation of their political ideas emerged at different periods in their lives. However, I have presented these thinkers in this order to demonstrate an analytical progression in how the work of Plutarch was read and applied to reflection in political theory. There is also a general and shared presumption in these thinkers that the public realm is centred on and largely, though not fully, defined by the actual office holders in the state, most specifically the king. Still, despite the focus on the monarch, we also see through these thinkers the progressive expansion of the relevant boundaries of the public, with exclusive focus on the person of the king in Budé to the broader and more complex notion of the public realm found in Seyssel that includes the king, *parlements* and the institutional network of *la police*. We also see emerging in this narrative an increasingly complex understanding of the ethical frameworks that govern action in the public domain; furthermore, these are frameworks that invoke distinctive but careful parsing of the categories of the good, the prudential, the pragmatic and the worst in understanding useful advice for those in public life. Whereas in Budé we saw the king praised and given broad parameters of action through the framework of a somewhat domesticated view of ancient heroism, we see emerging in his contemporaries a more nuanced articulation of the idea that the traditional frameworks of ethics in the private sphere do not always hold in the same way or to the same degree for public life, either due to the complexity of

---

[108] Despite his training and indeed his career as an academic in Turin teaching in the neo-Bartolist tradition of law, Seyssel did not take up the neo-Bartolist twist on the notion of imperium to bolster the claims of the absolutist monarch. See Skinner, *Foundations*, 260 ff.

competing demands on the ruler or to their specific public function. While Budé's conception of the king as a hero formally unbound by established rules and laws may seem a quaint and outmoded notion of public action, it is this model that resonates with later ideas (i.e. Arendtian) of a broader and more inclusive sphere of public action where it is precisely the public nature of the forum that allows for the manifestation of authenticity of the political subject.

In the work of Seyssel, the broadening of the notion of the public to include recruitment to administrative office and the need for class mobility marks a shift in thinking about public practice. There is no longer the need, as in Budé, for the ruler to instantiate or to seek to exemplify heroic and charismatic qualities as a normative measure of the qualification for leadership and monarchical rule. Instead, the notion of the public introduced with Seyssel's work begins to incorporate the concerns of a wider population to be given opportunities for personal advancement within the public structures of governance, not through considerations of justice but for reasons of efficacy. The notion of bridles on the king also ushers in a conception of a public realm where the imposition of singular higher judgement is replaced by a dynamic of give and take and the constant management of political relations as a necessary condition for public action. In this context, the privileged modes of discourse in public action become justification (in the light of the bridle of religion), constitutionalism (in the light of the bridle of justice) and appeasement (in the light of the bridle of *la police*).

CHAPTER 5

Tudor Plutarch

This chapter sheds light on some of the complexities associated with the intercultural transmission of texts. It lays out the general contours of the differential uptake of Plutarch's work in the French and English contexts of political reflection, then offers an overview of key moments of Plutarch reception in England in the sixteenth century, ranging from the echoes of Plutarch in More's *Utopia* to an analysis of Queen Elizabeth I's 1598 translation of Plutarch's essay "On Curiosity."

5.1 The Complexity of Tracking Traditions of Renaissance Reception: France vs. England

A comparison of Plutarch reception in sixteenth-century England and France helps to underscore the competing trajectories of classical transmission (something that was surely not unique to Plutarch) as well as to highlight some of the nuances in the relation between traditions of political reflection and the challenges of state development in competing political contexts. Of course, there was a great deal of intellectual interchange within courtly and elite circles and beyond, so there is no need to surmise that each state had its own fully independent tradition of reception. Indeed, the best example of the complex web of cultural ties between the two states in the early-modern period comes from one of the best-known moments of Plutarch reception itself, namely the translation of Plutarch's *Lives* by Jacques Amyot into the French vernacular (1559) and the subsequent translation of Plutarch's *Lives* from Amyot's French into English by Thomas North (1579). As is well known, North's translation served as an important reference for England's most celebrated writers, including Shakespeare. Indeed, Francis Matthiesen suggests that North's translation from Amyot's Plutarch must be considered one of the earliest great masterpieces of English prose after Mallory's *La Morte d'Arthur* and the *Book of*

Common Prayer.[1] We have also seen how the work of Erasmus was in many ways pan-European, although with a somewhat different uptake in the vernacular traditions of France and England.

The extent of interchange of people and ideas between England and France and with Europe more broadly in the early-modern period makes the singling out of distinct and independent intellectual traditions an artificial and misleading enterprise.[2] Nonetheless, regarding political thought and commentary there is some basis for acknowledging different tendencies. One stems from the distinct institutional histories of the two countries, though both marked steps towards the deeper historical process in the consolidation of the modern state.[3] Even before the Reformation, institutional paths and strategies differed across the Channel and were linked in part to diverging ways of coping with the challenges of dynastic succession and revenue raising. This was reflected to some degree in political commentary. So, for example, while the English chose to bolster the crown through landed assets (including seizure of monastery land), the French sought revenue through taxation. John Fortescue in *The Difference between an Absolute and a Limited Monarchy* (c. 1471) argued that the English were better off than the French because the English monarchy extended their domain to the point that the state could avoid taxation of

---

[1] Francis Matthiessen, *Translation, an Elizabethan Art* (Cambridge, MA: Harvard University Press, 1931), 58.

[2] As one very important example, Anne Coldiron acknowledges the central importance of francophone traditions in both the content and form of early printing in Britain and across all fields: "early print culture in Europe was a radically international phenomenon; as we know, continental printers such as Aldus, Jean de Tournes and Plantin worked in multiple languages and aimed at transnational audiences from the very start. In England, however, the situation in early print was different and transnationalism in early English print takes a particular form that has long-term consequences for literary culture … it is important to note that the world of early printing in England was an intensively francophone subculture at every level. The Act of 1484 allowed foreigners to work unrestricted in the book trade, and the people, the gear, the technical habits and the aesthetic tendencies in book production were largely francophone. The dominance of francophone texts and technology diminished gradually from the 1530s on towards mid-century but never vanished....The early printed books of England- physically, visually, right down to the woodcuts, typefaces, bookbinding techniques and the paper itself, not to mention the words- very often reveal themselves to be directly drawn from French works either in manuscript or recently put into print. This is true across genres: French poems, romances, histories, religious books, legal works and practical works, all came to English readers in early printed translations, often made by the printers themselves. Beyond the francophone foundations of early printing in England, which is itself a remarkable phenomenon, many books were imported into England from francophone places (Paris, Rouen, Burgundian territories), both in Latin and in French translations. It would be hard to overestimate the weight of medieval French/francophone, French translated and French-printed materials that, because of these conditions, came into English print during the century after Caxton." See A. E. B. Coldiron, "The Mediated 'medieval' and Shakespeare," in Helen Cooper et al. eds., *Medieval Shakespeare. Pasts and Presents* (Cambridge: Cambridge University Press, 2013), 61–62.

[3] Skinner, *Foundations*.

the peasantry.[4] In the history of political thought, Tudor period political thinkers tended to offer more concerted reflection on the nature of counsel, as well as on poverty and the methods towards its alleviation, than their French counterparts. The point here is not an in-depth discussion of causal explanations for differences of political reflection in sixteenth-century France and England, but only to suggest that such differences do exist.

In addition to institutional factors, religious and literary ones also shaped tendencies in political thinking. The different course of the Reformation in England influenced political reflection there, though many thinkers in the latter half of the century also had the upheavals of the continent on their minds.[5] We have also seen how the first translations of Plutarch's work in the vernacular French tended to focus on markedly political texts (through the translations of Tory, Budé and Seyssel), and that these translations make reference to a particular phrase, *la chose publique*. Through these texts Plutarch came to be regarded as a privileged author for insight into the nature of public life. Up to the end of the sixteenth century, the French Plutarch was a writer who offered heightened consciousness of the importance of public life and who provided readers with tools to make sense of the specific ethos associated with public matters, especially matters of state. Arguably, this contributed to one aspect of ongoing insight and sensibility within later French political thought among those who took inspiration from that tradition. Still, by the seventeenth century this early modern 'French' reading of Plutarch made its way to England.

The peculiarity of the early-modern tradition of Plutarch reception, as we have charted in Chapters 3 and 4, can be further highlighted through a contrast with the reception of Plutarch in England, at least through the first part of the sixteenth century. Up until the translations of North, the English sixteenth-century Plutarch in the vernacular was mainly the Plutarch of the *Moralia* with less attention being paid to his more overtly political teachings (except perhaps in the case of Thomas More, a subject we will return to later in the discussion).[6]

---

[4] David Starkey, "England," in R. Porter and M. Teich eds., *The Renaissance in National Context* (Cambridge: Cambridge University Press, 1992), 151. John Fortescue's work was published until the title *The Governance of England* in the nineteenth century. See John Fortescue, *The Governance of England Otherwise Called The Difference between an Absolute and a Limited Monarchy*, ed. C. Plummer (Oxford: The Clarendon Press, 1885), Online at https://archive.org/stream/governan ceenglaoofortgoog#page/n12/mode/2up. Accessed 5 November 2017.

[5] See, for example, Stephen Chavura, *Tudor Protestant Political Thought 1547–1603* (Leiden and Boston: Brill, 2011) and Paul Fideler and T. F. Mayer, eds. *Political Thought and the Tudor Commonwealth* (London: Routledge, 1992 and 2005).

[6] There were a few exceptions to this. A foremost early modern scholar of classical languages, Roger Ascham wrote a treatise on archery in 1545 called *Toxophilus* in which he drew from wide reading of the classics, including Plutarch, to document ancient variants on the bow and arrow. For the most

It may be that insofar as Plutarch was received as a political thinker in England, the reading of his work was shaped by a prior acquaintance with and wide English circulation of Cicero's reflections on the commonwealth. Cicero had been a reference in English political reflection since at least the 1450s with Worcester's *Boke of Noblesse*, and he stood as 'the great genius' of antiquity earlier acknowledged by Petrarch and other humanists.[7] As Starkey tells us, Worcester's invocation of Cicero to defend the priority of the collective good over the individual entwined with Christian ideals of sin and redemption, was a common" theme in the English Renaissance.[8] The background of deep immersion in Cicero led a number of humanists to suggest that the exercise of civic virtue was the only way to serve the common good and demonstrate one's true nobility. This is the larger framework within which many themes in Plutarch reception (including choices regarding which parts of Plutarch's opus to translate into the vernacular) can be made sense of. Thus, while Plutarch was presumed to have been the tutor to Trajan the general thrust of the uptake of his work in Renaissance England was as a study in the moral qualities

part, however, it was not until North's translation of the *Lives* in 1579 that Plutarch's *Lives* began to be a more common reference in English literature. As noted by Matthiessen, it became a particularly important reference for the field of drama. "Robert Garnier's *Marc Antoine* as translated by Signey's sister, the Countess of Pembroke, in 1590, drew the attention of Elizabethan dramatists to Plutarchan themes. Samuel Daniel wrote his Cleopatra (1594) confessedly in the desire to provide a companion piece to the *Antoine* of his patroness. Kyd translated another of Garnier's dramas in *Pompey the Great, his faire Cornelia's Tragedie* (1595). Fulke Greville attempted a play on 'the irregular passions' of Antonie and Cleopatra, who 'forsook empire to follow sensuality' but burnt it, fearing that an unfortunate analogy might be suggested to Essex and the Queen. The Scotchman William Alexander issued, in 1607, *The Monarchicke Tragedies*, including closet dramas on Alexander and Julius Caesar. Beaumont and Fletcher's *False One* (c. 1619) which deals with the stay of Caesar in Egypt, is also indebted to Plutarch." In *Translation an Elizabethan Art*, 56. While these accounts harboured important political implications (notably how passion can lead a hero to their downfall), they were not presented as systematic reflections in political theory.

[7] "Worcester's linkage of the Ciceronian ideal of the subordination of the individual to the collective good with Christian concepts of sin and redemption was ... to become universal." See Starkey, "England," 150. Petrarch's praise of Cicero is cited in Skinner, *Foundations*, 84. Robert Whittington published an English translation of *De Officiis* in 1534. See *The three books of Tullyes offyces* (London, 1534). On the predominant influence of Cicero in early English Renaissance thought, see Neal Wood, "Cicero and the Political Thought of the Early English Renaissance," *Modern Language Quarterly*, 51.2 (June 1990), 185–207.

[8] Starkey, "England," 150. Jonathan Scott also argues that the 'commonwealth' tradition in England can in part be traced to a Christian form of humanism. As he states: "Certainly the greatest shortcoming of the existing literature on English republicanism has been its relative neglect of the religious dimension. The consequent need is not simply to recover the radical protestant republican religious agenda. It is to explain why, when classical republicanism came to England, it did so in the moral service of an explicitly religious revolution. One long-term context for the answer was in Christian humanism. Another was the reformation, both magisterial and radical. Both informed the practical identity of the republican experiment as an attempted reformation of manners." Jonathan Scott, "What were Commonwealth Principles?" *The Historical Journal* 47.3 (2004), 591–613.

recommended for those embarking on a career of public service, rather than on the particular dynamics uniquely associated with the public realm and governance.[9] And while Cicero also served as a key reference for French humanists, there is no tradition of translating Cicero into vernacular French by those with direct access to the king and court and associated with the political theory canon, as we find with Budé, Seyssel and to some degree Tory for Plutarch. Cicero's *De Officiis* was translated into vernacular French in several editions over the course of the sixteenth century, but it appears that this work was read in France of the early sixteenth century in the way that Plutarch was read in England – that is, largely as a general moralist. So, for example, the preface of the 1501 vernacular translation of Cicero's *Des Offices* sold by the Parisian bookseller Jean Petit and translated by David Miffant suggests that through this work "chascun homme pourra prendre vrays enseignemens de bien et honestement vivre en societe humaine selon vertu morale" [each man can find true lessons regarding how to live well and honourably in human society according to moral virtue].[10] By the 1540s, Cicero's speeches, letters and editions of the *Tusculan Disputations* multiplied in vernacular French editions, thus confirming Marc Fumaroli's suggestion that French Renaissance debates invoking Cicero also often centred on forms of rhetoric and eloquence and their importance in all forms of civic life.[11] There appears to be no privileged invocation of Cicero in French Renaissance political thought, or not in the way that is notable in England. Nor is there any parallel in England to the presence of Plutarch in French political reflection with a focus on the notion of the *chose publique* and the social psychological dynamics in the public realm.

Dauber suggests that this vision of the requisite moral qualities for public service was challenged with the Reformation in England. A salient problem was that the political institutions were acknowledged to be ineffective in generating the pure devotion to public service that the model required. As a result, English thinkers began to reflect more systematically on how the notion of personal honour might be used more

---

[9] Fred Shurink suggests that this is a form of humanist political advice and of course from a certain perspective it is. The contrast that I am trying to develop here is that the English moralists who took up Plutarch were more concerned about how his writings could inform basic questions concerning the development of good character, something that was thought as an added benefit to help inform and inspire those who wished to enter public life; whereas in the French case Plutarch was often used, as we have seen, to provide insight into the particularities of interrelations in the public realm. See Fred Schurink, "'Scholemaister and Counsailour unto Traianus': Plutarch, the *Institutio Traiani*, and Humanist Political Advice in Renaissance England," unpublished paper, 2017.

[10] Cicero, *Le Livre Tulles des offices* (Paris: Jean Petit, 1501).

[11] Marc Fumaroli, *L'Age de l'éloquence* (Geneva: Droz, 1980).

effectively to defend forms of public service.[12] So there were arguably some shifts in political discourse in England in the sixteenth century as the initial language of humanism gave some way to a more concerted reflection on how to achieve effective rule and how to appeal to more varied motives and characters of political actors. By the 1530s the language of humanism which had invoked a form of civic consciousness may not have dissolved completely, but it also had to make space for more stark theoretical defences of consolidated monarchical rule under the growing absolutism of Henry VIII.[13] This shift from a somewhat devotional ideal of public service, to a model taking into account the self-regarding motivations of public figures served as a background to the English sixteenth-century reading of Plutarch at least up until the translations of Thomas North.

Thus, Plutarch was not often invoked by more strictly political thinkers (i.e. those we have come to associate with the political theory canon) in the first half of sixteenth- century England, as their concern for the commonwealth was largely driven by reference to other important classical sources, predominantly Cicero. However, Plutarch's moral essays and adages were translated offering certain *implications* for political reflection. In some cases, reference to themes of virtue and character could be seen as a general way to approach the more specific question of the motivations appropriate for office holders and more broadly of the means to advance the common weal or common good. Subsequent humanist appeals to Plutarch, still focused on themes of moral virtue, appeared to play more directly into the theological and political priorities of Henry VIII's regime. Still, the appeal to Plutarch as a source for thinking about the link between character and service was distinct from the tendency in France (as we saw especially in Chapter 3), where Plutarch was a source for reflection on the nature of the public realm and the ways in which pursuit of the public good might be governed by its own ethos and rules of appropriateness.

Further light can be shed on this dynamic by acknowledging Starkey's point that humanism in England was disseminated largely by the gentleman amateurs educated at Oxford. While they did travel to Italy, they also wrote in English (though inspired by Latin) and were not considered to be scholars on the same level of either Budé or Lascaris in France.[14] And despite the fine

---

[12] Noah Dauber, *State and Commonwealth. The Theory of the State in Early Modern England, 1549–1640* (Princeton NJ: Princeton University Press, 2016).
[13] Markku Peltonen, *Classical Humanism and Republicanism in English Political Thought, 1570–1640* (Cambridge: Cambridge University Press, 2009), 11–12.
[14] Starkey, "England,"153–154. Nonetheless, Skinner suggests that the arrival of key Italians was also important in the spread of humanism in England. In particular, Pietro del Monte (d. 1457) who

quality of scholarship by men such as Roger Ascham (1514–1568), among the English writers associated with the humanist movement, few had a deep knowledge of Plutarch's work and even fewer read it in the original Greek. Indeed, as suggested by Raisch, there was only a relatively small circle of humanists in early sixteenth-century England actively promoting the learning of Greek, a group More called the *Graecistes*.[15] This group was opposed by others who saw the new focus on ancient Greek language and traditions as an assault to conventional forms of learning. This stands in evident contrast to France where there was an appeal to Greek traditions as having a special status either (as in Tory) because of perceived links between Greek and French or because of a circulating myth that the French could trace their lineage to the Trojans. While Lazarus has recently suggested that the account of heavily circumscribed knowledge of Greek and Greek literature in the English Renaissance period has been highly exaggerated, this does not preclude the fact that its perceived value was not as prominent as in the French case.[16]

Nonetheless, one should also be careful to distinguish between access to the texts in the original ancient Greek and access to those in translation. There is no doubt that students did have relatively easy access to Plutarch's work in Latin translation, copies of which were in Duke Humphrey's library.[17] Through translations of Italian humanists and Erasmus as well as Budé, Plutarch's work was certainly more accessible to the English than had been previously thought, and within the educated elite, Plutarch was one author among many whose texts were used in translation to teach Latin.[18] Insofar as his work was a source for deeper reflection, it often took the form of a compilation of passages and observations that were written by the reader in commonplace books which served as a resource for future speeches and

arrived in 1435 as a collector of papal revenues, who wrote a treatise on the difference between the virtues and the vices and who advised Duke Humphrey of Gloucester on his book collection. In addition, he names Stefano Surigone, who was lecturing on grammar and rhetoric at Oxford 1454–1471, as well as Cornelio Vitelli, known as the first public instructor of Greek in an English university in the 1470s. Skinner, *Foundations*, 194–195.

[15] Jane Raisch, "Humanism and Hellenism: Lucian and the Afterlives of Greek," *English Literary History* 83.4 (2016), 935–936. See also Goldhill, *Who Needs Greek?*, and Eric Nelson, "Greek Nonsense in More's Utopia," *The Historical Journal* 44(2001), 889–917. As noted by Raisch (953 n. 11) the question of the influence of Greek thinkers in the English Renaissance cannot be boiled down to strands of Platonism found in English Renaissance thought. Still, the Francisation of the term by More further reinforces the association of more learned scholarship in Greek in France.

[16] Micha Lazarus, "Greek Literacy in Sixteenth-Century England," *Renaissance Studies* 29.3 (2014), 433–458.

[17] Famously, this was to become the foundation of the Bodleian library of the University of Oxford. Skinner, *Foundations,* 195.

[18] Cox Jensen "Popularity."

public interventions.[19] This was another way in which the reading of Plutarch largely served an already existing ethos of politics and service that was derived from broadly Ciceronian principles, one that praised a spirit of public service but did not engage with the broader social and moral psychology of public life. So to a large degree reception of Plutarch was shaped in the first part of the sixteenth century in England by already established modes in the reception of classical thought and through more general reflections on the nature of virtue and political service.[20] Apart from the work of Thomas More, Plutarch was not a central reference for many thinkers associated with English political thought of the early sixteenth century, despite relatively wide circulation of his books in translation (or his inclusion in collections of sayings and anecdotes from a variety of ancient authors at the time). Therefore, while a study of Plutarch reception in early sixteenth-century England will not offer us a picture of the full range of political argument in the English Renaissance, it can still serve to illustrate some broader assumptions about politics and public service that were prevalent in educated circles.

Erasmus is one scholar whose Latin translations played a role in both English and French traditions. Nonetheless, Erasmus's work had a somewhat different contour in each of these contexts, especially in vernacular editions. In the English case, for instance, a wider number of Plutarch's moral essays on various matters of education and health appear which are not as prominent in the French case. Erasmus's Latin translations of select Plutarchan moral essays (offered as gifts to his actual or expected English patrons in the early 1500s) were retranslated into English

---

[19] According to one pedagogical manual, Degory Wheare's *De ratione et method legend historias* (written in 1623 and translated into English for the 1685 edition) students were encouraged to read their history, largely Roman, with the following focus in mind: "enquire into the Causes of every action and counsel; let him consider the circumstances of it, and weigh the success; and let him in each of these search out wherein any thing is well or prudently, ill or imprudently managed; and let him from thence draw up to himself a general Precept, Rule or Direction, and then prove or illustrate it with many Sentences or Examples. For there is a two-fold use of Examples: the first for our imitation of what is done by good men, and that we may learn to shun the ill actions of wicked men: the second is, that from particular Stories we may deduce and extract some Sentence, which may be generally usefull to us." Cited in Frejya Cox Jensen, *Reading the Roman Republic in Early Modern England* (Leiden and Boston: Brill, 2012), 6. As also noted by Cox Jensen in the general model of common placing, it was suggested that each student use two books at the same time. In the first the student would take all their notes in sequence, but in the second the student would order their notes by theme and enter passages or observations under a series of established headings such as Love, Duty, Betrayal. It was these latter books that were meant to serve as a future reference when preparing public interventions. Cox Jensen, *Reading the Roman Republic*, 40.

[20] This was facilitated by a general practice of translation in the Tudor era which, despite being driven by an ideal of literalism in theory, tended in practice to involve a visible degree of modification through addition, subtraction and an imposition of new terms and metaphors. Massimilano Morini, *Tudor Translation in Theory and Practice* (London: Ashgate, 2006), 4.

vernacular more quickly than they were into French. These patterns may have been related to what could sell. For example from the works or excerpts of Plutarch translated by Budé, the moral essays rather than the political reflections were subsequently translated into vernacular English for the English book market. The broader implication is that despite Erasmus's important work in the translation and popularising of Plutarch, the subsequent patterns of the translations of Erasmus's own work into vernacular French and English diverged to a certain degree. Because of this, Plutarch's moral essays, including his "Precepts of Good Health", "On Anger", "On Curiosity" and "How to Tell a Friend from a Flatterer" enjoyed a great deal more prominence in England in the sixteenth century than they did in France.

It is also relevant to note that greater complexities in reception may be linked to variants and shifts in translation practice over the course of the sixteenth century. Massimiliano Morini suggests that with regard to England in particular there were different conceptions of translation coexisting in the period: namely, a practice of imitation that allowed for some significant departures from the original (both in extending some medieval habits and reaching towards a seventeenth-century idea of domesticating the text), and a humanistic and philological outlook that at least in theory aspired to more of a literalist approach.[21] We should understand this as a spectrum rather than a dichotomy, with the added recognition that the same work translated from the Greek to the Latin, and then from the Latin into the vernacular, could be subject to translation inspired by different sides of the spectrum. For example, Erasmus harboured to a large degree the latter modernist and humanist approach to translation, but even in his own practice, and with Plutarch's *Sayings*, he added his own commentary in a seamless way that was integral to the translation from Greek to Latin to enhance his readers' understanding of the text. Furthermore, as we will see, when some of those passages from Erasmus were integrated into Taverner's *Garden of Wisdom*, Taverner is both highly selective in his choice of sayings and anecdotes and exercises an even higher degree of discretion in commentary.

Thus, while some of Plutarch's essays did appear in the French case, such as in Budé's 1510 Latin translation of Plutarch's "On Tranquility of Mind", these works, especially those in the vernacular, never received the same prominence in France as the works that focused on political commentary, notably the *Sayings*, the essay "Political Precepts" and excerpts from the *Lives*.

---

[21] Morini, *Tudor Translation*.

A cursory review of the Universal Short Title Catalogue reveals that while in France there were at least twenty-eight editions or partial editions (some just reproducing the first part of the work where Erasmus integrates most of his Plutarch translations and commentary) of vernacular copies of Erasmus's *Sayings* (translated into French as *Apophthegmes*) from 1539 to 1574. There were fewer vernacular editions and translations of the same work in England, and it was only Taverner's selective presentation of the material from 1539 that highlighted its more strictly political commentary.[22] The English tradition tended to focus on Plutarch as a moral thinker, with Thomas Wyatt taking up Budé's 1510 Latin translation of Plutarch's "On the Tranquility of Mind" as the basis for his own English version. Erasmus, apart from being a translator of Plutarch's moral essays, was also associated with the popularising of moral sayings, under the title of *Proverbs or Adagies,* which were taken in part from Plutarch through vernacular translations of his *Adagia.*[23] That same work had been placed on the Index by the Council of Trent and may explain its much more prominent place in the English tradition than in France. So, as suggested by Susan Brigden, Plutarch took hold in the English context as a thinker who was recommended as part of the broader humanist educational agenda partly for language acquisition but also for a deeper understanding of basic moral issues and only collaterally or indirectly to provide insight into political matters.[24]

5.2 Plutarch Reception in Early Sixteenth-Century England

That the preponderance of Plutarch translations in English in the early English Renaissance were taken from his collection of moral essays did not imply a complete absence of political overtones. Even in the most overt

---

[22] See Agnes Juhász-Ormsby, "Erasmus' *Apophthegmata* in Henrician England," *Erasmus Studies* 37 (2017), 45–67. Also see E. J. Devereux, *Renaissance English Translations of Erasmus* (Toronto: University of Toronto Press, 1983) that offers full bibliographic evidence of all the English Renaissance translations of both the *Adagia* and *Apophthegmata.* It appears that there were two subsequent and distinct translations of the *Apophthegmata* in 1542 and 1564. However, it is significant that Taverner's translation of selections from Erasmus never gave credit to either Erasmus or even Plutarch.
    There was also at least one other edition and translation from the Greek to French of apophtheg-mata from Plutarch's *Lives* that was published in Antwerp under the title *Le Tresor des vies de Plutarque* (1567) translated by the abbe de Bellomane. This is cited by Cox Jensen in "Popularity." It reinforces my suggestion that the historical content of Plutarch was circulating, albeit with a great amount of curation and commentary, much more extensively in the vernacular French than the English up to the late sixteenth century.
[23] According to Olive White the *Proverbes* or *Adagies* went through at least six editions. See "Richard Taverner's Interpretation of Erasmus in *Proverbes* or *Adagies,*" *PMLA* 59.4 (December 1944), 928.
[24] Brigden, *Wyatt,* 135.

ways, as Fred Schurink acknowledges in agreement with previous scholars, these vernacular translations in Tudor England were effected not only to spread knowledge of classical ideas to middle-class readers, they were also often presented as motivated by a sense of devotion to the commonwealth.[25] In addition, with more narrow political intent, it is clear that the dedications accompanying these translations, as well as the translations themselves, often presented for the occasion of the New Year, were meant to be instrumental in either establishing or maintaining a relation or possible employment in the service of a powerful patron. In a context of shifting power dynamics, declaring loyalties could be a risky game. While a focus on the motivation of a public servant was certainly an ongoing theme of Tudor political thought, it did not carry the same analytic insight into the very nature of public office offered in the French tradition.

To help make deeper sense of these broad characteristics of Plutarch reception in Tudor England, and while there are links between the French and English traditions of the reception of Plutarch in shared Latin culture, the importance of Erasmus and his translations, and the works of French humanists subsequently translated into vernacular English, it is best to divide our discussion of Plutarch reception in sixteenth-century England into two parts. The first part covers the translation of selected moral essays by poets and prose writers who depicted Plutarch as a moralist with insight into various matters of practical and domestic import and, in the light of a humanist agenda, could offer some critical perspective on political life. This also includes an analysis of the place of Plutarch in More's *Utopia* (1516). While it is true that More never translated Plutarch, he is included here because he is a sixteenth-century political theorist based in England who engaged directly with Plutarch's work, drawing on various features to conceptualise a new form of political community. I suggest that a close reading of the first section of More's work indicates his awareness of the subtleties of argument that were beginning to emerge in the French context discussed in Chapter 3. Reading More's *Utopia* as in part a dialogue with the work of Plutarch also sheds new light on the main thrust and significance of More's enterprise.

---

[25] See Fred Schurink, "Print, Patronage, and Occasion: Translations of Plutarch's Moralia in Tudor England," *Yearbook of English Studies* 38.1–2 (2008), 86–101; H. S. Bennett, *English Books and Readers 1475 to 1557*, 2nd ed. (Cambridge: Cambridge University Press, 1969) and H. S Bennett, *English Books and Readers 1558–1603* (Cambridge: Cambridge University Press, 1965), Louis B. Wright, *Middle-Class Culture in Elizabethan England* (Chapel Hill: University of North Carolina Press, 1935).

The second period I examine can be identified with uses of Plutarch that more directly served the cause of consolidating the Tudor monarchy, starting with Henry VIII up to and including the reign of Elizabeth I, and ending with Elizabeth's own translation of a Plutarch moral essay five years before her death.

5.2.1   Plutarch and His Vernacular Reception in England Prior to 1550

Reception of Plutarch in the vernacular in early sixteenth-century England (hence prior to the famous North translations of Plutarch's *Lives*) can be represented by three writers, the three Thomases: Wyatt (1503–1542), Elyot (1490–1546) and More (1478–1535). The first two were translators of Plutarch's work in the vernacular, and the latter contributed to the broader tradition of reception and interpretation of Plutarch. I look to Wyatt and Elyot and subsequently to More, even though More's contributions come first chronologically. The reason is to place greater emphasis on the choices of direct reception and transmission of Plutarch's work. While More may have prepared his countrymen for some of the themes associated with Plutarch's *Lives*, these were not introduced by him with any direct transmission of the writing of Plutarch, and thus the themes he drew from the work were not dominant in the subsequent reception of Plutarch by his countrymen, at least not until the *Lives* were better known by the English.

I seek here to give an overview of the ways in which Plutarch was introduced to English *political* thought, and thus my narrative is not meant to provide an exhaustive account of Plutarch reception in Tudor and Elizabethan England nor indeed to offer a comprehensive account of political argument in this period, but rather to demonstrate a distinction in how Plutarch was initially read and received in relation to political matters.

Thomas Wyatt (1503–1542) is largely known as a poet (the inventor of the sonnet), but he was not at all removed from public matters. It is significant, then, that his role in Plutarch reception in England was through the English translation of Plutarch's moral essay, "On the Tranquility of Mind" (c. 1528), also widely known as "On the Quiet of Mind", presenting Plutarch as a commentator on Hellenistic philosophy. Wyatt was a key figure in the court of King Henry VIII, moving in and out of favour with the king (possibly because of his suspected relations with Anne Boleyn) and serving for a time as an ambassador at the court of Charles V.

As mentioned, the choice of translation, along with the content of the dedication, was often motivated by concerns of patronage as an attempt to curry favour with the powerful. In the case of this Plutarch essay, Wyatt took special initiative. Queen Katherine Howard had sent Wyatt a request to translate Petrarch's *Of the Remedy of Ill Fortune*. It was often the case that royalty and some of those in royal circles did not have the training or time to read classical texts in their original; however, Erasmus is said to have noted that Katherine was "remarkably learned," and she drew a number of humanists to her household.[26] Translations were prepared and most often read in court so that the king and his attendants could have easy access to their message.[27] In acting on the Queen's request, Wyatt found the text too dull – or perhaps too challenging – to translate, and he looked to another text with a similar message but more lively in presentation.[28] He settled on Plutarch's "On the Quiet of Mind", working from the Latin version which Budé had already completed shortly before (Wyatt did not know Greek).[29] The dedication is dated the last day of 1527 and the work was published the next year. It is reputedly the only work of Wyatt's published during his lifetime and with a secure attribution.[30] Schurink speculates that the Queen requested this text to provide her with philosophical solace at a time when Henry was seeking to separate from her.[31] As noted by Brigden, it was not an innocent act for Wyatt to declare his allegiance to the Queen openly and at a time when her status was being questioned by the king. In 1527–1528 when another champion of Plutarch, Richard Pace, dean of St Paul's, publicly defended Katherine's marriage to the king (having initially supported the king in this matter) – he was sent to the Tower.[32]

---

[26] Brigden, *Wyatt*, 144.

[27] We know that Henry VIII did read Latin, as Erasmus sent to the king his Latin translation of "How to Tell a Friend from a Flatterer," an essay which was greatly appreciated by the king. Brigden, *Wyatt*, 225.

[28] Brigden, *Wyatt*, 139. It is Robert Cummings suggestion that Wyatt turned to Plutarch over Petrarch because of the nature of Petrarch's Latin, which was so rich that its translation into the narrow confines of English posed a huge challenge. Budé's Latin proved to be more easily translatable into English. See his "Versifying Philosophy: Thomas Blundeville's Plutarch," in S. K. Barker and B. M. Hosington eds., *Renaissance Cultural Crossroads: Translation, Print and Culture in Britain, 1473–1640* (Leiden and Boston: Brill, 2013), 108.

[29] The version of the work I consulted is that accessible through the database Early English Books Online. http://eebo.chadwyck.com/search/fulltext?SOURCE=config.cfg&ACTION=ByID&ID=D00000998460380000&WARN=N&SIZE=69&FILE=&ECCO=param(ECCO). Date accessed May 2016.

[30] Brigden, *Wyatt*, 60   [31] Schurink, "Print, Patronage, and Occasion," 89–90.

[32] Brigden, *Wyatt*, 136–137.

The beginning of this essay reads like advocacy for Stoicism insofar as it suggests that the reader must prepare their soul for calamities before they happen to ensure navigation of difficulties with equanimity. However, Plutarch suggests that this does not mean having to disengage from all private and public concerns to embrace idleness. Indeed, he argues that, particularly for those of a restless disposition, the need for quiet is for the inner disposition. Plutarch counsels against taking offense too frequently to avoid being obsessed with the misdeeds of others and suggests that the reader in search of quiet of mind should focus rather on the present good. The reader also should try to avoid comparison with others above them. This includes not seeking comparison with the Stoic sage because even the Gods do not demand the same perfection in all matters of justice, speech, command, wealth etc. that the Stoics demand of themselves. Thus, the Plutarch who is presented to the English through the translation work of Thomas Wyatt is that of a moralist offering consolation and strategies for obtaining equanimity amid the vulnerabilities brought on by public life. Despite the Hellenistic overtones, one still finds in this essay a presumption of the need for an active life (though combined with a portion of philosophic *gravitas*).

A similar moralist theme is conveyed through Thomas Elyot's translation of Plutarch into vernacular English roughly three years after Wyatt's work. Thomas Elyot, like Wyatt, was no stranger to public life and the political fray, having served as a clerk to the Privy Council 1523–1530, a diplomat to the court of Charles V, as well as being a member of the circle of Sir Thomas More. Elyot took on the translation of the pseudo-Plutarch essay "On the Education of Children" a year before the publication of *The Boke named the Governour* (1531), which is thought to be the first treatise on education written in English and his best-known work. Elyot dedicated his translation to his sister Margery. He suggests in the dedication that there is nothing to be desired more in life than to raise children who are honest and courageous, and that there is no disease or grief so painful as to have abject or vicious children who not only consume the goods of their parents and friends, but who also undo the good name and reputation of the family. The difference, he goes on to suggest, is largely due to education: "the lacke of children shuld not be so payneful, as feare of having succession of heires, in whom shulde be lack of virtue and learning."[33]

---

[33] Thomas Elyot's *The Education of Children* (c. 1530) is accessible through the database Early English Books Online. http://quod.lib.umich.edu/e/eebo/A09790.0001.001?rgn=main;view=fulltext. Date

Elyot suggests in his dedication that his translation was prepared to help his sister in the education of her children. Pseudo-Plutarch's work suggests it is the woman who will oversee a child's education; and Elyot, still subscribing to the story of Plutarch serving as the tutor to Trajan, therefore deemed this essay to be a particularly good choice to guide his sister.

Still, to adapt the translation more fully to the situation and context, Elyot tells us that he understood his role as translator loosely, a stance that allowed him to make several changes and additions to the text. As he states:

> I have not only used therein the office of a translator but also have declared at lengthe dyvers histories only touched by Plutarch to the intent that difficultie of understanding shall not cause the matter to be to you fastidious as it often tymes hath happened to other. Also of pourpose I have omitted to translate some parte of this matter conteyned as well in the Greke as in Latin partly for that it is strange from the experience or usage of this present tyme partly that some vices be in those tonges reproved whiche ought rather to be unknown than in a vulgare tonge to be expressed.[34]

This refers in part to a section in the essay devoted to the theme of homosexuality, a section that Elyot chose to omit. Elyot goes on to suggest that he undertook this project in the spirit of a hobby: "I have this done for my pastyme without moch studie or travaile."

That this essay is now known as pseudo-Plutarch makes it no less important to understanding the tradition of the reception. For most early modern readers of Plutarch, this essay on education was considered one of his significant contributions, and it had an impact on their understanding of Plutarch's work as a whole. As summarised in Chapter 1, the work begins with a strong case for the significance of custom and habit in helping to modify the course of nature. The author invokes the famous Spartan anecdote of two dogs trained by Lycurgus being set before the people. When confronted by a rabbit and a bowl of meat, the first hound leaps up to hunt the moving prey, while the other hastens towards the prepared food. The takeaway lesson is that education through custom and habit is a deeper determining factor in the action of these hounds than what they might share in a common nature.

What is deemed important is to ensure the student not forgo honesty in seeking to satiate the appetites of others, a fate that can often befall those driven exclusively by seeking the grace and favour of the masses. These false

---

accessed 2 February 2017. This work was translated into the English vernacular by Elyot using Guarino Guarini's Latin translation of the pseudo-Plutarch essay as the base text.
[34] Elyot, *The Education of Children*.

motivations may also lead to careless speech and immoderate babbling. Good examples of moderation and discretion in public speech to follow are Pericles and Demosthenes who both refused to stretch the truth merely to curry favour with the crowd. Tutors must also seek to rid children of their propensity for arrogant and pompous speech as well as rudeness by encouraging gentleness without excessive fear, because like virtue, being well-spoken is an art of finding a mean.

In terms of a path of life, as noted, the author advocates the mixing of philosophy and the active life, thereby following the examples of Pericles, Archytas, Dion and Epaminondas. This is a message which became a standard trope of English humanism.[35] The discussion offered in chapter 7 of Elyot's translated version is also significant for this narrative. It offers a repudiation of one interpretation of Plato assuming the incompatibility of the active and the contemplative life. This widely circulated and well-known essay associated with Plutarch argues the opposite and suggests that the contemplative life on its own is of little value. While not here suggesting the merits of a public life in the narrowest of senses, the author recommends a life in the service of the "common weale of theyr country" without being motivated by mere subservience to the desires of the crowd. In contrast to the themes generally associated with the reception of Plutarch in France, focusing on the features of "la chose publique" and how action and speech should be adapted to it, we find in Tudor England a somewhat different message associated with the reception of Plutarch that is more inclined to a discussion of the moral make-up of the well-educated gentleman and the appropriate education, preparation, character and motivation for public service. Arguably the importance of the ideal of the public servant is the most important theme throughout the whole of Elyot's work and literary output,[36] but it is also a theme which binds the spirit of much of the vernacular translations of Plutarch's work in England up to the 1570s. For Elyot, as elaborated in *The Boke named the Governour*, education of the nobility was to be in service to the *publike Weal* which was seen as a social whole hierarchically ordered by a principle of equity or desert and governed by moderation and reason (distinguished from the *common weale* which harboured *for him* noxious intimations of democracy – or the types of radical politics invoked by More – and which he

---

[35] See Peltonen, *Classical*, 10. It is identified as an essentially Ciceronian doctrine.
[36] Cathy Shrank, "Sir Thomas Elyot and the Bonds of Community," in M. Pincombe and C. Shrank eds., *The Oxford Handbook of Tudor Literature 1485–1603* (Oxford: Oxford University Press, 2009). Online at www.oxfordhandbooks.com.myaccess.library.utoronto.ca/view/10.1093/oxfordhb/9780199205882.001.0001/oxfordhb-9780199205882-e-010. Date accessed 26 August 2017.

evokes through an association with the term *res plebeia*).[37] So the key to good governance, as gleaned in part from his translation of the pseudo-Plutarch essay and developed in his major treatise in political thought, is an education in the classics, including poetry and tragedy to put fear of tyranny in the minds of the young, and rhetoric and history to develop the traditional virtues. To reiterate the comparison developed here, Plutarch as distilled in French translations and appropriations in France of the early sixteenth century is one focused on *the particular relations and requirements of the public realm to which public figures must adapt in order to achieve their ends*, while the Plutarch represented by reception in England of the same time is focused *on the preparation of individuals entering public life through consideration of their motivation and state of mind*. So, to a certain degree both English and French reception of Plutarch in the early sixteenth century might be said to be characterised by tendencies to focus on and exaggerate the applied, or what Nikolaidis following Pelling calls the protreptic (as opposed to descriptive), forms of moralism in Plutarch, especially when drawing anecdotes from the *Lives*.[38] Still, the traditions tend to do so in two different ways, or with two types of focus, one more narrowly on the public realm and the specific work and place of prudence within that, and the other on the broader moral outlook or moral universe through which human affairs are to be considered more generally.

These two instances of vernacular translations of Plutarch in Tudor England demonstrate several things. Plutarch was not the most pre-eminent among classical sources in intellectual life in England in the early part of the sixteenth century. Plutarch was a not a central choice for translation and reception at the time, in part given his status as a Greek author and therefore the need to come to his work largely through the efforts of previous scholars and intellectual intermediaries such as Budé and Erasmus. Nor was Plutarch deemed to be central to most trends of political reflection at the time. The individuals we see here who chose to translate Plutarch from the Latin often did so as literary exercises. Furthermore, the pieces of Plutarch chosen for translation and dissemination in the vernacular were not the same central works of political reflection, such as *Political Precepts*, that were circulating more widely in the vernacular in France. Still, both Wyatt and Elyot offer these pieces not

---

[37] Thomas Elyot. *The Boke named the Governour* (London: J. M. Dent and co. 1998). Online at www .luminarium.org/renascence-editions/gov/gov1.htm. Date accessed 13 May 2019.

[38] Anastasios G. Nikolaidis, "Morality, Characterization, and Individuality," in Mark Beck ed., *A Companion to Plutarch* (Oxford: Wiley, 2014), 350–372; and Christopher Pelling, *Plutarch and History: Eighteen Studies* (London and Swansea: Bloomsbury, 2002).

as a repudiation of public life, but as counsel for those preparing themselves for entry into the public realm. They stand as versions of a moralist's advice to the politically inclined. In broader terms, the underlying appeal to service for the commonwealth suggests that Plutarch's moralism was received in England through a more general Ciceronian framework, which had already set many of the parameters of political reflection at the time.

This latter point can best be demonstrated if we look to an important moment in English political thought just prior to the vernacular translations of Plutarch by Wyatt and Elyot. Thomas More's *Utopia* (1516) provides us with an example of a thinker who was clearly knowledgeable about Plutarch's work and who drew on Plutarch in important ways in the development of his commentary. And while this work of More was written in Latin, as an important work in the tradition of political thought it merits consideration here as an important indication of the way in which Plutarch was taken up in political thinking in the English Renaissance. As we also can see, More's comment on Plutarch's thought in this treatise demonstrates a prior preoccupation with the themes of political reflection as set down earlier by humanists in their encounter with Cicero – namely, questions of how best to educate and predispose young gentleman for active and honest service to the commonwealth, avoiding the corruption that both status and wealth can bring to political activity.[39] More did not engage in the translation of Plutarch like his good friend Erasmus, but given his association with Erasmus (they met in 1499 and Erasmus stayed at More's home during his time in England) there is no doubt that More was introduced to Plutarch's work through this friendship.

While inspired no doubt by the age of exploration and by voyages to the "new" world, the ideal community constructed by More was also not without precedent.[40] As noted by numerous commentators, a long tradition of speculation on ideal worlds from ancient Greek thought to the Bible helped to inspire a number of the details in *Utopia* as well as the drive behind More's imagined community.[41] In particular, there has been a long

---

[39] For further discussion on More's dialogue with Cicero, see Gary Remer, "More's *Utopia* and its Ciceronian Roots," in D. Kapust and G. Remer eds., *The Ciceronian Tradition in Political Theory* (Madison: The University of Wisconsin Press, 2021), 55–85.

[40] Given that the character Hythloday acknowledges his connection with Amerigo Vespucci, links to the travel literature on exploration of the Americas is often noted. In addition, commentators have acknowledged More's probable inspiration by both Plato's depiction of ideal communities as well as the medieval Cockaigne myth. See, for example, Lawrence Wilde, *Thomas More's Utopia. Arguing for Social Justice* (London and New York: Routledge, 2017), 12–13.

[41] Susan Bruce, "Introduction," in S. Bruce, ed., *Three Early Modern Utopias: Utopia, New Atlantis, The Isle of Pines* (Oxford: Oxford University Press, 1999), xi–xii.

tradition tracing some of the features of More's utopia to the details of Plato's *Republic*. However, as noted by Susan Bruce, "one aspect of the Republic's difference from the early modern utopia can be apprehended when one considers how emphatically, even emblematically, embedded in reality the early modern utopia generally is."[42] More, mirrored by other of his contemporaries writing in the same genre, goes to certain lengths to mask the idealism of the enterprise, making both the occasion on which the details of this community are divulged, as well as the details themselves, as concrete and realistic as possible. If the tradition is ultimately driven by a previous genre of idealism and abstract philosophy, it makes little sense to go to extraordinary lengths to create an atmosphere of verisimilitude. However, if we think of these literary communities as inspired in part by historical examples, such as Sparta, then one might consider this as a reason for seeking to depict those societies with a greater and realist sense of possibility. The tension between the real and the unattainable that is provided by historical distance and the passage of time could be seen to be recreated on a new plane through a tension between the accumulation of detail demonstrating a realist urge and a simultaneous mocking of those details (through nonsensical names and outrageous features). In other words, it may be that the Greek tradition did have an impact on this work but less directly than through the rich lens of Plato and his idealised community, and more directly through the distilled form of Platonism running through Plutarch's account of Sparta. An intent to reference a stylised version of an actual community in the past as grounds for an idealised one in the present heightened the need and the case for verisimilitude even if impossible given both the philosophical and historical distance.

There is of course a long tradition of attributing Greek roots to More's ideal and many in this vein draw on the Greek words ironically invoked by More in the names of places, landmarks and people who inhabit his country (Polylerites, Achorians, Ademus, Anyder, Amaurot, Hythloday and of course the name Utopia itself). More recently Eric Nelson has argued that More was inspired by radical features associated with the model of commonwealth found in Greek *philosophy* and speculative thought and it was these features that made his project appear nonsensical, at least when viewed from within an alternative form of republicanism inspired by the Roman tradition.[43] Still, earlier lines of argument suggest

---

[42] Bruce, "Introduction," xii.
[43] Nelson, "Greek Nonsense," 889–917. Of course, this stands as an earlier statement of his treatment of More as found in *The Greek Tradition*.

that aspects of classical Greek *history* invoked by More in this work are features that render it more real and compelling rather than nonsensical. For example, R. Schoeck suggested many years ago that More could have been inspired by a reading of Plutarch's life of King Agis IV in his depiction of Utopia, in part because Sparta prior to Agis's ascent to the throne was depicted as suffering under some of the same challenges attributed to England by More in Book 1 of his work, and resolved by King Agis in ways similar to what More portrays in *Utopia* in Book 2.[44] Others note the resonance of the figure Utopus with the historical figure Lycurgus.[45] Indeed, we are told quite explicitly in the text that the Utopians "set great store by Plutarch's books" and that they have access to the Greek grammatical text of Lascaris, the Byzantine émigré who helped to spread the reading of Plutarch within the French court.[46] We are also told that the Utopians were able to develop the technology of printing from a study of the printed works of Aldus.[47] Given Erasmus's association with Aldus on the production of works of Plutarch, it can be surmised that those works of Aldus studied by the Utopians for printing technology may also have been those "Plutarch books" which had already been recognised as a valuable resource for the community.

Still, it may be most revealing to explore these questions thematically. In other words, what are some of the important themes that link More's text and Plutarch's work? Even if there are few explicit textual references, it is very clear on examination the large extent to which Plutarch stands as an important referent for More in the development of his political ideas.

There has been much discussion of the theme of counsel or public service around which the initial account of the meeting of Hythloday and the retelling of his first encounters with the Utopians is structured.[48] It is also significant to recognise the way in which this discussion of counsel

---

[44] R. Schoeck, "More, Plutarch, and King Agis: Spartan History and the Meaning of Utopia," *Philological Quarterly* 35 (January 1956), 366–376.

[45] Cathy Curtis, "Thomas More and Quentin Skinner," in Annabel Brett and James Tully eds., *Rethinking the Foundations of Modern Political Thought* (Cambridge: Cambridge University Press, 2006), 107. Martha Hale Shackford also claims that More was predominantly inspired by Plutarch's *Life of Lycurgus* and the Instituta Laconica in the drafting of his details of the Utopia regime. See her *Plutarch in Renaissance England* (Wellesley, MA: Wellesley College, 1929), p. 23.

[46] Thomas More, "Utopia," in Susan Bruce ed., *Three Early Modern Utopias* (Oxford: Oxford University Press, 1999), 86–87.

[47] More, "Utopia," 87.

[48] See, for example, C. B. Schmitt and Quentin Skinner, "Political Philosophy," in *Cambridge History of Renaissance Philosophy* (Cambridge: Cambridge University Press, 1988), 451. In particular, the focus on counsel was part and parcel of a feature of what Skinner came to call the neo-Roman tradition, a feature that defended an active life of *negotium* on the part of the citizen and public servant. See also his *Foundations*.

is raised; how there is in this discussion deliberation about the principles which should direct the exercise of counsel linked to competing understandings of counsel's purpose and nature. Peter Giles asks his new acquaintance why he does not choose to serve the king, something that Hythloday recharacterises as a form of slavery. Giles persists: "It is not my mind that you should be in bondage to kings, but as a retainer to them at your pleasure. Which surely I think is the highest way that you can devise how to bestow your time fruitfully, not only for the private commodity of your friends and for the general profit of all sorts of people, but also for the advancement of yourself to a much wealthier state and condition than you be now in."[49] Here the basic issues associated with the exercise of counsel are twofold: one is the potential loss of individual autonomy or independence in entering upon service to the king, and the second is weighing this possible cost against the potential benefit of the outcomes, both in terms of good public policy as well as one's own reputation and standing, which can be furthered by a good-willed offer of service to someone in power (hence Giles appeal to utility). In deeper terms, then, the focus of this short exchange is on the motivation of the individual contemplating entry into public service, and the possible benefits and disadvantages of offering oneself for public service. Hythloday suggests that the disadvantages of entry into public service are much greater than those suggested by Peter, partly because the motivations of those already at court are deemed corrupt and more attuned to self-promotion than to service, making them unreceptive to a voice of experience, truth and good-willed service. In more general terms, we see here juxtaposed two distinct versions or conceptions of the key motivations for public service. Hythloday is suggesting that an ethos of good public service necessarily entails a commitment of loyalty towards the king and hence a potential loss of independence; Giles is suggesting that the motivation needed to be a good public servant does not necessarily require a repudiation of self but that the benefits and motivation of serving a public function can be seen to be compatible with certain benefits of wealth and status to the self. These are two views centred on a conception of public service focused on the nature of the *motivation of the public servant*, a focus which we have already seen continued to be dominant in English discussions of the public good in the early Renaissance. In other words, contrary to the view that Giles represents the standard commonwealth and neo-Roman position with a defence of the active life in *negotium*, while Hythloday represents the

---

[49] More, "Utopia," 15–16.

position of *otium* or a defence of the contemplative life, I am suggesting that both sides in fact present conflicting visions of what *negotium* requires, for Hythloday is not looking at the stars in any Platonist contemplative sense, but merely suggesting that true public spiritedness requires a much more radical rethinking and reconstruction of standard public norms.[50]

Then the discussion evolves beyond a question of *what should motivate* one who counsels the king, to the *actual content of that counsel*. A broad number of policy matters are raised, including the managing of standing armies, approaches to punishment, and enclosures. In this second stage Hythloday is no longer talking to Peter Giles, but to More himself. At one point Hythloday excoriates the French and their policies towards standing armies as well as their foreign relations because first and foremost their deliberations are founded on questions of expediency: "Well, suppose I were with the French king, and there sitting in his council while in that most secret consultation, the king himself there being present in his own person, they beat their brains, and search the very bottoms of their wits to discuss by what craft and means the king may still keep Milan and draw to him again fugitive Naples; and then how to conquer the Venetians, and how to bring under his jurisdiction all Italy."[51] He imagines the various forms of counsel voiced based on competing conceptions of what is most expedient. Hythloday suggests that if he were party to these deliberations his recommendations would be based on uncompromising principle, though drawn from observation, that expansion itself is a misguided goal in matters of politics.

> Here, I say, where so great and high matters be in consultation, where so many noble and wise men counsel their king only to war, here if I, silly man, should rise up and will them to turn over the leaf, and learn a new lesson, saying that my counsel is not to meddle with Italy, but to tarry still at home, and that the kingdom of France alone is almost greater than that it may well be governed of one man, so that the king should not need to study how to get more ... if I should declare unto them that all this busy preparance to war, whereby so many nations for his sake should be brought into a troublesome hurly-burly, when all his coffers were emptied, his treasures wasted, and his people destroyed, should at the length through some mischance be in vain and to none effect, and that therefore it were best

---

[50] Here I am taking issue with the presentation of Cathy Curtis who states: "The authorial More in book I sets 'civic' or Ciceronian humanism, as articulate by the figure of More, against a Platonic notion of contemplative withdrawal, argued by Hythloday." See "Thomas More and Quentin Skinner," in Annabel Brett and J. Tully eds., *Rethinking the Foundations of Modern Political Thought* (Cambridge: Cambridge University Press, 2010), 100.

[51] More, "Utopia," 34.

for him to content himself with his own kingdome of France ... to make much of it, to enrich it, and to make it as flourishing as he could, to endeavour himself to love his subjects, and again to be beloved of them, willingly to live with them, peaceably to govern them, and with other kingdoms not to meddle, seeing that which he hath already is even enough for him, yea, and more than he can well turn him to: this mine advice, Master More, how think you it would be heard and taken?[52]

While some commentators have suggested that More invokes the French in this introduction as a foil or to exculpate himself from charges of criticising his own monarch, there is another way to consider this. One might consider that the invocation of the French state was a means for More to engage with what he considered to be a broader ethos of expediency that he saw as more strongly represented or emanating from the French case. Even if the Tory translation of Plutarch's *Precepts* post-dated More's work, it would not invalidate the idea of a spirit of expediency being present in the French case, for it was precisely elements of that tone that were inflected in Tory's translation. Of course, it does not mean that this form of reasoning was geographically limited to the case of France. Here, and in the continuing discussion over such matters as tax policy and collection, Hythloday challenges deliberations that weigh competing claims of various public constituencies and an evaluation of contextual considerations with his own set of absolute principles. He seeks to counteract an adjudication of equitable responses with a distinct vision of justice that modifies the basic rules and assumptions of traditional politics, most forcefully with his advocacy of the abolition of private property. It is the very way of thinking about the common weal that Elyot would later forcefully reject. The principles and absolutist rejection of politics-as-usual clearly link his reflections in this opening discussion to the more systematic depiction of a new regime and a new form of institutional refashioning that is exemplified by the state of Utopia.

Against the background of our broader discussion of the reception of Plutarch's work in France and England over the course of the first half of the sixteenth century it is possible to read the discussion that More provides for us at the outset of his work in a different light than is usually presented. More appears to be acknowledging here the clash between two different competing views of public life. The first is that which More centres on the notion of expediency, but in a more generous light could be depicted as the idea that public matters require a fine-tuned ethos which is specific to its nature.

---

[52] More, "Utopia," 34–37.

Matters of perception and concern for a broader good and multiple publics, both present and future, require a refined consideration of benefits and disadvantages in each matter subject to public decision. More acknowledges, however, that there are circumstances in which this first ideal of public service can clash with another conception of counsel. The crux of the matter is that Hythloday rejects the idea that the good-willed counsellor is one who demonstrates loyalty to their king or people of the court, but that the good counsellor can only be one whose sole focus and concern is the good of the broader public. The contrast between Hythloday and the Giles/More inter-locutor can be understood as a contrast between two conflicting visions of what an ethos of devotion to the public good requires.

Through this More, the author, is suggesting that the humanist focus on motivation as key to good public service, if understood through a different lens, can lead to much more radical and principled objection to the current structures of institutional life. So, in this initial discussion More opposes what he sees as a burgeoning French approach to the exercise of public office in England and counters what he sees as a deficient tendency in those trends. To highlight this picture, he provides us with a powerful reinterpretation and application of the English humanist view regarding the motivation of the counsellor as key, one which focuses solely on the vision of the broader good. This new application of the requirement that the measure of good public service is the good motivation of the counsellor results in questioning the basic parameters through which public matters have been designed and structured. As we are told, "Howbeit, doubtless, Master More (to speak truly as my mind giveth me), where possessions be private, where money beareth all the stroke it is hard and almost impossible that there the weal-public may justly be governed and prosperously flourish."[53] The good counsellor, the one with the best possible motivations, as modelled on Hythloday, has become a radical opponent to existing policy and socio-economic structures. The community of Utopia stands as the model or the beacon of the good society through which the inspiration for those challenges take shape. Thus, More is suggesting that there is a difference between loyalty to a public office and loyalty to the public good, and that the measure of a good public servant may in fact be their willingness to challenge the established political order of things. More takes on a Ciceronian theme, as often acknowledged by other scholars, while also challenging traditional invocations of it.[54] But as More

---

[53] More, "Utopia," 44.
[54] John Guy, *Thomas More* (London: Hodder Education, 2000); Quentin Skinner, "Thomas More's Utopia and the Virtue of True Nobility," in Q. Skinner ed., *Visions of Politics*, vol. 1 (Cambridge:

was to find out in 1534, loyalty to a principled conception of public good over loyalty to a public office can be a matter of life and death.

More's use of Plutarch does not structure his position in this work (for as we have argued the focus on the motivation of the public servant in English sixteenth century thought was driven largely by reference to other classical sources), but, as we shall see, reference to Plutarch does inform its shape in less central ways by offering material on which More draws to develop his argument in the text. As is well noted, Hythloday explicitly invokes Plato, thereby suggesting that his work inspired select features of the Utopian regime.[55] Alongside Plato there have been some, although much fewer, acknowledgements of More's debt to Plutarch. Plutarch's depiction of the regime of Sparta as discussed in the lives of Lycurgus, Agesilaus and King Agis IV can be recognised as a source, especially given the way in which Plutarch is well known to be reading Spartan experience through the lens of Plato.

The details that link Plutarch's *Life of Lycurgus* and More's *Utopia* are multiple: a founder inspired by a combination of Cretan principles of severity and simplicity with Ionian principles of comfort and pleasure, frugal and plain dress, few laws, common meals (enforced by general norms and principles of shame rather than penalties), recourse to bonds-men or helots for some of the daily manual labour, prohibition against unrestricted travel, mutual surveillance as a means to enforce morals, new customary practices of coinage and new uses for silver and gold so as to challenge and subvert the usual practices of wealth accumulation and commercial exchange, and the parading of young women in scant clothing in front of young men to encourage effective coupling.[56]

Of course, not all the details are the same. Most importantly, while the Lycurgan model of Sparta is as a community guided by the object of war and the production of good warriors, Utopia guides itself by more peaceful principles, again most likely inspired to a certain degree by Erasmus's hostility to combat and his stricture of only engaging in war for self-defence or to come to the aid of allies who are defending themselves against an aggressor.[57] And while some might suggest this distinction is crucial in distinguishing the two regimes, it is clearly important to acknowledge

Cambridge University Press, 2002), 213–244. For a revisiting and recasting of this interpretation, see John Guy, "Thomas More and Tyranny," *Moreana* 49.189–190 (2012), 157–188.

[55] "If so be that I should speak those things that Plato feigneth in his weal-public, or that the Utopians do in theirs, these things, thought they were (as they be indeed) better, yet they might seem spoken out of place." More, "Utopia," 42.

[56] More, "Utopia," 60–61, 65, 68, 71, 94.

[57] More, "Utopia," 97. Indeed they send few if any of their own citizens to war with a preference for hiring mercenaries, 100–101.

a more fundamental similarity in how the basic principles around which the regimes are structured are articulated. For Plutarch's Lycurgus it is this:

> It was not however, the chief design of Lycurgus then to leave his city in command over a great many others, but he thought that the happiness of an entire city, like that of a single individual, depended on the prevalence of virtue and concord within its borders. The aim, therefore, of all his arrangements and adjustments was to make his people free-minded, self-sufficing and moderate in all their ways, and to keep them so long as possible.[58]

For More, Utopia is the only form of true commonwealth:

> Now I have declared and described unto you as truly as could the form and order of that commonwealth, which verily in my judgement is not only the best, but also that which alone of good right may claim and take upon it the name of a commonwealth or public weal. For in other places they speak still of the commonwealth. But every man procureth his own private gain. Here, where nothing is private, the common affairs by earnestly looked upon.[59]

For both, it is the predominant ethos of virtue and concord that drives their ultimate design.

Of course, there is a great deal more going on in More's text than a commentary on Plutarch. Commentators have noted, for example, his important debt to Lucian among other Hellenistic writers.[60] There is clearly a syncretic exercise going on in this work with a combination of principles of Epicureanism, natural religion and civic republicanism.[61] It may also be that in his preoccupation with the ideal of virtuous public service More participates in a general tradition of what has famously been called neo-Roman thought, even though for More it is not clear that liberty as self-governance may be regarded as the supreme political good.[62] However, it is also the case that More is providing critical commentary on that same notion of service, and thus to some extent, in his partial deconstruction of it he stands apart from it in conventional terms. More's invocation of Plutarch, albeit sometimes in oblique ways, leads us to acknowledge the complicated strands of thinking woven into this work.

---

[58] Plutarch, *Life of Lycurgus*, 31.1.   [59] More, "Utopia," 119.
[60] On Lucian's influence on More, see for example, Raisch, "Humanism and Hellenism."
[61] For a discussion of More's mixture of Epicurean principles and those of natural religion, see Ana Claudia Romano Ribeiro, "Intertextual connections between Thomas More's *Utopia*, and Cicero's *De finibus bonorum et malorum*," *Moreana* 51.195–6 (2014), 63–84.
[62] For a discussion of this as well as of the distinction between the earlier invocation of a republican tradition and the later invocation of a neo-Roman tradition by Skinner, partly due to the pioneering work of Patrick Collinson, see Cathy Curtis, "Thomas More and Quentin Skinner," in Brett and Tully eds., *Rethinking the Foundations*, 91–112.

Nonetheless, the reading of More's *Utopia* with a broader tradition of Plutarch reception in mind may serve to highlight various things. In the first instance, as we have seen, More invokes in passing the very contrast we have been developing in our discussion of Plutarch reception, between, on the one hand, an English approach to public life which in rhetorical terms focused on the purity of the public motivation of the public servant, and, on the other hand, an approach to public matters represented by the French court where more realist considerations were at play. Secondly, we find in More's account a rather ambiguous analysis of the traditional Ciceronian focus on the quality of the public servant's motivation as a key to good political outcomes. We can consider this work as a form of commentary on thinking about politics through this lens. More suggests that the devotion to the public good, which should remain the ultimate measure of appropriate political motivation, can come into conflict both with demands for personal loyalty that often characterise public life and with practical policy options. True devotion to the public good, as argued through Hythloday, could only result in a radical reshaping of the most basic institutions and practices of the realm, eliminating the very structures that cause poverty for example. Still, these revisions are presented in a spirit that make them appear to be close to impossible. More appears not to be telling us that human motivation can never be truly public spirited (in the way that Dauber characterised the challenges of later English Renaissance political thinking as informed by Reformation thinking), because it remains within the power of our imaginations to think about and even to desire such changes; however, he may offer us a powerful indictment of the strength of the forces and institutions that serve to resist and even complicate such change. Plutarch's Lycurgus, in the widely circulated early modern apocryphal essay on education, served as a beacon and inspiration to the power of education. In the work of More, Lycurgus is now invoked, it would appear, in a more problematic way. In More's work it becomes no longer clear whether the required changes in both institutional reform and the education of mores to redress the deep and pressing problems of the contemporary socio-economic order come at a cost that is worth bearing.

5.2.2 *Plutarch and His Vernacular Reception in England 1550–1579: Humanists in the Service of the Consolidation of Monarchical Power*

As the Tudor era developed, the language of humanism in relation to political theory shifted in line with the political climate. It is generally recognised that the civic ethos of early Renaissance political thought in

England gave way to greater defence of established hierarchies and more subtle awareness of personal motivations and how they might be reconciled with a coherent political project. Whether this meant an abandonment of civic republican themes in political thought or merely a reconfiguration of them is something that does not concern us directly here.[63] However, in terms of Plutarch reception what we do see are two important examples of translations of Plutarch into the vernacular which offer a much more solid endorsement of established institutional arrangements and social orders.

Perhaps one of the most widely circulated versions of Plutarch in the vernacular in sixteenth-century England before the work of Thomas North is that of Richard Taverner (1505–1575) who provided his compatriots with distilled passages from Plutarch. Taverner is perhaps best known for his 1539 English translation of the Bible subsequent to the 1534 Act of Supremacy and Henry VIII's break from Rome, although he also taught Greek at Cambridge.[64] Taverner seized on Erasmus's compendium of passages from classical sources, including Plutarch, that made up his *Adagia* and *Apophthegmata* and worked in both translation and editing to provide his readers with a more accessible version of these texts published under the titles *The Garden of Wisdom* (1539), *The Second Book of the Garden of Wisdom* (1539) (with some evidence of a third), and *Proverbes or adagies* with the latter undergoing at least six editions, some with additions taken from Erasmus's *Chiliades*.[65] He is regarded as a key figure in the dissemination of Erasmus's work in England, and these were books found within a broader genre offering compilations of sayings and anecdotes of classical history and philosophy, presumably to provide insight that could be applied to contemporary life for the general reader. As we have seen in our discussion of Erasmus's own translations of Plutarch, there was already an important gap in how Erasmus took up the meaning of these passages (as is evident from his added commentary to the text). Taverner, in adding his own commentary to the passages and editing to a large degree the additions of Erasmus, provides us with yet another somewhat modified iteration of Plutarch. In other of Taverner's works it has been suggested that he was largely an agent of "propaganda," perhaps summoned by

---

[63] See, for example, the discussion of Dauber, *State and Commonwealth*, 10–11.

[64] For a brief discussion of Taverner's life, see Vivienne Westbrook, "Richard Taverner Revising Tyndale," *Reformation* 2.1 (1997), 191–205.

[65] D. T. Starnes suggests that the first edition of the *Garden of Wisdom* may have predated 1539, although 1539 is the date of the earliest extant edition. See " Richard Taverner's *The Garden of Wisdom*, Carion's *Chronicles* and the Cambyses Legend," *Studies in English* 35 (1956), 22–23. On possible evidence of a third Garden of Wisdom compilation, see E. J. Devereux, "Richard Taverner's Translations of Erasmus," *The Library* 5.19 (January 1964), 212–214.

Thomas Cromwell, his patron, to offer a strong defence of the newly reformed Anglican Church and the consolidation of political power that accompanied it.[66] Can this more diffuse moralistic work of translation be understood in the same light?

According to Agnes Juhász-Ormsby, the major thrust of Taverner's work in the *Garden of Wisdom* and *The Second Book of the Garden of Wisdom* was to offer a more easily accessible selection (it was a shorter work and in the English vernacular) of passages from Erasmus's *Sayings* to support a broader project of moral instruction in the wake of the Act of Supremacy (1534) and English reform, along with interjections offering mild admonition of the king.[67] This modifies an earlier reading by Baskervill who suggests that the additions of Taverner in his own words to the commentary on the *Adagia* are more narrow in intent, offering unquestioned praise and support for the crown and the reformed church.[68] Of note is the opening selection in *The Garden of Wisdom*. In relation to King Agasicles of Sparta who is reported to say that a prince can safely rule without any guards if he treats his subjects like he would his own children, Taverner adds the following commentary: "Certes this saying to be true" citing

> the experience at this day of the most excellent prince our sovereign lord king Henry the VIII. Lord god to what inward joy, with what hardy love and reverence do all his liege subjects embrace the majesty of his gracious person, and not only his liege subjects but also even the very rank traitors, which intended nothing else but sedition, yet the incomparable majesty of his own person they could not but have in wondrous reverence.[69]

We are far removed here from More's allusions to the Spartan example as a means to offer critical perspective on English politics. Still, Juhász-Ormsby

---

[66] Charles Baskervill, "Taverner's *Garden of Wisdom* and the *Apophthegmata* of Erasmus," *Studies in Philology*, (1932), 149–159. Westbrook confirms this view stating: "Taverner was therefore in place in the official Protestant propaganda machinery at the start of official Protestantism in England." Westbrook, "Richard Taverner," 191.

[67] Juhász-Ormsby, "Erasmus' *Apophthegmata*."

[68] Baskervill, "Taverner," 158–159. This is a view also argued by John Yost who notes several places in Taverner's commentary on Erasmus's translation that clearly give support for the principles of a Protestant humanism. See John K. Yost, "German Protestant Humanism and the Early English Reformation: Richard Taverner and Official Translation," *Bibliotheque d'Humanisme et Renaissance* 32.3 (1970), 613–625.

[69] Richard Taverner, ed. *The Garden of Wysdom, wherein ye maye gather moste pleasaunt flowres thath is to say, proper witty and quycke sayenges of princes, philosophers, and dyvers other sortes of men. Frawn forth of good authours, as well Grekes as Latyns by Richard Taverner*, 1539. Consulted through Early English Books Online, November 2017. Further reference to this work will be done with the title *The Garden of Wisdom*.

suggests that in the characterisation of the 'traitors' as nothing more than 'seditious,' Taverner is chastising the king for his execution of the leader of the 1538 Exeter Conspiracy and offering through both these comments as well as other comments regarding Augustus's treatment of Cinna, the need for the king to be merciful. The nuance is very subtle, however, and appears quite compatible with a broader purpose of giving historical and intellectual legitimacy to King Henry's ongoing work of political consolidation.

In subsequent comments, Taverner goes on the suggest that Englishmen of his own era should model themselves after the Spartan citizen solider who did not ask how many enemy soldiers there were, but rather where they were, suggesting that their "hardiness, courage, readiness and celerity" as well as loyalty to the king in whatever quarrel he was engaged in was a necessary and sufficient mark of good citizenship.[70] Yet again in the midst of a discussion of Dionissius (sic) he states:

> Demanded of a certain person whether he were idle. God forbid . . . that this thing should ever chance unto me: Meaning that it was a right foul thing for heads and ministers of commonweals not to execute diligently their office. But assuredly here our most . . . sovereign lord king Henry VIII may be a mirror and spectacle to all princes and other interior officers. For who ever either more prudently or more vigilantly hath governed a commonweal.[71]

It is no doubt curious that Taverner felt that various sayings of kings and commanders could be indiscriminately used as a basis for meting out praise for his own king. It is certainly not without some irony that both Spartans as well as Dionysius the Elder, the despot of Syracuse (430–376 BCE) might be considered equally good sources for identifying the virtues of public life in Tudor England. Political theorists will also note Taverner's extraordinary move in which the mirror for princes tradition is invoked and reversed such that it is no longer the virtuous political leaders of the past who are being raised as a means to educate and shape the virtue of the acting ruler, but the acting ruler, in this case Henry VIII, who is being invoked as the exemplar of virtue for all others. While this rhetoric may be a trope of

---

[70] Taverner, *Garden* "Agis."

[71] This saying is taken and translated from Erasmus's *Apophthegmata* drawing from Plutarch's "Sayings from Kings and Commanders" in the *Moralia*. The entirety of the Erasmus translation and commentary is as follows: "When someone asked Dionysius if he was at leisure, he said 'May that never befall me.' He realized that it was very shameful for a ruler ever to be at leisure from state business. So where are those men who spend a great part of the day in dicing and games of chance?" Of course, the quote itself is taken from Plutarch and the elaboration on its meaning is the commentary added by Erasmus. See Erasmus, *Apophthegmata, book 5 in The Collected Works of Erasmus, vol. 38*, eds. Elaine Fantham and Betty Knott (Toronto: University of Toronto Press, 2014), 5.62, 474.

dedicatory letters in the Renaissance, the remarkable feature of this praise is that it is embedded in the very midst of a supposed translation, thereby blurring the traditional lines between the textual and the paratextual material.

Juhász-Ormsby suggests Taverner's commentary on the Macedonian king, Antigonus, that "the king is not the rule of honesty and justice, but the minister of honesty and justice" is offered in the spirit of counsel and education for Henry VIII; but in terms of doctrine there is no version of absolutism which would hold anything different, despite Taverner's suggestion that certain flatterers might advocate otherwise.[72] Given the ongoing theme throughout this text of obedience to the king, as well as the depiction of the king as a model and mirror for others, it may be that the subtle invocations of policy and political practice are aimed at those who counsel the king and perhaps the king himself, not in a spirit of admonition but through a historically informed ideal of just rule.

It may also be pertinent here to compare this use of Plutarch for the glorification of an exercise in absolutism, with a previous figure we have briefly examined in the French case, namely Budé. As we saw, Budé uses elements of Plutarch's *Sayings* and places them in an interpretative context for a defence of developing absolutist power. Unlike Taverner, however, we do not see Budé ever suggesting a conflation of monarchical power with paternal power. Budé, as a committed humanist, argues that the king provides a favourable climate for learning with lessons drawn from classical thought serving as an invitation to study the classical age. It appears here and elsewhere that Taverner does little in terms of policy prescription and instead uses this selective account of classical figures to remind the court of the *supremacy* of justice as an ideal, even for absolute monarchs.

As an additional example of Plutarch translation being used towards a project of regime consolidation, we see a fourth Thomas – Blundeville (c. 1522–c.1606) – providing Tudor England with a vernacular version of Plutarch prior to the more famous contributions of North. In 1561 Blundeville published a poetic rendition of two of Plutarch's essays including "How to Profit from your Enemies," along with the translation of an additional Plutarch essay in prose. Blundeville wrote on various topics including astronomy, horsemanship and education (as well as being known for inventing the protractor). He provided his poetic rendition of Plutarch's famous essay in a work entitled *Three Moral Treatises* published in part, it is said, to commemorate the accession of Elizabeth I to the throne of

---

[72] Juhász-Ormsby, "Erasmus' *Apophthegmata*," 55.

England in 1558. Schurink, in referring to the collection of treatises by Plutarch translated by Blundeville, suggests, "while the work is, on one level, a simple celebration of the new regime by a previously unpublished author in search of patronage and preferment, it is also a skilful attempt to influence the future direction of the commonwealth by appealing to a shared past and present."[73] In this trilogy of verse translations, Blundeville places Plutarch's "The Learned Prince" (a verse translation of Plutarch's "To an Uneducated Prince") at the opening of the work alongside a dedication to Queen Elizabeth. Still, as Schurink suggests, he had translated "The Fruits of Foes" (otherwise known as "How to Profit from your Enemies") earlier and had given the new queen a copy as a New Year's gift shortly after her accession to the throne. These first two pieces were adapted and translated from Latin versions which had been translated earlier from the Greek by Erasmus.[74] The third piece included in the work is "The Port of Rest" or a translation of "Quiet of Mind" (also sometimes referred to as "On the Tranquility of the Soul" and the same essay from the same Latin source of Budé's translated earlier by his compatriot Thomas Wyatt).

Schurink suggests that these translations offered to the new queen were not only intended to present specific advice, but to more broadly endear the monarch to Blundeville and his collaborators as likeminded (both Blundeville and Queen Elizabeth were admirers of the work of Plutarch) and 'natural counsellors,' that is, well-suited to be chosen as administrators for the new regime. Still, it is somewhat curious that Blundeville considered that he could impress the queen with his skills for diplomacy and political acumen through the rendering of Plutarch into rhyming verse. According to Cummings the pitch may also have been merely stylistic to demonstrate to the queen, and to her tutor Roger Ascham, the translator's acumen and abilities in rendering Plutarch's message through another literary form, as an exercise in 'metaphrase'.[75] Whatever the case, it did not result in a posting.

In the rendering of Plutarch's essay in verse, Blundeville takes away some of the subtlety of the original but offers a pointed and clear message: "Hereby therefore we may perceive that of our foe right perilous, In this our lyfe we may receive, Such fruites as be commodious . . . .For though some thynges be very ill, To those, to whom they appertaine, Yet used they may be, with suche skyll; As losse shall easily turne to gaine." The general

---

[73] Schurink, "Print, Patronage and Occasion," 95.

[74] Cummings, "Versifying Philosophy," 104. Erasmus's Latin translation of "How to Profit from Your Enemies" was initially dedicated to Wolsey.

[75] Cummings, "Versifying Philosophy," 106.

thrust of the essay is a variant on Hellenistic moralism but with a social psychological edge. Given that we are sometimes blind to our own faults as well as to those of our friends, our enemies can be helpful in leading us to virtue, partly by indicating to us where our faults may lie, and partly by demonstrating to us certain virtues. In broader terms, given that social enmity is a fact of life, we can respond to that tension in productive or in destructive ways. Plutarch suggests that not only civil peace is possible through a productive response to social tension, but that it can even offer a means of individual moral development. It is of interest, nonetheless, in the broader context of the development of political thinking of the time, that the Plutarchan message being picked up and distributed publicly in this later Tudor period is no longer focused on a pure ethos of public service and devotion to the commonwealth, but one which acknowledges an array of motivations including strong personal honour which can lead to bitter rivalries and vicious tactics in public life. While Plutarch in this essay does advise his readers to take the high road so that their dealings in public life serve the improvement of their souls, he presumes a background of an awareness of overall moral weakness that resonates with contemporary scholarly accounts of the tone of political reflection at the time.

5.2.3 Epilogue to the Tudor Reception of Plutarch: Elizabeth I's Own Vernacular Translation

In 1598, towards the end of a long and tumultuous reign and five years before her death, Elizabeth I sat down to engage in a translation of Plutarch's moral essay "On Curiosity." This was not her first encounter with Plutarch. Her tutor in classical literature from a young age had been Roger Ascham, well known to have been acquainted with Greek sources, and indeed it was his knowledge of Greek that had given Elizabeth the skills to continue to translate Greek sources well into her old age. As we have seen also, Blundeville had rendered several of Plutarch's moral essays into verse as a gift to the queen.[76] Indeed, Blundeville's gift may have been in her mind as she worked on this translation, for while it was not presented in the identical poetic mode, it did present itself in the form of verse.

What were the queen's intentions as she embarked on the translation of this text? According to an early editor, the quality of this translation is not exacting, although it must be acknowledged that the queen was translating this essay directly from the Greek and was around sixty-five years old without

---

[76] Blundeville, *Three Moral Treatises*, London, 1561.

practice of her skills in ancient Greek given her preoccupation with the affairs of state.[77] The choice of this moral essay is curious in and of itself, due to its preoccupation with a line between private matters and an inquiring public. While the act of translating may have been an intellectual challenge to both test and rest the Queen's mind amidst pressing affairs of state, the essay invoked themes that were very much related to her role as a public figure.

Caroline Pemberton suggests that the thrust of Plutarch in general, including this essay, was of a Stoic bent, offering strategies for moral edification and the eradication of vices.[78] However, a more subtle reading of the essay and its translation offers a somewhat different lesson. Plutarch does not tell us to eradicate curiosity as a natural human impulse but to control the objects of our curiosity and to focus on knowledge of those matters which will incline to our good. There is also an interesting introduction to the lines between public life and private.

The first concern of Plutarch in "On Curiosity" is the eagerness of some to pry into the more hidden and private, and thus potentially more scandalous, facets of the lives of others. Indeed, this title is sometimes translated as "On being a Busybody". The broad complaint is that the desire to learn about the troubles of others and reveal them is driven by a deeper form of envy (like pain at the sight of good things happening to one's rival) and malice (or delight in the pain and evil brought to another) and "both spring from a savage and bestial affliction, a vicious nature."[79] To overcome a propensity for these vices, Plutarch suggest an inward focus on one's own faults and deficiencies. He suggests that this type of morbid curiosity into the secrets and faults of others can be destructive to the curious, especially in relation to the powerful. As Plutarch states:

> For only the most pleasant and most decorous attributes of kings are displayed openly – their banquets and wealth and festivals and favours; but if there is anything secret, do not approach it, but let it be! The joy of a prosperous king is not concealed, nor is his laughter when he is amused, nor his outlay on entertainment and favours; but it is time for alarm when something is hidden, something dark, unsmiling, unapproachable, a storehouse of festering wrath, or the meditation of a punishment indica-tive of sullen anger, or jealousy of a wife, or some suspicion against a son, or distrust of a friend. Beware of this darkening and gathering cloud! That

[77] Caroline Pemberton, "Forewords," in *Queen Elizabeth Englishings* (London: Kegan Paul, Trench, Trubner et Co. 1899).

[78] Pemberton, "Forewords."

[79] Taken from s. 6, 491 of the Loeb translation of the essay found online at http://penelope.uchicago.edu /Thayer/E/Roman/Texts/Plutarch/Moralia/De_curiositate*.html. Date accessed 9 November 2020.

which is now hidden will be disclosed to you when the cloud bursts forth amid crashes of thunder and bolt of lightning![80]

It would seem to suggest that the unpleasant aspects of those in power can also be destructive and that these more private features may be revealed in time. It has a slight air of menace. Those in public life have propensities they might try to keep more hidden, but in the end, those can be revealed in full force. As Elizabeth translates the latter part of this passage: "What hidden is fearful, woful, Sower and unknowen, the tresor of an Oveflowing, wasting Ire, Or rather habit deape in mynd to folle revenge, Or zelozie of wife, or Sons suspect, or dout of frind, Fly thou this darke and thikky mysty folded Cloude; A flasche and thoundar shal burst out whan hidden shewes."[81] If this offers any allusion to a display of anger in the face of perceived treachery, it is by all accounts not far off the mark as a description of periodic displays of extreme anger by the queen herself.

In the spirit of Plutarch's other essay "How to Profit from your Enemies," he describes a way in which this exercise of curiosity can be socially useful, not for those who exercise curiosity but for the objects of curiosity. As Elizabeth notes in her translation, "The Curius more profit yeldz his foes than good unto himself; that telleth them ther Lacks and where they do, and that bettar they may ware the warnid to correct."[82] So, as in the earlier essay, those who harbour ill-will towards us and who seek to illuminate our errors do us a good turn by showing us our faults and thereby motivate us to do better.

Despite its possible usefulness in social terms, Plutarch counsels his readers to avoid curiosity. The problem is not just curiosity's rootedness in vice, but also in its all-consuming energy that corrupts and makes it difficult for the busybody to focus on anything else but the faults of others and unfortunate events. In addition, this inclination to vice makes others shun the busybody, who is deemed untrustworthy and immoderate.

There is a point when Plutarch may sound like a Stoic in suggesting that his readers cultivate habits to soften their curious motivations, such as to decline to open messages immediately on notice of their delivery (good advice for a whole new technological era . . .). However, for the most part, Plutarch does not advocate repression of these curious motivations but instead for a redirection of the mind to such things as the secrets of nature or the historical display of personal faults and evils, where one may "Glut and enjoy yourself and cause no trouble or pain to any of your associates!"[83]

---

[80] Ibid., s. 4, 485. [81] Plutarch's "De Curiositate" in *Queen Elizabeth Englishings*, 126.
[82] Plutarch's "De Curiositate" in *Queen Elizabeth Englishings*, 123. [83] Ibid., s. 5, 487.

A more concerted effort to focus attention on things that matter and not on the trivial will help to develop a habit that could ward off the misuse of curiosity. "For as eagles and lions draw in their claws when they walk so that they may not ware off the sharpness of the tips, so, if we consider that curiosity for learning has also a sharp and keen edge, let us not waste or blunt it upon matters of no value."[84] The more basic point is not to deny these motivations, but to exercise them in appropriate ways that ultimately serves one's own interest.

What then was the political significance of Elizabeth's translation of this specific Plutarch essay in 1598? There is some possibility that this essay was chosen to reflect on the morals and manners of courtly life as they had been evolving in the latter part of Elizabeth's reign. There is commentary on an increasing sense of corruption within the Tudor court.[85] Plutarch here offers us an account of the origin of the term 'sycophant,' as one who tattled on others who illegally engaged in the export of figs when their trade was prohibited in ancient Greece. The shifting alliances of patronage and support as well as the revelation of secret affairs and marriages of those in court made it a hotbed of intrigue and gossip. This essay may have been translated with a wish to acknowledge the destructive facets of courtly culture. In addition, one cannot help but to reflect also on the curiosity of the courtiers and the broader English public on the life of the queen herself, especially in view of her efforts to keep her private self in many ways hidden and separate from the public persona she worked hard to develop. Her rage one year after this translation at the Duke of Essex's forced entry into her bedchamber when she had not yet dressed for the day was an indication of the importance she gave to her fashioning as an elegant and radiant ruler, especially in her declining years. Was this translation an attempt to chastise and potentially correct those who continued to try and reveal her secrets, or was this done in the spirit of seeking to correct a tendency she saw in herself as well as in others?

This vernacular translation of Plutarch by Elizabeth I was not published in her day and remained in her own handwriting until the late nineteenth century. As with her other translations, it remained a private exercise and ultimately a test of her own mental acuity. Nonetheless, the choice of theme reveals her ongoing preoccupation with the performative nature of public life and the danger of those who seek to reveal the private

---

[84] Ibid., s. 11, 503.
[85] See, for example, Felicity Heal, *The Power of Gifts* (Oxford: Oxford University Press, 2014) as well as the concluding chapter of Anne Somerset, *Elizabeth I* (London: Weidenfeld and Nicolson, 1991).

idiosyncrasies and faults of others, especially those in power. While framed by Plutarch as a moralist tale, for the English realm at the time it was also a matter of the very legitimacy of the crown and its occupant. It also perhaps demonstrates a growing awareness within the English political context that effective wielding of political power required not only attention to character and suitable disposition, but that one must, like the French, have a better understanding of the unique qualities of public life and how best to adapt to them.

5.3 Conclusion

This chapter has argued that work of Plutarch provided an important cultural reference for Englishmen in the early sixteenth century for a variety of reasons. In the first instance, as we saw, Plutarch's work served educational purposes and was often used in its Latin translations to help teach the young to develop their knowledge and skills to better exemplify the dominant model of the Ciceronian public figure who could speak and write well and play a commanding role in public life. Examples and anecdotes could often be culled from Plutarch's histories and placed in commonplace books to be invoked when needed to sustain an argument. In addition, Plutarch's moral essays were translated into the vernacular, helping to shed deeper light on some of the motivations to enhance the public good.

Thomas More stands as a special case in this period of the early sixteenth century in England. He was central to a discussion and re-evaluation of ideas stemming from Plutarch, but he did so in ways that did not always make his dialogue with Plutarch explicit. In addition, he uses Plutarch not only to repudiate the more pragmatic reception of his ideas in the French case, but also to put forward a much more radical alternative to political community. Through the lens of Plutarch's Spartan lives, More's Plutarch becomes a radical antithesis of the politics of the status quo, rather than a source that illuminates its nature (as it had figured in France).

With the turn in later Tudor thought we see a full inversion of this, and while it may not be intentional there is certainly a degree of irony in seeing through the work of Taverner the new invocation of More's Spartans to enhance the glory and legitimacy of the king despite his increasingly authoritarian policies. The malleability of examples and exemplars here may threaten to undercut the textual integrity and coherent legacy of the works.

Nonetheless, when we explore the next thread of Plutarch reception in England through the translations of Thomas North and Philemon

Holland, who provide a bridge to understanding the place of Plutarch in the work of both Shakespeare and Hobbes, we can see the return of one common thread. Through all these thinkers we see some form of engagement with Plutarch's work in order to shed greater light on the make-up of the individual immersed in public life, and the social psychology of politics. We see the introduction of considerations that move beyond the Ciceronian adage of concern for the public weal to move towards engagement with the themes of conflict, personal vice and religious dissent that can make public life a challenge. Thus, we can see in the move to the later sixteenth century in England a desire to take up Plutarch in a more realist spirit. What I mean by this is that the invocation of Plutarch and his work going into the seventeenth century in England was adapted in ways to help make sense of politics as actually lived. The concern was to shed light on a reconciliation between the demands for public service, which had always been apparent in the overriding Ciceronian ideal, and the more tangled and challenging features of collective life.

CHAPTER 6

Plutarch in Later French Humanism and Reformation: Georges de Selve, Jacques Amyot and Jean Bodin

There has recently been a good deal of attention paid to the evolution of juridical terms in French political theory of the mid- to late Renaissance.[1] Commentators have explored the way in which key legal minds took up concepts of Roman law, combined with some of the tools of scholastic thought, to derive new understandings of property that could be applied to the holding of office; that is, long-standing concepts governing *civil law* were used to derive authoritative lessons about *public law*. Many of these Renaissance jurists (e.g. Bodin and Charles Du Moulin) were employed by the king and sought new concepts for thinking about kingly authority, measures that challenged a long tradition of patrimonial office. This was regarded as urgent given both the pervasiveness of bureaucratic corruption, posing an obstacle to effective collection of needed revenues (especially given the early modern French state's reliance on taxation as opposed to landed wealth as in England), and increased conflict within France stemming from religious tensions. While initially allied to efforts to bolster the legal and political authority of monarchs, legal doctrines of sovereignty were later recast in intellectual terms (as popular sovereignty) to challenge those same monarchical claims.[2] In some contemporary theory, there is an attempt to burden this Renaissance turn with responsibility for many contemporary political ills, with efforts to dismantle the idea of sovereignty itself.[3]

---

[1] For a broad overview of the challenges of governance in France in the sixteenth century, especially as related to fiscal matters, and the ideological moves to articulate a new conception of the state to bolster monarchical claims in a context of crisis, see Howell A. Lloyd's *The State, France and the Sixteenth Century* (London: George Allen and Unwin, 1983). One of the key scholars of this approach is Donald Kelley. See his chapter "Law" in J. H. Burns and Mark Goldie eds., *The Cambridge History of Political Thought 1450–1700* (Cambridge: Cambridge University Press 1991). See also Daniel Lee, *Popular Sovereignty in Early-Modern Constitutional Thought* (Oxford: Oxford University Press, 2016), esp. chap. 3 and Richard Tuck, *The Sleeping Sovereign* (Cambridge: Cambridge University Press, 2016).

[2] Tuck's *Sleeping Sovereign*.

[3] See, for example, Arash Abizadeh, "Popular Sovereignty vs. Democracy: Or How Rousseau Killed Democracy," unpublished paper delivered to the Political Online Theory Seminar, University of

Despite its importance, aspects of the history of political thinking are overlooked by this tendency to collapse together political thought and jurisprudence. Conceptual innovation, while one source of political argument, cannot account for the central importance of the invocation of history and historical precedent that remained central to the political thinking in this period. In addition, a focus on the conceptual development of a discourse on sovereignty does not directly address the most pressing issue for those living in sixteenth-century France, namely the political consequences of the Reformation, and not just how sovereignty should work in the context of divided religious loyalties but how the social psychology of how governance and living together might work. This chapter and the next look to the increasing relevance of Plutarch as a reference in political argument in Renaissance France of the late sixteenth century, often drawing from the monumental translations of Jacques Amyot, as political reflection explored how to manage in a context of violent civil war.

In general, as much as my own efforts could reveal, figures closely associated with the reception of Plutarch in Renaissance France range from a strong defence of Catholic orthodoxy (with concessions for advocating institutional reform) in the person of Georges de Selve (1508–1541), to a humanist defence of limited toleration, most famously in Michel de Montaigne (1533–1592). Jean Bodin (1530–1596) and Montaigne also drew from Plutarch to provide different accounts of history and historiography. Pre-eminent among scholars associated with the work of Plutarch in sixteenth-century France is Jacques Amyot (1513–1593), who is still renowned for the vividness and skill of his translation. This chapter explores Plutarch reception in the work of de Selve, Amyot and Bodin. Chapter 7 explores how Plutarch was invoked for competing questions of religious accommodation in the work of Bernard Gerard du Haillan (1535–1610), Etienne de la Boétie (1530–1563) and Montaigne.

Georges de Selve was the first translator expressly commissioned by François I to embark on a French vernacular version of Plutarch's *Lives*. The king's interest had already been piqued by Lazare de Baïf's gift and dedication of four translated *Lives*, as well as by the work of Simon Bourgouyn, valet-de-chambre to Louis XII, known as the first to produce a vernacular French translation of select *Lives* (just prior to Seyssel).[4] With

---

Toronto June 2020 and Peter Russell, "Sovereignty: A Pernicious Claim Whose Days are Done," unpublished talk delivered to the Faculty Club of the University of Toronto, September 2019. See also Russell's *Canada's Odyssey* (Toronto: University of Toronto Press, 2017).

[4] Elina Suomela-Härmä, "Simon Bourgouin, traducteur à l'avant-garde,"*Studi francesi* 176. 49.2 (2015). Online at https://journals.openedition.org/studifrancesi/321. Date accessed 23 June 2020.

his untimely death, de Selve was never able to complete his project. Determined to see the project through, François I commissioned a second young scholar to complete the translation that would come to be regarded as a monumental contribution to French language and culture. My purpose in discussing Jacques Amyot's translation is not to expound on the precise philological details of translation, but to explore the broader spirit in which the translation was presented, with particular attention paid to the paratextual materials, which give some indication of Amyot's intentions and the guiding principles of his translation. His prefaces also give us indices of his conception of *la chose publique*.

There are interesting questions and issues when looking at the history of ideas and Plutarch reception in a broader cultural context. Plutarch as a reference was peripheral to most theological concerns of the Reformation. That the production of editions of Plutarch's historical works went from being seventh in popularity among editions of ancient historians to first in the second half of the sixteenth century could mean several things, but its practical effect was that readers recognised the calamitous turn in their collective histories while they were engaging with Plutarch's historical work.[5]

In sixteenth-century Geneva, at least twelve different editions of Plutarch were published, the most famous being that of Henri Estienne who published both the *Lives* and *Moralia* in Greek with Latin translation in 1572. In Geneva, Plutarch's *Lives* were second in popularity only to the Bible.[6] In addition, one of Amyot's contacts in Bourges was a Scot by the name of Henry Scrimgeour who converted to Calvinism and by the end of 1561 was received as a burgess in Geneva and lectured there until 1568.[7] He produced a Latin translation of Plutarch's essay on the seven sages. In terms of book history, then, it appears that the work of Plutarch was an important presence for commercial purposes in Geneva as a key centre of Protestant worship. However, invoking Plutarch in political argument appears to have been less common among Protestant resistance theorists

---

[5] See Cox Jensen, "Popularity," Table 4. See also her Table 5 (and Figure 2) which illustrates that the height of Plutarch book production occurred in the three decades from 1560 to 1590. Of course, Cox Jensen's figures allude to editions of Plutarch in any language, including Latin and the original Greek. The pioneering work of Jacques Amyot and Thomas North, as we will see in this chapter, account for a great deal of this phenomenon.

[6] Olivier Reverdin, "Figures de l'hellenisme a Geneve," in Olivier Reverdin ed., *Homere chez Calvin* (Geneva: Droz, 2000), 83.

[7] Marie-Claude Tucker, "Henry Scrimgeour (1505?–1572), diplomat and book collector," in *Oxford Dictionary of National Biography*. Online at www.oxforddnb.com/view/article/24968. Date Accessed 8 April 2016.

than among the group of *politiques* who preached some form of religious accommodation. And, in at least one instance, as for Georges de Selve, immersion in Plutarch was combined with calls for institutional reform of the Church alongside militant rejection of toleration. Arguably, while difficult to reduce in historical terms, it appears that in the face of civil discord appeal to Plutarch was most often favoured by those who occupied the middle ground between two strands of intransigent religious and political absolutism. But perhaps the most lasting legacy of Plutarch reception from this period of the latter sixteenth century is an increasing tendency to see him as a proponent of a certain type of heroism celebrating the exceptional individual in a position of leadership (distinct from Budé's ascribing a persona of exceptionalism to one in a position of leadership or from the idea that Plutarch uses his historical subjects to depict recognisable facets of character common to all).

6.1   Georges de Selve (1508–1541)

Prior to the edition of Jacques Amyot was the partial translation of Plutarch's *Lives* into the vernacular by Georges de Selve. According to Billaut, the king called upon de Selve for a translation after the sample translation from de Baïf met with his disapproval.[8] De Selve managed to complete a small portion of the project prior to his untimely death at thirty-two.[9] His translation, *Les vyes des huict excellens et renommez personnages grecs et romains*, was first published (posthumously) in 1543 and went through five editions between 1543 and 1548. It included the lives of Themistocles, Camillus, Pericles, Fabius Maximus, Alcibiades, Coriolanus, Timoleon and Paul Emile.

De Selve was a prominent public official under François I. He was son of the first President of the Paris parlement who also had been instrumental in negotiating the terms of the Treaty of Madrid 1526. As a reward, the parlementaire was granted the privilege of having his eighteen-year-old

---

[8] Allain Billaut, "Plutarch's Lives," in G. Sandy ed., *The Classical Heritage in France* (Leiden: Brill, 2002), 220–221. Billaut also claims via Sturel, that the king had commissioned Arnaud Chandon de Pamiers to translate the lives of Agesilaus, Marcellus, Alexander and Pyrrhus, a work which was completed prior to 1547. While manuscript versions of this appear in the collection of the Bibliothèque nationale, there is no record of these ever having been published and no record of them on the USTC.

[9] "comme vostre bon Plaisir eust este, Sire, me commander de mettre en Francais les susdictes vies des Grecz et Romains escrites par ledit Plutarque." Mary Hervey suggests that the king ordered these Plutarch translations by De Selve when he was a youth. See *Holbein's Ambassadors* (London: George Bell and Sons, 1900), 145.

son take the title of Bishop of Lavaur (a position he could not take up in earnest until the age of twenty-five). The son also began work as a diplomat. He served as ambassador to the Republic of Venice (1533–1536), and to the Holy See (1537), and subsequently to Charles V of the Holy Roman Empire. In 1540 he asked to be relieved of his diplomatic duties to devote himself to his pastoral duties, dying shortly thereafter.

When an ambassador, de Selve performed his most famous act: posing for a painting at the English court. "The Ambassadors" by Hans Holbein is perhaps one of the best-known works of art produced in northern Europe during the Renaissance. De Selve is the often-overlooked figure on the right of the painting, a friend of the flamboyant Jean de Dinteville who was French ambassador to the English court in 1533.[10]

De Selve's work, his politics and his political writing intersected in many ways. He was known in humanist circles for his command of Greek and Latin, having studied with Pierre Danes (1497–1577). While serving in Venice he sought manuscripts of classical works to include in the royal library, thereby furthering François I's significant patronage of the arts.[11] Still, unlike Erasmus whose work demonstrates a reflective weighing of reformist sympathies and moderate repudiation of them, de Selve offers a rhetorically charged and unrelenting harsh, unsympathetic condemnation, foreshadowing the strand of Catholicism that became dominant in the 1540s and beyond at the Council of Trent.[12] De Selve's rather stern, unyielding and unwelcoming look in Holbein's painting, especially when juxtaposed with his counterpart, is reflected in the tone of his various religious and diplomatic writings. Their justification can be seen in embryo in the prologue de Selve wrote for his Plutarch translations.[13]

---

[10] For an interesting discussion of the composition of the painting and the way in which it evokes a close friendship between these two men Kate Bomford's see Kate Bomford's "Friendship and Immortality: Holbein's Ambassadors Revisited," *Renaissance Studies* 18.4 (2004), 544–581.

[11] M. Magnien, "Dolet Editeur de Georges de Selve, et le rôle de Pierre Bunel: un évangélisme cicéronien," in Gabriel-Andre Perouse ed., *Etudes sur Etienne Dolet: le théâtre aux XVIe siècle* (Geneva: Droz, 1993), 103–120.

[12] One need only compare Erasmus's "Diatribe or Sermon Concerning Free Will" (1524) with the tone of de Selve's writing (written probably sometime in the period 1524–1540). The Erasmus work can be found in Erasmus and Luther, *Discourse on Free Will*, trans. Ernst F. Winter (New York: Continuum, 1961, 1989 and 2002). The fact that Erasmus was writing as a scholar and de Selve as a representative of the French king (with interests relevant to social peace within the boundaries of France) may partly explain the difference in tone. However, it is revealing that de Selve's harsh tone of unrelenting condemnation carried over into his preface to Plutarch, when he was not beholden to the king's diplomatic and security interests.

[13] Curiously it appears that the Plutarch translation was published posthumously as de Selve died in 1541 at the age of thirty-two. The Plutarch translation did not appear until 1543. According to Hervey, de Selve's loyal secretary Bunel, who followed him from service in Venice to his pastoral

In broader terms, de Selve offers a challenge to those who would see in humanist approaches a single outlook or sensitivity. Of course, how one defines humanism may depend on who one identifies as a humanist. Still, de Selve offers an example of someone who was deeply immersed in the study of Latin and Greek, interested in classical texts for purposes of translation, clearly drawn to an interest in rhetoric through the colourful language of his sermons and nonetheless holds on to definite metaphysical assumptions of the scholastic period, expressing strong hostility to the Reformation and rejecting any possibility of toleration in the face of religious pluralism (though he does make some concessions for institutional reform). Is it possible to see how the immersion in Plutarch's work as required for the exercise of translation had an impact on his broader outlook? It may be that in the case of de Selve, the approach to the study of this classical author, like many of his time, was done in largely instrumental ways, serving to hone his language skills rather than offering new outlooks and perspectives.

In his prologue to the vernacular translation of eight of Plutarch *Lives*, de Selve provides an account of social order in the Ciceronian tradition that is grounded on a conventional tale of sociality but mixed with Catholic orthodoxy: given that human beings are unable to meet their material needs independently in the way that other species can, humans have joined together as a necessary means to provide for all.[14] Still, for de Selve a logic of domination appears to flow directly from this: division of labour is imposed with the hardy and strong using their bodies to supply goods, and the intelligent and animated becoming the adjudicators of human wellbeing, including instilling in human beings a sense of virtue and law through a reminder of rational principle. For the work of virtue to be possible, one must continue to acknowledge that each individual in their rational capacity (which is also a reflection of the divine) has the ability in principle to distinguish between good and evil, and what's more, to choose one over the other ("lelection estoit en la puissance de lhomme"), something that allows for the possibility of moral praise, blame and punishment ("ilz le iugerent digne de louenge de ce quil avoit bien et vertueusement fait, come de chose dont luy seul estoit cause et auteur et

---

duties in Lavaur, asked George's brother Odet (a person of note in his own right) to take on the task of publishing George's work, including both the translation as well as his various sermons and discourses. See Hervey, *Holbein's Ambassadors*, 192.

[14] Georges De Selve, "Le Prologue du Translateur, adresse au tres chrestien Roy Francoy premier de ce nom," in *Les Vies des huis excellens et renommez personnages Grecz et Rommains, mises au paragon lune de lautre* (Lyon: Jean de Tounres, 1548).

digne en punition en ce quil delinqueroit comme estant le mal semblablement chose dont il se pouvoit ayseement garder"). For this purpose, laws
were written by those who were deemed wise and just; and to govern the
internal lives of human beings, religion and the veneration of God was
instituted.

While on the surface the beginning of this story of human institutions is
a conventional European account, it is already structured as an assault on
both the uneducated and on many of the precepts of the reform movement. The emphasis on free will and on the ability of the individual to be
fully responsible for their moral choices, links to de Selve's strong criticism
of the Reformers' notions of justifications by faith (thereby presumably
eliminating the need for penitence) and predestination in his other works,
both of which he argues evade moral responsibility and serve in their effects
to perpetuate vice.[15]

De Selve goes on to explain the rise of so many different opinions in
matters of religion as the natural wedge between the sublime matter of the
divine and the inadequacy of human capacity in fully accounting for it.
Religious opinion is likened to the Tower of Babel, which was destroyed by
its diversity, just as the false and competing views in matter of religion
make it impossible for human beings to attain beatitude, a condition that is
only possible under the true religion.

De Selve's broader position, as discussed in his various speeches on his
missions to Germany, is that corruption is rampant in all branches of the
Church, including that still loyal to the pope. Furthermore, his view is that
the Lutheran schism does nothing to address that corruption and everything to exacerbate it. In his Prologue he suggests that a fundamental
condition for bringing humans to a state of beatitude is the maintaining of
the one true religion. Its dissolution in ancient times presents a frightening
scene of the effects of religious division:

> Nous trouvons donques que de leur temps na regne en lieu de religion, si
> non superstition et idolatrie: en lieu de iustice, rapines, meurtres, violences
> et tyrannies: en lieu de temperance, une licence, effrenee et abandonee
> a toute lascivete. Et a brief parler, de toutes leurs bonnes semences ils nont
> vue naistre que mauvaises herbes. Et si bien il y en ha eu aucuns eu qui ses
> pechez grossiers ne soient point apparuz, si est il a croire que au dedens ils
> ont este maculez de diverses sortes de vice ; comme il est force que ainsi
> adviene en nature corrompue, despourveue de la lumiere celeste. Au moyen

---

[15] Georges De Selve, *Œuvres* (Paris: Galliot de Pre, 1559), 14b–15.

de quoy les meilleurs dentre eux ont deu plustost estre appellez simulateurs,
que executeurs des œuvres de vertu.[16]

[We thus find that in their time in place of religion there only ruled
superstition and idolatry; in place of justice, ravages, murders, violence
and tyranny; in place of moderation, a wild licence open to all forms of
lasciviousness. And to summarise briefly, from all the good seedlings they
only saw weeds sprout. And so much that there were some whose great sins
were not apparent but it can be surmised that inside they were torn up with
all sorts of vice; as it inevitably happens to corrupt nature when it is deprived
of heavenly light. Thus even the best among them should only be called
simulators, rather than agents of virtue.]

From this perspective, the cause for the deep sinfulness evoked by
Reformist theologians is identified as the lack of true faith and correct
understanding of God. To have access to virtue, it only suffices to have the
true laws of God in one's heart. He goes on to reject a great deal of
philosophical discourse as merely forms of rhetoric, of the type that he
refers to later in the prologue as "frivolous disputations," that provide no
practical guidance. This hostility to traditional scholasticism might place
him in the humanist camp but, as we will see, de Selve was a humanist of
a particular stamp and one with a rather loose appreciation of antiquity.

In his later work prepared as speeches given in Germany to counter the
spread of the Reform movement, he goes further in his criticisms, suggesting that the move to split the Church in Europe has strengthened the
Ottomans and undermined the authority of Princes.[17] The remedy, he
suggests, is clear: a general act of penitence that would lead to the reunifi-
cation of the Christian Church under the pope, but a Church that would
undergo important administrative changes to eliminate corruption and
a council to discuss doctrinal challenges. As a gesture of reconciliation, it
clearly offered more admonition, fire and brimstone than understanding
and practical incentives.

So why Plutarch? What could Plutarch offer for de Selve among so many
false leads and erroneous doctrines, particularly if the ancients could in his
view at best only 'simulate' virtue? Going back to the Prologue to his
translation of eight *Lives*, de Selve suggests that all human beings exercise
some form of office, whether it is to teach children, honour parents, obey
'superiors,' etc. and that humans need to exercise moderation and reason in
the light of God's will. To effect this, one must search for good teachings

---

[16] De Selve, "Prologue," 7.
[17] De Selve, "Discours eu vray et seul moyen de faire une bonne et perpétuelle paix, entre l'Empereur et
le roy tres chrestien" and "Remontrances adressantes aux Alemans" in *Œuvres*, 36aff and 49aff.

wherever they can be found, much like the Israelites who were able to make use of certain utensils they had taken from the Egyptians on their flight out of Egypt. Hence, for de Selve, ancient books, including Plutarch, can be useful in parts for both good and bad Christians alike. The bad will learn to detest their vices, and if they have a sense of shame, to acknowledge the good acts of pagans even when ignorant of God. The good will be strengthened in their virtue, seeing the virtuous and praiseworthy actions of others as an incitement to further goodness, while knowing how much they could surpass them with the grace and help of God. And for the king himself, suggests de Selve, Plutarch's practical and proper philosophical bent (i.e. geared towards moral virtue) can be helpful.[18]

It is nonetheless significant that no reference to Plutarch makes it into de Selve's speeches and sermons; indeed, it is not just references to Plutarch that are notably lacking, but reference to any pagan or classical source. For de Selve and others of the Counter-Reformation, the history and philosophy of the ancient world was structurally deficient and could not live up to the standards of virtue that came later to surpass it.

Even in terms of more worldly wisdom there is no reference to the classics. In a speech written for top administrators in the kingdom, de Selve speaks of strategies for attaining a proper perspective in governance. He acknowledges that practical wisdom, or wisdom before the fact and before mistakes are made, is the most difficult kind to gain because even the wisest will not always see clearly in relation to themselves. This becomes exceedingly more difficult for princes and "aux plus grands" because no one will take it upon themselves to address their faults, and indeed many applaud them in those things that may lead to their demise. For those in power, de Selve advises three things: they should not flatter themselves or come to think too highly of themselves; they should try to avoid flattery from others; and they should try to think of possible threats and difficulties before they arise.[19] An added challenge raised by de Selve here, and one that addresses the challenges unique to a public servant, is what to advise an official when either their own disordered appetites lead them to act contrary to God's will while serving their administrative superior or king, or when their allegiance to God may clash with the wishes of a superior with disordered and unruly appetites. In the first instance de Selve recommends confession, both to God and to the superior for one's own vices,

---

[18] De Selve, "Prologue," 10–16.
[19] De Selve, "Discours contenant le seul et vray moyen par lequel un serviteur favorise et constitue en administration de son Prince, peut conserver sa félicité éternelle et temporelle et éviter les chose qui luy pourroient l'une ou l'autre faire perdre," in *Œuvres*, 26aff.

except when such a confession might put them in 'his' bad graces, or worse lead the superior 'himself' to sin, in which case a confession to God and the confessor are sufficient.[20] In the case of a superior with a disordered appetite who might lead the public servant to run up against the laws of virtue and religion, de Selve suggests that there is little here to worry about given that the power of shame for the powerful should keep them from ordering their charges in wantonness.

There is an obsession with sinfulness and sinful behaviour in de Selve's work, and the remedy he prescribes is complete submission to God and to the one Church. Classical history through Plutarch and others, it would appear, serves as a limited and ultimately inadequate source of insight into human affairs, reduced in his rhetoric to the usefulness of a second-hand utensil. In general terms, while de Selve may have noted *in theory* the usefulness of history (and thus Plutarch's work) to bridge political divides by recognising some of the virtues of adversaries as a path to more moderate politics, this was not a lead that he took in matters of more direct political advocacy. His abandoning of the translation of Plutarch's *Lives*, sealed by his untimely death, is also symbolic of a heightening intransigence of Catholic forces in the face of religious schism.[21]

6.2 Jacques Amyot (1513–1593)

Jacques Amyot's contribution to traditions of Plutarch reception, beginning fifteen years after the publication of de Selve's work, offers certain points of contrast. It is not hyperbole to claim that Michel de Vascosan's publication of Amyot's translation of Plutarch *Lives* in 1559 was a major watershed in European cultural life. It stands as a crucial contribution whose impact on subsequent authors has been incalculable.

---

[20] "Mais cela ne s'entend des faultes dont le maistre pourroit estre scandilize de quelqu'un, ou de luy mesme: et qui seroient cause de luy faire prendre en male grace: ou bien qui pourroient estre cause du péché du maistre, en quelque façon que ce soit. Car de celles la se doibt il taire: et suffit les dire à Dire et a son confesseur, avec ce propos, que si lon scavoit que ce fust le vouloir de Dieu, que lon descrouvrist aussi celles la a son maistre, on le feroit: et prendroit on la honte que lon en pourroit avoir, en pénitence du péché. Et se doibt accompaigner ceste confession, qui se fait au maistre, d'une honneste commémoration des bienfaict que lon ha receuz de luy: tant pour le devoir, que pour plus capter sa benevolence. Prenant aussi quelque manière de modeste excuse sur la fragilité, sur sa débilite de scavoir et de pourveoir sur les assauls du monde et de l'ennemy, et sur la grandeur des charges. Qui sont choses qui rendent les faultes plus legieres devant les hommes." De Selve, "Discours contenant le seul et vray moyen . . .", in *Œuvres*.

[21] Perhaps, a general analog is the case of one who has such unquestioned and absolute confidence in the justice of their principled commitment that neither theoretical lip-service to conciliation nor study of historical accounts of humaneness offer them any insight into the potential harshness and cruelty of their ways.

It is therefore impossible to do full justice to Amyot's influence in a survey of early-modern Plutarch reception such as this, especially since, paradoxically, his work is little studied in detail despite being deemed the "most accomplished version in vernacular."[22] Only a well-trained philologist could think to provide useful commentary on the modes and methods through which Amyot rendered his Plutarch into an elegant French. I rely on the judgements of specialists regarding the reliability of the translation for the most part and only explore a wider question, namely, how might Amyot himself have perceived the significance of his Plutarch translations in the political context of his time. I also shed light on what I claim is a particular debt to Tory and his pioneering translation of Plutarch's essay "Political Precepts", a translation which helped to set the tone and some of the rhetorical background for the significance of Plutarch's work through the language of *la chose publique*.

With this focus we can examine the various paratextual materials (dedications, prefaces, etc.) Amyot produced in conjunction with his translations, alongside his later work *Projet d'Eloquence Royale* that offers a commentary on the links between humanist learning and the exercise of political office. Reading these materials together offers an opportunity to explore the spirit in which Amyot issued his translations, the continuities between that sense of purpose and function in 1559 (date of the first edition of Amyot's translation of Plutarch's *Lives*) to 1579 (date of his piece *Projet d'Eloquence Royale*) all in the broader context of a troubled political climate in France.[23] In addition, we pay close attention to the ways in which Amyot invokes the idea of the public realm through the terms *la chose publique*, or *le bien publique* as a means to chart how these terms evolved throughout the early modern period in conjunction with Plutarch reception.

What drove Amyot to translate the vast opus of Plutarch into vernacular French?[24] The king, it appears, commissioned him after de Selve's untimely death. Still, it is reasonable to assume that Aymot could have

---

[22] Francoise Frazier and Olivier Guerrier, "Plutarch's French Translation by Amyot," in Sophia Xenophontos and K. Oikonomopoulou eds., *Brill's Companion to the Reception of Plutarch*, chap. 25, 421–435. Also see Françoise Frazier and O. Guerrier, eds. *La langue de Jacques Amyot* (Paris: Garnier, 2018).

[23] Jacques d'Amyot, *Projet d'Éloquence royale* (Paris: Belles Lettres, 1992)

[24] Apart from the very select works translated into the vernacular by the set of scholars discussed up to now, prior to Amyot individuals lacking a solid knowledge of Greek would need to read Plutarch's *Lives* from one of the various Latin editions available. Yet even many scholarly Latin editions postdate Amyot's, including those of Wilhelm Holtzman (Xylander) in 1561, Hermann Cruser (Cruserius) in 1564 as well as Henri Estienne's (Stephanus) edition of Plutarch's collected works published in 1572 offering both the Greek and Latin translation (the Greek edition princeps of the *Lives* was issued in Florence in 1517 and the Aldine edition in 1519). Denton, *Translation*, 46.

abandoned his project either after the death of François I (1547), or after the publication of the translation of the *Lives*. Instead, Amyot continued more than twenty years up to 1572, both completing his translation of the *Lives* and taking on the translation of all the essays of the *Moralia*. What was Amyot's internal motivation for this vast project, and what did he see as its significance? According to Sturel, Amyot was driven by ideals of humanist scholarship. He went to great lengths to ensure that he was working from a variety of sources including available manuscripts, using methods of scholarship that are regarded as thorough and careful, even while taking on an added responsibility as teacher to the sons of the new king, Henri II. Amyot was also aware of the possible broader political import of his scholarship. He states in the dedicatory preface to the first edition of his translation of the *Lives* that the work would be of great use and significance for the king (who could not access the original nor its Latin translations) and those seeking lessons from ancient history.[25] Clearly, he was convinced that serious humanist, literary and historical scholarship was neither irrelevant nor ineffective in offering understanding and guidance in his own circumstances.

Amyot's work is an important moment in a longer tradition of interest in ancient Greek texts in Renaissance France.[26] Tory laid the groundwork for Amyot in another sense, helping to popularise the idea of the king as a *Hercule gaulois*, an image invoked by Amyot at the outset of his *Projet d'Eloquence royale*. Nonetheless, and despite a longer tradition, it is evident that French reception of Plutarch in the Renaissance reached its apogee with Amyot's contributions.

Amyot was educated in classical languages at the Collège de France (founded in 1530 by François I precisely for the purpose of training humanist scholars). A student of Toussaint and Danès he was later hired as a tutor to the children of Jacques Colin before his appointment as lecturer in Latin and Greek at the University of Bourges. After embarking on selected translations from the Greek, including a few *Lives* of Plutarch, his work was brought to the attention of the king which led to the commission for Amyot to translate all the *Lives*, along with an appointment in 1547 as Abbot of Bellozanne to help compensate him for his efforts. The king died shortly after this appointment, but Amyot soldiered on in his efforts, reaching the first milestone with the publication of his translation of the *Lives* in 1559.

---

[25] Sturel, *Jacques Amyot*, 92.   [26] Billaut, "Plutarch's Lives," 220.

He is respected for his scholarly work (a contemporary classicist still calls it the "best translation of Plutarch ever made"), not only consulting numerous Greek and Latin editions of the work but also consulting various manuscripts of the text which were held in libraries in Venice and Rome.[27] He coupled his visits to Italy with diplomatic projects. He had risen in courtly circles to become tutor to the sons of King Henri II by the time his Plutarch translations were first published, sons who were soon to become kings themselves: Charles IX (in 1560) and Henri III (in 1574). He was appointed Bishop of Auxerre in 1570, and it was to his former pupil, now Henri III, that Amyot delivered his *Projet d'Eloquence Royale*. The prefatory remarks to his translations, not surprisingly, suggest a strong commitment to the institutions of monarchy and the established church. Still, by the time of his death in 1593 he had lost favour with both the Catholic League and King Henri IV and was ruined financially.[28]

How did Amyot face the task of translation? In a preface to his readers (*Aux Lecteurs*, thus taking up a dedicatory format also found in the earlier work of Geoffroy Tory), Amyot addresses the utility of his work. He begins with a general defence of historical knowledge as a necessary complement to the understanding. From this perspective, history is just another place name for memory, and without memory any learning and indeed ability to cope reasonably with the forces of nature would be impossible. Indeed, the passing on of accumulated knowledge and understanding is acknowledged to be part of human experience long before the existence of writing and letters. In a somewhat different vein, history is also understood as the eloquent celebration of the honourable and worthy, and it is this that Amyot praises, as historical memory through praise can serve to bring immortality more effectively than any statue or monument:

> Je laisse semblablement à deduire, que c'est la plus seure garde et le plus durable monument que les hommes puissant laisser de leurs faicts en ce monde, pour consacrer leur nom a immortalité: car il n'y a ny statues, ny trophees de marbre, ny arcs de triomphe, ny coulonnes, ny sepultures magnifiques, qui puissant combattre la duree d'une Histoire eloquente.[29]
>
> [I leave similarly to deduce that it is the surest guarantee and most durable monument that men can leave of their actions in the work, to offer their

---

[27] This judgement of Amyot's *Lives* as the best translation of Plutarch ever made is voiced by Jeff Tatum, "Lost in Translation," unpublished paper.

[28] Billaut, "Plutarch's Lives," 222.

[29] Amyot, "Aux lecteurs," in *Les Vies des hommes illustres, Grecs et Romains, compares l'une avec l'autre* (Paris: Vascosan, 1565). It is a line whose force resonates into the twentieth century through the famous statement of André Malraux, celebrating the festival of Joan of Arc in 1964: "O Jeanne sans sépulcre et sans portrait, toi qui savais que le tombeau des héros est le cœur des vivants."

name to immortality: for there are neither statues, nor marble trophies, nor triumphal arches, nor columns, nor magnificent tombs that can surpass the legacy of an eloquent history.]

This was an interpretation of what was most crucial to Plutarch's work. Amyot goes on to address the usefulness of history in helping one to make appropriate judgements regarding the present, especially to know which things to pursue and which to shun. History can be likened to a picture that offers an overview of things, individuals, people and actions that are worthy to be committed to memory. The benefit of history for moral judgement is that it not only instructs but also motivates, drawing on the natural inclination of all people to imitate that which is judged to be beautiful and good. In addition, history provides a particularly forceful mechanism for punishing the mean and unjust by casting them in the light of perpetual infamy. Similarly, history speaks to courageous and learned individuals who are seeking to perpetuate the memory of their name, leading them to abandon their lives in private obscurity and instead offer service to *la chose publique*, to give up their possessions, to engage in endless efforts to defend the oppressed, to build public buildings, to establish law and governments, and to invent arts and sciences; in short, history is portrayed here as both a product of and condition for some of the most foundational features of human life.

In addition, history is a school of prudence (*une eschole de prudence*) that often operates to inform judgement at the level of society as a whole. In this it defies the logic of Aristotelian virtue through which prudence is only developed in practice (and not through lessons learned by the experience of others). This is particularly relevant to public action, suggests Amyot, in an argument we have seen before in Renaissance authors, because in crucial matters where life and community are at stake one does not have the luxury to fail twice (on "ne peut pas faillir deux fois, pource que les fautes y sont de telle consequence, qu'elles apportent le plus souvent ruine d'estat ou perte de vie a ceux qui les font" [one cannot fail twice because the mistakes are of such consequence that they often undermine the condition or status or even lead to the loss of life to whose who commit them]). In these instances, learning from the experiences of others must take the place of one's own actions and experience to train judgement.

For those in a position of public responsibility, these benefits are greater still, a circumstance that leads Amyot to call history the mistress of princes ("la maitresse des Princes"). Those born into a hereditary lineage of power may be raised coddled and sheltered, and therefore learn little of the world through their own experience or from the flatterers around them. To compensate for these deficiencies of a princely education, Amyot calls for the reading of histories to give future rulers the knowledge and judgement they will need to govern effectively.

We should focus briefly on the title of Amyot's translation, a title which I believe has been inadvertently responsible for a longstanding general view of Plutarch's work. The title given to the work in French is *Les Vies des hommes illustres* (*The Lives of Illustrious Men*, presumably in the sense of those who are both honoured and deserving of honour). Of course, Plutarch did not attribute any title to his work and only referred to his genre as *lives* (*Bioi*). The chosen subjects of his parallel constructions were notorious and chosen in part because they were points of reference commonly known by his readers. However, as we have seen, Plutarch notes famously in his *Life of Alexander* that his intent was not to celebrate the actions or known exploits of his literary subjects (indeed, some were clearly negative exemplars), but rather to reveal who they were through an examination of their more hidden actions and to reveal their underlying character. This was intended to spark reflection and deliberation on more general questions of character, as was part of the broader literary genre in which Plutarch was writing. Regardless, there is a tendency to refer to Plutarch's subjects as 'heroes.'[30] While there can be some ambiguity in the term – it can mean in a novelistic sense a central focus of attention and character development – it is most often associated with a more celebratory rhetoric, particularly as far as ancient history is concerned. The title of Plutarch's moral biographies as translated by Amyot shifted focus to the notoriety of the subjects, or how they would be perceived and celebrated in the eyes of the readers for their actions, and away from the instrumental use of notoriety as a common point of reference which allows the author to talk about subtleties of disposition and character. In Budé, the selective excerpts from the *Lives*, absent the parallelism, highlighted the intended tone of singularity and exceptionalism. Aspects of this same spirit could be seen as carrying on into the work of Amyot, where the whole text of Plutarch's *Lives* might be perceived in its presentation as taking on greater qualities of a Pantheon. While this shift in how the work came to be perceived could not have been fully dictated by Amyot's choice of term, the logic that it invokes is the replacement of one practice of exemplarity – that is, using the example of another as a case study for moral insight into both positive and negative attributes – for use of the example as a sort of moral

---

[30] As one example, see Jacobs, *Plutarch's Pragmatic Biographies*.

and historical template for mimicry and replication. And while diverse readings and appropriations of Plutarch continued into the seventeenth century, there was a growing trend to think of Plutarch's work as a form of celebratory rhetoric. What this implied is that the formal qualities of the work were envisaged as separate from the content and moral analysis. Later thinkers in the tradition of reception suggested that the supposed formal qualities of encomium be taken on but filled with new content through the celebration of more contemporary heroes deemed to have contributed to the public welfare. By the eighteenth century a series of texts entitled *The British Plutarch* celebrated the exploits and actions of those deemed to be the most eminent statesmen and cultural leaders of England.[31] Thus, for some, Plutarch came to be read as a celebration of the powerful and extraordinary according to a certain measure of greatness. In this way, the focus on moral development and the challenges of the broader public brought to light through the examples of the famous (the spirit perhaps closer to Plutarch's initial intent), after Amyot's translation became for many a focus on the famous as a category of its own.

To return to the preface of the translation: in making a distinction between the recounting of the public face of events and actions and the more private account of the inner life of historical actors and their lives, Amyot mentions his own engagement with Plutarch and his *Lives* as the best literary exemplar of its kind. He also alludes to and even cites in full the aprocryphal letter from Plutarch to Trajan, although he expresses his doubts about its authenticity. Amyot alludes to this letter (and here the details are important) as being placed ahead of the Latin translation of the "Politiques" of Plutarch ("il est expressement porte par une missive, qui se lit au devant de la traduction Latine de ses "Politiques", la quelle a dire la verité m'est un petit suspecte, pour ce que ie ne l'ay point trouvee entre ses oeuvres Grecques, ioinct qu'elle parle come si le livre estoit dedié à Traian, ce qui est manifestement dedict par le commencement du livre, et pour quelques autres raisons" [it is directly expressed by a letter, that is found in preface to the Latin translation of his "Political Precepts", the veracity of which is a bit suspect to me as I have not found it among his Greek works, combined with the fact that it suggests that the book was dedicated to Trajan something which is manifestly not true given the opening of the

[31] The best known of these was written by Thomas Mortimer under the full title *The British Plutarch: or, biographical entertainer. Being a select collection of the lives at large of the most eminent men, natives of Great Britain and Ireland; from the reign of Henry Viii. to George II. Both inclusive: Whether distinguished as Statesmen, Patriots, – Warriors, Divines, – Poets, – Philosophers* (London: Edward Dilly, 1762), but the genre carried over into the nineteenth century and into last century.

book, along with other reasons]). This corresponds most directly to the Latin translation of this essay by Sekoundinos, translated into French by Geoffroy Tory with the title "Politiques", both of which were prefaced by the letter to Trajan. As Amyot notes, this is curious because while the prefatory letter suggests that the work is dedicated to Trajan, the opening passages of Plutarch's "Political Precepts" or "Politiques" indicate that the text is in fact addressed to Menomachus, a young aspiring politician in Plutarch's day. Amyot's discussion of the letter in this preface is important to demonstrate his awareness of the Geoffroy Tory translation of "Political Precepts" and its initial rendering into Latin by Sekoundinos.

Amyot produced three editions of his translation of the *Lives* through the publisher Vascosan in Paris (1559, 1565 and 1567). While there were other pirated or copied editions of the volume during his lifetime, none of those had the benefit of his direct input and guidance. In the three sanctioned editions, despite the fact that Henri II died in 1559 and handed the throne first to François II (1559–1560), then to Charles IX (1560–1574), and despite the beginnings of the Wars of Religion in France around the same time as the first edition of this work was published, the introductory dedication to the previous king and the essay for the readers remained the same throughout the various editions in his lifetime. A difference in the 1567 edition is that it included Charles de l'Ecluse's translations of the *Lives of Hannibal and Scipio Africanus*. These translations were subsequently produced by different editors with over a dozen separate editions of Amyot's *Lives* produced from 1559 to 1645.[32]

How might Amyot have conceived of the function of his translation work in the changing political circumstances in France? To gain some insight into this, we turn to a reading of the dedicatory letter to Charles IX, Amyot's former pupil, which precedes Amyot's translation of Plutarch's *Oeuvres morales*, a translation first published in 1572.[33] Amyot here is writing a dedication for Plutarch's moral essays, but we can find in this later letter his broader defence of the worth of Plutarch's opus as a whole. Amyot begins the letter discussing the role of wisdom in helping to restrain princes and to guide them in the way of justice. He invokes the fear of God as a useful and functional doctrine to keep kings focused on the demands of wisdom and away from the dictates of their own wills. This can in part be imparted with a daily reading from the Law of Moses (or the first five books

---

[32] Patricia Gray, "Subscribing to Plutarch in the Eighteenth Century," *Australian Journal of French Studies* 29.1 (1992), 30.

[33] Jacques Amyot, "Epistre au roi tres Chrestien Charles IX," *Les Œuvres morales et meslees de Plutarque* (Paris: Vascosan, 1572).

of the Hebrew Bible) in conjunction with interpretation from the tradition of the universal Church (surely a hint that his recommendation of daily and direct engagement with scripture was not meant to encourage espousal of doctrines associated with Reformed Religion). The importance of conduct driven, he suggests, by wisdom, virtue and fear of God ensures its consonance with justice and sets a good example for all subjects to follow:

> comme au contraire aussi depuis qu'il est ignorant et vicieux, il espand la contagion du vice et de l'ignorance par toutes les provinces de son obeissance, ne plus ne moins qu'il est force que toutes les copies transcrittes d'un original defectueux ou deprave retiennent les faultes du premier exemplaire.

> [just as, to the extent that he is ignorant and vicious he spreads the contagion of vice and ignorance in all provinces under his command, so neither more nor less all the transcribed copies of a defective or depraved original carry on the mistakes of the first example]

He cites Cyrus of Persia who is said to have noted that no one deserves to lead or command unless they are better than those they lead, and he invokes the example of Osiris, wise king of Egypt, who painted an eye on his sceptre to signify the wisdom needed to exercise power well: "n'appartenant pas a un qui fourvoye, de redresser; qui ne voit goutte, de guider; qui ne sçait rien, d'enseigner; et qui ne veult obeir à la raison, de commander." [it doesn't belong to someone who misleads to do justice; nor to him who doesn't see a thing, to guide; nor to him who knows nothing, to teach; nor to him who does not wish to obey reason, to command.] Second to the lessons in fearing God, Amyot invokes knowledge of antiquity, both the reading of history as well as books and essays on moral philosophy, as an important source of education for rulers. These help to motivate princes to the same end as justice but in different ways, including considerations of glory associated with virtuous action and infamy tied to those deemed vicious. Judgements are made of princes in both large and small matters given that their elevated status exposes their lives to the view of all. In broad terms, this appears to reiterate the lesson of his remarks in the 1559 volume.

Amyot acknowledges the more turbulent political climate and notes the challenges of governance facing the current king: "le commencement de votre regne a este fort turbulent et calamiteux" [the beginning of your reign has been very turbulent and calamitous]. He expresses hope that the unfolding of the reign will wield progress and suggests that it might be possible if the king holds to kingly wisdom inspired by Solomon and driven by allegiance to the Catholic Church acting in accordance with the virtuous and religious customs as befits the inheritor of the title of a Christian King. The invocation of wisdom here may be consonant with the earlier references to the need for prudence on the part of rulers, but it is also a clear endorsement of the privileged role of the Catholic Church in France. There is no invocation for peace above all, as will be found in the subsequent work of *politiques* thinkers drawing from Amyot's translations. Nor does Amyot venture to comment on how exactly the content of Plutarch's work might inspire a solution to the political challenges facing the king.

One thing that clearly distinguishes Amyot is his sense of the importance of the *Lives* for the education of rulers, a position that places his own approach to the text in a long line of French Renaissance interpretations and modes of reception. Still, how Amyot conceptualised the precise way in which the *Lives*, often in the spirit of descriptive moralism, was to be taken up in the more applied spirit of prescriptive or protreptic moralism, is not clear. In addition, it is not obvious how the actual events and circumstances of the classical world would offer direction for the precise challenges of Renaissance politics. While Amyot offered his readers the *possibility* of a political application of Plutarch's work, it may be that in effect he left it to authors taking up and commenting on his translations to fill in the very substance of those lessons.

What of the actual translations? Titles aside, Amyot practised adherence to the idea of fidelity as more literal rendering of the text albeit with little embellishment given the laconic style of Plutarch. While not offering any commentary in the body of the translation in the manner of Erasmus and the *Apophthegmata*, Amyot sometimes doubled up descriptions, partly to improve the cadence of the text, but also to emphasise certain details. He is also said to have 'Greekified' the French language, providing in French constructions that were more germane to the ancient Greek language but thereby transforming the French language for future usage. Various commentators have also noted the measures Amyot takes to make the text more familiar and accessible to his readers: for example, names of people and institutions are often Latinised.[34] Somewhat similarly, as in Tory's work, is the imposition of French cultural references, such as the rank of *capitaine générale* held by Alcibiades. He offers minimal explanatory notes, though later editions included marginal commentary by the Calvinist pastor Simon Goulart.[35]

---

[34] Billaut, "Plutarch's Lives," 223.
[35] Denton suggests that Goulart's notes tended to sway Amyot's text in a fundamentalist Protestant direction and offers this example: "At the point where the episode of Titus Latinus' dream of Juppiter is described, Goulart adds in the margin: 'Satan se fourre a la traverse tant pour attiser le feu

Amyot's invocation of the term "la chose publique" in the introductory letter to readers accompanying the 1559 translation of the *Lives* shows a continuity with Tory. In invoking *la chose publique* in his dedicatory letter to King Henri II, Amyot suggests that the king 'represents' *la chose publique* ("*lui seul représente la chose publique*") since his will can become law and his speech and his actions can shape norms.[36] We could say Amyot holds that in a monarchy the king is the effective agent of *la chose publique*, but also that the substance of it precedes sovereign power. A few lines earlier, Amyot refers to Aristotle, who invokes three sorts of government *de la chose publique* of which monarchy is the best.[37] Thus, in Amyot's invocation, *la chose publique* stands for the normative force of Aristotle's good governments, where rulers rule for the good of the whole rather than for themselves. However, this notion of *la chose publique* is not collapsible into the notion of *le bien public* which is also invoked here. *Le bien public*, as he implies a few lines earlier, serves as a moral target measuring the impact and worth of action applicable in principle to every subject of the realm.

It emerges from Amyot's introductory letter that *la chose publique* designates at least three things: (1) a locus of power where a larger or smaller set of individuals take on responsibility for matters of common concern and importance; (2) an obvious but rather unspecified expectation concerning the proper uses of power, namely that reason and religion will help to shape the way in which power is wielded such that the broader conditions for the welfare, honour and good of all will be an unquestioned priority in decision-making (so power or sovereignty itself is not sufficient

---

de division par ses prodigies et miracles de mensonge, que pour establir tant plus ses superstitions et idolatries.'" *Translation*, 46.

[36] "lui seul represente la chose publique, veu que sa volonté est loi, sa parole arrest et sa vie discipline exemplaire de bien ou de mal faire." [He alone represents the chose publique, given that his will is law, his word is binding and his life and discipline exemplary of what is good and what is bad to do.] Amyot, "Preface" to Plutarch, *Vies des Hommes illustres* (Paris: Vascosan, 1583). The first edition of the French translation of the Lives was published in 1559.

[37] *au iugement du Prince des Philosophers, la plus parfait des trois espèces du gouvernement de la chose publique, et la plus selon Dieu et nature, est celle de la Royauté, ceux qui par élection ou par nativitié y sont soumis, doyvent bien afectueusement esuertuer toutes leurs forces et de corps et d'entendement, pour faire chacun en son endroit et selon sa vacation, service à leur souverain: atendu que servans à un, ils profitent à tous, et qu'en lui seul gist l'heur et malheur de ses suiets*" [in the judgement of the Prince of Philosophers, the most perfect of the three types of government of the *chose publique*, and the best according to God and nature, is that of monarchy. Those who by choice or by birth are subjected [to a monarch] must lovingly exert their strength of body and mind, and for each in their place and according to their vocation, to serve their sovereign; given that serving one, they benefit everyone, and that in him alone rests the happiness or unhappiness of his subjects.] Amyot, "Preface" to *Vies des Hommes illustres*, i.

to be a representative of *la chose publique*); and (3), in the case of monarchy, an ethical conception of the ideals pursued through the wielding of public power that also works to justify the service and dedication of subjects.

We can also compare Amyot's vernacular translation of "Political Precepts" with the earlier one of Tory. In the opening passages where Plutarch discusses the initial motivation of those entering public office, we saw in Chapter 3 how Tory invoked the idea of public life at 798e of the essay as *la chose publique* (via the Latin *res publica*), thereby reifying the notion of public life and emphasising its status (as brought out in other ways in the essay) as a very particular type of association with its own ethos and norms. In translating directly from the Greek, Amyot initially invokes the French term *les affaires publiques* to refer more readily to the idea of matters that are common to all.[38] However, shortly after, Amyot also uses *la chose publique* in relation to a sense of stewardship over the whole.[39] This is all to suggest that Amyot is not invoking the term *la chose publique* with exactly the same broad connotations as in Tory's work, but that there is some degree of overlap. Amyot, it could be suggested, in drawing on a usage initiated by Tory, still acknowledges the relevance of denoting public matters using a noun in the singular, and through a term which grants to public life a special status governed by special norms.

The invocation of the term *la chose publique* carries through in the translation of the *Lives*. In the life of Caesar, for example, he expresses Plutarch's observation that at a certain point in the civil war some Romans were brought to the position, which they even dared to express openly, that "il n'y avait plus ordre de remédier aux maux de la chose publique que par le moyen d'un seul, auquel on donnât plein pouvoir, puissance et autorité souveraine," [there was no longer any other way to remedy the evils of the

---

[38] The Tory version reads thus: 798e "Il en y a plusieurs autres venans de cas daventure a la chose Publique qui souddain estant faschez de la grande fascherie des choses ont mervilleusement desire de eulx retirer du negoce en repos laquelle chose ils nont peu faire." Amyot's version of the same passage is as follows: "en a il qui se jettent aux affaires publiques, d'autant qu'ils n'ont que faire chez eux, prenans les affaires publiques pour autant s'amusement et de passe-temps. Il y en a d'autres qui s'y estans jettes, par cas d'aventure, et s'en estans bien tost saoule, ne s'en peuvent plus, au moins pas facilement retirer," *Œuvres morales*, 161.

[39] Again, here is the Tory translation of the passage at 798f: "Je t'asseure que ceulx qui entreprennent la superintendence de *la Chose publique* ny doivent aller comme ceulx qui vont aux feres et petites assemblees de marchandise. Comme nous avons entendu que Stratocles et Dromocleides se invitoyent l'un l'autre daller a la moysson dor. Ils appelloyent ainsi en raillerie le Parlement et la Souveraine court de Justice." and Amyot's translation of the same : "il ne fault pas venir au gouvernement de *la chose publique*, en intention d'y trafiquer, ny d'y faire bien ses besongnes, ainsi comme iadis a Athènes un Stratocles et un Democlides se convioient l'un l'autre d'aller a leur moisson d'or, appellans ainsi par manière de mocquerie, la chaire et tribunes aux harengues, de sur laquelle ils preschoient le peuple." *Œuvres morales*, 161.

chose publique but through the means of one to whom one would give full power and sovereign authority] thereby again suggesting that the idea of *la chose publique* stood prior to strict constitutional and regime identity and was an indicator of public affairs that also carried a need for promoting the good of the community.[40] It was also a use of the term that was extended into other commentary of Amyot's contemporaries. For example, Francois Sienois in his *De L'Estat et maniement de la chose publicque* as translated from the Latin by Jean le Blond in 1584 suggests: "J'apelle une chose publicque tres bonne quand un ou plusieurs ne gouvernent a l'arbitre de leur volunte: mais en laquelle la loy est maistresse et domine seulement."[41] [I call a *chose publique* very good when one or several people do not govern by the freedom of their wills but where the law is master and alone rules.] What I am signalling here is not the criteria of the rule of law that Sienois sees as crucial for good governance, but rather the more subtle invocation of the term "la chose publique," which is here suggested can take the form of a monarchy or a republic. Thus, it stands as a more abstract indication of a normative public realm that not only needs some form of management, but is subject to rules of good and poor ways of doing so, even where is some deliberation regarding what those rules might be.

How might Amyot's immersion in the works of Plutarch have impacted his broader approach to public life? The *Projet d'Eloquence royale* draws on Amyot's extensive knowledge of classical history to make the case for an ideal of kingship where the king demonstrates unmatched skill in the art of speaking. Amyot recognises at the outset that rhetorical expertise is more readily identified with classical republican states. Excellence in the art of speaking is not necessary in monarchies to maintain power and influence. Still, there are reasons linked to the special status of the king that make this skill highly desirable and that may mark the difference between a mere holder of office and a highly effective ruler. Eloquence adds a tool that can be effective where others fail, much like the saliva of an animal's tongue that alone has the healing properties to save a wound from infection.[42] Amyot then refers specifically to the tradition of the *Hercule gaulois*, suggesting that the gift of eloquence is particularly well suited to monarchs.[43] However, Amyot goes on to suggest that one must be aware of the type of eloquence that is suitable for the proper exercise of political office. Vulgar eloquence, which can be reduced to flattery and seeking

---

[40] Plutarch, "Caesar," *Vies des Hommes illustres*, trans. Amyot, vol 2 (Paris: Gallimard, 1951), 444.

[41] Francois Patrice Sienois, *De l'Estat et maniement de la chose publique, ensemble du gouvernment des royaumes et instruction des Princes*, trans. Jean Le Blond (Paris: Claude Micard, 1584), 6.

[42] Amyot, *Projet*, 48.   [43] Amyot, *Projet*, 49.

merely to please the people, must be rejected despite its periodic effectiveness in history. Instead, the eloquence of kings must be tethered to a good understanding (itself comprised of invention, judgement and memory) as well as good speech. Kings should not speak without good knowledge of that of which he speaks, and this appears to be associated with succinctness.[44] In addition, knowledge of the history of service of the family lineages at court will solidify their loyalty and good public service.

Much more work needs to be done on Amyot and the broader tradition of Plutarch reception, including the inflections of meaning in terms and key passages in the works. Nonetheless, given the degree to which most of the subsequent thinkers in this narrative draw from Amyot's contribution, to a certain degree anything coming after Amyot can be thought of as a tribute to his invaluable place in the tradition.

6.3   Jean Bodin (1530–1596)

Bodin drew in numerous ways on Plutarch who forms a frequent reference in his *Methodus* (1566).[45] Written early in Bodin's career, just after a period of teaching law at the University of Toulouse, it presents his general working principles linking the historical study of law to broader precepts of political theory.[46] The popularity of the *Methodus* can be partly measured by the fact that it underwent thirteen Latin editions from 1566 to 1630.[47]

Bodin's later work, *Six Livres de la République* (1576) is better known as the first work invoking the modern notion of sovereignty. Plutarch is also a pervasive influence here, perhaps most notably via a reference to the life of Solon to support Bodin's definition of citizenship (famously conceived quite inclusively as those living within a certain territory subject to the

---

[44] "le premier et principal point de l'éloquence gît a ne parler d'aucune chose dont on n'ait bonne intelligence; et ceux qui ont enseigné l'art de bien dire ne l'avoir autrement formé qu'avec la connoissance des belles sciences, sans lesquelles ce qu'on appelleroit éloquence ne seroit a la verité qu'une baverie indiscrète et ignorante." Amyot, *Projet*, 71–72.

[45] As Paolo Desideri argues, the only time Bodin mentions the Amyot translation of the *Lives* directly is to contest Amyot's interpretation of a passage, suggesting that Bodin most likely read Plutarch in Latin translation. See "*Les Moralia* dans la *Méthode* et les *Six Livres sur la République* de Jean Bodin," in Olivier Guerrier ed., *Moralia et Œuvres morales a la Renaissance* (Paris: Honore Champion, 2008), 200. For purposes of this analysis, I am drawing from the English translation of Bodin's text using the following edition: Jean Bodin, *Method for the Easy Comprehension of History* (New York: W. W. Norton, 1945).

[46] See, for example, Donald Kelley, *Foundations of Modern Historical Scholarship: Language, Law and History in the French Renaissance* (New York and London: Columbia University Press, 1970).

[47] Beatrice Reynolds, "Introduction," in Bodin, *Method*.

same authoritative power).[48] Because the later work addresses questions of
public power through a consideration of institutional and legal structures
of power rather than the more informal norms that shape the public
sphere, and because Bodin's invocation of Plutarch in the earlier work
led to a debate with Montaigne over the usefulness of Plutarch as a source,
I will restrict my commentary here to the *Methodus* with reference to
chapter four, which is dedicated to a discussion of the relative value of
the accounts of classical historians.[49]

The question of method in the adjudication of legal principles was
a pressing topic at the time. There were ongoing tensions by the late
sixteenth century between legal theorists who applied Roman law precepts
uncritically to French traditions, acknowledging their universal authority,
and those who argued that those precepts came from another historical
context and therefore had to be interpreted and applied carefully. Bodin's
position comes out in his dedication where he cites the examples of
Lycurgus and Solon. As good legislators, they did not just rely on old
codes to apply to their respective homelands but adjudicated among many
foreign examples to discern good legal and constitutional practice. The
'method' that Bodin elaborates in this work draws from a similar inspiration of offering ways in which one might sort through a broad array of
traditions and legal codes to find those principles of law and politics that
appear to have universal validity. In this process, the study of history is
essential because it offers a more vivid expression of precepts by showing
their complement in practice and application, as well as offering the
particulars of life from which general precepts are first generated through
reflection. Thus, history is referred to by Bodin as the 'master of life.' In
addition, as he notes in the opening pages of this work, emulation is an
important feature of political life; thus, the question of which historical
figure one honours and how they are honoured has directly shaped the
course of history.

Bodin suggests a study of history starting with the most general and
universal level before proceeding to the study of particular peoples and

---

[48] Howell Lloyd, *Jean Bodin, 'This Pre-eminent Man of France': An Intellectual Biography* (Oxford:
Oxford University Press, 2017), 123–124. Lloyd suggests that Bodin made 243 references to Plutarch
in his *Six Livres* alone. Still, given what we note below one cannot be certain that Bodin was getting
his Plutarch references firsthand. Paolo Desideri notes that Bodin's invocation of Plutarch's notion
of a right to citizenship involving taking part in the rights and privileges of a city appears to come
from the life of Solon. Solon granted citizenship rights broadly to the people while only allowing the
rich to hold public responsibility. See Desideri, "Les *Moralia*," 213.

[49] For a broader survey of Bodin's use of Plutarch in his work, see Desideri, "Les *Moralia*." He suggests
that reliance on Plutarch's *Political Precepts* is particularly evident in Bodin's *Six Livres*.

kingdoms.[50] The systematic coverage of historical writing is comple-
mented by Bodin's advocacy for the well-attuned reader to uncover the
principles and concepts that apply universally, leading to a revision in our
common understandings of what is a state and a citizen.[51] The state
famously comes to be redefined as that entity meeting the minimal conditions of people sharing one and the same rule (leaving aside the earlier
Aristotelian and Ciceronian consideration that people come together in
a state for the purpose of living well). Similarly, ruling that "virtue and
viciousness do not create a type of rule," he undermines the very basis on
which the ancients commonly distinguished regimes.[52] There is thus
a degree of realism filtering into Bodin's way of looking at political analysis.
This attachment to realism also helps to inform his adjudication of various
sources of classical history.

In Chapter 4, Bodin reflects on which historians can be deemed more
reliable or valuable than others. For Soll, following Koselleck, it is this spirit
of critical assessment and reflection applied to adjudicating sources and
writing history that would become the critical rational spirit of the
Enlightenment itself.[53] (It is somewhat ironic, then, that the critical rational
spirit born in the adjudication of historical sources in the Renaissance has
often become in the modern era a source of scepticism concerning any useful
lessons at all to be drawn from historical study.) Bodin is judging authors
based on how worthy they are as sources all the while recognising how crucial
an understanding of history is to an understanding of principles of social,
legal and political organisation. He singles out various factors, including
authors' access to official sources, their practical experience in matters of
public affairs that could inform their historical writing (again reflecting his
realist affinities), as well as their closeness to the subjects they write about
(some distance from the subject matter, such as Caesar writing about the
Gauls appears to be in principle more reliable than Polybius's passages where
he defends the valour of the Greeks).

In this reconsideration of ancient commentary to develop a new theory
of politics, Bodin draws directly on evidence from Plutarch (though
according to Howell Lloyd, Bodin also drew on Budé for some of his
reading of Plutarch and sometimes did so with a degree of
misunderstanding).[54] In general, Plutarch was used or cited not to further

[50] Bodin, *Method*, 15–24.   [51] Bodin, *Method*, 154–162.   [52] Bodin, *Method*, 179.
[53] See Jacob Soll, "Empirical History and the Transformation of Political Criticism in France from
Bodin to Bayle," *Journal of the History of Ideas*, 64.2 (April 2003), 297–316.
[54] Howell Lloyd suggests that Bodin misjudged what Plutarch said about the amount of tribute given
by Marc Anthony to his troops, but he suggests that is because Bodin was not reading his source,

an understanding of ancient modes of governance as *paideia* or to explore links between regimes and the good life, but rather as a source of information about the ancient world that might offer support for a very different agenda than that furthered by Plutarch himself. For example, Bodin suggests that Plutarch's account of Sparta vindicates Bodin's assertion that Sparta was not a mixed regime, contra Aristotle. With the demise of royal power Lycurgus created a senate, but all decisions had to be ratified by the people, making them the sole holders of sovereignty, something that was not modified until almost 150 years later when sovereignty passed to the senate as the regime switched from a popular state to an aristocratic one.[55] Plutarch's life of Lycurgus is used to support Bodin's more general argument that sovereignty cannot be divided.

As the text unfolds, a more complicated relation between Bodin and Plutarch appears. Despite using Plutarch as a source for claims regarding the nature of the state, Bodin also acknowledges that Plutarch's work should be approached with caution, at least as a historical source. Plutarch may have had an advantage as an historian given his direct experience of political and administrative life, or what Bodin calls 'civil training.' Indeed, he acknowledges and praises the tradition identifying Plutarch as a tutor to Trajan.[56] At the same time, however, he expresses concern about his weaknesses, suggesting that Plutarch's historical accounts were piecemeal and thematically (implicitly too narrowly) focused on leadership. Bodin also suggests that "he seems to be not so much a historian as a censor of princes" (of course Plutarch never claimed to be a historian) and that at times in his accounts he defends "unbelievable" and "clearly preposterous things," sowing doubt regarding his reliability.[57] One such example among several is the famous incident taken from the *Life of Lycurgus* regarding a Spartan boy who suffered in silence the pain of having his innards torn and mangled by a fox to avoid the shame of being discovered for having stolen the animal. Bodin also notes how Plutarch's comparisons of Greeks and Romans is misleading given the obviously mightier example of Rome: "what difference is there

---

Budé, carefully enough. Still, this was not an observation noted in the *Methodus*, but rather in a minor work of Bodin's entitled *Response a Malestroit*. See Lloyd, *Jean Bodin*, 101.

[55] Bodin, *Method*, 186.

[56] The sources for this are double. The first is the apocryphal letter included in the Sekoundinos translation, which may have originated in John of Salisbury's *Politicraticus*. The second is another letter addressed to Trajan found at the start of the "Sayings of Kings and Commanders" in the *Moralia* about which there is ongoing speculation regarding authenticity. See Beck, "Plutarch to Trajan."

[57] Bodin, *Method*, 63–64.

between comparing Agesilaus to Pompey and a fly to an elephant?"[58] Bodin (somewhat ironically, given Howell Lloyd's suggestion that Bodin himself was misled by Budé on Plutarch) even notes a number of details where Plutarch misled his readers regarding particular features of Roman law, custom and coinage, details which, he claims, also misled Budé.[59]

While Bodin sees some merit in Plutarch as a source of historical reflection, suggesting he had some experience in matters he was writing about, Bodin also suggests that Plutarch was sometimes inaccurate and that he tended to let his patriotic attachment exaggerate the merits of the Greek subjects and overwhelm his historical judgement.

These remarks would later spark Montaigne's defence of Plutarch, but to some extent they may have been talking at cross-purposes. In the first instance, Bodin was addressing the value of Plutarch for historical insight into the ancient world in relation to an array of classical historians. His concern was the accuracy of Plutarch's claims about ancient societies. Montaigne, while very learned in his way, was in no better a position to judge the historical veracity of Plutarch's claims. Indeed, as we will see, while Montaigne does draw on various examples and incidents in the *Lives*, his purpose in doing so most often is to back a moral argument rather than make empirical claims about the past. Montaigne's Plutarch was a thinker valued to a large degree for his insights into the perennial features and idiosyncrasies of human nature.

Arguably, as we will explore in greater detail in Chapter 7, Montaigne offers a watershed in the development of French political theory. Prior to Amyot's translation of the full *Moralia* into French and Montaigne's immersion in that text, political reflection as inspired by Plutarch in the early sixteenth century had been dominated by references from the *Lives* and to "Political Precepts" as translated by Tory. From Montaigne on, it can be argued that traditions of political reflection in France began to draw more heavily from the *Moralia*. This shift may be more reflective of perhaps a broader bifurcation in cultural tendencies. On the one hand, as we have seen, Amyot helped to position Plutarch's classical lives as a form of cultural encomium or Pantheon of heroes somewhat in the spirit of Budé; on the other, we see the growth of critical reflection on the criterion and standards through which good and great action should be judged. Montaigne, for example, begins to question the cruelty of Alexander in the opening essay of his work, and at times extols the common peasant as most exemplary of the finest Stoic equilibrium.

---

[58] Bodin, *Method*, 64.   [59] Bodin, *Method*, 64–65.

Thus, while heroism was elevated as a literary discourse, the invocation of the lives of heroic classical individuals became more suspect as a standard of public exemplarity. It may be that the Wars of Religion made the grand gestures of generals and classical political leaders questionable regulative norms for contemporary politics. Indeed, this may be a foreshadowing of a broader cultural trend in which the ideal of exemplarity itself, particularly exemplarity of the ancients, would be questioned.[60]

---

[60] As Sue Farquhar states about Montaigne: "His attentiveness to the problem of reader address reflects a growing scepticism regarding classical, especially Ciceronian, belief in ethical capacity. The *Essais* contribute, perhaps more than any other work of its time, to a crisis in exemplarity, undercutting the belief that classical ideas could provide a model for present times, that virtue could be learned by imitating heroic ideals." In "Michel de Montaigne: the Essais and a Tacitean Discourse," in G. Sandy ed., *The Classical Heritage in France* (Leiden: Brill, 2002), 211. In support of this account of the shift Farquhar cites: Timothy Hampton, *Writing from History: The Rhetoric of Exemplarity in Renaissance Literature* (Ithaca, NY: Cornell University Press, 1989); John Lyons, The Rhetoric of Exemplarity in Early Modern France and Italy (Princeton, NJ: Princeton University Press, 1989); and Karlhenz Stierle, "L'Histoire comme exemple, l'exemple comme histoire," *Poétique* 10 (1972), 176–198.

CHAPTER 7

Bernard de Girard Du Haillan and Michel de Montaigne on Thinking Through the Public Good in a Time of Civil Discord

The work of classical reception in early modern political thought has tended to focus on the place of Stoicism, Ciceronianism and Tacitism.[1] It has been suggested that in the wake of the French Wars of Religion, intellectuals and theorists turned away from the hegemony of Cicero as a model for both speech and thinking through civic humanism, and towards Tacitean and Stoic notions of political prudence along with "fortitude and withdrawal."[2] Although admittedly the strands of the uptake of classical thinkers in a shifting view of the world through the Renaissance is a highly complex and multifaceted mix, the degree to which previous studies have neglected the place of Plutarch reception in these narratives is noteworthy. As noted in the Introduction, there was greater circulation of Greek historians than previously assumed, making Plutarch one of the most widely acquired, if not read, authors of the early modern period.[3] In relative terms, this also

---

[1] See for example Fumaroli, *L'Age de l'Éloquence*; Peter Burke, "Tacitism," in T. A. Dorey, ed., *Tacitus* (London: Routledge and Kegan Paul, 1969); Kenneth Schellhase, *Tacitus in Renaissance Political Thought* (Chicago: Chicago University Press, 1976); Richard Tuck, *Philosophy and Government 1572–1651* (Cambridge: Cambridge University Press, 1993); D. R. Kelley, "Tacitus Noster: The Germania in the Renaissance and Reformation," in T. J. Luce and A.J. Woodman, eds. *Tacitus and the Tacitean Tradition* (Princeton, NJ: Princeton University Press, 1993), 152–167; Sue W. Farquhar, "Michel de Montaigne: The Essais and a Tacitean Discourse," in G. Sandy ed., *The Classical Heritage in France* (Leiden: Brill, 2002), 187–218; and Brooke, *Philosophic Pride*. I could also include both constitutionalism and Epicureanism, although the first can in part be subsumed by one tradition of Cicero reception, and the latter extends beyond a narrow domain of political reflection.

[2] See J. H. M. Salmon, "Cicero and Tacitus in Sixteenth-Century France," *American Historical Review*, vol. 85.2 (April 1980), 307. As argued by Kenneth Schellhase, it is nonetheless evident that there was an ebb and flow in the popularity of Tacitus from the early Renaissance to the eighteenth century, and among French, English and Italian traditions, but with a general tendency to invoke Tacitus in the Renaissance for guidance in practical issues concerning politics to a broader attempt to malign him by the early eighteenth century. See *Tacitus in Renaissance Political Thought* (Chicago: University of Chicago Press, 1977). Although Plutarch is acknowledged as a source for the constitutionalists (e.g. Hotman) as well as Bodin and Montaigne, Schellhase does not see Tacitus as contributing to a broader tradition of argument on a singular theme in the way Plutarch can be seen to be as sketched in this book.

[3] Cox Jensen, "Popularity."

modifies to a certain degree what had previously been thought by many to be a strong preference for Tacitus among classical historians.[4] It becomes more difficult to claim that by the end of the sixteenth century in France Tacitus was "the most popular ancient historian."[5] The predominance and increasing popularity of Plutarch in the long sixteenth century, thanks to a large degree to Amyot, engages us in a reassessment of what was at play in the early modern period in terms of classical reception, especially by the end of the sixteenth century when he was being read in new ways.[6]

Does "fortitude and withdrawal" actively capture the literary spirit of the thinkers of late sixteenth-century France? Themes of Hellenistic philosophy were clearly circulating, but Plutarch reception at this time suggests that many thinkers were rethinking the nature of their public commitments, and not necessarily through a repudiation of them. Bernard de Girard Du Haillan (1535–1610) and Michel de Montaigne (1533–1592) through the lens of their engagement with Plutarch, did not abandon public commitments. Both were professed Catholics, but their work attests to a deeper wish to learn from the social and political struggles of the classical era and to find resources through which strategies of accommodation of difference and hospitality might be possible.

It was clear by the 1560s that a peaceful settlement to the conflicts required some form of accommodation, but public leaders and intellectuals endorsing compromise, identified collectively as the *politiques*, did not always conceptualise the process of accommodation in the same way. Differences emerge via a comparison of two key thinkers alongside their influential predecessors – that is, Du Haillan alongside his important mentor Etienne Pasquier (1529–1615), and Montaigne whose work evolved through a dialogue with that of his friend Etienne de La Boétie (1530–1563).

---

[4] Cox Jensen, "Popularity," Table 3.

[5] Soll, "Empirical History," 305. Of course, some of this may rest on to what degree Plutarch can be considered an historian, as he never claimed to be writing history strictly speaking. Nonetheless, given that many thinkers of the sixteenth century had recourse to his work for historical detail, he was certainly a resource for early modern historians and by that measure could be classified as such.

[6] As argued earlier in an earlier chapter, with the early translations of Plutarch into the vernacular, by Geoffroy Tory, Claude de Seyssel and Guillaume Budé among others, political thinkers in France were often concerned about the very specific nature of the public realm as a special form of relation which often functioned according to its own distinct optics, norms and expectations. Given the historical context of the Wars of Religion, that notion of a public realm and public good now also had to be tested or revised in view of the reality of deep civil and political divisions. What sort of conceptual form would the notion of a public good take that could accommodate the religious differences if not resolve them? Presumably some notion of hospitality or accommodation needed to be a new consideration if civil peace was to be achieved. So, a key question is how Plutarch was used as a resource for thinkers in the late sixteenth century in France to rethink the challenges of public life in view of a new need for religious accommodation and hospitality.

With a focus on Du Haillan and Montaigne but in the light of their intellectual counterparts we can explore diverse invocations and use of Plutarch's work in thinking through the public realm.

These thinkers are chosen because of their direct translation, or publication, of Plutarch's work, or for their deep engagement with Plutarch's work in their concerted reflection on policy and political theory. While clearly there were also Protestants who were involved in both scholarship and reading of Plutarch, the work of political theory coming from Protestant sources demonstrate less explicit use of Plutarch's work as a basis for their arguments, despite the valuable editorial contributions of the Estienne family in Geneva and of Simon de Goulart, a Calvinist pastor who added explanatory notes to Amyot's translation and published various editions of this beginning in 1583.[7] Although a close study of the implications of their work is beyond the scope of this study, for documentary purposes we should note that a translation of Plutarch by Philippe des Avenelles was dedicated to Francois de Coligny d'Andelot (1521–1569), a respected military officer and brother to the Admiral Coligny. The volume of translated excerpts from the *Lives* was published and dedicated to Andelot in 1558, the same year that Andelot publicly declared his Calvinist commitments.[8]

Each of the thinkers addressed in this chapter invoke a distinct understanding of the purpose of the public realm and institutions, and they draw on Plutarch to help address the challenges of their era. Du Haillan followed his predecessor Pasquier to uncover in French history norms that were unique to France and not fully deduced from Roman law. While Pasquier looked to longstanding constitutional norms for guidance, for Du Haillan the path to peace appeared to reside in cultivating good leadership to help manage dissent before it could erupt into violence. This was voiced in a somewhat circuitous way. Through his translation of Plutarch, Du Haillan highlighted the special prudence (as opposed to heroism) of a good political leader in dealing with social conflict and national crisis. Through his selective choice of passages from Plutarch's *Lives* he offered his readers a portrait of how the good leadership of one can overcome the effects and danger of civil discord, partly through strategies of listening,

---

[7] James Denton, "Translation and Manipulation in Renaissance England," *Journal of Early Modern Studies* 1 (2016), 46.

[8] *Epitome ou abrege des vies de cinquante et quatre notables et excellens personnaiges tant Greco que Romains extraict du Grec de Plutarque de Charonee,* trans. *Philippe des Avenelles* (Paris: Paris. De l'imprimerie de Philippe Danfrie, and Richard Breton, 1558). As indicated in the dedicatory letter, Avenelles used the Latin edition of Tiberti as the basis for his French translations.

and partly through judicious selection of advisers and public officials. The most effective leader is one who does not overstep constitutional norms, but who works with them and through them in effective and productive ways, through consultation bringing about the desired effect of peace. Like much of the political theory in Plutarch reception, it offers insight into features of political and moral psychology (as opposed to constitutionalism for example) as key to responding to political challenges.

As another perspective addressing religious discord in France, Montaigne's work offers us a shift prepared by his predecessor La Boétie. Earlier Renaissance political theorists offered lessons to *kings* illuminating the specific nature of the public realm often via anecdotes from Plutarch. Montaigne, in contrast, offered advice on how *subjects* should perceive and adapt to the power structures within which they find themselves. We find in Montaigne's work in contrast to an account of historically effective constitutional principles and the wish for an accommodating and judicious leader to heal social divisions, a broader defence of a general spirit of humanity and goodwill to be spread civilly as a means of checking the institutional abuses that exacerbate conflict.[9] The authors invoked in this chapter, identified in general terms as *politiques*, offer different ways of calling for the management of civil conflict and the conceptualisation of the public realm, and in ways that depart from the notions developed earlier in the sixteenth century.

As a background to these theorists, it cannot be stressed enough how the status and availability of vernacular translations of Plutarch shifted considerably with the work of Amyot. At the same time, we also find a shift in the work of political theorists associated with Plutarch reception. By the latter sixteenth century, theorists were speaking to a wider audience. The vernacular translations of the early sixteenth century were often done specifically for the king and his court. With Montaigne especially, but also implied with the others, we see a broadening of the intended audience. The optics of public life had shifted, and commentary is staged to some degree from the outside in, offering advice for those who find themselves observers of public turmoil and intrigue.

All the thinkers studied in this chapter cited Plutarch in their work. Du Haillan published in 1578 the *Recueil d'advis et conseils sur les affaires d'estat, tire des vies de Plutarque* as a version of a commonplace book in which select

---

[9] This argument stands in certain contrast to the recent work of Douglas Thompson who argues that Montaigne's work stands as an exemplar of judicious diplomatic reasoning to position himself as a suitable candidate for public service and the resolution of conflict. See *Montaigne and the Tolerance of Politics* (Oxford: Oxford University Press, 2018).

anecdotes and quotations were presented to readers out of context from the narrative of the *Lives* to offer a form of perennial wisdom on matters of public importance.[10] La Boétie also translated Plutarch's moral essays. This analysis will allow us to discern how Plutarch's work was invoked to call for public accommodation of religious difference.

7.1   Bernard de Gerard Du Haillan (c. 1535–1610)

Du Haillan is a historian and political thinker who, like his predecessor Pasquier, is often identified with constitutionalist thought.[11] Again like Pasquier, who served as a lawyer for the Paris parlement, Du Haillan as historian explored the details of the origins of the monarchy in France from the time of the Gauls to provide a normative picture of French institutions as a mixed regime. His intention was to demonstrate the minor role played by Roman law while also rejecting any account of the Trojan origins of the French people.[12] The tradition reveals a shift away from the 'mirror for prince's' genre and opened the possibility for a more general discussion of

---

[10] Bernard de Girard, Seigneur Du Haillan, *Recueil d'advis et conseils sur les affaires d'estat, tire des vies de Plutarque* (Paris: Olivier de Pierre l'Huillier, 1578).

[11] Skinner, *Foundations. vol. 2*, 259ff. Pasquier is rightly considered a pre-eminent representative of a tradition of constitutionalism in early modern France. In situating this work within larger debates, Skinner pits the constitutionalists of late sixteenth-century France (in an intellectual movement he calls the "reassertion of constitutionalism") against the chorus of theorists, including Charles Du Moulin (1500–1566), who defended the emerging practice of absolutism under François I. Du Moulin on the plane of legal theory argued that the complex feudal system of overlapping rights and obligations was a late usurpation of the more fundamental idea of dominium which defined the French monarchy and which it had inherited from Roman Imperial law. The constitutionalists, with Pasquier prominent among them, saw the necessity of fighting the absolutists on the domain of history going back to the sources and seeking a better account of the origins of French institutions. While having recourse to Tacitus as one resource among many, the impetus was to counter those legal glossators whose accounts led to the consolidation of royal authority at the expense of other subordinate and dependent institutions within the monarchical structure.

[12] Pasquier's historical and theoretical work is vast in scope, and from the outset of his *Recherches de la France* (1560–1621) he offers a new approach to political reflection. [There was an Etienne Pasquier who translated five essays of Plutarch in work entitled *Opuscules de Plutarche Cheronee*, trans. E. Pasquier (Lyon: Jean de Tournes, 1546), but the translator Pasquier is identified as the rector of schools in Louhans, a town in the region of Bresse, and not the young law student that our own Etienne Pasquier would have been at this time.] In facing the crisis of the Wars of Religion, his focus in 1561 was on convincing established powers, especially the king in council, that the policy of suppression of religious minorities was unsustainable and ultimately detrimental to the welfare of the regime. Thus, it does represent continuity with themes associated with public utility voiced earlier in the century, but in the case of Pasquier it is peace and the elimination of sedition which emerges as the most important task of public power.
    The first volume of *Les Recherches de la France* was published in 1560 – thus, prior to Du Haillan. [Etienne Pasquier, *Les Recherches de la France*, 3 vols. (Paris: Honoré Champion, 1996)]. In the initial chapters of the work, Pasquier sets about rehabilitating the reputation of the ancient Gauls given their vilification by various historians including Livy. The intent is to trace the roots of French

the origins and nature of the French national community and its institutions, acknowledging the importance of the rule of law, the parlements and
judicious domestic and international policy as a basis for good government. Indeed, for both Pasquier and Du Haillan one of the contributions
of addressing issues of politics through the lens of a national history was to
demonstrate how ancient Gaul emerged in its origins from a diverse
mixture of cultural and social forces and whose institutions emerged
autonomously but with longstanding practices of internal dialogue and
consultation.[13]

Pasquier's *Recherches* focuses on how French history can illuminate key
political norms, but he does appeal to classical history as a lesson for the
present in another work entitled *Exhortation aux Princes et Seigneurs du*

---

    political traditions to the practices of the ancient Gauls, thereby questioning those who claim deep
historical insight that allows them to trace French monarchy to the Trojans (a long-circulated
account) or to Hercules and the Greeks. For a discussion of Pasquier in relation to theories of the
Trojan origins of France, see James Dahlinger, *Etienne Pasquier on Ethics and History* (New York:
Peter Lang, 2007), chap. 4. See also Pasquier, *Recherches*, 1, 14, 315. Benoit de Sainte Maure's *Roman
de Troie* was the medieval text that sparked the historiographical tradition suggesting Trojan origins
for the French nation in a broader account of the founding of leading dynasties across Europe and
Turkey by epic heroes. Of course, as we have seen earlier, this could play into deeper sensibilities
stressing the relative autonomy of French political and legal traditions from ancient Roman sources.
A juxtaposition of this Trojan origins theory with that of the Gauls was found in Jean Lemaire de
Belges's *Les Illustrations de Gaule et singularitez de Troye* (1509). In his *Recherches*, Pasquier carried on
the discussion of the two competing accounts but suggested that no evidence existed to support the
Trojan origins theory, gesturing towards the more convincing status of the Gaullist account.

[13] From the outset of Pasquier's *Recherches* is a view of the interdependency of king and parlement from
the very roots of the founding of French monarchical institutions. The parlements are seen as
emerging from the ruins of (as opposed to a continuation of) Roman rule. Tweaking an ancient
trope, he suggests that the French monarchy owes its success and longevity partly to Fortune and
partly to the wisdom of its people. The principle on which his defence of the distribution of power is
based is not directly liberty, but the need to mitigate the possibility of internal division and
dissension by ensuring consultation with a broad spectrum of notables across the territory.
(*Recherches*, 11, 2, 326). In a time of clear internal division and conflict, Pasquier, while not remaining
blind to periods of division and dissent within the nation's history, is also clearly focused on the
institutional and legal ways in which division can be managed peacefully. The managing of
difference and division within the territory of France was modeled on earlier institutions of the
Gauls. "Estans doncques ces grands Seigneurs ainsi lors unis, se composa un corps general de tous les
Princes et Gouverneurs, par l'advis desquels se vuideroient non seulement les differends qui se
presenteroient entre le Roy et eux, mais entre le Roy et ses sujects. Qui fut une institution notable
pour contenir cette France en union, laquelle estoit ce neantmoins divisee en plusieurs Ducs et
Comtes, qui amoindrissoient l'authorite du Roy de tant plus, que hormis le baisemain, que par
prerogative ils luy devoient, ils en dependoient au surplus que de leur authorite et grandeur.
Tellement que maintes-fois ils guerroyoient particulierement le Roy mesme, et le reduisoient en
grandes angusties. Toutesfois apres plusieurs guerroyemens, chacun se soumettoit a ce commun
Parlement. Laquelle usance (Presque de la mesme facon) avoit este observe par les anciens Gaulois,
lesquels combine qu'ils fussent partialisez en ligues, si avoient-ils tous ensemble un general resort de
la Justice, qui se manioit au pays Chartrain par leurs Prestres, qu'ils nommoient Druydes."
Recherches, 11, 2, 330.

Conseil privé du roy, pour obvier aux séditions qui semblent nous menacer pour le fait de la Religion (1561).[14] He suggests the attempt to eradicate Protestantism in France is futile and ill-advised, given the number of committed Protestants, their importance to the economy of France, and the dangers, including ongoing corruption and degradation, associated with a continued campaign of violence. He advises the king and his council to think of their public role in terms of assuring the basic social conditions of peaceful coexistence through which the community can begin to prosper and thrive, and not to favour one religious group over another but to allow each to worship in their own way. His advocacy in this regard is largely about the need for peace and an expression of the cost and devastation of war, particularly for the peasants.[15] In the closing pages of the exhortation he invokes Julius Caesar as a cautionary tale for a continued policy of war. Just as Caesar, initially motivated by patriotic ambitions in his campaign in Gaul, was led through his continued campaign of war to develop more ambitious plans for overtaking the republican institutions of Rome, so continued war within France could incite certain notables to embark on a campaign leading to the subversion of the regime.[16] Pasquier raises the spectre of Caesarism as a possible outcome if a negotiated solution to the religious differences is not found, and this derived from the very psychology of factional struggle. The more general point being offered by this anecdote is that the exercise of extraordinary powers in times of war can have a corrupting influence on those who wield power. The idea of public power having its own special and unique qualities as developed in the early part of the century is here presented in a much more sinister light.

Pasquier's follower Du Haillan is best known for *De l'estat et succez des affaires de France* (1570) [*State and Success of the Affairs of France*] and *Histoire generale des rois de France depuis Pharamond jusqu'a Charles IX* (1576) [*General history of the kings of France from Pharamond to Charles IX*]. The status of some of Du Haillan's historical work has been questioned,

---

[14] Etienne Pasquier, *Exhortation aux princes et seigneurs du Conseil privé du roy. Pour obuier aux seditions qui occultement semblent nous menacer pour le fait de la religion.* (np, 1561) Online at: https://archive.org/details/exhortationauxproopasq/page/n1. Date accessed 30 October 2018.

[15] Dorothy Thickett, *Etienne Pasquier* (London: Regency Press, 1979), chaps. 5–7.

[16] "Quand Jules Cesar entreprint la grande conquest des Gaules, il imaginoit seulement la vengeance de ceux d'Autun allies de la Republique Romaine, son dessein n'estoit pour lors autre que le profit de sa patrie: mais apre que la fortune eut conduit ses entre princes a effet et qu'il se veid avoir une grande partie des armes de Rome en sa main, il commenca de bastir Nouvelles imaginations au dommage de sa Republique, et de vouloir reduire souz sa seule dition et puissance toute la maieste du Peuple. Je n'offense encores personne, car je n'apprehende point qu'aucun de vous ait iamais basty telz discours au desavantage du Roy: mais tant y ha, que nous sommes hommes, et l'ambition selon les offres et evenemens fait quelquefois grandes bresches en noz esprits." Pasquier, *Exhortation*, 47.

however. Indeed, Pasquier is said to have complained that Du Haillan directly copied parts of his work. To be fair, in later editions of his work Du Haillan acknowledged his debt to Pasquier (and others).[17] It certainly did not impede Du Haillan from being appointed the king's official historiographer under Charles IX and Henri III.[18] How ever we judge this in hindsight, Du Haillan's translation and presentation of Plutarch offers a political sensibility that is palpably distinct from that of Pasquier.

Skinner offers us an interpretation of Du Haillan's work as in line with other moderate Catholic writers, or the *politiques*, of his day, including Pasquier and Bodin of the 1560s.[19] This, it is argued, was structured in part as a return to some of the constitutionalist doctrines of Seyssel in particular. In Book III of *De l'estat et succez* he counters a new line of thinkers who claim it a crime of lèse-majesté to argue for constitutional checks on the king. He invokes Seyssel's *Monarchy of France* and suggests that the bridles of religion, justice and police, following Seyssel, structure the way in which kings exercise their authority.

In addition to his historical and constitutionalist work, Du Haillan published translations, including Cicero's *De Officiis* and a selection of translated passages from Plutarch's *Lives,* as matters for reflection and advice for political leaders. This latter was published as *Recueil d'avis et conseils sur les affaires d'estat tire des vies de Plutarque* (1578).[20]

---

[17] Paul Bonnefon, "L'Historien Du Haillan," *Revue d'Histoire Littéraire de la France* 22.3–4 (1915), 453–492.

[18] See Chantal Grell, "History and Historians in France, from the Great Italian Wars to the Death of Louis XIV," in J. Rabasa et al. eds., *The Oxford History of Historical Writing, volume 3: 1400–1800* (Oxford: Oxford University Press, 2012), 390.

[19] Skinner, *Foundations vol. 2.* 268ff.

[20] There is evidence that Du Haillan had knowledge of Plutarch's work long before the publication of those excerpts. The evidence comes from Du Haillan's *Promesse et Desseign de l'Histoire de France* published in 1571. This is a work which provides an overview of Du Haillan's plans for his broader history of France to be published many years later. Here Du Haillan praises the work of exemplarity, suggesting that rulers can benefit from the reading of history to find examples of good princes and rulers to learn how to govern, driven largely by the principle of public utility. In addition, at the outset of this essay, Du Haillan cites a passage from Plutarch's *Life of Theseus* without acknowledging Plutarch as the source. He suggests there is a parallel between certain maps where unknown territories in the margins are often indicated with illustrations of strange beasts or multiple hazards and his own notion that the time that precedes the start of his own historical account can only be thought of as a strange fiction: "pouvons dire, que tout ainsi que les historiens qui descrivent la Terre en figure, ont accoustume de supprimer aux extremitez de leurs Cartes, les Regions dont ilz n'ont point de cognnoissance, et mettent au marge; que outre ces pays descritz, il n'y a plus que profondes sablonnieres sans eau pleines de bestes venimeuse, ou de la vase que lon ne peult naviguer, ou la Scithie deserte pour le froit, ou bien la mer glacee: aussi en ceste mienne histoire ie puis bien dire des temps plus anciens et plus esloignez du present que ce qui est au paravant, n'et plus que fiction estrange et qu'on ne en trouve que fables monstrueuse, semblables a celles des Poetes." From

What does the collection of excerpts tell us? We should first ask whether these were translated by Du Haillan himself, or whether these were taken from an already extant translation, most obviously that of Amyot. There is no indication of who did the translation in the text. If we compare select passages with that of Amyot we find that the translation, though not the same, does follow it extraordinarily closely. Although pure speculation, I would venture to say that whoever produced these translations – Du Haillan or another – based their work largely on that of Amyot, making relatively minor changes to the wording. What this means in terms of my analysis is that the selection or choice of passages, rather than their wording, as well as the paratext, including preface and dedication, may be most significant in discerning Du Haillan's intentions in publishing this compilation.

A first observation in reading through the paratext and prefatory material is that there is a clear shift in the invocation of *la chose publique*. Unlike the connotation in Tory's translation of "Political Precepts", or even in Amyot's preface, in Du Haillan's preface its reference is limited to a singular type of regime – a republic, which is clearly distinguished from a monarchy. Still, he does acknowledge that lessons about politics gained from a study of republican forms may be relevant for a monarchical setting, even making the rather surprising suggestion that the turmoil in France exposes a need for the moral philosophy of republican practices and mores.[21] This, it might be suggested, speaks to the resonance of themes of collective psychology and the working of moral leadership that appears to link many of the invocations of Plutarch's work to political reflection in the French tradition.

Instead of any definitive notion of public good common to all in the way that appeared to be a supposition of political thinkers and readers of Plutarch earlier in the sixteenth century, we find a notion that political leadership is effective and praiseworthy insofar as it can achieve concord and serve "public utility." Political accommodation is attempted here in conjunction with an avoidance of any direct discussion of religious

---

Du Haillan, Bernard de Girard, *Promesse et Desseign de l'Histoire de France* (Paris: Olivier de Pierre l'Huillier, 1571), 3–4.

[21] This can be contrasted with its invocation in the body of the translation, where we find a return to the earlier invocation of the term "la chose publique" such as is found in Amyot's translation, for example in a passage from the *Life of Aristides* where it is noted that he did not want to be in league with any other person in the administration of "la chose publique." This usage is repeated at various places throughout the body of the translation. The contrasting invocation of the term in the preface versus the body of the translated work may be further indication of Du Haillan adapting his translation from that of Amyot.

differences. Instead the focus is on a set of practical maxims of governance concerning what constitutes good leadership skills but silence on the salient issues of conflict, as well as silence on any appeal to empathy, sympathy or individual sentiments of subjects to encourage accommodation.

Du Haillan orders his excerpts from the *Lives* in rough chronological order, starting with the founders of Athens, Rome and Sparta and then works through to figures of the final years of the Roman Republic. In so doing, he is eschewing Plutarch's own wish to consider these figures as paired with one another along with an associated moral deliberation. Du Haillan was extremely selective in the passages he culled from various *Lives,* sometimes only restricting his choice to a single one from any life. The few principles informing the selection of passages are apparent.

The selections reflect the intent expressed in the title of his translated excerpts – in other words, to shed light on more practical questions of how to exercise power and rule effectively. In line with some other early compilations, Du Haillan offers material for more generalisable maxims in public life (rather than insight into virtue or the character of any figure). Given this thrust, one of the upshots of the compilation is an emphasis that the work of accommodation and concord relies on the skills of leadership and education.

One issue treated is dealing with the pressures of popular opinion and temptations involved in one-person rule. A passage from the comparison of Romulus and Theseus tells us that the first erred by seeking to be swayed too strongly by popular forces and the second erred by becoming a tyrant and ignoring the people, neither of which were effective forms of kingly rule.[22] In a similar vein, Du Haillan selects a passage from Plutarch's *Cicero* that speaks to the holding of public office as the ultimate test of character given that power often stirs the passions that rest within and brings into full view the vices which had before remained secret.[23] It would appear,

---

[22] "Romulus et Theseus tous deux eu la nature propre a commander et gouverner, ne l'un ne l'autre ne retint les facons de faire d'un vray Roy, ains en sortirent tous deux, l'un se changeant en homme Populaire, et l'autre en tyran. Si que par diverses passions ils tomberent tous deux en mesme inconvenient et erreur, car il fault qu'un Prince devant toutes choses conserve son Estat, lequel se conserve non moins en ne faisant rien qui ne luy soit bien seant, qu'en faisant tout ce qui luy est bien convenable. Mais celuy qui se roidist ou relasche plus ou moins qu'il ne doit, ne demeure plus ne Roy ne Prince, ainx deviant ou Populaire flatteur, ou maistre superbe, et fait que ses subiets le mesprisent ou le haissent. Toutesfois il semble que l'un soit erreur de trop grade bonte et humanite, l'autre d'arrogance et de fierte." (s. 9).

[23] "ce qui plus espreuve et plus decouvre la nature de l'homme, comme lon dict et comme il est vray, cest la licence et l'authorite d'un magistrat, laquelle remue tout ainsi qu'il y a de passions au fond du cueur dun homme et fait venir en evidence tous les vices secrets qui y sont cachez." (s. 237).

drawing from the example of Lycurgus, that Du Haillan thinks that it is worthy of note that the obedience of people to their king and commander may not rest ultimately with popular wills (in the way Du Haillan's contemporary La Boétie had written) and instead with how well and effectively power is actually wielded.[24] Du Haillan chooses only one passage from *Pelopidas* which provides a strong indictment of popular rule, suggesting that those who do not have the skills to preserve and defend themselves need to submit to the person who can do so on their behalf, just like passengers on a ship who need a sailor with expertise to guide them, especially in times of rough weather.[25]

From the passages chosen by Du Haillan, the effectiveness and the quality of rule appear to have a direct impact on civil life. In selections taken from *Lycurgus* there is consistent emphasis on Spartan concord, both through the imposition of virtue within the city and through the diplomatic influence wielded by the Spartans throughout Greece to settle the quarrels, divisions and seditions that ravaged their neighbours (ss. 16–18). In a somewhat similar fashion, Du Haillan singles out the passages from *Numa* that emphasise the diversity, roughness and warlike nature of the first inhabitants of Rome who thrived on continuous conflict among themselves and against which Numa had to work (s. 19). And just as effective rule can help to forge a peaceful state, so too can incompetent and ineffective rule exacerbate civil discord, as brought to light by Du Haillan's noting of Plutarch's comments regarding the Argians and Messenians.[26] In the few passages from *Alexander* he ignores any commentary on the issue of the nature and development of Alexander's character and instead cites a reference speaking to the theme of concord: "La

---

[24] "Les homme ordinairement dedaignent d'obeyr a ceux qui ne scavent pas bien commander, de manière que la fidelle obeyssance des subiets depend de la suffisance de bien commander du bon Prince. Car qui bien conduict fait qui lest bien suivy. Et tout ainsi que la perfection de l'art d'un bon escuyer d'escurie est rendre le cheval obeisant et le scavoir renger a la raison, aussi l'effect principal de la science d'un Roy est de bien enseigner l'obeissance a ses subiets."

[25] "Aussi est ce la premiere et souveraine loy de nature, a mon advis, qui vault que celuy qui de soy mesme ne se peult garder et deffendre, se soubsmettre a celuy qui peult et a bien moyen de ce faire: ne plus ne moins que sur la mer, ceux qui sont dedans un navire, encores qu'en beau temps durant que la mer est calme, ou aussi semblablement pendant qu'ils sont a l'ancre en quelque bonne rade, ils se portent fierement et audacieusement envers les pilotes. Incontinent toutesfois que la tourmente se leue, et qu'ils se voyent en danger ils iettent les yeux sur eux, et n'ont aucune esperance de salut qu'en eux mesmes. Au cas pareil aussi les Eliens et Argiens, encores qu'ez assemblees de conseil ils querrellassent et debatissent alencontre des Thebains pour la superiorite et l'honneur de presider en l'armee, toutesfois quant ce venoit a donner battaille, et la ou ils congnoissoient bien qu'il y avoit du peril et danger, ils se rangeoient et se soubsmettoient volontairement a la conduitte de leurs capitaines." (s. 81).

[26] "qui voudra de pres considerer le seditions et mauvais gouvernements des Argiens et Messeniens autant des peoples que des Rois, trouvera que l'arrogance des Rois d'Argos et de Messe et la desobeyssance des peoples fut cause que les Argiens et Messeniens entrerent en guerres civiles les uns contre les autres." (s. 12).

où discord règne en une cité, le plus méchant a lieu d'autorité" (s. 148)
[Where discord reigns in a city the most vicious emerges as more powerful.]
Of all that could be noted from *Antony* only one remark stands out that has
nothing to do with Plutarch's commentary on Antony's character: "Pluralité
de Caesars n'est point bonne."[27] He also includes a passage from *Agesilaus*
suggesting that some level of disharmony, such as the tension between
Ulysses and Achilles, could do good as long as the quarrel and dissent was
not excessive, since quarrels taken to excess become dangerous to the
community.[28]

The passages noted above reflect a more general preoccupation with
division in a political community. It is not surprising that Du Haillan was
drawn to these passages given the context of civil war in France. Indeed, he
already noted in the preface how the politics and challenges of France in his
own era formed a major impetus for him to seek guidance in the texts of the
ancient world. Thus we see in the context of *Romulus* a note that good
kings are those who listen fully to all before pronouncing a judgement on
a public matter that is dividing the people.[29] Also in the context of *Numa*
he records that in the face of a major division of the people into two
opposing parties, Numa sought to emphasise factors that would break that
major cleavage down into more particular ones, thereby trying to minimise
the social costs of the divide.[30] With regard to Solon he notes Solon's
comment that the best governed city is one that rejects the politics of
revenge, and he notes Fabius Maximus's policy of dealing softly with
uprisings and rebellions.[31] He also notes Phocion's strategy of promoting

---

[27] "Pluralite de Caears n'est point bonne. Faisant allusion a un certain vers d'Homere ou il a, 'Pluralite de seigneurs n'est point bonne.'" (s. 239).

[28] "toutesfois cela n'est pas sans soubet et ne se doit pas a l'adventure confesser simplement pour ce que les querelles et dissentions excessives entre les citoyens sont tres dommageables et dangereuses aux Choses publiques." (s. 156).

[29] "celuy est digne d'estre Roy (comme dit Remus a Numitor) qui enquiert et escoute devant que de condemner non celuy qui condamne avant qu'ouyr les parties" (s. 5).

[30] "Rome sembloit encore ester composee de deux nations et pour mieux dire ester divisee en deux ligues, tellement qu'elle ne pouvoit ou ne vouloit aucunement se reduire en un, n'estant pas possible d'en oster entierement toutes partialitez, et faire qu'il n'y eut continuellement des querelles, noises et debats entre les deux parties. Parquoy il pensa que quand on vault meslter deux corps ensemble qui pour leur durte ou contrariete de nature ne peuvent recevoir meslange l'un avec l'autre on les brise et concasse le plus menu que l'on peult, car alors pour la petitesse des parties ils se confondent mieux l'un avec l'autre: ainsi pens ail qu'il valloit mieux diviser encore tout le people en plusieurs petite parcelles: par le moyen desquelles il les jetteroit en autres partialitez, lesquelles viendroient a effacer plus facilement celle principale et premiere quand elle seroit divisee et separee en plusieurs petites. Si fiest ceste divisions par métiers." (s. 20).

[31] "Estant interrogue quelle cite luy sembloit la mieux police, il respondit, celle ou ceux qui ne sont point oultragez poursuivent aussi asprement la reparation de l'iniure d'autruy, comme ceux mesmes qui l'ont receue." (s. 28) and (s. 66).

those who are peace-loving and good natured while ensuring that those deemed seditious, trouble-makers are denied public appointments.[32]

A final theme is the need for those in a position of power to stand up for the good, especially in dangerous times.[33] There are multiple passages taken from *Cicero*, *Cato* and others who were considered defenders of the republic in the face of Caesar's tactics. If anything emerges from this collection of passages from Plutarch, however, it is not republican sympathies but the defence of a singular authority who can help to quell divisions in a political community and institute a state of concord. Like Plutarch himself, it may well be that in the end Du Haillan was a mild supporter of Caesar for bringing peace to Rome.

Of course, Du Haillan is not explicit that his choices in translation were driven by the need to sketch the contours of a political solution to the challenges facing France. I do not suggest that this is the only factor to consider. Still, the translation of these selective nuggets of political wisdom teased from Plutarch's *Lives* while ostensibly carrying on a tradition established much earlier in the century with Budé and others, also diverges in noteworthy ways from it. We see less of an emphasis on and celebration of the extraordinary personalities of ancient history, and instead a consideration of the political prudence of their actions and decisions. In addition, we see an implicit shift (from de Selve for example) toward thinking about the challenges facing France as on a political plane, rather than a theological one. The implicit idea is that if classical history is read in the proper spirit, one can meet the challenge of pervasive civil discord through strategies that focus on political utility, and that offer political prudence and effective administration are sufficient to manage rather than resolve the issues that create conflict. Plutarch proved to be a helpful resource in reframing the challenges from religion and ideology to more narrow politics, and it may be that despite all his intellectual faults Du Haillan, at least in some respects, had some positive insight into how to

---

[32] "Phocion gouvernant ceulx qui estoient demeurez dedans la ville en grande iustice et avec grande humanite, quand il en cognoissoit aucuns doux et paisibles de nature, il les tenoit tousiours en quelque magistrat, mais ceux qu'il scavoit estre remuans, seditieux, et amateurs de nouvelletes, il les engardoit de pouvoir parvenir a office quelconque et leur ostoit tout moyen dexciter troubles, de sorte qu'ils se senoient d'eux mesmes, et apprenoient avec le temps a aimer les champs, et s'adonner au labourage." (s. 135).

[33] Re Marcus Cato Du Haillan cites this passage: "Quant aux actes civils en matière de Gouvernement il semble que Caton avoit ceste opinion, que poursuivre les meschans en iniustice estoit l'une des principals choses a quoy devoit vacquer et s'appliquer un homme de bien et bon gouverneur de chose publique." (s. 97) et re Caius Marius "C'est dit Metellus, chose trop facile et trop lasche que de mal faire, et que de faire bien la ou il n'y eust point de danger c'estoit chose commune, mais que faire bien la ou il y eut danger, c'estoit le propre office d'un homme d'honneur et de vertu." (s. 116).

approach the conflict in a new way (prior to Henri IV's accession to the throne in 1589).

7.2 Michel de Montaigne (1533–1592) via La Boétie (1530–1563)

How does Montaigne fit in to these patterns of reception? We have seen how Budé and to some degree Erasmus, used history to offer a model or vision of ideal kingship. With Amyot we have seen how this approach shifted to a celebration of the illustrious and extraordinary men of history. With the onset of intense religious conflict in France we have also seen how Du Haillan sought to forge much more prudential maxims of political life geared to reconciliation from a study of Plutarch. These maxims were somewhat different from the spirit of prudence discussed earlier via Tory, for the focus was not now fully on the special nature of public life for the effective exercise of power, but on how the exercise of public office should be managed given the challenging features of the social order in which concord needed to be forged (rather than simply preserved).

La Boétie's *Discours de la Servitude Volontaire* (written sometime between 1546 and 1548 – earlier than the work of Pasquier and Du Haillan) offers some insight into Montaigne's work. While his focus is on the question of what sustains rule and leadership, the inquiry is in a different spirit than earlier humanists inspired by or drawing from the work of Plutarch. The focus is no longer on the psychology of the ruler and approaches to governance power, but on the psychology of the public and how their mindset can serve to sustain the ruler. The work of radical Protestant thinkers may have played a role in this shift in perspective. Still, while the later monarchomachs (c. 1573–1584) worked largely within an idiom of French law and history, La Boétie draws on the humanist texts with which he was clearly well acquainted. He invokes the famous account in Plutarch of Lycurgus demonstrating the power of education through the example of two dogs from the same litter (as noted in Chapter 2, the essay "On the Education of Children" where one version of the anecdote is found, is now regarded as spurious).[34] In the hands of La Boétie it is still the

---

[34] "Licurge le policeur de Sparte, avoit nourri ce dit on deux chiens tous deus freres, tous deux allaites de mesme laict, l'un engraisse en la cuisine, lautre accoustume par les champs au son de la trompe et du huchet, coolant montrer au people lacedemonien que les hommes sont tells que la nourriture les fait, mit les deux chiens en plain marche, et entr'eux une souple et un lievre; l'un courant au plat et lautre au lievre; toutesfois, dit-il, si sont ils freres. Oncques, celui la avec ses loix et sa police nourrit et feit si bien les Lacedemonien, que chacun deux eut plus cher de mourir de mille morts, que de reconnaistre autre seigneur que la loy et la raison." Estienne de la Boétie, *Œuvres complètes*. 2 vols. ed. Louis Desgraves (Paris: William Blake and co., 1991), 78–79.

education and hence the power of habit and custom that can explain the behaviour of the disciplined animal, but he also suggests there is a cost to this power of habit. In the broader perspective of the quality of political life and the apparent willingness of vast numbers of individuals to acquiesce under tyrannical rule, the power of custom and habit can be nefarious, leading us to act in ultimately irrational ways that may serve to destroy our liberties rather than enhance our virtue. Here, insight into the psychology of power leads to a questioning of the mechanisms from below through which power can be sustained. Thus, we see a widening of the analytical lens. Plutarch's work is used to develop insight not only into the nature and dynamics of good and bad leadership, but more broadly on the wider social psychology structuring political life.

Of course, Plutarch's work is not responsible for this shift. Still, Olivier Guerrier does make the intriguing suggestion that, as hinted by Montaigne in a 1588 addition to the *Essais,* it may have been an observation made by Plutarch in an essay that offered a spark and suggestion for La Boétie's famous piece.[35] There are a myriad of factors beyond the scope of this work that might explain how La Boétie came to develop his political ideas in the way that he did. And clearly, as we have already seen, Plutarch's work was invoked and adapted in multiple ways so that its effective uptake carried a broad number of possibilities.

By the late sixteenth century a more varied uptake of Plutarch work is apparent. While the political challenges facing France and the need to come up with more creative or adaptive responses to the continued descent into civil war and unrest is a factor in this, most important is the growing availability of a wider selection Plutarch's work than in the earlier part of the century. In La Boétie and Montaigne, a wider array of Plutarch's moral essays, beyond the essay "Political Precepts", become sources for political reflection. The broader perspective on politics advocated so forcefully by La Boétie corresponds to a wider selection of resources from Plutarch's opus. While the *Lives* lend themselves easily to a relatively narrow conception of leadership and political rule, in terms of thinking about the subjects and the moral psychology which governs them, Plutarch's moral essays may indeed offer more trenchant and relevant material for broader perspectives on social and political psychology and of how citizens are educated for virtue and political life. In this light, it is not surprising to know

---

[35] See Olivier Guerrier, "Aux Origines du Discours de la Servitude Volontaire," in *Moralia et Œuvres Morales à la Renaissance* (Paris: Honore Champion, 2008), 237–251.

that in fact La Boétie was the translator of two of Plutarch's moral essays, most notably "The Rules of Marriage" and "A Letter of Consolation."[36]

Montaigne was twenty-six years of age when Amyot published his first edition of the translation of the *Lives*. It had a tremendous impact upon him, but it may be the *Moralia* which is most significant for Montaigne's work. In the *Essais*, more than half of the more than 500 direct references to Plutarch allude to the *Moralia* over the *Lives*.[37] This marks a distinct shift in Plutarch reception in France. Indeed, the very format of the *Moralia* as a series of short pieces offering philosophical reflection on varied topics, some more trivial than others, may have inspired the very concept and structure of Montaigne's famous work.

Despite the clear importance of Plutarch for Montaigne, a study of these two thinkers in tandem is not without its challenges and paradoxes. In terms of challenges the most prominent is that Plutarch's influence plays out in so many levels in Montaigne's work, be it stylistically or thematically, with continuity and discontinuity. For example, while education and the education of children has an important place in the legacy of Plutarch (through the apocryphal essay highlighted at the outset of this book), and through this finds an important presence in Montaigne's own reflections, the status of what figures become exemplary shifts considerably as Montaigne, in the essay "By diverse means we arrive at the same end", reconfigures the tradition of the exemplarity of Alexander. Montaigne depicts the emperor now as the anti-hero and as a leader whose example is to be avoided. In the slaughter of the population at Thebes, Alexander demonstrates his utter ruthlessness and incapacity for pity. This is no longer the depiction of a philosophic soul, but of one driven by excess if not fanatic cruelty. In Montaigne we see a clear dynamic where ancient norms begin to break apart against modern sensibilities.

One question that continues to drive my reflections, given that Montaigne has often been associated with major strands of both Stoic and Epicurean philosophy (sometimes distilled as his work passing from a 'stoical' period from 1572 to 1574 followed by a sceptical crisis and then an 'epicurean' period from 1578 to 1592), is how can he also be so closely associated with Plutarch who wrote polemical essays attacking those same philosophical schools? One central question that flows from this

---

[36] "Les Règles de Mariage de Plutarque," and "Lettre de Consolation de Plutarque a sa femme," in *Œuvres complète de la Boétie*, vol. 2, 9–45. Both Plutarch translations by La Boétie were included in Montaigne's edition of his friends works published in 1870.

[37] Oliver Guerrier, "Plutarque," in P. Desan ed., *Dictionnaire de Montaigne* (Paris: Honore Champion, 2007), 922.

admittedly rather abstract and complex issue is exactly where Montaigne can be said to stand (or what various stands did he take) on the question of the nature and priority of public life? Arguably one of the central issues that differentiates Plutarch from the Hellenistic schools of which he was a critic, is the question of the stance one takes regarding the nature and importance of public commitments. In a nutshell, while the Stoics and Epicureans did not always abjure or disregard public life, their central priority to enhance the happiness or tranquillity of the individual soul meant that much of their theorising about public commitments is understood in instrumental ways. As we have seen, Plutarch offers criticism of these schools for a lack of insight into the central importance of political and public commitments as not only good for individual happiness but as an extension of human nature. In approaching Montaigne and the tradition of Plutarch reception in his *Essais,* I will pay particularly close attention to the theme of the nature and place of public life.[38]

Even if we allow Keohane's assertion that Montaigne offers us the first truly modern articulation of individualism, recent scholarship on Montaigne has questioned whether his writing can be understood as guided by fundamentally private considerations.[39] While at times in his work Montaigne suggests that the *Essais* is really a book about himself, and while commentators stress his prudence in choosing not to comment on pressing matters of public importance, seeking instead an alternate emphasis on the anecdotal and personal, Philippe Desan suggests that when we look at his work in a broader context there are clear choices related to public considerations that are salient and indeed fundamental for understanding it.[40] Of course, the work was written and published in various stages, and different considerations may have directed changes and content each step of the way. Desan suggests that overtly political considerations, directed largely by Montaigne's own political ambitions, were predominant in the first editions of the work starting from 1580, especially but not isolated to version A of the manuscript.[41] The first essays

---

[38] For a more general overview of Plutarch and Montaigne, see the thoughtful essay by Christopher Edelman, "Plutarch and Montaigne," in Sophia Xenophontos and K Oikonomopoulou eds., *Brill's Companion to the Reception of Plutarch*, 479–492.

[39] Keohane, *Philosophy and the State.*

[40] Philippe Desan, *Montaigne, A Life* (Princeton, NJ and Oxford: Princeton University Press, 2017).

[41] For purposes of this analysis, I rely on two editions of Montaigne's Essays. In the original French I have consulted the Pléaide edition, i.e. *Les Essais*. ed. Jean Balsamo et al. (Paris: Gallimard, 2007). However, this French edition does not give a good indication of the differing variations on the manuscript, indices which are crucial to understand the text through the lens of the evolution of Montaigne's own public career. Thus, I also have consulted Montaigne, *The Complete Essays*, ed. M.

of Book 1, which were not subject to a much revision in subsequent editions, address political questions directly. Precisely because he was using this text to curry favour and be chosen for diplomatic service, they were composed to obscure where Montaigne stood on matters, and to demonstrate that he was aware of the stakes and could be judicious in his depiction of political issues. While not expressed by Desan, it might be suggested that the 1580 edition of the *Essais* was Montaigne's own Machiavellian moment, in the sense that he displayed his knowledge and wise treatment of political issues to gain a prestigious appointment. However, this meant that Montaigne had to be careful not to be explicit about his allegiances in the highly polarised context of the Wars of Religion. A certain constancy of circumspection in the *Essais* can be contrasted with Montaigne's own shifting convictions. As the mayor of Bordeaux in the early 1580s he was a concerted enforcer of laws of suppression and repression of Protestants. By the time he had shifted to the camp of the *politiques* or Catholics who favoured a policy of compromise and toleration, he was becoming rather disillusioned with his own public role and the capacity of well-intentioned political actors to fight against the forces of enmity and decline. Through this, he came to express in his writing in 1588 a much more complex understanding of the nature of the public realm than previously articulated. By reading some selections from the *Essais* I demonstrate here how his depiction of the public realm reflects a shift, but with some continuities, from that earlier discourse about the public realm developed in the earlier part of the sixteenth century in France in dialogue with the work of Plutarch.

There is a large breadth of material to draw from in assessing both Montaigne's debt to and engagement with Plutarch.[42] Montaigne himself famously expresses his debt to Plutarch in several passages of the *Essais*.

A. Screech (Penguin: London, 1987), which offers a comprehensive and accessible account of the variations in the manuscript and editions.

[42] This includes Gisèle Matthieu-Castellani, "Plutarque chez Montaigne et chez Shakespeare," *Actes des congrès de la Société française Shakespeare* [http://journals.openedition.org/shakespeare/671; DOI: 10.4000/shakespeare.671]. Date accessed 1 November 2018; Isabelle Konstantinovic, *Montaigne et Plutarque.* (Geneva: Droz, 1989); Nicola Panichi, "Montaigne and Plutarch: A Scepticism that Conquers the Mind," in G. Pagannia and J. Maia Neto eds., *Renaissance Skepticisms* (Dordrecht: International Archives of the History of Ideas and Springer, 2009), 183–212; Paul Smith, *Dispositio. Problematic Ordering in French Renaissance Literature* (Leiden and Boston: Brill, 2007), chap. 8; Robert Aulotte, *Amyot et Plutarque: la tradition des Moralia au* XVI*e siècle* (Geneva: Droz, 1965). Pierre Villey, an important editor of Montaigne's works suggests that Montaigne borrows from Plutarch close to 500 times in the *Essais*, and equally from the *Lives* and the *Moralia*. Pierre Villey, ed. *Les Essais de Michel de Montaigne* (Paris: Presses universitaires de France, 1965), 363. Still, it could be surmised that given the great extent to which Plutarch had a role in the intellectual development of Montaigne, this area of commentary is still at a rather early stage

Most famously, he explores his appreciation for Plutarch's work and his debt to his thought and writing In ii, x "Des livres" [On books]. Again, later in the work he states:

> Mais je me puis plus malaisément deffaire de Plutarque: il est si universel et si plain, qu'à toutes occasions, et quelque suject extravagant que vous ayez pris, il s'ingere à vostre besongne, et vous tend une main liberale et inespuisable de richesses, et d'embellissemens. Il m'en fait despit, d'estre si fort exposé au pillage de ceux qui le hantent. Je ne le puis si peu racointer [rechercher], que je n'en tire cuisse ou aile.

> [But I cannot free myself from Plutarch so easily. He is so all-embracing, so rich that for all occasions, no matter how extravagant a subject you have chosen, he insinuates himself into your work, lending you a hand generous with riches, an unfailing source of adornments. It irritates me that those who pillage him may also be pillaging me. I cannot spend the slightest time in his company without walking off with a slice of breast or a wing.][43]

Indeed, it has been suggested that as his favoured author, Montaigne preferred Plutarch to both Tacitus and Seneca: "Plutarque est admirable par tout: mais principalement, où il juge des actions humaines." [Plutarch is amazing in every respect but especially where he makes judgements on human actions.][44] Montaigne's knowledge of his writings is so deep he claims to know his very soul "Les escrits de Plutarque, à les bien savourer, nous le descouvent assez; et je pense le cognoistre jusques dans l'ame" [The writings of Plutarch, to savour them well, adequately reveal him to us; and I believe I know him down to his soul.][45]

of development. While scholars have mapped out some of the sections of the manuscript where the reference to Plutarch's work is either obvious or explicit, there is also the question of the role of broader and deeper questions as they play out in Montaigne's work, such as his conceptualisation of questions of character, ethics, emotions and public life. The relation is complex. While it is clear that Montaigne is often seen as a champion of the 'ordinary life,' his predilection for reporting the idiosyncrasies of life is not so far removed from the instincts of Plutarch, even in the *Lives* where he focuses on the less visible in order to reveal the substance of the character he is discussing. My hunch, however, is that a thorough study would find greater influence of Plutarch's *Moralia* for Montaigne than the *Lives*. Just in matters of form alone the lineage is clear. It was only recently in 2020 that researchers were able to locate one of Montaigne's copies of the *Lives* with annotations. See Alain Legros, "Plutarque annoté par Montaigne," MONLOE: Montaigne à l'œuvre, https://montaigne .univ-tours.fr/notes-de-lecture-de-montaigne/plutarque-annote-par-montaigne/. Date accessed 24 May 2022.

[43] Montaigne, "Sur des vers de Virgile," in Balsamo et al. ed., *Les Essais*, iii, v. 918. Translation into English taken from Montaigne, "On Some Lines of Virgil," in *The Complete Essays*, 989.
[44] Billaut, "Plutarch's Lives," 228–229; Montaigne, "De la cholere," ii, xxxi, 750. Translation from Montaigne, "On Anger," in *The Complete Essays*, 809.
[45] Montaigne, "De la cholere," ii, xxxi, 752.

Still, Montaigne could not read Greek well ("je n'entens rien au Grec" II, 4). Thus, the Plutarch of Montaigne is also Amyot's Plutarch. Montaigne greatly admired Amyot and even met with him, as he reports in I, 24. In his travel journal Montaigne recalls a dinner he had in Rome with the French ambassador and the scholar Marc-Antoine Muret where they discussed the fidelity of Amyot's translation, of which Montaigne was the sole defender. To illustrate the case, the hosts documented two examples from the text with the original Greek collated next to the French translation to demonstrate that Amyot had gone astray, something which Montaigne in the end could not deny.[46] Regardless, his defence of Amyot in the *Essais* suggests that Amyot was able to capture the essence and spirit of Plutarch's work. As suggested by Billaut in his analysis of II, 4: "Montaigne considers Amyot's Plutarch a book of wisdom where he reads some truths which are as important to him as the divine truths which a priest can find in a breviary."[47]

So how did Montaigne draw on Amyot's Plutarch to develop an account of the public realm (or an evolving account of the public realm)? Here I limit myself largely to passages from "De la Vanité." This essay made its first appearance in the 1588 edition and directly addresses the theme of public life. By the time this essay was published Montaigne was declining in health and had suffered a series of disappointments in his public career, making him pessimistic about the possibilities of his own contributions to public life, at least insofar as politics was concerned. While some have suggested that this essay speaks directly to the influence of Tacitus on Montaigne, I suggest here that it represents less an advocacy for political 'withdrawal,' as is often associated with late sixteenth-century Tacitism, and more a broadening of attitude towards public life for those who may traditionally have found themselves on the margins.[48] While not embracing public life enthusiastically, in this essay Montaigne demonstrates a need for individuals to acknowledge the possible benefits of public action and the need to temper public work with a spirit of humaneness and relative civility.

In this essay Montaigne characterises public life as suffering from a high level of corruption from which he willingly distances himself: "Car en mon voisinage, nous sommes tantost par la longue licence de ces guerres civiles, envieillis en une forme d'estats si desbordée ... qu'a la verité, c'est merveille

---

[46] Billaut, "Plutarch's Lives," 227.   [47] Billaut, "Plutarch's Lives," 228.

[48] This counters the reading of Sue Farquhar "Michel de Montaigne: The Essais and a Tacitean Discourse," in G. Sandy ed., *The Classical Heritage in France*, 187–218.

qu'elle se puisse maintenir." [The prolonged licence of our Civil Wars has already hardened us to a form of government so overflowing with evil ... that it is a miracle that it can endure][49] and "Le plus juste party, si est-ce encore le membre d'un corps vermoulu et vereux" [even the juster[sic] party is itself a limb of that rotten, worm-eaten body].[50] The idea developed earlier in the political thought of the French Renaissance, that political and public norms can take on aspects that are distinct from private ones becomes radicalised in Montaigne's thought, given his experience through the religious wars. Hence, public life not only requires different norms, but at times irreducibly vicious ones:

> De mesme, en toute police: il y a des offices necessaires, non seulement abjects, mais encores vicieux: Les vices y trouvent leur rang, et s'imployent à la cousture de nostre liaison: comme les venins à la conservation de nostre santé. S'ils deviennent excusables, d'autant qu'ils nous font besoing, et que la necessité commune efface leur vraye qualité: il faut laisser jouer cette partie, aux citoyens plus vigoureux, et moins craintifs, qui sacrifient leur honneur et leur conscience, comme ces autres anciens sacrifierent leur vie, pour le salut de leur pays: nous autres plus foibles prenons des rolles et plus aysez et moins hazardeux: Le bien public requiert qu'on trahisse, et qu'on mente, et qu'on massacre: resignons cette commission a gens plus obeissans et plus souples.

> [in all polities there are duties which are necessary, yet not merely abject but vicious as well: the vices hold their rank there and are used to stitch and bind us together, just as poisons are used to preserve our health. If vicious deeds should become excusable insofar as we have need of them, necessity effacing their true qualities, we must leave that role to be played by citizens who are more vigorous and less timorous, those prepared to sacrifice their honour and their consciences, as men of yore once sacrificed their lives: for the well-being of their country. Men like me are too weak for that: we accept roles which are easier and less dangerous. The public interest requires men to betray, to tell lies and to massacre; let us assign that commission to such as are more obedient and more pliant.][51]

Under the framework of utility, the trade-off between public interest and virtue could not be made more starkly, at least in certain extreme cases. There is a harshness of tone here that may be due less to the more strict moral compass of earlier writers in the century, and more to the extreme political measures undertaken by public authorities in the context of civil

---

[49] Montaigne, "De la vanité," III, ix, 1000. Translation into English is taken from Montaigne, "On Vanity," in *The Complete Essays*, 1082.
[50] Montaigne, "De la vanité," 1039; "On Vanity," 1123.
[51] Montaigne, "De l'utile et de l'honeste," 830; "On the Useful and the Honourable," 892.

war. The notion that the public realm might be subject to a special and sometime unique form of ethical consideration and calculation is radicalised by Montaigne and depicted as the necessity of not only vice but also viciousness (with the invocation of massacre – a clear allusion to the events of 1572), all in the name of the public interest.

Still, in the face of the recognition of the public viciousness of his time he decries efforts and advocacy for radical change as further invitation to injustice and tyranny, given that in public matters the shifting in an institutional edifice often makes bad things worse, such as what befell the Roman Republic after the assassination of Julius Caesar. In terms of his relations with current leaders, he seeks no deep reciprocity: "Les Princes me donnent prou, s'ils ne m'ostent rien: et me font assez de bien, quand ils ne me font point de mal: c'est tout ce que j'en demande." [Princes give me plenty if they take nothing from me and do me enough good if they do me no harm. That is all I ask of them.][52] In a similar spirit he turns away from national bonds to espouse the primacy of a cosmopolitan one, and citing Plutarch (on the theme of exile) states: "Nature nous a mis au monde libres et desliez, nous nous emprisonnons en certains destroits: comme les Roys de Perse qui s'obligeoient de ne boire jamais autre eau, que celle du fleuve de Choaspez, renonçoyent par sottise, à leur droict d'usage en toutes les autres eaux: et assechoient pour leur regard, tout le reste du monde." [Nature brought us forth free and unbound: we imprison ourselves in particular confines, like those kings of Persia who bind themselves to drink no water but that of the river Choaspes, foolishly renouncing their right to use all other waters, making, so far as they are concerned, all the rest of the world a desert.][53] What Plutarch invoked as a set of arguments to reconcile his target audience to enduring a very specific and taxing form of punishment is now invoked by Montaigne as a more generalised justification for a stance of civic disengagement.

The extremely negative judgement regarding the politics of his own era merges into a problematic portrayal of the nature of public life itself. His tone is one of pessimistic resignation regarding the pervasiveness of vice in public life. Indeed, even Cato himself is depicted as driven by vanity, since his demand for justice did not match the norms of his time.[54] Part of the challenge is that public virtue is "meslée et artificielle; non droitte, nette, constante, ny purement innocente." [complex and artificial, not straight,

---

[52] Montaigne, "De la vanité," 1013; "On Vanity," 1095.
[53] Montaigne, "De la vanité," 1018; "On Vanity," 1101.
[54] Montaigne, "On Vanity," 1121. "Cato's virtue was excessively rigorous by the standards of his age; and in a man occupied in governing others and destined to serve the commonwealth, we could say that his justice, if not unjust, was at least vain and unseasonable."

clear-cut, constant, not purely innocent].[55] Indeed, he suggests that the norms of life that he had learned for life as a private citizen were not only inapplicable in public life, but also dangerous.[56]

> Celuy qui va en la presse, il faut qu'il gauchisse, qu'il serre ses couddes, qu'il recule, ou qu'il avance, voire qu'il quitte le droict chemin, selong ce qu'il rencontre: Qu'il vive non tant selon soy, que selon autruy: non selon ce qu'il se propose, mais selon ce qu'on luy propose: selon le temps, selon les hommes, selon les affaires.

> [Anyone who goes into the throng must be prepared to side-step, to squeeze in his elbows, to dodge to and fro, and, indeed, to abandon the straight path according to what he encounters; he must live not so much by his norms but by those of others; not so much according to what he prescribes to himself but to what others prescribe to him, and according to the time, according to the men, according to the negotiations.][57]

The implication is that public life cannot be driven by a set of principles established internal to the self; rather, to function well in public life one must constantly reassess and recalibrate one's ideals and normative expectations in part based on the expectations, principles and considerations that others bring to the table: "De conclure par la suffisance d'une vie particuliere, quelque suffisance a l'usage public, c'est mal conclure: Tel se conduict bien, qui ne conduict pas bien les autres." [To infer a capacity for the affairs of State from a capacity for private affairs is to make a bad inference. A man may control himself but not others.][58] Thus public life is not based on a coherent and pre-determined set of principles but appears as a process that is always driven by forms of compromise and reassessment. Montaigne is critical of the worth of deliberations about ideal states and governments, and there is resignation to the fact that a functioning lawful society may not always need the purest motivations and that human society can hobble along even if its members are wicked and depraved.[59] He resists the vocation of more concerted public service because he acknowledges how difficult it can be and is aware of his own limitations.[60]

[55] Montaigne, "De la vanité," 1037; "On Vanity," 1121.

[56] "Once I made an assay at using in the service of some political manoeuvrings, such opinions and rules of life as were born in me or instilled in me by education – rough, fresh, unpolished and unpolluted ones, the virtues of a schoolboy or a novice, which I practice, if not conveniently at least surely, in my private life. O found that they were inapplicable and dangerous." Montaigne, "On Vanity," 1121.

[57] Montaigne, "De la vanité," 1037; "On Vanity," 1121–1122.

[58] Montaigne, "De la vanité," 1038; "On Vanity," 1122.   [59] Montaigne, "On Vanity," 1083.

[60] "where I am concerned I renounce my share, partly from self-awareness (which enables me to see both the weight attached to such vocations and the scant means I have of providing for them)- even

From singular and unbending standards of individual virtue the need for constant reassessment and accommodation in view of the standards and expectations of others may appear to be corrupt. We might also consider this to be a more radical restatement of a vision of politics that had been handed down to Montaigne from French political thinkers of the first half of the sixteenth century who reflected on the nature of *la chose publique* or public life and on the special qualities it demanded of an effective monar- chical ruler in conjunction with insight into the social and moral psych- ology of politics and governance. For those earlier thinkers, it is precisely the special play of perceptions that made public life a more complicated ethical terrain, but not by necessity a more corrupt one. Montaigne addresses those earlier commentaries directly and condemns them for promoting vice in the language of fine ethical distinctions:

> Qui se vante, en un temps malade, comme estuy-cy; d'employer au service du monde, une vertu naifve et sincere: ou il ne la cognoist pas, les opinions se corrompans avec les moeurs (De vray, oyez la leur peindre, oyez la pluspart se glorifier de leurs deportemens, et former leur reigles; au lieu de peindre la vertu, ils peignent l'injustice toute pure et le vice: et la presentent ainsi fauce a l'institution des Princes)

> [Anyone who, in an ailing time like ours, boasts that he can bring a naïve and pure virtue to this world's service either has no idea what virtue is, since our opinions are corrupted along with our morals- indeed, just listen to them describing it; listen to most of them vaunting of their deeds and formulating their rules: instead of describing virtue they are describing pure injustice and vice, and they present it, thus falsified, in the education of princes][61]

In the context of the violence of the religious wars, attention to the specific demands and rules of public life appeared to offer great license to those with destructive intentions and impure motivations. Montaigne offers a radical critique of that earlier tradition of thinking about the special qualities of *la chose publique,* and he offers instead a philosophy that is

---

that master-theoretician of all political government Plato did not fail to abstain from it himself- partly from laziness. I am content to enjoy the world without being over-occupied with it and to lead a life which is no more than excusable, neither a burden to myself nor to others." Montaigne, "On Vanity," 1078. He states again later: "If I had thoroughly to prepare myself for such occupa- tions [in public life], I know that I would need many changes and adjustments. Even if I could manage it (and why should I not do so, given time and trouble?) I would not want to. The little I have assayed of such a vocation was quite enough to put me off. Sometimes I do feel some temptations towards ambition smoldering in my soul. But I tense myself and obstinately resist." Montaigne, "On Vanity," 1122.

[61] Montaigne, "De la vanité," 1039; "On Vanity," 1123.

highly sceptical regarding the benefits possible in and through specifically public life, while nonetheless keeping his readers open to alternative ways in which valuable social ends might be pursued.

Ultimately, and despite this apparent pessimism, it can be argued that Montaigne adopts what is in essence a dual approach to public life. While on the one hand, public life is rejected and the vicissitudes of public action, both in his own day and throughout history, are cast in grey with deep reservations regarding the possibility of reconciling public life and virtue, there is nonetheless a lingering element of concern for a broader social and public good.

First, though expressed in a negative way, Montaigne suggests that to a certain degree it is impossible to separate oneself completely from the corruption of public life. He tells his readers, for example, that they are all implicated in the corruption of their time: "Les uns y conferent la trahison, les autres l'injustice, l'irreligion, la tyrannie, l'avarice, la cruauté, selon qu'ils sont plus plussans: les plus foibles y apportent la sottise, la vanité, l'oiseiveté" [some contribute treachery, others (since they are powerful) injustice, irreligion, tyranny, cupidity, cruelty: the weaker ones like me contribute silliness, vanity and idleness.][62] While those in a narrower public realm may do the most damage, each bears some responsibility for the deterioration in the quality of their common life. (This corresponds to a certain degree to the notion of statesmanship developed by Plutarch in his essay "Old Men in Public Affairs" in which he offers broad conception of the contours of public service.)

Further along Montaigne admits to his readers that he has been actively engaged in serving his prince.[63] Indeed he goes so far as to cite Cicero saying: "Je suis de cet avis, que la plus honorable vacation, est de server au publiq, et estre utile a beaucoup." [I do believe that the most honourable vocation is to serve the commonwealth and to be useful to many.][64] Still, in most of his interjections he appears to encourage novel and more nuanced forms of social and public intervention. For example, drawing on the general theme of Plutarch's essay, "How to Profit from your Enemies" Montaigne muses that perhaps the vice of the times as evident in public affairs does serve inadvertently to heighten appreciation for moral goodness and to enhance the determination of the upright.[65] In the midst of a spiral of deterioration, and despite a general pessimism regarding

---

[62] Montaigne, "De la vanité," 990; "On Vanity," 1071.   [63] Montaigne, "On Vanity," 1118.
[64] Montaigne, "De la vanité," 996; "On Vanity," 1078.
[65] "Just as some gardeners say that roses and violets spring up more sweet-scented near garlic and onions which attract and draw to themselves all that is foul-smelling in the soil, suppose those

wholesale change towards the better, Montaigne nonetheless offers the
suggestion of a more positive strategy: "La plus honnorable marque de
bonté, en une telle necessité, c'est recognoistre librement sa faute, et celle
d'autruy: appuyer et retarder de sa puissance, l'inclination vers le mal:
suyvre envis ceste pente, mieux esperer et mieux desirer." [In such straits
the most honourable mark of goodness consists in freely acknowledging
your defects and those of others, while using your powers to resist and
retard the slide towards evil, having to be dragged down that slope, while
hoping for improvement and desiring improvement.][66] And he acknowledges in "On Cruelty" that "we owe justice to men" thereby condemning
the gratuitous violence of the religious war and more broadly a lack of
respect that humanity can demonstrate to other living beings.[67] Thus,
distinct from the type of affection and appreciation that Montaigne
associates with friendship, he also advocates for a series of general civil
norms dictating basic humane treatment of fellow subjects and fellow
human beings. In "On the Useful and the Honourable," he denounces
judges who use fraud and false hopes in order to elicit confessions from
criminals and describes himself as "moderately devoted to public affairs,"[68]
and suggests in addition:

> De se tenir chancelant et mestis, de tenir son affection immobile, et sans
> inclination aux troubles de son pays, et en une division publique, je ne le
> trouve ny beau, ny honneste . . . Ce serait une espece de trahison, de le faire
> aux propres et domestiques affaires, ausquels necessairement il faut prendre
> party . . . Toutesfois ceux encore qui s'y engagent tout à faict, le peuvent,
> avec tel ordre et attrempance, que l'orage debvra couler par dessus leur teste,
> sans offence. N'avoins nous pas raison de l'esperer ainsi du feu Evesque
> d'Orleans, sieur de Morvilliers? Et j'en cognois entre ceux qui y ouvent
> valeureusement à cette heure, de moeurs ou si equables, ou si douces, qu'ils
> seront, pour demeurer debout, quelque injurieuse mutation et cheute que le
> ciel nous appreste."

> [to remain vacillating and mongrel, or to keep one's affections in check,
> unmoved by civil strife in one's country and having no preference when the
> State is divided, is neither beautiful nor honourable . . . it would be a species
> of treachery to act thus in civil strife at home, in which of necessity we must

---

depraved characters similarly suck up all the venom in the air of our climate, rendering me better and
purer by their proximity, so that all is not loss. But things are not so. Yet there may be something in
the following: goodness is more beautiful and attractive when it is rare, while the determination to
act well is stiffened by contradiction and concentrated in us by opposition, being enflamed by glory
and a jealous desire to resist." Montaigne, "On Vanity," 1099.

[66] Montaigne, "De la vanité," 1039; "On Vanity," 1123.   [67] Montaigne, "On Cruelty," 488.
[68] Montaigne, "On the Useful and the Honourable," 894.

decide to join one side or other … . Even those who become totally committed can still do so with such order and moderation that the storm may pass over their heads without battering them. Were we not right to think that way about the late Bishop of Orleans, the Sieur de Morvilliers? And some others that I know, who are now struggling valiantly, have manners which are so equable and gentle that they are the kind who will remain upright no matter what destructive upheavals and collapses Heaven may have in store for us.][69]

The basic lesson here is that despite the often compromising and impossible nature of public commitments, particularly in a time of civil war, there are still better and worse ways to be engaged in public matters. Montaigne offers a plea for moderation and a modicum of honourable behaviour even in the most difficult of contexts and circumstances.

> Rien n'empesche qu'on ne se puisse comporter commodément entre des hommes qui se sont ennemis, et loyalement: conduisez vous y d'une, sinon par tout esgale affection (car elle peut souffrir differentes mesures) au moins, temperée, et qui ne vous engage tant à l'un, qu'il puisse tout requerir de vous: Et vous contentez aussi d'une moienne mesure de leur grace: et de couler en eau trouble, sans y vouloir pescher.

> [Nothing stops us from behaving properly even when among mutual enemies – nor loyally either. Comport yourself among them not with an equal good-will (for good-will can allow of varying degrees) but at least with a temperate one, so that you do not become so involved with one of those mutual enemies that he can demand of you your all. Be satisfied too with a modest degree of their favour: do not fish in troubled waters, glide through them!][70]

Thus, despite the broadly negative depiction of public life and its compromises with virtue, there always appears to be a more honourable and humane pathway to follow. It is that more moderate pathway that cannot substitute for all the ethical challenges and compromises of public life but could serve as a limit to an acquiescence to its worst abuses.[71] In this way, Montaigne does not deny the earlier sixteenth-century arguments for

---

[69] Montaigne, "De l'utile et de l'honneste," 832–833; "On the Useful and the Honourable," 894–895.
[70] Montaigne, "De l'utile et de l'honneste," 833; "On the Useful and the Honourable," 895.
[71] By this analysis I diverge from the interpretation of Biancamaria Fontana who argues that the division between the public and the private is a distinction that does not make much sense for Montaigne's thought given that he seeks to blur the difference between the two. See Biancamaria Fontana, "The Political Thought of Montaigne," in Philippe Desan ed., *The Oxford Handbook of Montaigne* (Oxford: Oxford University Press, 2016). Online at www.oxfordhandbooks.com.myaccess.library.utoronto.ca/view/10.1093/oxfordhb/9780190215330.001.0001/oxfordhb-9780190215330-e-10?print=pdf. Date accessed 14 June 2018. From the perspective I develop here, Montaigne is less concerned about promoting "individual needs and choices" (as argued by Fontana) than the diffusion of norms of striving for

the unique features of public life and the resulting moral compromises that may be needed, although he does put them in a different and darker light. While giving his readers a sense of the potential dangers of that outlook, he offers some check in suggesting that it must be coupled and regulated with a background sense of humanity and decency to mitigate its worst effects.

7.3   Conclusion

Montaigne's reflections on public life as demonstrated through this admittedly narrow window represents a shift away from earlier strands of political reflection and uses of Plutarch's thought. Thinkers like Budé, Seyssel and Erasmus as they appeared in the French vernacular often drew from Plutarch to give lessons to those in power and to shed light on the ethos specific to the public realm, with explicit reference to the idea of the *chose publique*. By drawing on the anecdotal events in the lives of Plutarch's subjects, those earlier authors distilled maxims to inform kings and those in court how to adapt and conform to the expectations of public life. As the century progresses, the idea and even the very term *chose publique* appears to be dropped, until it is relegated in Du Haillan to the connotation of a specific type of political regime – that is, as a republic narrowly conceived.

Along with this shift in the connotation of the term, concern is no longer centred on the particularities and features of the narrow public realm but rather on the broader dynamics of subjects in their relation to power, and of both the merits and dangers of political power. In addition, we see greater attention being paid to the complicated dynamics of life at the margins of power in both the reinforcement and hence the acquiescence to established norms, as well as the resistance in reiteration of the same. I am not suggesting that the development of Plutarch reception is responsible for such shifts, but that the changing nature of Plutarch reception may reflect a deeper shift that involved a broadening perspective on the psychological basis of politics within a larger social order, along with more contested views concerning the nature and ethics of the public realm and the appropriate scope of royal power. The broader lesson here is that it is not the case that we can characterise the broader direction of political theory in France in the latter sixteenth century as one of withdrawal from the public sphere (as if participation had even been the norm in political

peaceful coexistence and acceptance of difference that give a public face and goal to civil relations, thereby expanding the scope of the public rather than blurring its contours.

discourse before this time), but rather, that through the various examples noted here we see new forms of perspective on the public realm and how subjects can orient themselves to it in a prudential and judicious manner.

We have seen how Du Haillan offers both an extension and refinement of the earlier sixteenth-century tradition, most notably invoking Plutarch and examples from his *Lives* in literature addressed directly to those in positions of political power – albeit while teasing out new arguments and applications of his thought.

In contrast, Montaigne invokes public life not through classical examples but largely through reflections on his own experience of it, and his perceived audience of readers is not those in power but those subjected to power (in line with the spirit of the previous work of La Boétie). He offers advice on how subjects should perceive and adapt to the power structures within which they find themselves. There is some carry-over of lessons and general depictions regarding public life (especially the idea that a position of power often has a magnifying effect on vices, and the way in which power can distort the dynamics of friendship and companionship).[72] Still, we find a new dynamic in which, on the one hand, the politics of his own time is judged to be irredeemably corrupt, spreading to a view of the challenges of public life in general and the possibility that it is impossible to navigate public life with a firm set of unchanging ethical principles; on the other hand, there is a lingering sense in his commentary that each individual is implicated by their own disposition and actions in the quality of the whole, implying a much broader notion of public responsibility. The stance implied by this dual notion is that the individual should avoid the narrow public sphere due to its consistent deviations from conventional ethical norms but still remain public-minded in a localised and small-scale ethics of respect and virtue for fellow human beings and neighbours.

Montaigne's openness to the broader opus of Plutarch offered him resources for a broader reflection on the nature of public life. We might suggest that Montaigne offers a perspective that further problematises the notion of the public from its iterations earlier in the century, while not fully abandoning it. So whereas (as was demonstrated in a Chapter 6) both

---

[72] "Every man loathes being spied on and having his actions recorded: but kings are spied on, down to their facial expressions and their thoughts, the entire people reckoning that they have the right and privilege of making judgements upon them. The higher and brighter the spot, the bigger the stain: a mole or wart on your forehead shows up more than a scar does elsewhere." Montaigne, "On the Inequality There Is Between Us," in *The Complete Essays*, 296. On the issue of power and friendship, see 297.

Amyot and Bodin appeared to give the monarch the benefit of the doubt, recommending wider perspectives in historical sensibility and a deeper sense of one's visibility as a means to encourage the responsible exercise of power, Pasquier sought to entrench the monarch's understanding of their power in a historical narrative that highlighted institutional checks and the effective interdependencies of power, and Du Haillan sought to tether public authority to a judicious ethos of prudence. Montaigne, while continuing that earlier historical narrative of the specificity of a public ethos, also radicalised that discourse by suggesting that that ethos was tinged with vice, bringing to it a deeper critical sensibility. His ultimate argument, however, was not to erase or delegitimate the idea of an independent public ethos, but rather to bring to bear upon it an independent and regulative set of pragmatic, moderate and humane considerations to mitigate its worse effects.

PART III

Seventeenth- and Eighteenth-Century Plutarch

CHAPTER 8

Shedding New Light on Thomas Hobbes's Leviathan *(1651)*

Thomas Hobbes (1588–1679), and Francis Bacon (1561–1626) before him, are often associated with the roots of modern sensibilities including individualism, anti-scholasticism, and a defence of scientific knowledge and method. Still, as is also acknowledged, they did so as notable scholars in a cultural context where classical texts and classical learning were pervasive and highly valued. A study of Plutarch's work in the structure and development of their ideas may offer insight into how this common cultural heritage was entangled with the development of innovative and challenging perspectives on social and political life. Both drew in significant ways from Plutarch's work, adapting his attention to social psychology and the circulation of honour, which was perceived by Plutarch as part of a very precise niche within a specific political situation (Greece under Rome), to their own context. Both Bacon and Hobbes extended the application of these insights as a starting point for comment on more fundamental questions of social and political order.

8.1 A Brief Prelude on Francis Bacon (1561–1626)

I begin briefly with Bacon to demonstrate an early seventeenth-century English use of Plutarch in the service of a contemporary outlook. Bacon is a difficult case because he demonstrated highly ambitious and largely self-serving political strategy in his own life, while engaging in political commentary that demonstrated a mixture of pragmatism, traditional classical humanism and what appears to some as Machiavellian republicanism.[1] To state it another way, it is a challenge to determine a singular interpretative framework for Bacon's life and thought that can easily make sense of his

---

[1] See Perez Zagorin's *Francis Bacon* (Princeton, NJ: Princeton University Press, 1998) as well as Markku Peltonen, "Bacon's Political Philosophy," in M. Peltonen ed., *The Cambridge Companion to Bacon* (Cambridge: Cambridge University Press, 1996), 283–310.

politics as a whole. Given this challenge, I offer only a partial analysis of his thought, and focus on a few examples of interest where Bacon invokes Plutarch to demonstrate how modern sensibilities brought new insights into a reading of Plutarch's work.

On the level of *genre*, the fact that Bacon wrote a great deal of his reflections in political and social thought in the form of *Essays* gives us a clue to the centrality of Plutarch as a reference, just as for Montaigne. But beyond the form, what of the substance of Plutarch can be said to have inspired Bacon? Both were keen observers of human moral psychology, and both eschewed a systemic approach to engage in piecemeal moral philosophical reflection addressing specific themes and examples. Bacon's collection grew from ten to fifty-eight essays over the course of almost thirty years, essays that underwent constant revision. For this analysis I consult the available published editions and cite the text of the 1612 edition (sidestepping any chronological analysis of the theme).[2] There is a long history of scholarship on Bacon, and editors have done the pains-taking work of documenting a number of classical allusions, including those of Plutarch, throughout the *Essays*.[3] I will content myself with shedding light on a few of the themes associated with Bacon's references to Plutarch, as they may be significant for traditions of reflection in political theory and the strands of thought I am tracing here.

Although his reputation is as a visionary and defender of modern science, Bacon was trained as a lawyer and spent much of his career as a public servant, serving in parliament for many years and rising to the office of Lord Chancellor in 1618 under James I. His public career ended abruptly in 1621 in the context of a parliamentary anti-corruption cam-paign. Bacon's dishonourable treatment of his former patron, Robert, the earl of Essex, and at the end of his career, his admission that he accepted bribes, have cast a shadow over his public reputation.[4]

The resonance of Plutarch is spread broadly throughout Bacon's work. His complex position vis-à-vis the world of classical literature is evident in one of his early and most famous works from 1605, *The Advancement of Learning*. Here Bacon offers an overview of the fields of knowledge while

---

[2] I draw from three editions of Francis Bacon, each with a slightly different selection of writings: *Essays and Colours of Good and Evil*, ed. W. Aldis Wright (New York: Macmillan, 1899); *The Essays*, ed. Brian Vickers (Oxford: Oxford University Press, 1999); *The Major Works*, ed. Brian Vickers (Oxford: Oxford University Press, 1996).

[3] Francis Bacon, *Essays and Colours of Good and Evil*; also Myrta Goodenough, "Bacon and Plutarch," *Modern Language Review Notes* 12.5 (May 1897), 284–286.

[4] Zagorin, *Francis Bacon*, chap. 1.

placing them in a new light that repudiates scholasticism as well as certain key aspects of traditional Renaissance humanism. Yet the work abounds with classical references. It begins with a defence of learning as fully consistent and supportive of the active life.[5] Alexander and Julius Caesar are celebrated as leaders who drew on great knowledge in their exploits. As he notes, knowledge, understood as a storehouse to offer "relief of man's estate," was dignified when it united contemplation and action.[6]

Despite the obvious link to Plutarchan themes of bringing together contemplation and action in learning as associated with the pseudo-Plutarch essay "On the Education of Children," the trope is also transformed. In effect, Bacon replaces Plutarch's focus on knowledge of virtue with praise of new methods, thereby harnessing the motivational force of key references in classical history to a defence of modern scientific reasoning.

In his essays Bacon tackles the broad civil and moral issues that overlap with his classical predecessor; he also attempts to coordinate and organise these topics. This more comprehensive coverage of moral questions responds to Bacon's point of advocacy in *The Advancement of Learning* that one should provide full commentaries on the work of ancient philosophers, laying out what aspects of their work are still valid and useful. He argues against the types of compilations associated with Plutarch's work (and Montaigne) where there is no order to the essays and where thought may appear inconsistent and dissonant.[7] The broad effort to systematise moral insight, as evident in the *Essays,* stems directly from Bacon's engagement with Plutarch's work and his dissatisfaction with the framework of the *Moralia.*

One of the first essays in the collection which draws on themes from Plutarch is "Of Envy." Harkening back to a discussion in Plutarch's *Table Talk*, here envy is likened to the evil eye, an active force that can almost poison its object in a glance.[8] Bacon focuses on the difference between public and private envy.[9] To follow on his interest in moral psychology in the public realm, he notes, suggestive of passages in "Political Precepts", that equals in office are often more subject to envy given that in that context relative accomplishments and virtues will invite more direct comparison.[10]

Still, in a certain acquiescence to pervasive Aristotelian inspired doctrines of distributive justice, honour and desert, he concedes that those of

---

[5] Francis Bacon, "The Advancement of Learning," in Vickers ed., *The Major Works*, 127.
[6] Bacon, "Advancement," 148.   [7] Bacon, "Advancement," 204.
[8] Bacon, *The Major Works*, notes 726 (citing Reynolds 1890 edition of the *Essays*).
[9] Bacon, "Of Envy," in *The Major Works*, 354.   [10] Bacon, "Of Envy," in *The Major Works*, 355.

pre-eminent virtue may be less subject to envy, while monarchs (or chief executives) are especially prone to envy their sovereign peers. Those who are perceived to advance suddenly in status are often the objects of envy and, in contrast, those who are perceived to undergo hardship and who are subject to pity may be less subject to envy. The latter helps to explain why sometimes the favoured and the powerful outwardly bemoan their lives, not as an honest expression of their state of mind but so as to "abate the edge of envy" and thus make others better disposed towards them.[11] He notes that those who parade their fortunes with pomp and who seek to belittle others in their pride are the most subject to envy, which is why the wise will often suffer other burdens in order to avoid it; or arrange matters so that envy is deflected onto someone else who may not fear and who may even crave the envious eye.

Reminiscent of the spirit of Plutarch's "How to Profit from your Enemies," Bacon nonetheless suggests that there can be good outcomes to public envy in ways not possible in private. He suggests, for instance, that envy can serve as a harness or bridle on those who gain excessive pre-eminence, and function as a sort of equivalent to ancient ostracism to hinder power and influence.[12] The presumption here is that those subject to envy may be led to self-regulate and to make concessions to retain earnest favour. However, there is a danger even in public life of envy becoming more generalised and tainting all public action to the point of encouraging contempt of all in a position of influence and power. A generalised sense of envy, Bacon tells us, can risk the spread of sedition.

In this treatment of envy, then, we see Bacon drawing in part on Plutarch to offer a deeper analysis of the moral psychology of public service, and as part of a wider project to work through the principles on which to base a new conception of public office suited for modern times.[13] What is distinct about Bacon's treatment of these issues is that Plutarch's discussion largely revolves around the working of envy within a small class of public officials or those of public pre-eminence, while Bacon enlarges the scope to include the psychological consequences of large inequalities of wealth along with power, while at the same time identifying a strategy of deflection as a new modern response to public envy.

---

[11] Bacon, "Of Envy," in *The Major Works*, 356.

[12] Bacon, "Of Envy," in *The Major Works*, 357: "There is yet some good in public envy, whereas in private there is none. For public envy is as an ostracism, that eclipseth men when they grow too great. And therefore, it is a bridle also to great ones, to keep them within bounds."

[13] For an analysis of Bacon's work in the context of revising principles of appointment and desert in matters of public office, see Dauber, *State and Commonwealth*, especially chap. 4.

A subsequent essay "Of Great Place" (i.e. of public eminence) also offers reflections on the nature of obtaining and maintaining public office and draws in part from Plutarch's "Political Precepts". Bacon notes that those in a position of public authority are servants in three ways: servants of the sovereign or state, servants of fame and servants of business. By seeking power such individuals lose liberty over their lives and become dependent on the opinions of others for their own happiness.[14] Given the potential of public office as a platform to do good as well as evil, a person would do well to study examples of those preceding them in office, especially when they offer evidence of what to avoid. One should avoid the vices and even the suspicion of vices of authority, identified as delays (including restricted access), corruption of oneself and one's servants through the taking of payments and bribes, roughness and taunting which breeds hatred from others, and facility, meaning to be easily swayed.[15] In an echo of Plutarch (and later Erasmus) Bacon acknowledges in quotes that the spotlight can reveal and even can exaggerate the character of the office holder: "A place sheweth the man" to which Bacon adds his own commentary "And it sheweth some to the better and some to the worse." This suggests that the public sphere not only provides greater transparency of latent character, but that the exercise of holding power itself can transform some for the better (those with a "worthy and generous spirit"), and others for the worse (those for whom exercise of authority precipitates a moral decay).

Bacon also gives advice on how to come to terms with the legacy of your predecessor in office: "Use the memory of thy predecessor fairly and tenderly; for if thou dost not, it is a debt will sure be paid when thou art gone."[16] In broader terms, Bacon acknowledges that an effective office holder will cultivate a longer term view and recognise how their actions may be perceived within a broader historical perspective, also suggesting that they do not act with an overblown sense of their importance with colleagues and interlocutors. Thus, Plutarch can be seen to serve Bacon in coming to an articulation of some of the norms and ethos of public life. While this is a sensibility first nourished in the French vernacular reception of Plutarch, we see here how some of that was subsequently taken up more broadly.

---

[14] Rousseau's diagnosis of the modern condition as individuals living outside themselves may be a move through which the growing force of public opinion allowed the condition of public officials to become generalised as a broad force of publicity, thereby subjecting all to the same fate without the honour and perks of office.

[15] Bacon, "Of Great Place," in *The Major Works*, 360.

[16] Bacon, "Of Great Place," in *The Major Works*, 361.

While the account in this book has often steered away from the study of how Plutarch's work was used in discussions of religious belief (a subject worthy of a separate book on its own), it should be noted how Plutarch is used by Bacon in argument deliberating over the status of atheism and idolatry. In his short essay "Of Superstition," Bacon explicitly endorses Plutarch's famous statement that no opinion of the deity is better than an opinion or superstition that is unworthy of that same deity. As Bacon develops it, a stance of atheism, as guides to forms of moral virtue, can still offer avenues for natural piety and philosophy, whereas superstition, "dismounts all these, and erecteth an absolute monarchy in the minds of men."[17] The further suggestion, is that atheism can still make men reflective and can encourage ongoing civility, whereas superstition can discourage solid argumentation and lead wise men to follow fools, thereby upending civil order (presumably with a strong sense of self-righteousness). It is a position that aligns Bacon with the later famous statements of Bayle on matters of civil religion.

In sum, Bacon drew on Plutarch in his *Essays* (part of his more extensive classical learning) to shed light on normative and experiential facets of public life. With Bacon's work we become aware that an institutionalised and more secular vision of public office seeking greater recourse to principles of merit instead of patrimony has to come to terms with new challenges of moral psychology in public life, such as envy.[18] His *Essays* reveal to some degree how selective recourse to a classical source, such as Plutarch, to identify challenges of public life can serve the management of vice in a tempered response to them, and the cause of the scientific world view, rather than the direct promotion of ancient virtue.

8.2   Hobbes (1588–1679)

In 1603 Philemon Holland (1552–1637) published a translation of Plutarch's *Moralia*, the first English vernacular translation of the work in its entirety. While of broad significance for English intellectual life as well as specifically for Thomas Hobbes (1588–1679), the Holland vernacular translation of the essay "How a man may receive profit from his enemies" also had a special impact on Hobbes's work in ways undetected by previous scholarship.[19] More specifically, I argue here that the significance of

---

[17] Bacon, "Of Superstition," in *The Major Works*, 373.
[18] On the broader import of Bacon's thought for shifting considerations of how to conceptualise public service, see Dauber, *State and Commonwealth*, chap. 4.
[19] Skinner argues that the Holland translation of the essay "How a man may discerne a flatterer from a friend," helped to stir discussion concerning some of the ambiguities in the relation of virtue and

Hobbes for Plutarch reception is threefold: first, Holland's translation of Plutarch's essay helped to shape the wording of one of the most famous phrases in the Western tradition of the history of political thought; second, Hobbes's use of Plutarch's essay is indicative of a broader innovation in English political thought whereby the previously independent genre of moral psychology is incorporated into political reflection more systematically than had been achieved by Bacon (Hobbes's former employer); and third, attention to this tradition of moral psychology, now made central to political reflection, offers insight into the subsidiary place of virtue in Hobbes's thought. To articulate this differently, we have seen how the work of Plutarch in English reflection throughout the Renaissance was in many ways focused on moral psychology first, and its application to political questions only second and derivatively. This goes hand in hand with the recognition that the select moral essays of Plutarch were more readily circulating in the sixteenth century. Hobbes's significance from the perspective of Plutarch reception was to bring a long tradition of reflection on moral psychology (for which Plutarch continued to be an important reference) to bear directly on matters of political submission and political right.

Hobbes's knowledge of Plutarch's work would have been both direct and indirect. In terms of Plutarch's *Moralia*, there is evidence that a copy of the 1603 Holland edition was purchased in 1605 for the library at Hardwick Hall where Hobbes (and William Cavendish) would have had the opportunity to read and study the work (Hobbes worked as tutor, secretary and librarian there from 1608). As Skinner has argued, the work informed William Cavendish's own writings on flattery.[20] In addition, Hobbes would have had exposure to Plutarch during his studies at Oxford and been able to read Plutarch in Greek.[21] As is well documented, Hobbes's early education was a humanist one and that, in addition to his work as a secretary to Francis Bacon, offers ample support for the supposition that he was acquainted with Plutarch's work, more than likely from an early age.[22] According to Noel Malcolm, Hobbes is not always known for citing his sources, and in the case

---

vice, and indeed informed the 1611 treatise entitled *A Discourse Against Flatterie* attributed to William Cavendish, Hobbes's patron. See Quentin Skinner, *Reason and Rhetoric in the Philosophy of Hobbes* (Cambridge: Cambridge University Press, 1996), 168–169.

[20] See footnote 17 in this chapter. The presence of the Holland translation in the library of Hardwick Hall was confirmed by Noel Malcolm in correspondence with me.

[21] Timothy Raylor, *Philosophy, Rhetoric and Thomas Hobbes* (Oxford: Oxford University Press, 2018), 42.

[22] See, for example, Skinner, *Reason and Rhetoric*. Still, for Skinner, in the light of Fumaroli, Hobbes's humanism was largely a rhetorical and Ciceronian one. There are others (including Raylor) who

of ancient writers such as Plutarch one can readily assume that he is working from memory in his references and allusions to examples.[23] In his allusions to Plutarch, Hobbes was of course tapping into a deep well of cultural capital for the era. A search on the Early English Books Online database suggests that roughly 1,400 sources from the period between 1600 and 1650 include at least one reference to Plutarch, for a total of 7,000 references altogether. Of these, the vast majority are found in works of ancient history, theology, or moral psychology, with noticeably less in the field of jurisprudence as the dominant language of political theorising of the age. Particularly relevant to my argument, is that some of the key works of moral psychology of the era include an important number of Plutarch references, including Robert Burton's *Anatomy of Melancholy* (1621) with eighty-three references and Edward Reynolds's *A Treatise of the Passions and Faculties of the Soul of Man* (1640) offering up seventy references to Plutarch's work. Thus, Hobbes would have had direct knowledge of Plutarch's work as well as an understanding of his significance in more general terms for both the fields of history and moral psychology.

As noted, Skinner has invoked the significance of this Holland translation, and more precisely the essay "How a Man may discern a Flatterer from a Friend," for Hobbes. He suggests that in the same spirit that informed the treatise of Cavendish on flattery, restating some of the central themes of the essay, especially regarding the creative re-description through which flatterers seek to shape perception, Hobbes picked up the idea of paradiastolic speech – namely, the idea that behaviours could sometimes be characterised by competing descriptions, depending on the disposition of the speaker. This is most famously invoked in the last paragraph of chapter 4 "Of Speech" in *Leviathan*: "for one man called *wisdom*, what another calleth *fear*; and one *cruelty*, what another *justice*; one *prodigality*, what another *magnanimity*; and one *gravity* what another *stupidity*, etc."[24] The more general point made clear by this analysis is that Hobbes was aware not

---

dispute the overriding significance of this strand of humanism in Hobbes's education. In another work, Skinner acknowledges Hobbes reading of Plutarch from an early age given that Hobbes cited Plutarch in a work entitled "On the Beginning of Tacitus" published in 1620. Perhaps even more significant for the purposes of my argument, is that Skinner suggests in the same footnote that Hobbes's account of Solon in chapter 27 of Leviathan is not only derived from Plutarch but from the English translation of Plutarch by North. This suggests that he did not read all of his Plutarch in the original Greek and may indeed have consulted the moral essays through Holland's comprehensive English translation. See Quentin Skinner, "Hobbes and the *studiea humanitatis*," in *Visions of Politics, vol. 3. Hobbes and Civil Science*, chap. 2, 44, n 49.

[23] Noel Malcolm, *Thomas Hobbes Leviathan. 1. Introduction* (Oxford: Oxford University Press, 2012), 108.

[24] Thomas Hobbes, *Leviathan*, ed. Edwin Curley (Indianapolis, IN: Hackett, 1994), 1, 4, s. 24, 22.

only of Plutarch's *Morals*, but of the Holland translation of the essays to which can be attributed, at least in part, the circulation of the theme of creative re-description of the virtues and vices in early modern England.

To further develop the general theme of the presence of Plutarch in Hobbes's work, I provide a brief overview of how Plutarch is reflected in Hobbes with a central focus on *Leviathan*. From there I explore the link between Plutarch's moral essay "How to Profit from your Enemies" as translated by Holland and the depiction of the state of nature as expressed in *De Cive* and subsequently *Leviathan*. Next, I reflect on the significance of this new finding for our current understanding of Hobbes's work.

8.2.1　Plutarch in Leviathan: A Broad Picture

As noted, in *Leviathan* Hobbes rarely offers the source from which he has taken his examples. More contemporary editorial work has contributed a great deal in offering suggestions regarding the textual sources from which his examples are culled. The work of both Noel Malcolm and Edwin Curley allows us to identify at least twelve places in *Leviathan* where Hobbes drew from a Plutarch source, in addition to the four places where Hobbes directly invokes Plutarch. A majority of these are specific examples from the *Lives*, such as the apparition of the ghost of Julius Caesar to Brutus after his slaying, as relevant for Hobbes's reflection on the working of the imagination in 1, 2. Some also are taken from select passages of the moral essays. So, for example in his discussion of the intellectual virtues in 1, 8 (where a discussion of madness and excess passion constitutes more than half the chapter), Hobbes relates an example taken from Plutarch on the virtues of women. A rash of suicides by hanging committed by young women in the city of Miletus led citizens to believe that the young women were possessed by the devil; however, one leading figure of the city attributed the acts to some disease of the mind and ordered that the dead bodies be stripped naked and displayed in public, something that worked to curb the behaviour (if not the melancholy). Hobbes's point is that there is a better internal psychological explanation for shocking behaviour than that attributed to evil spirits, although it is surprising that his materialism did not lead him to reflect on the objective circumstances that may have contributed to mass suicides. Of course, given that the act of suicide appears to counter a supposition of an internal impulse of self-preservation, it was evident that Hobbes could only characterise such actions as a form of madness from a poorly curated train of thought, and that fear of shame served to put an end to the practice may have been for him evidence of that.

It is evident that Hobbes was acquainted with Plutarch's work and was able to draw specific examples from both the *Moralia* and the *Lives* that spoke to the precise point he was making. We also see references to actors thinking of themselves through the lens of an historical exemplar, such as Alexander (1, 2), and a reference to the cobweb laws of Solon (11, 27). We also find looser allusions to the role of the Delphic oracle ("Know thyself") and systematic reflection on the crucial way in which religion, when organised in particular ways, can help foster or preserve a sense of community in politics. In short, there are a wide array of references to Plutarch's work in Hobbes's writing, some more elusive than others but none given the benefit of a precise reference.

It is not surprising, therefore, that Hobbes also did not cite Plutarch in his famous depiction of the state of nature in 1, 13 of *Leviathan*. The culminating description of the state of nature comes in section 9 of that chapter:

> whatsoever therefore is consequent to a time of war, where every man is enemy of every man, the same is consequent to the time wherein men lie without other security than what their own strength and their own invention shall furnish them withal. In such condition there is no place for industry, because the fruit thereof is uncertain, and consequently, no culture of the earth, no navigation, no use of the commodities that may be imported by sea, no commodious building, no instruments of moving and removing such things as require much force, no knowledge of the face of the earth, no account of time, no arts, no letters, no society, and which is worst of all, continual fear and danger of violent death, and the life of man, *solitary, poor, nasty, brutish, and short.*

According to the editorial work of Edwin Curley, this passage refers to the opening passages of Thucycides's *History of the Peloponnesian War*, a text which Hobbes translated at an early age.[25] While those passages from Thucydides offer a very general account of the pervasiveness of piracy and lack of security in Greece prior to the establishment of cities, there is no sense of the sheer devastation or the degree to which life is rendered to its bare minimum in such a state. Through Plutarch we can discern another and more convincing account of the genesis of Hobbes's vision.

Plutarch's moral essay "How a man may receive profit from his enemies" as translated by Holland may be of key interest here. In the first instance,

---

[25] See Hobbes, *Leviathan*, note 4, 76.

while Hobbes develops his concept of the state of nature through various avenues, this essay of Plutarch offers a brief depiction of the historical development of human life from a natural or 'pre-civilised' state to a more 'civilised' one. Furthermore, it does so in obvious secular, or pre-Christian terms, something that the dominant early modern accounts of the pre-lapsarian state of nature did not.[26] In addition, the transition that is depicted by Plutarch (though admittedly very brief), a transition that brings human beings from a more primitive condition to a more civil one, is not due to changes in external factors or even technology but rather to attitudinal changes among human beings regarding what sort of existence could render their lives easier. The broader point of the essay in Plutarch is that we cannot rid our societies and our communities from forms of human envy, rivalry and enmity, but we can choose how we respond to both the hostile sentiments of others directed towards us and to the hostile sentiments towards others that we may see arising in ourselves. If, as Plutarch suggests, we can seek to harness that contentiousness in ways that not only advance our own moral standing, but also that contribute to a more peaceful civil life, then we can see those forms of rivalry not as forms of social evil but as necessary conditions to propel us toward a better life.

Plutarch begins the essay with a reflection on how human beings lived at the origin of human society, and this story of the origins of civil society serves as a structural metaphor for rethinking approaches to competition and conflict in organised civil life. He suggests that initially humanity was fearful of the power and danger of wild beasts and the element of fire and sought to avoid them. However, subsequent generations began to understand how wild beasts could be used for food and that their life in common soon depended on their sustenance, so much so that without them (in the words of the Philemon Holland translation) "their life should become brutish, poore, needie and savage." (The relevant Greek phrase at 86 E of the essay is *ο βίος αυτου γένηται και άπορος και ανήμερος*.) We may recall that the concluding words of the famous Hobbes description is "solitary, *poor*, nasty, *brutish* and short." We see not only the invocation of some of the same words but also their placement in a line of adjectives with a similarity of cadence and sound.

Plutarch then goes on to suggest that his readers use this account as an analogy for thinking about how to deal with enemies – that is, to use enemies' competition and ill will for purposes of moral edification. He

---

[26] See James J. Hamilton, "The Origins of Hobbes's State of Nature," *Hobbes Studies* 26.2 (January 2013), 152–170.

discusses various ways in which social competitors, at first glance noxious, can also be instructive. In the first instance he suggests that enemies make one more susceptible to self-examination. Competitors can shake one from a sense of complacency and lead one back to circumspection in living, an important pre-condition for virtuous habits. With potential enemies one becomes more careful about not saying anything careless or inconsiderate, lest it be used against you, but this in turn ensures that you live an unassailable life.

> for like as those cities by ordinary warres with their neighbour cities, and by continuall expeditions and voiages, learning to be wise, take a love at length unto good lawes and sound government of state; even so that they by occasion of enmity be forced to live soberly, to save themselves from the imputation of idleness and negligence, yea, and to do everie thing with discretion and to a good and profitable end, through use and custome shall be brought by little and little (ere they be aware) unto a certeine settled habit that they cannot lightly trip and do misse, having their manners framed in passing good order, with the least helping hand of reason and knowledge beside.[27]

In addition to the analogy of war, Plutarch invokes the competitiveness of musicians who can often be led to greater virtuosity when faced with the performing skills of their rivals in the art.

He also suggests that honourable living is not only the best form of defence but also of offence against those who may seek to impugn your reputation. Thus, for motives not only of self-protection but also of outshining one's neighbour, the existence of enmity and ill-will may prompt the fair-minded individual to offer an even higher standard of virtue in their own behaviour so they can more readily and honestly be in a state to judge the actions and characters of others:

> If thou chance to upbraid thine enemie with ignorance, and call him unlearned, take thou greater paines at thy booke, love thou thy studie better, and get more learning: if thou twit him with cowardice, and name his dastard, stirre up the vigour of thine owne courage the rather, and shew thy selfe a man so much the more: hast thou given him the tearmes of beastly whoremaster or lasvicious lecher, wipe out of thy heart the least taint and spot that remaineth hidden therein of concupiscence and sensuallitie; for nothing is there more shamefull or causeth greater griefe of heart, than an opprobrious and reprochfull speech returned justly upon the author thereof.[28]

---

[27] Plutarch, "How a Man may Receive Profit by his Enemies," in *The Philosophie commonlie called, The Morals*, trans. Philemon Holland (London: Arnold Hatfield, 1603), 238–239.

[28] Plutarch, "How a Man may Receive Profit by his Enemies," 240.

A third insight into the usefulness of enmity and contentiousness in civil life for Plutarch is that the testimony of potentially hostile individuals can sometimes offer more truth about the self than the testimony of friends. For reasons of kindness, fear or flattery, those well disposed towards us may not always engage in frank speech. Thus, it can often be that those who are less well-disposed can offer greater insight into our true nature, or into ways in which our actions might be misperceived by others as vicious.

An additional benefit of having enemies or competitors is that it offers us opportunities for exercising restraint, especially for practising anger control. The idea is that only difficult relations and circumstances offer real opportunities to develop higher capacities for compassion, forbearance and control of anger, capacities which are marks of higher virtue. He cites the example of Caesar who in offering to preserve the statues of his political rival Pompey came to be judged in a more favourable light.

Finally, insofar as each human being must feel ill will of some kind or another, the existence of enemies offers an outlet for negative feelings, thereby sparing friends and relatives from the worst excesses of hostility:

> for if there be no other way or meanes to be delivered wholy from contentions, envies, jealousies, and emulations, acquaint thy selfe at leastwise to be stung and bitten at the good successe of thine enemies; whet the edge and sharpen the point (as it were) of thy quarrellous and contentious humour, and turne it upon them and spare not: for like as the most skilfull and best gardiners are of this opinion, that they shall have the sweeter roses and more pleasant violets, if they set garlicke or sow onions neere unto them, for that all the strong and stinking savour in the juice that feedeth and nourish the saide flowers, is purged away and goeth to the said garlick and onions; even so an enimie drawing unto himself and receiving all our envie and malice, will cause us to be better affected to our friends in their prosperitie, and lesse offended if they out go us in their estate[29]

To summarise, Plutarch acknowledges that human conflict, competition, envy and hostility, due to a variety of motivations and causes, is a perennial feature of social life. To meet hostile sentiments with hostile behaviour is largely a dysfunctional and regressive approach. However, finding ways to act more thoughtfully and creatively in the face of initially hostile intent can serve to improve one's own moral standing while also resulting in broadly positive social benefit. Social competition can thus provide a useful background and impetus for moral improvement. More generally, Plutarch's message in this essay comes down to this: a presumption of

---

[29] Plutarch, "How a Man may Receive Profit by his Enemies," 244.

certain levels of social hostility can paradoxically serve the cause of civility by pushing individuals with the appropriate mindset and outlook to cultivate and put forward their better selves.

So how might this message have played into Hobbes's understanding of the transition from the state of nature to civil society? There are two separate features of interest here. The first relates to the conceptualisation of the state of nature and the transition to civil society in conceptual terms, and the second relates to the moral psychology that helps to characterise the shift in behaviour and attitude. I will begin with the first before addressing the second.

8.2.2   Thinking about the State of Nature

It is of interest here to trace the evolving description of the state of nature from the *Elements of Law* to *De Cive* and *Leviathan* with attention to the shifts in the language used. In the first instance we must see if it is possible to distinguish the direct circumstances of the changes of wording in *Leviathan* to the description of the state of nature as famously "nasty, brutish and short" in a way that echoes the Holland translation of Plutarch. *The Elements of Law* first appeared in manuscript form in 1640. Prior to *Leviathan*, Hobbes had already published two editions of *De Cive* (the first with a very limited circulation in 1642 and the second in 1647), so a central question is how and why did Hobbes's depiction of the state of nature shift from his first writing to *Leviathan*, and how might the Holland essay have factored into this?

As is well known, Hobbes only came to conceptualise his grand three-part philosophical project in 1637, with treatises on the body, man and the citizen initially planned in that order. Soon after, it was clear that his philosophical ambitions had come up against the hard political realities of his time: his exile in 1640 and the execution of Charles I. All this meant that his major writings on political life, that is, *De Cive* (1642 and 1647) as well as *Leviathan* (1651), were penned under more pressing circumstances than originally planned.

As noted by Jean Terrell, in each depiction of the natural state, Hobbes never ignores the humanity of human beings, granting them both imagination and desire which allow them to collectively overcome and rise above the challenges they face.[30] The state of nature is first described in chapter 14

---

[30] Jean Terrell, *Thomas Hobbes: Philosopher par temps de crises* (Paris: Presses Universitaires de France, 2012), 67–68.

of *The Elements of Law*, albeit with few of the rhetorical flourishes that characterise subsequent depictions.[31] This first iteration emphasises the unlimited right of nature that all individuals exercise in the state of nature if one extrapolates hypothetically from the passions embedded in human nature and perceived signs of contempt. That state of hostility and war is also identified with the current state of "savage nations" as well as "the old inhabitants of Germany and other now civil countries" prior to the arrival of the comforts of life. The broad logic is that of self-defence, and therefore individuals should not perceive the more powerful person who controls them as an 'enemy.' Still, the dictates of natural law and the need to seek peace suggest the need for a collective and reasoned solution. While there is a kernel of Hobbes's key interest in moral psychology in this account in the need for self-preservation and security as a motivating driving force, in subsequent iterations we will see further emphasis on the desire for commodious living, the same motivation clearly present in Plutarch's discussion of his central analogy.

In the Preface to *De Cive* (absent from the first 1642 edition) Hobbes discusses one of the first principles of the work, that "men's natural Disposition is such that if they are not restrained by fear of a common power, they will distrust and fear one another."[32] He then invokes the image, repeated in chapter 13 of Leviathan, of subjects who demonstrate their mistrust of others by arming themselves and locking their doors and chests. Arguing that this does not imply that human nature is evil (as basic emotions such as fear and anger are not), he nonetheless claims that the condition of men in the state of nature or outside civil society would be a state of war of all men against all men.[33] The 'miserable' conditions of nature is what drives human beings out of it.

Returning to a deeper description of the state of nature (or 'the state of man without civil society') in chapter 1, he begins by refuting the general Aristotelian adage of man as a political animal, suggesting that it is not the case that all men love others equally but indeed that men tend to seek out the company of those they find most prestigious and useful to them. Thus, as he notes, "by nature, then, we are not looking for friends but for honour or advantage from them."[34] His model of social order is one structured by

---

[31] Thomas Hobbes, *Human Nature and De Corpore Politico*, ed. J. C. A. Gaskin (Oxford: Oxford University Press, 1994), 77–81.
[32] Hobbes, *On the Citizen*, eds. Richard Tuck and Michael Silverthorne (Cambridge: Cambridge University Press, 1998), 10.
[33] Hobbes, *On the Citizen*, 12.   [34] Hobbes, *On the Citizen*, 22.

the search for honour, reputation or self-affirmation (*gloria*) rather than personal connection.

Hobbes, then notes that the search for honour and recognition in various sectors of civil life will in most instances pit one individual against another over goods which are structurally scarce. Against this picture Hobbes acknowledges the fundamental right of nature that "each man protect his life and limbs as much as he can" followed by the "right to use any means and to do any action by which he can preserve himself."[35] He acknowledges that the natural state could not have been anything but "a war of every man against every man," and then invokes an image of indigenous communities in the Americas: "Past centuries show us nations, now civilized and flourishing, whose inhabitants then were *few, savage, short-lived, poor and mean*, and lacked all the comforts and amenities of life which peace and society afford." (my emphasis)[36] He notes that just as the Americans "now civilized and flourishing" moved beyond that natural state, so anyone should acknowledge that seeking one's own good is necessary and thus that we are driven by mutual fear to move beyond the war of all against all. What this *De Cive* passage suggests is that despite a logic that would make the Plutarch essay relevant to the underlying logic of the transition from the state of nature to civil society, the wording of the Holland translation was consulted and taken up in part by Hobbes in the drafting of *De Cive* and then carried over into *Leviathan*. *The Elements of Law* demonstrates a preoccupation with principles of political right alone. With *De Cive* and *Leviathan*, Hobbes supplements his rules of rational political prudence with a more concerted understanding of human psychology and political practice and behaviour and with a rhetoric that is designed to persuade through images and cadence as well as logic.

What is particularly significant about this passage in relation to the substance of the Plutarch essay summarised above, is that here Hobbes is making an analogy between the transition to a more flourishing and 'civilised' life among the indigenous nations in the Americas, and the transition between the natural state and civil life in the same way gestured to by Plutarch. What is left understated in the text is that the lack of comfort and amenities of life that characterised the previous life was transcended in part through the work and efforts of harnessing the potential of features that they encountered. So indigenous communities initially lived in mutual fear, by implication, like all in the state of nature, but that fear itself drove the individuals to associate and through

---

[35] Hobbes, *On the Citizen*, 27.   [36] Hobbes, *On the Citizen*, 29–30.

association to build a more prosperous life. Seen through the lens of Plutarch's essay, Hobbes shares the image of a natural state where fear is pervasive. For Hobbes the fear is directed at other human beings as potential enemies, while for Plutarch the fear is directed at other external threats to security such as animals or fire. What drives the transformation in Plutarch's picture is the dread of the continued prospect of a life in fear and the wish to live better, something that also drives those early human beings to harness the power of fire and use the animals to their advantage. In the case of Hobbes in *De Cive*, it appears that a parallel in the first, namely the dread of a life continuously in fear as well as desire for comfortable living, plays a major role in motivating individuals to seek a transformation away from the state of nature. Thus, while Hobbes tells us that mutual fear is the motivating factor in moving beyond the state of nature, in both the case of Plutarch and of Hobbes in *De Cive*, it appears that it is more precisely a fear of a continued state of mutual fear, as well as a clear desire for a more comfortable life, that impels individuals internally to seek change.

There is a shift in the status of indigenous communities when Hobbes comes to allude to this in *Leviathan*. Here "savage peoples in many places of America (except the government of small families, the concord whereof dependeth on natural lust) have no government at all and live at this day in that brutish manner as I said before" (1, 13). One can see by this that Hobbes may have acknowledged that the initial logic of the Plutarch essay (as translated by Holland) can apply to a broad transition from pre-civil to civil life but would not apply when one seeks to emphasise the need for structures of state governance. Thus, given his need to stress political order in the face of civil war (and by implication a lack of real consideration for the reality of indigenous societies), Hobbes removes his depiction of indigenous peoples from the category of the civilised and alludes to them as 'savage' (as he had done initially in *The Elements of Law*) because they do not have what he identifies as traditional state structures. This might serve to obfuscate the original Plutarch reference unless one understands the genesis and evolution of the description in Hobbes's work. It also offers insight into Hobbes's rhetorical practice, reflection and curation in his writing.

8.2.3   The Transition from the State of Nature to Civil Society: The Moral Psychology of Civil Life

In terms of exploring the significance of the Plutarch essay and the Holland translation for a depiction of the moral psychology underpinning the shift from the state of nature to civil society in Hobbes, it should be first acknowledged that for Hobbes the transition can be regarded as overdetermined. A great deal of scholarship has focused on the juridical transformation, namely, the covenant as the renouncing of an unlimited right of nature by individuals in the state of nature, a right which is then transferred to Leviathan, or the more powerful figure who is given the legal authority to ensure that peace in the social order is preserved. Still, the covenant described takes place at the same time as a moral transformation and a psychological one. In terms of moral thinking, the autonomy of individuals to determine their own sense of right as predicated on an extension of the right of self-preservation, is now policed by Leviathan who himself/herself conditions both the possibility and the content of justice (of course, the possibility of a female sovereign is acknowledged in chapter 20). While individuals retain a limited right of self-preservation, the content of the duties required of each citizen to maintain the good of the whole is predicated fully on the dictates of the sovereign. The moral transition, then, is one in which people delegate to the sovereign the ability to determine the content of the good insofar as the preservation of the social order is concerned and as it relates to external actions.

However, alongside the legal (or juridical) and the moral transition, we can also discern what we might call a social psychological one. In the trope of the state of nature, we are presented with an exaggerated realisation of an ongoing but latent and perhaps partially sublimated sense of insecurity as it exists in organised civil life. Hence, while readers can identify with the fear that Hobbes depicts in the state of nature, because readers themselves lock their doors and arm themselves on a journey, this sense of fear does not descend into social pathology in the way that it does in the state of nature precisely because the force of Leviathan or the state offers a counterbalance and relative degree of security that offsets the threat of violence from others. The transition from the state of nature to civil society in Hobbes offers a complex condition of psychological transformation. What begins as an overall climate of extreme mutual fear, given the strength of the fear of violent death and the desire for commodious living in the context of complete insecurity, evolves through rational reflection to an awareness of a need for an attitudinal change as represented by the first precepts of the law of nature (i.e. to seek peace). Thus, all agree to renounce violence by placing the almost absolute power of enforcement in the hands of one, in order to pursue the goods of living and its associated desires. In this climate, one does not fully overcome the sense of insecurity vis-à-vis the other, but this very sense of unease and lack of transparency (for one can speculate what the other *might* do in the context of no common power to enforce the law) leads one to live not only in ways that involve not harming others, but in a civil manner.

A question arises related to this psychological framework of how civil interaction with one's fellow subjects is to be conceived in civil society, and the relation of this interaction to other motivations of obedience to power and fear of punishment. Aspects can be clarified in examining Hobbes's account of the law of gratitude in chapter 15. There Hobbes tells us that individuals, through reason and the need to avoid a condition of war, should practice gratitude to those who do them benefit, that is to demonstrate a demeanour of trust and goodwill even if they acknowledge the self-regarding impetus of all such gestures.

> that a man which receiveth benefit from another of mere grace endeavour that he which giveth it have no reasonable cause to repent him of his good will. For no man giveth but with intention of good to himself, because gift is voluntary, and of all voluntary acts the object is to every man his own good; of which, if men see they shall be frustrated, there will be no beginning of benevolence or trust; nor, consequently, of mutual help, nor of reconciliation of one man to another; and therefore they are to remain still in the condition of war, which is contrary to the first and fundamental law of nature, which commandeth men to seek peace. The breach of this law is called ingratitude, and hath the same relation to grace that injustice hath to obligation by covenant.[37]

Hobbes tells us that "no man giveth but with intention of good to himself," so that each of us should acknowledge that gifts are self-regarding rather than disinterested. Yet in the face of that stark recognition of selfishness and self-promotion, the recipient should nonetheless acknowledge that to repudiate the gift based on awareness of the selfish motivation would rule out the possibility of any benevolence or trust or indeed reconciliation, however meagre. Thus, reason suggests that recipients of gifts should practice and express gratitude, not out of recognition and reverence for the kindness and goodwill of the giver, but out of an understanding that to deny gratitude, despite the selfish conditions of the gift-giving, would raise tensions and create a hostile environment. What this means is that gratitude is not a virtue which is directly dependent on the safe conditions of a civil order, but rather that a civil order is constituted in part by individuals who still recognise the vices and possible hostility of others, but react to them in ways that demonstrate the capacity for noble behaviour that also serves their interests in constructing and

---

[37] Hobbes, *Leviathan*, 1, 15, s. 16, 95.

maintaining a peaceful environment. Both recipients and givers pretend that they are better than they are, and thus they can be made to appear virtuous while being largely self-interested. An underlying climate of self-regard, if broached with the appropriate attitude, can serve to cultivate a practice of virtue, and actions that were once a source of contentiousness (self-regarding 'gifts') become an almost theatrical occasion to act in noble and virtuous ways.

This depiction of the law of gratitude may offer support for the argument of Peter Berkowitz who depicts Hobbes as a virtue theorist.[38] Berkowitz acknowledges that Hobbes rejects a perfectionist teleology, but this does not preclude some commitment to a set of necessary virtues. His position is that the status of authority does not do all the work of maintaining the peace and guarding the civil order. Indeed, even the commitment to peace itself, which also entails an understanding of the means to peace through, as Hobbes states, "justice, gratitude, modesty, equity, mercy and the rest of the laws of nature" are determined through principles of right reason and are deemed moral virtues because of their goodness. While Hobbes may appear to mock the language of moral virtue in the earlier chapters of *Leviathan*, this may ultimately be an attempt to dismantle the reader's attachment to the full force of Aristotelian perfectionism. In other words, Berkowitz sees no contradiction here but an attempt by Hobbes to replace one use of the language of virtue with another more precise one. It may be that for Hobbes there is no longer human good in pure wisdom and perfection, but given that human beings can still strive for "lesser" goods, or goals, such as peace, then Hobbes does participate in an Aristotelian-like sensibility in which some modes of mind and character that are more conducive to those ends.[39] In broad terms this is also a position shared by Skinner who acknowledges that subjection to the laws of the state is not sufficient for Hobbes's vision of how civility should be managed. In addition, as Skinner tells us, Hobbes provides his readers with guidance concerning the virtues needed to live a "peaceable, sociable and comfortable" way of life.[40] So really the question here is not *if* Hobbes has a theory of virtue, but rather how we can characterise it, especially in relation to classical theories of virtue which he appears to be hostile to in their more general thrust. In broad terms, it may correspond to

---

[38] Peter Berkowitz. *Virtue and the Making of Modern Liberalism* (Princeton, NJ: Princeton University Press, 1999).

[39] Berkowitz, *Virtue*, 38–50.

[40] Quentin Skinner, "Hobbes on Civil Conversation," in *From Humanism to Hobbes. Studies in Rhetoric and Politics* (Cambridge: Cambridge University Press, 2018), 177.

a similar logic in Bacon – that is, recourse to Plutarch avoiding an overarching theory of virtue but replaced with an awareness of a need for continued reference to civil and politically useful virtues. The insights of classical culture are fused here on to more fundamental suppositions of modern individualism.

This appears to be the case at least with Hobbes's description of the law of gratitude. Continuing with his discussion of the virtues in chapter 15, Hobbes's subsequent natural laws of complaisance, pardon and the out-lawing of injury are predicated on a slightly different dynamic because they do not involve a redescription of self-regarding acts as generous for pur-poses of a noble response, but only suggest that injuries not be perpetrated or taken as the cause of hostilities. This is a call for the direct promotion of peace by neither asking for more than one's share, nor by avoiding injuring and insulting others in ways deemed unsociable, intractable and stubborn.[41] Further laws dictate the need to acknowledge other human beings (Hobbes uses the term 'man') as equals by nature, exercising moderation, equity, etc. and all these are considered to be binding on the conscience (*in foro interno*) even if a breach of them is not considered strictly a crime.[42] Still, the deeper logic is that the subject is driven through force of reason and self-interest to be socially cooperative and complaisant despite and indeed because of an underlying feeling of mistrust (for otherwise the breakdown of the civil order would not be envisaged as a distinct possibility). The recognition of potential enmity serves as a negative regulative ideal pushing subjects to greater cooperation to avoid the worst. At the same time, good will and mutually supportive and constructive social relations are tinged with a triple sense of necessity, instrumentality and contingency. In short, one's potential enemy is to be treated as a fellow citizen and in a virtuous way because it is in everyone's self-interest to do so and so that competition is channelled in more socially productive modes.

It is thus evident that the structure of Plutarch's argument regarding the independent social dynamic that characterises the transition to a civil order, maps onto a similar dynamic in Hobbes's great work. Of course, there is a great deal more going on in Hobbes and it is not suggested here that Plutarch was the only or even the most important inspiration for Hobbes's argument; some of these observations may have been channelled through a reading of the French moralists. Nonetheless, I think that it is reasonable to suggest that this essay by

---

[41] Hobbes, *Leviathan*, I, 15, s. 17, 95–96.   [42] Hobbes, *Leviathan*, I, 15, ss. 16–41, 95–100.

Plutarch served as one interlocutor in the development of Hobbes's conceptualisation of the argument of *Leviathan*, both in terms of the distinction between the state of nature and civil society in secular terms, as well as a vision of social order in which hostility and competition is sublimated but not fully overcome and in which the very premise of potential hostility serves the effective function, through complex psychological reasoning, of strengthening social bonds and civility. The one important difference between the two is that for Plutarch competition was predicated of a specific class of elite individuals seeking prominence in public life, whereas through a more modern social lens Hobbes's idea of competition incorporates all individuals in a modern order and thus is a more broadly civil dynamic not only operative in public life.

8.3   Summary and Broader Significance

In thinking this parallel through it may first be useful to summarise points of comparison and contrast in three key aspects of the structure. In the first instance, as we have noted, both Plutarch and Hobbes set their arguments in the context of the overriding and pervasive presence of social conflict. For Hobbes, of course, the broad fear which informs the text is that of civil war, so the degree and level of social conflict is greater than that suggested by Plutarch. The subjects of Plutarch's essay may face the danger of a ruined reputation if their enemies prevail, and thus the experience of shame, but in the case of Hobbes's vision of social conflict it is the very survival of the subjects that is at risk. Hobbes provides us with a vision of social conflict in which a great deal more is at stake. Nonetheless, as Hobbes lays out in chapters 10 and 11 as well as in *De Cive*, while violent conflict is the endgame that is of concern to him, the root of such violent conflict is most often competition for honours. This is precisely the type of conflict that Plutarch himself has in mind in his essay. Thus, both Plutarch and Hobbes agree on the main motivation for social conflict, but Hobbes radicalises the repercussions of that motivation leading to much more dire stakes than those presupposed by Plutarch. Building on this we could even suggest, that the sphere of life that was pre-eminent in Hobbes's mind in envisaging conflict declining into civil war, was that of the public sphere.

A second important feature through which Plutarch and Hobbes can be compared is consideration of the effects of thinking through the perennial threat of conflict, especially over honours. In both instances the fact of conflict, if considered in the appropriate way, can lead to deeper reflection on one's own long-term advantage in behaving in ways that are conducive to greater civility and peace, leading to greater self-control. For Berkowitz, Hobbes adopts a revised (or perhaps distilled) form of virtue theory from Aristotle. The logic as depicted in this interpretation is still distinct from that of Plutarch. According to Berkowitz, Hobbes calls on subjects and his readers to pursue a path in virtue education largely due to fear of the consequences if they pursued their instincts and let their worst impulses take over. The broader logic is one of avoiding the worst. For Plutarch, as we have seen, the incentive to virtue cultivation is still a positive argument drawing on the same attachment to honour that may have sparked competition and conflict in the first place – namely, that one can better outdo one's rival by acting more conscientiously in favour of the virtues. Despite these differences, reading Hobbes in the light of virtue theory does serve to align these pieces in ways that might have previously been considered problematic. To recognise that Hobbes is still not fully out of the grips of traditional moral virtue theory makes the possibility of his dialogue with Plutarch here all the more plausible.

A key sticking point between Plutarch and Hobbes's understanding in this regard is the ongoing place of honour in the normative model of social life. For Plutarch, honour plays a key role in self-policing and self-discipline. The logic of seeking to outdo your rival, at least as a motivating force for some, continues to be central to Plutarch's notion of how to keep ambitious young public figures in line. In contrast, Hobbes suggests that pride, arrogance, vanity, self-regard and honour, taken to a certain level, can continue to act as threats upon civil life, a position that informs his condemnation of the duel as an extreme form of defence of one's honour, as well as his condemnation of laughter and ridicule as a form of informal civil policing.[43] Ultimately, Hobbes is most interested in how one could control and police outer expressions of contempt, as it is those actions which have the impact he fears. And even here, as Skinner acknowledges, Hobbes notes in *De Cive* that "because all pleasure and exaltation of the mind consists in being able to think highly of oneself by comparison with others, it is impossible for people to avoid exhibiting some mutual contempt, whether they express it by laughter, or by words or by some gesture or other sign."[44]

---

[43] Skinner, "Hobbes on Civil Conversation," 180–181.
[44] Skinner, "Hobbes on Civil Conversation," 181. Nonetheless, Hobbes goes on to argue in *Leviathan*, as noted by Skinner, that in the end scornful laughter reflects a lack of inner confidence in one's

Furthermore, despite Hobbes's denunciation of pride, vainglory and the like, in a social world and especially in a public realm where individuals struggle for influence, recognition and power, the motivation and seeking for honour may never be fully overcome. His plea for "complaisance" as a social virtue in chapter 15 is recognition that there will always be those individuals who seek out more than their share and who create an added burden on others. His appeal to various forms of self-discipline again preaches forbearance in the face of possible insults.[45] Finally, his appeal throughout the text to reform the curriculum and teach the young new ways, of course not at odds in any way with the appeal to self-discipline, suggest challenges to civil life that cannot be fully resolved through laws and political obedience alone.[46]

A third and final significant point of comparison is a consideration of the class of potential enemies or rivals. In the case of Plutarch, we are to consider political and social rivals existing in an actual public setting, but then to remind ourselves of humanity's response to difficulty in the past as a way to deal with conflict in the present in creative and socially and morally useful ways. In the case of Hobbes, we are asked to imagine our current social and political rivalries in the light of hypothetically and potentially more violent actions in the past, and then by acknowledging the dysfunction of that scenario to think of how our contemporary allegiances and actions should play out to avoid that worst scenario in the future.

Regardless of the grey areas and questions on the margins, the broader thrust of this understanding of Hobbes is that the force and authority of *Leviathan* in the end is not sufficient as a glue for the social order. Instead, it is contended that Hobbes acknowledged both the force and importance of thinking through a form of collective enlightened self-interest that would lead subjects and readers to acknowledge the importance and normative force of many of the traditional moral virtues that contributed to civil peace. To a degree, it might be suggested that Plutarch was one, up to now overlooked, contribution that allowed Hobbes to move from a dire vision of the outcomes of competition, to one in which we can seek from the very depths of the logic of that competition the reasons and motivation for a practice of civility.

---

worth, as laughter can be understood as a means of seeking to act out one's superiority through the derision of others precisely because one is uncertain of one's own worth.

[45] Julie Cooper, "Vainglory, Modesty and Political Agency in the Political Theory of Thomas Hobbes," *The Review of Politics* 72 (2010), 241–269.

[46] Skinner, "Hobbes on Civil Conversation," 185–189.

From a broader perspective of the evolution of ideas, what is also significant about this meeting of Plutarch and Hobbes is the way in which the literature of moral psychology in which Plutarch and his writings often figured, came to be integrated into the work of political reflection. We have seen in previous chapters how Plutarch was initially received in England as a thinker identified with a tradition of reflection in moral psychology with only subsequent application to questions of political life. The main tradition of political reflection in England in the early 1600s focused to a large degree on juridical questions expressed in the language of common law and the ancient constitution. One of Hobbes's innovations was not just bringing a scientific and mathematical mindset and materialist suppositions to the world of political reflection, but to offer a new vision of human life with its own language describing the nature of human psychology. At around the same time that Hobbes was bringing in a long tradition of moral psychology to bear on issues of political order and governance, works of French political theory that drew more heavily on Plutarch's work (such as the work of Jean Bodin, Louis Le Roy, Pierre Charron, Innocent Gentillet and Michel de Montaigne) were being translated into English and published in England. Of course, this followed the greater circulation of Plutarch's own work through the English vernacular translations of both the *Moralia* and the *Lives*. Because of this, it is no surprise that Plutarch, once regarded as a somewhat marginal thinker for traditions of political reflection in England, became by the mid-seventeenth century much more central to it. Aspects of Plutarch's work were drawn upon to devise a political theory that repudiated the classical visions of full virtue. While accepting the propensity of modern societies for conflict and struggle, Hobbes forged a theory he believed was better suited to modern times, championing a set of civil virtues to ensure the keeping of social peace.

CHAPTER 9

Plutarch on Stage: Shakespeare, Pierre Corneille and Jean Racine

Plutarch continued to be an important reference for political thinkers throughout the sixteenth century in France, going into the seventeenth, though we begin to see definite shifts as the century progresses. His importance is indicated by the continued popularity of Amyot's famous translations into the seventeenth century; however, by the end of that same century Bayle in his critical dictionary of 1647–1706 declares Tacitus as the most important of the ancient historians and, while offering a short entry on Jacques Amyot, he neglects to include Plutarch at all (although, as we have seen in our commentary on Bacon, Bayle's preference for the lesser evil of atheism over superstition sounds very much like Plutarch's own general stance on the issue). What we begin to see in France is a more diffuse spread of various themes from across Plutarch's moral essays (which were first offered in their entirety in the vernacular by Amyot) and a greater take-up of the dramatic and literary potential of the *Lives* and some sceptical commentary on the heroic status of the individuals featured there (such as was first offered in Montaigne's critical take on Alexander at the opening of the *Essays*). The thrust of all these developments was that Plutarch's work was coming to be regarded as valuable for a broader audience beyond the court. It could offer insight into more general questions of moral and political life by treating Plutarch's exemplars with greater critical reflection and flexibility. This means that Plutarch began to wane as a direct reference in political discourse by the latter seventeenth century in France, and by the early eighteenth century, as we will see in a later chapter, his work was taken up in new ways. By the late eighteenth century, there was a new tone in the most famous moments in the reception and appropriation of his work such that in matters of political reflection his authority was often put to the service of moral absolutism, a far cry from the tradition of political humanism we sketched earlier.

Much of the work of Budé and Seyssel was written to be read directly to the king, thereby providing those in power with food for thought regarding the nature of public life. By the time of Montaigne, we see reflections on the nature of power for a broader audience, including nobles contemplating how to navigate both the temptations as well as the dangers of public life in a time of civil war. And beyond those reflections on power, the messages taken from Plutarch by Montaigne offered ideas on a wide array of matters both public and private. Thus, to a certain degree, through Montaigne, the work of Plutarch was distilled for the use of a broader public, helping to cultivate and shape their perspectives on an array of issues. In that same spirit of widening the relevant audience, dramatic traditions carried on the task of sparking reflection about the nature of power and public responsibility.

This chapter explores a couple of highlights in Plutarch reception in the dramatic traditions in France and England in the seventeenth century as related to the history of political ideas. I provide a cursory comparison and contrast of the ways in which Plutarch's work helped key dramatists (Shakespeare on the English side, and Corneille and Racine on the French side) develop themes related to public life. The uptake of Plutarch in drama, while often studied independently, has been less explicitly invoked for its links to traditions of political reflection. This analysis not only ties dramatic pieces to longer traditions in political reflection as related to classical reception, but also compares specific instances of this in both French and English traditions. Plutarch in these dramatic traditions is here explored from a much wider perspective than is generally the case, and this may offer possibilities for new insight.

A second reason for including this focus is that it helps to underline a metaphor often invoked in Plutarch's work, one which may be linked to a narrative style that makes his narration of lives particularly well suited for dramatic adaptation. As we noted in our study of Tory's translation of Plutarch's "Political Precepts" in 1530, there are passages where Plutarch invokes the theatre as a metaphor for public life. Other commentators have noted passages where Plutarch's invocation of the theatre is done to cast a negative commentary on his subject, in the spirit, it is suggested, of Plato who was suspicious of dramatic representations.[1] While this link is open to various avenues of investigation, I am most interested in reflecting on how this shapes Plutarch's message and its reception concerning the nature of public life. There are numerous levels of mediation here (not including the

---

[1] Herve-Thomas Campagne, "Poétique de l'instant tragique: la place et l'influence des Vies de Plutarque dans la définition du tragique en France, 1600–1645," in Olivier Guerrier, ed. *Plutarque de l'Age classique au XIXe siècle* (Grenoble: Jerome Million, 2012), 55–56.

fact that these playwrights largely worked from vernacular translations, and in the case of Shakespeare, a vernacular English translation from a vernacular French edition!). I offer here no claim of exhausting the many areas of analysis, but I hope at least to illuminate how the use of Plutarch's work in crafting drama meant for the stage deepens our understanding of the evolution of conceptions of public life in the early modern period.

Sixteenth-century England saw increased interest in Plutarch by various poets and moralists, such as Lyly and Philip Sydney in addition to those we have discussed in Chapter 5, but it was not until the century's end and the start of the seventeenth that there was a notable trend for dramatists to turn to Plutarch for inspiration.[2] There may be multiple reasons for this, including a developing interest in classical culture for its own sake as well as growing interest in ancient history as a source of moral instruction for contemporary subjects: "The imaginative presentation of classical heroes was part of the emancipation of the English drama from insularity and medievalism."[3] What this involved in the case of England was a shifting of attention and inspiration from Plutarch of the moral essays to Plutarch of the *Lives*, stemming to a large degree from the new translations of Amyot into French and subsequently by North into English. This trend was also shaped by the translation of several French plays of the late sixteenth century which had been inspired by various lives of Plutarch, including the Countess of Pembroke's translation of Robert Garnier's *Marc Antoine* (1578 and 1592) and Thomas Kyd's translation of Garnier's *Cornelie* (1574 and 1594). Samuel Daniel also wrote *Cleopatra* (1594) and *Philotas* (1604) based on the lives of Antony and Alexander respectively, among other dramatic adaptations of Plutarch of the period, including those of William Alexander and George Chapman.[4]

In approaching this brief discussion of the dramatic adaptations of Plutarch's work in Shakespeare as well as Corneille and Racine it may be helpful to spell out in more precise terms the thrust of the analysis. I explore the ways Plutarch's work was reflected (or refracted), or more precisely how conceptions of the public realm were expressed in a select few passages of select plays. As not only vernacular representations but also dramatic ones, these examples will offer insight into how Plutarch's depictions and conceptions of public office were translated, portrayed,

[2] Shackford, *Plutarch*, 31.   [3] Shackford, *Plutarch*, 31.
[4] On Roman plays of the sixteenth century in both France and England, see M. W. MacCallum, *Shakespeare's Roman Plays* (London: Macmillan, 1925), chap. 1.

disseminated, and potentially transformed through drama. I relate these iterations of power and public position to traditions of political reflection and Plutarch reception analysed in previous chapters. I am interested in contrasting Shakespeare's depiction of public life in the classical world in *Titus Andronicus*, a play he wrote without consulting Plutarch, with passages from four of his later plays, *Julius Caesar*, *Antony and Cleopatra*, *Coriolanus* and *Timon of Athens*, for which Plutarch was clearly a source.[5] Through this comparison and contrast I seek to articulate in very general terms what the study of Plutarch might have brought to Shakespeare's understanding and depiction of the practice of being a public persona or office holding and responsibility for a public constituency. I try here also to be sensitive to chronology (though not engaging in questions of authorship or deep debates about when the plays were written but following respected scholars on these matters) for indeed it may be the case that what Shakespeare took from Plutarch and how he engaged with Plutarch's work may have evolved over the period from 1599 (when he is believed to have written *Julius Caesar* although the play was not published until the First Folio in 1623) to c. 1608 (when he is believed to have written *Coriolanus*).[6]

9.1 A Brief Commentary on Thomas North's Translation as a Prelude to Shakespeare

As is well-known, Shakespeare consulted the Thomas North English translation of Plutarch's *Lives* for the writing of his later Roman plays. The first edition of his translation appeared in 1579 with six subsequent editions over the course of the century. It was the first full English translation of the *Lives* and indeed prior to this only a few single lives had been

---

[5] Shakespeare is thought to have written different plays simultaneously, so some have also suggested there is evidence of Plutarch's influence on *Henry V* (thought to have been written at the same time as *Julius Caesar*) as well as *Macbeth* (showing some evidence of influence from Plutarch's *Antony*, as argued by James Shapiro) but those links will not be pursued here. See James Shapiro, *The Year of Lear. Shakespeare in 1606* (New York: Simon and Shuster, 2015), 230. Thanks also goes to Misha Terramura who gave me insight into the possibility of links between Shakespeare's Roman plays and others he was writing at the time. For example, in *Henry V*, written contemporaneously with Julius Caesar, the captain Fluellen offers a long comparison between Henry and Alexander the Great, the figure that Plutarch of course paired with Caesar. This suggests a broader dialogue happening among the plays of this period. For a discussion about some of the presence of Plutarch in the non-Roman and Greek historical plays, see Miryana Dimitrova, "Taking Centre Stage: Plutarch and Shakespeare," in Sophia Xenophontos and K. Oikonomopoulou eds., *Brill's Companion to the Reception of Plutarch*, 493–511.

[6] Shapiro, *The Year of Lear*, 225 and 305.

translated into English but remained in manuscript form, most notably that of Lord Morley during the reign of Henry VIII.[7]

It is first important to recognise that Thomas North translated Plutarch from Amyot's French translation into English, either due to a lack of confidence in his command of classical languages or due to his respect for Amyot's scholarship. Still, this meant that any passages where Amyot did not adequately capture the meaning of the original Greek text, or where his wording may have been ambiguous, may have been more fully obscured. The spirit in which North translated and dedicated his treatise appears to follow the same path as Amyot, celebrating heroism and indeed praising the ruling queen Elizabeth for living up to the standards of Plutarch's own central characters. This demonstrates a continuation in North of the panegyric qualities of the Amyot translation, illustrated in part by the very invocation of the term 'illustrious' in the translation. Still, in an important pivot from the commentary on Plutarch as found in a figure like Budé, North insists that the utility of the translation is no longer for princes or queens to help model their aspirations and behaviour but for the queen's subjects. The goals of honour and courage are now ascribed to subjects in the service of their political leader. Through this we see a widening of the relevant public and thus a more capacious view of who matters when making sense of political life. North reproduces Amyot's note to the reader where he praises the educational benefit of stories over analytical philosophical accounts because it can address central questions of importance for life in ways that can appeal to a much wider group of people. As noted by Denton, there was a clear intention to widen the relevant public to a middle class, although the cost of North's editions (three times the weekly salary of a skilled carpenter) ensured that it would only be affordable for those in the upper echelons of the social scale.[8] The broader target audience of the translation did impact the substance of the translation for both Amyot and North, as both felt the need to 'domesticate' the text – that is, to render some of the practices and institutions more understandable by invoking rough equivalents in European sixteenth-century terms, something that Latin versions generally did not need to do given the greater scholarly training of the readers.[9]

---

[7] See for example James Carley, "'Plutarch's' Life of Agesilaus: A Recently Located New Year's Gift to Thomas Cromwell by Henry Parker, Lord Morley," in Felicity Riddy ed., *Prestige, Authority and Power in Late Medieval Manuscripts and Texts* (Cambridge: Cambridge University Press, 2000), 159–170.

[8] Denton, "Translation," 48.

[9] Denton, "Translation," 49. In documenting some of the liberties North took in translation, see Michele Lucchesi, "The First Editions of Plutarch's Works and the Translation by Thomas North,"

North's more Puritan sensibilities were evident in his rendition of religious themes, and there are debates concerning the accuracy of North's and subsequently Shakespeare's depictions of the various social forces at play in the Roman republic and in Plutarch's representation of it.[10] The details of these debates are beyond the scope of this study. What I seek to do is to focus in a more general way on the depiction of the public realm as it appears through a variety of seventeenth-century dramatic adaptations of Plutarch.

9.2 Shakespeare from *Titus Andronicus* to *Coriolanus*

It is not known how or exactly when Shakespeare became first acquainted with Plutarch (although the first edition of North's translation of the *Lives* appeared when Shakespeare was a teenager), nor indeed when he took inspiration from him for the drafting of some of his plays, but it is known that one early play *Titus Andronicus* represents a depiction of Roman politics and culture that is quite distinct from the more historical treatments found in the later Roman plays. It is surmised by many commentators that the later Roman plays were written in close consultation with Plutarch's commentary on Roman politics of the late republican period. Shackford speculates that the 1603 edition (the third) of North's translation of Plutarch's *Lives* edited by Richard Field may have sparked renewed interest in Plutarch for Shakespeare and helped to inspire the writing of those later Roman plays, although Spencer suggests that Shakespeare's later turn to Roman history began earlier in 1599 and that his *Julius Caesar* had already been written by 1603.[11]

In *Titus Andronicus* Shakespeare's Roman characters, including the Emperor Saturninus, were fictional creations. So the first discernible lesson in tracing the impact of Plutarch on Shakespeare's dramatic writings is that

---

in. Sophia Xenophontos and K. Oikonomopoulou eds, *Brill's Companion to the Reception of Plutarch*, 436–457.

[10] Denton takes on Christopher Pelling's somewhat more positive assessment of Shakespeare's ability to capture the gist of Plutarch's reading of Roman republicanism. See Denton, *Translation*, chap. 5, as well as Christopher B. R. Pelling, "The Shaping of Coriolanus: Dionysius, Plutarch, and Shakespeare," *Poetica* 48 (1997), 3–32.

[11] Shackford, *Plutarch*, 37. T. J. B. Spencer, "Introduction," in T. J. B. Spencer ed., *Shakespeare's Plutarch* (Harmondsworth: Penguin, 1964), 14 and 18. There are hints of references to North's Plutarch in earlier plays, including *Titus Andronicus*, but these are few and scattered and do not bear evidence of a systematic study of Plutarch's text in the way that the later Roman plays do. Shakespeare seems to have known of North's translations soon after their publication but did not take them up with the same concerted attention as for his later work until 1599. See Gordon Braden, "Shakespeare," in Mark Beck ed., *A Companion to Plutarch*, 577–591.

it shifted his focus to a somewhat more concrete historical plane for dramatic treatment of the lives of *Julius Caesar*, *Timon of Athens*, *Antony and Cleopatra* and *Coriolanus* (of course, *Timon* was set in Greece and the others at various points of history in ancient Rome). While not all the minute historical, personal and dialogical detail found in Plutarch's account of the various lives that informed Shakespeare's writing can be validated, there is a key kernel of truth in Plutarch's narratives (that of Coriolanus is placed so far back into the early history of Rome that it more than likely bears a faint relation to historical fact), verified in certain instances by similar accounts in a number of contemporaneous sources and from which Plutarch partly drew. Arguably, the relative veracity of the material, or at least the historical accuracy of the general historical context and narrative that Shakespeare gleaned from Plutarch, added to the intensity of the drama and convincing psychological feel of the plays. Still, as noted by commentators, Shakespeare did exercise a degree of poetic licence in adapting some of the historical details of Plutarch's account.[12]

As a contextual feature of interest, at the same time as the Roman plays were being written, appeal to the classical world, not just as a broad motif, but through more concrete historical detail, was directly at play in the public sphere. Warren Chernaik suggests, for instance, that James I drew explicitly on the presentation and example of Augustus to bolster his kingly aura at the time of his 1604 entry into London, calling himself "England's Caesar."[13] Here was a king following to a certain degree the prescription offered to François I by Budé in the previous century, only instead of being offered in a spirit of an endorsement of humanist learning, the Jacobean appropriation served as a symbol of legitimation and unity in the face of religious divide and political subversion. More precise historical reading of the classical heritage was becoming a currency of contemporary public life,

---

[12] For example, MacCallum acknowledges that Shakespeare transformed some of the chronology of Plutarch's account of the life of Julius Caesar, placing his defeat of the sons of Pompey five months later than it happened in order that Shakespeare could have it coincide with the celebration of the Lupercalian Festival in 44 BCE, as just one example among many where basically three years of events have been compressed into five days. As MacCallum states: "Shakespeare thus greatly alters the character of Plutarch's narrative by his ceaseless activity in sifting it, ordering it afresh, and reading into it an internal nexus that was often lacking . . . . The more carefully one examines the finished fabric, the more clearly one sees that the dramatist has not merely woven and fashioned and embroidered it, but has provided most of the stuff." (196–197) See MacCallum, *Shakespeare's Roman Plays*, 188 ff. Again, this level of detail in the transformation of the original narrative is not my focus here.

[13] Warren Chernaik, *The Myth of Rome in Shakespeare and His Contemporaries* (Cambridge: Cambridge University Press, 2011), 4.

at times for the purposes of legitimation and consolidation, and at others for possibilities of more critical commentary.

Along with historical detail, Shakespeare drew from North's Plutarch selective phrases and images. As demonstrated by J. T. B. Spencer, Shakespeare at various places in his play integrated some of North's words, adapting them to the style of his dramatic verse, especially in *Antony and Cleopatra* and *Coriolanus*.[14] The close mirroring of the language of North's translation in these later Roman plays as well as in *Timon of Athens* and especially in the life of Antony into passages of *Antony and Cleopatra*, as well as the synthesising of some of Plutarch's analysis and judgements in key dialogues of the plays are documented convincingly by various scholarly commentators.[15]

For our narrower purposes, we first turn to an early play not written with Plutarch in hand. *Titus Andronicus* was one of Shakespeare's early plays published and performed for the first time reputedly in 1594.[16] While Shakespeare appears to have had knowledge of Plutarch's work prior to this date, he did not write this play with the more intense interaction that we find in his later plays. Still, Shakespeare did consult multiple Roman sources while writing *Titus Andronicus,* which contains invocations of Seneca, Horace, Livy and other Latin texts generally taught in schools.[17] While the differences between this earlier play and the later Roman plays cannot all be explained by Shakespeare's recourse to Plutarch as a key source in the later instances, part of the shift may indeed be understood as mediated by his later study of Plutarch's work, at least insofar as his depiction of public life in Rome is concerned. Despite his knowledge of many Latin sources in the drafting of *Titus Andronicus*, there are several key features that stand out in contrast to the later treatments of Roman political history.

First is the notable bloody and violent course of events in the play, which has been a standard trope of commentary. While it may be understood as an attempt by a young playwright to capture the attention of popular classes of London in an outright physical expression of dramatic action (as Coleridge said, "obviously intended to excite vulgar audiences by its scenes of blood and horror,"), its force as a depiction of classical history would nonetheless rely on broad popular conceptions of life in ancient Rome as dominated by brutal and violent behaviour.[18] As both a foreshadowing of

---

[14] Spencer, "Introduction," 13.
[15] Shapiro, *The Year of Lear*, 230–247. Braden, "Shakespeare," 578 ff. Spencer, *Shakespeare's Plutarch.*
[16] Shakespeare, *Titus Andronicus*, ed. Jonathan Bate (London and New York: Routledge, 1995).
[17] Chernaik, *The Myth of Rome*, 61.   [18] Coleridge cited by Chernaik, *The Myth of Rome*, 69.

the violence to come in the play and a critical commentary on it, Chiron (the captured son of the Gothic queen Tamora) exclaims "Was never Scythia half so barbarous!" thus accusing the Romans of moral hypocrisy in acting more brutally than the enemies they deride, in the end becoming victims of their own brutality. It is a central message of the play. In more general terms, the actions and the historical and mythological allusions participate in a broader theme of vengeance: Tamora and the Goths seek vengeance for their capture and the killing of Alarbus, the eldest son; Saturninus for the killing of his brother Bassianus; Titus and his sons for the rape of Lavinia and the plotting of Aaron (for which Titus tricks Tamora into an act of cannibalism). As Tamora states near the end of the play in feigning an alliance with Titus to further carry out her plotting:

> I am Revenge, sent from th'infernal kingdom
> To ease the gnawing vulture of thy mind
> By working wreakful vengeance on thy foes.
> Comes down and welcome me to this world's light,
> Confer with me of murder and of death.
> There's not a hollow cave or lurking place,
> No vast obscurity or misty vale
> Where bloody murder or detested rape
> Can couch for fear, but I will find them out,
> And in their ears tell them my dreadful name,
> Revenge, which makes the foul offender quake.[19]

A second feature of the play is an overwhelming stream of competing historical and mythological allusions in the classical tradition. This includes Titus Andronicus's initial refusal to allow for the proper burial of the son he killed for defying orders; Lavinia who, like Lucretia, is raped in revenge for the killing of the captured son of Tamora; and, Lucius's political revolution in response to the rape of his sister and the tyranny of the emperor, which is an invocation of Ovid's Philomela.

A third feature is the combination of various aspects of Roman political history in one dramatic moment to form a sort of distilled version of the life of Rome, or as Braden suggests "an ahistorical phantasmagoria."[20] As just one example, at the opening of the play we are told that the reigning emperor has died and that both of his sons (purely fictional characters) lay claim to the throne. Alongside their claims, a Tribune (Marcus Andronicus) pronounces that the people have elected Titus Andronicus, a Roman nobleman and general, to be emperor. These few examples evoke

---

[19] Shakespeare, *Titus Andronicus*, 254–255.   [20] Braden, "Shakespeare," 579.

a practice of combining features of the early, republican and imperial institutions of Rome contemporaneously. Clearly the play was written with broad disregard for historical accuracy.

A final consideration in characterising the treatment of Roman history in *Titus Andronicus* is exploring its verdict on Roman public life. *Titus Andronicus* revolves around a tension within the ideology of Rome and its principled commitment to the ideal of *virtus*, alongside devotion to militarism, imperialism, and bloody conflict. The play ends in a veritable orgy of violent actions, perhaps to drive home the message of the utter incapacity of Roman public ideals to bring about ordered and peaceful civic and political life. It demonstrates that the military ethos through which the Roman rulers were able to expand their empire made peaceful governance at home an impossibility.

To a large degree, then, we might consider *Titus Andronicus* to be a critical commentary on the ethos conveyed by classical history (despite its lack of attention to more precise historical detail) and a concern for the underlying brutality of the ancient world, which allows little or no room for moderation, reconciliation and forgiveness. And as the dramatic energy in the play is driven by a struggle over succession, it should also not be forgotten that this play was written at a time when the aging Queen Elizabeth had yet to name a successor, a situation that made many Englishmen nervous over the possibility of war in the event of competing claims to the throne. In contemporary terms, however, the play can be read as Shakespeare's caution against recourse to ancient models of imperial expansion and military virtue in his own era.

If Shakespeare was denouncing the brutality of the classical military ethos as a mode of politics, why then did he return to classical themes beginning in 1599 with the play *Julius Caesar*? There may be multiple reasons for this. For one, it had since become a popular choice for staging dramatic writing at the time.[21] The setting of drama in the distant past, be it classical Greece or Rome, or medieval England, offered Shakespeare and his contemporaries a historical proxy which allowed writers to broach issues while skirting restrictions or masking their contemporary relevance.

Even here dramatists needed to tread carefully. As Shapiro tells us, Shakespeare's contemporary Fulke Grenville was convinced by his friends to destroy his play *Antony and Cleopatra* written late in Elizabeth's reign because of the clear danger in depicting an unflattering portrait of an aging queen and her lover, now a fallen soldier, just at the time when the Queen had sent her close friend and reputed lover Essex to be executed following

---

[21] MacCallum, *Shakespeare's Roman Plays*, chap. 1.

his failed military campaign in Ireland.[22] With a changing political climate in the Jacobean era after the death of the queen in 1603 it became safe to place Cleopatra on stage where her dramatic presence now could be interpreted as a gesture of political nostalgia.[23]

The need to choose an historical setting to avoid questions of loyalties and partisan struggles within England became particularly acute after the uncovering of the Gunpower Plot in November 1605. It is thought that Shakespeare had already written *Julius Caesar* in 1599, but subsequent political and security circumstances may have led him to see the benefit of continuing to write a series of plays in a similar mode. Even the choice of dramatic setting can be read as evidence of prudent public judgement.

Added to this, the 1606 Act "To Restrain Abuses of Players" outlawed any form of blasphemy on stage. One express way to avoid that dramatic temptation, which had been a common trope in earlier plays for Shakespeare, was to set plays in non-Christian contexts. For Shapiro, this also helped to influence the choice of plays that were written after the passing of this act, namely *Antony and Cleopatra, Coriolanus* and *Pericles*.[24]

Which themes or features in Shakespeare's later classically themed plays were influenced by the work of Plutarch? In the first instance, Plutarch's influence can be seen in some expositions and development of moral character. In *Titus Andronicus* the escalation of violence and horror appears to be the result of circumstances taken advantage of by those with malign and evil intentions. What we find in the later plays set in a classical context are attempts to portray the developing character of key figures as a form of moral journey. For example, *Timon of Athens* might be read as the fall of a moral absolutist, someone who is driven by a vision and by expectations of purity of motivation and action and when disappointed becomes a misanthrope through the same moral absolutist logic. As Braden notes, Shakespeare's depiction of character development offers it up as a highly personal account, making ethical decisions the outcome of intense and very individualised and privatised internal dialogues, rather than as the result of a pattern of education and training. He suggests that the enormous influence of Plutarch in the fashioning of these plays is reflected in the concern for character but with a modern twist: that is, in terms of a model of moral personhood Shakespeare offers up a much more privatised and individualised model.[25]

---

[22] Shapiro, *The Year of Lear*, 227.   [23] Shapiro, *The Year of Lear*, 266 and 271.
[24] Shapiro, *The Year of Lear*, 218.
[25] Braden, "Shakespeare," 580. See also C. Marshall, "Shakespeare, Crossing the Rubicon," *Shakespeare Survey* 53 (2000), 73–88; and G. B. Miles, "How Roman are Shakespeare's Romans?" *Shakespeare Quarterly* 40 (1989), 257–283.

What does this mean for an understanding of public life? Some have suggested that a Stoic ideal of constancy is invoked repeatedly by Amyot and North as the key virtue to denote a series of qualities including courage and gravity in Plutarch (thus a subtle process of Stoicising Plutarch in translation) and that this corresponds to an understanding of public power that holds its vicissitudes and effects as morally irrelevant to the character of one who occupies a position of power. The notion that character should be steadfast and the full responsibility of the moral agent, whatever the course of fortune, is a key feature of Stoic ethics and, as argued by Braden, an approach to moral understanding that is directly transferred into Shakespeare's later Roman plays.[26] The public realm then becomes the arena where individual and internal qualities are exposed and tested, the domain of fickle fortune. Of course, this way of characterising the moral message of the Roman plays would set them apart from earlier French traditions of Plutarch reception where light was shed on the qualities and features of public life that offer their own unique ethical challenges for the one seeking to wield that power appropriately and effectively.

Still, *Timon of Athens* may also be read as a more sober message, namely, that any attempts to achieve virtue, be it in the course of private, civic or public behaviour, will be caught up in inevitable human inconstancy and hypocrisy (As Timon states in despair: "There's nothing level in our cursed natures But direct villainy").[27] If there is a lesson to be distilled by Timon's example then perhaps it is that a more compromising and less absolutist Stoicising approach is to be favoured. ("The middle of humanity thou never knewest, but the extremity of both ends.")[28]

In the same play, a speech by Alcibiades offers another challenge to the Stoic model. In Act III, Scene V, Alcibiades is deliberating with senators regarding the fate of a soldier who resorted to violence to right his reputation. The First Senator suggests that a Stoic stance is the appropriate one to take in the face of public insult: "He's truly valiant that can wisely suffer, The worst that man can breathe, And make his wrongs his outsides, To wear them like his raiment, carelessly, And ne'er prefer his injuries to his heart, To bring it into danger." In response, Alcibiades disagrees offering a justification for acting on public injury: "Why do fond men expose themselves to battle, And not endure all threats? Sleep upon't, And let the foes quietly cut their throats Without repugnancy? If there be Such

---

[26] Braden, "Shakespeare," 581.
[27] Shakespeare, *Timon of Athens*, ed. H. J. Oliver (London and New York: Routledge, 1959), 90–91.
[28] Shakespeare, *Timon of Athens*, 108.

valour in the bearing, what make we Abroad?"[29] With regard to the soldier who resorted to violence, Alciabiades suggests that mercy is appropriate given the various situations, including public and political ones, in which an angry and active response to injury is warranted. This challenges a Stoic ethos in favour of an ethics weighing situational factors as well as public circumstances. Of course, none of the precise details of this exchange or situation are derived from Plutarch who only offers the mention of Timon's misanthropy in the *Life of Antony* as the starting point for Shakespeare's dramatic work on this character. But it is of interest that while Braden suggests that Amyot and North tended to Stoicise Plutarch (Plutarch, as we have seen earlier, was a critic of Stoicism), when taken up by Shakespeare as a source he was not fully swept up in those same tendencies.

Related to this, but on a different plane, is a questioning of the Stoic ideal of virtue as singular and unchanging, that regardless of the context and circumstances the demands of virtue would be identical. Contrary to this, we find in Shakespeare's later Roman plays a tendency to consider the unique ethos and demands of public life, illustrated through closer consideration of *Julius Caesar* and *Antony and Cleopatra*. Of course, these plays are first and foremost compelling unveilings of character, but alongside there are subtle indices suggesting a distinct conception of public life and the ways in which its normative demands may lead actors to behave in ways that contravene central tendencies of their character, i.e. where they may feel the push of public requirements or demands despite themselves and their own specific natures (or vice versa). This is not a depiction of the public realm as a realm of fortune, but rather the public realm as one in which the choice of good action is shaped by different sorts of considerations.

Key figures in this reading are Brutus and Antony. Brutus's personal history and loyalties make him a friend of Caesar, yet for public reasons, or reasons that he understands as public duty, he is compelled to plot against him. In contrast stands Antony, who is thrust into in a leading position of authority and influence following the death of Caesar but who, through his own personal loyalties, reneged on the responsibilities and calling of his public office. A study of these contrasting examples reveals the special demands and requirements of public life as depicted by Shakespeare and refracted through the lens of Plutarch.

---

[29] Shakespeare, *Timon of Athens*, 73.

The reason for Brutus's agonising when we meet him first in the play is revealed quickly with Cassius's study of his words. Recognising Brutus's less than warm reception for the people's growing inclination to claim Caesar for their king, Cassius asks "Ay, do you fear it? Then must I think you would not have it so." And Brutus replies: "I would not, Cassius; yet I love him well." This serves to reveal the tension in Brutus's mind between private loyalty and his sense of public exigencies,[30] a tension that is reflected in his later speech to the Roman people: "If then that friend demand why Brutus rose against Caesar, this is my answer: Not that I loved Caesar less, but that I loved Rome more."[31]

And what sort of reasoning leads his sense of public duty to act against someone to whom he had many reasons to be loyal? Brutus offers us a reflection on the nature of public authority and its specific ethos. There is the question of how the wielding of political power may impact certain individuals, as well as the question of the basis for Brutus's own sense of public duty. Brutus muses how holding public office can itself have a negative impact on character (or bring out latent and destructive aspects that might have otherwise remained hidden). Thus, when contemplating the rumour that Caesar will be crowned king the next day in the Senate, Brutus muses: "He would be crown'd: How that might change his nature, there's the question. It is the bright day that brings forth the adder, And that craves wary walking."[32] The broad meaning here is that the effect of being in the political spotlight, or the transparency alluded to by Plutarch, is not only an opportunity to see corrupted aspects that were already there, but can itself have a corrupting influence to the point of forcing others to watch their steps (i.e. in fear of that power being weaponised against them). Brutus goes on to reflect: "Crown him? – that; – And then, I grant, we put a sting in him, That at his will he may do danger with. Th'abuse of greatness is when it disjoins Remorse from power... ". Here, then, he notes that the granting of power may be an occasion for Caesar to work mischief and engage in unjust things, harming others without a sense of compassion. He goes on to reinforce his sense that power may change the nature of the man by suggesting that while he has known him to be driven by his reason up to now, the achievement of his ambitions will change him and lead him to excesses, "that what he is, augmented, Would run to these and these extremities." Brutus ends the soliloquy with a repetition of the image of Caesar as a budding poisonous snake, a danger for which there is

---

[30] Shakespeare, *Julius Caesar*, ed. T. S. Dorsch (London and New York: Routledge, 1955), 12.
[31] Shakespeare, *Julius Caesar*, 79. [32] Shakespeare, *Julius Caesar*, 34.

only one possible resolution: "And therefore think him as a serpent's egg, Which, hatch'd, would, as his kind, grow mischievous, And kill him in the shell."[33] While there is some sense here of a latent tendency in Caesar's person to be tempted to abuse power, there is also some suggestion that the "bright day" or the dynamics of visibility and power itself can lend itself to certain things. Brutus's decision to partake in the conspiracy against Caesar appears not to be dictated by the materials sent his way by Cassius, but rather by his own understanding of the nature of power and of its potential for corruption. What he does not see, however, is how that power of corruption can also infect those who are jealous of those achieving popularity, such as Cassius, who seeks to destroy Caesar less from a fear of tyranny and more from resentment regarding Caesar's political success, a motivation confirmed by a later speech in the play.

This soliloquy is raised by MacCallum by virtue not only of its clear departure from details of the Plutarchan source (i.e. no such speech appears in Plutarch's *Brutus*), but also in relation to Coleridge's concern that it appears to debase Brutus by suggesting that Brutus is not opposed to one-person rule or monarchy per se, but rather to the abuse of power that was expected to come with Caesar at the helm, something that seems at odds with deeper historical preconceptions of Brutus as a defender of republicanism on principle.[34] If one considers that the commentary by Brutus is not just regarding the character of Caesar in the position of monarch but rather the nature of unrestrained political power itself and how it may have an impact on the bearer of that power, then the passage becomes less alarming and stands as a principled rejection of unimpeded one-person rule. The reading presented above suggests that anyone in that position, regardless of their previous exercise of self-discipline, will have to exist in a structure of power that allows them to attack enemies without consequences and to act with no need for compassion or justification, and this possibility, while likely with Caesar, could corrupt almost anyone. In other words, while Brutus's remarks are consistent with the idea that Caesar's character may make him more susceptible to abusing power, there is also here a hint that there is a feature of singular political power itself when wielded without restraint that structurally tends to shield its holder from the pangs of pity and remorse, as a sort of internal moral bridle that may begin to fall away and facilitate abuse of power and political excess. This is not the same thing as an unqualified rejection of one-person rule on the basis of republican sympathies, but it does move in that direction.

---

[33] Shakespeare, *Julius Caesar*, 34–35.   [34] MacCallum, *Shakespeare's Roman Plays*, 201.

Of course, this soliloquy may not articulate Shakespeare's own understanding of the potentially corrupting nature of power, but only a depiction of how Brutus conceives of it and what might be merely Brutus's imagination getting the better of him. Be that as it may, as a representation of the corrupting possibilities in the holding of power it does mark a shift from the Plutarchan source. For Plutarch, abuse of power is rooted in poor character traced to inadequate education.

With regard to the question of tyranny, according to Stephen Greenblatt, *Julius Caesar* represents Shakespeare's most morally complex and politically complicated stance.[35] While his plays set in early English history depicting tyrannical moments, e.g. *Richard III*, *Macbeth* or *King Lear*, focused on dysfunctional inner psychology, social pathology or political havoc associated with the tyrant, with obvious normative implications, *Julius Caesar* depicts a set of circumstances where it is more difficult to find a space of moral purity from which to judge the just and appropriate course of action. As Greenblatt suggests, the moment of catharsis which earlier may have arisen with the death or murder of the tyrant is no longer operative in the account of *Julius Caesar* because that late republican context of mixed motivations and selective corruption makes the act of resistance to tyranny itself the final blow to collective liberty. *Julius Caesar*, we might say, offers conflicting normative accounts that make the final verdict on the assassination a difficult one. While one can sympathise with what appear to be Brutus's pure principles of a need to avoid tyranny, if the effective result of acting on that motivation is a descent into further conflict and deeper tyranny, then the question of which public principles are to be followed become less clear. We are faced with a tension between a seemingly good motive in a sense of public duty and the actual collectively destructive public consequences of acting on that motive. The suggestion, it would appear, is that when it comes to public life, purity of motive is not a sufficient guarantee of good action. It is perhaps here in coming to terms with Brutus where Shakespeare approaches the ethos of Plutarch of "Political Precepts".

Just as *Julius Caesar* can be read as illuminating the tensions between individual justifications through a sense of public duty and the effects of public action given the dynamics of public life, *Antony and Cleopatra* remains to a certain degree a reflection on the consequences of reneging on one's public duties. Perhaps the most symbolic action in the play, as well as in Plutarch's *Antony*, is the moment in the battle of Actium when

---

[35] Stephen Greenblatt, *Tyrant* (New York and London: Norton, 2018), 154.

Antony as commander refuses to continue his fight against Octavian's fleet and instead flees the battle scene in pursuit of Cleopatra. By turning his back on the pre-eminent public task at hand when control over the Roman state and empire was at stake, Antony reneges on his claims to power and authority. For Plutarch this was clearly a moment of weakness and representative of a broader deficiency of character in Antony when his desires and need for indulgence clouded his better judgement and undermined his efforts for political dominance. Does Shakespeare see Antony's turn away from public duty toward private indulgences in the same way? Not fully. For one, we are presented with a much more sceptical vision of the possibilities within the public realm. As Cleopatra tells us closer to the end of the tragedy, "'Tis paltry to be Caesar. Not being Fortune, he's but Fortune's knave, A minister to her will."[36] The suggestion here is that no principled commitment can really hold sway in public life which moves largely according to the random forces of fortune. Indeed, in a somewhat ironic twist of theme, and perhaps even to the denigration of the theme of the public, it seems that the realm of command most evident in the play (apart from the final acts of suicide) was the realm of love through which Cleopatra was able to control a good deal of Antony's decisions and actions. This inversion of public and private priorities is further reinforced by the fact that despite Antony's clear public ambition, the scenes where he returns to Rome and negotiates an initial alliance with Octavian hold much less intensity and energy for the characters than those in Egypt where the geographical divide between him and Rome is matched by psychological dislocation from his public duties due to preoccupation with his love interest. As commentators have shown, the narrative is shorn of Plutarch's clear condemnation of Antony's indulgence in a love affair, and replaced by a spirit of celebration of their love not despite but partly because of the broader context of their public tragedy. Despite the divergences in their accounts, both Plutarch and Shakespeare base the dramatic tension of the narrative on the conflicting demands of public duty and private desire.

As Stephen Greenblatt tells us, *Coriolanus*, based in part on Plutarch's account, was the last tragedy written by Shakespeare.[37] The historical context of *Coriolanus* being a very early period of ancient Rome when the poor were suffering from a long period of food shortages, had a parallel

---

[36] Shakespeare, *Antony and Cleopatra*, ed. John Wilders (London and New York: Routledge, 1995), 276.
[37] Greenblatt, *Tyrant*, 155.

in the conditions of Elizabethan England in the early 1600s. For Greenblatt, as a parallel to his earlier portrayal of Richard III, Coriolanus provides us with another example of the Shakespearean tyrant:

> here we are dealing . . . with an overgrown child's narcissism, insecurity, cruelty, and folly, all unchecked by any adult's supervision and restraint. The adult who should have helped the child achieve maturity has either been completely missing or, if present at all, has reinforced the child's worst qualities.
>
> The suite of traits brought forth by his upbringing – a proneness to rage, a merciless penchant for bullying, an absence of empathy, a refusal to compromise, a compulsive desire to wield power over others – helps to explain Coriolanus's success in war. But the question on which the plot turns is what happens when such a personality seeks to wield supreme authority not on the battlefield, at the head of the Roman army, but in the state.[38]

For Greenblatt, the play demonstrates the ill-suited nature of the haughty and tyrannical man for public office. Yet for Plutarch, Coriolanus is not understood as a fully negative model, and certainly not in the way that Antony is meant to be. There is an ambiguity in Coriolanus in Plutarch's narrative, and one of the central questions is whether those virtues for which Coriolanus was praised as a military commander both entitles him to political influence and makes him effective as a public leader. It is precisely Coriolanus's conviction that political influence is owed to him due to his military record that makes his political ambitions fall to pieces. Coriolanus fails in his attempt at election for consul due largely to his ignorance of and ultimate contempt for the people, something that is revealed further in the attacks of the tribunes. It is the spread of the truth of Coriolanus's disdain for democracy that sinks him in the end with the people. The lesson here may be that the qualities needed to best meet key demands of public life are not the same as those that bring success in other domains, especially military command. Related to this, the dominant ethos of each sphere is distinct. While military leaders may be due respect, public leaders need constantly to earn it.

In the wake of rejection Coriolanus becomes unhinged, seeking to undermine the Roman constitution, and eliminating the tribunes and the social benefits meted out by the state. When charged with treason he is unable to suitably defend himself and is sentenced to banishment. He uses the opportunity to take revenge on the city and join forces with Rome's enemies, demonstrating above all his lack of love for the homeland.

---

[38] Greenblatt, *Tyrant*, 166.

Only an appeal from his mother leads him to spare the city from slaughter. The Volscians then turn against Coriolanus cognisant of all the damage and hurt he has inflicted on their families.

According to Shakespeare, Coriolanus's failure comes from his own character weaknesses, while for Plutarch it may be a mismatch between character tendencies and political ambitions. Aspects of his personality that aided him as a military commander became liabilities in public life and politics. The nature of the public sphere, as we have seen in Plutarch, highlights the sharpest aspects of moral character, and the unwillingness to compromise and be more flexible can often bode ill in public life. Furthermore, the underlying nature of Coriolanus's ambition and his propensity for rage at any perceived slight demonstrated that his self-regard trumped concern for the public good, and this disposition meant that he could not effectively persist in his political aspirations.

Despite the multiple and intricate ways that Plutarch's narrative helped to inform Shakespeare's dramatic retelling of various moments in classical history, regarding the theme of the nature and function of public life, we can nonetheless discern a shift between Plutarch and Shakespeare's renditions. In the shift from *Titus Andronicus* to his later Roman plays, I noted how historical validity held greater importance for Shakespeare. At the same time, he appeared to better appreciate features of the classical heritage which offered resources for dramatic tension and for a veiled treatment of themes relevant in his own day. There is a sensibility shared with Montaigne in how these themes are taken up, for in highlighting the special dynamics of public life he suggests that public life can not only shed light on deficiencies of character but has the capacity to worsen them.

Furthermore, while not explicit, it becomes apparent that the way in which a life might be redeemed under these circumstances is through the commitments and virtues demonstrated in civil matters or everyday life, such as Antony's commitment to Cleopatra, or Brutus acknowledging his personal ties of loyalty to Caesar even when choosing public duty. These are contrary to the spirit in which Plutarch drafted his *Lives*, but they demonstrate a shifting sensibility and they channel the spirit in which Plutarch's material was read in the early modern period.

9.3   Corneille's *Pompée*

Comparing these dramatic adaptations of Plutarch's work in England with those of French playwrights Pierre Corneille and Jean Racine, will offer some, albeit limited, insight into how Plutarch was taken up by French dramatists in the seventeenth century. As noted by David Clarke, Plutarch's work, as popularised by Amyot, was a primary source for no less than *a fifth* of all the historical tragedies written in the century.[39] I focus on two plays by pre-eminent writers inspired in part by Plutarch's work to illustrate my key theme of the moral complexity of public life: *Pompée* by Corneille and *Mithridate* by Racine.

Corneille and Racine wrote their plays in what might be called the apogee of absolutism in France. Cardinal Richelieu's famous *Testament politique*, seen by many as a definitive statement of absolutist principles, remained incomplete at the time of his death in 1642.[40] What the *Testament* reveals is an approach to governance based on a set of key principles including an appeal to reason as the rule of public conduct, and the overriding importance of the public interest over the private, with an express repudiation of the passions and recourse to a strong sense of realism.

There are conflicting views of how Corneille's dramatic work relates to absolutist thinking. Michel Prigent, following earlier interpretation, suggests that Corneille's plays should not be analysed as cultural and ideological manifestations of seventeenth-century state hegemony. The tragic tensions depicted in Corneille's work often work to discredit a crude Machiavellianism, interpreted as a stand-in for reason-of-state politics of the era. In addition, the play of emotions, poetry, tragedy and heroism are seen as contributing to an anti-political thread running throughout Corneille's work.[41] This is distinct from but similar to Paul Bénichou's earlier argument that the celebration of honour, pride and glory in Corneille's work (including celebration of the duel) was at odds with the ideology of absolutism and the efforts of Richelieu to ensure the supremacy of the administrative and military state over the nobility.[42]

Others disagree. Claude Haas argues that Corneille's early plays in general and his *Horace* in particular are an unqualified assertion of absolutist sovereignty given that the deaths of Corneille's figures are not really tragic deaths (insofar as they harken back to a feudal and therefore outmoded notion of honour) but serve rather to consolidate the new

[39] David Clarke, "Plutarch's Contribution to the Invention of Sabine in Corneille's *Horace*," *The Modern Language Review*, 89.1 (1994), 40.

[40] Richelieu, *Testament politique ou Maximes d'Etat de Monsieur le Cardinal de Richelieu*, ed. Daniel Dessert (Paris: Éditions Complexe, 1990).

[41] Michel Prigent, *Le Héros et l'État dans la tragédie de Pierre Corneille* (Paris: Presses Universitaires de France, 1986). See especially p. 28 for the reference to Hobbes.

[42] Paul Bénichou, *Morales du Grand Siècle* (Paris: Gallimard, 1948), 55.

model of absolutist sovereignty (symbolised by the exclusion of mourning in the play).[43]

While Corneille is best known for his play *Le Cid* (1636), in the wake of the quarrels it raised (how suitable the topic was for dramatic treatment and whether he treated it appropriately), he turned, as did many of his contemporaries, to studies of eminent historical public figures. For some this trend in seventeenth-century French drama is understood as a sort of ideological turn, i.e. to convey "a lesson intended to ensure for France its own glorious future in emulation of Rome's ascent to a universally civilizing exercise of military power."[44] Indeed, Clarke suggests Plutarch was often left unacknowledged as a source in this tradition because of Plutarch's more cautious evaluation of historical figures and imperialist themes (as opposed to, for example, the more overtly Augustan ethos found in Dionysius of Halicarnassus, i.e. the *Roman Antiquities*).[45] Clarke argues that explicit praise of Plutarch did not fit with what was regarded as a hagiographic project to glorify Richelieu's state-building project.[46]

In a more nuanced way Katherine Ibbett also suggests a clear link between French neoclassical theatre of the seventeenth century, especially the later dramatic works of Pierre Corneille, and the broader reason-of-state ideology that informed the political culture and the legal and political frameworks through which plays and playwrights were allowed to function.[47] Despite a rhetorical rejection of a crude Machiavellianism, she suggests that Corneille's plays demonstrate in theoretical terms an embracing of the efficient, thereby reinforcing the general ethos of Richelieu's politics.[48]

---

[43] Claude Haas and Michael Auer, "The Dramaturgy of Sovereignty and the Performance of Mourning: The Case of Corneille's *Horace*," *Yale French Studies*, no. 124 (2013), 121–134.

[44] Clarke, "Plutarch's Contribution," 39.   [45] Clarke, "Plutarch's Contribution," 41.

[46] Clarke, "Plutarch's Contribution," 42.

[47] Katherine Ibbett, *The Style of the State in French Theatre, 1630–1660* (Farnham: Ashgate, 2009).

[48] A clear statement of her argument is thus: "in suggesting Corneille's implication in the political rhetoric he has often been thought to oppose, I mean not to argue he was a covert support of Richelieu himself. Rather, in asserting that he draws upon the same rhetorical or epistemological tools as figures such as Richelieu, I wish to show how their shared preference for the efficient over the universally good, or in Ciceronian terms for the *utile* over the *honestum*, undermines the standard of Corneille's relation to political authority and nuances our picture of the professional path of a neoclassical dramatist." Ibbett, *The Style of the State*, 125. I would come to a slightly different conclusion. My argument is that this issue is much better understood if we look at the longer picture of Plutarch reception within French political culture. Richelieu's *Testament* represents a radicalisation of some of the themes in that tradition with a hyper-emphasis on interest and efficiency over a notion of the good and honourable. Arguably Corneille, at least as far as *Pompée* is concerned, offers a nostalgic look at what he sees as an older and more honourable form of politics. He also embraces engagement with the new that does not fully repudiate a moral centre or conception of the universal good but nonetheless seeks to come to terms with some of the ongoing moral ambiguities of public life.

It might be asked whether the emotions associated with tragic drama are in tension with principles of interest-driven rationalism. In what way might we conceptualise the dialogue between what was going on in drama and the ideas informing the broader ruling climate? In addition, how might we come to terms with the way in which Plutarch's work was taken up as a key dramatic source by these authors and what complex transformations and iterations the work was subject to might make it compatible with that same political climate? To begin to answer these complex questions it is necessary to explore concrete details of a play.

Corneille expressly and for the first time acknowledges drawing on Plutarch for the writing of his play *Pompée*. It was first performed, it is thought, in 1643, that is one year after the death of the Cardinal Richelieu. The play is set in the final day of the life of Pompey leading also to the death of Ptolemy, Cleopatra's brother and political rival. Pompey (who never appears in the work) has arrived in Egypt seeking refuge after his defeat by Caesar at Pharsalus. The play explores what led to the death (though in contrast to Shakespeare and much of French sixteenth-century drama the French classical approach rejected staged violence) and its aftermath, and through this it sheds light on the competing forms of ambition harboured by key players in the drama. In his commentary on the play, or *Examen*, Corneille acknowledges that he has indulged in a small amount of poetic license vis-à-vis the historical sources, but he suggests it was done largely to adhere to the three unities of classical theatrical form (i.e. unity of action, unity of time or within twenty-four hours, and unity of place).[49] He acknowledges his use of Plutarch for the writing of this play, along with Lucan's *Pharsalia*.

This is Corneille's first play in which he deals with the Roman republican era, and the first play for which a major historical source is Plutarch. Perhaps coincidentally, it also marks, at least according to Prigent, a major shift in Corneille's depiction of tragedy in the evolution of his work.[50] Up to this point, with perhaps the most famous example being *Le Cid*, the tragic drama depicted in the plays of Corneille was internal to the hero as a tension between two deep commitments or claims, such as love and duty. Prigent argues that with Pompey the tragedy takes on a broader dimension in which the tragic hero is no longer torn between two competing claims but becomes the victim of a fate driven by political forces beyond his

---

[49] Pierre Corneille, "Examen," in H. T. Barnwell ed., *Pompée* (Oxford: Oxford University Press, 1971), 147–150.
[50] Prigent, *Le Héros et l'État*, 180ff.

control. Pompey does not even need to appear in the play, yet one can acknowledge that his demise is the result of a broader shift away from more noble and fair-minded norms in Roman public sensibilities. Plutarch himself appears to acknowledge this, for in his treatment of Pompey, despite recognising his faults, Plutarch also suggests that Pompey had good qualities especially as a public figure. These qualities can be seen in his early rise to fame, and the idea that Caesar's success was due to an ability to pursue his interests in a more crafty, rationalist way – for example, extending his campaign in France so as to commandeer more resources for good political effect and thereby engineering his advance over Pompey.[51] That approach to public life is raised initially by Cleopatra when we first meet her at the beginning of Act II:

> Les princes ont cela de leur haute naissance.
> Leur âme dans leur sang prend des impressions
> Qui dessous leur vertu rangent leurs passions;
> Leur *générosité* soumet tout à leur gloire:
> Tout est *illustre* en eux quand ils daignent se croire,
> Et si le peuple y voit quelque dérèglements,
> C'est quand l'avis d'autrui corrompt leurs sentiments.[52] (my emphasis)

> [This to their high extraction Princes shew,
> That by th' assistance of their Royal Blood
> Their Passions are more easily subdu'd.
> Their honour still the Victory will have;
> And whilst they trust themselves, they still are brave.
> All the disorders which in Kings we see,
> To others Counsels must imputed be.][53]

The general theory presented here by Cleopatra suggests that princes who are born to the expectation of achieving glory are naturally disposed to repress other immediate desires and passions in the service of a broader vision of service and a self-image of being, as in Amyot's words, "illustre." It is the mark of the upright and noble to practice *la générosité*, that is to reject narrow self-interest and to act in honourable ways without seeking any reward. This trope of seventeenth-century classicism is what Bénichou calls aristocratic pride.[54] However, sometimes flatterers and others around

---

[51] For a good overview of Plutarch's treatment of Pompey, see Jacobs, *Plutarch's Pragmatic Biographies*, chap. 6.

[52] Corneille, *Pompée*, 91.

[53] Corneille, *Pompey a tragedy*, trans. Katherine Philips in *Poems by the most deservedly admired Mrs Katherine Philips The Matchless Orinda. To which is added Monsieur Corneille's Pompey and Horace Tragedies* (London: Printed for Henry Harringman, 1678), act II, scene I.

[54] Bénichou, *Morales*, chap. I.

them can corrupt those high-minded visions and lead princes to become vicious (like her own brother Ptolemy). The suggestion is that the very ideal of becoming an illustrious ruler serves as its own form of bridle, similar to the vision defended by Budé earlier. Arguably, this was the model of a public figure exemplified by Pompey, a model that in other public figures is already eroded by the start of the play. Thus, the play can be read as a tragedy of the decline of an older political ethos.

It begins with a key political deliberation: Ptolemy holds the fate of Pompey, now a desperate defeated man, in his hands and he can grant him mercy at the risk of angering Caesar, or finish Caesar's work to destroy his rival. Ptolemy follows the advice of Photinus and Septimus to dismiss notions of justice and law in their clear statement of a crude Machiavellianism:

> Photin: Quand par le fer les choses sont vidées, la justice et
>   le droit sont de vaines idées . . .

> [Photinus: When things, Sir, are determin'd by the sword,
> Justice is nothing but an empty word]

and

> Photin: . . . la justice n'est pas une vertu d'Etat;
> Le choix des actions ou mauvaises ou bonnes
> Ne fait qu'anéantir la force des Couronnes;
> Le droit des Rois consiste à ne rien épargner.
> La timide équité détruit l'art de régner:
> Quand on craint d'être injuste on a toujours à craindre,
> Et qui veut tout pouvoir doit oser tout enfreindre,
> Fuir comme un déshonneur la vertu qui le perd,
> Et voler sans scrupule au crime qui lui sert.[55]

> [Photinus: 'Tis not a Statesman's Virtue to be Just.
> When Right and Wrong are in the Ballance laid,
> The Interest of Kingdoms is betray'd.
> Extreamest Rigour is the Right of Kings,
> When Timerous Equity their Ruine brings.
> Who fears a Crime shall ever be afraid,
> But he'll fule all, who all things dares invade.
> Who dangerous virtue, as disgrace, does shun,
> Ans to a useful Crime as swiftly run.][56]

They calculate what the force of circumstance, fortune and the weight of Roman wishes for vengeance against Pompey dictate, summed up in what

[55] Corneille, *Pompée*, 78–80.
[56] Corneille, *Pompey a tragedy*, trans. Katherine Philips, Act 1, scene 1.

Ptolemy calls "le torrent," as opposed to the principle of the justice of the matter, and resulting in Ptolemy issuing an order for Pompey's death. In response, the character Achillas notes that the action is a just one because the king has ordered it.[57]

Cleopatra declares herself on repeated occasions to be driven largely by her own ambition; however, her goal is not glory but power (she takes centre stage as a more developed political villain in Corneille's later work *Rodogune*).[58] Still, she demonstrates, unlike her brother, the power of self-regulation and independence of thought. Caesar is described as having a complex reaction to the death of Pompey by demonstrating outward sorrow but also some inward joy; however, Caesar ensures that his virtue triumphs in a demonstration of sympathy that involves crying for his former rival and taking vengeance on Pompey's killers.[59] This rivals the earlier version of the prince (invoked by Cleopatra), for whom a vision of glory serves as a moral bridle. Caesar's struggle for virtue in this case suggests that vision contains some degree of weakness and ambiguity.

As a departure (one of many) from Plutarch's narrative, Ptolemy dies due to his own foolishness and rash behaviour even though Caesar intended to spare his life out of love for Cleopatra. Cornélie, Pompey's widow and perhaps the most noble character of all in the play, declares both her respect for Caesar as well as her intention to spare no effort in educating her sons to take vengeance on him for Pompey's demise.

What is the broader lesson of this play in terms of a commentary on public life? One feature is clear, that the crude form of Machiavellianism represented by Ptolemy and his flatterers does not pay. And despite Prigent's thesis that the plot is a commentary on the tragic nature of political life itself, given that Pompey as the representative of the noble ethos is the central victim of public conflict, the play in the end does not advocate withdrawal from public matters. Cornélie will counsel her sons to engage in public life. Indeed, in one of the final monologues of the play she displays an astute awareness of the noble ends of public life alongside a recognition of the prudential and sometimes pragmatic considerations that must also come into play. She declares that she both admires Caesar for his virtue and hates him for what he has done to Pompey, and thus her sons will seek to avenge their father's death. This demonstrates a somewhat

---

[57] Corneille, *Pompée*, 83.
[58] Ibbett has a chapter devoted to this later play where she argues that Corneille flirts with reason-of-state themes and the Machiavellian ethos of mastering *fortuna*. The link drawn to Pocock's civic humanist Machiavelli may be a bit stretched here.
[59] Corneille, *Pompée*, 108.

nuanced judgement, and with it a rejection of both moral and political absolutism. Here, then, in the hands of Corneille, the matter of Pompey is less about individual character and moderation through self-regulation, and more about the complicated terrain of public life itself where Caesar, played in different ways by Ptolemy and Cleopatra, faces the murder of his former more virtuous ally and tries to do right. The politics here walk a tightrope between the heinousness of sheer cruelty and opportunism (as exemplified by Ptolemy and his advisors) and what is portrayed as the growing ineffectiveness of older models of nobility (in the person of Pompey himself). It is telling that the voice of reason and good character in the play is that of a woman who is forced to take on a public role through tragic circumstances and whose ultimate action in the public realm will be felt only indirectly through the actions of her sons. The other public figures are all tainted to a certain degree. One might suggest that Corneille has taken the careful and wry commentary on the paradoxes of public life in Montaigne's appropriation of Plutarch and elevated it to a worldview of somewhat epic proportions.

There are two more general and important issues here. In terms of the context of seventeenth-century French politics and the performance of this play in the wake of the death of Cardinal Richelieu the message is not fully evident. While detractors might seek to reduce the doctrine of *raison d'état* famously championed by Richelieu to a form of Machiavellianism and thus see in Corneille's treatment here both a caricature and rejection of the doctrine through its representation in the character of Ptolemy, a more serious reading of Richelieu's work would acknowledge that there is a key place for both divine law and reason in his approach to public life, as well as a concern for the public interest and the repudiation of flatterers. While the *Testament* does not invoke glory as a motive in public life in the way that it appears in the classical context, and so for Richelieu princes are to be bridled more by their sense of interest than by their need for glory, it does reflect a certain understanding of a special ethos in public matters.[60] While the exact parameters among the good, prudent, pragmatic and the bad may not map clearly onto the ambiguities of public life as highlighted by Corneille in the play, the acknowledgement that ambiguities do exist is something that both texts share. Nonetheless, the idolisation of Pompey that results from his unfortunate end and the clear admiration he received from Caesar and others may also be an expression of a sort of political nostalgia for a time of greater moral clarity in public life on the part of

---

[60] Richelieu, *Testament politique.*

Corneille. While espousing a form of political realism at the end of the play, one that is still circumscribed by its clear rejection of a heinous model of public life and corrupt motivation, Corneille also does not hide a sense of nostalgia for a less complicated, perhaps feudal, model. I will not enter into the argument as to whether Corneille's later plays demonstrate a judgement that politics is inherently tragic, or whether they offer a more positive exploration of contemporary currents of political realism.[61] I am only suggesting here that the first play in which Corneille draws explicitly upon a Plutarch text can also be seen to engage with a much more nuanced tradition of discussion of public ethics in the French case, one that acknowledges the coexistence of the good, prudent and pragmatic and seeks to navigate an honourable public course with certain realist assumptions without falling victim to the worst in public ethics.

The broader message to be found here is that concern about the potentially vicious or even corrupting nature of public life is not a revelation of the contemporary era, but something that was acknowledged in the early modern period. The answer in that era was not to deride and discount all those in public office, nor to turn away for the most part from the realm of the public, but to acknowledge the moral complexity of that world and to seek to navigate it with better intentions in mind while at the same time recognising that it is within one's power to identify, call out and avoid what is worst.

9.4　Racine's *Mithridate*

As a final piece of the analysis, I look to a play by Racine also inspired by the same life of Pompey from which the details of Corneille's play *Pompée* were drawn. Here we see an interesting shift in the subject matter. While in Corneille's play we saw a certain decentering of Pompey in that, despite being the main subject, he never appears (technically his ashes appeared in an urn but not the full man). For Racine, we are led beyond Pompey to a full dramatic treatment of one of his most notorious enemies in the east, the mighty King Mithridates VI. It is part of a more general trend found in Racine's work of creating dramatic narratives around figures who were Rome's enemies or the women often mentioned in passing in the *Lives*. This is not to say that those historical figures around whom Plutarch

---

[61] The first is a statement of the overall position of Prigent in *Le Héros et l'État* and the second that of Ibbett in *Style of the State*.

centered his *Lives* were not the subject of dramatic representations throughout the period. One author notes that in France between 1550 and 1650 there were four adaptations of the death of Antony and three of the death of Caesar in tragedy and other tragic dramas that included the death of Pompey, and the lives of Camma and Coriolanus.[62] What also is clear is that by the mid-seventeenth century there was a new sensibility that looked with greater interest and curiosity at what might have initially been described as the supporting characters of Plutarch's narrative. For example, while Bacon could only muse in his essays about which female historical figure Plutarch could possibly compare with Elizabeth I, several decades later in France a remarkable number of Plutarch's female heroines are taken up as a focus for the theatre. This was part of a broader cultural movement from roughly 1630–1650 that celebrated female heroism.[63] Given the laconic treatment accorded these heroines in Plutarch's account, those narratives, as Mazouer argues, were often taken up with a healthy dose of poetic licence. Nonetheless, this demonstrates both the centrality of the work of Plutarch as an important cultural resource, and the creativity and elasticity of the tradition in making space for newer sensibilities. The question that concerns us here is whether in these moves we also see any shifting representation of the nature of public life.

Racine had read Plutarch from an early age and indeed had annotated Plutarch's works when he was a teenager as part of his education at Port-Royal. He more broadly shared a close affinity with ancient authors and was able to read them in both Latin and Greek. He appeared to distill clear lessons from the psychological depictions of Plutarch, acknowledging parallels with figures in French history, both medieval and modern.[64] If we accept Bénichou's assessment that there is a clear distinction in the portrayal of politics in Racine as opposed to Corneille, filtered in part through Racine's immersion in Jansenism and their broadly noted presumption of the pervasiveness of self-interest in part through the triumph of absolutism that left no more space for the imaging of a heroic politics, what aspects of the Plutarchan source were still a matter of inspiration?

In his preface to the play, Racine explicitly acknowledges his use of Plutarch as a source in his dramatic rendering of the life of Mithridates VI,

---

[62] Charles Mazouer, "Les Mulierum virtutes de Plutarque et la tragédie française du XVIIe siècle," in Olivier Guerrier, ed., *Plutarque de l'Age classique au XIXe siècle* (Grenoble: Jerome Million, 2012), 45–54.

[63] Mazouer, "Les Mulierum virtutes de Plutarque." The key historical figures taken up by seventeenth-century dramaturges include Aretaphila, Camma, Chiomara and Timocleia.

[64] On Racine's notes on Plutarch, see Ranum, *Artisans of Glory*, 282–285.

the famous king of the Pontus who valiantly resisted Sulla, Lucullus and Pompey, three of Rome's best generals. Indeed, Mithridates appears in those three *Lives* of Plutarch. Along with Plutarch, Racine is acknowledged to have consulted Florus, Dion Cassius and Appian. It is suggested that in historical terms Plutarch was most important for introducing Racine to the figure of Monime, Mithridates's favourite of the harem, who provides the lynchpin of dramatic tension in the play.[65] Of course, Plutarch's psychological insight was also valuable.

A curious quid pro quo is evident in the setting of this play. Of course, Pompey and Mithridates were pitted against each other as enemies and warriors. Corneille devotes a play to one and Racine to the other, and both draw in part from the same Plutarch source. One play offers an expression of nostalgia for a lost ideal of good and noble political action, while the other concerns tyrannical rule. Both plays also begin with the announcement of the death of the central character and in the aftermath of a major battle where they were defeated. Yet for Racine the apparent death of Mithridates, like many of the character's tactics of deception in governance and on the battlefield, is revealed as a ruse. Mithridates, revived by Racine, appears and declares his defeat at the hands of Pompey. Both characters share a similar fate in the end with their final personal demise brought on by betrayal by those they most trust – Ptolemy in the case of Pompey and Pharnace in the case of Mithridates. Through recourse to the same Plutarch source while writing with the spotlight on Pompey's rival Mithridates, it might appear that Racine is (once more) sparring with Corneille.[66]

There is an epic aspect to Racine's depiction of the last bulwark against the imminent triumph of Greco-Roman civilisation. As noted by Mitchell Greenberg:

> Mithridate garbs itself in the most spectacular of rhetorical displays, where politics and desire, arrogance and cruelty, and narcissism and megalomania create the image of this last wounded but still dangerous and magnificent "father" whose defeat represents not only his own ruin but the inevitable obliteration of an entire world order. Mithridate will be defeated, the Orient will fall under the sway of Rome, and the course of world history will be changed. Racine's new Oriental tragedy portrays the death throes of not

---

[65] Gustave Rudler, "Introduction," in Racine, *Mithridate* (Oxford: Basil Blackwell, 1943), vii–viii.

[66] It is acknowledged that Racine in previous instances, such as regarding *Bérénice*, sought to compete with and outdo the dramatic writing of Corneille. On this point see, for example, Gerard Defaux and Michael Metter, "The Case of Bérénice: Racine, Corneille and Mimetic Desire," *Yale French Studies* 76 (1989), 211–239.

only a defeated warrior but an entire world, a world that has resisted Roman tyranny and that here, in its last stand, is about to be engulfed. A man, an empire, and a man who is an empire are about to be wiped off the map of the world, and in their stead, we are led to believe, Rome will finally establish her dominion over the last vestiges of those Eastern barbarians who have resisted and threatened the onward march of (Western) civilization.[67]

Was it this that made it one of Louis xiv's favourite tragedies?[68] Along with the momentous political circumstances and clear Orientalist implications for traditions reaching on and past Montesquieu's depiction of despotism, what is the lesson we can draw from Racine's play in terms of the theme we focus on here – namely, the specific ethos of public life?

We are told that Mithridates has been killed in a battle setting up the dramatic tension between his two sons Xiphares and Pharnace. Xiphares is at odds with his brother, given their opposing attitudes towards the Roman enemies (Pharnace is more well disposed and Xiphares very hostile), but most significantly because both love their father's betrothed, the Greek woman Monime. It is largely from Plutarch that Racine has gathered details about Monime and her unhappiness as the wife of Mithridates, although Racine has spun those relatively few details into his own invented version of drama and intrigue. Among other things the tragedy offers a case study in tyranny, both domestic and political, and is made more dramatic through the depiction of the tyrant's unravelling.

Once it is made known that Mithridates is in fact alive, his tyrannical and cruel nature is understood in the reaction of sheer horror from his son Pharnace who remarks that both sons will be executed if the king knew of their desire for Monime. He describes his father thus: "Amant avec transport, mais jaloux sans retour,/ Sa haine va toujours plus loin que son amour." (353–354) Earlier in the play they acknowledged his skills as a warrior and enemy to the Romans and paid tribute to his "prudence ordinaire" (4).

Mithridates does not trust his sons and asks for a full account of their behaviour during his absence, and in extreme anger he denounces Pharnace's supposed treachery. In a long soliloquy ushering in Act III, he reveals his general state of paranoia (literally all surrounding nations he perceives are out to get his treasures) and his delusional mentality as well as

---

[67] Mitchell Greenberg, *Racine: From Ancient Myth to Tragic Modernity* (Minneapolis: University of Minnesota Press, 2009), 153. ProQuest Ebook Central, http://ebookcentral.proquest.com/lib/utoronto/detail.action?docID=496590. Date consulted 8 June 2019.

[68] As noted by Greenberg, *Racine*, 162, citing the notes of Georges Forestier in his Pléaide edition of Racine's theatre and poetry.

his colossal ambition, deciding that his only favourable option is to march on Rome itself, a campaign which he envisages will be joined by all of Rome's enemies. Further, through deception he elicits a confession from Monime that she is in love with Xiphares, setting up the final drama of Mithridates's vengeance. Xiphares tries to warn Monime: "je n'ose vous dire à quelle cruauté/ Mithridate jaloux s'est souvent emporté." (1205–1206) Monime accepts her fate with dignity and refuses Mithridates's advances. Pharnace convinces the troops to rebel against Mithridates's plans for further war, seeking instead to negotiate a peace with Rome. The tyrant rages with vengeance and vows to punish both his sons as the Romans invade the palace.

In Plutarch's account of Mithridates there are only a few clues concerning the psychology of the tyrant, including a suggestion he had mortally poisoned another of his sons, his refusal of titles of honour because he wanted grander expressions of veneration, and his suicide in the face of Pharnace's mutiny. These are taken up by Racine and given greater psychological texture and depth.

While to some extent a love story (which is why some critics suggest it fails as a tragedy), the play also offers clear models of honourable and dishonourable conduct. Xiphares strives to be the good man in the bad regime, refusing to renege on his father's demands, but in doing so embarks with him on a wildly imprudent campaign. Pharnace is the corrupt man and bad son, but his political calculations to ally with the Romans demonstrate a degree of good political pragmatic judgment unmatched by his kin. In the middle stands Mithridates who embodies the worst pathologies of bad leadership. Here deception and manipulation are used to an extreme (he appears to have been the source of the rumours concerning his own death and he deceives Monime into declaring her love for Xiphares). The narrative demonstrates the paradox of how in a position of absolute political power Mithridates remains a victim to his own impulses of anger, rage, jealousy and sense of inadequacy as well as a pressing need to dominate and control all who surround him. His inability to live up to his need for control pressures him into greater and greater political delusion with what is here portrayed as an impetuous and foolish plan to march directly on Rome. (In historical reality, Mithridates's plan to march on Rome in alliance with Rome's enemies and his effective use of guerrilla tactics came close to being successful.)[69] In the play as Mithridates demands more he

---

[69] See Adrienne Mayor, *The Poison King* (Princeton NJ: Princeton University Press, 2010).

commands less. By the end of the play, he is not even able to control the
condition of his own existence, failing in his attempt to poison Monime
and initially failing even to kill himself. Racine's play and his loose
appropriation of Plutarch offers his readers insight into the pathologies
of the despotic personality and the dangers of personal rule taken to an
extreme.

So how does this depiction relate to traditions of reflection on the
public realm and the broader account of Plutarch reception?
Mithridates provides an exemplary case of an egregious violation of
the norms of public life. As we have seen, Plutarch himself did not
disavow the need for some form of theatrical dimension in public life,
minimising the visibility of one's faults and putting one's best face
forward. However, Mithridates uses deception in the service of consolidating his own crumbling power and pursuing his own private fantasies
rather than promoting the good of his people for whom he never
appears to give a thought. While he may claim to fight for liberty
(816, 821) in the face of what he calls the "tyranny" of Rome (804,
861, 1659), as noted by H. T. Barnwell, there is nothing in his most
important speech that reveals adhesion to any political principle or
principled objective.[70] In consequence his appeal to liberty appears to
be nothing more than a rhetorical ploy to secure his own position,
confirmed by the fact that he is willing to risk the life of his already
exhausted soldiers (many follow Pharnace in mutiny at the end of the
play) and subjects in a highly imprudent campaign to conquer Rome.
His reputation for cruelty to the point of poisoning his own son offers
further evidence of his abuse of power as he seeks popular and familial
loyalty through fear rather than affection. We are left with another clear
contrast: while Corneille uses the life of Pompey and the work of
Plutarch to put forward tentatively a morally complicated politics in
the wake of a fading idolised vision, so Racine looks to Plutarch to help
shed light on a clearly tyrannical and ineffective approach to governance. In the wake of Jansenism and the dismantling of the heroic ethos,
given that any seemingly high-minded motive was now regarded as
a manifestation of more deeply rooted vices, Plutarch's work still could
help to demonstrate that some vices were worse than others and that the
nature of the political realm could exacerbate and indeed make more
visible those vicious tendencies despite all attempts of dissimulation.

---

[70] H. T. Barnwell, "'Moins roi que pirate': Some Remarks on Racine's *Mithridate* as a Play of
Ambiguities," *Seventeenth-Century French Studies* 24.1 (2002), 182.

9.5   Conclusion

In this chapter we have explored the ways in which Plutarch's work was taken up by early modern dramatists, notably Shakespeare, Corneille and Racine. Of course, this in no way exhausts the extraordinary number of dramatic adaptations of Plutarch's work in the sixteenth and seventeenth centuries. The concern throughout this chapter has been to explore how some of the most iconic adaptations of Plutarch were used to develop themes that were already circulating in political reflection, namely the nature of the public sphere and the ethos that was specific and appropriate for it. This was done sometimes through a rejection of a stance of moral absolutism as a basis from which to judge political and social life (e.g. Shakespeare's *Timon of Athens* and Corneille's *Pompée*), sometimes in the acknowledgement of how the occupation of public office can have a certain effect on personal psychology (Shakespeare's *Julius Caesar* and to some extent Racine's *Mithridate*), and sometimes through reflection on how ambition goes wrong and becomes tyrannical (Shakespeare's *Coriolanus* and Racine's *Mithridate*). Apart from demonstrating the dramatic potential of Plutarch's narratives, these various adaptations tend to offer a complex portrait of public life. Contrary to a dominant ethos of Stoicism, public life was not seen as the exclusive arena of Fortune, immune or morally neutral to the effects of carefully considered action by individual characters. We see in the representation of Brutus, Antony and other characters, proof of the possibility and impact of individual deliberation and action on public life that is not just driven by fate. We also see in these plays recognition of the distinct ethos of public life, whether from the unsuitability of military norms in public life, as in the example of Coriolanus, the disconnect between private loyalty and public duty, as in the case of Brutus, or in a combination of respect for Augustus Caesar while educating sons to bring about his demise, in the case of Cornélie. In addition, we see that the type of appropriate action in the sphere of public life should not be reduced to a form of Machiavellian cynical calculation but a weighing of considerations that does not repudiate a notion of public good and subjects its effective implementation in a set of hard choices and an understanding of certain constraints.

Plutarch in the Long Eighteenth Century with a Focus on British and Irish Political Thought

Plutarch's place as a reference in the literary culture of the English-speaking world of the eighteenth century is extensive. A search in the digital catalogue of Eighteenth-Century Collections Online (ECCO) reveals just under 15,000 references to texts where Plutarch is mentioned explicitly at least once. His name is invoked for reasons ranging from the offer of anecdotal evidence from ancient history (such as strict Spartan building codes and the harshness of a Spartan child's education mentioned by Mandeville in *The Fable of the Bees*, Remarks S and X) or the filling out of historical detail for dramatic representations of ancient figures; the history of morality and the study of character; a defence of publicly sponsored education for reasons of citizenship; the denouncing of a pursuit of universal monarchy largely targeted at the expansionist policies of Louis xiv; and for various discourses on natural religion and superstition.[1]

This chapter offers an analysis of a few examples of this broader set of English and Irish encounters with Plutarch's work over the course of the long eighteenth century. The aim is to shed light on how Plutarch's work was used in political argument with special reference to conceptualising the public realm. These usages will be compared to features of the previous centuries in the history of early modern political thought, as well as to developments in French political thought of the same period.

---

[1] See, for example, Bernard Mandeville, *Fable of the Bees*, 3rd ed. (London: Tonson, 1724), 247–248 and 277–278; Nathaniel Wanley, *The history of man; or, the wonders of humane nature in relation to the virtues, vices and defects of both sexes* (London: R. Basset, 1704) in terms of a history of morality; Erasmus Saunders, *A domestick charge, or the duty of household governors* (Oxford: Lichfield, 1701), which offers a defence of public education drawn from Plutarch's description of Lycurgus's Sparta (130); George Smyth, *The Vanity of Conquests and universal monarchy: being a succinct account of all the great conquerors and heroes* (London: R. Smith, 1705); John Wilkins, *On the Principles and Duties of Natural Religion* (London; 1715) and Edward Stillingfleet, *Origines sacrae: or, a rational account o the grounds of natural and revealed religion* (London: R. Knaplock, 1662 and 1724).

Recourse to Plutarch as a source was in no way indicative of an author's position on the debate known as the Battle of the Books or the ongoing question of the Ancients vs. the Moderns.[2] Despite being an ancient source, the distilled lessons and wisdom from Plutarch were deemed by select English and French authors to be transferable in various ways to a modern context. While Jonathan Swift and Abbé Mably draw from Plutarch in a broader championing of the ancients over the moderns, Abbé de Saint-Pierre combines recourse to Plutarch with an allegiance to modern principles. Where a distinction might be perceived between French and Anglo-Irish reception of Plutarch in this period, what will be borne out here and in Chapter 11, is that thinkers like Dryden and Swift took up their positions in a selective and piecemeal way in a relative spirit of cautious commentary, while in France the versions taken up and championed by Mably, Saint-Pierre and Rousseau all tended in their own way towards a strident plea to refashion established practices and norms.

In continuation of themes going back to the sixteenth century, abundant citation of Plutarch is found in works in English in the tradition of popular moralist commentary. For example, *The Gentleman's Library* drawing heavily on Plutarch offers an overview of the rules of behaviour in areas of life, including friendships, how to handle oneself in marriage, and the dangers of impertinence.[3] We will limit the analysis here to the *Lives* as a reference for commentary on public life. This is perhaps to the detriment of commentary on Plutarch in the work of key intellectuals in the American colonies, including Benjamin Franklin, John Adams and Alexander Hamilton, to name a few. Some headway has been made in this field, but the subject remains open to further investigation.[4]

10.1   John Dryden (1631–1700)

Many eighteenth-century authors working in English owe their knowledge of Plutarch to John Dryden's 1683 translation *Lives of the Ancient Grecians and Romans Compared*. In reality, forty different translators were sought

---

[2] Michael Werth Gelber, "John Dryden and the Battle of the Books," *Huntington Library Quarterly*, 63.1 and 2(200), 139–156.

[3] Anonymous, *The Gentleman's Library: containing rules for conduct in all parts of life*, 4th ed. (London: S. Birt, 1744).

[4] See Philip Stadter, "Alexander Hamilton's Notes on Plutarch in his Pay Book," *The Review of Politics* 73 (2011), 199–219. In footnotes 2–6 Stadter offers a helpful review of some of existing literature on these figures in relation to Plutarch.

out by Dryden to translate the text directly from the Greek (and for the first time into English) according to Judith Mossman, a noted Plutarch scholar.[5] Dryden, who by then had already distinguished himself as an eminent literary figure, having been appointed England's first Poet Laureate in 1668 did not do any of the translation (although he was an avid translator especially from Latin), but he set the tone in which the work was received. Dryden provided a *Dedicatory Letter* in praise of his patron James Butler, first duke of Ormond (1610–1688), and composed a *Life of Plutarch* which was given a place of pre-eminence in the collection. It was not new to attach a life of Plutarch to translations of the *Lives* (Dryden himself mentions that of Rualdus in his piece), but the tone of Dryden's life was new to the tradition. Translation of the work was justified by Dryden for reasons of form, but arguably issues of substance also played a role, as reflected in Dryden's version of Plutarch's life.[6]

The association between Dryden and Ormond dated to at least 1671.[7] In its defence of his patron against charges of betrayal of the Stuarts in civil war Ireland, the *Dedicatory Letter* demonstrates Dryden's loyalty to the Stuart monarchy against political pressures from both Roman Catholics (though Dryden became a convert to Roman Catholicism later in his life) and radical Protestants. Further, Dryden defends Ormond's personal integrity as well as his effective management of public matters.

Dryden begins the *Dedicatory Letter* in defence of the ancients over the moderns, lavishing praise on Plutarch in the process.[8] He notes the need for a new English translation of the *Lives* given that North's was based on a French version which itself was "lamely taken from the Greek original." In addition, he notes that the English language has become more polished, hence the need for a more intelligible and grammatical version of the work.

Praise of Ormond is couched in a condemnation of both radical Protestant and Catholics striving to subordinate the Crown and principles of succession to spiritual considerations and sectarian preferences. His

---

[5] Judith Mossman, "Plutarch and English Biography," *Hermathena*, 183 (2007), 92.

[6] As the *Dedicatory Letter* notes in reference to North's translation: "His *Lives*, both in his own esteem, and that of others, accounted the Noblest of his Works, have been long since render'd into English: But as that Translation was only from the French, so it sufffer'd this double disadvantage, first, that it was but a Copy of a Copy, and that too but lamely taken from the Greek Original: Secondly, that the English language was then unpolish'd, and far from the perfection which it has since attain'd: So that the first Version is not only ungrammatical and ungraceful, but in many places almost unintelligible." Note here the lack of appreciation for the quality of Amyot's translation.

[7] Jane Ohlmeyer and Steven Zwicker, "John Dryden, the House of Ormond and the Politics of Anglo-Irish Patronage," *The Historical Journal* 49.3 (2006), 679.

[8] John Dryden, "Dedicatory Letter to Plutarch's Lives," in *The Works of John Dryden, vol. 17. Prose 1668–1691* (Berkeley: University of California Press, 1971), 228.

concern is especially focused on the political and religious wings of the Revolution, given that both Republicans and Schismatics "hold Kings to be Creatures of their own making, and by inference to be at their own disposing."[9] The duke is praised for having prevented the spread of revolutionary politics and radical Protestant fervour to Ireland amid the upheaval of the English Civil War.

In his *Life of Plutarch* Dryden is not, for the most part, engaging in the same sort of analysis of soul-craft that is found in Plutarch's larger opus. The type of evidence available to Dryden is almost exclusively statements from Plutarch's own work. The analysis of his written work will not necessarily reveal deeper insights into the nature of his person, even if it may reveal his moral aspirations (e.g. the famous passage cited again by Dryden: "I had rather be forgotten in the memory of Men, and that it should be said, there neither is, nor was a Man called Plutarch, then that they should report, this Plutarch was inconstant, changeable in his temper, prone to anger and revenge on the least occasions.") Its status is closer to a panegyric than a life. He offers insight into the character of Plutarch's father through the anecdote in "Political Precepts". Dryden remarks on the wisdom and humanity of the father who gave the young Plutarch the advice not to trumpet his own diplomatic achievements but to share recognition for completion of a mission with a colleague, prizing collegiality, and defusing envy and self-effacement over self-promotion.[10]

While raising doubt, as Amyot before him, concerning the veracity of the letter to Trajan, Dryden nonetheless includes a translation of it for his readers. He acknowledges that the writing of lives can only give us a partial account of events historically speaking, a judgement which may have contributed to the lowering of Plutarch's cachet in the modern era. Nonetheless, Dryden concedes that this approach offers better moral instruction. He suggests instruction largely works by exemplars, through the force of moral examples that "allure rather than force" people to virtue, as akin to basic principles of Aristotelianism.

While dominant in the Enlightenment, this account sidelines the recognition of character flaws in many of Plutarch's characters, as well as the function of parallels in his biographies (although Dryden does acknowledge the presence of tensions within individual characters of Plutarch).[11] The use of examples is not solely or even predominantly that the reader imbibe and reproduce those examples through habit prior to reflection,

[9] Dryden, "Letter," 232.   [10] John Dryden, "The Life of Plutarch," in *Works*, 239–288.
[11] This is noted about Sylla in particular. See Dryden, *Works*, 282

rather Plutarch calls upon the reader to actively engage in deconstructing the parallels he builds and to draw through analysis the lessons of the comparison to gain deeper understanding of the qualities and disposition of the person studied (among other things). This is an aspect of Plutarch's work that was well understood by Montaigne, though it appears to have been lost to many Enlightenment readers.

According to Rebecca Nesvet, the most important contribution of this *Life of Plutarch* read in tandem with the *Dedicatory Letter* was to make this classical and pagan author more palatable for Christian orthodoxy, and to support Charles II's policy of religious toleration.[12] Whereas North identified Plutarch as a pagan author with no insight for matters of faith, and others went so far as to almost call Plutarch a Christian, Dryden insists on Plutarch's paganism as a priest of Apollo but also makes the suggestion that there is some overlap between Plutarch's monotheism and certain tenets of a Christian outlook. He furthermore draws parallels between the ability of both Ormond and Plutarch to combine colonial administration at the periphery (in Ormond's case, Ireland) and loyalty to the centre, (i.e. the Stuart monarchy and the Roman Emperor). As Nesvet states: "By confirming Plutarch's paganism and paralleling his political career with that of his own patron, Dryden demonstrates that adherence to a faith outside the one his readers were expected to follow should not disqualify a rational individual from political involvement or leadership."[13] This was a vision of toleration, albeit a limited one, because it depended on all accepted religious faiths to be loyal to established political authority and was limited to monotheism. It also reflected an understanding of faith that was not exclusively fideist but acknowledged the possibility of rationally grounded spiritual understanding or of natural religion.[14]

The broader significance of Dryden's presentation of the new translation of the *Lives*, a presentation through which a great deal of the work was to be perceived and received, is that it appeared to largely enforce the thrust of Plutarch's contribution as a panegyric and emulation model. This is not surprising given the background of decades of political upheaval in which a response of unqualified praise in defence of a besieged political patron was prudent for reasons of both personal status and principled commitment to ideals of toleration. As Plutarch reception carried into the eighteenth century, the model of critical assessment of character continued to

---

[12] Rebecca Nesvet, "Parallel Histories: Dryden's Plutarch and Religious Toleration," *The Review of English Studies* 56.225 (2005), 424–437.
[13] Nesvet, "Parallel Histories," 425.   [14] Nesvet, "Parallel Histories," 431.

give way to panegyrics as the core of Plutarch's work in the *Lives*. It was, in turn, a double logic of emulation that inspired and gave rise to *The British Plutarch* (1762), which was used to give an account of and celebrate the achievement of heroes from more recent times.[15] It went through at least four editions by the end of the eighteenth century. While sharing the spirit of education, the new genre dropped the parallelism and thereby also the subtle art of comparison that could serve to incite deeper and more thorough reflection on the content of the *Lives*.

In the wake and popularity of the Dryden edition of Plutarch's *Lives*, a plethora of translations began to be seen in England over the course of the eighteenth century. The first to appear in 1727 was an English translation that sought to correct or perfect that of the Dryden through further recourse and reference to the French translation by André Dacier (1651–1722).

Patricia Gray has noted, that on the French side after the huge wave of editions of the *Lives* in Amyot's vernacular translation, some supplemented with Charles de l'Ecluse translations of the lives of Hannibal and Scipio Africanus, after 1645 no further edition of Amyot's translation of the *Lives* appeared after 1645 until the 1780s.[16] The mid-seventeenth century did see three editions of a translation of the *Lives* by Abbé Tallemant. Thus, the key edition for much of eighteenth-century commentary was that of André Dacier (a Huguenot hired to become the king's librarian after his conversion), although some of the work of translation should also be attributed to his wife, Anne Dacier, who was an accomplished and famous classicist in her own right. Anne Dacier also offered an influential contribution as a strong defender of the ancients against the moderns with here stinging criticism of Alexander Pope's translation of Homer.[17]

The Dacier edition appeared under the same title as Amyot's *Les Vies des hommes illustres*. First published in 1694, it appeared again in 1721 on a subscription basis, with new editions in 1734, 1735, 1762 and 1778. In Chapter 11, I will remark briefly on the spirit in which this translation was issued, as the extensive marginal notes made it an important contribution for the interpretation of the text. Still, the Amyot translation had not been

[15] Thomas Mortimer, *The British Plutarch; or biographical entertainer. Being a select collection of the lives at large of the most eminent men natives of Great Britain and Ireland; from the reign of Henry VIII to George II*, 12 vols. (Perth: R. Morison, 1762); also, Joseph Cradock, *The life of John Wilkes, esp. in the manner of Plutarch* (London: J. Wllkie, 1773).

[16] Gray, "Subscribing to Plutarch."

[17] Anne Dacier, *Remarks upon Mr. Pope's Account of Homer prefixed to his translation of the Iliad* (London: E. Curll, 1724).

fully repudiated, for it was again reissued in 1783, 1784 and 1801. According to the re-issuing publisher, the Dacier translation was no longer speaking to the new generation (Dacier's editorial comments written in the 1690s were by then were almost 100 years old) whereas the direct and simple rendition of the text by Amyot was thought to have a more universal appeal.[18] An upshot of this history of edition is that many large private libraries had at least one copy of either the complete works of Plutarch or his *Lives*, though some not in the vernacular French.[19]

The English translation, which merged the Dryden edition with corrections from Dacier claimed to incorporate findings of further research that had offered new insight into existing manuscripts and provided a better account of certain passages that had been obscure in previous versions. It also included some of the comparisons omitted in previous versions, as well as Dacier's own composition of comparisons which had been lost. Given that the Dryden edition had been shared by forty some translators, the work was uneven; thus, the Dacier edition was defended as being based on better manuscript sources as well as providing a consistent and better translation throughout. In addition, Dryden's own life of Plutarch, while included in the Dacier edition, was also accompanied by Dacier's own version of the life of Plutarch in which he sought to correct what he perceived to be Dryden's many errors in his account of the career and trajectory of Plutarch (e.g. whether or not he travelled to Egypt or to Sparta, when he travelled to Rome and whether he was given the dignity of consul in Rome).[20] In a similar spirit of clarity, Dacier offers extensive footnotes to his translation of the *Lives* through broader and deeper historical and cultural background so that the reader might better understand the text. Further, the editor of Dacier's translation into English (whose name remains unidentified in the edition consulted) wrote not only a new preface comparing Dacier's life of Plutarch to that of Dryden, but also offers commentary on the historical and linguistic accounts and explanations offered by Dacier in the notes. In later editions of the same compilation editors explicitly state that with each new edition more corrections and revisions were made with diligent review in comparison to the Greek text.[21] These editions were printed with corrections and improvements almost each time: 1727, 1749, 1758, 1763, 1769, 1774. Also, in 1762 an abridged version of the text appeared.

---

[18] Gray, "Subscribing," 36.   [19] Gray, "Subscribing," 37.
[20] "Preface," In *Plutarch's Lives in eight volumes* (London: J. Tonson, 1727).
[21] *Plutarch's Lives in six volumes* (London: J. and R. Tonson, 1758), vi.

By the end of the eighteenth century in England the reworked Dryden version of the *Lives* was surpassed by a new translation, again directly from the Greek, by John and William Langhorne (with five editions in twenty-four years).

The sheer number of editions of the *Lives* printed in English in the eighteenth century provides ample evidence of the centrality of Plutarch for literary culture. Indeed, the preface of the first Langhorne edition in 1774 claims that Plutarch's *Lives* has been "more generally sought after" and "read with greater avidity" than any other book.[22] As Pierre Briant notes in his study of the historiography of Alexander throughout the long eighteenth century, the *Lives* remained throughout the period a key source of exempla for all manner of argument in history, politics and morals, an observation borne out by the data cited earlier from ECCO.[23] So what are some of the distinctive ways his work was used or invoked for reflections in political argument and political theory related to the theme of the nature of the public sphere?

10.2   Jonathan Swift (1667–1745)

Plutarch has been identified as one of Swift's favourite authors, and it shines forth in his work.[24] Plutarch appears to inform Swift's basic orientation to politics in considering the central questions of public life to discern how both institutions and leaders can and should impact the ethical temper of a community.

At the time of the Restoration (1660) and despite a population of 5.5 million in England and Wales, only roughly 300,000 had a right of suffrage (that is, one fourth of the adult male population and restricted to those owning a certain amount of property).[25] In this context, Jonathan Swift's politics have been a matter of contention. He approved of 1688 and

---

[22] *Plutarch's Lives, translated from the original Greek, with notes critical and historical and a new life of Plutarch*, eds. John Langhorne and William Langhorne (London: Edward and Charles Dilly, 1774).

[23] "Since antiquity, exempla drawn from the Lives of Illustrious Men had regularly and abundantly nourished books of history, politics and morals, and inspired the elaboration of collections made in the manner of the ancients." Pierre Briant, *The First European. A History of Alexander in the Age of Empire* (Cambridge, MA: Harvard University Press, 2017), 21. As my discussion demonstrates, by the eighteenth century it appears that many intellectuals had moved on from North's translation and were no longer wedded to that title adapted from Amyot.

[24] J. H. Hanford, "Plutarch and Dean Swift," *MLN* 35 (1910), 181–184; William Halewood, "Plutarch in Houyhnhnm land: A Neglected Source for Gulliver's Fourth Voyage," *Philological Quarterly* 44.2 (1965), 185–194 and William Eddy, *Gulliver's Travels: A Critical Study* (Princeton, NJ: Princeton University Press, 1923).

[25] J. A. Downie, *Jonathan Swift. Political Writer* (London: Routledge and Kegan Paul, 1984), 8.

the 1701 Act of Settlement as necessary to secure liberties and thwart tyranny, yet he also was a close associate of the Tory leaders in the final years of Queen Anne's reign and saw himself as a champion of the ancient constitution. While he sometimes called himself a Whig, both parties were subject to his searing satire, and so to some degree he is better understood as standing some distance from both and more clearly identified with 'old Whig' principles (which nonetheless placed him closer to his contemporary Tories than Whigs, perhaps somewhat akin to how political theorists perceive Edmund Burke at the end of the eighteenth century).[26] What appears to resonate most clearly in both his journalistic tracts on contemporary politics as well as in his literary works, is an appeal to a version of model of virtue politics, where instead of ancient classical philosophy Swift shows a knowledge and sympathy for Plutarch in repeated examples. He acknowledged that he had been "long conversant with the Greek and Roman authors" and found himself "a lover of liberty."[27] Indeed his first published political work was entitled *A Discourse of the Contests and Dissensions between the Nobles and Commons in Athens and Rome, with the Consequences they had upon both those States* (1701) where, through a parallel history, he comes to defend Whig lords collaborating with the Crown in making treaties with Louis XIV's France over the heads of the Commons.[28] Swift invokes Plutarch directly to suggest that the cause of the civil war in Rome can be traced to the populist-like strategies of both Pompey and Caesar, drawing on popular support to pull down the nobles. This strategy, he argues, led to "all encroachments of the people" as well as Caesar's eventual tyranny.[29]

Thus, Swift voices his preference for a balance of power among Commons, Lords and monarch and his wariness towards unrestrained popular power, especially in the wake of the English Civil War. He was also critical of the use of royal prerogative to infringe on the rights and privileges of property owners and opposed a standing army in times of peace. While garnering Whig acclaim for this work, and with some overlap with Whig positions on certain issues, in other matters, such as Swift's lack of support for Dissenters in the Church, Swift did not align himself fully with Whig principles, hence his own description of himself as an "old Whig."

Swift wrote a series of articles in support of the Harley ministry (1710–1714) policy in a publication called *The Examiner*, in which he invokes

---

[26] Downie, *Swift*.   [27] Downie, *Swift*, 67.   [28] Downie, Swift, 67.

[29] Jonathan Swift, *A Discourse of the Contests and Dissensions between the Nobles and Commons in Athens and Rome, with the Consequences They Had upon Both Those States* (London: John Nutt, 1701), 36.

Plutarch's work on several occasions. In one instance Swift suggests he will apply Plutarch's principle of biography to show the essence of character in the quieter actions and behaviour, but it is a method he uses to demonstrate the character or spirit of the contemporary English parliament.[30] Through this he defends the decency of the parliament in their decision to denounce the attempt upon the minister Mr Harley, as well as their decision to adjourn for a week when it was heard that the Speaker of the House had lost his eldest son. Later on, writing anonymously for *The Examiner,* he defended his own record and responded to criticisms he was writing to pursue his own ambitions by invoking Plutarch's discussion of Pompey in battle with Caesar "when it was not his Interest; merely because he was a man of that honour and modesty, he could not bear a reproach; neither would he disoblige his friends; but broke his own measures, and forsook his prudent resolutions, to follow their vain hope and desire."[31] He then suggests that it might have been better to act like a Phocion who refused to take up battle with the enemy. Still, his journalistic interventions in political debate can be regarded somewhat suspiciously given how close Swift seems to have been with the prime minister and his associates, to the point of being allowed to attend inner cabinet meetings on occasion.[32] This position of influence was, of course, short lasted when the death of Queen Anne in 1714 ushered in the reign of King George I and Harley and Bolingbroke were subject to impeachment (under charges of treason for having wished to alter rules of succession in favour of the Jacobite line) at the hands of the House of Commons now under the influence of the Whigs.

Swift was at odds with Walpole, not only due to Walpole's possible implication in the South Sea Bubble Scheme, which had disastrous effects on Ireland, but also on the grounds of basic constitutional positions.[33]

---

[30] Jonathan Swift, *Political Tracts. By the author of Gulliver's travels,* 2 vols. (London: C. Davis, 1738), vol. 1, 237–238.

[31] Swift, *Political Tracts,* vol. 1, 341.   [32] Downie, *Swift,* 148.

[33] "To Swift, the Revolution had restored the equilibrium of the 'ancient constitution' of King, Lords and Commons, re-establishing the balance between the three elements crucial to the Gothic concept of mixed monarchy. In common with other 'Country' thinkers, Swift argued that, far from endorsing the effects of the Revolution, Whig politicians had pursued the further corruption of the constitution to the situation which obtained in 1726. Walpole and 'upstart monied men' like him, having 'ousted the traditional rulers' – the 'natural aristocracy' which 'governed in the national interest' – 'governed entirely for their own self-interest'.

Walpole's attitude was far different. He believed that the Revolution of 1688, far from restoring an ancient constitution, had established a mixed monarchy for the first time, removing the threat of absolutism posed by successive Stuart kings. These gains had to be consolidated at all costs, and so his main energies were devoted to defending the achievements of 1688 from the, largely imaginary, Jacobite threat. He was unable to appreciate Swift's concern for the rights and privileges of the Irish,

Opposition to Walpole's ministry fuelled a great deal of the satire in Swift's *Gulliver's Travels* (1726) where he also builds upon themes and literary modes rooted in Plutarch. Indeed, according to F. P. Lock, *Gulliver's Travels* represents a shift in Swift's interjection in political debates. From a position of critic of personalities and policies in contemporary political life, Swift also demonstrates in *Gulliver's Travels* a deeper conversation with broader philosophic traditions; that is, an engagement on more fundamental issues of character, virtue, and faction in politics.[34]

In form, Swift's work portrays various parallel societies to engage the reader in a thoughtful consideration of the ethical strengths and weaknesses of each. It continues the genre of parallel history first used by Swift in the 1701 *Discourse*.[35] In terms of the substance of commentary, given Swift's rejection of a specialised administrative class, Lock regards More's *Utopia* as an inspiration for Swift over and above Plato.[36] While it is true that both More and Swift's model societies are committed to peace rather than war, in contrast to Sparta, the added and distinct allusions to Plutarch are evident in both (as shown in my discussion of More in Chapter 5 and through affinities in Swift's work with themes of Plutarch as developed in this chapter). The Platonic spirit in both can well be understood via the common thread of Plutarch.

The race of Houyhnhnms, more horse than man, function as the Stoic ideal privileging reason, friendship, and benevolence, but rejecting all emotional motivation as legitimate, hence their inhuman form.

> As these noble Houyhnhnms are endowed by Nature with a general dispos-
> ition to all virtues, have had no conceptions or ideas of what is evil in
> a rational creature; so their grand maxim is to cultivate reason, and to be
> wholly governed by it. Neither is reason, among them, a point problemat-
> ical, as with us, where men can argue with plausibility on both sides of
> a question but strikes you with immediate conviction; as it must needs do,
> where it is not mingled, obscured, or discoloured by passion and interest.[37]

The narrative of this stage of Gulliver's saga, all the while invoking Plutarch's polemics against the Stoics, also invokes the thrust of his

---

or his fears for the Englishman's liberty and property. His main political objective was to achieve stability so that a Stuart restoration would be impossible. Far from endangering liberty, Walpole believed he was safeguarding it, even in Ireland, from the threat posed by Popery and the Pretender. His own position as Prime Minister confirmed the security of the Protestant Succession." Downie, *Swift*, 258–259.

[34] F. P. Lock, *The Politics of Gulliver's Travels* (Oxford: Clarendon Press, 1980).

[35] Downie, *Swift*, 275.   [36] Lock, *Politics*, 20.

[37] Jonathan Swift, *Gulliver's Travels* (London: Collins, 2018), 261.

moral essay "Gryllus" in which a shipwrecked Ulysses embarks on a conversation with Gryllus (a sailor who had been transformed by Circe's magic into a pig) and deliberates on the respective virtues of their different conditions. In Gryllus, the aptitude of animals for virtue, with a natural tendency to moderation and the avoidance of human extremes, is displayed in the same way through Swift's race of intelligent horses. Both authors appear to be offering the portrait of ideal features of virtue through the example of a living animal, while suggesting in the same portrayal that such an ideal is too much for humans to aspire to.

Examined in a slightly different way, Halewood and Higgins have suggested that the Houyhnhnms offer a clear parallel to Lycurgus's Spartans as virtuous republicans for which all aspects of life are regulated through a lack of money and luxury, a lack of foreign entanglements, very little book learning and a moderate and simple lifestyle, and who rule over a subjected and brutalised class, the Yahoos (compared, of course, to the Spartan subjection of the helot farmers).[38] For Halewood, this appears to suggest that Swift approved of the Houyhnhnms, given that some have suggested Plutarch regarded the Lycurgan experiment as praiseworthy for offering a model of *achievable* human perfection.[39] For Higgins, Swift's depiction of the Houyhnhnms as horses suggests that while he approves of the vision, he acknowledges it as an unattainable ideal.[40] However, as I have shown in Chapter 1 of this book, Plutarch's judgement of Lycurgus and Sparta in general was ambiguous, and to a certain degree he offered criticism of the regime and its people for being too harsh despite their noble aspirations. Thus, in the same way that Plutarch depicts the Spartan regime as harsh, Swift's clear highlighting of the cruelty of the regime, with the equine masters meeting to consider the genocide of their Yahoo slaves, demonstrates his acknowledgement of the deficiencies and moral blind-spots in a regime that would prefer to see itself as replicating the highest moral principles.[41]

This reading also falls in line with Swift's high church of Ireland commitments, which is clearly at odds with the notion that the pagan Spartans are exemplary of the best possible human life. In addition,

[38] Halewood, "Plutarch in Houyhnhnm Land," 186–187 and 194. The importance of the Spartan example for Swift is also argued by Ian Higgins "Swift and Sparta: The Nostalgia of *Gulliver's Travels*" *The Modern Language Review* 78.3 (1983), 513–531.
[39] Halewood, "Plutarch in Houyhnhnm Land," 194.   [40] Higgins, "Swift and Sparta," 529.
[41] "One of these grand assemblies was held in my time about three months before my departure ... the question to be debated was whether the Yahoos should be exterminated from the face of the earth?", Swift, *Gulliver's Travels*, 263.

Houyhnhnm political life bears little resemblance to Swift's advocacy for a well-structured and balanced constitutional authority rooted in a strong historical legitimacy to guard against corruption. A community of largely self-regulating and independently virtuous individuals is far removed from his advocacy for a strong church and state. Whichever the ultimate determining factor, read in this way Swift shows himself to be a particularly astute reader of Plutarch, as is evident in other of his invocations. What is especially noteworthy when we understand the Houyhnhnm land in this light is that in contrast to his French Enlightenment counterparts in their adaptation of the Spartan example – particularly Mably as we will see – Swift appears to offer an appropriation of Plutarch that is closer to the critical and inquiring spirit of Plutarch's own position.

We also see in Swift's appropriation of Plutarch themes an aspect that is more fully modern. The concern about the Spartan regime for Plutarch demonstrated not a pessimism regarding the possibility of achieving a moral ideal, but rather an understanding of some of the ways in which human actors had faltered in their attempt to attain a moral ideal. In the hands of Swift, the motif of a politics of virtue as a self-sustaining principle of a regime is subject to double criticism. With the leadership of horses who exercise a consistent and passionless ethos that is insensitive to the well-being of other sentient beings, Swift infuses the Plutarchan motif with greater scepticism regarding both its desirability and its viability as a political model. We leave Swift not thinking how we might soften the harsh edges of a politics of virtue, but with a deeper questioning of where to rank virtue in relation to liberty, humanity and indeed sensibility, as features of political life in the present.

10.3 Further Invocations of Plutarch in Eighteenth-Century Commentary

In other debate in political theory, Plutarch was often invoked in matters related to metaphysics, the genealogy of religion (especially in relation to Egypt in his Isis and Osiris) as well as civil religion, by such writers as Ralph Cudworth and William Warburton.[42] He also was regarded as a good source for education in practical ethics.

Some drew direct lessons from Plutarch's accounts of the ancient world. As one example, Edward Wortley Montagu distilled from Plutarch an ethos of republicanism to serve as a remedy for decline and corruption in his own

---

[42] See Ralph Cudworth, *The True Intellectual System of the Universe* (1743).

political context. He advocated that Great Britain establish a national militia following the practices of Sparta and Rome for which a military spirit brought discipline, independence and the mitigation of factionalism.[43]

Others, including David Hume (1711–1776), read Plutarch with a greater sense of historical distance. Hume suggests that Plutarch's subtle and complex portrayal of the mixed qualities of his subjects combines with a more general ancient sensibility that virtue or qualities and deficiencies were not a direct emanation of the individual will, but emerged indirectly through the qualities of character through which the will was habituated. For Hume, then, despite Plutarch's defence of philosophical education, Plutarch's work offers doubt about whether virtue could be shaped by institutional means. The modern alternative (presumably seeing individual interest as a prime motivation) presents strategies to shape behaviour through sanctions of reward and punishment, treating morals in the same manner as civil laws.[44] Hume's discussion raises the question of the continuing relevance of Plutarch's approach to modern sensibilities in ethical and political theory.

L. M. Stretch also draws on Plutarch to transform and cast a more critical eye for the modern era on the theme of public ambition.[45] He begins an analysis of Plutarch's account of Marius, a talented and successful soldier who rose in power and influence in Rome throughout his life, marrying Julia, the aunt of Caesar, and becoming consul seven times. Still, the force of his ambition led him to seek more glory even at the age of seventy in taking on the war against Mithridates. He was opposed in this by the consul Sulla, resulting in civil war and Sulla's seizure of power. Marius suffered a humiliating fall from privilege, slaughtered in the swamp to which he had fled. For Stretch, the example of Marius serves not only to shed light on the pitfalls of excessive ambition, a repeated theme through-out the *Lives*, but offers an occasion to rethink the category of heroism itself. He brings his readers to acknowledge that there is little that separates the vices of Marius and that of other ancient and modern so-called heroes such as Alexander the Great, Julius Caesar or Louis XIV. Despite their somewhat different fates, Stretch suggests that they are all tainted by the same pernicious degree of vice and he questions the broader weakness of

---

[43] Edward Wortley Montagu, *Reflections on the rise and fall of the ancient republicks. Adapted to the present state of Great Britain* (London, 1769).

[44] David Hume, *A Dissertation on the Passions* (Oxford: Oxford University Press, 2014), section IV, 438.

[45] L. M. Stretch. *The Beauties of History or pictures of virtue and vice, drawn from real life: designed for the instruction and entertainment of youth* (Dublin, 1788), 2 vols.

humankind who ascribe the category of hero to such individuals who stake the fulfillment of their ambition on the "fatal art of destroying their species."[46] Stretch critically deconstructs the very idea of heroism, which had become the lens through which much modern reading understood Plutarch. It demonstrates a greater contemporary sensibility to the welfare of ordinary subjects and citizens, and an epicurean spirit questioning the worth of public ambition. This mirrors the tone in which William Temple invokes Plutarch reflecting critically on the dangers of a love of power.[47] Thus, for a certain number of thinkers, Plutarch's work offered a cautionary tale, less of examples to follow than of pitfalls to avoid in the spirit of curtailing ambitions.

It is doubtful Plutarch himself was advocating such levels of ambition for his own readers, especially given his context living in a province under Roman imperial rule in first century CE. The prominence of his subjects served as assurance that all his readers would know of those exemplars that served as a common reference point in a practical discussion on character and action. Nonetheless, Stretch's approach exemplifies and perhaps explains the epicurean spirit in which not only Plutarch, but a more general concern regarding the importance and specificity of public life became increasingly vilified and reduced to a veiled projection of power-hungry impulses. While this modern sensibility has the benefit of turning attention to those groups and individuals who are victims of the abuse of power, it also suffers from its own blind-spot in not recognising a need for continued discussion on what constitutes an appropriate wielding of power. Given an ongoing need for public life, along with greater sensitivity not only to its misuse but also its potentially malignant impact, it might appear even more imperative to reflect on the ethos that could sustain its most responsible and effective functioning.

10.4 Conclusion

This chapter has offered a brief look into how Plutarch was taken up in eighteenth- century English political thought. We see here a divide in tendencies. While some follow the lead of Bacon and Hobbes taking up the

---

[46] Stretch, *The Beauties of History*, 59.
[47] "although this love of power be so general, when it is possessed beyond a certain degree and measure, it is almost constantly fatal to interest, virtue and felicity. It inflames the most criminal and destructive passions, it corrupts the most humane and gentle natures. What, indeed, so adverse to moderation, to humanity, to equal justice as the dangerous and stimulating consciousness of being above all account or control." William Temple, "Of Unrestrained Power" in *Moral and historical memoirs* (London 1779).

theme of the public realm, leading to greater and greater cynicism regarding the nature, purpose and possibilities of public life and ambition, others extend earlier Renaissance traditions of reflection and read Plutarch as a more general moralist. With Dryden, Plutarch was read as a resource of political reconciliation through a broad moralist lens. With Swift, Plutarch is invoked largely in the spirit of commenting on the possibilities and limits of legislating public morality within a modern context. Other British writers took up Plutarch in the spirit of a cautious moralism, using his account of well-known public figures in the ancient world to denounce strong public ambition and gesturing towards a contemporary ethos of moderation and restrained gratification.

As we turn to Enlightenment France in the final step of this study, we will see a greater tendency to see in Plutarch a source of institutional models for public life and policy, while at the same time a revision or rejection of Plutarch's philosophical approach to the nature of good character and its development.

CHAPTER 11

Plutarch in French Enlightenment Thought: The Abbé de Saint-Pierre, the Abbé Mably and Jean-Jacques Rousseau

As a final piece of the narrative, I explore in this chapter three important iterations of Plutarch and his political thought as received in French Enlightenment thought. Each in its own way amounts to an odd mix of reverence and subversion. Overall, I suggest that the innovations in reception ushered in by these theorists demonstrate a notable departure from some of the foundational principles of the tradition of public humanism. I assess some of the broader significance of this departure here and in my conclusion.

Charles Irénée Castel de Saint-Pierre, best known as the Abbé de Saint-Pierre, (1648–1753), Gabriel Bonnot de Mably (1709–1785) and Jean-Jacques Rousseau (1712–1778) all bear witness to the extraordinary impact of reading Plutarch on the intellectual development of their generation, and all looked to Plutarch as a central component of their political teaching. Yet in the process of articulating and coming to terms with that impact, each thinker engages with Plutarch's legacy with new considerations and ideals. We find through these different ways of appealing to Plutarch not only a more capacious reading of his message, but also, of more significance for this study, a departure from the principles of 'political humanism' through which Plutarch was first received in the early modern European tradition. Each of these figures represents a distinct challenge to that tradition. For the Abbé de Saint-Pierre the most salient measure of public good is utility as defined by measurable contributions of human benefit in all areas of culture and philosophy, thereby minimising the distinct contributions of governance or the distinct nature of the public realm. For Mably, the measure of effective political rule and the nature of political justice is a singular vision of personal virtue, often making the work of politics a matter of sorting out those of good faith and commitment from those of bad faith, and promoting the former against the latter, risking the weaponisation of virtue. This replaces an earlier model of addressing policy challenges with a complicated process of seeking justice, reconciliation, and concord. The broader complexity of Rousseau's model of governance, while offering benefits of a theory of liberty as autonomy, also harbours inadequate means toward achieving public good More specifically, Rousseau's approach risks obfuscating the need for concerted deliberation and a process of trial and error as well as attention to how policy is implemented, how public expectations come into play and how they are managed. This model of government minimises the centrality of political judgement in governance and appears to reduce the work of the public realm to periodic expressions of the general will.

Of course, this admittedly selective array of eighteenth-century appropriations of Plutarch in political thought in no way covers the many ways in which Plutarch's thought was taken up with significant implications for politics. As one leading example, Pierre Briant has masterfully traced interpretations of Alexander the Great throughout the long eighteenth century, showing how various thinkers drew on classical sources, including Plutarch and Arrian.[1] These interpretations ground the competing arguments concerning imperialist practices that were being intensified by European powers. Central to this account is Montesquieu, who despite his rejection of despotism and cruel practices of conquest, does draw from Plutarch's work "On the Fortune or Virtue of Alexander" to develop a defence of the 'civilising' and 'humane' work of Alexander in Persia and India, setting forth part of the ideological background of contemporary Orientalism.[2] Other thinkers, such as Mably, were highly critical of Montesquieu's defence of Alexander and drew on other classical sources to demonstrate the weakness of Montesquieu's account. Indeed, Plutarch, as we have seen, singles out some of Alexander's moral failures in his life of Alexander, in contrast to the celebratory tone of the essay that is used as a source by Montesquieu. Thus it is important to remember that Plutarch was not accessed as a source in isolation, and often part of the work of appropriation meant sorting through various accounts and assessments by classical authors on similar themes or events. Through this process there can be no one version of Plutarch that emerges. What I am seeking to achieve in this chapter is more modest than a broad account of Plutarch in eighteenth- century political reflection. I demonstrate that in relation to reflections that offer a depiction of the public realm while drawing on Plutarch, select thinkers of the French Enlightenment veer away from the vision of politics associated with Plutarch in an earlier century. Perhaps this

---

[1] Briant, *The First European*.
[2] This defence of Alexander in Montesquieu is found in chapter 14, Book 10 of the *Spirit of the Laws*. See Montesquieu, *Œuvres complètes* 11, ed. Roger Caillois (Paris: Gallimard, 1951), 388–391.

is to be expected. Nonetheless, I will articulate these shifts more explicitly so that we are in a better position to assess both the losses and gains associated with them.

11.1 Eighteenth-Century French Editions of Plutarch's *Lives*

Some background on the editions and vernacular translations of Plutarch's work circulating in the eighteenth century may be helpful in setting the stage for the analysis. As noted in Chapter 10, after a flurry of editions of Amyot's translations of both the *Lives* and *Moralia* in the late sixteenth and early seventeenth centuries, the pace of the issuing of these editions slowed down considerably by the mid-seventeenth century. In the wake of the decreasing uptake of this translation, there were two alternative translations of the *Lives* issued. The first, by the Abbé Tallemant, appeared in the latter seventeenth century. The second, as mentioned earlier in connection with later iterations of the Dryden translation, was a more popular eighteenth-century translation accompanied by expansive explanatory notes by André Dacier (1651–1722). Dacier's position as Royal Librarian helped to encourage a new generation of readers of Plutarch's work in Enlightenment France, harnessing the moral utility of the *Lives* with its poetic and agreeable facets to the cause of enlightened absolutism.[3] His wife, Anne Dacier, was also an accomplished translator and there is some evidence that she also contributed to the Plutarch translation but was given no explicit credit for her work in this regard.

In analysing the paratextual writing of this translation we can better discern the driving principles which helped to inform it. In the *Dedicatory Letter* provided for readers in the 1721 edition, Dacier offers his translation to Louis XV, who was about to come of age and ascend to the throne. He notes how the reading of Plutarch's *Lives* can offer useful insights about leadership and politics for the new king. He compares a king's rule to a majestic river, suggesting that it does not just enrich the soil of its origins, but can bring benefits wherever it goes.[4] It is therefore important that the king act for the good of all. In this regard, knowledge of the *Lives* can serve as a mirror to help the king make their morals and actions conform to the most beautiful, worthy, and dignified standards, in other words,

---

[3] Eric Foulon, "Le Plutarque de Dacier," in Olivier Guerrier ed., *Plutarque de l'Age classique au XIXe siècle* (Paris: Jérôme Million, 2012), 161–172.

[4] André Dacier, "Au Roy," in *Les Vies des Hommes Illustres de Plutarque reveues sur les mss. Et traduites en français* (Paris: Clousier et al, 1721). Online at https://books.google.ca/books?id=CJpmAAAAcA AJ&printsec=frontcover&source=gbs_ge_summary_r&cad=0#v=onepage&q&f=false .

mimicking what is admirable in Plutarch's accounts, and repudiating what is defective. Dacier sees the major thrust of the work as providing models of moral insight for the powerful, as a sort of bridle of virtue, rather than ideals of grandeur and glory, which had been the thrust of Budé's presentation of the *Lives* for the king in the sixteenth century.

In his Preface, appealing to a tradition stemming at least from Montaigne, Dacier also suggests that in terms of the general readership there is an even greater case for a broader utility of the work for the reader and common man, not just political elites.[5] He invokes Democritus who spoke of the importance of instruction in history to avoid repetition of error. Plutarch's insights into the morals and internal psychology of his subjects bring the otherwise calcified actors of the ancient world to life.

Dacier also defends his offer of a new translation despite the grand work of Amyot. He suggests that the language of Amyot's translation is elegant but outdated. This not only affects the spirit in which the work is received, but can also distort its meaning for the reader, thus making the earlier version "dangereux pour les moeurs" [dangerous for morals] due to the imprecision and licence in the language of the sixteenth century.[6] This is in addition to the various mistakes and hazy translations found in Amyot's text. Furthermore, as he proudly notes, Dacier adds commentary to his translation to make it more accessible to even the least versed in classical history. His effort is one of widening and deepening the readership, to make it accessible to young adults. A more accurate translation can shed better light on the text's more subtle nuances and meaning for a wider audience. The broader implication here, of course, is that Plutarch's lessons are largely applicable to all spheres of life, and not oriented in any unique way to the morals and actions of public life.

In terms of his approach to translation, Dacier remarks that where the expression may appear too terse or subtle, he has completed it to make the meaning more understandable to the reading public. He also takes greater license than many translators might allow in deciding to make up for the four comparisons or *synkriseis* missing from the manuscripts by drafting and including those as an integral part of the translation. In broader terms, Dacier's justification of more extensive historical contextualisation and commentary on the text in the form of notes is an indication that

---

[5] For my analysis of the Preface and notes on the text I have consulted a later printed edition of the work for easier access than the online version (the later one being printed after the Revolution did not include the original letter of dedication). André Dacier, "Préface," in *Les Vies des Hommes Illustres de Plutarque traduites en français, vol 1* (Lyon: Amable Leroy, 1803).

[6] Dacier, "Préface," *Les Vies*, xiii.

knowledge of and insight into the classical past was no longer taken for granted. The ancient world was to some degree both an enigma and a source of moral inspiration.

As one indication of the tone of translation and commentary it is of interest to see how Dacier treats the life of Lycurgus, especially give the pervasive and influential place of this life in eighteenth-century commentary in France. The first notable place where his presence is felt is in the note on the first actions of Lycurgus when taking the throne. Plutarch tells us that one of the first things Lycurgus did when he took office by popular demand was to travel to Delphi to consult the oracle about the constitutional design he had in mind (forged in part after his travels to Crete and elsewhere). Plutarch tells us nothing more than that Lycurgus sought Apollo's judgement on his plans. However, in the editorial note, Dacier takes a blunter civil religion approach suggesting that Lycurgus's motivation was to give the appearance of a sanction from the god for his legislative project, much like Minos before him did in Crete. Thus, as Dacier notes "La superstition a de tout temps eu tant d'empire sur les hommes, qu'il n'est aucun Législateur qui n'ait persuadé aux peoples à qui il vouloit faire recevoir ses loix, qu'il était en commerce immédiate avec la Divinité."[7] [Superstition has had in every time such power over men that there is no legislator who has not persuaded people over whom he wished to rule and have accept his laws that he was in direct communication with God.] It is a much more sceptical take on the veracity of appeal to religion for political purposes, an attitude, while not originating with Dacier, that informed a current of discussion concerning the role of religion in political life throughout the eighteenth century, culminating famously in Rousseau's *Social Contract*.

Another of Dacier's interventions is important in relation to the ongoing theme of thinking about the public good. At the point in the narrative where the people begin to resist the imposition of great constitutional changes Archelaus, the co-reigning king of Sparta (a system with a dual monarch), bears testimony to Lycurgus's gentle nature, suggesting that he does not even have the force to be "méchant aux méchans" [mean to the wicked]. Dacier's editorial note for this passage suggests a much different normative code for those holding political power. As he states: "C'est un défaut à un Prince d'être trop bon, et de n'avoir pas la force d'être méchant aux méchans; car alors c'est foiblesse. Pour un Prince, c'est être véritablement bon que d'être méchant avec justice." [It is a defect of a

---

[7] Dacier, note i in *Plutarch*, trans. Dacier, "Lycurgue," *Les Vies, vol. 1*, 220.

Prince to be too good, and to not have the strength to be mean to the evil; for then it is weakness. For a Prince, it is to be truly good to be mean with justice.][8] The passage marks both a basic and a fundamental commitment to justice while acknowledging that the public sphere requires that those who have a commitment to justice carry themselves with strength of purpose and permit leeway in action.

In commenting on the famous attributes of Lycurgus's regime especially as related to the regulation of property and luxury, Dacier repeatedly suggests how fragile and ultimately unworkable many of these regulations became: heavily weighted currency made commerce difficult; regular meals in common and exceptions to sumptuary laws for the Ephors created resentment from other classes and undermined the laws' efficacy.[9] Dacier's anxiety over how this constitutional ideal could destabilise basic precepts of commercial society can also be seen in Plutarch's later commentary on the role of the helots and how the Spartan citizen was discouraged from taking on manual labour and seeking wealth. Dacier suggests here that Socrates was opposed to this feature of the Spartan model, and that he regarded manual labour as in no way dishonourable for a free man, an observation further endorsed by Dacier with the words, "et il n'y a rien de plus vrai." [… and there is nothing truer.][10]

In broad terms, then, we might say that Dacier's Plutarch opened avenues of moral reflection for a wide breadth of the literate population in France. Furthermore, it attempted to reconcile the Plutarchan discourse of virtue and good character with a defence of commercial society and the principles of governance associated with enlightened absolutism. The translation was re-edited numerous times throughout the eighteenth century, and like Amyot before him, rendered into English.[11]

11.2   Abbé de Saint-Pierre

The Abbé de Saint-Pierre offers a curious case of Plutarch reception. In general terms and despite an interest in classical history, he is known as an innovator who clearly favoured the moderns over the ancients, and who

---

[8] Dacier, note n in *Plutarch*, trans. Dacier, "Lycurgue," *Les Vies, vol. 1*, 222.

[9] Dacier, notes f to l in *Plutarch*, trans. Dacier, "Lycurgue," *Les Vies, vol. 1*, 232–234.

[10] Dacier, note x in *Plutarch*, trans. Dacier, "Lycurgue," *Les Vies, vol. 1*, 279.

[11] Plutarch, *The Lives in eight volumes. Translated from the Greek. With notes historical and critical from M. Dacier.* (London: J. Tonson, 1727). This English version, as either a direct English translation of Dacier's work, or a translation from the Greek to which English translations of Dacier's notes were added, appeared in 1758, 1763, 1769 and 1774, and eventually succeeded by the Langhorne translation of the *Lives* in the later eighteenth century.

had various schemes for the improvement of governance, society, education and even spelling.[12] In his dogged pursuit of innovation and candid criticism of the French regime, he was expelled from the Académie française in 1718.[13] His *Projet pour rendre la paix perpétuelle en Europe* (1713) advocating confederal institutions at the international level to replace the traditional balance of powers is deemed to have been inspirational for twentieth- century initiatives such as the United Nations and the European Union.[14] His political writing relating to institutional reform within France defended a sort of 'technocratic absolutism' which looked to the rule of administrators informed by scientific reason with a goal of maximising public happiness.[15]

In addition to his famous scheme for securing peace in Europe, a scheme which drew the attention and commentary of both Rousseau and Immanuel Kant, he provided commentaries on Plutarch, including a guide to the reading of the *Lives*, as well as commentaries on various specific lives and a guide for those who planned to write in the same idiom. While claiming great familiarity with the work and using it as a focus for his own writing on numerous occasions, his engagement with the *Lives* is often in tandem with an advocacy of new priorities.[16] And while each case of reception, as we have seen, may involve to some degree an

---

[12] His various essays that come together to fill sixteen volumes include the "Discours sur la polysynodie," offering a new model of governance of the king in conjunction with councils, (and which resulted in his expulsion from the Académie française) as well as essays arguing for new forms of economic management, for the abolition of duels, for reform of education, and for a new spelling system based on phonetics, among others.

[13] The "half philosopher, half mad" description comes from Saint Beuve who attributed this description of Castel de Saint-Pierre to Voltaire. Cited in Keohane, *Philosophy and the State,* 363, n. 8.

[14] Simone Goyard-Fabre, "Je ne suis que l'Apothicaire de l'Europe," in *Les Projets de l'abbé Castel de Saint-Pierre (1658–1743)* (Caen: Maison de la Recherche en Sciences humaines, université de Caen Basse-Normandie, 2011), 19–37.

[15] Carole Dornier and Claudine Poulouin, "Introduction," in *Les Projets de l'abbé Castel de Saint-Pierre (1658–1743)* (Caen: Maison de la Recherche en Sciences humaines, université de Caen Basse-Normandie, 2011), 12–14.

[16] Sarah Gremy-Deprez identifies a number of titles in Castel de Saint-Pierre's collected works that harken back to Plutarch, including: *Observations pour diriger ceux qui écrivent la vie des hommes illustres, Sur le grand homme et l'homme illustre, Observations pour rendre la lecture des hommes illustres de Plutarque beaucoup plus agréable et plus utile, Thémistocle et Aristide ou Modèle pour perfectionner les Vies de Plutarque* and *Lycurgue et Solon.* In addition, she also claims that Castel de Saint-Pierre's most famous work, the *Projet de paix perpétuelle* may have in fact have been indirectly inspired by the Epicurean philosopher Cyneas, as he is presented in Plutarch's *Life of Pyrrhus,* as a staunch critic of Philip's campaigns of conquest and war. See Sarah Gremy-Desprez, "De l'Homme illustre au grand homme: Plutarque dans l'œuvre de l'abbé Castel de Saint-Pierre," in Carole Dornier ed., *Les Projets de l'abbé Castel de Saint-Pierre (1658–1743)* (Caen: Maison de la Recherche en Sciences humaines, université de Caen Basse-Normandie, 2011), 158–167. Her suggestion is that Castel de Saint-Pierre was using the Dacier translation for his commentary.

appropriation if not idiosyncratic reading, the Abbé de Saint-Pierre offers a particularly strong case. This may be in large part related to his concern for the practical application of his message in view of his forward thinking and advocacy of benevolence, an approach which may at times get in the way of an appreciation of the subtlety and deeper philosophic engagement with the classical source. I suggest that in the Abbé de Saint-Pierre we begin to see an understanding of public good that becomes reducible to certain tangible institutions, educational facilities, discussions for diplomatic councils, to give it a stronger sense of materiality and the possibility of more quantifiable impact. Politics becomes the means through which public goods are instituted and managed with the overriding goal of public happiness or utility.

In "A Discourse on the Distinction between a great Man and a Man of illustrious or shining Character" the Abbé de Saint-Pierre demonstrates how thinkers began to take up Plutarch with greater discernment for the passing of time and questions concerning the importance of classical examples for their own contemporary era.[17] His analysis also demonstrates how over the course of French intellectual history the work of Plutarch had shifted from being judged to offer privileged insight and guidance for the conduct of leaders and kings in the narrow public realm, to become a text of more general moral guidance. The status of Plutarch's literary subjects was less important than how one should judge their exploits. He revisits and unsettles questions of public honour, starting with a discussion on how to distinguish among great, powerful, and illustrious historical figures. While sometimes power and rank appear to require outward respect, it is only great men who, due to the specific features of their person, deserve our praise and inward regard or a more general attitude of esteem. He makes a further distinction between a great man, distinguished for their virtues, talents and deeds, and an illustrious man (invoking Amyot's term) who may achieve good things for the broader community, but who does not demonstrate great virtue. He subtly shifts questions of public ethos towards a measuring of utility through extrinsic contributions while not rejecting the initial Plutarchan concern to understand inner moral psychology.

---

[17] Abbé Seran de la Tour, *The Life of Scipio Africanus and of Epaminondas; intended as a supplement to Plutarch's Lives … To which is prefixed A Dissertation on the Distinction between a Great Man and an Illustrious or Eminent Man*, by the Abbe de Saint-Pierre (London: Richardson, 1787). Here I am using an eighteenth-century English translation of the original essay written in French by Castel de Saint-Pierre.

In the context of early modern debates on the ancients and moderns, a focus on the theme of greatness allows the author to combat strands of his own contemporary culture that tended to the veneration of ancient heroes, and to offer a revised version of how society should measure social and political contributions. He posits three criteria by which true greatness can be assessed: skill in overcoming difficulties; the nature and strength of personal motivation (be it personal ambition or zeal to procure the public good); and the extent of advantages or benefits actions have procured to humanity or to fellow subjects. He notes explicitly that his remarks are suited for printing at the beginning of Plutarch's *Lives* presumably to guide their reading according to his own preoccupations. But in his criteria, there is an emphasis on motivations, actions, and outcomes, as opposed to the qualities of soul, such as moderation and self-discipline, that are often thought to be characteristic of the ideal of *paideia* informing Plutarch's work. A palpable and new consequentialism, discerning the greatness of an individual by principles and measures of beneficence, while not the entirety of greatness, certainly makes itself felt as the Abbé lays the groundwork for his analysis.

Having articulated these principles the Abbé goes on to compare the merit of Alexander and Epaminondas (a life that Plutarch wrote but which was lost in antiquity and which the author Seran de la Tour sought to recreate in the volume to which the Abbé de Saint-Pierre's guide was attached). The Abbé argues that Epaminondas had to overcome much greater difficulties than Alexander but without the same strength of ambition. He praises Epaminondas as somewhat selfless and gaining pleasure in procuring the safety and happiness of his fellow citizens, while bringing to his country many more advantages than Alexander did to Macedonia. Alexander is demoted and deemed "no more than an illustrious man" who is replaced in high estimation by Epaminondas. While it is certainly clear, as we noted in our introduction and discussion of Plutarch's *Life of Alexander*, that Plutarch made no claim that Alexander lived an exemplary life, the flaws highlighted in Plutarch's account are attributed to a lack of self-control and desire for the wrong things. Montesquieu's later praise of the benefits of Alexander's rule (compared favourably to Julius Caesar) in Book x, chap. 14 of *The Spirit of the Laws* can be seen as a direct conversation with the Abbé de Saint-Pierre's scepticism regarding his legacy.[18]

---

[18] Montesquieu, *L'Esprit des lois*. Montesquieu was drawing on Plutarch's essay "On the Virtue of Fortune of Alexander" for this praise, as noted by Pierre Briant.

What the Abbé de Saint-Pierre appears to be doing with this analysis, is appropriating the powerful scaffold of moral assessment found in Plutarch but infusing it with new criteria and giving voice to new sensibilities associated with the burgeoning idea of utility, as also found in the work of contemporaries such as Shaftesbury and Hutcheson. The measure of virtue becomes a question of whether the interest of others or the public good, now seen as a vision of public happiness, was a driving motive.[19] The Abbé regards the effects of Alexander's rule as nugatory, thus any admiration for him should be at the same level as any act of daring or feats accomplished in the face of great risk; a rope dance is invoked explicitly here. In short, his actions are deemed comparable to a daring trapeze act.

Greater praise is reserved for Epaminondas and Solon, who are said not only to have overcome great difficulties with talent and constancy but who were also motivated by beneficence and whose accomplishments that measurably improved the lives of their fellow citizens. The new criteria invoked by the Abbé led him to villainise Caesar, thought to be a common criminal on a large scale, and to elevate Scipio, the general responsible for Rome's victory over Carthage, above even Cato, given that many more benefitted from his actions.

The final twist is the Abbé de Saint-Pierre's invocation of Descartes alongside these traditional historical heroes. He asks the reader to consider the contributions of Descartes and in the light of the three criteria posed at the outset of his analysis, Descartes appears not only to be great, but to be one of the "greatest men who ever lived"! To Descartes is due the most veneration, given his aim to serve society by perfecting human reason, his ability to overcome the difficulties in doing so and the outcome of his work which rendered invaluable insight to humankind.

So, to usher in a framework that we still invoke today, the Abbé de Saint-Pierre provides his readers with a new largely consequentialist framework for the judgement of figures in history and society. As he notes: "a great man must be a great benefactor, either to the world at large, by maxims or truths, most important in themselves, well demonstrated; or a great benefactor to some particular country either by a wise and virtuous conduct, through a long course of years, or by rules and establishments of vast moment, or by great advantages gained over its enemies."[20] In closing, he suggests that if Henry IV had succeeded in his plan for universal peace he

---

[19] "Exploits which are neither praise-worthy, nor virtuous, because they have not the interest of others, or the public good for their motive, may yet sometimes have a seeming greatness from extraordinary successes, like those of Alexander." Abbé de Saint-Pierre, *A Dissertation*, 13.

[20] Abbé de Saint-Pierre, *A Dissertation*, 26.

would replace Descartes as the greatest. Hence, in not-so-subtle ways the ethos of military leadership and political dominance that set the stage for Plutarch's assessment of character becomes the very antithesis of the conditions for flourishing. What we ultimately find in the work of the Abbé de Saint-Pierre is a Plutarch identified with a celebration of conquest and war and used as a foil to condemn advocates of the ancients in the face of new considerations of beneficence and utility. It is not a long stretch from this to Benjamin Constant.

The perspective is deepened in another guide to reading Plutarch. He begins "Observations pour rendre la lecture des *Hommes illustres* de Plutarque beaucoup plus agréable and plus utile" with a similar rhetorical strategy of redescription, suggesting that he prefers to read Plutarch among all ancient authors because it strengthens a desire in himself to be distinguished as very just and beneficent.[21] This characterisation suggests that instead of offering insight into the complicated dynamics of character, Plutarch's work partakes of celebratory or epideictic rhetoric more than anything else (or perhaps hagiography). He suggests that the genre of celebratory rhetoric should be taken up in his own time, and through the model of Plutarch used to honour the most beneficent and exemplary citizens and leaders of his own day. He then proceeds to give an example of what this would entail.[22]

He makes suggestions for new editions of Plutarch's *Lives* that offer condensed versions of the *Lives,* that is, dropping all that is deemed extraneous to the work of moral edification (the parallel structure included) and providing a preface as well as a set of observations following each life to highlight the appropriate moral lessons. This is something he proceeds to do in relation to a few select lives in the latter part of the essay (e.g. Theseus and Romulus). In addition, he suggests carrying on with the Plutarchan legacy by continuing the project with more contemporary figures. Of course, adding other figures to the *Lives* (including the figure of Plutarch himself) has a long tradition in reception, but in Abbé de Saint-Pierre's mind this enterprise was not just a series of limited additions but a whole-scale reworking.[23] This project would indeed improve the

---

[21] Abbé de Saint-Pierre, "Observations pour rendre la lecture des Hommes illustres de Plutarque beaucoup plus agréable et plus utile," in *Ouvrages politiques, vol. ii* (Rotterdam: Beman, 1737), 173–256.

[22] "Il faudroit les écrire pour nos contemporains a peu prez comme Plutarque lui-même lus eut écrites s'il avait vécu de notre tems, tant pour plaire aux Lecteurs que pour leur être plus utile à eux et à leur patrie," Castel de Saint-Pierre, "Observations," in *Ouvrages politiques,* 174

[23] Mossman, "Plutarch and English Biography," 78.

Plutarchan legacy as it might rid the genre of the extraneous, tendential and distracting prose in Plutarch's original work and replace it with more a specialised focus on what could most effectively give life to Plutarch's assumed intent, enhancing his discussion of the various rewards of virtue and the ill effects of vice. In short, the Abbé de Saint-Pierre seeks to appropriate the Plutarchan tradition but leaving no space for the reader's independent judgement.

Indeed, in a subsequent work devoted to his long-standing preoccupation with improving the utility of the Académie française, he proposes that in addition to ongoing work on the French dictionary, the members of his reconstituted Academy should be given the task of writing the lives of men who can be deemed to have most benefitted humankind. Given that the Academy exists in and through the favour of the Crown, in essence he is recommending a government sponsored appropriation and reconstruction of an updated and highly reductive iteration of Plutarch to enhance the civic virtue of subjects.[24] Arguably this attempt by the Abbé de Saint-Pierre, who invented the term *bienfaisance* to reinvent Plutarch, did little to enhance Plutarch's legacy. From the Abbé de Saint-Pierre on, we can see other examples where Plutarch's work is invoked for enterprises that are quite new. Clearly following in this tradition is the Abbé de Mably.

11.3   Gabriel Bonnot de Mably (1709–1785)

In opposition to the so-called sophists who seek to explore some of the distinct features and modes of public life, the Abbé de Mably offers a universal and uncompromising defense of a specific vision of virtue. His idea of virtue is predicated on the notion of the ruling of reason over passion in the soul, and this in turn is deemed the source of both individual happiness and the pursuit of justice that is an expectation of good rule and citizenship alike. While this in principle might be considered an admirable vision, his account also suffers from weaknesses in some of the details.

---

[24] "les vies des hommes illustres, qui ont procure les plus grans bienfaits à leur patrie. Ces sortes d'ouvrages quand ils sont vivement et sagement écrits peuvent plus contribuer, que tous autres à rendre les lecteurs tous les jours plus sensés, plus laborieux, plus vertueux et la nation entière plus heureuse. Tel doit être le but du bon gouvernement et d'un bon gouverneur." From Castel de Saint-Pierre, *Ouvrages politiques, vol. 4*, 165–166. Cited in Carole Dornier, "La Politique culturelle dans les Projets de l'abbé de Saint-Pierre," in C. Dornier and C. Poulouin eds., *Les Projets de l'abbé Castel de Saint-Pierre (1658–1743)* (Caen: Université de Caen, 2011), 109. The work in which he proposes this is called "Projet pour rendre l'Académie des bons écrivains plus utiles a l'Etat," which is speculated to have been written sometime between 1730 and 1733.

The figure of Phocion is central to Mably's vision. He was a well-known figure in the eighteenth century as a leading statesman in classical Athens and was praised by Plutarch. As noted in our summary of Phocion's life in Chapter 1, he is best known as the political opponent of Demosthenes, particularly over the question of how to respond to the emerging power of Macedonia. Phocion opposed direct confrontation with the armies of Philip I, but his advice was rejected, leading to the famous defeat of the Athenians at Chaeronea in 338 BCE. Again, despite stances that were sometimes wary of Macedonian motives, he opposed entreaties to help Thebes in its battle against Alexander, a battle famous for its cruel treatment of the Thebans. When the Macedonians, being more lenient towards Athens, allowed its democratic institutions to continue despite the defeat, democratic forces within the city charged Phocion with complicity, a charge for which he was found guilty and put to death. Given this, Phocion gained the reputation of an unbending public figure motivated by a strong sense of right and public good. Though his name was invoked by forces across the political spectrum in France (Mably for example is known as a key inspiration for revolutionary ideology), Phocion's name was often cited by aristocrats on the way to the guillotine during the French Revolution as a symbol of their own sense of martyrdom.

Mably is perhaps best known as an admirer of the Spartans. He is mentioned by Benjamin Constant in the famous lecture on the "Liberty of the Ancients Compared to that of the Moderns" as one of those theorists, along with Rousseau, who mistakenly (at least in Constant's estimation) believed in an ancient model of liberty.[25] Mably's praise of an agrarian economy guided by a basic principle of enforced economic equality was deemed anachronistic by Constant who argued that the modern world now structured by modern commerce should protect individual liberties as best defined by the individuals themselves in their own private pursuits. Still, while being identified as a proponent of the Spartan model in the history of ideas, in fact Mably's most popular work in the eighteenth century was not devoted to praise of a Spartan but to praise of the Athenian Phocion. *Entretiens de Phocion* was published in 1763 and through Phocion in this work Mably provides an expression of his own vision for the future of political life in France. The fact that Mably believed that he could most effectively present his political vision for his

---

[25] Benjamin Constant, *Political Writings*, ed. Biancamaria Fontana (Cambridge: Cambridge University Press, 1997).

contemporaries through the words of an ancient Athenian public figure may suggest that Constant was correct in his judgement of Mably's anachronistic normative measure for politics; however, the details of the text will allow us to discern the degree to which ancient notions were prescribed through Mably's fictional reconstruction.

It appears that in his own politics, at least as presented by Plutarch, Phocion saw himself as a trustee or steward of the interests of the Athenian people. He sometimes took unpopular positions, ones that were rejected by the democratic assembly but which he believed to be in the long-term interests of the state. In one sense we can see Phocion as a defender of a certain notion of the public good.

Mably's work is presented as a manuscript (clearly fictional) relating five conversations between Phocion and his friends, a manuscript the narrator purports to have found in in an Italian monastery. This literary structure allows Mably to draw on the story of Phocion, a known and respected defender of the public good in Athenian history and infuse it with Mably's own more clearly defined philosophy of politics and public matters. The link with Plutarch's own life of Phocion is made explicit in the eighteenth-century English translation of this text, as Plutarch's *Life of Phocion* directly follows Mably's piece.[26]

So how does Mably draw on both the good name of Phocion as well as the details of his life as provided by Plutarch to develop his own theory of public life? All the conversations revolve around issues of the relation between morality and politics. The first conversation is prefaced by a commentary on the increasing corruption of the age; noting that the existence of a figure like Phocion means that not all hope is lost and that there may be ways to improve the polity. It is mentioned at the outset of the conversation that the policies of war and conquest have only served to weaken the Greeks. The speakers turn to Phocion for guidance who notes that there are unchanging principles of good government throughout history, given that human nature remains the same. Phocion offers unreserved praise for the work of Lycurgus in Sparta and suggests that the main thrust of his constitutional innovations was to ensure the rule of virtue through reason and moderation and to restrain the passions, since passions are the source of all that is vicious in politics and social life. The upshot of this position is that there are no distinctive normative standards in the

---

[26] Mably, *Phocion's Conversations or the relation between morality and politics* (London: Dodsley, 1769). Online at https://go-gale-com.myaccess.library.utoronto.ca/ps/i.do?ty=as&v=2.1&u=utoronto_ma in&it=search&p=ECCO&dblist=ECCO&qt=BIB_ID~0043801000&lm=&sw=w.

ethos of public and private life.²⁷ The prescription becomes even more explicit at the start of the second conversation: "the establishment of morality is the principal object of politics." A similar message is reasserted in the close of the final conversation: "the public morals are formed by the domestic virtues. Be it your leading maxim, that it is only by virtue a state can enjoy settled happiness and prosperity."²⁸

What vision or idea of virtue does Mably have in mind here? In the first instance Mably, through Phocion, denounces any politics that panders to popular opinion. He conflates such politics with the instruments of "craft, injustice and violence."²⁹ A good political goal, it appears, is to rule in a way that teaches all citizens to restrain their passions and to strengthen the force of reason in their soul so as "to give a superior activity to the virtues." While ostensibly an expression of classical theories of moderation, it should be noted that the vision here is not of a fully tamed soul, but one in which the passions are kept "under strict subjection" (indicating a less than perfect model, since the ideal model of Platonic moderation is that in which the passions themselves may be considered moderate). While presumably wary of the passions, in a later passage Phocion does concede that in a time of decline and corruption the passions can serve more positive ends, as they sometimes work to express indignation at the presence of vices in other citizens and nations.³⁰ In later conversation, Phocion also suggests that an appeal to the passion and love of glory may effectively serve to focus citizens' efforts and sights on actions that promote the good of the country and distract from lesser and debilitating concerns.

Mably's Phocion praises Lycurgus and his Spartan reforms, interpreted as an attempt to instill the 'honest' virtues in the domestic morals of his countrymen. The shift clearly visible here is that the Spartans are no longer regarded as embodiments of skill on the battlefield and the pre-eminence of warrior virtues, but as engaged in a largely civic enterprise. In later passages Phocion invokes the Spartan military force but regards it as an

---

²⁷ "The prosperity of states is the never failing and stable reward of their virtues; and adversity and declension, the sure punishment of their vices." Mably, *Phocion*, 35.

²⁸ Mably, *Phocion*, 209.   ²⁹ Mably, *Phocion*, 45.

³⁰ "my dear Aristias, for the politics of our Sophists to make a people lastingly happy, the human heart must be totally changed. Were it only from our bare reason that we hate injustice, deceit, violence, ambition, avarice etc. possibly there might be a way of dazzling it, deceiving it, and hoodwinking it with prejudices which it would never be able to remove; but it is likewise from our very passions, which detest those vices in our equals, kindle at any appearance of them, and inveigh against them with implacable indignation, that an unjust, an insidious man is looked on with an evil eye by his fellow citizens, whilst a grasping, ambitious and haughty republic is suspected and hated by its neighbours; that is, whilst the nature of man continues as it is, persuade yourself that politics is not to look for the source and foundation of prosperity out of virtue." Mably, *Phocion*, 78.

instrument for managing peace and order among the Greeks and rejecting the work of conquest and war. Phocion's Spartans are thus no longer trained to be traditional warriors but rather good magistrates and good citizen judges of the morals of political candidates who seek their support.[31]

In terms of Mably's vision of politics and the public realm there may initially appear to be some ambiguity. In the first instance, Mably's espousal of virtue is identified with basic ideals of moderation, advocating self-control and the rule of reason, though not in all circumstances and not dogmatically such as when love of glory can be a good civic motivation. From this perspective it appears that Mably is advocating basic forms of reasonable self-governance that are necessary for any well-functioning social and political order regardless of its goals. His attack on vices in the social order seem to address those theories stemming from the seventeenth-century moralists, subsequently taken up by Mandeville, suggesting that a functional social order can be based on self-interest and vicious motivations. In dismissing those motivations, Mably's main thrust is that any social order dominated by vice cannot sustain itself.

However, as the conversations unfold, he develops the further principle that not only is virtue an important element of a social order that sustains good political order, it is also the primary and fundamental work of politics to establish and maintain the moral basis of the social order. Mably then invokes Lycurgus as a leader who was involved in the regulation and shaping of the domestic morals of his countrymen. The stark discipline imposed through public institutions in turn helps to shape individuals who are well suited for public office due to a love for justice and probity. Still, it becomes clear that Mably instills his invocation of collective virtue as a goal of politics with a certain self-righteous and dogmatic sense that the social and political requirements for virtue are obvious to almost all and can be legitimately imposed. By dismissing any discussions of the more complicated moral ground of the public terrain, Mably comes to conflate any calls for adjudication or equivocation, including aspects of what I have been calling 'political humanism,' suggesting that the language of political effectiveness (even presumably the consequentialism of an Abbé de Saint-Pierre) is all part and parcel of advocacy for vicious methods and motivations in public life. Justice, prudence, and courage are deemed key

---

[31] "People need a love for justice, as then they will take care to have a magistrate who on all occasions will be just, consistent, and inflexible as the law itself. Corrupt citizens will dread such a magistrate; his probity would be an insupportable curb to them. They would reject him for a Cleon, who foments their vices, whose heart is open to selfishness and in whose remiss and weak hand the scales of justice are not duly balanced." Mably, *Phocion*, 50–51.

virtues in both private and public life and these in turn are said to rest on a further four: temperance, love of labour, love of glory and respect for the gods.[32] Mably, in the name of an idea of public good suggests that the well-being of the whole should be subsumed in a broad project of instilling a singular vision of virtue for all individual citizens. Rigorous training for virtue in the domestic realm would be a sufficient condition and preparation for the citizen's proper performance of public duties.

The final piece of Mably's vision involves his understanding of the material conditions for his moral vision to be instilled, and it is through this that Constant's characterisation of his thought is confirmed. While Mably does not expound on the vision of agrarian economic autarky he explores in other work, he does here advocate for strict controls on luxury and wealth. The overriding reason for this advocacy is not concern for the injustice of economic inequality or educational opportunities etc., but rather a concern that the wrong moral priorities are projected through inequality and luxury. This feature of Mably's work offers some insight into the shifting historical terrain of ideologies. While from a contemporary perspective we might be inclined to place Mably on a line of political advocacy associated with radical politics of the left with an interest in policing wealth and income, from the perspective of the world of ancient Greece, Sparta served as an icon and model for defenders of aristocratic, rather than democratic, politics.

In broad terms, then, we can see how an initial appeal to general and non-controversial principles of self-control and collective moderation becomes increasingly radicalised throughout the text. Politics becomes subsumed by a project of deep transformation and the reform of citizens according to a singular and rigorous moral vision, which in turn requires specific controls on commerce and the circulation of wealth as well as an array of domestic practices. One might suggest that in Mably the unique ethos of the political realm as explored by thinkers of earlier generations is overwhelmed by a rigorous and uncompromising moralism – indeed a form of moral absolutism – imposed to reform both private and public spheres alike. Arguably the discourse gives rise to a strongly critical outlook that is no longer willing to make compromises with the existing order nor adapt to the nature of longstanding social and political relations. While Mably does suggest that political methods may need to be adjusted in accordance with the circumstances, he does not shift at all in his conception of the ends and goals of politics. The more general model of politics in

---

[32] Mably, *Phocion*, 83–84.

relation to an idea of public good in Mably is that an understanding of the requirements for justice are easily discerned if citizens are all educated in a shared vision. It suggests that a proper motivation and sense of priorities as virtue is not only accessible to all citizens, but also a sufficient condition for identifying and determining what justice requires in a public sense. The implication is that there is no need for a special and unique form of political prudence or judgement because political justice is a matter of identity and commitment. The weakness of such a view is less in the exacting material conditions associated with it as criticised by Constant, and more in the supposition that political justice is reducible to an issue of personal virtue. It not only offers the pitfall of leading to the dismissal of political opponents as individuals of general bad faith and character (and indeed a weaponisation of virtue), but it also can lead to an outright rejection or misguided view of the work of public concord and ongoing conciliation that is part and parcel of public good.

11.4   Jean-Jacques Rousseau (1712–1778)

The thinker in the French tradition perhaps best known as an avid reader of Plutarch is Jean-Jacques Rousseau. Rousseau famously called Plutarch his "maître et consolateur,"[33] and consulted his works throughout his life.[34] As is evident from his narrative in *The Confessions*, his encounter with Plutarch shaped his emerging sense of self as a child as well as his intellectual development and many features of his moral and political philosophy. Given the extent of Plutarch's place in Rousseau's thought it would be impossible to exhaust the topic of Rousseau's Plutarch here. A central focus for this study is the *patterns* of Rousseau's uptake of Plutarch given the long history of reading and reflection on his work, and through that the *significance* of that for subsequent politics.[35]

---

[33] This reference to Plutarch is made by Rousseau in his letter to Louise Florence Petronille Lalive d'Epinay dated 26 May 1754. Mme D'Epinay had asked to borrow one of Rousseau's volumes of Amyot's *Vies des hommes Illustres*. Rousseau granted the request but only on the condition that she not pass it on to anyone else.

[34] As Rousseau notes in the *Rêveries*: "dans le petit nombre de livres que je lis quelquefois encore, Plutarque est celui qui m'attache et me profite le plus. Ce fut la première lecture de mon enfance, ce sera la dernière de ma vieillesse; c'est presque le seul auteur que je n'ai jamais lu sans en tirer quelque fruit." Further evidence of Rousseau's reading of Plutarch after his early years in Geneva comes from several sources, including his poem *Le Verger de Mme de Warens* giving an account of authors he read while at Les Charmettes. References to Plutarch throughout his written work, of which we will mention only a few here, also demonstrate ongoing consultation of his work. Plutarch's *Vies des hommes illustres* was one of only several volumes found in his possession at the time of his death. Rousseau, *Œuvres complètes*, ed. B Gagnebin et al. (Paris: Gallimard, 1964).

[35] There are several monographs exploring Plutarchan themes in Enlightenment thought but no recent book devoted exclusively to Rousseau and Plutarch. E.g. Martial Lamothe, "Montaigne et Rousseau

In 1719 Rousseau and his father began to read through some of the books that his mother had inherited from her own father, including *Les hommes illustres de Plutarque*, through the Amyot translation.[36]

> Above all Plutarch became my favorite reading. The pleasure I took in rereading him ceaselessly cured me a little of the Novels; and I soon preferred Agesilaus, Brutus, and Aristides to Orondates, Artamens, and Juba. From these interesting readings, from the discussions they occasioned between my father and myself, was formed that free and republican spirit, that indomitable and proud character, impatient with the yoke and servitude which has tormented me my whole life in situations least appropriate for giving vent to it. Ceaselessly occupied with Rome and Athens; living, so to speak, with their great men, myself born the Citizen of a Republic, and son of a father whose love of the fatherland was his strongest passion, I caught fire with it from his example; I believed myself to be Greek or Roman; I became the character whose life I read: the account of the traits of constancy and intrepidity which had struck me made my eyes sparkle and my voice strong.[37]

Three key facets stand out here considering his later reflection: education, exemplarity as an important feature in the development of character and ethical intuitions, and the republican ideal. These are key themes through which Rousseau draws on Plutarch. I will explore each of these in turn and then focus on the broader implications of his thought for conceptions of public life.

Rousseau's childhood reading of Plutarch offers a natural foundation for thinking through moral development in terms of education. Rousseau's methodological emphasis on experience in education, like his empiricist predecessors Locke and Condillac, singles him out as a moderniser. We see some of these methods applied concretely in the

---

lecteurs de Plutarque," unpublished dissertation, City University of New York, 1980; André Oltramare, *Jean-Jacques Rousseau* (Geneva: na, 1920) and Georges Pire, "Du Bon Plutarque au Citoyen de Genève," *Revue de littérature comparée*, vol. 32 (1958), 510–547. All these works tend to trace Rousseau's love of Sparta to Plutarch, but while Plutarch had some admiration for the founder, Lycurgus, there were also many aspects of the Spartan system that he found cruel and excessively harsh. See also Jean Morel, "Jean-Jacques Rousseau lit Plutarque," *Revue d'histoire moderne* 81(1926). Some of my own analysis of Plutarch's relation to Rousseau as noted here is also found in part in my piece, "Rousseau's Debt to Plutarch," in Eve Grace and C. Kelly eds., *The Rousseauian Mind* (London and New York: Routledge, 2019), 23–33.

[36] There is no indication of the actual edition of this Amyot translation consulted by Rousseau and his father, but given that it was something first owned by Rousseau's grandfather it was likely an edition of the seventeenth century or earlier. It is probable that this remained the dominant source for Rousseau, as he gives us no indication of any knowledge of Greek, and while he read Latin his knowledge of it was not excellent.

[37] Jean-Jacques Rousseau, *The Confessions and Correspondence, Including the Letters to Malesherbes*, trans. Christopher Kelly (Hanover and London: University Press of New England, 1995), 8.

education of Emile.[38] However, Rousseau's insistence on educating the whole person for virtue in the tradition of *paideia* does tap into the spirit of Plutarch.[39] A staunch individualist in many ways, he is still acutely cognisant of the dynamics of moral psychology as they work collectively and through the individual. Rousseau's concerted attention to the inner life, of himself, his compatriots and his characters is evidence of his longstanding knowledge of Plutarch's work. It also helped to foster an outlook that offered important new insights into social and political theory. To a large degree, Plutarch is fundamental to Rousseau's vision, even if those fundamentals were adopted and adapted in many new ways.

One of the interesting aspects of the dialogue between Plutarch and Rousseau is their approach to exemplarity. We can see in Rousseau's life and work the use of two forms of exemplarity in relation to moral education, forms which were identified in an earlier chapter. In the first, the example of valued moral action in the life of one individual is a measure for the character development and behaviour of another. This form of mirroring in practice characterises the moral psychology of a number of Plutarch's heroes (e.g. Caesar taking Alexander as a model) and provides insight into human possibilities as well as a tool of self-discipline in attaining them. The second type of exemplarity is to use the lives and actions of various individuals as a source for moral lessons. Here readers are told by Plutarch or are given the task of adjudication to sort out which aspects of character and behaviour are praiseworthy and those which are not. A focus on actual individuals and the ways in which they thought and acted under certain circumstances adds a degree of realism to moral deliberation and can deepen moral commitment.

These two forms of moral insight using exemplarity, found in Plutarch, are also given importance in Rousseau's work. The approach, which finds a source for higher moral goals in the worthy examples of others to supplement what may be limited in the individual intuition, is articulated in Rousseau's *Julie ou la nouvelle Héloïse*:

> Sitôt qu'on veut rentrer en soi-même, chacun sent ce qui est bien, chacun discerne ce qui est beau; nous n'avons pas besoin qu'on nous apprenne à

---

[38] Jean-Jacques Rousseau, *Emile ou de l'Education In Œuvres complètes*, vol. 4.

[39] This is even accounting for broad agreement among classicists that the moral essay "On the Education of Children," often attributed to Plutarch throughout the eighteenth century and certainly thought by Rousseau and his contemporaries to be one of Plutarch's moral essays, is now considered to be pseudo-Plutarch (in the style of Plutarch but written by someone else). In other words, Plutarch's known works including the *Lives* demonstrate a sustained interest in the importance of education in a broad Hellenistic vein, and Rousseau in his discussions of education throughout his opus engages with Plutarch broadly on this question.

connaître ni l'un ni l'autre, ... Mais les exemples du très bon et du très beau sont plus rares et moins connus; il les faut aller chercher loin de nous. La vanité, mesurant les forces de la nature sur notre faiblesse, nous fait regarder comme chimériques les qualités que nous ne sentons pas en nous-mêmes; la paresse et le vice s'appuient sur cette prétendue impossibilité; et ce qu'on ne voit pas tous les jours, l'homme faible prétend qu'on ne le voit jamais. C'est cette erreur qu'il faut détruire ce sont ces grands objets qu'il faut s'accoutumer à sentir et à voir, afin de s'ôter tout prétexte de ne les pas imiter. L'âme s'élève, le cœur s'enflamme à la contemplation de ces divins modèles; à force de les considérer, on cherche à leur devenir semblable, et l'on ne souffre plus rien de médiocre sans un dégoût mortel.

N'allons donc pas chercher dans les livres des principes et des règles que nous trouvons plus sûrement au-dedans de nous. Laissons là toutes ces vaines disputes des philosophes sur le bonheur et sur la vertu; employons à nous rendre bons et heureux le temps qu'ils perdent à chercher comment on doit l'être, et proposons-nous de grands exemples à imiter plutôt que de vains systèmes à suivre.[40]

[Retreating into oneself, each one feels what is good and judges what is beautiful; we have no need for others to teach us to know one or the other, ... But examples of the very good and the very beautiful are more rare and less well known; we need to go and look for them outside ourselves. Vanity, measuring the forces of nature through our weakness, makes us think that the qualities that we do not find in ourselves are chimeras; laziness and vice reinforce this prejudice; and the weak man believes that that which is not seen daily does not exist. It is this error that must be demolished. One must accustom oneself to feel and see great objects so as to remove all pretext for not imitating them. The soul rises up, the heart is enflamed in contemplating these divine models; in studying them, one seeks to become like them, and one will no longer suffer anything mediocre without mortal disdain.

Let us therefore not look in books for principles and rules that we can find more easily inside ourselves. Let us abandon all the vain disputes of philosophers on happiness and virtue; let us use our time to make ourselves good and happy, instead of losing time seeking how one should be, and let us suggest great examples for imitation rather than vain systems to follow.]

As stated here by Saint-Preux in his letter to Julie, the problem here is neither books nor even theory but abstract *systems* of moral philosophy. Examples of the highest ethical order (as opposed to rules) are a necessary form of moral education because they engage the sentiments and the faculty of wonder as well as reason. Examples coming from both life and history can lead us out of ourselves and bring us to acknowledge ideals higher than what our own intuition may offer. While Rousseau via Saint-Preux does not

---

[40] Jean-Jacques Rousseau, *Julie ou la Nouvelle Héloïse* (Paris: Garnier Flammarion, 1967), 30.

cite Plutarch by name, the dynamic of exemplarity and its work in cultivating an awareness and hence a model of higher ethical aspirations is something that Rousseau learned in his reading of Plutarch's *Lives* at a young age.
The depths of the import of Rousseau's encounter with Plutarch forms a
pillar of his understanding of moral development.

Saint-Preux informs Julie of questions in matters of taste and manners, but as for the virtues he will offer her only an array of examples of
individuals to admire. Indeed, he goes on to suggest that in this regard
the ancients offer a much richer array of outstanding individuals for
inspiration and education than his contemporaries.[41] Still, it is significant to note that the first book to be read by Emile is not that of a
classical hero, but a literary one, namely Robinson Crusoe.[42] Just as
Rousseau in his early years developed his sense of identity through an
identification with heroes he discovered in his reading of Plutarch, so
too does Emile takes Robinson Crusoe as a model of his moral aspirations; Sophie in turn looks to Eucharis (from Fenelon's *Télémaque*).[43]
The logic of exemplarity as derived from Plutarch is operative here, but
in line with Rousseau's analysis in Book 1 (and indeed with perhaps a
gesture towards the innovations in this regard of the Abbé de Saint-
Pierre) it is no longer taken from the annals of the history but from
those heroes representing natural and civil independence.[44] Indeed, the
choice of Crusoe is significant because in terms of the Abbé's set of
three criteria, Crusoe illustrates for Rousseau the prime importance of
surmounting difficulties and showing a certain strength of character in
doing so, while jettisoning the third criteria of social utility or beneficence. The selection of Crusoe also speaks, we might suggest, to the
tradition of anti-heroes forged in the Enlightenment as was often the
case in the novels of Defoe.

In the spirit of the second form of exemplarity, examples are the material
for moral reflection and adjudication in a later stage of Emile's

---

[41] "L'histoire la plus intéressante est celle où l'on trouve le plus d'exemples de mœurs, de caractères de
   toute espèce, en un mot le plus d'instruction. Ils vous diront qu'il y a autant de tout cela parmi nous
   que parmi les anciens. Cela n'est pas vrai … Enfin ils diront que les hommes de tous les temps se
   ressemblent, qu'ils ont les mêmes vertus et les mêmes vices ; qu'on n'admire les anciens que parce
   qu'ils sont anciens. Cela n'est pas vrai non plus ; car on faisait autrefois de grandes choses avec de
   petits moyens, et l'on fait aujourd'hui tout le contraire." Rousseau, *Julie*, 31.

[42] Rousseau, *Emile*, 454–455.   [43] Rousseau, *Emile*, 762–763.

[44] Rousseau, *Emile*, 249–255. There is speculation by Burgelin that the name Emile itself may have
   been inspired by Plutarch, either directly through the life of Aemilius or through Plutarch's account
   of Numa's own gesture to give one of his sons the surname Emilius to connote a gracious and noble
   demeanour. See Burgelin's editorial preface to the same set of volumes, p. 1314.

development. Rousseau has Emile embark on the study of individual lives as a foundation for his understanding of moral psychology.[45] As we are reminded, not all of Plutarch's lives were meant to be praiseworthy or models for emulation, but like the narratives of Antony and Demetrius they were to serve nonetheless as examples for the purpose of edification.[46] In this aspect of Emile's education Rousseau is following the Plutarchan model also endorsed by his disciple Montaigne:

> Ceux, dit Montaigne, qui écrivent les vies, d'autant qu'ils s'amusent plus aux conseils qu'aux événemens, plus à ce qui se passe au-dedans qu'à ce qui arrive en dehors, ceux-là me sont plus propres; voilà pourquoi c'est mon homme que Plutarque.[47]

> [Those, says Montaigne, who write lives, insofar as they take more pleasure in giving advice than unpacking the succession of events, more interest in what is happening inside than what is happening outside, those are more to my liking; that is why Plutarch is my man.]

In accordance with this second type of exemplarity, examples of individual lives and behaviour are invoked to *make sense of* both the good and the bad in human conduct, rather than as an aspirational ideal. Rousseau states a preference for ancient history, as he suggests that modern historians are not as frank regarding human defects.[48] He waxes poetic on the mastery of Plutarch in revealing character through small details.[49] Of course, the use of examples is not the only method through which moral growth and moral insight is possible for Rousseau. He draws indiscriminately from

---

[45] It is generally thought that Plutarch's drafting of the *Lives* was done in his later years after writing most of his moral essays and with the sense that it was a more effective way to encourage moral deliberation.

[46] G. Lepan, "De la Morale a l'Éthique: Plutarque dans *Emile* et les *Rêveries*," in Olivier Guerrier, ed., *Plutarque de l'Age classique au xixe siècle* (Paris: Jerome Million, 2012), 203–219.

[47] Rousseau, *Œuvres complètes*, 530.   [48] Rousseau, *Œuvres complètes*, 530.

[49] "Plutarque excelle par ces mêmes détails dans lesquels nous n'osons plus entrer. Il a une grâce inimitable à peindre les grands hommes dans les petites choses, et il est si heureux dans le choix de ses traits que souvent un mot, un sourire, un geste lui suffit pour caractériser son héros. Avec un mot plaisant Annibal rassure son armée effrayée, et la fait marcher en riant à la bataille qui lui livra l'Italie; Agésilas à cheval sur un bâton me fait aimer le vainqueur du grand Roi; César traversant un pauvre village et causant avec ses amis décèle sans y penser le fourbe qui disoit ne vouloir qu'être l'égal de Pompée; Alexandre avale une médecine, et ne dit pas un seul mot; c'est le plus beau moment de sa vie; Aristide écrit son propre nom sur une coquille, et justifie ainsi son surnom; Philopœmen le manteau bas coupe du bois dans la cuisine de son hôte. Voilà le véritable art de peindre. La physionomie ne se montre pas dans les grands traits, ni le caractère dans les grands actions: c'est dans les bagatelles que le naturel se découvre. Les choses publiques sont ou trop communes ou trop apprêtées, et c'est presque uniquement à celles-ci que la dignité moderne permet à nos auteurs de s'arrêter." (Rousseau, *Œuvres complètes*, 531.)

both Plutarch's *Lives* and his *Moralia* for insight throughout his writing; however, it is fair to say that Rousseau favours exemplarity in its various forms as a desirable and effective mode of moral education.

Exploration of the theme of Brutus can shed further light on how deep the recourse to exemplarity runs in Rousseau's work, as well as the way Rousseau shifts the meaning of his classical master. The status of Marcus Brutus (and descendent of the republican Junius Brutus) as a hero for Rousseau is significant especially when viewed alongside Plutarch's account.[50] In the *Lives* Marcus Brutus is presented in parallel with the Greek hero Dion who deposed the Sicilian tyrant Dionysus. In the *synkrisis* Plutarch first suggests, as he can often do, that the life of the Greek hero compares favourably to that of the Roman. Dion, he tells us, acted alone and was able to build his forces autonomously against a tyrant whom many had cause to hate for his cruelty and violence. Furthermore, Dion was a more successful military tactician than Brutus. Brutus, in certain contrast, acted with the goading of an ally, Cassius. In the case of the plot against Julius Caesar they were resisting a popular and, at least in Plutarch's eyes, perhaps much needed monarch, and in their final violent confrontation with Octavian they had little choice but to resort to war. Furthermore, despite the lengths to which Plutarch goes to emphasise Brutus's moderation and avoidance of cruelty towards enemies and kindness to his own soldiers, the killing of Caesar was a dramatic betrayal given that Caesar had previously saved his life and become his friend and honoured him above many.

Nonetheless, Plutarch suggests there is one significant aspect in view of which Brutus compares favourably: his disposition as a man of principle, opposing tyranny and cruelty and risking his life for the common liberty, and thereby acting from concerns for the public good even when he had no cause for grievance on personal grounds against his declared enemy. Similar motivations determined his friendship with Pompey: "it was the public good that made Brutus a friend even to Pompey, who was his foe, and an enemy to Caesar, since he determined both hatred and friendship by justice alone." A preference for Brutus over Dion, and indeed over several other exemplars in Plutarch's pantheon, a preference certainly felt

---

[50] Early in *The Confessions* Rousseau acknowledges that Brutus was one of his childhood heroes (20–21), but the context does not allow us to identify whether he is referring to Junius Brutus or to his descendent Marcus Brutus. In any case, the point he is making with the invocation of Brutus is that the hero served as a means of aspiring to virtue through the denial of self. It was not until the watering experiment with the tree that he became cognisant of how public action could also be motivated by a quest for personal glory and recognition.

by Rousseau despite Plutarch's overall assessment, demonstrates Rousseau's greater commitment to republican forms, and the strong appeal of deeply principled motivation even in the face of conflicting personal ties and interests.

The link between a fascination for Brutus and broader principles of moral psychology and moral theory is made more explicit through the voice of Julie in *La Nouvelle Héloïse*. When Julie reaffirms her commitment to follow her father's wishes and renounce her desire to stay with her lover, she invokes Brutus.[51] She suggests in her letter that all human beings are capable of what she calls the *impartiality of the heart* which allows individuals to prefer the exemplars of men like Brutus over those of Caesar and of Nero. Even though Caesar's wealth and glory and Nero's power may have given them subjectively more pleasure and hence happiness, human beings in the face of historical exemplars seek not to emulate or at least praise the happiest but rather the most beautiful. Here the examples of Brutus among others such as Socrates and Cato gain more admiration, despite their final unhappy fate, due to the deeper fulfillment associated with acts of virtue. Julie refers to a sort of innate moral compass shared by all individuals that leads them to admire such virtuous individuals despite themselves, and this admiration often entails our emulation of them.

The significance of this passage is threefold. In the first instance, this suggests that the Plutarchan form replicates a basic impulse in moral thinking. In other words, moral thinking in general is said to proceed in the form of exemplars and through the adjudication of lives taken as a whole. The passage implies that the assessment of lives in this exemplary way is not only an insightful procedure for moral deliberation but is in fact how individuals deliberate. Still, if we place this insight in the context of Rousseau's whole oeuvre, we can see that presumably there are productive and pathological ways in which this can occur. The dynamic of invidious comparison highlighted in the *Second Discourse* is a clear example of how a comparative process is at the root of moral thinking but also of how this can be destructive for the individual. The distinction between beneficial and destructive forms of exemplary and comparative psychology is partially addressed in the classical distinction between jealousy (seeing the good qualities or accomplishments of another and seeking to emulate them in oneself) and envy (seeing the good qualities or accomplishments of another and wishing them misfortune). Avoiding the more pathological iteration of this dynamic of living outside oneself can perhaps be mitigated by giving

---

[51] Rousseau, *Julie*, 157.

ourselves a specifically historical point of reference, for envy or wishing misfortune on someone because of their accomplishments can only occur psychologically and meaningfully with one's broad temporal peers.

In the second instance, the passage suggests that a specifically *historical* perspective on the adjudication of lives on basic questions of how to live provides a better method for broad moral judgement, as it reveals the possibility of *impartiality* in our moral judgements through *agreement* on basic questions of which lives are to be seen as more worthy of emulation than others. Recourse to historical examples, then, reveals the nature and grounds of broad moral judgements – that is, we prefer the virtuous over the vicious due to its beauty, and we need to differentiate between the happiness of pleasure and true happiness or fulfillment. It also helps to mitigate a dynamic of social competition and envy that can occur through comparison with one's own contemporaries. A privileged place for historical analysis in helping us to sort out our moral intuitions in a productive way is another aspect that Rousseau here shares with Plutarch.

In the third instance, we find here a shared source of inspiration. While not articulated in the same terms as Plutarch, Rousseau's account of the principles guiding moral judgement shares with Plutarch an appropriation of a basic Platonic framework regarding our assessment of character (with the identification of the beautiful and the good in terms of virtue and an understanding of happiness or fulfillment that subverts the centrality of pleasure).

What this demonstrates overall is just how deep the force of Plutarch's inspiration can be found in Rousseau. The taking to heart of some of the very examples praised by Plutarch is done for insight into basic questions of moral judgement while perhaps, as we have seen, eschewing some of the subtleties and ambiguities of Plutarch's own analysis in his assessment of such lives. While Rousseau leaves out Plutarch's more tempered judgement of Brutus and his actions, he also develops the account in new ways, using the example of Brutus as an opportunity to invoke the Enlightenment tools of insight into the very mechanics and dynamics of moral psychology (by invoking or implying such terms as impartiality, agreement, as well as a version of moral sense theory where it is our hearts and sentiments that lead us to the proper moral outlook).

The example of Brutus also invokes Rousseau's strong commitment to the republican ideal. Rousseau gave an important normative boost to details of republican governance found in Plutarch. Sparta, as Rousseau famously notes in the *First Discourse* and indeed throughout his writing, represents a model of practical virtue, courage and good citizenship undistorted by the vanity of polite, commercial, and learned society. While the details of Lycurgus's regime are clearly drawn from Plutarch's work, the normative preference for Sparta over Athens is not, since Plutarch condemns Sparta's imperialism among other features.[52] Rousseau selects features of Spartan life that Plutarch appears to praise and singles them out as facets of an ideal form of political life in a wider exercise of what has been called the mythologising of antiquity.[53]

To better understand the mythologising of antiquity as allied with the study of Plutarch reception, I return to Rousseau's own narrative of his shifting engagement with *The Lives* and reflect on the sources through which his later interpretations of Plutarch may have been mediated. While Rousseau drew from a wider range of ancient sources, including Livy and Tacitus, it is certainly the case that Plutarch served as an important source for Rousseau in working through his political vision.

Initially we are told in *The Confessions* that Rousseau's childhood fascination lies first and foremost with personalities such as Brutus, Agesilaus and Aristides who served as exemplars through which his own self-image and deep features of his disposition were shaped: "I had had fits of pride at intervals when I was Aristides or Brutus. This was my first well-marked movement of vanity."[54] He also notes a developing fascination

---

[52] Pire, "Du Bon Plutarque," 510–547.

[53] Denise Leduc-Fayette, *J.-J. Rousseau et le Mythe de l'Antiquité* (Paris: Vrin, 1974). As noted earlier, it is true that Plutarch offered praise for Lycurgus as an individual who demonstrated moderation in his own person, but this goal of moderation was better met by others in the pantheon. Furthermore, Plutarch's regard for the good temperament and accomplishments of the Spartan founder do not always carry over to the highest regard for the state he founded, given the cruelty (especially vis-à-vis the helots) and harshness embedded in the Spartan way of life. In the life of Lycurgus, Plutarch suggests that the worst injustices regarding the helots (especially the Cryptia) were a product of post-Lycurgan reforms and that therefore the concern voiced by Aristotle regarding this practice should not be used to judge Lycurgus's project. However, at the outset of the *synkrisis* of the lives of Lycurgus and Numa he suggests that it is possible that the barbarous and cruel practices concerning the helots were due to Lycurgus. It is in part for this reason that Numa is judged to be a more humane and ideal Greek legislator with a more obvious commitment to justice and moderation. Plutarch, *Les Vies des hommes illustres*, trans. Jacques Amyot (Paris: Gallimard, 1951), 123–124 and 164. While virtue was a central standard by which to compare individuals, and while Plutarch often expressed a more Hellenistic appreciation for the virtues as practiced rather than contemplated or dialectically parsed, his judgement of Sparta was mixed. Indeed, at the level of the individual, Plutarch praised a life of moderation informed by philosophy, and at the level of the state he was less a defender of liberty and unquestioned allegiance than equity and justice. It is for both these reasons that Numa appears more favourable for Plutarch in the comparison with Lycurgus. According to Morel, Plutarch's moral essays "To an Uneducated Ruler" and "The Dinner of the Seven Wise Men" were crucial for Rousseau's defence of democracy at the time of his writing the *First Discourse*, including the identifying of the Spartan regime as a democracy. Morel, "Jean-Jacques Rousseau lit Plutarque."

[54] Rousseau, *Confessions*, 20–21.

with the republican histories of Athens and Rome, with no mention of Sparta, though Agesilaus is cited as one of his most notable heroes. Sparta as a focus for critical perspective on the emotional and psychological economy of modern commercial society appears to be for Rousseau a product of subsequent reflection.

As we proceed along in *The Confessions*, despite his early fascination with Plutarchan heroes, in his account of his years as a young man after leaving Geneva, we become aware of how *unlike* his early heroes he was. During his Annecy and Chambery years his concerns focused on making a living and managing the complicated relations in which he was entangled, and apart from his short-lived administrative posting in Venice he demonstrated little interest in public matters. Indeed, his praise for the Romans on his visit at the Pont du Gard is remarkable precisely for how out of step it appears with his concerns and discourse up to that point in the narrative.

> This time the object surpassed my expectation, and this was the only time in my life. It belongs only to the Romans to produce this effect. The sight of this simple and noble work struck me all the more since it is in the middle of a wilderness where silence and solitude render the object more striking and the admiration more lively; for this so-called bridge was only an aqueduct. One asks oneself what force transported these enormous rocks so far from any quarry, and brought together the arms of so many thousands of men in a place where none of them live. I wandered about the three stories of this superb edifice although my respect for it almost kept me from daring to trample it underfoot. The reverberation of my steps on these immense vaults made me believe I heard the strong voices of those who had built them. I lost myself like an insect in that immensity. While making myself small, I felt an indefinable something that raised up my soul, and I said to myself while sighing, "Why was I not born a Roman?" I remained there several hours in a ravishing contemplation.[55]

The tone and tenor of this reflection invoking classical Rome appears in stark contrast with that of other accounts of his adventures and travels, including the decidedly anti-heroic tone in what are sometimes indulgent accounts of his shortcomings and vices. The lyrical call to Rome serves in part as a reawakening or as a harkening back to some of his first experiences as a child when he was immersed in the reading of Plutarch with his father.

It also recalls an early story of Rousseau's narrative. After his father was exiled from Geneva in the aftermath of a violent quarrel, Rousseau was sent to live with the Lamberciers in Bossey under the guardianship of his uncle

---

[55] Rousseau, *Confessions*, 214.

Bernard. Over his two-year stay there he and his cousin built a hidden tributary which watered their own young willow tree in the garden, diverting water from a recently planted walnut tree. This covert attempt to find their own path to glory in a newly planted tree, while surreptitiously parasitic on the nourishment of the first, was celebrated with the phrase: "An aqueduct! An aqueduct!" It is noteworthy that the return of the high-minded language of classical heroism returns in Rousseau's narrative with an account of his visit as an adult to the famous Roman aqueduct in southern France. In this thematic continuity there is a curious intermingling or over-determination of nostalgia for the classical past and a longing for childhood innocence.

Significantly, the language of heroism re-enters the narrative once more in a slightly different form when Rousseau reflects on his first experience of mature writing in response to the famous question posed by the Academy of Dijon:

> With the most inconceivable rapidity my feelings raised themselves to the tone of my ideas. All my little passions were stifled by enthusiasm for truth, for freedom, for virtue, and what is most surprising is that this effervescence maintained itself in my heart during more than four or five years to as high a degree perhaps as it has ever been in the heart of any other man.[56]

Here the ideal of heroism is transposed onto a literary plane, hence more closely aligned with what we saw as the Abbé de Saint-Pierre's reformulated version of modern greatness. This is confirmed by Rousseau a few pages later when he discusses hearing the news of winning the prize for his *Discourse on the Arts and Sciences*.

> The following year 1750, when I was no longer thinking about my discourse, I learned that it had won the prize at Dijon. This news reawoke all the ideas that had dictated it to me, animated them with a new strength, and finished setting into fermentation in my heart that first leaven of heroism and virtue which my Father and my fatherland and Plutarch had put there in my childhood. I no longer found anything great and beautiful but to be free and virtuous, above fortune and opinion, and to suffice to oneself. Although false shame and the fear of hisses kept me from behaving upon these principles at first and from brusquely quarreling openly with the maxims of my century, from then on I had the decided will to do so, and I delayed executing this only for the amount of time it took for the contradictions to irritate it and render it triumphant.[57]

---

[56] Rousseau, *Confessions*, 295.   [57] Rousseau, *Confessions*, 298–299.

Here themes associated with Plutarch play an important role not only in the theoretical commitments of Rousseau the thinker but help to shape his self-understanding (insofar as *The Confessions* can be read as a roadmap of this and with all the challenges of what a retrospective account can reveal). The features of a good life that Rousseau had associated with Plutarch's depiction of certain characters of his *Lives* are identified in *The Confessions* as qualities of *freedom, virtue, eschewing fortune and opinion* and *sufficing for oneself.* These are also the outstanding qualities Rousseau seeks to make his own guiding principles.[58] Yet instead of an active life of service like a public figure such as Brutus (a path admittedly not available to an eighteenth-century exile from Geneva), Rousseau appears to embrace this path through writing. While writing did offer Rousseau an escape from the crowd in one sense, in another sense it was a more practical public role. In the framing of the start of his literary career, Rousseau suggests that again, as he did in his youth, he is taking on the persona of a Plutarchan hero, but in another guise and without the need to build the aqueducts. Instead, Rousseau dreams of building his "great system."[59] The construction of a theoretical project which will span the realms of education, politics and moral psychology becomes the enduring monument to which he aspires as a writer.

Rousseau's literary ambitions are depicted in the light of a new form of classical grandeur and defended through notions of freedom and virtue, so in a sense reclaiming the measure of greatness in utility as offered by the Abbé de Saint-Pierre as a universal application of ancient values. The founding of this project in the *First Discourse* starts from a clear parsing of the classical legacy where the critical force of Sparta is used to cast aspersions on commercial and polite society and to celebrate ideals of moderation and self-sufficiency. Here Rousseau shares a great deal with Mably. Ancient Sparta is described as "unique and sublime" in *Du Contrat Social*, but in a line of praise that is also granted to the institutions of Rome and Athens in their attempts to promote equality and prevent faction among citizens. Emblematic of Rousseau's mythologising of the Spartan case is his project of writing a history of Sparta. However, burdened

---

[58] It should be acknowledged that these ideals as found in classical literature are not unique to Plutarch and it may be, as by Oltramare in *Jean-Jacques Rousseau*, that Plutarch served Rousseau as an able compiler and advocate for some of these older and broader Hellenistic ideals, at least insofar as some of the essays of the *Moralia* are concerned.

[59] Shortly after his account of winning the prize from the Academy of Dijon, Rousseau tells his reader: "I dreamed about my great system, I threw some of it onto paper with the aid of a blank booklet and a pencil which I always had in my pocket." (Rousseau, *Confessions*, 309).

perhaps by the demands of veracity in historical writing (and the lack of real sources), the work exists only as a fragment.[60]

What currents or considerations mediated Rousseau's account of Sparta? In the first instance Rousseau's invocation of Plutarch in his early writing seemed shaped in part by his nostalgia for the innocence of his own youth as well as for the bond with his father when this first reading occurred.

In addition, as is evident from *The Confessions*, Rousseau read Plutarch through the lens of his own father's political allegiance to Geneva.[61] Plutarch is generally regarded as endorsing the imperial structures of the first century CE. The celebration of republican heroes in Plutarch's work, is done in view of the ethical outcomes of educational regimes rather than the political institutions themselves. As a loyal subject of the Roman Empire at the time of "Greece under Rome" Plutarch makes no suggestion that Rome or Greece return to its republican past. An early allegiance to republican Geneva allowed Rousseau to focus on the republican heroes of Plutarch and to suggest, counter to Plutarch's intention, that they represented advocacy for republican ideals alongside a model of ethical excellence.

Another mediating influence is Montesquieu's depiction of 'virtue' as love of the republic, independent of its classical association with the content of character.[62] The identification of virtue with pure republican patriotism allowed Rousseau to equivocate between the strength of Spartan patriotism and the goodness of an ideal of self-sufficiency, moderation and plain spokenness. While Plutarch acknowledged that love of the republic was an important condition for the more favourable effects of the Spartan constitution, this devotion was itself never identified as synonymous with virtue itself in the way that Rousseau sometimes invoked it.

Of course, another element of mediation to consider is the longer tradition of reception sketched out in previous chapters. The Renaissance tradition in France as we have seen placed particular emphasis on the nature of public life and the public good, with Amyot, following

---

[60] Rousseau, "Histoire de Lacédémone," in Gagnebin et al. ed., *Œuvres complètes*, 544–548.

[61] As Rousseau notes in the Dedication to Geneva at the start of his *Second Discourse*: "Qu'il me soit permis de citer un exemple dont il devroit rester de meilleures traces, et qui sera toujours présent à mon Coeur. Je ne me rappelle point sans la plus douce émotion la mémoire du vertueux Citoyen de qui j'ai reçu le jour, et qui souvent entretint mon enfance du respect qui vous étoit du. Je le vois encore vivant du travail de ses mains, et nourrissant son âme des Vérités les plus sublimes. Je vois Tacite, Plutarque et Grotius, mêlés devant lui avec les instrumens de son métier. Je vois à ses côtés un fils chéri recevant avec trop peu de fruit les tendres instructions su meilleur des Pères." (Rousseau, *Œuvres complètes* III, ed. B. Gagnebin et al. (Paris: Gallimard, 1964).

[62] Montesquieu, *De L'Esprit des Lois*, in *Œuvres complètes* II, III, 3, 251–25.

predecessors in this regard, using the French term *chose publique* to translate the various Greek terms invoking politics. While not initially or predominantly an institutionally republican discourse, this tradition of reception was an approach to monarchical politics that could find some common ground with republican themes. One finds in Rousseau through his comments on Plutarch's *Lives* in the *Confessions*, one of the first (along with Mably) explicit and overt associations of Plutarch with expressly and often exclusively republican themes, and this despite Plutarch's own imperial commitments.

Indeed, we see at least one instance where Rousseau invokes the notion of the *chose publique* in the same generic connotation and tradition as Amyot and others of the sixteenth century. This is found in Book 11, chap. 12 of the *Social Contract* where Rousseau states: "pour ordonner le tout, pour donner la meilleure forme possible à *la chose publique*, il y a diverses relations à considérer." [to order the whole, to give the best possible form to the *chose publique*, there are several relations to consider.][63] While his theory is inspired by republican principles, here he is not talking about one of several forms of possible government, but of the public realm itself, where citizens relate in different ways depending on whether they are exercising sovereignty or subject to the laws. The Legislator in particular, is given the difficult task of ordering this whole in proposing a set of laws that adapt ideal aspirations to very particular, contingent, and often flawed, contexts. There are rules that apply to the Legislator's work that are unique to their public role and station. Rousseau is suggesting here that *la chose publique* is something that exists in abstract, prior even to the identification of the type of government, and can take several competing institutional expressions, though some do better justice to its nature than others.

Rousseau infuses an understanding of the ancient republican past with a modern notion of popular sovereignty that extends equality and political power to all citizens, thus, it would appear, claiming Sparta for democracy (rather than aristocracy). Developing from the Erasmian depiction of the body politic, which we examined in Chapter 3, Rousseau reconstrues his political order through the metaphor of the body, suggesting that sovereignty, as the source of legislative power, is the *heart* of the state – its most important life-giving source – with the executive power now in the place of the *head*.[64] While for Erasmus making the heart the principle of life also

---

[63] Rousseau, *Du Contrat social* in B. Gagnebin et al. ed., *Œuvres complètes*, III (Paris: Gallimard, 1964), 393.

[64] Rousseau, *Du Contrat social*, III, II, 424.

implied that the ruler should be in a constant state of worry and concern for the welfare of citizens, Rousseau's sovereign appears to be shorn of emotive qualities and relies on encompassing every citizen in a structural guarantee (along with an internal cognitive appeal to the idea of the general will) that ensures the general welfare is targeted in decision-making. The distinction, I think, does point to a more important foundational question concerning how the public good is to be considered.

11.5 Thinking through Rousseau and Plutarch in the Light of Public Humanism

Despite mediation through a tradition of Plutarch reception, Rousseau also leads political reflection in new directions. Arguably, this also includes an important challenge to the tradition of 'political humanism': articulation of the unique ethos of public life combining robust ethical demands for those in a position of public responsibility as to the ends of public life with attention to the interpersonal features and social psychology of a life in the public eye, including the workings of visibility, responsibility, attentiveness and collegiality.

To demonstrate this in greater detail we need to explore the key features of Rousseau's political thought. There are two important axes of debate in contemporary trends of scholarship on Rousseau in political theory. The first axis centres on the challenge of how to characterise Rousseauian freedom and republicanism, and the second centres on the nature of Rousseauian sovereignty and its constitutional implications for both governance and the possibility of plurality.[65] In both, contrary to interpretations that Rousseau argues for the homogeneity of the citizen body (akin to the Spartan citizenry), supplemented by procedures that appeared to coerce individuals to conform to majority opinion, contemporary trends have tended to see greater possibilities for the protection and promotion of individual liberties in his work. Current scholarship tends to argue that Rousseau offers safeguards against arbitrary power by the privileging of popular sovereignty while also curbing the extensive power of that sovereignty through various procedures that restrict how and when sovereignty is exercised. In general, then, this recent work explores the significance of

---

[65] See, for example, Annelien de Dijn, "Rousseau and Republicanism," *Political Theory* 46.1 (2018), 59–80; Dan Edelstein, "Rousseau, Bodin and the Medieval Corporatist Origins of Popular Sovereignty," *Political Theory* (2021), 1–27; Antong Liu, "Youthfulness and Rousseau's Anti-Pluralist Realism about Political Pluralism," *Political Research Quarterly* 5 (2021), 1–13; Tuck. *The Sleeping Sovereign.*

Rousseau's solutions to the challenges of modernity with an examination of the juridical and institutional structures through which his model of self-government is defined.

A focus on the legacy of Plutarch for Rousseau, in the light of the tradition of political humanism developed in earlier chapters, leads us to shift attention away from the juridical and institutional plane and to consider the features of social and political psychology and the ethos of the public realm associated with Rousseau's vision. From this perspective, and despite some degree of tension in Rousseau's text, it could be suggested that Rousseau called into question several key facets of political humanism.

The play of social psychology in the public realm in Rousseau's *Social Contract* works at several different levels: the interpersonal relation among citizens in the act of constituting and exercising sovereign judgement; the work of government in relation to the citizenry; and the broader conditions for and effect of public procedures on a longer-term experience of the whole.

In terms of motivational perspectives, the *Social Contract* has been fruitfully studied as a coming together of three idioms in the history of political thought: the language of interest, the language of virtue (or republicanism) and the language of natural law.[66] What is perhaps most intriguing about this text is less the separate idioms in which the argument proceeds, but the discussion of psychological transformation that occurs in the process of the formation and exercise of sovereignty between the force or dominance of one or the other. Rousseau suggests that he begins with "les hommes tels qu'ils sont" [men as they are], presumably driven by interests, but that important transformations will occur in the formation of political community.[67] Of course, not all such transformations necessarily happen for the better. As his readers know, there are psychological transformations that are unjust and illegitimate in the history of peoples, such as the way in which people can become habituated to servitude (and Rousseau here alludes to Ulysses sailors in Plutarch's Gryllus who have become so used to their existence as pigs that they refuse to be transformed back to men).[68] Rousseau seeks to replace an account of illegitimate psychological transformation with one that is legitimate and on which a practice of a politics informed by the principle of freedom can be based. At the passage from the state of nature to the civil state, when all alienate their

---

[66] See, for example, Anthony Pagden, ed. *The Languages of Political Theory in Early-Modern Europe* (Cambridge: Cambridge University Press, 1987).
[67] Rousseau, *Du Contrat social*, 351.   [68] Rousseau, *Du Contrat social*, 353.

rights simultaneously to the whole community and submit themselves to the general will, the person becomes a "citizen," or an indivisible part of the whole (and in the true sense of the word as suggested by Rousseau in a footnote).[69] In that juridical transformation, which is also a psychological one, as he tells us, the impulsive force of appetite and instinct can allow itself to be overridden by a stronger sense of moral imperative and justice, driven by a wider sense of obligation to the whole.[70] A new civic identity precipitates a moral transformation. Arguably the sensitivity in Rousseau to the complexity in social and moral psychology (as we noted previously regarding Hobbes) may have in part been shaped by his early immersion in the work of Plutarch.

Still, as Rousseau noted, a complexity arises in relation to the new sovereign. The associates as a whole are called the 'people' collectively, 'citizens' when they are participating in sovereign authority and 'subjects' when they are subjected to the laws of the state.[71] It would appear then that not only their name but also how they perceive their relation to others in the association shifts and is directly impacted by their sense of whether they are being active in the formation of law or passive in obedience to it (even though this is deemed to be compatible with freedom). It is in the combination of active sovereignty with not only obedience to the law assented to but also the form of government established by the sovereign as a representative in the Hobbesian sense (rather than the liberal-democratic sense), that Rousseauian sovereignty has been more recently recast as limited (with roots going back to Bodinian ideas of constrained sovereignty). In this sense it can only be active in certain ways and at precise intervals, thereby mitigating the potential force of the tyranny of the majority.[72]

The question of how limited or constrained the exercise of sovereignty may be in the Rousseauian picture, influenced as it is largely by a concern for the primacy of liberty as a political good, may partially obscure the additional objective for Rousseau in this account, which is also to offer a picture of governance able to respond to the needs of the whole in order to be a valid mechanism for achieving the public good. Rousseau had already shown us in the *Second Discourse* how consent (e.g. with the introduction of property) can be an insufficient condition for justice, and how collective dynamics in which all participate can have deleterious effects. An added

---

[69] Rousseau, *Du Contrat social*, 361.   [70] Rousseau, *Du Contrat social*, 364.

[71] Rousseau, *Du Contrat social*, 362.

[72] See again, de Dijn, "Rousseau and Republicanism"; Edelstein, "Rousseau, Bodin and the Medieval Corporatist Origins"; and Tuck, *The Sleeping Sovereign*.

question to the adjudication of the mechanisms of the contract is how well they can assure us of a policy and practice that promotes the public good.

The central feature of Rousseau's sovereign people is the distillation of many popular voices into one. There are certain limitations on the way in which sovereignty is exercised in the Rousseauian picture, but the guiding principle is that collective popular assent is an authoritative and final measure of both liberty and legitimacy. Furthermore, the sovereign vote is voiced in the absence of deliberation, so the exercise of sovereignty offers a particular way in which the judgement of all is exercised (though Rousseau is not clear on the question as to whether any consultation or deliberation can occur prior to the act of voting). An important question, then, is whether this portrayal shifts a fundamental understanding of the essence of public good to something that is directly and immediately voiced by the people with little deliberation or mediation. Is there possibly a category mistake in that it is a notion of the common good, as an articulation of popular perception of the good, that is taken as the stand-in for the idea of public good, in the presence of a concern for liberty?

The concern is whether these guarantees for political freedom as established by Rousseau are also *sufficient* to ensure that the public good is achieved. It might be argued that the exercise of collective liberty is itself a measure of public good, but in a somewhat less procedural sense, concern to identify and further those policies that will truly be for the benefit and well-being of the whole, in an abstract sense, are not necessarily an outcome of a process in which people target the general will. While the supposition is that people may themselves be the best judges of their own collective welfare and good, even granting this, the exercise of Rousseauian sovereignty is not an absolute or *sufficient* guarantee that the exercise of collective judgement, filtered through the concept of the general will, will in fact achieve this.

What this depiction does offer is the impression that the exercise of the collective will, subject to clear qualifications and as an exercise of liberty, can be deemed a sufficient condition for the public good. It suggests that what is most important in ascertaining this idea of what is best for the whole is that it is willed by all with the right motivation, regardless of the knowledge, deliberation or judgement that might inform those wills. By implication, this vision fuels suspicion towards a long tradition of political stewardship.

There are sincere attempts by Rousseau to ensure the singularity or unity of the general will, as a signifier of its true generality. He tells us in Book II of two ways to deal with what he calls 'partial societies' in the state. The first method is to follow the lead of Lycurgus, who banned partial associations in the founding of Sparta so that each citizen can only consult within themselves. The second method is to multiply these associations, following the lead of Solon, who divided citizens into four relatively equal classes, or Numa who divided Romans by profession, or Servius whose innovations he expounds upon in Book IV, chap. 4.[73] Rousseau suggests, in a rather puzzling remark, that these methods can be the only way to ensure that the general will be enlightened ("toujours éclairée"). While it is true that these examples, all taken from Plutarch's *Lives*, are noted as methods to prevent destructive factionalism and division, there is in fact a fair leap between suggesting that a sense of civility and relative unity can keep a community focused on seeking the welfare of the whole, and the idea that the same mechanisms will ensure that the people are aware or will always recognise the measures that are necessary to achieve that welfare.

The broader question here is whether the measures needed to further the good of the whole can be identified through conditions of relative consensus and a strong sense of social unity and concern. While it is true that in some instances these may serve as sufficient conditions to reach a good decision on matters of policy, it may also be that in other matters, which are more complicated and require some forms of specialised knowledge (e.g. public health, environmental protection, etc.), they may not be sufficient. Enlightened decisions in such matters may require partial communities who specialise in such knowledge, offering citizens better awareness of the stakes involved in voting one way or another.

Linked to previous commentary on Rousseau's general move to undermine mediation in its numerous ways, cultural, ethical and personal, we can see here another extension of the same broad logic with an assault on practices of stewardship, especially in politics.[74] My concern here is less on Rousseau's demand for transparency and authenticity of the individual subject and more on his idea of the primacy of the individual will in political life, one for which a need for good information, valuable advice, the wisdom of experience, etc. seem to have a secondary place, even if not fully eliminated, given the constraints on the exercise of sovereignty as noted. Instead of considering maxims as a source of ethical education (they are replaced by an internal consultation with the individual heart), community leaders as a source of social education (partial associations are generally frowned upon), and experienced participants in public life as a

---

[73] Rousseau, *Du Contrat social*, 372.
[74] Jean Starobinski, *La Transparence et l'obstacle* (Paris: Gallimard, 1971).

source of political education (the government proposes but it is not really clear if any ongoing discussion and deliberation is encouraged), Rousseau's emphasis on the political primacy of the will appears to reject various modes of mediation and reciprocity between governors and governed. We have gained a powerful vision of political liberty as popular rule, and what appears to be a regulative ideal that offers imaginative potential for people to think of ways to overcome traditions of oppression, tyranny and unjust rule. However, the model, even in its imaginative state and prior to any discussion of its possibility, is arguably not without its costs.

More generally, Rousseau offers his own unique spin on the reading and uptake of Plutarch and in doing so he advances an important departure from the spirit of the previous legacy of Plutarch reception and from the ethos of 'political humanism.' Rousseau invokes a strong sense of political agency for citizens in the modern era, along with measures intended to ensure that this agency is voiced in ways corresponding to the interest of the whole. If we look at the mechanisms of government in the *Social Contract* more closely, we see how this is partially promoted through the separation of sovereign from government. The importance of this separation, as highlighted in recent commentary on Rousseau, and also seen more abstractly as the separation of willing from judgement, could be read as an attempt to democratise the tradition of political humanism inherited by the eighteenth century; in other words, to keep the elaboration of policy in the government (now perceived as delegates), while enhancing the power of willed consent for the people who themselves vote directly as a sovereign.[75] These readings place new emphasis on Rousseau as a theorist of legitimacy requiring popular input at least in the formal enactment of law, if not in its content. The people, when politically active, are willing citizens who voice yea or nay on the proposals placed before them. The suggestion is that willing consent, regulated by the concept of the general will, is a guarantee of not only legitimacy but also of respect for the public good.

Does the separation of the political functions of willing and judging have the effect intended by Rousseau? Hélène Landemore suggests that this separation serves to isolate popular and democratic voices from the actual policymaking process (or processes of judgement), which is where true political power is exercised.[76] While this is clearly true, my point is a

---

[75] See here Nadia Urbinati, *Representative Democracy* (Chicago: University of Chicago Press, 2006), Tuck *The Sleeping Sovereign*, and Hélène Landemore. *Open Democracy* (Princeton, NJ: Princeton University Press, 2020), chap. 3.

[76] Landemore, *Open Democracy*.

somewhat different one. A legacy of Rousseau's political thought may be in giving greater popular credence to the idea that the power of assent, consent and willing is the essence of political power, and that the work of judgement and policy elaboration is by necessity subordinate, messy and a proper object of suspicion. In Rousseau, the sphere of meaningful politics is made narrow and projected through a largely voluntarist lens. The power of the people resides in whether they decide to adhere or not to decisions made elsewhere, yet the arguments and reasons which may be considered to shape those positions appear to be of less importance than the expression of the yea or nay. The politics that can be seen to emerge from this is one where deep concern for the public good and deliberation about what it requires is lost amidst a theatre of both assertion and denunciation. Thus, while Rousseau could be perceived as drawing from the tradition of public humanism in seeking to construct a theory where deliberation about the public good might be protected from the worst forces of social and political corruption, his elevation of the will expressed merely as a yes or no, and in a response to policy pronouncements, may encourage a tendency of strident declaration of position as opposed to a willingness to engage in dialogue to probe what may be better for the whole. While Rousseau did go to great lengths to ensure that his notion of a legitimate public and collective will met further criteria of broader measures of public good, the upshot of Rousseau's work was to give greater credence and independent legitimacy to the act of political willing (in the name of autonomy and freedom) over the mechanisms through which the public good might be discerned.

We should also acknowledge that in his political vision at least, Rousseau appears to be presenting a dialogue on these issues as opposed to a dogmatic assertion of the pre-eminence of individual judgement. So, while presenting the ideal of an unmediated politics in the outset of his *Social Contract*, many interpreters have acknowledged that in the course of that same work Rousseau recognised and sought to come to terms with reservations and doubts concerning his ideal. While he continued to espouse the normative force of the general will as a sole source of political legitimacy in the modern era, and this as a coming together of all citizen wills on general questions of law, he also had to come to terms increasingly with the problem of citizen education. His invocation of the classical legislators, again inspired in many ways by Plutarch's lives of Lycurgus, Numa, Theseus and Solon acknowledges that, at least in initial stages, a broad minded and informed political leader may be necessary for a polity to get on its feet and to function for a limited while. For Rousseau, an underlying anxiety apparent in the text is the cultural changes associated with the modern era, the spread of commercial society and the growing strident pull of the rhetoric of self-interest that appeared to threaten a sensibility for the collective good that the spirit of good citizenship required, a force he sought to mitigate with an appeal to patriotism in his work on the constitution of Poland.[77] While acknowledging the possibility of a public good that is discernible in all policy decisions, Rousseau also recognised the difficulties of having the public actually come to this vision unanimously and unaided. In consequence, for modern readers, if not for Rousseau himself, the procedural primacy of popular political power and a presumed need that a majority expression of will could be akin to an expression of the public good, arguably came to replace the qualitative considerations by which a substantive ideal of the public good could be discerned.

The gist of the concern I express here is not new. As others have noted, a danger in a politics of direct appeal to a singular popular will is that it repudiates the function of traditional mediating institutions and organisations such as political parties.[78] Rousseau banned such partial associations in his own brand of popular politics only to seek other means of educating the popular will. However, in the current age of liberal democracy, political scientists have recognised the important and indeed crucial role that political parties and traditional mediating organisations play. Not only do they help to educate popular opinion; they also help to build coalitions and construct unity among individuals through the political process. To deny the legitimate role or to undermine their place in policy discussion and the formation of political wills can be damaging to the political process of contemporary liberal democratic states.[79]

Secondly, the delegitimating of traditional modes of mediation, aggregation and opinion formation, along with the recognition that political wills only form through some process of mediation, leaves the door open for new surreptitious avenues of opinion formation (through social media or otherwise) of which participants remain largely unaware. In other words, while thinking that political opinions are shaped through their own reflection and agency, in actual terms and with growing mistrust in political elites and political parties, voters and participants in the political process are prey to new insidious forms of opinion formation that are

---

[77] Rousseau, *Considérations sur le Gouvernement de la Pologne*, in B. Gagnebin et al. ed., *Œuvres complètes*, III (Paris: Gallimard, 1964), 951–1041.

[78] See, in particular, Frances McCall Rosenbluth and Ian Shapiro, *Responsible Parties* (New Haven, CT: Yale University Press, 2018).

[79] Rosenbluth and Shapiro, *Responsible Parties*, chap. 1.

linked to private (or foreign) interests but whose sources and intent are highly obscured.

Thus, while Rousseau represents a powerful vision of political liberty, one that continues to have a hold on our contemporary democratic imagination, his apparent rejection of agency of mediation in the formation of opinion, and his mistrust of the possibility that specialised, well-informed and well-minded citizens might offer articulations of what can be in the best interests of all, has perhaps left us with a questionable model of what constitutes good politics.

In short, Rousseau offers us a very complex, engaging but, I would argue, a case of reception that offers cause for worry. In many ways, while we might think of Rousseau – the thinker so enamoured with Plutarch that he claimed him as his master – as an important force of cultural transmission and a monument to Plutarch's ongoing legacy, the reality is much more complicated. The insights of individual psychology as they come to bear on a narrative of social and political life are certainly a lasting tribute to Plutarch that can be found in Rousseau. Nonetheless, in relation to the impact on contemporary political discourse, arguably the very rhetoric of praise and loyalty, much like the cases of the Abbé de Saint-Pierre and Mably, hide a more complex case of reception, particularly in relation to the tradition of political humanism through which Plutarch was first received in European political culture.

11.6 Conclusion

In broad terms the place of Plutarch in Enlightenment political thought appears to be both foundational (in both historical and principled terms) and limited. Plutarch serves as the *sine qua non* through which various political theorists developed central themes of their own political thought, and so his work continues to be an important reference throughout the tradition in both England and France. Several facets of various Enlightenment thinkers overlap with key themes from Plutarch, beyond those discussed in this chapter, of which there are too many to mention. These include fascination with regime founders, the status of animals in relation to humans, the ethical issues surrounding vegetarianism, the civic function of religion, and balancing concerns for the public good with the conflict among individuals in public life. The reading of the works of Plutarch is the means through which many of the thinkers here developed central tenets of their political theory.

In carrying through with fundamental Plutarchan themes such as moral education, exemplarity as a central aspect of moral thinking and political right as the pursuit of justice and the common good, many of these thinkers come to theoretical conclusions that toy with authoritarianism (the Abbé de Saint-Pierre, Mably) or seem to favour a politics that centres on momentary consultations of the popular will as a sole measure of political right (Rousseau). Arguably, in broad terms these repudiate the tradition of political humanism forged during the Renaissance in Plutarch reception. What this means in principle is that they not only reject the more subtle adjudication of character found in Plutarch's own work, something which is often in a great deal of early modern reception, but that they also appear to reject a conception of public governance that explores how politics might be conceived as an exercise in reciprocity between the governors and the governed to seek what is acceptable, possible and conducive to the promotion of public good, as far as it can be articulated. The conception of stewardship ushered in in conjunction with attention to Plutarch's work would have favoured, of course, in an early modern context, a definite (and gendered and colonial etc.) political elite and their ability to make decisions on behalf of the whole. A key question, then, is the degree to which a notion of stewardship is appropriate to a model and practice of more inclusive politics. An underlying presumption of my analysis in this chapter is that it can be possible, in part due to the same problem and question faced by Rousseau and other subsequent political thinkers of the modern era who wrestled with the question of citizen education.

Contemporary liberal democratic politics must always be centred on respect for collective political preferences. But instead of a politics driven uniquely by either a momentary snapshot of where political preferences lie or on an imposition of a highly theoretical and idealised notion of a public good, there is perhaps still ongoing relevance for a notion of reciprocity between the governors and the governed. This entails the continuance of an aspirational politics that does not reject the notion of public welfare and the public good, while also acknowledging that the existing tendencies and characteristics of the population pose constraints to what is achievable. Is it possible to conceive of a politics that advances in a spirit of reconciling political ideals and popular mores, while being part of wider effort of individual and social development?

Plutarch the historian, though admittedly an ally and defender of imperial elites, was also a subtle and measured judge of character who assesses the good and bad in each example and offers sceptical reflection on the relative strength of nurture in the face of natural dispositions, guided by a regulative ideal of the humane. In the hands of his most passionate and famous Enlightenment disciples, as we have seen, Plutarch was often used to construct a much more dogmatic and reductionist account of the nature of public life, judged either by a narrow concept of utility, a rigorous ideal of virtue, or an uncompromising idea of the individual will as the crux of legitimacy, liberty and the political good.

Conclusion

I have a distinguished colleague who is always prodding his fellow political theorists to offer practical examples of the concepts and ideas that they are developing in abstract and to express in more down to earth form the concerns that drive or animate the broader project. In this spirit, I offer a brief invocation of some of the more general considerations that inform this book.

There are several overlapping motivations for this book. As a student of the history of French political thought I am aware of an overwhelming number of references to the work of Plutarch in the primary sources, and yet I never found that the commentary adequately came to terms with its significance for political reflection. This work is my effort to redress the balance on this topic. My work does this in conjunction with new tools in research, including digital catalogues and records that allow for better study of classical reception in early modern thought and create a more accurate picture of the distribution and translation of relevant texts. The status and uniqueness of the way in which Plutarch was picked up in France is highlighted in contrast with an account of reception in the England.

As I proceeded, I recognised that the study of the history of political thought through the lens of Plutarch offered opportunities for new insights into important texts of the tradition. I have demonstrated in a number of these chapters how attention to the work of Plutarch as a source gives us fresh perspectives on several canonical thinkers, including Erasmus, More and Hobbes. Still, there is a great deal left to explore in this regard, especially with lesser-known figures in political reflection.

There was, however, another compelling motivation for this project that developed along the way. Attention to Plutarch reception serves to shed light on some unique features of the ethos of public service and offers resources for thinking about the concept of the public good. To put this in a slightly different way, the account I offer here serves as a form of intellectual resistance to a broad somewhat populist discourse driven by an attitude of anti-politics.[1] There are, perhaps, three key manifestations of this in the contemporary era. A first expression of anti-politics is the rise of new initiatives seeking to escape public regulation and intervention, circumventing the state in the drive for greater profits. Such initiatives are often justified with recourse to a narrow conception of freedom conceived of as not only distinct from but indeed in opposition to state and political power as it is narrowly conceived. These strategies are consciously designed to escape their subjection to any meaningful deliberation of how the same technologies might be harnessed for the public good. Alongside this, a second manifestation of anti-politics can be found in progressive circles, which are often guided by a deep mistrust of state institutions and a rise in advocacy for direct resistance, direct action, and public protest directed towards government actors and elected officials rather than corporate ones. The ethos of this resistance is often informed by a model of agonistic democracy, with the presumption that there is a value in the public theatre of denunciation and resistance to radicalise and raise consciousness. This is accompanied by a broader social attitude of cynicism towards public life and public officials. Finally, a third manifestation of anti-politics in the contemporary era may be driven in part by the political classes themselves who have taken on a model of public administration that is driven increasingly by principles of corporate management. It often serves public officials to depict themselves as standing outside the political class as a feature to enhance their popularity. The discourse of corporate management is sometimes even used to legitimate forms of service delivery. While not always detrimental, the broader impact of the shift may have unintentionally served to reinforce an attitude of anti-politics.

All these tendencies (and other more localised ones within individual states, such as the weaponising of local governments against the federal centre) work in concert to oppose and undermine confidence in public life, not in relation to specific policies and actions but as a needed feature of collective life. These developments feed into cynicism toward the idea of public service. At a certain point, they erode public trust and deepen the fragility of modern democratic institutions, and indeed, they weaken popular commitment to the very institutions of liberal democracy. This is particularly worrying at a time when the actors responsible for some of the worst damage to collective life in the form of environmental devastation, overproduction, colonisation of our time and attention, the

---

[1] Glaser, *Anti-Politics*.

generation of mental health pathologies, addiction promotion, corrosion of the book industry and spread of misinformation, to name just a few, tend to be corporate actors, or those in public life who demonstrate no deep commitment to public good. Should not the charge of corruption in contemporary society be levied first at those who seek to maximise their profits at the expense of public welfare? For better regulation of these social pathologies, a robust conception of the public good is needed. This project is partly motivated by this awareness.

In opposition to presumptions of rampant corruption and self-serving behaviour in public life, attention to the tradition of Plutarch reception demonstrates the importance of both good motivations for the public servant and proper assessment of those motivations and actions on the part of the broader public. While there is clearly a place for the critical study of the actions and character of those in public life, and for acknowledgement of the place of self-interest, both in the narrow sense of self-promotion and the broader sense of attachment to the interests of a somewhat larger constituency or group, attention to the tradition through Plutarch's prism offers insight into the limits of thinking about politics *only* in that anti-politics way. Those narrowly self-regarding motivations can end up being ineffective and self-defeating, and the effects of actions fuelled by such motivations can be deeply damaging. Where an ethos of public-mindedness is lacking, we find leaders whose actions have tended to the detriment of their citizens, either through wavering and erratic leadership or through transparently self-serving behaviour that has dodged responsibility, corroded public trust, and undermined concerted efforts of harm reduction. In the contemporary context, the nature and disposition of the person in public office and the quality of their commitment to public service can quite literally be a matter of life and death.

Acknowledging the importance of public service can be coupled with a strong defence of a logic and discourse that is centred around a concept of the public good (again in the broadest sense) and more generally justice, for a variety of reasons. First, even when the exact content of these ideas cannot be precisely elaborated it expresses a willingness for conciliation and does not close off avenues for dialogue. In the face of a lack of a conception of public good one can easily see how ideological stances in the public realm become entrenched, with little possibility for concession or compromise, because each modification is no longer conceived as a broader and shared win, but only as a loss. The cost of excessive scepticism vis-à-vis a notion of public good, or denial of its possibility, can not only lead to hardened and uncompromising stances in public life but also to citizens shunning the political realm altogether in a hopelessness about its capacity to solve shared challenges justly. Despite a lack of precise parameters and often disputed features, linking policy proposals to a broader appeal to a notion of the public good forces adjustments, negotiations, and a consideration of the good of the whole, integrating new perspectives, weighing respective burdens and adjudicating among a wider array of considerations than would otherwise be done.

In addition, it is important to have concepts to make sense of stances in public life that do not reflect the position of any one existing limited constituency. What of someone who acts with less concern for their reputation or who even risks their public reputation seeking reconciliation for a public purpose they see as more important and bigger than themselves? What of proposed policy options that seek to improve existence through broad visions of public welfare, whether it be through enhancing the status of the marginal so as to ensure greater inclusiveness and justice in the community, devoting their purpose to find a way to better manage the challenges of key issues (e.g. economic downturn, health challenges, economic disparities) in the community involving all stakeholders, or seeking a way to enhance the beautification of public spaces, contributing to the preservation of heritage and art and the regulation of development in private spaces, all for a broader sense of the good of the community? While there is a good deal in public life that can be understood through the rubrics of interest and interest maximation and the wielding of power for its own sake, there is fundamental importance in acknowledging possibilities in public life where actions are not always cynically construed and where individuals can make decisions and engage in action, not just for reasons that go beyond their narrow interest, and not just for reasons that favour a compromise with the expressed interests of other citizens, but also for reasons of a perspicacious view of what might actually make life better for future generations as well as for others of the polity. These are motivations we can ascribe to many in established professions of civil society (teaching, medicine, etc.), so why deny the same possibilities for those in public life? If public service is an extension of our humanity and better capacities, then we should allow for the recognition and possibility of valuable and indeed essential acts in view of the public good. This does not preclude the need for keen analysis to guard against the abuse of the idea in rhetorical terms, but such critical analysis does not make sense without an underlying acknowledgement of the deeper motivational concern that there is a substance to the notion of public service.

It is evident that groups and individuals who feel marginalised in a social and political order may be wary of the notion of a monolithic goal, or singular telos, through which politics is thought to tend in normative terms. The appeal of a model of agonistic politics is that it offers an easy solution to the reality of pluralism and conflicting agendas, and it may allow those devoted to an idea of social justice to prioritise the traditionally marginalised in absolute terms. Yet, again, this same ideal of social justice itself only makes sense when harnessed to a concept of public good in a deeper sense. Without an attachment to the possibility of an ideal where the community is restored, even in some incremental sense, there is only a clash of powers, and thereby no good-willed basis nor acceptance of an epistemological opening that might overcome the imminent challenges. Also, if the possibility of the productive and positive work of politics is denied, then commitments to the democratic process may themselves be weakened. Thus, there is a connection between motivational, epistemological and institutional reasons that make a notion of public good important for modern politics.

Part of the thrust and concern in this historical narrative is an attempt to revive and bolster a notion of the public good as a longstanding, useful and indispensable concept in our ongoing discussions on the nature and normative features of public life. My book does not make a claim to precisely articulate all that it entails, although some effort is made in my discussion of Rousseau to distinguish it from the idea of the common good. At the same time, this book explores the special features of the public realm where actors can be judged for both their motivations and the effects of their decisions. Plutarch, whose work has long been associated with the notion of *la chose publique* in the French tradition of reception, offers us insight into the history and usages of the idea of the public realm and the regulative and associated notion of public good, or *le bien public*, that forms part of the conceptual background to this idea.

There are many ways in which Plutarch's thought was appropriated and adapted to the dominant concerns of the times, and some thinkers drew more extensively on his thought than others. Still, many of these efforts can be seen as driven by an effort to avoid heavily abstract speculation, to bring historical examples to bear on practical concerns and on the active life, and to use history and practical advice to advance some understanding of the public realm and practice of public good. This was an idea not intrinsically associated with any type of institutional configuration, republican or otherwise, nor did it prioritise a conception of liberty but rather a *pursuit* of conciliation, concord and – ultimately – justice.

These varied appropriations at the outset of the tradition share a sense of the importance and dignity that can be associated with public service. As we have seen, they also offer some account of what distinguishes public life – both in terms of special responsibilities and demands and the challenges of seeking acceptable solutions among competing points of view – sometimes requiring compromise but in a spirit of concord and pursuance of public good. It is a loose 'tradition' (if I can call it that, given its wide parameters and variations) that I have called 'public humanism' due to its emphasis on the public figure and the unique features and challenges of public life (as opposed to the motivations in the realm of the citizenry).

Another contribution of a focus on this tradition is the insight that it offers into the moral psychology of public life. It explores not just the inner psychology of the public figure, as we have seen, including questions of character, but also aspects of the social psychology related to public life and how best to manage and govern perceptions and expectations. With a moralist thrust, it restores to the public a reading of Plutarch that is reflected in much of classical scholarship, but with a more inclusive moral framework and in direct contrast to blind celebrations of military heroism and conquest, or to loose appropriations for scripts of insurgent politics.

The tradition developed here rejects an idealist conception of perfected philosophical virtue, and promotes particular virtues, such as courage, prudence and moderation, with the idea that an individual in public life may be judged to be better when they are able to bend to some degree to the needs of their communities and the expectations of their era. An elevated understanding of a value in public service as an expectation in those seeing public office can help ensure that even mundane tasks of public service will be undertaken with a sense of dignity and dedication. Those who engage in public service must be seen as fallible individuals and who are indeed at times corruptible. Thus it is important to be able to discern between those features, qualities and actions that can be tolerated in view of broader public goals and those which indicate unsuitability for public office.

An idea of the motivations of an individual is not sufficient in assessing their suitability for public life. There are skills and dispositions that make some individuals better suited to the task of public service and they involve facets such as commitment to the community, an ability to work with others to seek solutions, good judgement and a sense of justice. Zacka has argued that those on the front line of public service need to be able to judge effectively when to prioritise certain roles of public service delivery, most notably those of efficiency, indifference and care-giving, and that the proper disposition is to be able to judge which stance is more appropriate in which context.[2] While those in the tradition of Plutarch reception have more often than not focused on those in higher office of public service, the more general point that good public service is not only possible but that it requires a certain degree of responsiveness and flexibility in different contexts, is a principle that can be traced back to that tradition. At a minimum, it involves the recognition that there are types of motivation, personality, as well as the lack of certain skills that make some individuals ill-suited for public office and that overly abundant self-concern, ignorance and lack of proper judgement can often inflict lasting damage on both the community and the institutions.

The ethos of the tradition stemming from Plutarch, as I have sketched it here, invokes an idea of the specificity of public life. A commitment to justice is combined with an understanding of the work of practical reason and prudence in which not all solutions consonant with justice are clearly visible, and for which both trade-offs and concessions may be necessary, with the possibility of a longer term give and take between governors and citizenry so that expectations are managed but also concerns heard. To consider the position of the public in terms of a snapshot of the public will (as one may find, for example, in Rousseau's notion of the general will, despite all the caveats of curation that I have acknowledged through a study of the more recent literature in political theory on his work), ignores the work of ongoing give and take that makes the notion of public service and its delivery a process of communication, education and readjustment in light of popular opinion. Good judgement through reflection and recon-sideration in public matters is necessary, alongside appropriate motivation, if power is to be exercised effectively. Aspirations to further the public good go hand in hand with a commitment to justice, and in a contemporary liberal-democratic order that also means adjusting one's ideals to the capacities and limits of the relevant public. However, it also should also not disregard the welfare of future generations.

I have shown over the course of the intellectual history covered here how the idea of public good has been subject to shifts. In Part II covering the period of the French Renaissance starting with the work of Geoffroy Tory I demonstrated a tendency for writers to identify the public good with the power and well-being of the monarch and for which the glory of the monarch was synonymous with the glory of the state. This was challenged

---

[2] Zacka, *When the State Meets the Street.*

in the period of the Wars of Religion as there was greater need to seek some form of accommodation for minorities and a means of peaceful coexistence, whether through judicious leadership, negotiation and compromise, or the exercise of civil virtues of humaneness and respect. We see then a different conception of the means to achieving the public good with ongoing reflection, consultation and negotiation to ascertain what might serve the better interests of the whole, while also acknowledging a possible need for compromise.

Part III includes consideration of competing accounts of public good in various thinkers of the Enlightenment. In the work of the Abbé de Saint-Pierre we see a developing logic and language of utility, and through this, as distilled in other writings, comes a notion of public good that is no longer associated with a collective state of justice but rather the existence of tangible services, such as roads, distribution networks and educational services; we might understand *choses publiques* (although the Abbé de Saint-Pierre does not use the term, it has come to be identified with the consequentialist logic of utility in matters of governance) as literally *public things* (à la Bonnie Honig, recognising her stance as a defender of agonistic democracy) or services offered by the state in view of enhancing the general welfare, on which citizens may come to rely as conditions for their material flourishing, despite also serving in certain contexts as matters for contestation.[3] In contrast, Mably pictured the public good as all citizens adhering to a singular vision of private virtue, thereby reducing good citizenship to ideal character and motivation, a notion that is not without its dangers for a weaponisation of virtue. As demonstrated in our discussion of Rousseau, yet another notion of public good was developed which sought to make its content relative to what was assented to by a snapshot of a singular common or general will.[4] I suggested that this Rousseauian notion risked marginalising the practices necessary for achieving conciliation around an idea of public good and demoting an idea of public service, despite the background work of curation in his thought. Rousseau points us in the direction of a politics fundamentally dictated by willing, thereby ignoring the hard work of assessment, judgement, conciliation, adjustment, citizen education, prudential consideration, reconsideration, and communication that goes into the fashioning of a political response that

---

[3] Bonnie Honig, *Public Things. Democracy in Disrepair* (New York: Fordham University Press, 2017).

[4] For a discussion of this view and its danger for liberal democracy, see Nadia Urbinati's *Representative Democracy* (Chicago: University of Chicago Press, 2008).

aims to serve the needs and longer-term well-being of all in the community together.

Rousseau's solution may have been fuelled in part by anxiety arising from the claimed necessity of degrees of prudence and pragmatic realism in public life. By offering a political solution that appeared to limit this by making it subject to periodic collective pronouncements of the general will, he offered a powerful and compelling ideal of the grounds for political liberty and collective popular autonomy. As I have argued here, while a worthy and important contemporary political ideal, it is not clear that his solution offers a sufficient guarantee of achieving an optimal outcome, and it carries the risk of ushering in a politics of generalised denunciation.

According to the Plutarchan tradition of reception, prudence and pragmatism were necessary features of public life. The keys to ensuring a responsible and effective use of power included appeal to the good qualities of the public official, along with knowledge of the characteristics, challenges and parameters of public responsibility and understanding of the social characteristics, aspirations and limitations of the general public. This must be framed by an underlying commitment to some understanding of the good for the polity and a sense of justice, which is further reinforced by a regulative sense and limiting power of bad and corrupt examples. The public official is cautious and often anguished in the face of the challenges. Without a solid and earnest sense of what sorts of political behaviour may be unacceptable, it is difficult to envisage a public official who can keep within the bounds of what is appropriate.

And while this may appear to be a narrative for the use and reflection of those thinking of embarking on public life, or those who study it, it is also intended to be informative for those who vote and help to choose public officials. Without a deeper sense and understanding of what is required of public life, and the sensibilities, commitments and priorities that make for good public service, it is difficult to envisage how a voter can easily discern who makes for a better candidate competing for public office. A basic take away from this account is that a rhetorical appeal to the popular will is an insufficient measure of political propriety. In a liberal democratic setting where campaigns may offer an array of competing conceptions of the good of the community, candidates should be required to articulate a version of the idea of justice that fuels their understanding of public service and be challenged regarding the contours of prudence and pragmatism that they associate with a position of public service.

In broad terms the demand for a more nuanced and variegated understanding of the nature and expectations of public life and public service constitute a major impetus for this book, drawing on long traditions of translation and reception. It suggests that regardless of the constitutionalist and legal parameters on the holding of office, part of the broader picture supporting the practice of good politics is an understanding of and certain respect for the general norms that help underlie and define the work of a public official, regardless of the specific contours of the regime in which they function.

Finally, this project seeks to revive and reorient our understanding of the evolution of the history of ideas, allowing the tradition of pre-revolutionary French political thought to become a point of reference in ongoing discussion and commentary. The tradition resuscitated here, one that looks neither to constitutions and institutions as the key to politics, nor to citizens and their republican virtues, but instead focuses directly on the ethos of public office, allows for greater attention to be paid to the broader and deeper contributions of political reflection in France to liberal democratic traditions today. And while we are at a crossroads where those liberal democratic traditions find themselves increasingly on the defensive, it may be appropriate to reconsider what is most central and worth defending in that conglomeration of ideas. While we would not wish for a full-scale return to the politics of Plutarch, reflection on the tradition that his work generated within France and England of the early modern period may be a helpful resource in allowing us to reflect on the politics we should aspire to have, rather than the politics we must suffer.

Bibliography

Primary Sources

Alciatus, Andreas. *Livret des emblèmes mis en rime francoyse*, trans. Jacques LeFevre. Paris: 1536.

Amyot, Jacques d'. *Projet d'Éloquence royale*. Paris: Belles Lettres, 1992.

"Avis aux lecteurs," *Les Vies des Hommes Illustres grecs et romains compares l'une avec l'autre par Plutarque*. Paris: l'Imprimerie de Ieremie des Planches, 1583.

Anonymous, *The Gentleman's Library: containing rules for conduct in all parts of life*, 4th ed. London: S. Birt, 1744.

Appian of Alexandria, *Wars of the Romans and Plutarch, Life of Mark Antony*. Paris, Bibliothèque Nationale, MS Fr. 713–714 (1507?).

Bacon, Francis. *The Major Works*, ed. Brian Vickers. Oxford: Oxford University Press, 1999.

Essays and Colours of Good and Evil, ed. W. Aldis Wright. New York: Macmillan, 1899.

The Essays, ed. Brian Vickers. Oxford: Oxford University Press, 1999.

Bodin, Jean. *Method for the Easy Comprehension of History*. New York: W. Norton, 1945.

Boétie, Estienne de la. *Œuvres complètes* 2 vols. ed. Louis Desgraves. Paris: William Blake and co., 1991.

Budé, Guillaume. *De l'Institution du prince*. Paris: Maistre Nicole Park, 1547 and Farnborough: Gregg Press, 1966.

Extrait ou abrégé du Livre de Asse. Lyon: Thibauld Payne, 1534.

Budé, Guillaume and D. Erasmus. *La Correspondance d'Erasme et de Guillaume Budé*, trans. M. de la Garanderie. Paris: Librairie Philosophique J. Vrin, 1967.

Castiglione, Baldesar. *The Book of the Courtier*. London: Penguin, 1967.

Cicero. *Le Livre Tulles des offices*. Paris: Jean Petit, 1501.

On Duties, eds. M. T. Griffin and E. M. Atkins. Cambridge: Cambridge University Press, 1991.

Tusculan disputations, trans. J. E. King. Cambridge, MA: Harvard University Press, 2014.

Cocteau, Jean. *Théâtre*. Paris: Grasset, 1957, vol. 1.

Constant, Benjamin. *Political Writings*, ed. Biancamaria Fontana. Cambridge: Cambridge University Press, 1997.

Corneille, Pierre. *Pompée*, ed. H. T. Barnwell. Oxford: Oxford University Press, 1971.

Cradock, Joseph. *The life of John Wilkes, esp. in the manner of Plutarch*. London: J. WIlkie, 1773.

Cudworth, Ralph. *The True Intellectual System of the Universe*, 1743.

Dacier, Anne. *Remarks upon Mr. Pope's Account of Homer prefixed to his translation of the Iliad*. London: E. Curll, 1724.

Diodorus Siculus, *Books* XVIII, XIX, XX *of Bibliotheca and Plutarch, Life of Demetrius*. Paris, Bibliothèque Nationale, Ms. Fr. 712 (1511).

    L'Histoire des successeurs de Alexandre de Grand extraicte de Diodore Sicilien et quelque peu de vies escriptes par Plutarque, trans. Claude de Seyssel. Paris: Iehan Barbe et Claude Garamont, 1545

    A Righte noble and pleasant history of the successors of Alexander surnamed the Great, taken out of Diodorus Siculus, and some of their lives written by the wise Plutarch, translated out of French into English by Thomas Stocker. London, Henrie Bynneman, 1569.

Dryden, John. "Dedicatory Letter to Plutarch's Lives," in *The Works of John Dryden*, vol. 17. Prose 1668–1691 (Berkeley: University of California Press, 1971).

Elizabeth I. *Queen Elizabeth Englishings*, ed. Caroline Pemberton. London: Kegan Paul, Trench, Trubner and Co. 1899.

Elyot, Thomas. *The Education of Children* (c. 1530). Online http://quod.lib.umich.edu/e/eebo/A09790.0001.001?rgn=main;view=fulltext Date accessed 2 Feb 2017.

    The Boke named the Governour. London: J. M. Dent and co. 1998 www.luminarium.org/renascence-editions/gov/gov1.htm Date searched 13 May 2019.

Emerson, Ralph Waldo. "Introduction," in *Plutarch's Morals*, ed. William Goodwin. Boston: Little, Brown and Company, 1874.

Erasmus, Desiderius. *The Education of a Christian Prince*, ed. and intro. Lisa Jardine. Cambridge: Cambridge University Press, 1997.

    Collected Works of Erasmus. The Apophthegmata, vols. 37 and 38, ed. Betty Knott and trans. Elaine Fantham and Betty Knott. Toronto: University of Toronto Press, 2014.

Erasmus and Luther. *Discourse on Free Will*, trans. Ernst F. Winter. New York: Continuum, 1961, 1989 and 2002.

Fortescue, John. *The Governance of England Otherwise Called The Difference between an Absolute and a Limited Monarchy*, ed. C. Plummer. Oxford: The Clarendon Press, 1885.

Haillan, Bernard de Girard Du. *Promesse et Desseign de l'Histoire de France*. Paris: Olivier de Pierre l'Huillier, 1571.

    Recueil d'advis et conseils sur les affaires d'estat, tire des vies de Plutarque. Paris: Olivier de Pierre l'Huillier, 1578.

Hobbes. Thomas. *Human Nature and De Corpore Politico*, ed. J. C. A. Gaskin. Oxford: Oxford University Press, 1994.

Leviathan, ed. Edwin Curley. Indianapolis, IN: Hackett, 1994.

On the Citizen, eds. Richard Tuck and Michael Silverthorne. Cambridge: Cambridge University Press, 1998.

Hume, David. *A Dissertation on the Passions*. Oxford: Oxford University Press, 2014.

Mably, *Phocion's Conversations or the relation between morality and politics.* London: Dodsley, 1769.

Mandeville, Bernard. *Fable of the Bees*, 3rd ed. London: Tonson, 1724.

Montagu, Edward Wortley. *Reflections on the rise and fall of the ancient republicks. Adapted to the present state of Great Britain.* London, 1769.

Montaigne, Michel de. *Les Essais.* ed. Jean Balsamo et al. Paris: Gallimard, 2007.

The Complete Essays, ed. M. A. Screech. Penguin: London, 1987.

Les Essais de Michel de Montaigne, ed. Pierre Villey. Paris: Presses Universitaires de France, 1965.

Montesquieu, *Œuvres complètes II*, ed. Roger Caillois. Paris: Gallimard, 1951.

More, Thomas. "Utopia," in *Three Early Modern Utopias*, ed. Susan Bruce. Oxford: Oxford University Press, 1999.

Mortimer, Thomas. *The British Plutarch: or biographical entertainer.* London: Edward Dilly, 1762.

The British Plutarch; or biographical entertainer. Being a select collection of the lives at large of the most eminent men natives of Great Britain and Ireland; from the reign of Henry VIII to George II, 12 vols. Perth: R. Morison, 1762.

Pasquier, Etienne. *Les Recherches de la France*, 3 vols. Paris: Honoré Champion, 1996.

Pizan, Christine de. *The Book of Peace*, ed. Karen Green et al. University Park, PA: 2008.

Le Livre du corps de policie, Geneva: Droz, 1967.

Plutarch. *Collected Works, Loeb edition*, 26 vols. Cambridge, MA: Harvard University Press, 1936–1980.

Les Apophthegmes, c'est-à-dire prompts subtilz, et sentencieux dictz de plusieurs Roys, chefz d'armées, Philosophes et autres grands personnages, tant Grecz que Latins, trans. Antoine Macault from Erasmus. Paris: Estienne Grouilleau, 1551.

Caesar, trans. and ed. Christopher Pelling. Oxford: Oxford University Press, 2011.

Épitomé ou abrégé des vies de cinquante et quatre notables et excellens personnaiges tant Greco que Romains extraict du Grec de Plutarque de Charonee, trans. Philippe des Avenelles. Paris: Paris. De l'imprimerie de Philippe Danfrie, et Richard Breton, 1558.

"How to be a Good Leader" [also known as "Political Precepts"] trans. J. Beneker in *How to Be a Good Leader*. Princeton: Princeton University Press, 2019.

The Lives in eight volumes. Translated from the Greek. With notes historical and critical from M. Dacier. London: J. Tonson, 1727

Les Œuvres morales et meslees de Plutarque, trans. J. Amyot. Paris: Vascosan, 1572.

The Philosophie commonlie called, The Morals, trans. Philemon Holland. London: Arnold Hatfield, 1603.

Plutarch's Lives, translated from the original Greek, with notes critical and historical and a new life of Plutarch, eds. John Langhorne and William Langhorne. London: Edward and Charles Dilly, 1774.

Politique ou civiles institutions pour bien regir la chose publicque, trans. Geofroy Tory. Lyon: Boulle, 1534.

Les Vies des hommes illustres, Grecs et Romains, compares l'une avec l'autre. trans. J. Amyot. Paris: Vascosan, 1565 and 1583.

Les Vies des Hommes Illustres de Plutarque reveues sur les mss. Et traduites en français, trans. André Dacier. Paris: Clousier et al., 1721.

Les Vies des Hommes Illustres de Plutarque traduites en français, trans. André Dacier. Lyon: Amable Leroy, 1803.

Les Vies des hommes illustres, trans. J. Amyot, 2 vols. Paris: Gallimard, 1951.

Opera moralia. Basile: Mich. Isingrinium, 1541.

Pseudo-Plutarch. *Essays on the Life and Poetry of Homer*, eds. J. J. Keaney and R. Lamberton. Atlanta, GA: Scholars Press and American Philological Association, 1966.

Racine, Jean. *Mithridate,* ed. Gustave Rudler. Oxford: Basil Blackwell, 1943.

Richelieu, *Testament politique ou Maximes d'État de Monsieur le Cardinal de Richelieu*, ed. Daniel Dessert. Paris Éditions, Complexe, 1990.

Rousseau, Jean-Jacques. *Julie ou la Nouvelle Héloïse*. Paris: Garnier Flammarion, 1967.

Œuvres Complètes, ed. B. Gagnebin. Paris: Gallimard, 1964.

The Confessions and Correspondence, Including the Letters to Malesherbes, trans. Christopher Kelly. Hanover, NH and London: University Press of New England, 1995.

Saint Pierre, Abbé de. *Ouvrages politiques*. Rotterdam: Beman, 1737.

Salisbury, John of. *Policraticus*, ed. C. Nederman. Cambridge: Cambridge University Press, 1990.

Salutati, Coluccio. "On Tyranny," in *Political Writings*, ed. Stefano Baldassarri, trans. Rolf Bagemihl. Cambridge MA and London: Harvard University Press, 2014.

Saunders, Erasmus. *A domestick charge, or the duty of household governors*. Oxford: Lichfield, 1701.

Selve, Georges de. "Le Prologue du Translateur, adresse au tres chrestien Roy Francoy premier de ce nom," in *Plutarch. Les Vies des huis excellens et renommez personnages Grecz et Rommains, mises au paragon lune de l'autre*. Lyon: Jean de Tounres, 1548.

Œuvres. Paris: Galliot de Pre, 1559.

Seran de la Tour, Abbé. *The Life of Scipio Africanus and of Epaminondas; intended as a supplement to Plutarch's Lives . . . To which is prefixed A Dissertation on the Distinction between a Great Man and an Illustrious or Eminent Man*, by the Abbe de Saint Pierre. London: Richardson, 1787.

Seyssel, Claude de. *La Monarchie de France*, ed. Jacques Poujol. Paris: Libraire d'Argences, 1961

    La Grant Monarchie de France. http://gallica.bnf.fr/ark:/12148/btv1b8626309q/ f7.item.zoom. Date consulted 22 May 2016.

Shelley, Mary Wollstonecraft. *Frankenstein*. Berkeley: University of California Press, 1984.

Sienois, François P. *De l'Estat et maniement de la chose publique, ensemble du gouvernment des royaumes et instruction des Princes*, trans. Jean Le Blond. Paris: Claude Micard, 1584.

Shakespeare, William. *Antony and Cleopatra*, ed. John Wilders. London and New York: Routledge, 1995.

    Julius Caesar, ed. T. S. Dorsch. London and New York: Routledge, 1955.

    Timon of Athens, ed. H. J. Oliver. London and New York: Routledge, 1959.

    Titus Andronicus, ed. Jonathan Bate. London and New York: Routledge, 1995.

Smyth, George. *The Vanity of Conquests and universal monarchy: being a succinct account of all the great conquerors and heroes*. London: R. Smith, 1705.

Stillingfleet, Edward. *Origines sacrae: or, a rational account o the grounds of natural and revealed religion*. London: R. Knaplock, 1662 and 1724.

Stretch, L. M. *The Beauties of History or pictures of virtue and vice, drawn from real life: designed for the instruction and entertainment of youth*, 2 vols. Dublin, 1788.

Swift, Jonathan. *A Discourse of the Contests and Dissensions between the Nobles and Commons in Athens and Rome, with the Consequences they had upon both those States*. London: John Nutt, 1701.

    Gulliver's Travels. London: Collins, 2018.

    Political Tracts. By the author of Gulliver's travels, 2 vols. London: C. Davis, 1738.

Taverner, Richard, ed. *The Garden of Wysdom, wherein ye maye gather moste pleasaunt flowres thath is to say, proper witty and quycke sayenges of princes, philosophers, and dyvers other sortes of men. Frawn forth of good authours, as well Grekes as Latyns by Richard Taverner*, 1539. On Early English Books Online, November 2017.

Temple, William. "Of Unrestrained Power," in *Moral and historical memoirs*. London 1779.

Tory, Geofroy. *Champ Fleury*. East Ardsley, New York and Paris: S. R. Publishers, Johnson Reprint Corporation and Mouton and Co, 1970 and 1529.

    Champ fleury, trans. and ed. George Ives. New York: The Grolier Club, 1927.

Wanley, Nathaniel. *The history of man; or, the wonders of humane nature in relation to the virtues, vices and defects of both sexes*. London: R. Basset, 1704.

Wilkins, John. *On the Principles and Duties of Natural Religion*. London; 1715.

Secondary Sources

Abizadeh, Arash. "*Popular Sovereignty vs. Democracy: Or How Rousseau Killed Democracy*," unpublished paper delivered to the Political Online Theory Seminar, University of Toronto, June 2020.

Ahmed, Eshan. "Wisdom and Absolute Power in Guillaume de Budé's *Institution du Prince.*" *Romanic Review* 96.2 (2005), 173–185.

Allen, J. W. *A History of Political Thought in the Sixteenth Century.* New York: The Dial Press. 1928.

Altman, William. ed., *Brill's Companion to the Reception of Cicero.* Leiden: Brill, 2015.

Aulotte, Robert. *Amyot et Plutarque: la tradition des Moralia au XVIe siècle.* Geneva: Droz, 1965.

Balot, Ryan. "Virtue and Emotional Education in Ancient Greece," in *Emotions, Community and Citizenship*, eds. Kiran Banerjee et al. Toronto: University of Toronto Press, 2017, 35–51.

Barnwell, H. T. "'Moins roi que pirate': Some Remarks on Racine's *Mithridate* as a Play of Ambiguities." *Seventeenth-Century French Studies* 24.1(2002), 179–190.

Baron, Hans. *Crisis of the Early Italian Renaissance.* Princeton, NJ: Princeton University Press, 1966.

Baskervill, Charles. "Taverner's Garden of Wisdom and the Apophthegmata of Erasmus." *Studies in Philology* (1932), 149–159.

Basset Bérengère et Christine Bénévent. "Les apophtegmes de Plutarque et la tradition des miroirs du prince au XVIe siècle: l'exemple de l'Institution du prince de Guillaume Budé." *Littératures Classiques* 84.2 (2014), 63–96.

Beck, Mark, ed. *A Companion to Plutarch.* Oxford: Blackwell, 2014.

Beneker, Jeffrey. *The Passionate Statesman: Eros and Politics in Plutarch's Lives.* Oxford: Oxford University Press, 2012.

Bénichou, Paul. *Morales du Grand Siècle.* Paris: Gallimard, 1948.

Bennett, H. S. *English Books and Readers 1475 to 1557*, 2nd ed. Cambridge: Cambridge University Press, 1969.
 English Books and Readers 1558–1603. Cambridge: Cambridge University Press, 1965.

Berkowitz, Peter. *Virtue and the Making of Modern Liberalism.* Princeton NJ: Princeton University Press, 1999.

Berry, Edmund G. *Emerson's Plutarch.* Cambridge MA: Harvard University Press, 1961.

Bershin, Walter. "Plutarque en France XIVe–XVIe siècle," in *Traduction et adaptation en France. Actes du colloque organisé par l'Université de Nancy II 23–25 mars 1995*, ed. Charles Brucker. Paris: Honoré Champion, 1997.

Bizer, Marc. *Homer and the Politics of Authority in Renaissance France.* Oxford: Oxford University Press, 2011.

De Blois, Lukas et al. *The Statesman in Plutarch's Works.* 2 vols. Leiden: Brill, 2004.

Bolgar, R. R. "Humanism as a Value System, with reference to Budé and Vives," in *Humanism in France at the end of the Middle Ages and in the early Renaissance*, ed. A. H. T. Levi. Manchester: Manchester University Press, 1970.

Bomford, Kate. "Friendship and Immortality: Holbein's Ambassadors Revisited." *Renaissance Studies* 18.4 (2004), 544–581.

Bonnefon, Paul. "L'Historien Du Haillan." *Revue d'Histoire Littéraire de la France* 22.3–4 (1915), 453–492.

Boone, Rebecca. "Claude de Seyssel's Translations of Ancient Historians." *Journal of the History of Ideas* 61.4 (2000), 561–575.

War and Domination and the Monarchy of France. Claude de Seyssel and the Language of Politics in the Renaissance. Leiden and Boston: Brill, 2007.

Boucher, Warren. "The Renaissance," in *The Oxford Guide to Literature in English Translation*, ed. Peter France. (Oxford: Oxford University Press, 2000), 45–55.

Bourrilly, V. L. Jacques Colin. *Abbé de Saint-Amboise (14?–1547)*. Paris: Société nouvelle de Librairie et d'Edition, 1905.

Bradshaw, Brendan. "Transalpine Humanism," in *The Cambridge History of Political Thought 1450–1700*, ed. J. H. Burns. Cambridge: Cambridge University Press, 1991.

Brett, Annabel and James Tully, eds. *Rethinking the Foundations of Modern Political Thought.* Cambridge: Cambridge University Press, 2010.

Briant, Pierre. *The First European. A History of Alexander in the Age of Empire.* Cambridge, MA: Harvard University Press, 2017.

Brigden, Susan. *Thomas Wyatt. The Heart's Forest.* London: Faber and Faber, 2012.

Brooke, Christopher. *Philosophic Pride. Stoicism and Political Thought from Lipsius to Rousseau.* Princeton, NJ: Princeton University Press, 2012.

Bruce, Susan, "Introduction," in *Three Early Modern Utopias: Utopia, New Atlantis, The Isle of Pines*, ed. S. Bruce. Oxford: Oxford University Press, 1999.

Burke, Peter. "A Survey of the Popularity of Ancient Historians, 1450–1700." *History and Theory* 5.2 (1966), 135–152.

"Cultures of Translation in Early-Modern Europe," in *Cultural Translation in Early-Modern Europe*, eds. Peter Burke and Po-Chia Hsia. Cambridge: Cambridge University Press, 2007, 7–38.

"Tacitism," in *Tacitus*, ed. T. A. Dorey. London: Routledge and Kegan Paul, 1969.

Canfora, Davide. *La Controversia di Poggio Bracciolini e Guarino Veronese du Cesare e Scipione.* Florence: L. S. Olschki, 2001.

Carley, James. "'Plutarch's' Life of Agesilaus: A Recently Located New Year's Gift to Thomas Cromwell by Henry Parker, Lord Morley," in *Prestige, Authority and Power in Late Medieval Manuscripts and Texts*, ed. Felicity Riddy. Cambridge: Cambridge University Press, 2000, 159–170.

Carley, James and Myra D. Orth, "Plus que assez: Simon Bourgouyn and his French Translations from Plutarch, Petrarch and Lucian." *Viator* 34 (2003), 328–363

Charité, Claude la. "Henri III rhéteur, nouvel Hercule gaulois," in *New Chapters in the History of Rhetoric*, ed. Laurent Pernot. Leiden and Boston: Brill, 2009.

Chavura, Stephen. *Tudor Protestant Political Thought 1547–1603.* Leiden: Brill, 2011.

Chavy, Paul. "Les Traductions humanistes au début de la Renaissance française: traductions médiévales, traductions modernes." *Canadian Review of Comparative Literature* (Spring 1981), 302.

Chernaik, Warren. *The Myth of Rome in Shakespeare and His Contemporaries.* Cambridge: Cambridge University Press, 2011.

Clarke, David. "Plutarch's Contribution to the Invention of Sabine in Corneille's *Horace*." *The Modern Language Review*, 89.1 (1994), 39–49.

Coldiron, A. E. B. "The Mediated 'medieval' and Shakespeare," in *Medieval Shakespeare. Pasts and Presents*, eds. Helen Cooper et al. Cambridge: Cambridge University Press, 2013.

Collins, James. "Dynastic Instability, the Emergence of the French Monarchical Commonwealth and the Coming of the Rhetoric of l'état, 1360s to 1650s." in *Monarchy Transformed*, eds. Robert von Friedeburg and John Morrill. Cambridge: Cambridge University Press, 2017.

Collinson, Patrick. "The Monarchical Republic of Queen Elizabeth I." *Bulletin of the John Rylands Library*, 69.2 (1987), 394–424.

Connolly, Joy. *The Life of Roman Republicanism.* Princeton NJ: Princeton University Press, 2017.

Cooper, Julie. "Vainglory, Modesty and Political Agency in the Political Theory of Thomas Hobbes." *The Review of Politics* 72 (2010), 241–269.

Cox Jensen, Freyja. "The Popularity of Ancient Historians, 1450–1600." *The Historical Journal* 61.3 (2018), 561–595.

Reading the Roman Republic in Early Modern England. Leiden: Brill, 2012.

Cummings, Robert. "Versifying Philosophy: Thomas Blundeville's Plutarch," in *Renaissance Cultural Crossroads: Translation, Print and Culture in Britain, 1473–1640*, eds. S. K. Barker and B. M. Hosington. Leiden and Boston: Brill, 2013.

Dahlinger, James. *Etienne Pasquier on Ethics and History.* New York: Peter Lang, 2007.

Dauber, Noah. *State and Commonwealth. The Theory of the State in Early Modern England, 1549–1640.* Princeton NJ: Princeton University Press, 2016.

Defaux, Gerard and Michael Metter. "The Case of Bérénice: Racine, Corneille and Mimetic Desire." *Yale French Studies* 76 (1989), 211–239.

Denton, John. *Translation and Manipulation in Renaissance England.* Florence: Firenze University Press, 2016.

"Translation and Manipulation in Renaissance England." *Journal of Early Modern Studies* 1(2016).

Desan, Philippe. *Montaigne, A Life.* Princeton, NJ and Oxford: Princeton University Press, 2017.

Devereux, E. J. *Renaissance English Translations of Erasmus.* Toronto: University of Toronto Press, 1983.

"Richard Taverner's Translations of Erasmus." *The Library* 5.19 (January 1964), 212–214.

Dijn, Annelien de. "Rousseau and Republicanism." *Political Theory* 46.1 (2018), 59–80.

Dornier, Carole and C. Poulouin, eds. *Les Projets de l'abbé Castel de Saint-Pierre (1658–1743).* Caen: Maison de la Recherche en Sciences humaines, université de Caen Basse-Normandie, 2011

Downie, J. A. *Jonathan Swift. Political Writer.* London: Routledge and Kegan Paul, 1984.

Duff, Timothy. *Plutarch's Lives Exploring Virtue and Vice.* Oxford: Oxford University Press, 1999.
 "Models of Education in Plutarch." *The Journal of Hellenic Studies* 128 (2008), 1–26.

Duval, Edwin. "Erasmus and the 'First Renaissance' in France," in Christopher Prendergast, ed. *A History of Modern French Literature: From the Sixteenth Century to the Twentieth Century.* Princeton, NJ: Princeton University Press, 2017.

Eddy, William. *Gulliver's Travels: A Critical Study.* Princeton, NJ: Princeton University Press, 1923.

Edelstein, Dan. "Rousseau, Bodin and the Medieval Corporatist Origins of Popular Sovereignty." *Political Theory* (2021), 1–27.

Edwards, M. J. *Plutarch. The Lives of Pompey, Caesar and Cicero.* London: Bristol Classical Press, 2003.

Eichel-Lojkine, Patricia. *Claude de Seyssel. Ecrire l'histoire, penser le politique en France, à l'aube des temps modernes.* Paris: Presses Universitaires de France, 2010.

Fideler, Paul and T. F. Mayer, eds. *Political Thought and the Tudor Commonwealth.* London: Routledge, 1992 and 2005.

Fontana, Biancamaria. "The Political Thought of Montaigne," in *The Oxford Handbook of Montaigne*, ed. Philippe Desan. (Oxford: Oxford University Press, 2016).

Frazier, Françoise and O. Guerrier, eds. *La langue de Jacques Amyot.* Paris: Garnier, 2018.

Fumaroli, Marc. *L'Age de l'éloquence.* Geneva: Droz, 1980.

Geanakoplos, Deno. "Erasmus and the Aldine Academy of Venice." *Roman and Byzantine Studies*, 3.2 (1960), 107–134.

Gelber, Michael Werth. "John Dryden and the Battle of the Books." *Huntington Library Quarterly*, 63.1 and 2(200), 139–156.

George, Robert Lloyd. *A Modern Plutarch: Comparisons of the Most Influential Modern Statesmen.* New York: Overlook Duckworth, 2016.

Gilmore, Myron Piper. *Humanists and Jurists.* Cambridge, MA: Belknap Press, 1963.

Glaser, Eliane. *Anti-politics: On the Demonization of Ideology, Authority and the State.* London: Repeater Books, 2017.

Goldhill, Simon. "The Value of Greek. Why Save Plutarch?" in *Who Needs Greek? Contests in the Cultural History of Hellenism.* Cambridge: Cambridge University Press, 2002.

Goodenough, Myrta. "Bacon and Plutarch." *Modern Language Review Notes* 12.5 (May 1897), 284–286.

Goyard-Fabre, Simone. "Je ne suis que l'Apothicaire de l'Europe," in *Les Projets de l'abbé Castel de Saint-Pierre (1658–1743)*. Caen: Maison de la Recherche en Sciences humaines, université de Caen Basse-Normandie, 2011, 19–37.

Gray, Patricia. "Subscribing to Plutarch in the Eighteenth Century." *Australian Journal of French Studies*, 29.1 (1992), 30–40.

Green, Jeffrey. "Solace for the Frustrations of Silent Citizenship: The Case of Epicureanism." *Citizenship Studies*, 19.5 (2005), 492–506.

Greenberg, Mitchell. *Racine: From Ancient Myth to Tragic Modernity*. Minneapolis: University of Minnesota Press, 2009.

Greenblatt, Stephen. *Tyrant*. New York and London: Norton, 2018.

Grell, Chantal. "History and Historians in France, from the Great Italian Wars to the Death of Louis XIV," in *The Oxford History of Historical Writing, volume 3: 1400–1800*, eds. J. Rabasa et al. Oxford: Oxford University Press, 2012.

Guerrier, Olivier, ed. *Moralia et Œuvres morales à la Renaissance*. Paris: Honoré Champion, 2008.

  ed. *Plutarque de l'Age classique au XIXe siècle*. Grenoble: Jerome Million, 2012.

  "Plutarque," in *Dictionnaire de Montaigne*, ed. P. Desan. Paris: Honoré Champion, 2007.

Guy, John. *Thomas More*. London: Hodder Education, 2000.

  "Thomas More and Tyranny." *Moreana* 49. 189–190 (2012), 157–188.

Haas, Claude and Michael Auer, "The Dramaturgy of Sovereignty and the Performance of Mourning: The Case of Corneille's Horace." *Yale French Studies*, no. 124(2013), 121–134.

Hale, David. "Intestine Sedition: The Fable of the Belly." *Comparative Literature Studies*, 5.4(1968), 377–388.

Halewood, William. "Plutarch in Houyhnhnm Land: A Neglected Source for Gulliver's Fourth Voyage." *Philological Quarterly* 44.2(1965), 185–194.

Hamilton, James J. "The Origins of Hobbes's State of Nature." in *Hobbes Studies* 26.2 (January 2013), 152–170.

Hampton, Timothy. *Writing from History: The Rhetoric of Exemplarity in Renaissance Literature*. Ithaca, NY: Cornell University Press, 1989.

Hanford, J. H. "Plutarch and Dean Swift." *MLN* 35(1910), 181–184.

Hankins, James. *Virtue Politics*. Cambridge, MA: Belknap Press, 2019.

  Humanism and Platonism in the Italian Renaissance, 2 vols. Rome: Edizioni di Storia et Letteratura, 2003.

  "Humanism and the Origins of Modern Political Thought," in *The Cambridge Companion to Renaissance Humanism*, ed. Jill Kraye. Cambridge: Cambridge University Press, 1996.

Heal, Felicity. *The Power of Gifts*. Oxford: Oxford University Press, 2014.

Hervey, Mary. *Holbein's Ambassadors*. London: George Bell and Sons, 1900.

Higgins, Ian. "Swift and Sparta: The Nostalgia of Gulliver's Travels." *The Modern Language Review* 78.3(1983), 513–531.

Hirzel, Rudolf. *Plutarch*. Leipzig: Theodor Weicher, 1912.

Honest, Marie-Luce. "Antoine du Saix, Pédagogue humaniste émule d'Erasme." *Bibliotheque d'Humanisme et Renaissance*, 54.3 (1992), 661–689.

Honig, Bonnie. *Public Things. Democracy in Disrepair*. New York: Fordham University Press, 2017.

Humble, Noreen. *Xenophon of Athens: A Socratic on Sparta*. Cambridge: Cambridge University Press, 2021.

Ianziti, Gary. *Writing History in Renaissance Italy. Leonard Bruni and the Uses of the Past*. Cambridge, MA: Harvard University Press 2012.

Ibbett, Katherine. *The Style of the State in French Theatre, 1630–1660*. Farnham: Ashgate, 2009.

Jacobs, Susan. *Plutarch's Pragmatic Biographies*. Leiden and Boston: Brill, 2018.

Jardine, Lisa. *Erasmus, Man of Letters: The Construction of Charisma in Print*. Princeton, NJ: Princeton University Press, 1993 and 2015.

Jaeger, Werner. *Paideia: The Ideals of Greek Culture*. Oxford: Basil Blackwell, 1939.

Jones, C. P. *Plutarch and Rome*. Oxford: Oxford University Press, 1971.

Juhász-Ormsby, Agnes. "Erasmus' *Apophthegmata* in Henrician England." *Erasmus Studies* 37 (2017), 45–67.

Kantorowicz, Ernst. "*Pro patria mori* in Medieval Political Thought." *The American Historical Review* 56.3 (1951), 485.

Kapust, Daniel and Gary Remer, eds., *The Ciceronian Tradition in Political Theory*. Madison: University of Wisconsin Press, 2020.

Keaney, J. J. and R. Lamberton, "Introduction," in *Essays on the Life and Poetry of Homer, by [Plutarch]*, eds. J. J. Keaney and R. Lamberton. Atlanta, GA: Scholars Press and American Philological Association, 1966.

Kelley, Donald R. *Foundations of Modern Historical Scholarship: Language, Law and History in the French Renaissance*. New York and London: Columbia University Press, 1970.

"Law," in *The Cambridge History of Political Thought 1450–1700*, eds. J. H. Burns and M. Goldie. Cambridge: Cambridge University Press, 1991.

"Tacitus Noster: The Germania in the Renaissance and Reformation," in *Tacitus and the Tacitean Tradition*, eds T. J. Luce and A. J. Woodman. Princeton, NJ: Princeton University Press, 1993, 152–167.

Keohane, Nannerl. *Philosophy and the State in France*. Princeton, NJ: Princeton University Press, 1980 and 2017.

Kingston, Rebecca. "Rousseau's Debt to Plutarch," in *The Rousseauian Mind*, eds. Eve Grace and C. Kelly. London and New York: Routledge, 2019, 23–33.

"Thinking about the Public Realm in Early Sixteenth Century France through Plutarch and Geoffroy Tory (1480–1533)," in *Brill Companion to the Legacy of Greek Political Thought*, eds. David Carter et al. Leiden: Brill, forthcoming.

Knos, Borje. *Un Ambassadeur de l'Hellénisme Janus Lascaris et la Tradition Greco-Byzantine dans l'Humanisme Français*. Uppsala and Paris: Almquist and Wiksells and Les Belles Lettres, 1945.

Konstantinovic, Isabelle. *Montaigne et Plutarque*. Geneva: Droz, 1989.

Kovtun, George. "John Lascaris and the Byzantine Connection." *The Journal of Library History* (1974–1987), vol. 12, n. 1 (winter 1977), 17–26.

Kristeller, Paul O. *Renaissance Thought the Classic Scholastic and Humanistic Strains*. New York: Harper and Row, 1955.

Lamberton, Robert. *Plutarch*. New Haven, CT: Yale University Press, 2001.

Lamothe, Martial. "Montaigne et Rousseau lecteurs de Plutarque." Unpublished dissertation from the City University of New York, 1980.

Landemore, Hélène. *Open Democracy*. Princeton, NJ: Princeton University Press, 2020.

Larsen, John and Gianni Paganini, eds. *Skepticism and Political Thought in the Seventeenth and Eighteenth Centuries*. Toronto: University of Toronto Press, 2015.

Lazarus, Micha. "Greek Literacy in Sixteenth-Century England." *Renaissance Studies* 29.3 (2014), 433–458.

Leduc-Fayette, Denise. *J.-J. Rousseau et le Mythe de l'Antiquité*. Paris: Vrin, 1974.

Lee, Daniel. *Popular Sovereignty in Early-Modern Constitutional Thought*. Oxford: Oxford University Press, 2016.

Legros, Alain. "Plutarque annoté par Montaigne," MONLOE: Montaigne à l'œuvre, https://montaigne.univ-tours.fr/notes-de-lecture-de-montaigne/pl utarque-annote-par-montaigne/. Date accessed 24 May 2022

Lewis, Michael. *The Fifth Risk*. New York: Norton, 2018.

Liebert, Hugh. *Plutarch's Politics*. Cambridge: Cambridge University Press, 2016
"Plutarch's Critique of Plato's Best Regime." *History of Political Thought* 30.2 (2009), 251–271.

Liebeschütz, H. "John of Salisbury and Pseudo-Plutarch." *Journal of the Warburg and Courtauld Institutes*, 6 (1943), 33.

Liu, Antong. "Youthfulness and Rousseau's Anti-Pluralist Realism about Political Pluralism." *Political Research Quarterly* 5(2021),1–13.

Lloyd, Howell A. Howell Lloyd, *Jean Bodin, 'This Pre-eminent Man of France': An Intellectual Biography*. Oxford: Oxford University Press, 2017.
The State, France and the Sixteenth Century. London: George Allen and Unwin, 1983.

Lobbes, Louis. "Les Apophtegmes d'Erasme." *Seizième Siècle* 1(2005),85–97.

Lock, F. P. *The Politics of Gulliver's Travels*. Oxford: Clarendon Press, 1980.

Lyons, John. *The Rhetoric of Exemplarity in Early Modern France and Italy*. Princeton, NJ: Princeton University Press, 1989.

MacCallum, M. W. *Shakespeare's Roman Plays*. London: Macmillan, 1925.

Magnien, M. "Dolet Editeur de Georges de Selve, et le rôle de Pierre Bunel: un évangélisme cicéronien," in *Etudes sur Etienne Dolet: le théâtre aux XVIe siècle*, ed. Gabriel-André Pérouse. Geneva: Droz, 1993, 103–120.

Malcolm, Noel. *Agents of Empire: Knights, Corsairs, Jesuits and Spies in the Sixteenth-Century Mediterranean World*. London: Allen Lane, 2015.
Thomas Hobbes Leviathan. 1. Introduction. Oxford: Oxford University Press, 2012.

Margolin, J.- Cl. "Guillaume Haudent, poète et traducteur des Apophthegmes d'Erasme." *Revue de Littérature comparée*, 52(1978), 202–222.

Marshall, C. "Shakespeare, Crossing the Rubicon." *Shakespeare Survey* 53(2000), 73–88.

Martin, Janet. "John of Salisbury as Classical Scholar," in *The World of John of Salisbury*, ed. Michael Wilks. Oxford: Blackwell, 1994.

Matthiessen, Francis. *Translation, an Elizabethan Art*. Cambridge, MA: Harvard University Press, 1931.

Matthieu- Castellani, Gisele. "Plutarque chez Montaigne et chez Shakespeare," *Actes des congrès de la Société française Shakespeare* http://journals.openedition.org/shakespeare/671; DOI: 10.4000/shakespeare.671

Maxson, Brian J. "Kings and Tyrants: Leonardo Bruni's translation of Xenophon's Hiero." *Renaissance Studies* 24.2 (2010), 188–206.

Mayor, Adrienne. *The Poison King*. Princeton NJ: Princeton University Press, 2010.

McNeil, David O. *Guillaume Budé and Humanism in the Reign of Francis I*. Geneva: Droz, 1975.

Miles, G. B. "How Roman are Shakespeare's Romans?" *Shakespeare Quarterly* 40 (1989), 257–283.

Moatti, Claudia. *Res publica: histoire romaine de la chose publique*. Paris: Fayard, 2018.

Mombello, Gianni. "Du Doute à la conscience du succès: Le Cas de Claude de Seyssel (1504–1514)," in *Traduction et adaptation en France. Actes du Colloque organisé par l'Université de Nancy II 23–25 mars 1995*, ed. Charles Brucker. Paris: Honoré Champion, 1997.

Morel, Jean E. "Jean-Jacques Rousseau lit Plutarque." *Revue d'histoire moderne* 81 (1926), 81–102.

Morini, Massimilano. *Tudor Translation in Theory and Practice*. London: Ashgate, 2006.

Mossman, Judith. "Plutarch and English Biography." *Hermathena*, 183(2007), 75–100.

"Tragedy and Epic in Plutarch's Alexander," in *Essays on Plutarch's Lives*, ed. Barbara Scardigli. Oxford: Clarendon Press, 1995, 209–228.

Nederman, Cary J. "Aristotelianism and the Origins of 'Political Science' in the Twelfth Century." *Journal of the History of Ideas* 52.2 (1991), 179–194.

"Introduction," in *John of Salisbury, Policraticus*. Cambridge: Cambridge University Press, 1990.

Nelson, Eric. *The Greek Tradition in Republican Thought*. Cambridge: Cambridge University Press, 2004.

"Greek Nonsense in More's Utopia." *The Historical Journal* 44 (2001), 889–917.

Nesvet, Rebecca. "Parallel Histories: Dryden's Plutarch and Religious Toleration." *The Review of English Studies* 56.225 (2005), 424–437.

Norton, Glyn. *The Ideology and Language of Translation in Renaissance France and their humanist antecedents*. Geneva: Droz, 1984.

Ohlmeyer, Jane and Steven Zwicker. "John Dryden, the House of Ormond and the Politics of Anglo-Irish Patronage." *The Historical Journal* 49.3 (2006), 677–706.

Oltramare, André. *Jean-Jacques Rousseau*. Geneva: Unknown publisher, 1920 and 1972.

Pade, Marianne. *The Reception of Plutarch's Lives in Fifteenth-Century Italy, 2 vols.* Copenhagen: Museum Tusculanum Press, 2007.

"'I Give You Back Plutarch in Latin': Guarino Veronese's Version of Plutarch's Dion (1414) and Early Humanist Translation." *The Canadian Review of Comparative Literature.* 41.4 (2014), 354–368.

Pagden, Anthony, ed. *The Languages of Political Theory in Early-Modern Europe.* Cambridge: Cambridge University Press, 1987.

Panichi, Nicola. "Montaigne and Plutarch: A Scepticism that Conquers the Mind," in *Renaissance Skepticisms*, eds. G. Pagannia and J. Maia Neto. Dordrecht: International Archives of the History of Ideas and Springer, 2009, 183–212.

Paul, Joanne. *Counsel and Command in Early Modern English Thought.* Cambridge: Cambridge University Press, 2020.

Pelling, Christopher B. R. "The Moralism of Plutarch's Lives," in *Plutarch and History: Eighteen Studies.* London: Classical Press of Wales, 2002 and 2011.

"Introduction," in *Plutarch Caesar*, ed. C. Pelling. Oxford: Oxford University Press, 2011.

Plutarch and History: Eighteen Studies. London and Swansea: Bloomsbury, 2002.

"The Shaping of Coriolanus: Dionysius, Plutarch, and Shakespeare." *Poetica* 48 (1997), 3–32.

Peltonen, Markku. *Classical Humanism and Republicanism in English Political Thought, 1570–1640.* Cambridge: Cambridge University Press, 2009.

"Bacon's Political Philosophy," in *The Cambridge Companion to Bacon*, ed. M. Peltonen. Cambridge: Cambridge University Press, 1996, 283–310.

Penwill, John. "Expelling the Mind: Politics and Philosophy in Flavian Rome," in *Flavian Rome. Culture, Image, Text*, eds. A. J. Boyle and W. J. Dominik. Leiden: Brill, 2003.

Philippides, Marios. "The Fall of Constantinople 1453: Classical Comparisons and the Circle of Cardinal Isidore." *Viator* 38.1 (2007), 361–362.

Pire, Georges. "Du Bon Plutarque au Citoyen de Genève." *Revue de littérature comparée*, vol. 32 (1958), 510–547.

Pocock, J. G. A. *The Machiavellian Moment.* Princeton, NJ: Princeton University Press, 1975.

Popova, Ivayla. "Manuel Chrysoloras (1350–1415), Erudit et Diplomate Byzantin, et Sa Syncrisis." *Etudes balkaniques 3 and 4* (1998), 153–157.

Preston, Rebecca. "Roman Questions, Greek Answers: Plutarch and the Construction of Identity," in *Being Greek Under Rome*, ed. Simon Goldhill. Cambridge: Cambridge University Press, 2001.

Prigent, Michel. *Le Héros et l'État dans la tragédie de Pierre Corneille.* Paris: Presses Universitaires de France, 1986.

Raisch, Jane. "Humanism and Hellenism: Lucian and the Afterlives of Greek." *English Literary History* 83.4 (2016), 935–936.

Ranum, Orest. *Artisans of Glory*. Durham: Univeristy of North Carolina Press, 1980.

Raylor, Timothy. *Philosophy, Rhetoric and Thomas Hobbes*. Oxford: Oxford University Press, 2018.

Reverdin, Olivier. "Figures de l'hellénisme à Genève," in *Homère chez Calvin* ed. Olivier Reverdin. Geneva: Droz, 2000.

Ribeiro, Ana Claudia Romano. "Intertextual Connections between Thomas More's Utopia and Cicero's De finibus bonorum et malorum." *Moreana* 51.195–6 (2014), 63–84.

Rigoulot, Robert B. "Guillaume Budé." *Sixteenth-Century French Writers of the Dictionary of Literary Biography*, vol. 327 (2006). http://go.galegroup.com/p s/retrieve.do?inPS=true&userGroupName=oxford&prodId=DLBC&docI d=GALE|PKJAGR102182797. Date consulted 6 May 2016.

Rosenbluth, Frances McCall and Ian Shapiro. *Responsible Parties*. New Haven, CT: Yale University Press, 2018.

Rummel, Erika. *Erasmus as a Translator of the Classics*. Toronto: University of Toronto Press, 2012.

Rundle, David. "Book Review of Marianne Pade's *The Reception of Plutarch's Lives in Fifteenth-Century Italy*." *Renaissance Studies* 23.1 (February 2009), 129–131.

Russell, Peter. "Sovereignty: A Pernicious Claim whose Days are Done," unpublished talk delivered to the Faculty Club of the University of Toronto, September 2019.

Salmon, J. H. M. "Cicero and Tacitus in Sixteenth-Century France." *American Historical Review*, vol. 85.2 (April 1980), 307.

Sanchi, Luigi. "Budé et Plutarque," in *Moralia et Œuvres morales à la Renaissance*. Paris: Honoré Champion, 2008.

Sandy, Gerald, ed. *The Classical Heritage in France*. Leiden: Brill, 2002.

Schadee, Hester. "Caesarea Laus: Ciriaco d'Ancona praising Caesar to Leonardo Bruni." *Renaissance Studies* 22.4 (2008), 435–449.

Schellhase, Kenneth. *Tacitus in Renaissance Political Thought*. Chicago: University of Chicago Press, 1977.

Schmitt, C. B. and Quentin Skinner. "Political Philosophy," in *Cambridge History of Renaissance Philosophy*. Cambridge: Cambridge University Press, 1988.

Schoeck, R. "More, Plutarch, and King Agis: Spartan History and the Meaning of Utopia." *Philological Quarterly* 35 (January 1956), 366–376.

Schurink, Fred. "'Scholemaister and Counsailour unto Traianus': Plutarch, the Institutio Traiani, and Humanist Political Advice in Renaissance England." Unpublished paper, 2017.

"Print, Patronage, and Occasion: Translations of Plutarch's *Moralia* in Tudor England." *Yearbook of English Studies* 38.1–2(2008), 86–101.

Scott, Jonathan. "What were Commonwealth Principles?" *The Historical Journal* 47.3 (2004), 591–613.

Shackford, Martha. *Plutarch in Renaissance England*. Wellesley, MA: Wellesley College, 1929.

Shapiro, James. *The Year of Lear. Shakespeare in 1606*. New York: Simon and Shuster, 2015.

Shrank, Cathy. "Sir Thomas Elyot and the Bonds of Community," in *The Oxford Handbook of Tudor Literature 1485–1603*, ed. M. Pincombe and C. Shrank. Oxford: Oxford University Press, 2009. www.oxfordhandbooks.com.myac cess.library.utoronto.ca/view/10.1093/oxfordhb/9780199205882.001.0001/oxfor dhb-9780199205882-e-010. Date accessed 26 August 2017.

Skinner, Quentin. *The Foundations of Modern Political Thought*, 2 vols. Cambridge: Cambridge University Press, 1978.

From Humanism to Hobbes. Studies in Rhetoric and Politics. Cambridge: Cambridge University Press, 2018.

Hobbes and Republican Liberty. Cambridge: Cambridge University Press, 2008.

Machiavelli. Oxford: Oxford University Press, 2019.

Reason and Rhetoric in the Philosophy of Hobbes. Cambridge: Cambridge University Press, 1996.

Visions of Politics, 2 vols. Cambridge: Cambridge University Press, 2002.

Smith, Paul. *Dispositio. Problematic Ordering in French Renaissance Literature*. Leiden and Boston: Brill, 2007.

Somerset, Anne. *Elizabeth I*. London: Weidenfeld and Nicolson, 1991.

Soll, Jacob. "Empirical History and the transformation of political criticism in France from Bodin to Bayle." *Journal of the History of Ideas*, 64.2 (April 2003), 297–316.

Sowerby, Robin. "Thomas Hobbes's Translation of Thucydides." *Translation and Literature*, vol. 7, no. 2 (1998), 147–169.

Spencer, T. J. B., ed. *Shakespeare's Plutarch*. Harmondsworth, UK: Penguin, 1964.

Stadter, Philip. "Alexander Hamilton's Notes on Plutarch in his Pay Book." *The Review of Politics* 73 (2011), 199–219.

Stadter, Philip and Luc van der Stock, eds. *Sage and Emperor: Plutarch, Greek Intellectuals, and Roman Power in the Time of Trajan (98–117 ad)*. (Leuven: Leuven University Press, 2002), 163–174.

Starkey, David. "England," in *The Renaissance in National Context*, eds. R. Porter and M. Teich. Cambridge: Cambridge University Press, 1992.

Starnes, D. T. "Richard Taverner's *The Garden of Wisdom*, Carion's *Chronicles* and the Cambyses Legend." *Studies in English* 35 (1956). 22–23.

Starobinski, Jean. *La Transparence et l'obstacle*. Paris: Gallimard, 1971.

Steel, Catherine ed. *The Cambridge Companion to the Reception of Cicero*. Cambridge: Cambridge University Press, 2013.

Stefano, Guiseppe di. "L'Hellénisme en France à l'Orée de la Renaissance," in *Humanism at the End of the Middle Ages and in the Early Renaissance*, ed. Anthony Levy. Manchester and New York: Manchester University Press and Barnes and Noble, 1970, 29–42.

La Découverte de Plutarque en Occident. Turin: Accademia delle Scienze, 1968.

Stevens, Linton. "A Re-evaluation of Hellenism in the French Renaissance." *Studies in Philology*, 58.2 (April 1961), 115–129.

Stierle, Karlhenz. "L'Histoire comme exemple, l'exemple comme histoire." *Poetique* 10 (1972), 176–198.

Straumann, Benjamin. *Crisis and Constitutionalism.* Oxford: Oxford University Press, 2016.

Sturel, René. *Jacques Amyot traducteur des Vies parallèles de Plutarque.* Paris: Joseph Flock, 1908 and 2006.

Suomela-Härmä,Elina. "Simon Bourgouin, traducteur à l'avant-garde." *Studi francesi* 176. 49.2 (2015). https://journals.openedition.org/studifrancesi/321. Date accessed 23 June 2020.

Swain, Simon. *Hellenism and Empire.* Oxford: Clarendon Press, 1996.

Talbot, A.-M. "Sekoundinos, Nicholas," in *Oxford Dictionary of Byzantium* 3. Oxford: Oxford University Press, 1991, 1865.

Taylor, Andrew. "The Translations of Renaissance Latin." *Canadian Review of Comparative Literature* 41.4 (2014), 332–333.

Taylor, Craig. "The Ambivalent Influence of Italian Letters and the Rediscovery of the Classics in Late Medieval France," in *Humanism in Fifteenth Century Europe*, ed. David Rundle. Oxford: The Society for the Study of Medieval Languages and Literatures, 2012, 203–236.

Terrell, Jean. *Thomas Hobbes: Philosopher par temps de crises.* Paris: Presses universitaires de France, 2012.

Thickett, Dorothy. *Etienne Pasquier.* London: Regency Press, 1979.

Thompson, C. R. *The Translations of Lucian by Erasmus and Sir Thomas More.* Ithaca NY: The Vail-Ballou Press, 1940.

Thompson, Douglas. *Montaigne and the Tolerance of Politics.* Oxford: Oxford University Press, 2018.

Thomson, Ian. "Manuel Chrysoloras and the Early Italian Renaissance." *Greek, Roman and Byzantine Studies,* 7 (1966), 63–82.

Thomson, Patricia. "Classical Philosophy and English Humanism," in *Sir Thomas Wyatt and His Background.* London: Kegan Paul, 1964.

Torrens, Philippe. "Claude de Seyssel traducteur des historiens antiques," in *Claude de Seyssel, Ecrire l'histoire, penser le politique en France, à l'aube des temps modernes,* Paris: Presses universitaires de Rennes, 2010, 183–200

Trego, Christine. "Do as I say and as I do: lessons on the use of history for the civic statesman in Plutarch's Praecepta." *Classical World* 109.3 (2016), 357–379.

Tritle, Laurence. *Phocion the Good.* Beckenham: Croom Helm, 1978.

Tuck, Richard. *Philosophy and Government 1572–1651.* Cambridge: Cambridge University Press, 1993.

The Sleeping Sovereign. Cambridge: Cambridge University Press, 2016.

Tucker, Marie-Claude. "Henry Scrimgeour (1505?–1572), Diplomat and Book Collector," in *Oxford Dictionary of National Biography.* www.oxforddnb.com/view/article/24968. Date Accessed 8 April 2016.

Urbinati, Nadia. *Representative Democracy.* Chicago: University of Chicago Press, 2006.

Vasunia, Phiroze. "Plutarch and the Return of the Archaic," in *Flavian Rome. Culture, Image, Text*. eds. A. J. Boyle and W. J. Dominik. Leiden: Brill, 2003, 369–390.

Villey, Pierre ed. *Les Essais de Michel de Montaigne*. Paris: Presses universitaires de France, 1965.

Walzer, Michael. "Political Action: The Problem of Dirty Hands." *Philosophy & Public Affairs*, 2.2 (Winter, 1973), 160–180.

Westbrook, Vivienne. "Richard Taverner Revising Tyndale." *Reformation* 2.1 (1997), 191–205.

White, Olive. "Richard Taverner's Interpretation of Erasmus in Proverbes or Adagies." *PMLA* 59.4 (December 1944), 928–943.

Whitmarsh, Tim. *The Second Sophistic*. Cambridge: Cambridge University Press, 2005.

Wilde, Lawrence. *Thomas More's Utopia. Arguing for Social Justice*. London and New York: Routledge, 2017.

Wilson, Catherine. *Epicureanism at the Origins of Modernity*. Oxford: Oxford University Press, 2008.

Wood, Neal. "Cicero and the Political Thought of the Early English Renaissance." *Modern Language Quarterly*, 51.2 (June 1990), 185–207.

Worth, Valerie. *Practicing Translation in Renaissance France*. Oxford: Clarendon Press, 1988.

Wright, Louis B. *Middle-Class Culture in Elizabethan England*. Chapel Hill: University of North Carolina Press, 1935.

Xenophontos, Sophia. *Ethical Education in Plutarch: Moralising Agents and Contexts*. Boston and Berlin: de Gruyter, 2016.

Xenophontos, Sophia and Katerina Oikonomopoulou, eds. *Brill's Companion to the Reception of Plutarch*. Leiden: Brill, 2019.

Yolton, Jean S. "John Locke as Translator," in *Studies in Voltaire and the Eighteenth Century*. Oxford: Voltaire Foundation, 2000.

Yost, John K. "German Protestant Humanism and the Early English Reformation: Richard Taverner and Official Translation." *Bibliotheque d'Humanisme et Renaissance* 32.3 (1970), 613–625.

Zacka, Bernardo. *When the State Meets the Street*. Cambridge, MA: Harvard University Press, 2017.

Zagorin, Perez. *Francis Bacon*. Princeton, NJ: Princeton University Press, 1998.

Index

438

Milton Keynes UK
Ingram Content Group UK Ltd.
UKHW020721280124
436796UK00022B/112